CONTENTS

INTRODUCTION   xv

HOW TO GET TO THE ORIENT AND ASIA   1

    All About Air Travel   2
    Making Travel Arrangements   7
    Passports and Visas   14
    What to Take   22
    Telling Time and the International Date Line   29
    Weather   33
    Money   38
    Health   40
    The U.S. Customs   45
    PATA (The Pacific Area Travel Association)   49

JAPAN   50

    Background   50
    When to Go   56
        Weather Strip: Tokyo   58
    Visa Requirements   58
    Customs   58
    Health   59
    Time   60
    Currency   60
    Price Level   60
    Tipping   61
    Transportation   62
    Airport and Tourist Taxes   66
    Communications   67
    Electricity   68
    Food Specialties and Liquor   68
    Time Evaluation   75
    Capital City: Tokyo   76
        ORGANIZED SIGHTSEEING   82
        SIGHTSEEING ON YOUR OWN   83
        SEVEN TRIPS ON YOUR OWN   84

ACCOMMODATIONS   91
RESTAURANTS   96
SHOPPING   101
ENTERTAINMENT   112
SPORTS   127

Short Trips from Tokyo   135
Kamakura   136
The Hakone District   143
Fuji Lake Area   145
Nikko   150

Longer Trips from Tokyo   156
Nagoya   156
Iseshi   162

Kyoto   165
HOTELS   172
RESTAURANTS   173

Sidetrips from Kyoto   173
Nara   173
Weather Strip: Osaka   175
Osaka   176
Kobe   179
Inland Sea   183
Beppu   186
Fukuoka   187
Nagasaki   188
Unzen National Park   190

Northern Japan and Hokkaido   191
Sendai   192
Aomori   193
Weather Strip: Sapporo   194
Hokkaido Island   195
Daisetsuzan   196
Shikotsu-Toya   196
Akan   197

Miscellaneous   197

Myra Waldo's
Travel Guide

ORIENT AND ASIA

Newly Revised

Collier Books
A Division of Macmillan Publishing Co., Inc.
New York

Collier Macmillan Publishers
London

ISSN 0195-7759
ISBN 0-02-098960-1

Macmillan Publishing Co., Inc.
866 Third Avenue, New York, N.Y. 10022
Collier Macmillan Canada, Inc.

First Collier Books Edition 1977
Second Printing 1978
Third Printing 1979

Revised and Updated Edition 1980, 1981, 1982

Designed by Jack Meserole

Printed in the United States of America

General Editor: Robert Schwartz

       LANGUAGE   197
       GETTING AROUND IN JAPAN   198

KOREA   208

    Background   208
       Weather Strip: Seoul   211
    When to Go   211
    Visa Requirements   212
    Customs   212
    Health   212
    Time   213
    Currency   213
    Price Level   213
    Tipping   213
    Transportation   214
    Airport and Tourist Taxes   214
    Communications   215
    Electricity   215
    Food Specialties and Liquor   215
    Time Evaluation   217
    Capital City: Seoul   218
       ACCOMMODATIONS   221
       RESTAURANTS   222
       SHOPPING   223
       ENTERTAINMENT   225
       SPORTS   226

    Short Trips from Seoul   226
    Longer Trips from Seoul   227

TAIWAN   231

    Background   231
    When to Go   232
       Weather Strip: Taipei   232
    Visa Requirements   233
    Customs   233
    Health   233
    Time   234
    Currency   234

Price Level   234
Tipping   234
Transportation   235
Airport and Tourist Taxes   235
Communications   235
Electricity   236
Food Specialties and Liquor   236
Time Evaluation   239
Capital City: Tapei   239
   ACCOMMODATIONS   242
   RESTAURANTS   243
   SHOPPING   246
   ENTERTAINMENT   248
   SPORTS   249

Short Trips from Tapei   249
   Grass Mountain   249
   Green Lake   249
   Wulai   250
Longer Trips from Taipei   250
   The Taroko Gorge   250
   Sun-Moon Lake   251
   Orchid Island   252
   Kaohsiung   253

HONG KONG AND MACAO   255
Background   255
When to Go   257
   Weather Strip: Hong Kong   257
Visa Requirements   258
Customs   258
Health   258
Time   259
Currency   259
Price Level   259
Tipping   259
Transportation   260
Airport and Tourist Taxes   261

Communications   261
Electricity   262
Food Specialties and Liquor   262
Time Evaluation   263
The Crown Colony: Hong Kong   263
Hong Kong Island   264
Kowloon   269
  New Territories: Sidetrip From Kowloon   272
  Hong Kong's Other Islands   276
  ORGANIZED TOURS   277
  ACCOMMODATIONS   278
  RESTAURANTS   281
  SHOPPING   283
  ENTERTAINMENT   292
  UNDERSTANDING THE LOCAL TALK   292

Macao   293
When to Go   293
Visa Requirements   293
Currency   294
Accommodations   294
Health, Customs   295
How to Get There   295
Restaurants, Food Specialties and Liquor   296
  MACAO SIGHTSEEING   296

CHINA   300
Background   300
When to Go   302
Visa Requirements   303
Customs   303
A Special Note about Traveling in China   304
The Actual Entry   304
Health   305
Time   306
Currency   306
Price Level   307
Tipping   307

Transportation 308

Communications 309

Electricity 309

Food Specialties and Liquor 309

What to Wear 310

What to Take Along 311

A Few Thoughts on Behavior in China 312

Hotels 313

Shopping 313

The Principal Cities and Tourist Areas 314

  Kwangchow (Canton) 314

    Weather Strip: Kwangchow (Canton) 315

  Nanking 316

    Weather Strip: Nanking 316

  Shanghai 317

    Weather Strip: Shanghai 317

  Kweilin 318

    Weather Strip: Kweilin 319

  Peking (Beijing) 320

  Kunming 320

  Hangchow (Hangzhou) 321

  Wuhan 321

  Sian 321

  Shenyang 322

THAILAND 323

Background 323

When to Go 325

    Weather Strip: Bangkok 326

Visa Requirements 326

Customs 326

Health 326

Time 327

Currency 328

Price Level 328

Tipping   329
Transportation   329
Airport and Tourist Taxes   330
Communications   330
Electricity   331
Food Specialties and Liquor   332
Time Evaluation   333
Some Local Customs   334
Capital City: Bangkok   334
ACCOMMODATIONS   338
RESTAURANTS   339
SHOPPING   341
ENTERTAINMENT   345
SPORTS   346

Short Trips from Bangkok   347
Rose Gardens   347
Ayudhya   347
Nakorn Pathom   350
Longer Trips from Bangkok   350
Pattaya   350
Lopburi   351
Surin   352
Phuket   352
Chiengmai   353
Weather Strip: Chiengmai   354

BURMA   355
Background   355
When to Go   357
Weather Strip: Rangoon   357
Visa Requirements   358
Customs   358
Health   358
Time   359
Currency   359
A Special Note about Traveling in Burma   359

Price Level   360
Tipping   360
Transportation   361
Airport and Tourist Taxes   362
Communications   362
Electricity   362
Food Specialties and Liquor   362
Time Evaluation   363
Capital City: Rangoon   364
   ACCOMMODATIONS   366
   RESTAURANTS   366
   SHOPPING   367
   ENTERTAINMENT   368
   SPORTS   368

   Pegu   368
   Pagan   369

INDIA   370

Background   370
When to Go   373
Visa Requirements   374
Health   374
Customs   376
Currency   376
Price Level   377
Tipping   377
Transportation   378
Communications   380
Electricity   380
Food Specialties and Liquor   380
Language   383
Approaching India and Its Cities   384
   SUGGESTED ITINERARIES   385
Calcutta   386
   Weather Strip: Calcutta   387
   Andaman Islands   393

Darjeeling   393
  Weather Strip: Darjeeling   394
Bhubaneswar   395
Benaras (Varanasi)   396
Delhi   398
  Weather Strip: Delhi   399
  ACCOMMODATIONS   401
Agra   404
  Weather Strip: Agra   405
Jaipur   408
  Weather Strip: Jaipur   408
Udaipur   409
Kashmir   411
  Weather Strip: Srinagar   412
Bombay   414
  Weather Strip: Bombay   415
The Ellora and Ajanta Caves   419
Goa   421
The South   422
  Weather Strip: Madras   423
Nepal   424
  Weather Strip: Kathmandu   427

SRI LANKA (CEYLON)   429
Background   429
When to Go   430
Visa Requirements   430
Customs   431
Health   431
  Weather Strip: Colombo   431
Time   432
Currency   432
Price Level   432
Tipping   432
Transportation   433

Airport and Tourist Taxes   433
Communications   433
Electricity   434
Food Specialties and Liquor   434
Time Evaluation   435
Capital City: Colombo   436
    ACCOMMODATIONS   437
    RESTAURANTS   438
    SHOPPING   438
    ENTERTAINMENT   439
    SPORTS   439

Short Trips from Colombo   440
A Tour of Sri Lanka   442
    Trips to the Seychelle Islands   444

SINGAPORE AND MALAYSIA   446
Background   446
When to Go   448
    Weather Strip: Singapore   449
Visa Requirements   449
Customs   449
Health   449
Time   450
Currency   450
Price Level   450
Tipping   450
Transportation   451
Airport and Tourist Taxes   451
Communications   452
Electricity   452
Public Holidays   452
Food Specialties and Liquor   453
Time Evaluation   454
Singapore   455
    ACCOMMODATIONS   460
    RESTAURANTS   461
    SHOPPING   464
    ENTERTAINMENT   468

Sports   469
Short Trips from Singapore   469

Malaysia   470
A Tour of the Country   470
Other Interesting Sidetrips   473
Miscellaneous Notes About Malaysia and
    Singapore   475

INDONESIA   476

Background   476
When to Go   477
    Weather Strip: Jakarta   478
Visa Requirements   478
Customs   478
Health   479
Time   479
Currency   479
Price Level   480
Tipping   480
Transportation   480
Airport and Tourist Taxes   481
Communications   481
Public Holidays   481
Electricity   481
Food Specialties and Liquor   482
Time Evaluation   484
Capital City: Jakarta   484
    Short Trips from Jakarta   487

Bali   488
Some Other Islands of Indonesia   492
    Shopping   493
    Entertainment and Restaurants   496

INDEX   499

INTRODUCTION

Fifty years ago, only the very wealthy could afford the expense and almost unlimited time required for a trip to the Orient and Asia; to almost everyone else, that continent was a far-off romantic place, to be read about but unlikely to be visited.

A decade or two ago, the continent of Asia was opened to the tourist by the advent of regular plane service, often on an infrequent basis, however. Then came the jet planes, and the enormous distances immediately shrunk. A month's voyage by sea was reduced to a matter of twelve hours, new hotels were built, and the traveler's comfort became a matter of great concern to the various countries of the Orient. It can now be flatly stated that tourist accommodations are generally better in most of the Orient than they are in Europe.

Travel to foreign lands has become a way of life for Americans, the greatest tourists in the history of the world. In my opinion, the Orient offers more to the traveler than any other region in the world: the food is good, often superb; as mentioned previously, hotels are more luxurious than many to be encountered in Europe, or for that matter, elsewhere in the world. And best of all, the people and the sights are far from hackneyed, anything but tourist-ridden, and offer fresh vistas and pleasures for American sightseers.

You'll certainly enjoy your trip to this part of the world. Just be sure to allow sufficient time, so that the schedule is comfortably paced. It becomes tiresome to keep on the move day after day— allow for a little rest and relaxation. When tourists return, if they have a complaint to make, it is inevitably about too tight a schedule which failed to allow time to absorb the atmosphere of a country. Merely seeing the sights involves just a few days; getting the "feel" of a foreign land takes more time. Be sure to allow enough time for your trip so that you can enjoy to the fullest the wonderful world of the Orient.

MYRA WALDO

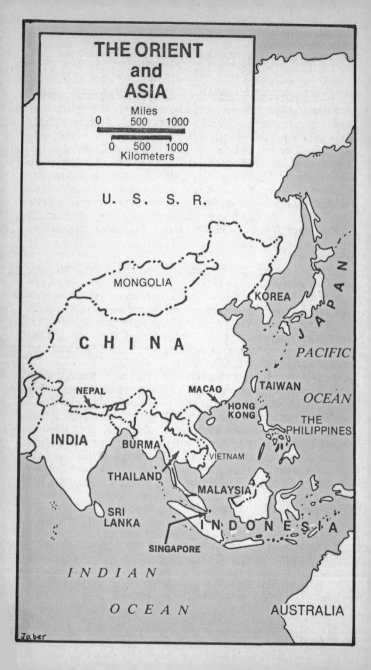

HOW TO GET TO THE ORIENT AND ASIA

What a wonderful age we live in! Aren't we fortunate in being able to see the far-off lands of Asia and the Orient, making the trip by jet plane in a matter of hours? All of us have hundreds of thousands of ancestors, covering a span of many thousands of years, and we are very likely the first in our entire family line to see the Orient.

Now that you've decided to make the trip, I can promise that you will never regret your decision. The first problem, of course, is the method of getting there.

BY SHIP OR PLANE? There are many who think an overseas vacation involves a ship, or it isn't a vacation. There are far many others, attuned to the 20th century, who wouldn't want to waste a minute sitting aboard a ship traveling at 14 knots when they could be flying to their destination at 600 miles per hour; they simply can't wait to get there. It is perfectly obvious that the ship group will never get together with the plane group, and each can present valid arguments conclusively proving the advantage of one method of travel over the other. The ship enthusiasts argue (and with reason) that shipboard life is luxurious, it offers a vacation en route, the meals are paid for, and the traveler rests in both directions, arriving at his destination completely relaxed and refreshed after the ocean voyage. Air travelers argue (and with reason) that tedious, time-consuming days of shipboard travel are compressed into merely hours, the swiftness of the trip leaves you refreshed rather than bored and stagnant from the long crossing, and furthermore, there's no other way to travel in the 20th century. Both groups obviously have their points.

Of course, ships are not suitable for the traveler with less than six weeks unless he intends to visit only one or two places—Japan and Hong Kong, for example. It would be extremely difficult to arrange a shipboard schedule that would encompass a half-dozen or more Oriental countries unless the visitor could spare about four months. Of course, some cruises do visit the highspots, but the stops are quite brief. There are steamship services between almost all ports in the Orient, but the scheduled sailings are often widely separated, sometimes by as much as a month. On the other hand, almost every point in the Orient has frequent plane service, sometimes even daily. A combination trip consisting of a sea voyage plus air travel may often be arranged; if you do decide to go partly by ship and partly by plane, consult your travel agent or steamship company or airline and request a combination fare. If you want to take a tip—fly out to the Orient and return by ship. The reason: people are always anxious to get some place when they commence a trip and usually dislike returning; by taking the ship for the return portion, you'll enjoy the long delay in reaching home. Besides, going away your baggage is light, but returning (with loads of purchases) your baggage will have increased. In this way, you'll pay no overweight returning by plane.

However, the vast, overwhelming majority of travelers to the Orient make the entire trip by plane. The distances involved are staggering—Los Angeles to Hong Kong is over 8,000 miles, from New York about 11,000 miles! The great advantage of air travel lies in the fact that practically nothing (only a day each way) need be deducted for ordinary travel time. Almost your entire vacation trip can be spent in the Orient, less perhaps one day's travel each to and from your home. Round-trip shipboard travel would involve an absolute minimum of five or six weeks, which would have to be deducted from your allotted trip.

⨎ All About Air Travel

A matter of only fifteen years ago, plane travel to the Orient was considered as being conducted on a large scale. Flights were scheduled by the various airlines on a twice-a-week basis between the U.S. and most points on the continent of Asia. But along came the jet plane, the 600-mile-an-hour monsters of the air, and travel to the Orient really took off (in more ways than one). All that had gone before was as nothing; travel increased by the proverbial leaps and bounds, and instead of empty seats aboard Tokyo-bound planes, it became difficult for travelers to make reservations.

One great advantage of air travel is that you know in advance precisely what the cost of the trip will be. Air fares are definite, and there are no "extras" except for transportation charges (usually quite nominal) from the airport to your hotel. Aboard ship, you'll have to pay out a fairly substantial sum in tips, averaging slightly under 10% of your steamship fare, in addition to all of the more or less concealed extras which are customary aboard ship—deck chairs, bar bills, landing charges—all of which can run up your expenses quite alarmingly.

SELECTING YOUR AIRLINE Most Americans, probably about 80% of them, travel to the Orient via American carriers, and this is the way it should be, what with our ever present problem about the stability of the dollar—that is, about keeping too many of them (dollars) from going out of the country. All airlines charge the identical price for the same service, so there can be no question of shopping around for air travel bargains (except for charter flights and package tours). Asia and the Orient are served from the west coast of the United States by several important airlines—Pan American, Northwest, Japan Airlines, and British Airways. The first two airlines are American, Japan Airlines is Japanese of course, and, quite naturally, British Airways is British.

Pan American World Airways, to use its full corporate name, is the giant of this group and usually manages to secure the bulk of Pacific travel business. It has the largest network of routes, the most frequent service, and all in all, lives up to its claim of being the world's most experienced airline, having pioneered the first Pacific flights with regular service decades ago, before any other airline had even attempted a trial run. The great advantage of Pan American, in my opinion, lies in this great, complex network of services. Some smaller airlines should theoretically be able to offer more personal service (although in actual fact they don't as a rule); however, with jets costing from six to twenty million dollars each, many small airlines just have a very few planes. When planes require sudden or emergency servicing, and they do because planes are just pieces of machinery, the airline has to come up with another plane in a hurry. As can be imagined, the smaller airline with its limited facilities finds it extremely difficult to locate an extra plane; the giant airline with dozens and dozens of planes is almost always able to put a standby plane into service so that your schedule is not disrupted. Furthermore, most of Pan Am's customers think quite fondly of the airline for a very personal reason—it is the one airline that always keeps pressing for lower fares (over the opposition of its competitors). At present, Pan Am is the only airline using 747SP planes on its services from New York to Tokyo; the SP designation means Special Performance, and this means an exceptionally large fuel capacity, permitting the planes to fly nonstop. First class has reclining seats that are almost like beds.

China Airlines is now flying from the west coast of the U.S. They use wide-bodied planes and the flights are just about on a par with those of important western airlines. They have a very good on-time record and the food is quite good.

Air India concentrates, as you might expect, on its service to India. It uses 747s, which fly out of New York and always stop at London en route to India. (There is no service across the Pacific.) From India, the airline continues to various destinations in Asia, including Bangkok, Singapore, Hong Kong, and Tokyo. All flights from New York to London are non-stop, but from London to either Delhi or Bombay, they may make stops en route; on certain days, they fly non-stop. By all means study the timetable and try to fly on one of the non-stop flights. The service on board is excellent and the food surprisingly good. In first class, travelers will find considerable luxury and far more personal attention than is customary on competitive airlines. In tourist class, passengers will also find a great deal of courtesy and service from the stewardesses, who are dressed in native costumes.

Singapore Airlines has built itself a reputation for service. It also uses wide-bodied planes and flies from the west coast of the U.S. to Singapore. The airline is well regarded for its food, and as previously mentioned, for its excellent service. Many experienced passengers, who regularly fly from the U.S. to the Orient, seem to prefer Singapore Airlines.

Northwest Orient Airlines is the other American carrier that covers Asia, although its service is limited mostly to flights from the west coast of the U.S. to Tokyo and Hong Kong; it does not serve areas past this point. The airline features a service from New York and Chicago to Japan, via Anchorage, Alaska, which is quite direct. Personally, I have never had very good luck on board Northwest Orient; more often than not the flights have been delayed for substantial numbers of hours, and their flight personnel seem singularly disinterested. But I must admit that these statements are based on no more than somewhat over a dozen trans-Pacific flights, so perhaps you will do better.

British Airways is the English airline; it has a large network of Oriental services leaving from San Francisco for Honolulu, Tokyo, and Hong Kong. They also head south toward southeast Asia, Australia, and New Zealand. As you might expect, the British are crisp and efficient, and their flight personnel are extremely courteous and willing.

Japan Airlines is a medium-sized, excellent airline with frequent service from the U.S. west coast to Tokyo. The service also covers Taipei, Hong Kong, Singapore, and Bangkok. It also serves Japan very well, with frequently scheduled flights from Tokyo to Osaka and Sapporo, the first service being especially important for tourists. Aboard the aircraft, passengers receive quite personalized service from the stewardesses, charmingly attired in native costume.

SELECTING YOUR CLASS ABOARD THE PLANE Over the years, the airlines serving the Orient have experimented with various classes, ranging all the way from the most luxurious service with cocktails and champagne, personalized attention, fruit, gifts, and almost every imaginable type of luxury, all the way to the other extreme, a type of bare-bones service (particularly from the U.S. west coast to Honolulu) in which the fare is cut to the minimum and not even a sandwich is served in flight. Most of the time, however, there are three classes of service which may be designated by various names, but which inevitably add up to First Class and Economy (also called Tourist), and then there's an in-between class called Executive or Business class, or whatever name the airline chooses to use.

What is the difference among the three services? you rightly ask. Forget the difference in price for the moment so that you can find out what you're going to be paying for if you select the more expensive class. All of the following represents generalizations, because the various airlines have somewhat different personalities, arrange their planes somewhat differently, and are almost always engaged in some type of experimentation in an effort to improve passenger comfort. Planes are so flexibly designed that the very same aircraft can carry say 300 passengers, and can also be arranged so that it can handle 375 passengers in the same space. Sometimes an airline will maintain the same space between rows of seats during the off-season when the plane is half-empty, whereas another airline will remove several rows of empty seats and give the smaller number of passengers greater comfort.

In any event, First Class service has two seats on each side of the aisle, making each row nine or ten seats abreast. In Economy Class, there are usually nine seats abreast. To translate this into personal terms, it means that 1½ Economy passengers take up the space that is used by 1 First Class passenger, or to restate it once again, the First Class traveler gets 50% more seating space. The same rule holds roughly true with regard to leg room, and the First Class passenger has about 50% more space in which to stretch his legs than the Economy traveler. (I won't bother mentioning the fancier groceries, the constant offers of free drinks and wines in First Class —we'll confine this discussion to space, weights, and measures, for the moment.)

Now, turning to Executive or Business class, or whatever the airline chooses to call this service, it may consist of fewer seats across than Economy class. Usually it does, and some airlines only have banks of two seats at a time, repeated four times across the width of the plane. In this class, there is no charge for the headphones, nor for liquor (often, however, no movie is shown in this class). It's become very popular with the public, however, because Executive class usually has its own check-in line, which saves quite some time. Although the airlines like to say that they serve "special" meals in this class, it really isn't true, because it consists strictly of Economy class meals, although perhaps you might be offered a choice of entrees. The fare in this class is usually somewhat higher than Economy but considerably lower than First Class.

Over the last few years, many attempts have been made to reduce fares to the Orient, so it's impossible to quote fares exactly. One fact will probably remain the same, however; that is, First Class will be very much higher than Economy. Should you spend the extra money or not? I hate to give an evasive answer, but it all depends on many circumstances—your personality, finances, mood, etc. I've traveled many times by both classes and I don't suppose it takes very much thought on my part to say unequivocally and flatly that First Class is extremely luxurious and delightful, and puts you into the perfect mood to begin, and subsequently to end, your vacation.

But I hasten to add that Economy Class is perfectly bearable, particularly now that jet travel has so shortened distances. From the west coast of the U.S. to Honolulu is only a matter of about 5 hours; from Honolulu to Tokyo involves about 8 hours flying time; most other flights in Asia will be even shorter. Direct flights from New York to Tokyo, on Pan Am's non-stop 747SPs, takes 14 hours.

The question obviously presented therefore is: inasmuch as travel times are comparatively short, is it worth all that extra money? The answers are very surprising, often unexpected. One person (of limited means) who has saved for the trip will declare that it's the vacation trip of his lifetime and he wants everything first-class, at any cost. Another person (quite affluent) will say that he can't see the value of First Class and never travels other than by Economy Class.

Well, where are we now? The record shows that more than three-quarters of all Pacific travelers use Economy in preference (well, maybe not preference) to First Class. It isn't because they prefer a simple meal to an elaborate gourmet-type meal; it isn't because they would rather pay for their own drinks and wines than receive them free. It is simply and plainly because when a couple arrives in Tokyo (to use the previous example) they will have saved a considerable amount of money, or to put it another way, a good deal of money. Whatever the decision, make it yourself.

AIR FARES TO THE ORIENT   If you're going from the west coast of the U.S. to one particular destination or perhaps two in the Orient and then returning home, it is a simple matter to look up the fare in an airline timetable, and that is all there is to it. However, if you're planning to circle the Pacific, visiting Japan and Hong Kong, then returning home via a different route, the precise fare is too difficult for you to ascertain and is something for a travel agent to compute. The airlines are very liberal about stopover privileges, but you must keep going in a westerly direction (there are a few exceptions) before returning and the fare for the most westerly point you reach is the total fare, including the previous stopovers. Is that confusing?

𝄢 Making Travel Arrangements

What sort of person are you really like? Do you enjoy being with crowds of people, do you belong to numerous clubs and organizations, and do you like large family groups? Or, at the other extreme, do you think that anyone but your husband or wife would be in the way when you take a Sunday afternoon drive? Human beings have their own individualistic personalities, to restate the obvious, and the type of travel arrangements to be made should (in fact, must) take this into consideration. If you're the jovial, garrulous, hail-fellow-well-met sort, a solitary trip may be completely lacking in pleasure if there's no one around to share it with. Most of us, I would imagine, fit into a median category, enjoying the company of other people at times, and equally enjoying a reasonable degree of privacy on other occasions.

Let's consider the various possibilities, step by step. To begin with, we must make a flat and definite statement—there is nothing complex about making your own arrangements, if you wish to do so. Merely because your trip is to the Orient, don't for a moment think that you'll be facing language problems, once there, with regard to hotel reservations, airline tickets, or local transportation. You're going to be absolutely astonished at the enormous number of people who speak English, not only intelligibly, but often completely without an accent.

Here are the three possible choices presented: (1) the conducted group tour, (2) the independent but planned trip, and (3) traveling completely on your own. If you've been to Europe before, the chances are that you know almost exactly the method you wish to follow this time. At the risk of being repetitious, I want to reiterate that traveling through the Orient presents no additional complications as compared to Europe, and in many respects, may be even simpler.

(1) *The conducted tour.* There are people who love them, and equally there are those who despise them. A group tour is one in which a travel organization collects a group of people, arranges for their travel from place to place always as a group, arranges for their hotel accommodations, sightseeing, and meals, and in general makes the trip almost effortless from beginning to end. The net result is that the personal wishes of the individual are subordinated to that of the group. This is not necessarily the fault of the travel organization, because they must take people as they come, and in catering to a large number, the individual must be put in second place, behind the prior rights of the group.

I have spoken to dozens of people who have been taken on whirlwind tours of the Far East and who have complained loudly that it was a terrible mistake and that never again would they become part of a group tour. I know many others, rugged individualists at heart, who have experienced difficulty with their hotel reservations, and arrived late at an airport and found local transportation hard to come by, who have equally complained, and said they would never travel alone again. Of course, the simple answer is that nothing in life is absolutely perfect, and that both the conducted tour and the independent type of travel have their respective advantages and disadvantages.

The basic, almost inevitable problem with organized tours is— somewhat surprisingly—that they do too much for you, show you too many sights you'd just as soon not bother about seeing, and keep you on the move almost continuously, actually far too much. This all comes about in a rather peculiar way. The travel agents are engaged in a competitive business, and being good businessmen, are out to sell you on *their* tour, in opposition to the tour of another travel agency. What better way to attract the potential traveler than by means of elaborate, beautifully illustrated folders in which the travel agent outlines in considerable detail every single sightseeing attraction that you will be shown if only you will take this particular trip? The folder outlines continuous days of activity, one after the other, packed with morning tours of Tokyo, afternoon tours of Nara, night tours of Kyoto, and so on, and more of the same. This is not evil, nor even wrongful, on the part of the travel agent. I am convinced that he is doing his level best to show you the most that can be seen, and to help you do the most that can be accomplished, on a visit to the Orient. Tours must inevitably be set up for what the travel agent regards as the common denominator of tourist interest—that is, what the travel agent thinks you're going to be interested in, not necessarily what you're *really* interested in. Like as not, he could be wrong. Getting tourists up very early in the morning and rushing them from one Buddhist temple to another Shinto shrine is emphasized, because those are specific, definite "sights" and everyone will probably want to see some of them. When the travel agents are preparing their folders, they can't very well say that they will spend the day in letting you understand Japan. No—by force of circumstances, they must list all the "sights" to be seen during the day. But by the time you get to your third or fourth country, perhaps just seeing the one most important Buddhist temple in that country will be sufficient for you (often it will be more than sufficient). But as we know, the schedule has been previously arranged for the group, and no allowance can be made for the individual tourist who reaches a saturation point on a particular type of sightseeing. There are tourists who can go from temple to monument to statue (and so on) all day long. Other travelers can take one long look at a particular sight, absorb all they care to, and then completely lose interest in endless repetitions (with only slight variations) on the same subject.

Another problem involves the very tight schedule kept by most tour groups. They are on the go, as a rule, from morning to night, so much so that the average tourist is perfectly happy to collapse into bed after dinner. This suits many people, who like to keep going at full steam all day long. But other people are cast in a different mold. They like to pace themselves, sightseeing furiously on Monday and then getting up to a luxurious late breakfast on Tuesday and wandering about the town on their own. Then there is the question of weather. If a prearranged schedule calls for sightseeing on Wednesday and shopping on Thursday, the schedule cannot usually be altered. If it rains on Wednesday, most people would rather go shopping on that day because good weather would be comparatively unimportant. With a clear day on Thursday, for example, spending the day shopping indoors would equally be foolish.

Now obviously the same arguments for or against organized tours cannot be made about every tour group. They vary, much as people vary. Some tour groups make their chief pitch on a price basis, offering a certain number of days in the Orient for what is apparently an attractively low price. Other tours attract in the opposite fashion, by charging the highest prices on the basis of luxury hotel accommodations, private automobiles for sightseeing, and the like. But in between are the vast majority of tours, in which the travel agent in all good faith seeks to offer the most for your money, but at a medium price level. A further refinement, much needed in my opinion, is an attempt to appeal to people having "special interests," such as gardening, photography, or antiques, to give a few examples; this has been done, but only on a limited scale. Another way to assemble a more homogeneous group is based upon age groups, so that very young people are not on the same tour with older, more mature people, on the theory that people in similar age groups will have more or less related interests. The fact remains that any tour group is a rather mixed bag, and no two groups are exactly alike, and you could have a marvelous time with one group and a disastrously dull time with another.

However, conducted tours are absolutely recommended for those who must travel alone, whatever the reason. For single tourists, in any event, there is the important automatic companionship brought about by merely being with other people. Rare indeed and of unusual personality is the traveler who can find very much pleasure in lonely and solitary travel. In any miscellaneous group, composed even by pure chance, there are usually at least several people with whom one can find a set of common interests and establish a pleasant relationship, perhaps even friendship of a sort. Gone, too, are the problems of arriving alone in a strange airport and of finding one's own transportation to a hotel, only to have a solitary meal. The tour conductor leads his group about, telling them what they should see (or what he thinks they should), perhaps patronizingly telling them what to admire or not admire, but nevertheless and in all seriousness, saving them from much of the routine strains and stresses of travel. On the other hand, in such groups the traveler actually misses direct *contact* with the people of the country, speaking directly only to porters and waiters. The group traveler *sees* the country, but he rarely *feels* it.

(2) *The independent planned trip.* This is something like a conducted tour but without a large group and only in company with the other person (or persons) you select in advance. This is obviously not an especially good arrangement for a solitary traveler, but is ideal for a husband and wife, or two good friends, or perhaps for two couples. Travel agents call this type of travel F.I.T. (Foreign Independent Travel).

On an F.I.T. trip, you select the countries you wish to see, decide how many days to spend in each one, and whether to travel Economy, First Class, or even in super-luxury. In effect, you tell your agent how many days you have available, your proposed date of departure, and how much money you wish to spend; as a result, the trip will be tailored to your individual needs. You'll be handed a precise, fixed itinerary, specifying each plane, ship, or train you're to take, the names of the hotels where reservations have been made in your name, whether someone will meet you at the airport and help you through customs, the time your sightseeing bus or private car (depending upon how much you spend) will meet you at the hotel, and so forth, in complete detail. Actually, you're on a conducted tour, in a manner of speaking, except that it's *your* own trip, and is obviously more luxurious because you're traveling alone, or with just a few people. As it is obviously cheaper to arrange transportation and accommodations for larger groups than for two people, the F.I.T. is naturally, and must of necessity be, somewhat more expensive. The tremendous advantage of F.I.T. is that *you* see exactly what *you* want to see, that is, if you've given your travel agent the proper specifications and told him of your interests (for example, lots of beach resorts and girls in bikinis) and lack of interests (archeological ruins, for example). On the contrary, if you're burning with a desire to see every ruined temple in Asia, you'll undoubtedly chafe and grow restless sitting on the beach, soaking up sunshine, and wasting precious time. Obviously, the F.I.T. offers special advantages to the traveler, but only if he knows the kind of trip he wants to take and (equally important) tells his travel agent, and he, in turn, knows how to translate your wishes into an itinerary. Most travel agents can do so, but it's up to you to furnish him with the basic information.

(3) *Traveling on your own.* I suppose everyone dreams of being free from care, responsibility, and commitments and wandering about the face of the earth without a single bit of advance planning or prearranged schedule. This may be possible if you have unlimited money and also unlimited time. The vast majority of us earthbound people must usually travel within reasonably fixed time limits, and we rarely have access to unlimited funds. All in all, traveling on your own may mean doing away with tight schedules, fixed days of sightseeing, and rigorous advance plans difficult to alter or unravel, but it does not usually mean that *some* advance planning should not be made.

First of all, this type of travel is only suitable for two people or more. Individual travelers will do better, in my opinion, to find a traveling companion; in the alternative, join up with a small group tour. To reiterate, it's not too enjoyable being all by yourself, and sharing the pleasure (although a well-worn cliché) is half the fun. If a sight is beautiful, you'll want to talk about it; if a particular dish in a restaurant is delicious, you'll feel the same way. You definitely can, however, travel on your own in Asia, as well as in Europe. There are a few thoughts that go with this. No matter how free-wheeling you plan to make the trip, at least get started on a few basic plans. Naturally, you'll buy your ticket to Asia, but don't make the mistake of buying it for only one way, because you'll lose the round-trip discount. Should you decide to continue around the world, the unused portion can always be refunded without any financial loss. And no matter how free and easy you wish to travel, be sure and make a hotel reservation at your arrival point, so that at the very least you have a roof over your head to start with.

This type of "no planning" trip is perfectly acceptable if you're not going to visit too many countries, for example, an arbitrary limit of three countries. If you're planning to visit a half-dozen countries, I'd think that you'd do much better to make some hotel reservations and get booked on almost all your flights. The reason is far from complicated. The hotel situation can often get quite tight, with rooms at a tremendous premium during the height of the local tourist seasons; furthermore, hotel rooms can often be difficult to come by, even in the "off-season," because the local people use their own hotels, and sometimes you'll encounter a convention which will take up just about every room in a town. In addition, the airlines flying the various routes throughout Asia are frequently heavily booked, sometimes for days (or weeks) in advance. What this means is that all of your hopes of traveling as free as the birds will go down the drain, because you'll have to remain for several extra days waiting for plane space to open up. Inasmuch as the whole theory of "no planning" was to leave when the mood struck, it can be seen just how impracticably the whole plan works out. Then, too, when the airline space comes through, how do you know you'll have hotel space awaiting you at your destination? The answer is simple, you don't know until you get there, short of very expensive telephone calls. (There's seldom time to cable under these circumstances, and receive a reply.) There are few things more discouraging than to arrive at a hotel in some far-off place at midnight (or even later) and be told there's nothing available. It's not too enjoyable in your home country, and it's doubly so in a foreign land.

Do I have you talked into some advance planning? I sincerely hope so. If you're the independent type, and enjoy traveling on your own (with your spouse or perhaps with a good friend), by all means plan your own trip, make your own hotel reservations, and just go and have a marvelous time!

Isn't it terribly difficult to plan a trip to the Orient and do it all on your own? Wouldn't it be much easier to have a travel agent take care of all the details? The answers to these questions are No to the first, and Yes to the second. No, it's not difficult to plan a trip, but it is even easier to have someone else do it for you. As far as selecting the countries you want to visit, that's what this book is for. It should help you decide what interests you, and where you want to go. There are several tried-and-tested trips outlined in this book under the heading of Suggested Itineraries, and one of them should suit you to the proverbial T. How many days to allot to each country is a personal matter, although under the respective sections in this book called Time Evaluation (for each country), you'll find my personal recommendations. Take a sheet of paper, and place a calendar in front of you. Now, starting with your date of departure, write down the proposed itinerary along the following lines:

> Leave San Francisco, May 17
>   Arrive Tokyo, May 18.
>
> In Japan, May 18–26
>
> Leave Japan, May 26
>   Arrive Hong Kong, May 26.
>
> In Hong Kong, May 26–June 5.

And so forth. Next, go to your overseas airline, and show them your proposed schedule. In some cities, there may be no direct representative of the overseas airline, such as Pan American for example. You then have the choice of writing to the airline, enclosing your schedule and asking them to advise you; or in the alternative, you could have the ticket issued by a travel agent, paying only for the airline tickets.

Next, you will be told if your schedule can be executed with the dates you have furnished. The problem lies in the fact that sometimes there are no daily flights, perhaps only three or four times weekly (occasionally only twice a week), and it may be that you will have to leave a particular place a day before or a day later than your original schedule. However, there is so much airline traffic in the Far East that delays of more than a day or so are comparatively rare.

Once your schedule is confirmed, hotel space should be requested. Your travel agent or airline will do this for you or, if you prefer, write a letter yourself along the following lines:

"Will you kindly reserve a double room, preferably facing the front, with private bath for my wife and myself. We expect to arrive on July 16 via Pan American flight #211 in the early evening, and will stay for eight nights. Your prompt airmail reply, confirming this reservation, with the rate, will be appreciated."

Forty-nine times out of fifty, you will receive a confirmation within a reasonable length of time, assuring you of your reservation. Keep all your hotel confirmations together, and take them along on your trip, presenting them at the hotel desk when you arrive. Of course, none of this applies to the Republic of China—you must go with a group.

✒ Passports and Visas

To travel abroad, you must have a valid passport, of course. It's that familiar booklet issued by the State Department in Washington, D.C., and is required for almost every single country on your trip through the Orient. What is a passport? It's a document issued by your government which in effect tells other countries that you are a citizen of the United States. It is an extremely important document, and if you lose it en route, it will be necessary to go immediately to the nearest U.S. Embassy or Consulate and obtain another one (with some delay occasionally), so it is important to hang on to that passport. There is some indication that the present passports will be reduced in size in the near future.

At one time, passports were valid for three years, and renewable for two additional years. But now, all passports are issued for a period of five full years.

To obtain your first passport, it is necessary to apply in person —your travel agent cannot do it for you, nor can anyone else. However, if you wish, you can obtain the form in advance before going, fill it out at home, and thus save a little time. To obtain your first passport, you'll have to bring along a birth certificate (which is actually the best evidence), a baptismal certificate, or an expired passport. If these are not available, they will usually accept an affidavit as to your birth, signed by someone, preferably a relative, who has actual knowledge of your birth; the affidavit must be signed before a notary public. In order to use the affidavit as to your birth, you must also obtain a letter from your local Bureau of Vital Statistics certifying that your birth record cannot be located. You will also need two passport pictures, measuring about 2½–3 inches square, front view, with a white background, and you can even smile if you wish to. (While on the subject of passport photos, be sure to order at least a dozen, because you will sometimes need them to obtain visas, and sometimes even need them when you arrive in the particular country.) If you have a passport not more than 8 years old and produce it, the cost of a new passport is $10. If it's your first passport, the charge is a total of $14. Incidentally, bring cash to the passport office rather than a check. A husband and wife, and their children, too, may travel on one passport; sometimes husbands and wives obtain their own individual passports, but this doubles the fees for issuance, and also for visas. However, if it is anticipated that it will be necessary for the husband and wife to separate during the trip (as, for example, the husband may be called back home for business, and the wife wish to continue on the trip), two passports might be advisable. At the passport office, they'll tell you to expect your passport in the mail within ten days or two weeks; however, it rarely takes over a few days. In real emergencies, if you explain the problem, passports can sometimes be issued in a matter of hours.

If you live in or near one of the following cities, the document may be obtained at the local passport office of the State Department:

BOSTON: 148 Tremont Street
CHICAGO: U.S. Courthouse, 219 S. Clark Street
HONOLULU: 217 Federal Building
LOS ANGELES: 500 S. Figueroa Street
MIAMI: 320 S. E. First Street
NEW ORLEANS: 124 Camp Street, International Trade Mart
NEW YORK: 630 Fifth Avenue (50th Street)
SAN FRANCISCO: Airlines Terminal Bldg., 375 O'Farrell Street
SEATTLE: 1410 Fifth Avenue
WASHINGTON: Passport Office, Dept. of State, 22nd and E Streets, N.W.

If you don't happen to live close to one of the above cities, inquire about the nearest Federal (District) Court; if there is no Federal Court near you, call the clerk of the local county courthouse in the county seat, and he'll tell you where to apply. One court in the county seat of every single county of the United States is authorized to accept passport applications, if there is no other issuing authority.

When you've received the passport, sign your name and address in it at the proper place, and afterwards, don't ever write in it yourself, or otherwise change anything in it; it's against the law. When traveling, the passport belongs in your pocket or purse, never in a suitcase. There's no point in endangering the passport—your suitcases may get lost, but you won't. Also, inasmuch as the pass-

Asia Document and Regulation Checklist

Country	Entrance Papers	Medical Requirements	Currency	Tobacco
BURMA	Visa required (fee $4.85) valid for 7 days; 4 pictures required; must have proof of onward transportation, letter from travel agent stating applicant is bona fide tourist*	Smallpox and cholera shots required; yellow fever shot required if coming from infected area	No Burmese currency in or out; foreign currency must be carefully declared on arrival	200 cigarettes or 50 cigars
CHINA	Visa required (fee $6); duplicate forms, 2 pictures	Smallpox	No Chinese currency in or out; carefully retain currency exchange vouchers	3 cartons cigarettes
HONG KONG	No visa required on visit of up to 1 month	Smallpox; yellow fever and cholera if coming from infected area	No restrictions	200 cigarettes or 25 cigars
INDIA	No visa required for tourists for a 30-day stay; otherwise visa valid for 3 entries within 6 months of issue for 3-month stay; $2.15 fee, onward ticket	Smallpox; yellow fever and cholera if coming from infected area	No Indian currency may be taken in or brought out	200 cigarettes or 50 cigars
INDONESIA	Visa required (fee $3.50 plus $2.20 extra for joint passport) with 2 pictures; valid for 30-day visit; letter from travel agency that traveler is a bona fide tourist	Smallpox and cholera	No *rupiahs* may be taken in or brought out; when changing money, be sure appropriate entries are made to avoid difficulties when leaving	200 cigarettes or 50 cigars

Asia Document and Regulation Checklist (*Cont.*)

Country	Entrance Papers	Medical Requirements	Currency	Tobacco
JAPAN	Visa required (no fee), valid for 4-month visit	Smallpox; cholera if coming from infected area	No limit on *yen* if personally brought in; no yen may be taken out	200 cigarettes or 50 cigars
KOREA	Theoretically a visa is not required for a 5-day visit but better get one; no charge; valid for 15 days	Smallpox and cholera shots required	Any amount of currency may be brought in, but must be declared; all transactions must be entered on currency form	200 cigarettes or 50 cigars or 1 pound of tobacco
MACAO	Visa required ($5.85 fee), may be obtained readily in Hong Kong or at any Portuguese Consulate or on arrival in Macao	Smallpox and cholera	No restrictions	No restrictions for all practical purposes
NEPAL	Entry visa good for 15-day visit; fee $5, 2 forms, 1 photograph; also obtainable at the Kathmandu Airport, but it takes an hour	Smallpox	Subject to change, but Indian currency not permitted for foreign tourists	200 cigarettes or 50 cigars
SINGAPORE AND MALAYSIA	No visa required for 3-month visit	Smallpox	500 Malaysian dollars or the equivalent of £250 sterling in other currencies	200 cigarettes or 50 cigars
SRI LANKA (CEYLON)	No visa required for visits of up to 1 month	Smallpox; yellow fever and cholera if coming from infected areas	Only 40 English pounds and 75 Indian and Pakistani *rupees* may be brought in	200 cigarettes or 50 cigars

Asia Document and Regulation Checklist (*cont.*)

Country	Entrance Papers	Medical Requirements	Currency	Tobacco
TAIWAN	Visa required (no fee) valid for up to 30-day visit; proof of onward transportation required	Smallpox and cholera	No restrictions	200 cigarettes or 25 cigars
THAILAND	No visa required for stay of up to 15 days; may usually be extended locally for 15 more days, sometimes up to 60 days	Smallpox; yellow fever and cholera if coming from infected area	Only $500 U.S. in or out if in cash; no limit on traveler's checks	200 cigarettes or 50 cigars

NOTE: The information on this checklist is accurate at the present time, but rules change frequently; inquire of your travel agent or airline.
* At present, only group travel visas are being issued for travel in Burma.

port must be presented when entering or leaving foreign countries, it would be time-consuming to have to locate your luggage and take out the passport. There are passport cases for sale which aren't a bad investment, because they'll keep your passport clean, and are also suitable for holding tickets, small amounts of cash, etc.

VISAS   This is nothing more or less than the permission given to you in advance by a foreign government to enter a particular country. The permission takes the form of a stamp placed in your passport. In Europe, visas are now largely a thing of the past except for iron-curtain countries, but they are still required in almost all of the Asiatic countries. Sometimes they are quite simplified, and the visa is issued in a matter of minutes while you wait. Most of the countries, however, for reasons known only to themselves, require that your passport be left overnight and picked up the following day. Why this should be so, when the clerical work involved can be taken care of in five or ten minutes, is beyond our ken. (Special note: Foreign consulates are usually open weekdays, and closed on Saturday and Sunday. Even when open, many of them keep very short hours, often only 2–3 hours per day. Before visiting a consulate, phone ahead and ask when they are open. The consulates are also closed on U.S. holidays and their *own* national holidays, so be sure to check this point when leaving your visa application.) But, since we must obtain visas, let's consider the problems involved.

To obtain a visa for any country, you'll need your *passport* (in which the foreign government stamps the visa); a health certificate (more about this later) showing that you have been vaccinated against smallpox, and possibly one or two other diseases; an application form furnished by the government in question, completely filled out and signed by the applicant. Sometimes one (or more) pictures of the applicant (you) may be required. Sometimes there is a fee, and sometimes it is free. Always be sure that you are applying for a "Tourist Visa," otherwise you'll be bothered by customs officials when entering or leaving the particular country. Several countries require proof that you have onward transportation; if so, you must theoretically submit your airline or steamship ticket, but this is always a mistake. Instead, obtain from your transportation company (airline, steamship, or travel agent) a group of "To Whom It May Concern" letters stating that you are a bona fide tourist and that your tickets are being prepared but are not yet available. There is always a danger of your tickets being soiled, damaged, or lost, and the letter from the transportation company or travel agent will serve the same purpose.

When obtaining your tickets, ask if they have a set of visa application forms available. They usually do have, or in any event, should obtain them for you. Most travel agents will obtain the visas for you, although there is inevitably a service charge. If your tour will take you to a half-dozen or more countries, it may be necessary to allow a minimum of several weeks to round up all the necessary visas, particularly if you plan to obtain them yourself by mail.

Can you obtain them yourself and save the service charge? You certainly can, but it will cost money for the registered mail, and it will take time, assuming you live any distance from the various consulates. Of course, if you live in or near large cities like New York, Chicago, or San Francisco, and can make the rounds yourself (or coax a good friend into doing it for you), you can obtain a visa every day on the average by phoning for the forms, filling them out at home, and visiting one office every day, then picking it up the following day and taking it to the next consulate, and so forth. In a week or so, you'll have collected all of the necessary visas.

But what if you don't live in one of the big cities? As previously mentioned, your travel agent can take care of it for you, although at an added charge. If you're in a great hurry, American Express, 374 Park Avenue, in New York City, has a special visa department which will secure them for you, also for a fee, based upon the number required. If you wish to obtain them yourself and live out of town (meaning away from the various consulates), it may take several weeks, as mentioned previously. As soon as you know which countries you intend to visit, write to all of them *immediately,* enclosing a self-addressed envelope, and request their application forms. Send off your request for a visa (enclosing all of the required documents) to the first country by registered mail. Generally, the foreign consulate will have previously advised you of the amount of money (or stamps) required to return your passport and visa back to you, again by registered mail. (This will appear, as a rule, in the instruction sheet which accompanies the visa application form.) It would be convenient and helpful if you could request that the consulate send your passport (together with the next application form) along to the second country, but alas, this is seldom possible and not advised. It will have to go back and forth between you and the various consulates involved.

In an emergency, if you have not obtained all of the necessary visas, and are perhaps short only one or two, these missing visas could be obtained en route. Your time is so precious while on a trip that every effort should be made in advance to obtain all of the necessary visas, and not place this undue burden upon yourself when you should be enjoying your trip, and not be bothered with routine matters. But once again, if it's a matter of an emergency, the visas can be obtained en route.

Here is a list of the various sources of visas, if you wish to obtain them yourself. They are all consulates, except in Washington, where the visas are issued by the embassies. If there is no listing for Washington, that indicates the particular embassy does not issue visas.

HONG KONG
No visa required for less than a month's stay.

INDIA
No visa required for 30 days' stay. (Exception: If you're going to visit Sri Lanka or Nepal and return to India, a visa is usually needed.)

JAPAN
CHICAGO: 520 N. Michigan Avenue
HONOLULU: 1742 Nuuanu Avenue
LOS ANGELES: 510 W. Sixth Street
NEW ORLEANS: 411 International Trade Mart
NEW YORK: 235 East 42nd Street

PORTLAND: 632 American Bank Building
SAN FRANCISCO: 346 California Street
SEATTLE: 520 Union Pacific Building
WASHINGTON D.C.: 2514 Massachusetts Avenue N.W.

KOREA
LOS ANGELES: 5455 Wilshire Boulevard
NEW YORK: 9 East 80th Street
SAN FRANCISCO: 3500 Clay Street
WASHINGTON, D.C.: 2322 Massachusetts Avenue

MACAO
(Portuguese Consulates)
BOSTON: 31 Commonwealth Avenue
HOUSTON: 2202 Nance Street
LOS ANGELES: 724 S. Spring Street
NEW ORLEANS: 808 Queen & Crescent Building
NEW YORK: 630 Fifth Avenue
PHILADELPHIA: 521 Bourse Building
SAN FRANCISCO: 3298 Washington Street
WASHINGTON, D.C.: 2125 Kalorama Road N.W.

MALAYSIA
No visa required for 3 months' visit.

SRI LANKA
No visa required for visit of up to 1 month.

TAIWAN
CHICAGO: 205 West Wacker Drive
HONOLULU: 1634 Makiki
HOUSTON: 4808 Austin Street
LOS ANGELES: 448 South Hill Street
NEW YORK: 1250 Sixth Avenue
SAN FRANCISCO: 551 Montgomery Street
SEATTLE: 607 Third Avenue
WASHINGTON, D.C.: 2311 Massachusetts Avenue N.W.

THAILAND
No visa required for a 15-day visit; can usually be extended to 60 days, if you wish, while in Thailand.

POINTER:
   The term "jet lag" is used to describe the out-of-phase feeling experienced by travelers who fly swiftly in jet planes from their hometown to the Orient where the difference in time may be anywhere from 8 to 12 hours. That means, in effect, that when it's lunchtime in Tokyo (for example), you would ordinarily be asleep if you were home. And so it goes, with every part of the day having an upside-down, topsy-turvy relationship to hours at home.
   There are certain things that can be done to alleviate this situation and make the adjustment easier. If you arrive in the Orient in the morning, check into your hotel, perhaps have a little breakfast if you're hungry, get undressed, put a "Do Not Disturb" sign on your door, and go to sleep for a few hours. (Don't sleep for 7 or 8 hours. You'll only compound the problem.) Get up, have a bath, dress, and go out. It's lunchtime, so have something to eat in order to start getting back on schedule.
   In the evening, you may find yourself getting sleepy; fight off that feeling. Don't give in, or you're lost. If you go to sleep at 8 or 9 P.M., you'll awaken at 3 or 4 A.M. You'll be completely wide-awake, and it will be impossible to fall asleep again. For the next few days, if you're unbearably sleepy, take a nap for an hour or so (but not too long!) at about 5 in the afternoon, but then get dressed and go out; don't stay in your hotel. It takes about a week to adjust to large time differences, so follow the above suggestions for that length of time.

🧳 What To Take?

   I'm talking about clothing, of course. Naturally, the method of travel selected is important, and steamship passengers can practically disregard the problem of baggage weight because it is of little concern to them; however, there is a practical limit—even for steamship passengers—because an excessive number of suitcases can be a tiresome problem when making transfers ashore. But the vast, in fact overwhelming, majority of travelers to the Orient go by air, and the clothing selection becomes important because of its weight.
   Almost everyone takes too much clothing along, particularly first-time travelers. Unless you plan to stay at one particular place —such as a resort hotel—for a week or more (where repetitions

might prove tiresome), extensive changes of clothing are quite un-necessary because you'll be on the move every few days and meeting new people. You'll dress quite casually during the day because most of Asia is not very formal. But I should explain what I mean by "casually." Women should avoid very large, loud, splashy prints; small designs are better and they are not remembered so much by the people you encounter. No one can ever forget a red dress with enormous poinsettias splattered across it. By the same token, casual dress for men means plain (not Hawaiian-type) sport shirts during the day, worn with slacks, in places where this sort of apparel is customary—Bangkok, Singapore, and other warm weather spots. Even during the day, men should wear jackets in Tokyo, because that is the local custom. However, and this is most important, even in warm weather places, in the evening, a sport shirt is not accept-able in the majority of better hotels and restaurants, and that applies to Hong Kong, Singapore, New Delhi, and so forth, where daytime wear can be casual. It behooves all of us to dress in accordance with local custom; don't forget that every American tourist is a walking ambassador, and that foreigners judge us by our behavior—and appearance.

More important than almost anything else is the need for perfect-fitting shoes, absolutely the most comfortable that you can find. Don't bring along new, untried shoes, because sightseeing can quickly become tiresome and tedious if your feet hurt. (That is probably the understatement of the year.) A good deal of sightseeing consists of walking, and of course shopping involves a good deal of standing on one's feet.

In Japan, India, Burma, etc., you'll be asked to remove your shoes when entering certain temples; inasmuch as the floors are not neces-sarily free from miscellaneous objects like cigarette ends and the like, it is always a good idea to take along lightweight cloth slippers (they cannot be made of an animal hide—that is why you're asked to remove your shoes), or sandals of straw or plastic; in the alterna-tive, take along wool socks or something on that order. Airline slippers are perfect for this purpose. You don't need too many pairs of shoes (especially men), and don't forget that you're wearing one pair when you leave on your trip, in addition to those in your suitcase. Don't forget that in hot weather countries, your feet tend to swell, and therefore shoes that seem comfortable at home may be too tight in Singapore, for example. Slightly loose shoes are best in tropical countries. Shoes are the bane of a male air traveler's life, because they weigh about 4 pounds, and 2 pair weigh 8 pounds.

Wash-and-wear, drip-dry, miracle fibers, and the like? Of course, and by all means, because these permit you to travel with fewer blouses, shirts, socks, and underwear. It just so happens, however, that laundry services in Asia are very quick, very good, and often quite reasonable. Thus, although I urge you to take the wash-and-wear type of clothing, you'll probably find that it's often just as easy to send them to the laundry. While I think of it, be careful about doing any wash-and-wear laundry the night before your departure from any point—there's always the danger that the clothes will not be fully dry in the morning. Better plan on doing your wash-and-wear laundry when you *arrive* at a new destination. Although the new miracle fabrics are very helpful, they are not necessarily resistant to creasing and crushing, and I have found that lightweight men's suits made partly of wool (combined with dacron) often retain their appearance better than when made with 100% dacron. The same logic holds true for women's dresses. Silk crepes, for example, as well as many cottons, hold their shape better than when made exclusively from the new fabrics. Cottons are cooler in hot climates.

Let's get into particularities, as opposed to generalities, beginning with:

FOR WOMEN To simplify your wardrobe, select colors that can be worn with one particular color accessory. In this way, your clothing will be coordinated and you'll be able to wear all your shoes with all your dresses, all your blouses with all your suits, etc.

Where are you going? If every country on your trip has similar weather conditions, planning should not be too difficult. If you're ranging from warm to cool climates, however, a little more thought and planning will be required. The basic items you'll need on a month's vacation are set forth below; we suggest that wherever possible they should be of the wash-and-dry variety:

    2 nightgowns or pajamas
    3 bras
    3 girdles or panties
6–12 pair hose or pantyhose
    1 pair lightweight, comfortable walking shoes, and 1 pair sandals
    1 pair dressy shoes
    1 dressy handbag (this presumes you will be carrying the very large carry-all traveling bag so popular today)
    2 dressy dresses and 1 long informal dress
    3 daytime dresses
    1 suit or pants suit (you'll probably be traveling in another one)

2–3 blouses
 1 sweater
 1 scarf
 1 lightweight coat (tweed or all-weather type which you'll carry with you)
 1 folding nylon or plastic raincoat
12 handkerchiefs
 1 robe
 1 pair bedroom slippers (preferably the lightweight traveling type)
   Shower or bathing cap
   Bathing suit (if required)
   Jewelry
   Cosmetics, medicine and necessary toilet articles (Don't take too much, they're available everywhere.)
   Sunglasses
   Sewing kit

Obviously, a size 8 suit weighs less than a size 20, but in general, and just to give you an idea, an average medium-weight suit weighs about 2½ pounds; most dresses weigh under a pound or so, less when of silk, more when of wool; shoes are very variable, with dressy shoes running about a pound, whereas some larger size walking shoes might weigh 2 pounds. About the lightweight coat mentioned above; even in countries like Japan during what should be warm weather months, an occasional cold day will make you glad you brought a coat along. But taking along a coat during summertime trips is up to you—do you get chilly quickly? Incidentally, in very warm weather, cotton lingerie is far more comfortable than dacron, nylon, or silk.

POINTER:
  My personal tip, for which you'll thank me (after the trip) is to take along jacket dresses; when hot, omit the jacket, when the weather is chancy, wear the jacket. Even during periods of hot weather, the jacket will protect you from too much hot sun, and also is helpful in air-conditioned restaurants because they really believe in turning it down low in most of Asia so you'll *know* it's air-conditioned.

FOR MEN Of course, when and where you're going are the controlling factors.

Let's consider these consecutively, beginning with the season of the year. If you're traveling during the summer months, obviously very little will be required in the way of warm clothing. Even so, occasional cool days come along during what should normally be the hot weather season. In the spring or fall months, allowance must be made for the changeability of weather and the likelihood that some part of your trip will be warm, while another portion will be cool.

The next question under consideration is where you're going. If your trip involves only several large cities, you'll have to wear comparatively conservative clothing with little emphasis upon sportswear. Then, too, if you're going to a resort and plan to spend several weeks at one hotel, you'll need more changes than if you're going to spend only a few days each at numerous stops (when you'll be able to wear the same clothes over and over again). It is essential that you build your entire wardrobe around one color scheme. After talking about this with many travelers, it seems clear that the best color is blue, because it harmonizes with just about everything except brown. In the evening, a blue suit will look dressy, whereas a brown one will not. If your sport jacket and slacks match or harmonize with each other, that means you'll get full usage out of everything you take along. If, on the other hand, you bring a jacket that can only be worn with a particular pair of slacks, its usefulness will be limited. The following packing list is basic, and even though you may want to make some variations for individual tastes, you'll find it useful as a guide:

1 dark suit, preferably blue (or 2 suits, if you wish)
2 pair slacks, blue or gray or charcoal
1 lightweight sport jacket, to match slacks (and a heavier jacket for cooler climates)
1 lightweight topcoat or raincoat
5 shirts (3 if synthetic)
3 sport shirts (preferably synthetic)
4 ties
4 sets underwear
8 handkerchiefs
6 pair socks
1 pair shoes
1 sweater
2 pair pajamas
1 lightweight robe
1 pair slippers (preferably the lightweight traveling type)

1 pair swimming trunks (if you'll have any need for them)
  Shaving kit or electric razor (preferably international model)
  Miscellaneous items—sunglasses, medicine, etc.

How to Pack   Collect some tissue paper before you begin and stuff the sleeves of your suit and sport jacket with crumpled tissue. Begin with trousers, laying them flat, folded in two (with tissue paper between), across the bottom of the suitcase, then follow with the jackets, folded inside out and then in half. Place the shirts, underwear, and lighter articles on top.

Visit the 5-and- 10-cents store and buy several large plastic bags (the transparent ones, like cellophane); pack shoes in one of these to keep them from soiling your other clothing. (Take along a few extra ones for wet bathing suits, and laundry that didn't competely dry, etc.) Your shirts might well be packed in another of these plastic bags, because that will minimize wrinkling. Another advisable gadget is a plastic container, with a zipper or other closing device, large enough to hold your shaving gear, toothbrush, toothpaste, etc.; in this way, everything you need in the bathroom will be instantly ready. If your suitcase isn't completely full, add some crumpled tissue paper to take up the extra space, otherwise everything will be jumbled about when you arrive. Pack all your socks in one plastic bag, all your handkerchiefs in another, all your underwear in a third. Keep one large plastic bag always available for unwashed laundry. When you arrive, unpacking will involve only a few minutes.

Miscellaneous Items

Give some thought to taking along some of the following items which will brighten your trip. A transistor portable *radio* weighs only a few ounces but is worth having with you; be sure to take a few extra batteries. Of course, if you don't have one, they're plentiful in Japan and Hong Kong. Don't worry about film, it's available almost everywhere, although it will be expensive in Indonesia.

If you like American *liquor,* such as rye or bourbon, better bring a bottle or two because while scotch whisky is obtainable almost everywhere, rye and bourbon are often difficult to locate. Your favorite brand of *cigarettes* is worth taking because some Asiatic brands are unpalatable to Americans. A portable *travel clock* is often worth its weight in gold, because telephone operators have been known to forget early morning calls. An international-model travel *iron* with dial settings for 220 current will help you freshen up creased articles or touch up nylon or dacron blouses and shirts;

unfortunately these are fairly heavy (about three pounds) and not worth the excess baggage charge if you've exceeded the limit. (However, you could slip one in your coat pocket.) *Sunglasses* and an extra pair of your prescription glasses (if you wear spectacles) are essential. Be sure to bring along a large cake of *soap* in a plastic container; the hotels all supply soap, but it always comes in handy to have a large cake available. Liquid soap or soap flakes in individual paper envelopes are marvelous for doing your dacron shirts or blouses and underwear. Buy two folding *plastic hangers,* because wooden or wire hangers will stain your freshly washed shirts or blouses.

One of the most interesting extra items you can take along is a *Polaroid camera.* The new models weigh comparatively little and deliver a finished color photo in a minute; the impression made upon most people in the Orient, who have never seen this miracle, is very rewarding. Often, a picture of a driver or guide, or other person who has been helpful to you, can be a nice gesture on your part. On many occasions, I have found that an instant picture of this sort can be a remarkable ice-breaker and start up an entire new relationship with strange people.

Medical kits. In the vast, vast majority of cases, you won't get sick, but you might feel more comfortable if you have an accustomed prescription made up and take it along with you. Almost anything you use in the ordinary medical line is easily obtained and almost always far cheaper in Asiatic countries. Vitamin pills, toothpaste, drugs, and cosmetics are usually about one-third less than at home, so why pay excess weight charges when you can buy them for less in Asia? One good example is after-shaving lotion, weighing three-quarters of a pound, which could be duplicated or even bettered in many places and at moderate cost.

Most travelers to Asia are subject to only one disorder, and that is caused by changes in water content. Be careful about drinking tap water except where specifically approved (as in Japan). If there is any sense of discomfort, of impending or actual diarrhea, the best product to have on hand is a tiny pill called Lomotil. It generally stops the sensations and discomfort, and if one pill doesn't work, two almost always will. Be sure to get a prescription from your doctor and take the pills with you; you never know when you may need them. One of the mycins in capsule or tablet form is an excellent precautionary item, but your doctor will have to write a prescription for this. A few Band-Aids are handy in case of nicked fingers; a thermometer is worthwhile too.

⏱ Telling Time and the International Date Line

All of us are acquainted, to a greater or lesser degree, with the question of time around the world. For example, we realize that when it is 12 noon along the eastern seaboard of the U.S., it is 3 hours earlier, or 9 A.M., along the western coast.

However, traversing the Pacific involves something far more complex—the crossing of the International Date Line. Depending on the direction in which the line is crossed, it will become a day earlier or a day later. Confusing? You bet it is. So let's go through the whole matter slowly, from the beginning, and see if it can't be unraveled and made less confusing.

We must start with the fundamentals. To state the obvious, the world is round, like an orange for example, as Columbus once proved. During the three centuries that followed this momentous discovery, communities around the world began to fix their own local time as they wished, or as their governments wished, based upon rough calculations as to the position of the sun. At the beginning of the 19th century, it became apparent that more complex communication systems and growing international commerce required a change from the confusing situation caused by letting each locality fix time to suit itself. A conference was held in Washington, D.C., in 1884 and the governments of most nations attended, and they talked of how to determine time around the world.

But how to divide up the world into time zones? The scientists pointed out that there were 360 degrees in a circle and 24 hours in a day, and therefore, dividing 24 into 360 degrees gave a result of 15 degrees. It was clear that if the time zones were fixed at 15 degrees (written 15°) of longitude all around the earth, every part of the world could have the correct time, based on its position on the globe. (Longitude is an imaginary line drawn on the earth's surface from the North to the South Pole.) Inasmuch as the world is approximately 24,000 miles in circumference around the equator, each time zone would therefore measure about 1,000 miles. (Bear in mind, however, that as one goes farther north or south from the equator, the circumference is lessened, because the equator is the earth's widest part. Thus, at the distance of the United States from the equator, for example, the circumference around the world is about 17,000 miles, making each time zone equivalent to only about 700 miles in width.)

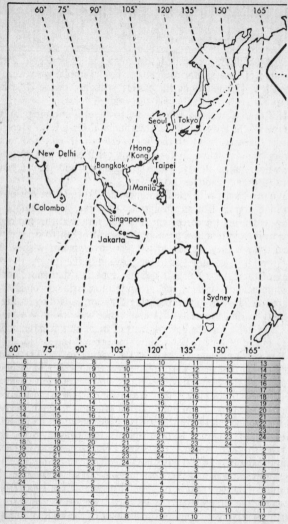

Telling Time *Dark Area* indicates the day before. For example, when it is 12 noon in Tokyo on Saturday, it is 10 P.M. in New York on Friday.

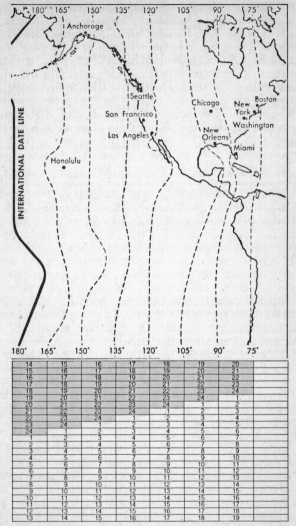

14	15	16	17	18	19	20	
15	16	17	18	19	20	21	
16	17	18	19	20	21	22	
17	18	19	20	21	22	23	
18	19	20	21	22	23	24	
19	20	21	22	23	24	1	
20	21	22	23	24	1	2	
21	22	23	24	1	2	3	
22	23	24	1	2	3	4	
23	24	1	2	3	4	5	
24	1	2	3	4	5	6	
1	2	3	4	5	6	7	
2	3	4	5	6	7	8	
3	4	5	6	7	8	9	
4	5	6	7	8	9	10	
5	6	7	8	9	10	11	
6	7	8	9	10	11	12	
7	8	9	10	11	12	13	
8	9	10	11	12	13	14	
9	10	11	12	13	14	15	
10	11	12	13	14	15	16	
11	12	13	14	15	16	17	
12	13	14	15	16	17	18	
13	14	15	16	17	18	19	

Light Area indicates the day following. For example, when it is 12 noon in Los Angeles on Wednesday, it is 4 A.M. in Hong Kong on Thursday.

Much of the work with regard to making the calculation of time into an exact science had taken place at a British observatory located in Greenwich, England. It was therefore decided that an imaginary line drawn from the North Pole to the South Pole and cutting through Greenwich would be the starting point for all measurements, that line being fixed as 0° longitude. The half of the world to the west of this line is called the Western Hemisphere; the half of the world to the east is called the Eastern Hemisphere.

They set up twelve time zones to the west, designated as *minus zones;* for example, New York is minus 5, because it is five time zones to the west of Greenwich, England, the starting point. San Francisco, being eight time zones to the west, is designated as minus 8. The scientists also set up twelve time zones to the east of Greenwich, designated as *plus zones.* Paris, being one hour ahead of Greenwich, was designated as plus 1, Istanbul as plus 3, and so forth. Thus, by a simple calculation, it became possible to learn the difference in time between any two parts on the globe. The time differential between San Francisco and Istanbul can readily be determined as eleven hours (minus 8 and plus 3).

It now became necessary to select some point on the earth's surface to indicate the point at which one day ended and another began. Obviously it had to be at 180° of longitude, precisely on the other side of the world from Greenwich, which is situated at 0°. It is at this 180th parallel that Monday, for example, would become Tuesday, Tuesday would change to Wednesday, and so forth. The International Date Line is an imaginary line running more or less along the line of the 180th parallel of longitude. It does not follow it exactly and makes several sharp turns. The reason for the variations is so that the date line does not cross any land areas, otherwise there would be considerable confusion to the people residing there. Thus, if one looks at the map, the date line has been positioned between Alaska and Siberia, so that it does not cross any land area, having been diverted over water. All the way from the North Pole to the South Pole, inhabited land areas have been bypassed.

The date line, as previously mentioned, is the point at which a new day begins. At precisely one second after midnight, a new day commences. For example, when Tuesday begins in the time zone immediately west of the date line, it is still Monday in the time zone to the east of the date line. There are always two different days of the week around the world, except for one fleeting second of the day. That exception is the exact second, precisely at midnight, when it is the same day of the week all around the globe. One second later, it is a day later in the time zone west of the date line.

Anyone going from the U.S. to Asia must cross the date line, and by so doing theoretically "loses" a day. In turn, anyone going from Asia to the U.S., has two successive same days of the week and theoretically "gains" a day. Let's put this to a practical application and see how the date line works. Before me is a Pan American time-table. It shows that there is service from Honolulu to Tokyo, the flight leaving Honolulu at 1 P.M. on Wednesday. It makes the flight in about eight hours actual flying time arriving at 4 P.M. (The difference of five hours can be calculated readily because Honolulu is in the minus 10 time zone, and Japan is in the plus 9 time zone. From minus 10 to 12 is two, and from plus 9 to 12 is three.) But although the flight started at 1 P.M. on Wednesday and lasted eight hours, when the passenger alights in Tokyo it is Thursday, because the plane has passed the International Date Line. The reverse in time occurs when going from Tokyo to Honolulu. If a flight leaves Tokyo on Wednesday at say 12 noon and flies to San Francisco, arriving at 8 A.M., it will still be Wednesday, the passengers having had two Wednesdays in succession.

One other important question frequently comes to mind—a complete day may apparently disappear during a flight. For example, if a flight leaves California on Thursday evening and reaches Japan a half-day later, but on Saturday morning, what has happened to Friday? This question seems confusing on first thought but is really not too difficult to understand. A few hours after leaving California, the clock approaches midnight; then, one second after midnight, it becomes Friday. However, several hours later, you cross the International Date Line, and it becomes one day later than Friday, or Saturday. Friday has not disappeared, it is merely that it only lasted a few hours, perhaps while you were sleeping. On flights going westward which involve travel time extending through midnight, a day will apparently be "lost." But don't worry, you'll get it back.

You may recall the plot of Jules Verne's *Around the World in Eighty Days*, which involves a bet about whether Phineas Fogg could make the journey around the world in the specified time of the title. Our hero returned to London a day late (he thought) but actually in time to win his bet—he had overlooked the fact of crossing the International Date Line, and had "gained" a day.

↑ Weather

It would be wonderful, wouldn't it, if every day were bright and sunny with never a trace of rain during a trip? It would be, but don't count on it, because the one thing you can be sure of is that weather is always changeable. Even the stock market is more reliable, under certain circumstances, than the weather.

In all seriousness, no one enjoys cloudy days or rain, but a certain amount of preparation and advance planning can help to minimize the probability of bad weather. There are various guideposts which will be of great assistance in selecting the time of year of a proposed trip with emphasis upon being in those places where the weather is usually at its best. I have no hesitation in saying, however, that I would much rather be in Tokyo (for example) on a rainy day, than not be there at all. Nevertheless, if by advancing or delaying a trip it would be possible to arrive in a particular place during a season which usually has good weather, anyone would be well advised to do so. Of course, it isn't always possible to start a trip earlier or delay it, because of children at school, business commitments, scheduled vacation periods, and the like. But a little thought can sometimes help. Let us suppose a planned circuit of the Orient—say Japan, Hong Kong, Thailand and Singapore. Suppose further that a perusal of the weather section of this book indicates that a certain month is very rainy in Japan, whereas the weather will be improved during the following month. There is no necessity to follow the original schedule by beginning in Japan and ending up in Sri Lanka; it may be perfectly possible to reverse the trip, commencing in Sri Lanka and ending up in Japan. This is only an example, and the thoughtful traveler will spend a little time in trying to work out a schedule which will bring him to each country under better than average conditions with regard to weather.

Let me also add a few personal observations of my own. If you're planning an extensive trip of the Orient, visiting about ten countries, and covering vast areas, don't worry too much about weather, cross your fingers and just go, have a marvelous time, and the devil with the weather. The reason: it is almost impossible to cover a large area of the Orient in a continuous trip and expect to have good weather the entire time. For example, if you visit Japan during April when the weather is usually quite good, you'll probably hit the rainy season in Hong Kong and the hot season in Bangkok. So, you naturally say, why not go to Hong Kong and Bangkok during their good seasons? If you visit them during their periods of good weather —December, January, or February—then Japan has cold, wintry weather which you won't particularly enjoy. Many people, however, like to visit just one country and do a complete and thorough sightseeing job on the entire country, spending a month or so in the process. If this is the case, by all means try to go during the best-weather season. For example, March in Japan is usually somewhat raw and damp, whereas April is far better; anyone planning to spend a substantial period of time in Japan would be well advised to delay the trip for a few weeks. Again, and to conclude, if you're going to visit a dozen countries in Asia, just go, because the weather cannot be perfect in all of them.

UNDERSTANDING WEATHER STRIPS Throughout this book, there are weather strips for each country which set forth the average high and the average low temperatures. This is followed by the amount of rainfall usually experienced during the particular month on the average; then the number of days with rainfall exceeding a specified amount. Now obviously these represent composite averages, and as such, are just precisely that—*averages* covering a long period of time. (These figures have been reproduced by permission of the Controller of Her Britannic Majesty's Stationery Office from their *Tables of Temperature, Relative Humidity and Precipitation for the World.*) For most of us, statistics of this sort are almost completely meaningless. But, by comparing them to a similar set of figures for our own region, we gain what amounts to an overall *impression* of what the weather will be like. For example, let us assume that you want to know what the weather will be like in New Delhi, India, during your visit there; by noting the figures furnished for that city, and by matching them up as best you can with those of your home city, you will have a good general (although admit-

Jan.	Feb.	Mar.	Apr.	May	June	July	Aug.	Sept.	Oct.	Nov.	Dec.
EAST											
Boston											
36°	37°	43°	54°	66°	75°	80°	78°	71°	62°	49°	40°
20°	21°	28°	38°	49°	58°	63°	62°	55°	46°	35°	25°
3.6	3.3	3.8	3.5	3.1	3.2	3.3	3.6	3.2	3.3	3.6	3.4
12	10	12	11	11	10	10	10	9	9	10	11
New York											
37°	38°	45°	57°	68°	77°	82°	80°	79°	69°	51°	41°
24°	24°	30°	42°	53°	60°	66°	66°	60°	49°	37°	29°
3.7	3.8	3.6	3.2	3.2	3.3	4.2	4.3	3.4	3.5	3.0	3.6
12	10	12	11	11	10	12	10	9	9	9	10
Washington, D.C.											
42°	44°	53°	64°	75°	83°	87°	84°	78°	67°	55°	45°
27°	28°	35°	44°	54°	63°	68°	66°	59°	48°	38°	29°
3.4	3.0	3.6	3.3	3.7	3.9	4.4	4.3	3.7	2.9	2.6	3.1
11	10	12	11	12	11	11	11	8	8	9	10

	Jan.	Feb.	Mar.	Apr.	May	June	July	Aug.	Sept.	Oct.	Nov.	Dec.

SOUTH

Atlanta

Jan.	Feb.	Mar.	Apr.	May	June	July	Aug.	Sept.	Oct.	Nov.	Dec.
51°	54°	62°	71°	79°	86°	87°	86°	82°	72°	61°	52°
35°	37°	43°	51°	60°	67°	70°	69°	64°	54°	43°	37°
4.9	4.8	5.5	3.7	3.6	3.7	4.7	4.3	3.2	2.6	3.1	4.5
12	11	11	10	10	11	13	12	8	7	8	11

Charleston

Jan.	Feb.	Mar.	Apr.	May	June	July	Aug.	Sept.	Oct.	Nov.	Dec.
58°	59°	66°	73°	80°	86°	88°	87°	83°	75°	66°	59°
43°	44°	50°	57°	66°	73°	75°	75°	71°	61°	51°	44°
2.9	3.3	3.4	2.8	3.2	4.7	7.3	6.6	5.1	3.2	2.3	2.8
10	9	9	8	8	11	13	13	10	6	7	9

Miami

Jan.	Feb.	Mar.	Apr.	May	June	July	Aug.	Sept.	Oct.	Nov.	Dec.
74°	75°	78°	80°	84°	86°	88°	88°	87°	83°	78°	76°
61°	61°	64°	67°	71°	74°	76°	76°	75°	72°	66°	62°
2.8	2.1	2.5	3.2	6.8	7.0	6.1	6.3	8.0	9.2	2.8	2.0
9	6	7	7	12	13	15	15	18	16	10	7

New Orleans

Jan.	Feb.	Mar.	Apr.	May	June	July	Aug.	Sept.	Oct.	Nov.	Dec.
62°	65°	71°	77°	83°	88°	90°	90°	86°	79°	70°	64°
47°	50°	55°	61°	68°	74°	76°	76°	73°	64°	55°	48°
4.6	4.2	4.7	4.8	4.5	5.5	6.6	5.8	4.8	3.5	3.8	4.6
10	12	9	7	8	13	15	14	10	7	7	10

CENTRAL

Chicago

Jan.	Feb.	Mar.	Apr.	May	June	July	Aug.	Sept.	Oct.	Nov.	Dec.
32°	34°	43°	55°	65°	75°	81°	79°	73°	61°	47°	36°
18°	20°	29°	40°	50°	60°	66°	65°	58°	47°	34°	23°
2.0	2.0	2.6	2.8	3.4	3.5	3.3	3.2	3.1	2.6	2.4	2.0
11	10	12	11	12	11	9	9	9	9	10	11

Columbus

Jan.	Feb.	Mar.	Apr.	May	June	July	Aug.	Sept.	Oct.	Nov.	Dec.
37°	39°	49°	61°	72°	81°	85°	83°	77°	65°	50°	39°
22°	23°	32°	42°	52°	61°	65°	63°	57°	46°	35°	26°
3.1	2.7	3.4	2.9	3.5	3.4	3.6	3.2	2.5	2.5	2.8	2.7
14	12	14	12	12	12	11	10	9	9	11	13

Dallas

Jan.	Feb.	Mar.	Apr.	May	June	July	Aug.	Sept.	Oct.	Nov.	Dec.
55°	60°	67°	75°	82°	90°	94°	94°	88°	78°	66°	57°
36°	40°	46°	55°	63°	71°	75°	74°	68°	57°	47°	38°
2.5	2.4	3.3	4.2	4.5	3.8	2.8	3.0	2.7	2.8	2.7	2.5
9	7	7	9	9	7	5	6	6	7	6	7

Detroit

Jan.	Feb.	Mar.	Apr.	May	June	July	Aug.	Sept.	Oct.	Nov.	Dec.
31°	32°	42°	55°	67°	77°	82°	80°	73°	60°	46°	35°
19°	18°	27°	37°	48°	58°	63°	62°	55°	44°	33°	24°
2.1	2.1	2.5	2.5	3.3	3.6	3.3	2.7	2.8	2.4	2.4	2.3
13	12	13	11	13	11	9	9	10	10	12	14

Minneapolis

Jan.	Feb.	Mar.	Apr.	May	June	July	Aug.	Sept.	Oct.	Nov.	Dec.
22°	25°	38°	56°	68°	77°	83°	80°	72°	59°	40°	27°
6°	8°	22°	36°	48°	58°	63°	61°	52°	41°	26°	12°
1.0	1.0	1.6	2.3	3.4	4.4	3.4	3.4	3.4	2.1	1.4	1.2
8	7	8	10	12	12	9	9	9	9	7	8

	Jan.	Feb.	Mar.	Apr.	May	June	July	Aug.	Sept.	Oct.	Nov.	Dec.

Omaha

Jan.	Feb.	Mar.	Apr.	May	June	July	Aug.	Sept.	Oct.	Nov.	Dec.
30°	35°	47°	61°	72°	81°	86°	84°	76°	64°	48°	35°
13°	17°	28°	42°	53°	62°	67°	65°	57°	45°	30°	19°
0.7	0.9	1.3	2.7	3.7	4.6	4.0	3.4	3.3	2.3	1.2	0.9
7	6	7	10	12	11	9	9	9	7	5	7

Pittsburgh

Jan.	Feb.	Mar.	Apr.	May	June	July	Aug.	Sept.	Oct.	Nov.	Dec.
38°	39°	49°	61°	72°	80°	84°	82°	76°	64°	51°	41°
24°	23°	31°	41°	52°	60°	64°	63°	57°	46°	36°	27°
3.0	2.6	3.0	3.0	3.1	3.7	4.2	3.2	2.5	2.6	2.3	2.8
16	14	15	13	13	12	12	10	9	10	12	14

St. Louis

Jan.	Feb.	Mar.	Apr.	May	June	July	Aug.	Sept.	Oct.	Nov.	Dec.
40°	43°	54°	65°	75°	84°	88°	87°	80°	68°	54°	43°
24°	26°	36°	47°	57°	66°	71°	69°	62°	50°	38°	28°
2.3	2.5	3.5	3.8	4.5	4.5	3.5	3.4	3.2	2.9	2.8	2.5
9	9	11	11	11	11	9	8	8	8	8	9

WEST

Des Moines

Jan.	Feb.	Mar.	Apr.	May	June	July	Aug.	Sept.	Oct.	Nov.	Dec.
30°	33°	46°	61°	71°	80°	86°	84°	76°	64°	48°	34°
12°	15°	27°	40°	51°	61°	65°	63°	55°	43°	30°	18°
1.1	1.1	1.8	2.9	4.4	4.8	3.4	3.6	3.6	2.5	1.5	1.2
8	8	9	10	12	11	9	9	9	8	7	8

Los Angeles

Jan.	Feb.	Mar.	Apr.	May	June	July	Aug.	Sept.	Oct.	Nov.	Dec.
65°	66°	67°	70°	72°	76°	81°	82°	81°	76°	73°	67°
46°	47°	48°	50°	53°	56°	60°	60°	58°	54°	50°	47°
3.1	3.0	2.8	1.0	0.4	0.1	0.1	0.1	0.2	0.6	1.2	2.6
6	6	6	4	2	1	1	1	1	2	3	6

Phoenix

Jan.	Feb.	Mar.	Apr.	May	June	July	Aug.	Sept.	Oct.	Nov.	Dec.
65°	69°	75°	82°	91°	101°	104°	101°	97°	86°	75°	66°
39°	43°	47°	53°	60°	69°	77°	76°	69°	56°	45°	40°
0.8	0.8	0.7	0.4	0.1	0.1	1.0	1.0	0.7	0.4	0.6	0.9
4	4	4	2	1	1	5	6	3	2	3	4

Salt Lake City

Jan.	Feb.	Mar.	Apr.	May	June	July	Aug.	Sept.	Oct.	Nov.	Dec.
35°	41°	51°	62°	73°	82°	92°	90°	79°	66°	49°	40°
17°	24°	31°	38°	45°	52°	61°	60°	49°	40°	28°	22°
1.3	1.5	2.0	2.0	2.0	0.8	0.6	0.8	1.0	1.5	1.4	1.4
10	9	10	9	8	5	4	6	5	7	7	10

San Francisco

Jan.	Feb.	Mar.	Apr.	May	June	July	Aug.	Sept.	Oct.	Nov.	Dec.
55°	59°	61°	62°	63°	66°	65°	65°	69°	68°	63°	57°
45°	47°	48°	49°	51°	52°	53°	53°	55°	54°	51°	47°
4.7	3.8	3.1	1.5	0.7	0.1	0.1	0.1	0.3	1.0	2.5	4.4
11	11	10	6	4	2	1	1	2	4	7	10

Seattle

Jan.	Feb.	Mar.	Apr.	May	June	July	Aug.	Sept.	Oct.	Nov.	Dec.
45°	48°	52°	58°	64°	69°	72°	73°	67°	59°	51°	47°
36°	37°	39°	43°	47°	52°	54°	55°	52°	47°	41°	38°
4.8	3.7	3.1	2.3	1.8	1.4	0.6	0.7	1.7	2.9	4.8	5.6
18	16	16	13	12	9	4	5	8	13	17	19

tedly rough) idea of what the weather will be like. Of course, there are differences in humidity, and the rain may take a somewhat different form, for example, in Colombo, Sri Lanka, than it does in Topeka, Kansas. During certain times of the year, it rains very heavily for an hour each day in Ceylon, but the remainder of the day may well be bright and clear. On the other hand, it may rain all day long, steadily but rather lightly, in Topeka. In Colombo, the tourist might be able (during the clear period of the day) to go swimming or sightseeing in bright sunshine even on a so-called rainy day, whereas that would not be the situation in Topeka.

You may find that June in New Orleans may be quite a bit like March in Singapore (in temperature) by comparing the respective weather strips. Every resident of New Orleans has a fairly good general idea of what June is like in his home town, and that general impression would probably be more helpful than a page of description about Singapore's weather conditions. Cities located quite close to the equator have similar temperatures the year around—Singapore, for example.

In the figures which follow, the first line is the average high temperature, then the average low temperature, the amount of rain each month, and lastly, the number of days with .04 inches of rainfall.

💲 Money

There can be no doubt that *traveler's checks* are the best way to carry funds on a trip. Some people bring letters of credit issued by their banks, but the red tape involved in unsnarling $100 from a bank in Asia will cause you $200's worth of trouble, aggravation, and time. Some rugged individualists like to carry all cash, but this can hardly be recommended, although a moderate amount of cash should be carried (more about this later).

All in all, traveler's checks are still your best bet. The cost is not great, and in case of loss, the entire amount will be refunded. Be sure to obtain a proper breakdown of traveler's checks, because if you take only $10 traveler's checks, they will be tiresome to cash; and at the other extreme, if you carry all $100 checks, you'll often find yourself cashing far more than you actually need or want. There is a fine art in obtaining precisely the right assortment of traveler's checks (which come in denominations of $10, $20, $50, and $100), so that you always have the correct denomination available when you need it. I also think that every traveler should visit a bank before departure and obtain $100 in new bills divided as follows: 4 $10 bills, 5 $5 bills, and 35 $1 bills. (The reason for the new bills is that they take up less space in your wallet.) Often you'll need a few dollars to pay for transportation to the airport, and several countries levy departure taxes, and if you've used up all of your local currency, it may be inconvenient to cash a traveler's check at that time; your American money will be accepted wherever you go; and if you find yourself having to pay $4 in taxes, you can use the single dollar bills, or if you pay $5, you are entitled to receive change in U.S. currency. I can assure you that your small hoard of American currency will come in very handy during the trip, and there is no law against bringing American currency into any Asiatic country, although sometimes you may have to declare it. It is even a good idea to bring along about $5 in American quarters; these come in handy for tips when you reach a new country, in the event that you haven't had an opportunity to cash a traveler's check. American money somehow is known the world over, and is rarely, if ever, refused by the recipient. Of course, if you have the time, it's a good idea to cash a small amount of money at the airport prior to departure for a new country, or upon arrival, obtaining some small change of that country (not only large bills) so that you can pay for tips, airport transfer, and the like.

Let's get down to cases. For the sake of our discussion, let's assume that you (but assuming two people) are planning to take along $1500 on your trip. One person traveling alone would probably need much less, although, of course, it depends upon the person, his type of hotel accommodations, gifts purchased, and the like. Nowadays, most people rely upon credit cards which are accepted almost everywhere. Of course, it is a fact that in some areas one credit card company will be accepted whereas another will not. For this reason, it's often a good idea to have at least two different credit cards, thus increasing the odds.

There is a certain amount of thought required before cashing any traveler's check. When you arrive in a new country, try to estimate (very roughly of course) the probable amount of your expenses. For example, if you think that you'll need $50 for purchases and $100 for your hotel bill, cash only the $50 traveler's check to begin with. There's always time to cash the $100 traveler's check at the time of departure, and thus minimize the dangers of carrying too much cash with you at any one time. If you're buying substantial amounts of merchandise in a shop, ask if you can pay by personal check (a supply of which should always be carried). Wherever possible, pay by personal check; this will give you a reserve of uncashed traveler's checks, which is always a comforting feeling. In this way, you'll minimize the chances of developing that slightly uncomfortable feeling at the end of a trip about whether or not you'll have enough traveler's checks to see you through.

♥ Health

It would be foolhardy to sidestep this important question, but let's start off by saying that this problem should be considered as neither a black danger nor, on the other hand, something that can be completely disregarded. It doesn't take much knowledge of conditions around the world to know that the United States has the highest level of health and sanitation of almost any country. Food and water are carefully inspected, public health officials check for the slightest signs of disease, and in general, the health of our citizenry is closely watched. In certain parts of Asia, although efforts are being made, a somewhat lower level of public health control must be expected. At the opposite pole, it should be recognized that Japan, for example, is as health-conscious as our own country, and their standards of sanitation are almost the same as our own.

SPECIAL NOTE:
  As of this printing, The World Health Organization has declared smallpox to be universally eradicated; smallpox vaccinations are not required for visiting the nations in this volume.

VACCINATIONS When you receive your passport, there will also be enclosed a yellow form, issued by the World Health Organization (the initials of which spell out to an unbelievable WHO); it folds into four parts and provides for inoculations for (1) Smallpox, then (2) Yellow Fever, next (3) Cholera, and finally (4) Other Immunizations (Typhus, Typhoid-Paratyphoid, Plague, Tetanus, etc.). If you didn't receive one for any reason, ask your travel agent or transportation company for the form, or inquire of your local Health Department. You can't travel in Asia without it, so don't fail to obtain one. When you've been shot (to use the vernacular) by your doctor, he fills out the form and adds his name. Ask him if he will obtain the necessary "Approved Stamp." If he doesn't wish to do so, you'll have to obtain it from your local or state Health Department; every town or city has such an office, sometimes called a Commissioner of Health, Health Department, or the like. This is important: your physician's signature alone, without the "Approved Stamp," is not good enough. Many times, even though you've had the particular shot (but lack the "Approved Stamp"), you'll have to be reinoculated. If, while you're traveling, there is a smallpox or cholera scare, which occasionally occurs, your yellow WHO card will be carefully scrutinized, and if it lacks the approved stamp, may lead to your being led (against your wishes of course) to a local hospital and sometimes detained for several days. My unqualified advice is—get that approved stamp! And furthermore, don't lose the yellow WHO card, because no health officer is going to take your word for its contents and you might have to start the whole vaccination process over again. (A most depressing thought!)

The standard shot, and one that almost everyone has had on various occasions, is for *smallpox*. Almost all Asian countries require it, but it is no longer a requirement for re-entry into the United States. The smallpox shot does not become valid for entering a foreign country until eight days after the date of inoculation, so don't plan on having your smallpox vaccination the last day or so before your departure. Many Asian countries also require a *cholera* vaccination, and this becomes valid six days after the inoculation. *Yellow fever* inoculation always presents a problem; do you need it, or can you do without it? Even in the regulations of the various Asian countries, it is not listed as a requirement, but merely noted as "necessary if coming from a yellow-fever infected area." But what is such an area? What it usually means is that if there's a yellow fever epidemic under way, you need it, otherwise it may be waived. To play it safe, it is advisable to get the yellow fever shot if your trip takes you through India, Ceylon, and Southeast Asia. Better ask your doctor, who, however, cannot give you the yellow fever shot, because the serum has to be made up fresh every day; you'll have to obtain it at the U.S. Public Health Service; some insurance companies with health services also give the shot. If there isn't one in your city, ask your doctor for the location of the nearest source. The United States no longer requires that travelers returning home from cholera-infested areas of the world have a cholera vaccination in order to enter this country. It has been found that the cholera vaccine is of little use in preventing the spread of disease across international borders. Of course, this doesn't mean that other countries will necessarily follow this ruling, and you will still have to show a cholera vaccination when entering most Asiatic countries.

It is, in the opinion of most experts, not necessary to get other shots if your trip does not take you to Southeast Asia and India; thus, on an itinerary which takes you, for example, to Hawaii, Japan, Taiwan, and Hong Kong, no other shots are required. However, you should get typhus, tetanus, typhoid-paratyphoid, and perhaps polio too, if you're going on to Southeast Asia and India. Why be half safe? Get the whole works, as long as you're at it.

The various shots affect people differently; some have no after effects, others get headaches, sore arms, and perhaps even run a slight fever. The best bet is to take your vaccinations in the late afternoon and plan on an early bedtime. Smallpox and yellow fever involve only one shot; cholera, typhus, and tetanus need two each; but typhoid-paratyphoid requires *three* shots. The cholera, typhus, and typhoid-paratyphoid shots must each be separated by at least one week; that is to say, one week must separate each of the two cholera shots, for example. However, you could take a cholera and a typhus shot, for instance, on the same visit to your doctor's office. Some doctors like to give a whole group of shots at one time to save time, but you can usually expect a good headache and some aches and pains that night if you get such a group. Tetanus is a problem, for there should be one month between each of the two shots; be very careful about getting repeat shots of tetanus before at least six months are up, or you could get a nice mild case of tetanus, or a close facsimile thereof. Here is the way it sets up in tabular form:

Vaccination	Number	Interval	Valid for
Smallpox	1		3 years
Yellow fever	1		10 years
Cholera	2	1 week	6 months
Typhus	2	1 week	1 year
Tetanus	2	1 month	4 years
Typhoid-Paratyphoid	3	1 week	1 year

Once on your trip, remember that conditions vary a great deal in various countries. For example, in Hawaii health conditions are identical with mainland states, and no special precautions need be taken. In Hong Kong, the tap water is not safe, and so on, with varying conditions in different countries. It is therefore necessary to consult the appropriate Health section in each chapter of this book.

One of the most common problems of travelers is diarrhea, caused by an infection. All of the previous efforts to come up with a drug that will prevent or cure diarrhea have met with comparatively little success. However, there is now a prescription drug on the market called *doxycycline,* an antibiotic which is most effective. It is taken daily, in single 100-milligram doses, and seems to be nearly 100% satisfactory in preventing this common and annoying travelers' complaint. The drug is taken each day while in a foreign country, whether there are symptoms or not, and the protection offered seems to last for a week after the use is stopped; therefore, if taking doxycycline, you can stop taking it several days before your final departure for home. It does appear to have one side effect with some people (not all) taking the drug; it may cause an itching sensation.

WATCHING YOUR DIET Many people experience a type of malaise called "Hong Kong belly," or "Bangkok tummy" (or fill in your own city and name), on their trips. There are several reasons for this condition which generally may be described as an upset stomach, or even as a disturbance of the gastrointestinal tract. What it means, in plain language, is that you feel poorly, have various strange sensations in your stomach, complicated with a headache. The reasons for getting Bangkok tummy (to use one example) are manifold, but basically it is caused by the change in drinking water, change in the local bacteria, and too much living-it-up. What does all of this mean in plain language? To begin with, water has a somewhat different composition in various parts of the world, and even though you don't necessarily drink plain water, you do drink tea, coffee, and the like, which are made with local water. It is perfectly possible that the difference in mineral content may somehow throw your stomach out of kilter, although not necessarily always. Next, every part of the world has what might be called "local" bacteria, peculiar to one city or one country or even one portion of the world. There are foreign organisms present in say Bangkok, for example, which are not present in Duluth. In Bangkok, the local residents feel no effect from their own local bacteria, having become acclimated or immune to those microscopic organisms. In the same way, people in Duluth are not disturbed by *their* local bacteria. But bring a person from Duluth to Bangkok and you expose him to the strange organisms. It may (or in the vast majority of cases probably will not) involve a slight period of readjustment until the system is acclimated to the strange bacteria. Most of the strange bacteria can be killed off in advance by cooking, and therefore the tourist who sticks to cooked foods minimizes the possibility of taking in large quantities of strange bacteria. It is primarily the raw foods, the fruits and vegetables, that introduce these unwanted organisms into our body. Thirdly, and perhaps more important than either of the two previous items, is the tourist who changes his life completely. At home, he eats regular meals, takes it easy most evenings watching television, and sleeps eight hours nightly. On a vacation trip, nothing is too much for him in the way of eating and drinking and keeping on the go and staying out late. His overworked system naturally rebels, and the average tourist mumbles, "Must be something I ate," and whereas it could very likely be something he overate, or drank, it could also be because he did too much.

Of course, the tourist should particularly bear in mind that care in the selection of what he eats is important in certain countries. In those countries where this book (in the Health sections) cautions you against drinking the water (which also means ice in drinks), eating raw fruits and vegetables, etc., those suggestions should be *scrupulously* followed. Certain foods, in addition, provide almost ideal cultures for the development of bacteria (especially in warm weather countries) and these should be avoided. Particularly dangerous are meringues, custards, puddings, ice cream, ices, sherbets, butter, soft cheese, raw fruits with light or thin skins, uncooked vegetables, cake filled with whipped cream or cream mixtures, and unboiled milk or cream (even when used in coffee).

THE CHANGE IN TIME Another problem, not serious, but worth a brief discussion, involves the change in the accustomed day-night cycle. This means that human beings are almost completely indoctrinated into a set of time-based routines which have made the body a creature of habits. We almost all tend to arise in the early part of the morning, eat three meals spaced throughout the day, and then after a few hours of amusement or relaxation, retire for about eight hours of sleep. After say fifty years, to use a hypothetical age, this pattern is quite firmly ingrained, and the body would rebel against too much innovation in the way of hours. Thus, if we stay up too late, we're likely the next day to find our eyes closing; if we lose sleep, we're tired the next morning. This physiological day-night cycle has become a part of us, something our system retains partly out of habit and partly as an inheritance from our ancestors, from thousands of them who did the very same thing. When we travel via ship, the comparatively small amount of mileage covered involves a change (from one time zone to another) of only an hour each night, and thus our system makes a somewhat gradual adjustment to changing hours and times. But now, in these modern days of jet planes, New York is separated from the Orient by only a day's travel.

Let's imagine a theoretical New Yorker who flies to Hong Kong, arriving there at 8 A.M. local time in Hong Kong. But although he may recognize that it's early in the morning (in Hong Kong) and he may eat breakfast and look forward to the entire day which stretches before him, his body reacts quite differently. Perhaps, unbeknown to him, his system and bodily functions think it is about twelve hours later, and that in effect it is nearly 8 P.M. During the course of the day, such a traveler may find himself growing drowsy, or his metabolism fluctuates, or his thinking capacity may vary. He might find upon retiring at night that he falls asleep immediately (because he is tired) but awakens a few hours later because he is actually hungry (his stomach tells him that it is 3 P.M. and not 3 A.M. as the clock indicates).

As a rule, these physiological changes in the cycle of the human body take a day or so for adjustment. There is no cause for alarm if one awakens in the middle of the night and thinks with pleasure of a sandwich; equally, there is nothing disturbing about growing drowsy in the afternoon. In the matter of a few days, that remarkable mechanism, the human body, will make the necessary adjustments.

♟ The U.S. Customs

There are so many things to buy in Asia that even the most disciplined, budget-conscious traveler will find that he has exceeded the $300 limit, and soon begins to have small qualms of doubt about clearing the Customs. This mental hazard can easily be put into proper perspective, but first the regulations must be understood. Let's go through the various problems, item by item, because they are not terribly complicated.

(1) Every American is entitled to bring back $300 worth of articles purchased abroad free of duty; this is a basic statement of the rule, but as you know it has many exceptions. The exemption may be used every 31 days, so theoretically you could keep on making trips to the Orient and repeating your $300 exemption. (Then, too, the exemption of $300 is in force for even a child who goes on the trip, regardless of age, and members of a family traveling together may pool their exemptions. Discussed later on.) Incidentally, the law requires that baggage be examined at the first point at which your plane or ship reaches U.S. soil, so that if your plane, for example, stops at Alaska, or Honolulu, the customs inspection takes place at that point, even though you and the plane are continuing onward.

A recent ruling which is rather complicated permits a traveler to bring in articles purchased in certain foreign countries free of duty. It's called the Generalized System of Preferences (GSP) and is being used to help certain developing areas improve their financial condition. About 2,700 items have been designated as eligible for duty-free treatment, but certain items (such as footwear, watches, some electronic products, etc.) are excluded. The countries in the Orient which have been included in this preferential list include Burma, India, Korea, Nepal, Singapore, Sri Lanka, Taiwan, Thailand, Hong Kong, and Macao. In order to take advantage of GSP (that is, to go over the $300 exemption), you must have acquired the article in the country where it was grown, manufactured, or produced. You may carry it with you or ship it. If you buy more than $250, it's advisable to obtain a Certificate of Origin (called Form A), from the seller of the merchandise. They always tell you it's not necessary, but it is if you buy a fairly expensive item or items valued at $250 or more. If in doubt, call the U.S. Consul and ask for assistance. I should point out that liquor may still be subject to Internal Revenue taxes despite its special GSP status.

I hope this isn't too confusing, and I'll restate it briefly. You are still allowed your basic $300 worth of articles free of duty. Then, after the basic $300 exemption, comes the GSP. Many U.S. Customs officials are not fully aware of the provisions of the GSP, and if the inspector insists that the articles over your basic $300 exemption are subject to duty, ask him to call a supervisor. If you still are required to pay duty, you may write to the District Director of Customs where you entered the U.S., giving him the information concerned. He will then make a determination as to whether or not you are entitled to a refund.

If you exceed the limit of $300 exemption per person, you will have to pay duty assessed at a flat 10% on the first $600 worth of merchandise over the standard exemption.

Turning to wines and liquors, or alcoholic beverages if you prefer that less specific term, the situation is far more complicated. Even though the item in question was actually produced in a country on the GSP list, you are still subject to Internal Revenue Tax and Customs Duty if you bring in more than one bottle per person.

All of the above Internal Revenue taxes and Customs Duty are based upon a U.S. gallon containing 128 fluid ounces; they are not for each bottle. The above schedule is based upon a "proof gallon" if 100 proof or over.

	Int. Rev. Tax	Customs Duty
Brandy	$10.50	50¢ to $5
Gin	$10.50	50¢
Liqueurs	$10.50	50¢
Rum	$10.50	$1.75
Whisky	$10.50	51¢ to 62¢
Wine, sparkling	$2.40 to $3.50	$1.17
Wine, still	17¢ to $2.25	31½¢ to $1

(2) Members of a family traveling together, including young children, may pool their allowances together, so that a husband and wife can claim $600. This holds true even though the purchases consist of $595 worth of dresses from Hong Kong purchased by the wife and a $5 purchase by the husband, as is frequently the case.

(3) On board the ship or plane approaching the U.S., you'll be handed a declaration to complete. It consists of a few simple questions about your trip, and then requires you to list your purchases in reasonable (but not precise) detail. (Don't forget that the U.S. Customs is experimenting with new types of declarations, so this may change somewhat.) Write down the actual *retail* value of your purchases, using the sales slip to support the price you're using.

EXCEPTIONS AND VARIATIONS TO THE ABOVE   Each person (over 21 years of age) is entitled to bring in one bottle of liquor; if you bring more with you, and you can, duty will have to be paid. There is also a restriction against more than 100 cigars (or 3 pounds of smoking tobacco); any excess is subject to duty. It should be clearly understood that you are not prohibited from bringing in more than the permitted quantities of wines, liquor, or tobacco—merely that duty will have to be paid on the excess, and this holds true even though the value of your purchases is under the exemption.

All *antiques* may be brought into the country duty-free. For customs purposes, anything made before 1830 is an antique; this holds true even though the date is somewhat arbitrary. Antiques may include figures, furniture, art objects, porcelain, china, paintings, scrolls, or, in fact, any article which has artistic merit and value. It is always advisable to obtain a certificate from the dealer at the time the purchase of the antique is made, certifying to his appraisal and setting forth the age of the antique; if not, you'll find the burden placed upon you (on your return to the U.S.) to prove the exemption of the article from customs duty.

While on the subject of antiques, it is important to mention the need for a careful evaluation of all Chinese-type art objects, whether new or antique, purchased in Hong Kong. (This is discussed in considerable detail in the shopping section of the Hong Kong chapter of this book.) Be sure to have anything of value authenticated, because otherwise you might find you have bought a very clever copy rather than a valuable antique.

Certain other articles are prohibited under any circumstances; these include lottery tickets and narcotics. Cured or cooked meats, fruits, plants, and vegetables are extremely troublesome to clear and are never worth the trouble involved. Many foreign candies will not be allowed unless a list of ingredients is specified on the box, to comply with the Pure Food and Drug Law.

Some gifts may be sent home duty-free. Most of us want to bring or send small gifts to friends. The U.S. Customs has a ruling that is ideal for the average tourist. All purchases costing under $25 may be shipped directly from abroad to the American recipient without being included in your $300 exemption. For example, if you send ten $25 gifts to ten different friends (cost, $250), your $300 exemption still remains untouched. The vast majority of shops will take care of the shipment for a small additional postage charge, not only leaving your exemption free but relieving you of the burden of toting gifts in your already heavy baggage. When shipped via parcel post, the gift will arrive at the recipient's home in the regular mail, with no fuss or feathers. Be sure to have the shopkeeper write on the outside of the package: "Unsolicited gift under $25 enclosed."

Articles shipped to your home separately (that is, purchases not in your possession) are subject to duty, even though you remain under the $300 exemption. Thus, *anything* shipped home from abroad (except for $25 gift parcels) is subject to duty. Incidentally, when shipping anything fairly light from abroad, insist that it travel by parcel post; if sent as ordinary freight, the articles will have to clear through a customs broker, and you'll be astonished at how high the charge can be in relation to the original purchase price. If the package is too heavy for parcel post, request that it be shipped to you in care of the Railway Express Agency, who will be able to clear it for you. In this regard, it is essential that the documents (shipping papers) be mailed promptly to the Railway Express Import Department. You'll save quite a bit of money by following this advice; sometimes the customs brokers' charges, when used, are so high that the entire savings involved in the purchase is completely eliminated.

GOING THROUGH CUSTOMS Whether you arrive by ship or plane, keep all your purchases together in one suitcase for easy examination. Try to have the various sales receipts available, should the inspector wish to see them. Before the customs inspector arrives, have your bags open, ready for inspection. Don't ever, under any circumstances, offer a tip to the customs inspector; this is a serious offense.

There are two attitudes, both equally wrong, which definitely will slow up your customs examination. The first wrong way is to act as if the entire proceeding is an undue invasion of your privacy; the second is to act as if you have a fortune in narcotics hidden in your luggage. The best—and easiest—way to clear customs is to be responsive to the inspector's questions: look him right in the eye and answer his questions with frankness. Under normal circumstances, the entire proceeding should not take more than five or ten minutes.

PATA (The Pacific Area Travel Association)

The prospective traveler to Asia and the Orient has a remarkable source of information in PATA, a nonprofit organization which exists for the express purpose of developing tourism in those areas. The membership of PATA consists of the foreign governments involved, the various airlines and steamship companies, plus many hotels, travel agents, and others interested in Pacific tourism.

PATA's main office is at 228 Grant Street, San Francisco, California 94108. Write to them for any general or specific information —schedules, timetables, hotel rates—or travel suggestions about any country in the Pacific region. They will send you all sorts of promotional material and travel folders; of course, inasmuch as they are not a travel agency, they will not make up your itinerary, nor make travel or hotel reservations for you. Their function primarily covers the dissemination of travel information, and that is precisely what they do in very excellent fashion. Two 16-page booklets are available free on request. They are "Events in the Pacific," which lists in calendar form the festivals and other interesting happenings in 30 Pacific area countries, and "Discover the Friendly Pacific," which gives a brief sketch of the attractions in each of the 30 countries. Don't hesitate to write to PATA if you want travel folders or similar material for any country in the Pacific or Asia.

JAPAN

♀♂ Background

The would-be traveler to Japan has seen pictures of snow-capped Mount Fuji, dark-haired women in lovely costumes, feudal castles, Buddhist shrines, quaint rice paddies, and other sights calculated to make him think that the Land of the Rising Sun is a sort of never-never land, a re-creation of an unrealized childhood dream. In the imagination of most Americans, Japan is a land of courteously bowed heads, perhaps with a hint of servility, a background of glorious scenery, and in the distance the gentle music from *Madame Butterfly.* Fostered by the tales of soldiers who occupied the country at the end of the war, a large proportion of American men are subconsciously (or otherwise) attracted by the thought of acquiescent Japanese girls, and by the knowledge that men are regarded as superior beings, to whom women must always be subservient.

This whole package of preconceived ideas and dream sequences about Japan is the result of much calculated effort by the Japanese Tourist Office, by travel agents, and by calendar artists. Not all of it is exactly as depicted. Of course, Japan does have its beauty spots, as can be seen from the many color postcards for sale everywhere. It is also true that the unthinking tourist, carefully insulated in a protective, walled-in all-expense guided tour which rushes him from one shrine to another temple to a third ancient palace, may return home with a set of Kodachrome memories and pictures to match, fully convinced that modern Japan is a living set of color postcards.

If that is what you want to see, and if you look only in front of you (as the guide instructs), making sure not to look to right or left, travel only in large groups, never talk to a Japanese person other than a waiter, porter, or maid, it is perfectly possible to preserve this image intact, straight out of a nursery picture-book, the kind in which *you* fill in the colors. Imagine in reverse that a Japanese tourist was placed on an assembly-line tourist belt and shown only the picture-book sights of our country—the Capitol, the White House, Monticello, the Statue of Liberty, Mount Rushmore, and the Grand Canyon; imagine further that the Japanese tourist ate nothing but Japanese food and never spoke to an American other than a waiter, porter, or maid in a hotel. Would such a Japanese tourist be entitled to say that he had seen the United States, knew some-

N

HOKKAIDO

Sapporo

Hakodate

Aomori

Morioka

Matsushima

JAPAN SEA

Sendai

Nikko

Ursunomiya

HONSHU

Tokyo

Fuji Lakes
Mt. Fuji ×

Hakone

Gifu

Nagoya

Kyoto

Kobe

Nara

Himeji

Osaka

Hiroshima

INLAND SEA

Takamatsu

SHIKOKU

TO WEST COAST OF U.S.
VIA GREAT CIRCLE ROUTE

TO HAWAII

Beppu

Fukuoka

Unzen

Nagasaki

KYUSHU

TO
HONG KONG

thing of it, what made it tick, and why our country is the sort of nation it is? Of course not, and neither will any American who undertakes a spoon-fed tour of Japanese picture-book sights.

Japan is not really a picture-book country, although, as mentioned previously, it does have its fair share of old-world sights, and some people still wear the ancient costumes, and you may eat your dinner seated on the floor, if you wish. Japan is a 20th century country, dynamic, restless, energetic, pushing, overcrowded, and noisy. Japan itself is a vast traffic jam, with space at a tremendous premium for living as well as parking, with a confused, conflicting set of cultures all fighting for survival and expression. With almost 100,000,000 people crowded into an area about the size of California, the Japanese exhibit all of the energy and action of compressed air.

The tourist experiences this repressed energy when he first takes a taxi from the airport to his hotel, and it is an experience that leaves him breathless, white, and shaken at his destination. The frantic rush of the taxi as it snakes its way in and out of the undisciplined traffic, going at full speed towards intersections in an effort to beat the lights, makes the passenger think he is in the hands of a driver motivated by suicidal impulses. Not without reason have Tokyo's cabdrivers been dubbed *kamikaze,* after the suicidal pilots of World War II. Actually, though, the driver is driven by that restless energy which forces the Japanese to hurry wherever they are going whether there is a need or not.

Their energy has been a blessing to the Japanese, and also their downfall. It has also given the world a picture of a paradoxical character which is a blend of such opposites that many a would-be observer throws up his hands helplessly and calls them inscrutable. They aren't inscrutable, far from it, but they are confused.

Their energy helped them break out the bonds of an ossified, feudal society and become modern in a few decades. So advanced and modern that they were able to take on mighty Russia, then as now one of the world's great powers, and defeat them in a quick war less than forty years after the Japanese took the deep plunge from the warm waters of a decayed feudal society into the icy waters of the 20th century.

There have been people living in Japan for about 4,000 years, at a very minimum, although others say it may be closer to 10,000 years. The country began to be more or less unified about the 7th century B.C., when it acquired its first emperor. However, during the centuries that followed, Japan was never completely under the control of the emperor, for various family groups wielded almost uncontrolled power within their particular local districts. The next thousand years saw the development of a strong class of nobles and privileged people living in considerable splendor while the average person worked long hours in the fields and was completely without legal rights. In the year 710 A.D. the first permanent capital was built at Nara, and it remained there for only seventy-four years; then it went to Nagaoka for a decade, and subsequently to Kyoto, where it stayed for about 1,100 years. At various times, certain emperors attained considerable nationwide control over the people and nobles, but it never was a fully centralized power; at all times, the various clans and family groups vied for authority, sometimes actually dictating to the emperor, or even selecting the ruler themselves. At other times there were riots, civil wars, raids, and other demonstrations of discontent.

Most important of all, to comprehend the Japanese and their way of life, we must understand the Japanese social system, chiefly developed through life at the royal court, and the military hierarchy. Beginning about the 7th century A.D., social lines began to be rigidly drawn. At the top was the *shogun,* the military ruler. Beneath him was the aristocracy, consisting of those who had no land or estates, called the *kuge,* and the more powerful aristocracy with land—the *daimyo.* The territorial lords were anxious to maintain their power, and maintained groups of warriors, called *samurai.* The *samurai* were really paid mercenary troops, usually uneducated, who owed complete, unswerving loyalty to their *daimyo.* The aristocracy and the *samurai* together constituted less than 1% of the total population; the remaining 99% lived in abject fear of their lives from the capricious behavior of the *samurai,* who terrorized the countryside, stealing whatever pleased them. In the next half-dozen centuries, the *samurai* enforced rules of behavior for the common people, who were told what to wear, how to walk and sit, and what to say under almost every conceivable circumstance. It seems almost incomprehensible to us that every single activity of the day could be so prescribed that the most routine, ordinary actions had to be performed in only one way—the "Japanese way"—or swift punishment would follow. For even the slightest infraction, beatings, confiscation of property—and often death—would follow. Outward behavior was emphasized, and formal manners were to become so stylized that the inner meaning or content ultimately disappeared. When a medieval Japanese walked down the street and encountered a *samurai,* he had to fall to his knees and bend his head low, under pain of sudden death. Sometimes if the *samurai* was filled with *sake,* the Japanese liquor, he might take an unwarranted affront at

the behavior of a peasant, and the peasant's death might well
be the result.

Etiquette, and the proper rules for the public under almost all
situations, became the Japanese way of life. Why a particular behavior was expected, or what was behind it, became quite unimportant
to the mass of people. Why worry about the reasons for a certain
code of behavior if death was to follow an infraction—far better to
learn to follow the rule. Even a slight infraction of the social rules
of behavior meant, at the very least, total ostracism. More often, the
punishment was far more severe. Accidentally brushing against a
person of superior social status meant death, no matter how slight
or unintended the touch.

As a direct result of centuries of being ingrained towards a rigid
social behavior, the Japanese have developed certain formalized
traits greatly admired by visiting tourists, who find the bowing and
scraping most charming. It is delightful to see two Japanese bow low
to each other, but it is perhaps even more important to realize that
a thousand years of cruel, fiercely enforced laws were the forerunner
of today's bow. Tens of thousands of Japanese citizens died in the
enforcement of these barbaric rules of social conduct so that the
shogun and the aristocracy could more readily control the general
population.

But conditions do change, even though slowly in a country like
Japan, with its feudal system. Although the country had been almost completely sealed off from the remainder of the world for
many centuries, Admiral Perry, in 1854, forced the Japanese to sign
a treaty opening the country to trade with the remainder of the
world, and that was the beginning of the end. A merchant class had
always existed, but now it became increasingly important; the *daimyo* and the *samurai* disappeared, and Japan began its headlong,
unrestrained rush towards modern times. In 1868, the capital was
moved from Kyoto to its present location, the city of Edo, and the
name changed to Tokyo. (If you rearrange the letters that make up
Kyoto, you will find Tokyo.)

Their energy got the Japanese in trouble in the 1930's and 1940's
when it expressed itself in a desire to conquer their neighbors and
to rule the Asian world. Thwarted in this direction, postwar Japan
turned about completely and expressed its still unbounded energy
in the fine products now pouring out of this island and into the
world markets: the cameras, the transistor radios and television sets,
and, lately, the automobiles which are now beginning to catch on.

The Japanese are a conservative race like those other islanders,
the English. When their energy, which expresses itself in their burning desire to know and understand the world about them, conflicts

with their innate conservatism, the result is a puzzling, confusing head-on collision of cultures.

Their energy is also the source of that great Japanese puzzle which finds them, individually, a very courteous people and, collectively, very rude. On analysis, this paradox vanishes. When their energy is restrained under the very strict social regulations which control individual relationships, there is no person more courteous. Free it from these chains, however, as when the Japanese are in a crowd, and they are past experts at elbowing, shoving, jostling and pushing. Their homes are immaculate, every article in its precise place. On a train, however, they litter the floors with papers, orange peels, and empty candy boxes. The two social systems have met in a direct clash.

Examples of this clash are seen in the arranged marriages of today. Formerly, no proper boy or girl would ever think of marrying someone strictly of his own choice. Very often a go-between, or *nakodo,* was involved who would first bring the families together, and later the two marriage prospects. Nowadays, boy meets girl in the best Hollywood tradition; but, when they decide to marry, they still call upon a *nakodo* to attend at the wedding and perform his part as before in *Shinto* ceremonies.

There is the classical case, too, of the efficient Japanese businessman who wears a western suit, or *yofuku,* and runs his business with all the modern equipment and techniques available. Yet, when he returns home after a hard day's work, he steps out of his shoes and into slippers at the door, gets out of his *yofuku* and into a kimono and sits on the *tatami* (straw-matted) floor at the low *handai* (table). There he sips tea served by his outwardly obedient wife, who refers to him respectfully as *dannasan,* or "honorable husband," instead of "honey" or "sweetheart," while he watches his favorite television program.

In recent years, this small country has had a series of ups and downs, to say the least. Starting in 1969, the Japanese economy suddenly found itself running not only at full blast, but far too successfully for its own good. Predictions were being made widely that within a decade Japan would surpass the United States in the production of steel and would have a greater gross national product within 20 years. The Japanese people (as a whole, of course) became embarrassingly rich in the years from 1969 to 1978. The imbalance of trade grew so great that Japanese government leaders were searching for ways to return dollars to the United States, for a vast flood of American currency had been brought in by the nation's exports—mostly electronic equipment, autos, and steel. In the heart of Tokyo land prices had risen above the prices for New York real estate. And still the dollar continued to pile up, in alarming fashion. The Japanese people were urged to spend their money on imported items, to travel abroad, to purchase art held in European and American hands, and to buy property in foreign lands, particularly Hawaii. Various gifts were made by Japanese corporations to American universities. But suddenly, the Japanese economy received a mortal blow, following the Arab-Israeli war of 1973: The supply of oil was cut and also tripled in price. Japan was rudely awakened from the dream of becoming the world's number one industrial country. It was lovely while it lasted, but those 4 years ended with dramatic abruptness. The oil crisis caused a complete change in the Japanese way of thinking, for it brought to the people's attention that Japan produces less than one-third of one percent of its oil needs, and must rely almost totally upon the whims and moods of the Arabs, who could cut off Japan's supply of oil or raise its price whenever they chose to do so. This situation also involved a tremendous inflation, with prices rising daily, and the cost of living becoming astronomical. Food became wildly expensive, with the cost of fresh fish going to $12 a pound, and the best beef selling at $23 a pound!

Nevertheless, and this is quite inexplicable to the financial experts, everyone seems well fed and properly clothed. Indeed, the Japanese are pointing out that overweight is beginning to become a national problem. A look at Tokyo subway riders quickly shows that the people are better dressed than their New York counterparts. Many commentators, however, think that the gains achieved during the heyday of Japanese growth in the national economy are being wiped out by the new inflation.

Although these remarks are brief and cursory, and cannot hope to do more than serve as an introduction to Japan, perhaps the tourist will be made more aware of the nature of the country and its very interesting people. Of the many thousands of Americans who visit Japan, the vast, vast majority find it a fascinating and exciting country. Almost all departing tourists plan to return as soon as possible, and who can blame them?

◱ When to Go

A very good question, indeed. The Japanese have overpromoted the Cherry Blossom Season to such an extent that many would-be visitors think there is only one month in Japan—April—and only one thing to see—cherry blossoms. What a vast disappointment awaits the April cherry blossom tourist! For the pink blossoms are so fragile that any wind stronger than the mildest breeze denudes the trees of the delicate blooms and sends them cascading down like tinted snowflakes. The only cherry blossoms that last longer than a few days are those that you see on the Ginza and only because they are made of paper and tied so firmly to the trees that it takes a typhoon to blow them down.

Actually, every month has its charm in Japan. The bracing winter days of January and February send out a clear call to skiers and other nature lovers (a hardy breed!) to trek to the Japan Alps, where some of the greatest ski runs in the world can be found. Fujiyama, the great sacred mountain of Japan, is at its most beautiful in wintertime. And the place to see it is in the charming Fuji Lakes area at the base of this classic mountain. Its snowy head and perfectly sloping shoulders are etched clearly in the clean, dry air. One glimpse of this magnificent ex-volcano dominating the entire vista will make the viewer understand why the awestruck Japanese of earlier days—and even some today—regarded it as sacred. Nonetheless, it can be cold and raw in Tokyo; if you're properly dressed, it should be bearable.

March sees the beginning of the foreign tourist season, the time of year when the big tour groups come. The warming weather makes trips to the surrounding countryside enjoyable, although there is still a nip in the air, especially at night. As March heads into April, you can follow the cherry blossom season from southern Japan up to Tokyo, where they emerge about the first week of April and last about that long. Once again, April is a lovely month in Japan as a rule, but it's not the only month by a long shot.

May and June are excellent months in Japan, as they are in most countries in the North Temperate Zone. Some rain falls during these months; but it is what the Japanese call *harusame,* or spring rain, and their poems tell of the gentle caressing touch of the soft drops. It's wet, just the same.

In July it starts to get hot and in August comes the worst possible weather, hot and humid. This is the time that the residents who can afford it head for the hills and the others suffer away in the lowlands. This is also a good time for tourists to visit the northern island of Hokkaido with its rugged scenery, and deep, trout-filled lakes. Besides which, it's delightfully cool.

Now we come into the autumn, actually the loveliest time of the year in Japan. The leaves turn color; and the most striking example of autumnal magic is the leaf of the gingko tree, that modern relic of primeval botany. The gingko leaves change into a brilliant yellow, making the roadway through Tokyo's Meiji Park, for example, look like a street lined with gold. But wherever you may go in Japan, whether to Hokkaido, to the Inland Sea for a quiet cruise, or to the southern island of Kyushu, you will find the artistic brush of the season at work making the country's parks, forests, and countryside a many-hued wonderland.

Weather Strip: Tokyo

	Jan.	Feb.	Mar.	Apr.	May	June	July	Aug.	Sept.	Oct.	Nov.	Dec.
Average daily high	47°	48°	54°	63°	71°	76°	83°	86°	79°	69°	60°	52°
Average daily low	29°	31°	36°	46°	54°	63°	70°	72°	68°	55°	43°	33°
Monthly rainfall	1.9	2.9	4.2	5.3	5.8	6.5	5.6	6.0	9.2	8.2	3.8	2.2
Number of days with 0.04 inches of rainfall	5	6	10	10	10	12	10	9	12	11	7	5

To sum up, every season is worthwhile in Japan, although some are more so.

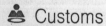 Visa Requirements

Tourist visas are obtained at Japanese consular offices and are valid for the life of your passport. They are of the multiple-entry type, which means you can re-enter if you want to leave Japan and return (say to make a sidetrip to Korea). If coming from Southeast Asia you may need two cholera shots less than six months old. This is most important, for the Japanese are mortally fearful of cholera and will quarantine anyone who has touched down at any Southeast Asian airport and looks ill. With Japanese health authorities, it is quarantine first and ask questions later.

Customs

You can bring in tax-free 200 cigarettes or 50 cigars or 250 grams (slightly over half a pound) of tobacco. More than these amounts will be subject to a tax of 355%! Three bottles of any kind of alcoholic beverage is the limit that can enter tax-free, the rest being subject to a 50% duty. When you purchase certain goods subject to tax during your stay (pearls and cameras, for example), the stores will make a notation in a special form issued by the government. Don't lose the form, because you will probably be required to show it on departure. After you pick up your baggage, be sure to head for that portion of the Customs area marked "Non-Residents." This is specifically intended for foreigners as opposed to Japanese nationals. If you stand in the wrong line, they will politely tell you to head for the correct line, so be sure to look for the signs that appear in English, and go through the correct Customs section.

⚕ Health

Water is good anywhere in Japan. In fact, it is so good that the Japanese claim that New York water makes them sick. Some go so far as to take water-purification tablets along when they go to the United States and use them when they cannot get bottled water.

The Japanese still laugh at a group of tourists who got off a ship at Yokohama lugging their own water in bottles with them. Each day they went back to the ship to get refills. What they didn't know was that after the first day the ship was replenishing its water supply from the Yokohama reservoir.

It is a fact that tests have shown Japanese water is among the purest in the world. So if you get a touch of stomach trouble, check your intake of alcohol and rich foods before you blame the Japanese water. Of course, there are those for whom even the mere change of water creates all sorts of digestive ills, due perhaps to the difference in mineral content. For them, bottled water, which is available at the hotels, is recommended.

There is no need to worry about eating in Japanese cities, from a health standpoint. All hotels and first-class restaurants are absolutely safe. It is not advisable to go wandering about the country dining off the land, though. Beware of raw foods in small rural villages especially. "Night soil," that delicate euphemism for an indelicate fertilizer, is still used in Japan and can cause a revolt in the digestive tract if consumed in a salad or uncooked vegetable which has not been thoroughly washed.

The Japanese are health bugs of the most enthusiastic kind. They are more afraid of what you will bring to them than they are of what they will give to you. This is evidenced by the close scrutiny which the immigration doctors give to health cards. Because they are such health nuts, there are pills for the various types of ills and diseases —and even some for all diseases. So if you come down with anything, you may be sure that the Japanese will have a pill for it. Whether the pill will kill or cure is another matter.

If you walk along the street and see numbers of people with white masks over their faces and mouths, do not panic! The black plague has not struck. Far from it, in fact. It means that the person has a cold and is thoughtful enough to protect others from catching it.

⏱ Time

Fourteen hours ahead of Eastern Standard Time (New York, for example) except when Daylight Saving Time is observed. Then Japan time is only 13 hours ahead of New York. There are two ways of calculating EST: by subtracting 14 hours from the Japan time or, in the rapid short-cut method, by adding ten hours to Japan time and making it the day before.

💲 Currency

The unit of currency is the *yen,* and there are hundreds of them to the U.S. dollar. Due to great fluctuations, it isn't possible to set forth any table of values showing precisely how many *yen* you'll receive for your dollars. Hotels offer the poorest rates of exchange; you'll do somewhat better (particularly important if you're changing substantial amounts of money) by reading the exchange rates usually shown in the windows of banks. Obviously, if you run out of money on weekends when the banks are closed, or during the evening, you'll have no choice but to exchange your money at your hotel.

🌐 Price Level

Tokyo has the dubious distinction of being the most expensive night life town in the world. A night out on the town that includes the top-class cabaret circuit will probably cause you to concur emphatically. Food prices in good restaurants are extremely high, although the individual menu prices look inoffensive enough at first. But, since everything is *à la carte,* you will find that the bill reflects everything you have ordered, including, you will swear, that glass of water. Even old Japan hands express shock at the bills that they are handed. Hotel prices are only moderately high, don't expect to find prices low in Japan; it is quite expensive, in fact. Economists say that Tokyo may well be among the most expensive cities in the world, including New York and Paris. Food is slightly higher here and housing costs approximately three times what it does in New York. Exaggerated? Far from it, probably an understatement. To keep the cost down, don't order imported liquors—have local drinks instead.

Tipping

As for tipping in Japan, the answer is still: Please DON'T. A few years ago that reply could have been given in a resounding, authoritative voice. Today, it is spoken a few decibels lower and with just the slightest quaver. For the influx of American tourists has tended to break down the barrier a bit. Now not only do you tip the boy who brought your bags up to your room (100 *yen* is enough) but you also tip the doorman who calls your cab (50 to 100 *yen* in this case).

As for everything else, cab, restaurant, and other hotel services, tipping is definitely OUT. A 10% service charge is added to your hotel and restaurant bill, and it takes care of the tip. Even the boy who rolls in the tray of room-service food should not be tipped. He expects nothing but a pleasant smile; so be sure and give him only that. In case you missed my statement about taxicabs, I'll repeat it —don't tip taxi-drivers.

As for train diners, the waiters and waitresses a few years ago showed a rare pride in deciding as a matter of policy that they did not want to be tipped. They have held fast to this decision. As for the porters who carry your bags on the train, there is a definite charge per bag, and they expect no more. The rate is posted on the station walls in English; it keeps changing, going upward from time to time, but isn't excessive.

There is one exception to the above rule: the Tokyo cabaret circuit. If you plan a night's entertainment at one of the capital city's plush nightspots which cater to foreigners, be sure you are well armed with (lots of) money and are prepared not only for a big bite out of your bankroll but also for heavy tips to all of the hostesses who sit at your table, and also for the waiter who has brought the drinks as fast as the girls could ask for them. But there is no problem here, either; for if you forget the hostess she will remind you and tell you how much and, as for the waiter, she will take the tip out of your change and give it to him. Oh yes, there is a 10% service charge added to your bill, but it is more in the nature of tradition than practice. You must still give the waiter 10% in addition.

⟳ Transportation

Although there is a subway in Tokyo, most tourists will get around by *taxi* more than likely. At one time, the local taxi-drivers were wild men, given to sudden turns and erratic driving patterns; happily, the situation has greatly improved and they now drive with a certain degree of decorum. Rates keep changing, so they can't be set forth here; however, they are generally about the same as at home. Also, you get a fairly long ride included in the first drop of the meter. (At various times there is a nighttime surcharge, but the cabbies, surprisingly honest, will tell you if it's in effect.) Don't forget, there's no tipping; you just pay what it shows on the meter.

The best way to get a taxi is to have your hotel doorman call one, telling the doorman where you want to go. He then instructs the driver. If you try hailing one yourself, you generally will find yourself unable to tell the driver where to take you. Even if you know the address, it won't do much good. There are such things as addresses in Tokyo, but their significance is obscure. The way Tokyoites find their way to their destinations is by going to the general area and then inquiring at the nearest police box. Or else they bring along the telephone number and call the place from a booth in the general area and get precise directions.

Cabbies in Tokyo act as though they have just arrived from the country, as far as knowing locations is concerned. But even if they don't know where they are going, they are in an awful hurry to get there. There are very few spots that a Tokyo taxi-driver can readily find. Among them are the major hotels, but not too many additional places. For any other destination, arm yourself with the telephone number and either have the cabbie call the place for directions or have the doorman do it and tell the driver.

No matter what community in the United States you live in, there is an address. Almost anyone in your town can generally direct a person to that address, and surely every local cabdriver knows how to get there. It may come as a great surprise to learn that this is definitely not the situation in Japan and that there are no street addresses. According to the ancient system, each city was divided into what we might call "wards," or small districts, measuring about a square mile. As each new house was built in the particular district, it was numbered 1, 2, 3 and so on, even though the houses might be on different streets and perhaps a half-mile away. On a given street, number 2 might be followed by 21, then by number 7 and next by number 64 ... but surely you get the idea. However, there are frequent fires in Tokyo, and when house number 34 burned down and was subsequently rebuilt, it might have to take a new number, let's say 223, for example. The result: absolute chaos and utter confusion, further aggravated by the fact that many houses do not even bear numbers. It was (and still is) the custom for taxi-drivers and even for residents of Tokyo to drive to the general area, and then make local inquiry: "Do you know anyone named Namura in the export-import business?"

When the American military authorities took over in Tokyo at the war's end, they were horrified to learn of the city's archaic system of addresses. They managed to get certain main streets named, such as X Avenue, Y Avenue, 4th Street, 5th Street, and other simple names. Thus it shouldn't be too difficult (you think) to get into a cab and ask for the corner of 5th Street and Y Avenue. But it won't work, for two reasons: first, the cabdriver will undoubtedly not speak English; second, even if he does speak English, he has never paid any attention to the street names and probably hasn't even noticed them.

If you do have a full Tokyo address, you'll probably notice that it has a certain name at the end, followed by the phrase -ku, which refers to the ward, or part of the city, where your address is located; thus, Chiyoda-ku gives your driver an idea of where to go in the first place.

Another problem is the use of the word *chome,* meaning block, which may, for example, appear as 6-chome; but *chome* may be replaced by *cho* or *cho-me.* Sometimes *banchi* is used to indicate the building number in the block, but as you know, this isn't too helpful. Furthermore (I have shielded you from some of the worst), it so happens that often (very often) there may be a half-dozen buildings in the same ward bearing the same number as the one you're looking for. How come? Because sometimes two buildings are built about the same time, or perhaps rebuilt, or perhaps some-one paid the local officials to get a "good" or "lucky" number, and so forth.

What to do? It isn't all that difficult, and the solution is extremely simple. Before leaving your hotel for a particular address, ask at your hotel desk for assistance; have them write out (in Japanese of course) your destination. Sometimes, at certain tourist hotels, the doorman can orally tell the taxi-driver where to go, but even an experienced doorman may not know a particular shop, or a small restaurant. However, there is no reason to hesitate about going out even to remote spots—just make sure you have the correct address, written in Japanese, plus driving instructions. If in doubt, call the store or restaurant on the phone (or better yet, have the hotel clerk do it for you) and obtain the necessary information.

> POINTER:
> If you want to go to a particular restaurant, you can obtain a Japanese and English card from either the City Information desk or the Public Relations desk at your hotel. They keep a stock of cards with driver's instructions for the most popular restaurants. Merely show the card to your cabdriver. When you are ready to leave, the restaurant will call a cab if you wish.

Taxis are very plentiful in Tokyo, and you shouldn't have any problem, except late at night or when it's raining. In the case of rain, it is impossible because the taxis seem all to be made of some soluble material that melts away with the first few drops. If you are in the Ginza area at about 11 P.M., however, you will see plenty of empty taxis cruising around. But, though you hail with all your might, they seem deaf and pay you no attention. The secret is to hail with your fingers, the number of fingers raised indicating the number of times the meter fare you are willing to pay. If one won't get you a taxi, two should and three positively will.

Tokyo has an excellent subway system and signs are in English. It's an inexpensive way to get around the enormous city.

Though self-drive *rental* cars are available in Tokyo, it is not the recommended thing to do. For traffic is not only capricious, it is downright dangerous. For most visitors, the problem of driving on the left side is a considerable problem in any event. Rental cars cost about $20 a day, including gas and oil. Cars with English-speaking drivers are available through any of the major hotels at a rate of about $10 an hour. If you are the kind who prefers to go it alone rather than joining a group, the self-drive price may be worth it to you. However, whether driving yourself or with an English-speaking driver, be prepared for the roads. Few meet U.S. standards, and most are very much substandard. So if you decide to go by car in Japan, be prepared in any case to rough it.

Train service is excellent in Japan, perhaps—at least as far as schedules go—the best in the world. The trains leave and arrive on the dot. There is First and Second Class Service on the Tokyo-Osaka limited expresses, roughly a 325-mile journey. On the trains there are diners with the leading hotels catering the food. The new Tokaido Line (Tokyo-Osaka) is said to be the fastest in the world. There are about 26 trains a day, and the elapsed time varies from 3–4 hours, depending upon whether they are super expresses or limited expresses. These times will probably be reduced in the near future, the railroad says.

The important station for the foreigner is Tokyo Station, which is in the central business district and only a short taxi ride from most hotels; from here, the southbound trains arrive and depart. From Ueno Station in north Tokyo, at least 30 minutes by taxi from Tokyo Station, the northbound trains arrive and depart, including those on the Tokyo-Nikko runs. But trains can be confusing.

Take the case of the group of brave tourists off a ship docked in Yokohama who decided to try to return from Tokyo by train. When they boarded, they had plenty of time. But after riding a few hours without arriving at Yokohama and especially after one of the group noticed that they had passed the same station several times, they became alarmed. Finding a Japanese passenger who could speak English, they told him their troubles. The root of their problem, they discovered, was the fact that they had taken the so-called Loop Line, which goes around Tokyo in a circle. Through the help of the Japanese, they got the right train and eventually arrived at their ship but not until they had delayed the sailing enough hours to make the captain, crew, and other passengers irate.

Airplane service to the major cities is provided by Japan Air Lines' domestic service and by All-Nippon Airways. The former is government-owned. Both use jets and propeller planes. The fares are relatively cheap, but the food leaves something to be desired, consisting of damp, cold sandwiches at the most (and pretty horrible at the least), and tea generally with sugar already added. Better take your own sandwiches.

There are also coastal *steamer* service and steamship service through the Inland Sea from Osaka to Beppu. The latter is a trip that should be taken, if time is available. It sails through the island-studded Inland Sea, providing the comforts of air conditioning, good food, and individual cabins for first-class passengers, who line the rails with cameras to snap the islands as they come up and obtain some of the best pictures they will have of their visit to Japan.

✊ Airport and Tourist Taxes

Tokyo now has a brand new airport, and if you've been to the old one, the new one is quite a change. It's the New Tokyo International Airport, popularly called Narita, and it's located a whopping, almost unbelievable 40 miles east of Tokyo. You've got to allow plenty of time to get from your hotel (perhaps anywhere from 1¼ to 1½ hours), and the ride out is quite expensive by taxi, even though Tokyo taxi rates are similar to ours—the mileage is enormous, and so is the fare. If you want to go out by train, the Keisei Electric Railroad runs six-coach expresses to and from the airport, using Ueno Station. You'll have to inquire at your hotel as to the schedules, which will vary from time to time. (Incidentally, if you're making the trip to and from Tokyo during rush hours, the train is far better than the airport bus, which often becomes snarled in automobile traffic.) A new line will be operated to the airport from downtown Tokyo by the Japan National Railroad. One thing is certain, you're going to find it necessary to allow plenty of time to get to the airport (or from it, for that matter). And don't forget, you're supposed to be at the airport one hour before departure time for international flights. Security at Narita is pretty tight, and there are at least two check points before you can even get into the airport itself. This takes a little time, and it might be better to allow more than the customary one hour arrival time at the airport before your flight.

Now, about the airport hotel situation. The Narita View Hotel is about 10 minutes from the airport, and the hotel is quite nice on all counts; it has four restaurants. The Narita Prince is probably the best and most luxurious of all the airport hotels; it is probably also the most expensive. The Nikko Narita Hotel is far more functional and not nearly so luxurious; the rooms are not very large. The Narita International is a bit removed from the airport, but it does have lovely grounds, 25 acres of them; it has an American air about it and the rooms are good-sized. The Narita Airport Rest House has the great advantage of being located within the airport itself; you can actually walk to it. Rooms are moderate in size, and rates are fair. The Holiday Inn Narita is something like a high-rise motel; the hotel somehow seems undignified and lacks any sense of elegance; however, it is perfectly satisfactory for an overnight stay. All the airport hotels have free minibus service to and from the airport, and most of them also have free service into the town of Narita, which is only about 15 to 20 minutes away from the airport by bus or taxi.

The town of Narita is worth a visit if you stay over at the airport and have some free time while waiting for your next plane. During the 10th century, Emperor Suzaku began the building of the Naritasan Temple. As the centuries went by, the community of Narita grew up around it, and it has become a pilgrimage spot, a very holy place, for the Shingon sect, a branch of Buddhism, in Japan. About 8 million worshippers come each year to worship Fudo, the god of fire, to whom the temple is dedicated. It's pleasant to walk through the temple and through the streets of the small town, where there are shops and places for lunch. The 45-acre Naritasan Park is just minutes away by foot from the buildings of the main temple, and it's beautifully planted with shrubs and plants.

The New Tokyo International Airport looks pretty good. Although it's planned primarily for international flights, it is possible that some domestic flights will continue to arrive at and depart from this new airport. The airport is shaped as an open "U" with four separate levels, from which four concourses will lead to four more separate boarding satellites, each able to accommodate eight large planes.

The old airport, Haneda, is now used primarily for domestic flights, with a limited number of exceptions, as mentioned above. Haneda is only 11 miles from town, and it ordinarily takes 40 to 45 minutes to get there by car, unless traffic jams up suddenly and without warning, something you must expect in the Tokyo area.

There is a passenger "service fee" (that's really a departure tax but the Japanese are too polite to say so) of about $7.50 per person at Narita Airport.

▌▌ Communications

Telephone service is fine in Japan, provided you have the hotel operator get the number for you. The language barrier being what it is, you also should have an interpreter standing by your side just in case there is nobody at the other end who can speak English. Overseas calls were a matter of chance until the cable between the U.S. and Japan was laid in May 1964; calls now go through in less than ten minutes as a rule. A U.S. call costs about $12 for three minutes. Have the hotel operator get it for you, or else, if she cannot, dial 109 and give the operator, who speaks excellent English, the number you want.

Every hotel has *telegram* and *cable* blanks. If you want to send a wire, be sure to ask the hotel desk for the blanks and be sure to print legibly. Remember, the person transmitting your message probably knows no English and can only go by the letters. A 10-word cable costs about $3.50. The cost of the telegram will be charged to your room. The hotel desk will also take care of mailing your letters, charging the stamp cost to your room. *Airmail* letters cost about 30¢ to the U.S. (can't be more accurate because of currency fluctuations).

POINTER:
  The Armed Forces maintains a radio and television network in Japan called the Far East Network, sometimes abbreviated FEN. Almost all the hotels receive their radio and TV programs by cable. Broadcasts can be heard in the early morning, are mostly off during the day, and return about 6:30 P.M. Incidentally, without commercials, you may be surprised to find that your favorite half-hour program lasts only 20 minutes. On the radio, there is American-style entertainment, with news broadcasts on the hour.

⚡ Electricity

No real problem in Japan, where the electric current is 100 to 110 volts A.C. All American appliances will work satisfactorily on the Japanese current except those where cycles play an important part. Eastern Japan, which includes Tokyo, operates on a 50-cycle basis, and western Japan on 60 cycles. You will need an adjustment in eastern Japan if you want to use your own phonograph or television set. But then, how many tourists bring their own phonographs and television sets? Practically none, to answer the question.

✕ Food Specialties and Liquor

Unfortunately, Japanese food has suffered from two major drawbacks: One, real Japanese food is only good in Japan because of the lack of the proper ingredients elsewhere. Thus, some Japanese restaurants in the U.S. tend to serve poor food; and two, there is a misconception abroad that Japanese food consists almost exclusively of raw fish and rice. The latter fact has caused foreigners to worry needlessly about what they will eat in Japan.

Actually, *sushi,* which is raw fish with specially prepared rice, and *sashimi,* which is raw fish without the rice, can be likened to the hot dogs of the Americans and the fish and chips of the Britishers, although this analogy courts the danger of oversimplification. *Sushi* and *sashimi* are eaten chiefly in conjunction with drinking and not so much as entire meals in themselves. But we will go further into this a little later.

In a word, if you like beef you will like Japan. For Japan produces what is considered by many gourmets the best beef in the world from the point of view of taste and tenderness. Why Japanese beef is so good is a matter of controversy. One school insists that it is because the cattle are fed beer with their meals and are rubbed down with straw nightly to knead the fat into the flesh. Supporting this view are the beef slaughterhouses in the village of Matsuzaka (near Nagoya). In some villages, the cattle are taken into the peasants' homes and the entire family takes turns in massaging the prize cattle. According to the beer-feeding school, Japan's cattle are really contented even unto death. They are given a beer bust just before slaughtering so that they go to their glory utterly happy and relaxed; and, as a result, their flesh, untoughened by tenseness, is all the more tender.

A second school insists, however, that beer-drinking and massaging, like the flowers of spring, have nothing to do with the case. The secret of the tenderness of Japanese beef lies in the breed, proponents of this view say. The name of the breed is Tajima, and Tajima beef are born with flesh prone to tenderness and tastiness. Also, they do not roam extensive ranges developing hard muscles where tender flesh should be. Theoreticians point out that tender young heifers are slaughtered rather than toughened steers, and this is also a major contributing cause. Compare the tenderness, they say, of a young girl living at home to that of a range-roaming cowboy.

But let the controversy rage so long as the beef is choice, and that is what it is at the best restaurants in Japan. Beef is chiefly served as steak; in *sukiyaki,* a kind of Japanese stew; in *oil-yaki,* which consists of a small steak broiled in butter or oil; *shogayaki,* or slices of beef about a half-inch thick marinated in a ginger sauce; and *teriyaki,* similar to *shogayaki* except that the meat is marinated in soy sauce. Roast beef is just beginning to be discovered in Japan; and you can get some excellent roast beef at certain hotels but especially at Players' Restaurant just below the Roppongi intersection in Tokyo.

The two Japanese dishes best known to the foreigner are *sukiyaki* and *tempura. Sukiyaki* is really sautéed vegetables and meat, and foreign residents in Japan tend to look down their noses at it as being more publicized than popular. It is prepared in an iron pan in front of the diner; soy sauce is mixed with sweet *sake* or *mirin* (a type of rice wine) and sugar is added along with thin slices of Japanese beef, onions, *tofu* (a custard-like substance made out of soybean curd), plus various greens and vegetables. A bowl, in which an uncooked beaten egg has been placed, is set before the diner. The bits of food are taken from the pot and dipped in the egg momentarily for cooling and added taste, and then eaten. Everyone, no matter how timid, likes *sukiyaki.*

Tempura is, briefly, french-fried, batter-dipped seafood and vegetables. It is quite different from the soggy fried shrimp generally served in restaurants outside of Japan. Prawns or shrimp, however, are only one course of this many-coursed dinner. For good *tempura* the batter must be just right—not too thick or too thin; and the temperature of oil must be just right—not too hot or too cold. The chef then lifts up the fish, prawn, vegetable, or gingko nut, places it in the batter and then into the oil. Meanwhile, the diner has mixed together some shredded white radish and soy sauce in a small bowl placed before him. When the *tempura* is ready, the chef places it before the diner who picks it up and places it into the radish-soy sauce mixture. This cools, and adds taste to, the piece of *tempura.* The foods in a *tempura* are cooked individually and are served separately, one at a time, so that each item is hot and appetizing.

Most tourists would enjoy *shabu shabu.* A large pot is placed before the diner and filled with broth. He is served with a platter of thinly sliced beef which is picked up with chopsticks, then placed in the broth which cooks it swiftly. The beef is then quickly dipped in a sauce. Later, vegetables, and perhaps noodles, are cooked. It is a delicious meal, one that almost everyone will enjoy.

Lesser known to the foreign visitors but more popular with the local residents are *yakitori* and *tonkatsu. Yakitori,* which is the name given to bits of chicken skewered together (*à la* shish-kebab) and barbecued over a charcoal fire, is an excellent accompaniment to *sake,* the Japanese drink made from fermented rice. At a *yakitori* restaurant, *sake* is not served in those delicate thimble-sized cups, but, instead, in huge mugs. *Sake,* though only about the strength of table wine, is more potent because it is drunk warm, and the alcohol takes immediate effect.

When you go to a *yakitori* dinner, be prepared to eat every edible part of the chicken, with delicious quail eggs added as an appetizer. *Yakitori* is so delicate in flavor that the chefs at the best restaurants refuse to serve more than three cups of *sake* because they feel that after three the customer loses his sense of taste.

In the same way that *yakitori* and *sake* seem made for each other, *tonkatsu* (Japanese-style pork cutlets) and beer are excellent companions. To make *tonkatsu,* a good-sized piece of pork tenderloin is dipped in batter and deep-fried. The chef then slices the tenderloin, puts some shredded cabbage on the same plate, and serves it up to the customer. Meanwhile, the customer has been drinking the excellent Japanese beer and munching on *mame,* boiled beans, cooled and mixed with a bit of soy sauce. Another variation of *tonkatsu* is *kushikatsu.* This consists of bits of pork placed on a skewer alternately with pieces of onion, dipped in the batter and deep-fried.

It must be emphasized that to get good *yakitori* and *tonkatsu* you must go to a restaurant which specializes in these courses. Otherwise, you will be eating inferior versions of them. To order these delicacies in an ordinary restaurant is a mistake; to repeat, you must go to a *yakitori* or *tonkatsu* restaurant.

Before going into the more exotic Japanese foods, let us hasten to assure the prospective visitor to Japan that he can get any kind of cuisine he wants in major Japanese cities, including hot dogs and hamburgers; although the former leave a little something to be desired. In Tokyo, for example, there are excellent French, German, Italian, Hungarian, Swedish, Korean, Mongolian, Siamese, Indonesian, Indian, and, of course, Chinese restaurants. All the leading hotels serve adequate (but not great) western-style food.

Many gourmets proclaim that Tokyo serves better Chinese food than any place else in the Far East outside of China, and Taiwan. This, naturally, is a matter of dispute. It is a fact that the Chinese cooks in Tokyo mostly come from Shanghai, which, in its day, was the food capital of China. Then the communists moved in, and the Shanghai chefs fled to Tokyo.

Be that as it may, Tokyo offers a wide variety of Chinese-style provincial food. You can get Peking, Shanghai, Canton, Szechuan, and Fukien cooking in Tokyo. The more ornate Chinese restaurants are literally food palaces, the buildings consisting of several floors with lavish decor and even, in one, a gong to announce the arrival of guests. The menus generally have over 200 listings; and it is often a problem for the novice to make a selection. A good clue: those which foreigners generally like are usually underlined. So you will be safe if you select the underlined dishes under the various sections into which the complicated menu is divided, such as beef, chicken, pork, vegetables, etc.

Since the visitor will be familiar with the different types of European cuisines, and in Tokyo they come as close to their original as in any other city in the world, it is not necessary to describe them. However, a word about the less familiar oriental styles from the Asiatic countries will probably not be amiss.

Korean cooking is spicy and is usually made in the form of a barbecue, especially in making *bul-googi.* A small brazier is placed on the table along with a plate of thin pieces of beef, well-marinated in a spicy sauce. The meat is placed on the grill until it is done to the diner's taste. It is then dipped into a sauce for added flavor. The Korean cuisine also offers excellent soups and a pickled cabbage, called *kimchi,* that is so highly spiced with red peppers and garlic that it will burn the tongue and palate of the uninitiated. A sort of tartar steak, Korean style, also can be ordered. This consists of chopped raw beef served on a bed of apple straws.

Mongolian fare is also barbecue-style, and is said to derive from the campfire meals of Mongolians on the march. Another name is "Genghis Khan barbecue," because it is said to have originated with the great conqueror's armies. The barbecue consists of lamb or pork, plus chicken and beef, cooked in front of you by a waitress. After the meat is done, it is dipped in a special sauce and served. Then vegetables—slices of onion, green pepper, and sweet potatoes—are grilled, dipped into the same sauce, and served. Who wouldn't like this? No one, I hasten to add.

Siamese and Indonesian cooking also are spicy, with the specialty of the latter being *nasi goreng,* or to describe it simply, Indonesian-style fried rice. Siamese food is extremely spicy and not for the uninitiated.

And now, the next several paragraphs are dedicated to those who have a curious palate, who seek adventures in eating, and who wish to probe the unknown to discover new taste sensations.

First on the list of exotic Japanese dishes is the previously mentioned *sushi,* an attractively shaped combination of raw fish, vinegared rice, and the grated root of the *wasabi* plant, whose cool-seeming greenness belies its pungent strength. There is a saying among westerners resident in Japan that once a foreigner acquires a taste for *sushi,* he becomes an addict, enjoying it even more than the Japanese. And once the taste is acquired, the eating of *sushi* approaches ceremony.

Each *sushi* devotee has his special *sushi-ya,* or *sushi* shop, which he contends is the finest. The true *sushi* lover never sits at a table, but insists on a place at the wooden counter, always spotlessly clean, so that the time between the making and eating of *sushi* will be minimal. For the *sushi* addict insists that the taste seems to dissipate once it is made, and the quicker it gets into the mouth the better.

Before the diner begins to eat, a damp cloth is placed before him along with a cup of specially brewed green tea, a small saucer of soy sauce, and a tiny cup of pickled ginger. The damp cloth is used for wiping the fingers, for only fingers are used by the inveterate *sushi* eater. The pickled ginger serves the same function as cheese in wine-tasting: it refreshes the palate and cleanses the taste buds for the next bite. The *sushi* is dipped into the soy sauce before eating to add to its flavor.

Sushi enthusiasts also know what fish is best. In the Tokyo area, *maguro,* or tuna, is best, with the richly larded ventral side considered the choicest part. To the southwest, in the Osaka area, *tai,* or sea bream, is unsurpassed. The reason for this, experts say, is because the *tai* in the Osaka region develops in texture from having to battle the swirling currents of the Inland Sea. The best *uni,* or sea chestnut, comes from Hokkaido, although there are some gourmets who claim the *uni* from Kyushu, the southernmost island, is just as good. All of this is probably only of theoretical interest to the westerner, who may never have tasted the dish, but it is a matter of serious discussion with Japanese gourmets.

The real specialty of Kyushu, by the way, is *fugu,* or blow fish, a form of gustatory Russian roulette, which is to say, there is a thrill with every bite. For *fugu* is a very poisonous fish. Actually, there is no real danger in eating this fish, for the *fugu* restaurants are licensed by the government after passing tests and proving their skill in extracting the poisonous portions of the fish. If they make a mistake and a customer dies, their license, of course, is removed, as some Japanese with a ghastly sense of humor like to say as they take a guest to a *fugu* restaurant. It really is not that bad. The only persons who die are those amateur fishermen who catch and clean the fish themselves. *Fugu* devotees say that the best parts of the *fugu* are those closest to the tainted areas, as you might expect they would. You know, the tastiest part of the meat is nearest the bone, as we sometimes say about chicken or steak. *Fugu* is served raw in thin slices that are so transparent you can see the plate underneath. A sauce made of spices, a sour citrus juice, and soy sauce is used to give character to the delicate taste of the fish. After this part of the meal is finished, other parts of the *fugu* are boiled with vegetables into a sort of stew, and then, finally, a soup is made of the residual liquid, if you're still with us.

Another Japanese delicacy is *kabayaki,* or broiled eel. Like all Japanese delicacies, freshness of the food is one of the prime requisites. In the case of eel, the creature must be alive immediately prior to broiling. The skilled *kabayaki* chef deftly extinguishes the life of the wriggler, splits it, and places it on a grill over glowing charcoal. When sufficiently broiled, it is then softened again by steaming. Afterwards, the eel is immersed in a specially prepared liquid, with soy sauce as a base, and broiled again. Throughout this last phase of the cooking, the meat is continually basted with liquid. The two methods of eating broiled eel are either as *kabayaki,* which is the eel alone with or without rice on the side; or as *unagi donburi,* where the meat is placed on top of the rice and the remaining sauce poured over the whole. The latter is the preferred way. The Japanese say that broiled eel is best during the summer months. The demand for eel is so great that it is raised commercially in small ponds. But gourmets insist that wild eel is tastier, because of the food it eats in its natural habitat.

Another favorite dish is *soba,* or noodles made from soy bean flour. The tourist probably will make his first acquaintance with *soba* by hearing about it. In the early morning hours, he will hear the curious wail of the *soba* man's flute curling up from the street. Though the sound may be slightly eerie to westerners, to Japanese and knowledgeable foreigners it is a call to the hungry, the somewhat drunk, and the curious to go to the *soba* man's stand, where a bowl of noodles cooked in a hot soup can be obtained. *Soba* is especially effective for the upset stomach and is said to be a sure cure for a hangover.

Speaking of alcohol, the Japanese have entered the world of hard liquor quite as effectively as they have grabbed a place for themselves in the fields of electronics and optics. Japanese beer, for example, is second to none and elicits praise from the most chauvinistic Germans. Even a Munich *braumeister* has been heard to comment favorably on the Japanese variety. The Japanese produce both the lager and the pilsner types and put out an especially fine draft beer. An interesting novelty is the Sapporo "black" beer, dark and rich. The most popular beer in Japan is surely Kirin, which is available almost everywhere; it's excellent, and a perfect accompaniment with Japanese food.

Sake (pronounced sakkey), mentioned before, is the delicate drink made from fermented rice, and thus, if we wish to be technical, is more a beer than a wine. Although it is generally warmed before drinking, a process which increases its potency, some *sake* is served cold. *Sake* is usually served in tiny cups, and several drinks wouldn't affect anyone. However, if continued, *sake* can sneak up on you before you know it.

If beer and *sake* are not strong enough for your tastes, try Japanese whisky. The best brand is Suntory, which vaguely resembles scotch in taste and has about the same alcoholic content. It is smooth and makes a good highball, and is available in ordinary and special brands. Stay away from Tory whisky unless you want to learn what liquid dynamite tastes like. Also in the line of liquid explosives is *shochu,* which is distilled from sweet potatoes, and, even more powerful, *awamori,* which is distilled from millet.

Special, although belated, mention should be made of Japanese strawberries which grow in the wintertime. These are called Fukuba strawberries after Dr. Fukuba, an agriculturist, who invented the process of growing them. The strawberries are planted with stone walls surrounding them—hence their other name, stonewall strawberries—and get their warmth from the heat of the stones as they are warmed by the sun. They are available only in winter and early spring and are as delicious as they are huge.

In summary, it is very difficult to classify Japanese restaurants. There are the *machiais,* literally "waiting rooms," which in reality are restaurants with many rooms which can be made larger or small by means of opening or closing the sliding doors. These provide geisha entertainment, meaning the geishas are called there from a central employment bureau. Then there are the specialty restaurants, the *sushi-yas,* the *tonkatsu-yas,* the *tempura-yas,* the *yakitori-yas,* and so forth. (*Ya* means shop.) There are the special steak restaurants where the steak is broiled on a grill in front of you and cut into bite-sized pieces which you pick up with chopsticks or, if you insist, with a fork. There are the westernized restaurants with tables and chairs downstairs and Japanese rooms upstairs, which provide menus with extensive lists of food. And there are those cozy establishments which also specialize in Japanese foods, have beautiful little gardens somewhere on the precincts, and can call geishas if you want them, or let you eat in pleasant intimacy with a companion in a private room.

∞ Time Evaluation

Being the fascinating place that it is, Japan is entitled to the largest single share of time during your trip to the Orient. On a quick 3-week trip, allow an absolute minimum of 7 days, but 10 would be better. On a 5- or 6-week trip, Japan should be allocated a minimum of 10 days, but 2 weeks would be more suitable. There is absolutely nothing wrong in coming to the Orient solely to see Japan, and many people do just that; however, as long as you're in this part of the world, Hong Kong is definitely worth your time; however, don't divide your time equally between Japan and Hong Kong. Allow two-thirds of your time in Japan, and one-third for Hong Kong.

🏛 Capital City: Tokyo

The place most travelers see is Tokyo, the capital, and many never leave there until it comes time to go home. This is a mistake. For Japan offers many attractions outside of Tokyo, and they are less expensive, too. There are the charms of the Inland Sea; history-filled Kyoto and Nara, the former capitals; Kamakura, and its huge Buddha; Hakone with its magnificent lake; Nikko, site of the splendid mausoleum of one of the Tokugawa shoguns; and let us not forget those other thriving cities of Nagoya, Osaka, and Kobe. No matter how long a visitor stays in Japan, he can spend his time enjoyably.

Tokyo, the capital of Japan, automatically draws visitors because practically all the international airlines land only there. Newcomers are almost immediately taken aback by the skyscrapers of this great sprawling city and its unending traffic. But somehow they inevitably leave with a feeling of affection for the enormous city and vow to return.

This giant metropolis, the largest in the world, contains well over 10,000,000 inhabitants, and although the birth rate has declined slightly, it seems certain that no other world city will catch up to it in the immediate future. It is busy, mobbed in fact, and the visitor may be shocked at the crowded pavements, the heavy, unceasing traffic, the heavily patronized shops, the continuous demand for transportation, and the never ending movement, movement. At first sight, Tokyo may superficially resemble other cities of Asia that have gone western, with American office buildings, luxury hotels, and other hallmarks of our civilization. But Tokyo is not an absorbed, assimilated city—although it has taken over western ideas, westerners have not taken over Japan. Despite the great influx of tourists, there are comparatively few westerners living in Japan, well under 10,000 permanent residents in the Tokyo area. This figures out to one-tenth of 1%, and for that reason, once off the well-trodden tourist beat, Americans will find themselves swallowed up by hundreds, even thousands, of local residents. Even on main streets, tourists seem engulfed by the mass of Japanese. For those who complain that they only see other Americans when abroad, this should offer a refreshing change.

Tokyo over the past 10 years has changed its appearance. Once an ugly city, it is now fairly attractive, and in certain areas very attractive. But it is also an unusual, exhilarating place, filled with dynamic ideas, supercharged with natural life and exuberance, and

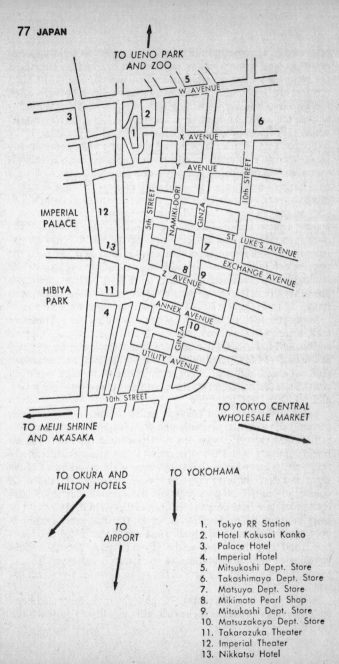

TO UENO PARK
AND ZOO

W AVENUE

X AVENUE

Y AVENUE

IMPERIAL
PALACE

5th STREET

NAMIKI-DORI

GINZA

10th STREET

ST. LUKE'S AVENUE

EXCHANGE AVENUE

HIBIYA
PARK

Z AVENUE

ANNEX AVENUE

GINZA

UTILITY AVENUE

10th STREET

TO MEIJI SHRINE
AND AKASAKA

TO TOKYO CENTRAL
WHOLESALE MARKET

TO OKURA AND
HILTON HOTELS

TO YOKOHAMA

TO
AIRPORT

1. Tokyo RR Station
2. Hotel Kokusai Kanko
3. Palace Hotel
4. Imperial Hotel
5. Mitsukoshi Dept. Store
6. Takashimaya Dept. Store
7. Matsuya Dept. Store
8. Mikimoto Pearl Shop
9. Mitsukoshi Dept. Store
10. Matsuzakaya Dept. Store
11. Takarazuka Theater
12. Imperial Theater
13. Nikkatsu Hotel

possessed of a great admiration for western ways. It picks up western ideas, and western music, and western bad habits. Sometimes the results are quite charming, as when western notions of hotel comfort are combined with gracious Japanese service; equally often the Japanese love for something new brings a repulsive hybrid— witness the local teen-agers' love for the worst in American music, which they make even worse than the original, if possible.

Tokyo is novel, it's original, and it's trying to be something— what, it doesn't quite know. Although it apes the west, nothing is ever absorbed completely and without a change. It seems off on a wild binge of newness, of willingness to *attempt* the new, which is more than can be said of westerners, who now apparently prefer to stick to the tried and true. What the future will bring to Tokyo is anyone's guess, but the fact remains that right now it is one of the most fascinating, lively, amusing cities in the world, provided you have the inclination to cope with newness and new ideas. In the pages which follow, you will find listings of sightseeing "musts" or highlights. See at least some of them, but Tokyo, perhaps more than any other city in the world, must be *absorbed* by the onlooker, who must add to his gaze a little contemplation about what he sees.

Many people think of Tokyo as one city with a central business area, a separate theatrical and entertainment section, a shopping region, and so forth. Of course, the Ginza (which may be regarded as the center of town) has a little of everything. But there are many regional areas, each with its own distinctive personality, and very worthwhile seeing. Don't go there with any plan—just take a taxi, and wander about at random.

I should like to say that Tokyo is almost completely free of crime, certainly of violent crime. Although the newspapers carry an occasional crime story, it always seems to have taken place in the countryside or away from the tourist areas. It is a great pleasure to say that tourists can wander about anywhere at almost all hours of the night and don't have to give any thought to personal danger. Of course, any intelligent person should use a certain degree of judgment, particularly in deserted sections of Tokyo in the late night or early morning hours. Happily, however, the incidence of crime is very low indeed in all of Japan. Here are the principal neighborhoods and what they're known for. If you have any questions about anything of interest to tourists, of any nature whatsoever, be sure to call the information number of the Japan National Organization, which is 502-1461.

Akasaka. A large percentage of the nightclubs are located here, which obviously means a night visit, although there's quite a bit to see in the daytime as well. You'll observe everything from the most elaborate (and expensive) places down to the smallest holes in the wall, coffee shops, discotheques, hostess bars, and so on.

Asakusa. You'll notice how similar the name of this area is to Akasaka, the one above. Asakusa (make sure you pronounce it clearly to the cabbie) has as its center the remarkable Asakusa Kannon Temple, which is particularly interesting on weekends. From the entrance, where your cab leaves you, there's a very long lane of shops. The general neighborhood surrounding the Temple is worth wandering about.

Ginza. Many people describe this as the equivalent of New York's Fifth Avenue, because the leading branches of the better department stores are here. It's a broad, long avenue lined with shops. Behind the main street, on both sides, are several smaller streets, filled with restaurants, small shops, bars, entertainment places—ideal for browsing. The main part of the Ginza is marvelous for walking on Saturday and Sunday, when autos are barred; tables are set up in the streets.

Shinjuku. The nearest equivalent and best way of describing Shinjuku is to call it Tokyo's Greenwich Village. You'll find Japanese hippies, homosexuals, swarms of people at almost all times of the day or night, and lots of things to watch and observe. There are plenty of places at which to eat, especially coffee houses. Shinjuku has hotels, bowling alleys, department stores, jazz spots, game parlors, and more and more of the same. This area is headquarters for the young people of Tokyo. When you go, tell the cab driver to let you off at Kabuki-cho, which is the center of the Shinjuku district. It's about 25 minutes from downtown Tokyo, and an expensive cab ride. However, it's a very inexpensive subway ride, and you can get precise directions at your hotel about which train to take.

Azabu Juban. Here you'll find thousands of small shops, partly indoors, partly outdoors. Loads of snack shops, offering all sorts of exotic delicacies, such as hot dogs and hamburgers (at least they're exotic to the Japanese), plus routine items like crackers made with seaweed, bean-paste buns, and so forth. During the summer months, there are many outdoor markets, colored lanterns, costumed parades, and if you're lucky, a local festival. Just off the Juban, you can see a little of what Old Tokyo must have been like, with tiny wooden houses, cheek by jowl, miniature lanes, and lovely small gardens.

Roppongi. A fascinating area filled with restaurants, boutiques, night clubs and food shops. It's centered around what's called Roppongi Crossing, and the streets lead off in four directions. Behind the main streets are smaller streets, almost alleys, which are also filled with restaurants and places of entertainment. Have dinner at one of them, and then wander about the area. I never fail to visit Roppongi at least once on a visit to Tokyo.

Tokyo is filled with many historic and interesting places. Listed here are just a few that should be on the tourist's list. (Special note: If you're more interested in shopping, eating and drinking, don't worry. Nothing will happen if you keep your sightseeing to a minimum. One half-day's tour will be enough for the vast majority of tourists. If you're on your own, just see the Imperial Palace, the Central Wholesale Market, and the Meiji Shrine. On a Sunday morning, pay a visit to the Asakusa Kwannon Temple.)

Imperial Palace. This was formerly the palace of the Tokugawa shoguns, or military dictators, who ruled Japan with an iron hand from 1603 until 1868, although in the last hundred years of its rule the iron became somewhat corroded. Before the Tokugawas, who built the Palace up to imposing size, it was the stronghold of a Japanese warrior, Ota Dokan, who began developing the group of mud flats at the mouth of the Sumida River into the world's largest city. Although tourists can get into the palace with special permission, they are limited as to where they can go. Anyway, the palace is much more imposing when seen from the outside. Be sure to notice the walls, built by carefully placing huge stones one against the other and letting their weight alone hold them in place.

Yasukuni Shrine. A Shinto shrine dedicated to those who lost their lives for their country, a sort of Arlington Cemetery without the graves; "cenotaph" may be the proper word. Shintoism is the original native Japanese religion and combines nature and ancestor worship.

Tsukiji Central Wholesale Market. The wholesale market covers 50 acres. Nearly 90% of the fish catch which is brought daily into Tokyo is sold here, but you have to stay up very late or get up before the break of dawn to see the auction, which is very worthwhile. Wholesale transactions also go on throughout the day in vegetables, meat, fruits, etc., in case the fish market is too early for you. The fish market itself, called *Uogashi* (very close to the downtown Ginza area) is at its best at 5 A.M.; later on, say by 8, the excitement is finished. In the fish market there are numerous simple, excellent, rather inexpensive fish restaurants.

Tokyo Tower. Tokyo's rival to Paris' Eiffel. It is 1,092 feet high and has a five-storied Modern Science Museum at its base, in which there are three science exhibition halls showing the latest developments in electronics.

Zojoji Temple. Built in 1605, the two-storied, red-lacquered Tower Gate is registered as an "Important Cultural Property" by the Japanese government. The temple itself was formerly the family temple of the Tokugawa shoguns.

Sengakuji Temple. One of the most famous temples in Japanese literature. It is here where the 47 *ronin,* or warriors without a master, are buried. These men all committed suicide in a dramatic gesture after avenging the death of their lord. Their graves are arranged in order of respective rank.

Akasaka Detached Palace. The temporary residence of the Emperor Meiji (who threw the Tokugawas out and made Tokyo the Imperial capital) from 1873 to 1888 while the present Imperial Palace was being rebuilt for his occupancy. The present building was constructed in 1909 and used to be the Crown Prince's residence. The Prince of Wales, famous later as the lovesick abdicator Edward VIII, stayed here in 1922. It now houses the National Diet Library and government offices.

Shinjuku Gyoen Gardens. Many rare varieties of cherry trees may be seen here. Open to the public from 9 A.M. to 5 P.M. daily with a slight admission charge.

Asakusa Kannon Temple. Kannon is the Goddess of Mercy. The approach to the temple is bordered with souvenir shops which are very colorful, day or night. It is supposed to have been founded by three fishermen in the 7th century when they found a tiny image of Kannon in their nets. It is also the temple where the prostitutes of the Yoshiwara used to worship before the red-light district was closed a few years ago.

Earthquake Memorial Hall. A three-storied pagoda built as a memorial to the 35,000 people who were killed in the earthquake and fire of 1923. They had flocked to this area, which was then an open place, as a place of refuge from the fires that followed the earthquake. But sparks from the surrounding blazes lit the piles of goods which the refugees had brought with them, and the people were caught in a trap.

Meiji Shrine. One of the holiest pilgrimage centers in Japan. The large *torii,* or gates, at the entrance are made of Japanese cypress wood, 1,700 years old. There is an iris garden with more than 80 varieties of the flower.

Museums in Tokyo are not like those you will find in the European capitals, although the same words of caution apply in visiting them: Take it easy, and don't overdo it. Here is a list for those devotees of the finer, artistic things in life.

National Museum. Open the year around except on Mondays and for a week at year's end. Hours: 9 A.M. to 4 P.M., with an entrance fee of only 30 *yen*. Twenty-five rooms exhibit archeological, religious, armor, weapon, and painting collections covering the years of Japanese history.

National Museum of Western Art. Open the year around also, except for Mondays. Hours: 9:30 A.M. to 4:30 P.M. Contains masterpieces of famous western sculptors and painters.

Meiji Memorial Picture Gallery. Dedicated to the Emperor Meiji, who, you will have gathered by now, was quite a person in modern Japanese history. Pictures illustrating incidents in his life are on display.

Gotoh Art Museum. Open daily, except on Monday, from 9:30 A.M. to 4:30 P.M. Contains hundreds of ancient art objects, including many designated by the Japanese government as national treasures.

Okura Museum. Open daily, except Sundays, from 9 A.M. to 4 P.M. Contains the late Baron Okura's collection of antiques from Japan, China, and India.

ORGANIZED SIGHTSEEING In other words, the tours. If tours are ever necessary, they are in Tokyo, where it is so difficult to get about because of the lack of street names and house numbers that even the native-born get lost. You can have any variety: the morning or afternoon, or both combined, and the night tours. The half-day tour takes about 4 hours, picks the tourist up at one of the leading hotels and returns him there afterwards. The whole-day tour lasts about 7½ hours, includes lunch and an hour and a half at a Japanese theatre. The former includes a visit to the Mikado, Tokyo's only theater-restaurant, preceded by a session of Japanese folk dancing at another establishment. The more expensive tour gives you a *sukiyaki* dinner, a visit to a theater, a geisha party, and a look-see at a nightclub. This is highly recommended as a good way to see Tokyo nightlife and still have money left over for shopping. But of course, it is regimented, and not everyone likes fun in a group. Use your own judgment.

If you want to make trips anywhere in Tokyo or anywhere in Japan for that matter, by all means do so through the Japan National Tourist Organization, which has offices in many of the principal hotels. The general information number is 502-1461, and they can be very helpful.

Those who aren't leaving Tokyo for a trip through the country, but would nevertheless like to see what old farmhouses look like, a satisfactory solution might be a visit to the Open Air Museum of Traditional Japanese Houses. It's located outside of Tokyo in Kawasaki City, and consists of 16 farmhouses, ranging from 200 to

300 years old, all numbered, along a path that leads the visitor through rural Japan of centuries ago. It's open daily except Monday, and there's a moderate admission charge.

SIGHTSEEING ON YOUR OWN   There is really no reason why you can't go sightseeing all by yourself, without the assistance of an organized sightseeing tour. To be perfectly frank, much of what you see on a tour is not all that thrilling (with a very few exceptions mentioned in the previous pages), and you can see them by yourself in any event. Just remember one thing: if you get lost, there's nothing easier than hailing a taxi and riding back to home base. That's the worst that can happen, so don't worry. Walking along the Ginza, the city's main shopping street, is as simple as can be. Walk down one side, then later on, cross over, and walk down the other side. Of course, you'll probably be in and out of a dozen shops on the way. Just remember that the streets which run parallel to the Ginza (on both sides of that main thoroughfare) are extremely interesting, both by day and night. Indeed, some of the most colorful shops, bars, and places of entertainment, as well as snack places and restaurants (far cheaper than those on the main street) may be found on those side streets. Or, just wander about at random, and keep going as long as your feet hold out. A strolling tour of Tokyo will reveal lovely little spots of beauty—so well hidden from the eye of the casual observer—which, when seen, give Tokyo a completely different character. These are the quiet little neighborhoods and the neighborhood shopping centers with their tiny open-front stores, their wares in full display, and the warmhearted people who seem always so willing to help, although hindered by the language barrier. Department stores are a sightseeing attraction too. Be sure to go to the basements of these large stores; there you'll see the largest food sections anyplace and be able to sample some of the prepared dishes.

To get about at low cost, don't hesitate to use the Tokyo subways (except during the rush hours). They are air-conditioned and comfortable even during the hot summer, and are quite safe to ride. You can reach every single district in Tokyo by subway very quickly, for the train service is fast and efficient. Don't worry about getting lost, for there are signs in both Japanese and English. If you have any doubts, speak to your hotel concierge or bell captain before taking the subway and he'll tell you which station is nearest, and where to get off. The main Ginza station is nothing short of enormous, with 48 separate entrances. Inside (and this is true of other major stations) there are fascinating shops and restaurants. Bring some coins along, although they have machines that change paper money to coins suitable for use on the subway. And on a hot day, just remember that the stations themselves and even the tunnels are air-conditioned, rather than the individual cars in the train.

For the traveler who likes to make his own plans, here are some suggestions. First of all, read the English-language newspapers published in Tokyo and, in particular, go through the entertainment pages, which list the shows available. It's very easy to get theater tickets through your hotel's representative in the lobby; it's his job to assist hotel guests. You'll surely want to see some Japanese theater, particularly *kabuki,* but perhaps also the *Takarazuka* group of all-girl shows. *Tokyo Weekender,* a free publication, appears on Fridays and lists pretty nearly everything that may be seen or heard in the Tokyo area, plus restaurants, bars, etc. And, if you dial 503-2911, there's a recorded 24-hour message about what's going on in the city. If you want some further assistance you can call the Japan National Tourist Organization, where they speak English and can be very helpful about a wide range of subjects; their number is 502-1461, and they're open from 9 A.M. to noon and from 1 to 5 P.M. The office is closed Saturday afternoon and all day Sunday.

SEVEN TRIPS ON YOUR OWN

Trip 1. Start from Hibiya Crossing. Hibiya Crossing, as it is known to the Japanese, is the intersection of Z Avenue, running east and west, and A Avenue, running north and south. The avenue names were applied by the U.S. Occupation Authorities and mean nothing whatsoever to the Japanese. As you stand at the crossing looking down Z Avenue westward, on your left is Hibiya Park, and on your right is the so-called outer moat of the Imperial Palace. Hibiya Park used to be a Japanese noble's residence, and, later, a military drill ground. Today it is planted with delicate wisteria and eye-tingling azaleas that flower in May, and spectacular chrysanthemums that bloom in November.

Now walk northward up A Avenue to Y Avenue, turn left and continue to the great plaza fronting the famous Nijubashi, or Double Bridge. It is here that the Japanese people regularly gather to pay homage to their emperor on January 2 (New Year's), and also on his birthday, April 29. The moat that runs around the palace grounds is the so-called inner moat. In the old days, the palace was much larger and was a defensive complex of moat-and-wall within moat-and-wall. Today much of the moat system has been filled in and the walls destroyed, leaving only the two remaining moat systems.

From the Double Bridge proceed southward along the broad street that fronts it. This is First Street, as named by the Occupation authorities, and it turns right, becoming a continuation of Z Avenue. As you turn right, you can look backward and see Z Avenue stretching eastward through the Ginza's heart. Now walk along until you come to a slight incline. A street running off to your left and up a small hill leads to an imposing building whose top seems to resemble a Mayan temple. This is the Diet (Legislature) Building, and it stands atop Kasumigaseki Hill. A three-storied structure, it is 215 feet in height and is a conspicuous landmark. It took 18 years to construct the building, which was completed in 1936. Foreign correspondents sometimes call it Tokyo's Madison Square Garden, because of the fist fights that have taken place there between Diet representatives of opposing parties when issues got too heated for words.

Continuing your trek, return to Hibiya Crossing. This time go eastward along Z Avenue. You are entering the fabulous Ginza area, which is a combination shopping and entertainment section. Drab though it may appear in the daytime, when the main lure is the goods displayed in the various shops, it is a mulitcolored display of neons in the nighttime. Tip: If you want to save wear and tear on your pocketbook, visit the Ginza in the daytime. Shopping is far easier on the purse than the cute little kimonoed girls in the various bars and cabarets. (By the way, the Ginza is really an area, although there is a Ginza street, which will be the starting point of the next walking tour.)

Trip 2. The best way to start on this tour is to take a taxi to the Mitsukoshi Department Store. It would be a good idea to go into the store first and visit its various departments. A department store expedition has never failed to interest and excite tourists. After your exploration, go southward down the street that fronts the building. This is called Ginzadori, or Ginza Street, one of the few exceptions which prove the rule that Tokyo streets have no names. Ginza Street divides the Ginza area into the Nishi-Ginza, or West Ginza, and the Higashi-Ginza, or East Ginza. (Just south of the department store is the Nihombashi Bridge, famous in the past as the absolute center of Tokyo and from where all distances from Tokyo are measured.)

As you walk southward along Ginza Street, you will pass many shops, some of the finest and most famous in Tokyo. There is Ando, known for its cloisonné; Mikimoto, whose cultured pearls have won world renown; and the Matsuya, Matsuzakaya, and Mitsukoshi department stores, all equally rewarding for the browsing shopper.

When you get to Z Avenue, to the left is a large building with a temple-like roof. This is the Kabuki-za, one of the most popular theaters in Tokyo. Reconstructed in 1950 at a cost of over three-quarters of a million dollars, it is a splendid example of modern Japanese architecture.

Turning left on Z Avenue and passing the Kabuki-za, continue until you get to Tenth Street and then turn right. You are now at the famous Central Wholesale Market of Tsukiji, where fruits, vegetables, and meat are sold at wholesale prices. The fish auction, where most of the daily catch brought into Tokyo is sold, takes place between 5 A.M. and 6 A.M.

Now return to Z Avenue and head down in the opposite direction, crossing Ginza Street again and continuing on. As you walk along, you will pass the many shops for which the Ginza district is famous. Cross Fifth and Fourth Streets; just beyond the latter, you will see a large building on your right. It is the Asahi Shimbun Building, which provides news flashes on top of the building, like the former Times tower in New York. The *Asahi Shimbun* is one of Japan's national newspapers, being distributed daily throughout the nation, with various local editions, and claims a circulation of four and a half-million a day. Just past the Asahi you will see on your right the Nichigeki Theater, Tokyo's largest movie theater. In this area, called the Yurakucho, you will find a cluster of theaters. Another cluster of theaters will be found on your left down the cross street just before Hibiya Crossing. This street goes to the Imperial Hotel. On the northwest corner from the Imperial is the famed Takarazuka Theater where the 'Zuka girls give their performances. This all-girl troupe gained international fame from James Michener's *Sayonara*. But long before the novel and movie, the 'Zuka girls were the darlings of the Japanese. They are the female of the Kabuki in that girls play both male and female roles, as opposed to the latter where all roles are played by men. The Takarazuka theater performances would interest psychiatrists. As you know, for thousands of years Japanese women have been dominated by their fathers, brothers, and husbands. Marriages were always arranged, and there was little in the way of a boy-and-girl courtship, love, or romance in the western sense. In the past few decades, romantic love has taken the fancy of Japanese girls, who dream of a knight on a white charger coming to take them by storm. The Takarazuka performances specialize in romantic operettas in which love, sex appeal, and romance are all that make life worth living. The young girls who make up the vast majority of the audience drink it all in, have an emotional binge, cry not a little, and go home steeped in romance.

Trip 3. Take a taxi, telling the driver to take you to Meiji Gai-en (May-jee Guy-en). This is the Meiji Outer Garden and consists of a park with an oval roadway. At the south end of the park is a broad avenue lined with gingko trees—whose leaves turn a deep green in spring and a brilliant yellow in autumn—providing a colorful approach to the Meiji Memorial Picture Gallery, which lies at the north end of, but within, the oval enclosure made by the encircling roadway. The gallery is dedicated to the Emperor Meiji and contains pictures painted by leading Japanese artists. Walking along the left side of the oval driveway away from the boulevard of gingko trees, you will see on your left, and opposite the Meiji Memorial Picture Gallery, the Olympic Stadium, built for the Tokyo Olympics.

Continue along the road, which branches just at the bend of the stadium, and take the left fork. You are now headed along another street lined with gingko trees and towards the Meiji Inner Garden, about a 15-minute walk from the Outer Garden.

The Inner Garden contains the Meiji Shrine, one of the holiest places for the Japanese. It was erected to the memory of Emperor Meiji, who died in 1912 and is credited with making a modern nation out of Japan. The grounds of the Inner Garden cover an area of about 179 acres and are filled with trees and shrubs contributed by people from all over the country. There is an iris garden here containing 80 varieties of the flower and a pond filled with water lilies. Both blossom in late June and early July.

Many festivals are held at Meiji Shrine, but the most important is that held on the anniversary of the Emperor Meiji's birthday on November 3, when *bugaku,* which is ancient court music and dancing with the dancers wearing colorful costumes, is performed on the stage in front of the sanctuary.

Trip 4. Take a taxi and tell the driver to take you to the Kokusai Gekijo (Koke-sigh Geh-kee-joe). It is in the notorious Asakusa area, famed for being a rough-and-ready playground for the great mass of people in Tokyo. In other words, it is a place where prices are lower and pleasures lustier. The Kokusai Gekijo boasts the largest stage in the Far East, on which, their advertisements say, three hundred or more girls gather in colorful stage spectacles. The stage is large, the spectacles are colorful but the number of girls appearing on the stage at one time is closer to seventy than three hundred. But more of this all-girl troupe, which is a rival to the Takarazuka troupe, under Entertainment.

Across from the Kokusai Gekijo is the Asakusa amusement area. The best way to explore this conglomeration of stores, theaters, pleasure palaces, and so forth is to follow your nose. Entering from the Kokusai Gekijo side, you will see on your left a covered arcade. This is fille d with all sorts of shops where the wares are as good and cheaper than in the Ginza. The large temple that lies at the end of a walk—also filled with little shops but not roofed over like the arcade—is the Asakusa Kwannon Temple. The real name of this structure, which is typical of Japanese temples, is the Sensoji Temple. However, because its main hall is dedicated to the Kwannon, the Goddess of Mercy, it is better known as the Asakusa Kwannon. The street along which you pass towards the temple is quite colorful. It is about 150 yards long and 10 yards wide and the shops are all gaily decorated.

At the western end of this area is the Shinsekai, or New World Cabaret. It is housed in a veritable oriental pleasure palace where the cabaret is only one of its activities. In this building there are restaurants, *pachinko* parlors, a turkish bath, and a movie house. It seeks to meet the varied demands of all who enter. Down the road to the east of the Shinsekai is a row of "strip tease" theaters. You might be able to get in, although these theaters generally are barred to foreigners. The same rule applies to many of the cabarets in the Asakusa. If you can get in, you will have an interesting time rubbing shoulders with Tokyo's very down-to-earth types and your bill will be small. But don't be disappointed if you are refused admittance.

Now go through the covered arcade until you come to the end, fronting a street. Cross the street and continue on until you come to an area where there are many turkish baths. This place is the Yoshiwara district, which until 1958 was the largest and busiest red-light district in the Far East. Japan's antiprostitution law closed the brothels down, but there is some suspicion that the girls that once worked for the houses took a quick (1 hour) course in massaging and are now the masseuses of the Yoshiwara. At any rate, as you walk along this area, remember that it was here that much of Japan's great literature and art was born. It was the gathering place of the rich and the poor, of the student, the artist, the writer, and the warrior in its time.

Trip 5. Take a taxi to Shibuya Station (it is pronounced exactly as spelled). Shibuya is one of Tokyo's many wards and consists of a sprawling area whose entertainment center is located around the station. You will see a huge department store when you arrive at the station. This is the Tokyo Department Store and would be a good place in which to browse, like all Japanese department stores, if you feel like it. In the plaza that is formed by the station and the store, look for a statue of a dog. This is the famous Shibuya dog, a favorite rendezvous for Tokyo residents, especially in the teen-age category.

Many a boy meets girl at this statue; "Meet me at the Shibuya dog at such and such a time" being the usual phrase. The statue is of a dog named Chuken Hachiko whose master went away and never returned. The dog waited here daily for his master to come back, fed by passers-by, until he died. In its memory, and out of respect for its faithfulness, the Japanese erected the statue.

For an interesting walking tour, go out to the main street that runs past the plaza and turn left. From here you are on your own. Just keep walking, going wherever fancy decides, and you will see a Tokyo that no formal tour can produce. Go into the little streets and see how they open into little squares. In some parts restaurants abound, and everywhere are the little shops presenting their wares in the open for your inspection.

Trip 6. This tour actually could be done in conjunction with Trip 4, because it is on the way to the Asakusa. Take a taxi to Ueno Koen (Oo-ay-no Ko-en), which means, in English, Ueno Park. It covers about 210 acres and once was the estate of a Japanese feudal lord, which was taken over by the Tokugawas (the military dictators that once controlled Japan) in the first half of the 17th century. The shogun built a Buddhist temple there and made it the family temple. During a battle between the forces supporting the emperor and those supporting the shogun, at the time of the Meiji Restoration, the temple was burned. In 1878, ten years after the Emperor Meiji made Tokyo his capital, the entire area was made into a park.

The taxi will let you off before a broad flight of stone steps. The area at the top of these steps is called Sakura-ga-oka, or Cherry Blossom Hill, because of the three thousand cherry trees planted there which burst forth into bloom in April, making Cherry Blossom Hill a gathering place for all who wish to view the delicate blossoms at their best.

At the other end of the park is a massive building. This is the National Museum, opened in 1938. There are twenty-five galleries in this two-storied building, which is the site of periodic exhibitions of paintings, calligraphy, textiles, ceramics, lacquerware, metal work, and sculpture. The museum is open throughout the year, except on Mondays, from about 9 A.M. to 4 P.M. Admission fee is 50 *yen.*

To the left of the National Museum is the Metropolitan Fine Art Gallery; and along the road running at right angles to the broad avenue will be found the Faculties of Fine Arts—and of Music— of the Tokyo University of Arts, the Japan Academy, and the Japan Science Conference. Behind the Japan Academy are the National Science Museum and the National Museum of Western Art. Next to the Faculty of Music is the Ueno Library. South of the University of Fine Arts are the Ueno Zoological Gardens.

As you return to the entrance along the avenue of cherry trees, on your right is the Toshogu Shrine and, near it, a pagoda. Nearby you will see an equestrian statue of Prince Komatsu of the Imperial Family. Behind the statue are a Japanese Cypress and a magnolia tree, both planted by General and Mrs. Ulysses S. Grant in 1879 when they visited the park with the Emperor Meiji during their stopover in Japan on their round-the-world tour.

A word about the Toshogu Shrine: It was founded in 1626 in the memory of the first Tokugawa shogun, Ieyasu. It was remodeled in 1651 and has remained unchanged since. It is now under the care of the Cultural Properties Protection Commission of the Ministry of Education. The stone and bronze lanterns lining the approach to the shrine were gifts of the *daimyo,* or feudal lords. Among the shrine's treasures are letters written by Shogun Ieyasu and a collection of weapons.

To the west of the main road is Lake Shinobazu. The temple on the island is the shrine of Benten, the goddess of good fortune. The lake is about a mile and a half in circumference and has boating facilities. The north third of the lake is the habitat of aquatic birds and animals and is a branch of the Ueno Zoo; crowds of people gather to watch when they are fed.

If you can finish this tour in time, you might take a cab out to the Asakusa and continue on with Trip 4 instead of returning to your hotel. The contrast between the two sections is great, and is an excellent way of seeing two sides of the many-faceted face of Japan.

Trip 7. Tell the taxi-driver to take you to—and this is a tough one but worth trying to pronounce—Sumidaku Ryogokubashi (Soo-mee-dah-koo Ree-yoh-gohk-bah-shee), which means "Ryogoku Bridge located in Sumida Ward." It is one of several bridges that cross Tokyo's Sumida River, which empties into Tokyo Bay.

Less than a mile to the north is the Kuramae Bridge. Near it is the Kuramae Kokugikan, the headquarters of Japanese *sumo,* the unique sport (something like wrestling) which is becoming more popular with the foreigners. *Sumo* tournaments lasting fifteen days each are held here in January, May, and September, in a hall which can seat 10,000 spectators. There is also a *sumo* museum, which is open from 9 A.M. to 5 P.M. daily except Sundays.

Not too far from the *sumo* headquarters on the east bank of the Sumida is one of the most tragic spots in Tokyo's history. At the time of the 1923 earthquake, it was an open space covering about eight acres. Here Japanese fled for safety from the fire that raged after the earthquake struck, bringing their belongings with them. About 40,000 people gathered and piled their goods on the ground.

Flying sparks from the surrounding buildings set fire to the people's belongings, trapping the victims. An estimated 35,000 died here. In the three-story pagoda of the Earthquake Memorial Hall erected in the middle of the area, the charred bones of the victims are kept in huge urns. In a corner of the hall is a temple bell consecrated by Chinese Buddhists to the souls of those who lost their lives in the disaster. The incense burning before the altar in the hall has never been allowed to go out since it was lit four days after the 1923 earthquake. Every year on September 1, the day when the catastrophe occurred, a service in memory of the dead is held here.

Adjoining the memorial ground is a small garden. It was donated by a Japanese nobleman in 1922 and at that time was one of the most elaborate landscape gardens in the capital. Many of its uniquely beautiful features were lost, however, the following year in the earthquake and fire.

A little over a half-mile away and after passing two more bridges, the Umaya and Komagata, is the Azuma Bridge. Just north of this bridge and stretching for a mile along both banks of the Sumida is Sumida Park, one of the three largest parks in Tokyo. Three lines of promenades and a motor driveway run along the bank, and rows of cherry trees and weeping willows border the walks and the driveway. The finest part of the park is in Mukojima, on the east bank of the river. This area formerly was the garden of a mansion belonging to a branch of the Tokugawa family.

ACCOMMODATIONS There are three hotels which can be considered in the luxury category: the Okura, Palace, and Tokyo Hilton. Actually, the Okura is in a class by itself, and should be considered as such, although that is not intended to put down the Palace and Hilton hotels, which are just fine. But the Okura is really one of the great hotels of the world, and should be in a separate category; its rates are comparatively reasonable, all things considered.

Staying at a luxury or first-class hotel in Tokyo is an interesting experience. There's usually a color television set in the room, and watching the programs (and particularly the commercials) can be very diverting even if you don't understand the language. However, there is almost always an English-language broadcast going on, and some hotels even have special cable programs in English. Each room should have slippers for both men and women, plus comfortable *yukata* (a type of robe) to wear; if by some chance it isn't in your room, the maid will bring it. Employees are not used to tips, and except for the baggage porter, don't bother to give them unless you've bothered someone for special services. Don't forget that there's a 10% service charge added to your room rate, and that takes care of almost all tipping. (Unfortunately, there's also a 10% government tax on your room as well.)

Okura Hotel. Located across the street from the American Embassy, in its own grounds, with a swimming pool and numerous restaurants. In my opinion, this is the best hotel in Tokyo, all things considered. The rooms are attractively decorated and spacious, the service is good, and the atmosphere pleasant. The hotel is about 10 minutes from the center of town, but taxis are usually available, and are quite inexpensive. There is a Starlight Lounge, where on clear nights a beautiful view of Tokyo may be had. The Okura has 980 western-style rooms, and 11 in the Japanese-style, and they're absolutely beautiful; even if you prefer to sleep in a western-style room, ask to see one of the Japanese rooms. The hotel is in two sections, consisting of Main Building and South Wing, but both are excellent.

Tokyo Hilton. Naturally, by any name, a Hilton hotel is the same all over the world, offering American tourists a taste of their homeland. It has 475 western rooms and 3 Japanese; all of these are well-decorated and pleasant. Good selection of shops in the arcade, and many restaurants from which to choose. There is, surprisingly enough for a Hilton hotel, a reasonable degree of Japanese atmosphere, and to my way of thinking, this may be one of the best Hilton hotels in the chain. It's about 10 minutes from the center of town.

Imperial Hotel. This hotel was originally designed by Frank Lloyd Wright. All traces of his original structure have disappeared having been replaced by several tower buildings, and one very new wing. It has a marvelous location in downtown Tokyo, convenient to everything. The layout of the hotel's wings is odd, and considerable walking is involved because of the sequential fashion in which additions to the hotel were added. The lobby bears an unfortunate resemblance to a busy airport terminal, and is very commercial and anything but attractive. The rooms are satisfactory, however.

FIRST-CLASS HOTELS: Some people may object to this classification because the prices and the quality of accommodations are not far behind those of the above-classified de luxe hotels. However, there is just the slightest difference between those about to be listed and those already named, enough of a difference to warrant the classifications.

Palace Hotel. This modern luxury hotel has a unique location, directly across the street from the Imperial Palace, affording its guests the opportunity to see the walls and moats from their window (if they face in the right direction). The Palace Hotel has an open, free-standing appearance because of its location in an area with no other tall buildings. It has 409 western rooms, just a trifle small, with soundproofed windows.

Keio Plaza Inter-Continental. This hotel is a giant—47 stories tall with two buildings—located somewhat out of the center of town in the Shinjuku district, noted for its entertainment, theaters, etc. The guest rooms are located on the 10th to 41st floors and have marvelous views. Rooms are somewhat small, service is good, and rates are moderate. The Keio Plaza is about a 25-minute cab ride from downtown Tokyo, which is expensive; it's a cheap ride by subway.

Pacific Hotel. Another large hotel, with 1,000 rooms in a most attractive 30-story building in its own gardens well set back from Tokyo noise. Rooms are moderate in size, fairly attractive, and rates are in the medium category. Excellent facilities for large gatherings, and the hotel concentrates on tours, conventions, etc.

New Otani Hotel. An absolutely enormous hotel with 2,050 western-style rooms and 2 in the Japanese fashion (so you can see what they look like). This 20-story hotel with a 40-story tower is located about 10 minutes from downtown Tokyo, and has very attractive rooms, a shopping arcade, and several restaurants.

Century Hyatt Tokyo. In the Shinjuku district, a 28-story hotel facing Shinjuku Park. Impressive 8-story lobby, many restaurants and shops. Guest rooms have color TV and refrigerator.

New Japan Hotel. From the standpoint of those who like night life, this may be the most conveniently located hotel. It has nice rooms, having 369 western-style and 131 Japanese-style accommodations. It caters to western and Japanese tourists at the same time, and has a certain Japanese flavor lacking in the other luxury hotels; there is a tea-ceremony room, which offers the tourist a chance to see the famous ceremony without going to a special teahouse.

Odakyu Century Hyatt Regency Tokyo. This is a large, 28-story hotel with 800 rooms. Most of them are of fair size, and the lobby is enormous. There are no less than 8 restaurants and many shops. (I think, however, the management should change the ponderous [and forgettable] name of the hotel.)

Kokusai Kanko Hotel. Near Tokyo Station, its claim to fame is convenient location. Rooms are fair enough, although the lobby has little or no personality. It also has a golf driving-range on the roof. It offers 88 western-style rooms, all with bath.

Ginza Tokyu Hotel. In the Ginza district, close to the theatrical area, and particularly handy for shopping, walking, etc., being near the heart of the city. All of its rooms are good-sized, all with bath, but in a somewhat noisy location.

Azabu Prince Hotel. A little away from the center of town, but with a charming atmosphere. It has a Japanese-style main building, and offers 31 western-style rooms, all with bath. It's usually quite tranquil and peaceful.

Tokyo Prince Hotel. This newish hotel is fairly well located. There are 510 western-style rooms, which are fairly large and reasonably well furnished. This is the most important convention hotel in Tokyo; about half of them are held here. It's near Shiba Park, in the shadow of Tokyo Tower. There are 7 restaurants, plus poolside barbecues in summer.

Takanawa Prince Hotel. Formerly a royal residence. Although far from the center of things, situated about midway between Tokyo Station and Tokyo International Airport, it has spacious grounds and two swimming pools to recommend it. It offers 96 western-style and 5 Japanese-style rooms, all with bath.

Akasaka Prince Hotel. Located in the Akasaka, the district of nightclubs and Japanese restaurants which cater to high-class geisha parties. Swimming pool. It has 51 western-style rooms and 1 Japanese-style room, all with baths. Rather inconvenient for most tourists, but lots of Japanese atmosphere.

Diamond Hotel. Away from the center of activity but not too far-off. Has an excellent Chinese restaurant. 162 western-style rooms, almost all with bath; most rooms are quite pleasant.

Miyako Hotel Tokyo. A 500-room hotel set in more than 5 acres of gardens, this is a very good place to stay, although not inexpensive. Near the Meguro Railway Station, and about a half hour from the Tokyo Central Station and Haneda Airport.

POPULAR-PRICED HOTELS:

Marunouchi Hotel. In the Marunouchi, or Central Business District; 3 minutes' walk from Tokyo Station. Offers 208 western-style rooms; 2 Japanese-style; all with bath.

Dai-Ichi Hotel. Tokyo's largest hotel with 1,238 rooms, 876 with baths; 23 Japanese-style rooms.

Shiba Park Hotel. The inexpensive version of the Imperial Hotel and run by a son of the Imperial's owner; 200 western-style rooms.

Tokyo Station Hotel. In Tokyo Station Building; 60 western-style rooms; only 23 with bath.

Fairmont Hotel. A modern hotel facing a small lake; has its own swimming pool. The new wing has very pleasant rooms. Altogether 195 rooms.

Tokyo Grand Hotel. Near the Japanese Diet (Legislature); 54 western-style rooms; somewhat busy, commercial atmosphere.

Hotel Toshi Center. Forty-one western-style rooms and 14 in the Japanese style. Modern, somewhat small rooms; rates are somewhat lower than the others in this category.

JAPANESE INNS: The Japan Ryokan Guide has a list of 26 *ryokans* (the name given to Japanese inns) in Tokyo with rooms suitable for foreign guests. A Japanese inn (in Tokyo) can only be recommended to the occasional tourist who really wants to live in the local fashion; you'll enjoy it, but decide for yourself if you want to sleep on the floor, etc. Although it is better to have your tourist agency make arrangements for you, after giving specific instructions as to what kind of accommodations you want, here is a list of a few that can be specially recommended:

Fukudaya. This *ryokan* is two minutes from Yotsuya Station and close to Sophia University. It has 5 rooms with private bath and the moderately high rates include two meals daily.

Kyoine. Not far from the Fukudaya (described above); it also has 5 rooms with bath, and medium rates include two meals daily. Friendly, charming atmosphere.

Seikoen Hirano. Another well-known Japanese inn that is accustomed to foreigners. It is situated in the Akasaka district and is close to many good restaurants in the Roppongi and Akasaka areas, as well as nightspots, although quite far away from the downtown area.

Honjin. On your way out to Shinjuku, one of the major wards of Tokyo, you may pass what looks like a Japanese castle. It will be the Honjin Hotel, which claims that in keeping with its castle-like appearance it treats all guests like *samurai,* up to, but not including, giving them swords. The Honjin is famous because of its castle style of architecture and its good service. It has 46 Japanese-style and 9 western-style rooms, all with bath, and the medium rates do not include meals.

RESTAURANTS It is not easy to write about restaurants in Tokyo, not because there are so many, but because it is difficult to list them. Many of the leading Japanese restaurants never come to the attention of foreigners. They are the ones to which geishas are called and which cater only to those Japanese with highly developed taste buds and/or expense accounts; westerners would surely feel out of place in them, and for this reason they have not been listed. I personally have only gone in the company of Japanese friends, and would not wish to go alone. Other restaurants specialize in a type of food, like *sushi, tempura, yakitori, etc.* The following list, therefore, will be divided into specialty restaurants and those with a national cuisine, the latter being foreign-style and not Japanese. We will not even attempt to list the restaurants that provide geisha entertainment, as previously mentioned. The reason is not based on any moralistic views, for you can take your wife to a geisha party, but on the fact that it would be impractical for any tourist to find his way to one and try to inquire of the bill of fare in a place where only Japanese is spoken. Also, you can't just say, "Let's have ourselves a geisha party." It's necessary to call ahead of time, tell them how many people will be in the party, how many geishas you will want and for how long, and all of this conversation must be conducted in Japanese. Furthermore, if the management of the restaurant does not know you, no matter how fluent your Japanese, he will be apt to turn you down politely by saying the place is full for the night. So you see why it is impractical to list this type of restaurant.

Getting to most restaurants involves little difficulty. Almost all of the most popular restaurants in Tokyo have supplied the leading hotels with medium-sized cards which include their names and addresses in Japanese as well as English. These cards may be obtained at the City or Information Desk in your hotel. When you step into a taxi, merely hand the card to the driver and he shouldn't have any trouble taking you to your destination.

The listing that follows will therefore be in accordance with the type of national cuisine served.

CHINESE: Tokyo has a host of Chinese restaurants, so many, in fact, that it would be impossible to count them. Almost every provincial style of Chinese cuisine is offered. For example, don't ask for Peking duck at a Szechuan restaurant or for Szechuan smoked duck at a Cantonese restaurant. They will oblige if you do order it, but you will be in for a disappointment. The following four Chinese restaurants are to be recommended on all counts.

The Szechuan, at Tamaracho, is the best of its kind. Here the smoked duck is as it should be, juicy with the right smoky flavor. Szechuan food is highly spiced, so be prepared for it. Try the shrimps in chili sauce if you want to have something different and delicious. But by all means order the smoked duck.

Sanno, at 77, 2-chome, Nagatacho, Chiyoda-du between the Hotel New Japan and the Sanno Hotel serves food in the Shanghai style. It is in a four-story building with private rooms, ornately decorated. The food is exceptionally good.

Liu Yuan, 9, 6-Gochi, Shiba Park, Minato-ku, another four-story food emporium offering Cantonese, Szechuan, Foochow, and Shanghai food. If you order Cantonese dishes, however, you will be more than satisfied. It is a big, elaborate affair with elevator doors shaped and colored like the full moon. Eat lunch here; the waitresses bring Chinese food (*dim-sum*) around in trays for you to pick what you want.

FRENCH: There are three restaurants deserving of the name of French, though there are many others which classify themselves as such. First and foremost is the *très élégant Maxim's de Paris,* located in the basement of the Sony Building at 3-1, 5-chome, Ginza, Chuo-ku, Tel. 572-3621. Maxim's of Paris created this restaurant giving its Japanese offspring its own name. The same cuisine as you will find in the parent restaurant is there along with the same service, both of which gave the Paris restaurant its five-star rating. Maxim's is expensive, very expensive. In fact, it may well be the most costly restaurant in Japan. The second excellent French restaurant is *Shido,* located in the basement of the Tokyo Broadcasting System's building at 3-3, 5-chome, Akasaka, Minato-ku, Tel. 582-5891/3. It offers delicious French dishes by Paris-trained chefs, with roast beef a specialty. Lunch is expensive, but nothing like the charges made at Maxim's. The third of the recommendable trio français is *Crescent,* 1, 8-gochi, Shiba Park, Minato-ku, Tel. 436-3211, located close to Tokyo Tower in an off-the-road setting which lends a peaceful, quiet atmosphere. Incongruously, the restaurant is in an English-cottage-style building. Prices are within reason.

GERMAN: *Lohmeyer* at 3-14, 5-chome, Ginza-nishi, Chuo-ku, is the better of Tokyo's two best-known German restaurants. Its prices are reasonable, and its dinners are plain German fare, but very good.

If you like sauerbraten or pig's knuckles, this is the place. *Ketel* at 5-15 chome, Ginza-nishi, Chuo-ku, located not far from Lohmeyer, is not quite so German or as good as its rival. However, if Lohmeyer is filled, Ketel is fairly good.

INDIAN: The *Ashoka*, at 1, 7-chome, Ginza, is worth trying, particularly if you aren't continuing on to India. It specializes in those excellent *tandoori* chicken preparations, as well as a range of good curries. The cooking is quite authentic and the decor is attractive.

ITALIAN: There are many Italian restaurants in Tokyo; or rather, should we say, restaurants that advertise themselves as Italian. Because of lack of proper ingredients Italian food in Tokyo does not taste the same as in New York or Italy. But the one that comes the closest is *Antonio's* at 1-20, 3-chome, Nishi Azabu, Minato-ku. Antonio is an Italian sailor who was stranded in Japan after the war. His dishes are good, the prices are low, the service terrible. *Chianti* at Iigura, Katamachi, near the Russian Embassy, is another small restaurant that tries its best and may even be better than Antonio's, on occasion. Prices reasonable; food good; service usually good.

RUSSIAN: *Manos* at Akasaka Tamachi, 4-chome, is open almost all day and night. Russian chefs cook borscht and blini, which are quite good. Prices reasonable; service good.

STEAKS: Now we reach a culinary treat which can be written about with superlatives and without exaggeration. For premium Japanese beef, if not the best in the world from the standpoint of tenderness and taste, at least is among the very best. The least you can say about it (assuming you're from Texas) is that it has no superior, though it may have its peers.

Akasaka Misono at 30, 3-chome, Akasaka, Shinmachi, Minato-ku, is one of several steak houses where the cook broils the meat on a large table-sized grill in front of you, cuts it up into edible pieces and pushes the pieces to your area of the table-grill for you to eat, along with Japanese vegetables, with chopsticks. The steaks are superb, the service excellent—insofar as each table-grill has its own chef—the prices are expensive, but the check won't be too astronomical if you don't drink scotch, or other imported liquors. *Suehiro,* behind the Matsuzakaya Department Store; the address is 3, 6-chome, Ginza, Chuo-ku. It has several floors serving steaks and *sukiyaki.* Some steaks are served whole, in the western style, and are quite good but like all steaks in Japan, expensive. Service is pleasant and efficient. They also serve many Japanese dishes.

Sakurammbo, located down a little alley in Akasaka at 14, 4-chome, Akasaka, Tamachi, Minato-ku, is a steak place where the meat is served differently. Here you sit at long bars, the top of which is an iron grill where the steak—or pork, lamb, or chicken—is barbecued in front of you. It differs from Misono (mentioned above) not only in the shape of the grill but also in the fact that you cook the meat yourself. A sauce is also furnished in which you can dip the meat after you cook it to your taste. Prices reasonable; service is good and the little girls who bring out the food you are going to cook are pretty, cheery, and make for better digestion.

Tsutsui is another good steak place that serves its steak a bit differently. It is up the street from Sakarammbo, at 16, 4-chome Shinmachi, Akasaka, Minato-ku. In addition to the regular thick, tender steak, try the *sogayaki,* or ginger beef. This is steak fried in a ginger sauce and it is excellent. Prices reasonable; service excellent. Try to get a Japanese room so that you can enjoy privacy and comfort (except for sitting on the floor) while eating your steak.

Club Rosier, located past Roppongi on the way to Tokyo Tower at Mikawadaimachi, Minato-ku; it has excellent steaks served in as pleasant and quiet a surrounding as you can find in Japan. Its bar is the best-stocked one in Japan, with all brands of scotches, bourbons, cognacs, etc. lined up behind the bar. Prices reasonable; service excellent.

SPECIALIZED JAPANESE RESTAURANTS: In this group I have included those restaurants which specialize in only one type of dish. Don't go there if you want to eat something different; very often, they won't be able to serve you.

Sukiyaki. For some reason, first-time visitors think that *sukiyaki* is the national dish of Japan; they could not be more wrong. *Sukiyaki* is nothing more or less than sautéed beef and vegetables. It is very good, but there are other dishes that are equally good. But if it's *sukiyaki* you want, try the Imperial Hotel's Japanese restaurant and the Kegon Hotel's dining room. (The Kegon is at 39, 1-chome, Yoyogi, Shibuya-ku.) Zakuro also serves perfectly prepared *sukiyaki.*

Tonkatsu. This is tenderloin of pork dipped in a batter and deep-fried. Done properly, it is delicious and tender; at the wrong places it's likely to consist chiefly of fat with just a little bit of very tough pork. The outstanding *tonkatsu* restaurant is Horaiya, at 6, 1-chome, Uenomachi, Daito-ku. Few foreign residents know about it, but those Japanese who know their *tonkatsu* swear by it. Have some of the excellent Japanese beer with *edamame,* soy beans cooked in the pod, before you dive into the pork. Prices reasonable; service good.

Tempura. There are several restaurants specializing in this dish, which consists of seafood and vegetables dipped into batter and deep-fried. Most of them are very expensive; the cook must be especially skillful, making the batter carefully and watching the temperature of the frying oil. Ten Ichi at 5-chome, Ginza-nishi, is one of the best with the most reasonable prices.

Crab. The Japanese regard fresh crab as one of their outstanding delicacies, and after eating it in Tokyo, I can only agree heartily. The best single place for crab is at a very attractive restaurant (located near Roppongi Crossing) called *Kani-Seryna.* Here you'll find a most unusual menu listing crab in more than a dozen different styles—for example, crab dumplings, crab soup, cooked crab, cold crab, and so forth. They also have a non-crab item on the menu consisting of steak cooked on a volcanic stone, but the real reason for coming here is to have a crab dinner. Fairly expensive, I must add.

Yakitori. This excellent dish consists of bits of chicken barbecued on skewers over a charcoal fire; it's a favorite with both Japanese and foreigners. Isehiro in Kyobashi, and Torigin at 5-chome, Ginza-nishi, are the best of many good *yakitori* restaurants. Prices very reasonable at both places: service very good.

Sushi. A great favorite among Japanese and an even greater favorite among those foreigners who have overcome their prejudice against raw fish. *Sushi* consists of raw fish placed over lightly vinegared rice with some grated *wasabi,* the root of a mountain plant and very spicy. *Sashimi* is raw fish without the rice. If you feel adventurous—try *sushi* at Ozasa, at 8-chome, Ginza-nishi. Although expensive, you will be giving yourself the best chance to learn to like the dish. Better try this first, before you attempt a complete meal.

Genghis Khan Barbecue. This is food prepared in the Mongolian style, with beef, pork, and chicken barbecued on a grill in front of you along with various types of vegetables. Chinzaso (a most attractive garden restaurant) is the most notable of this culinary genre. It is at 41 Sekiguchidaimachi, Bunkyo-ku (about 20 minutes out by taxi). Prices moderate to high; service good.

Wild Game. There are various restaurants offering wild game, but Akahane at Fukuyoshicho, Minato-ku, is the outstanding one. It offers wild duck, even sometimes including the pellets that killed it, and other game served barbecue-style. For an adventure, try the bees as an appetizer snack.

Shabu Shabu. This dish consists of thin slices of meat which the diner himself dips in boiling broth until cooked, then places in the special *gomadare* sauce; it's delicious. The best place is Zakuro, located in Akasaka in front of the American Embassy and just down the hill from the Okura Hotel.

Rabato. This is country-style Japanese cooking and is generally quite appealing to most Americans. The food is somewhat simpler than usual and consists of many broiled dishes cooked over open fires. The best place is Inakaya, in the Roppongi district.

SHOPPING   Anything said about shopping in Japan must be prefaced (again) with the warning that the tourist must be sure to obtain the proper discount on certain goods (like pearls, cameras, and optical goods) which are sold tax-free to tourists. Formerly on arriving in Japan, a certificate was attached to one's passport. But many tourists forget to carry their passports with them, so now the system is somewhat different. Stores authorized to sell tax-free merchandise have new forms. When you buy something tax-free, the shopkeeper will enter the item on a line in the certificate, and you will be required to sign the form. The purpose of this entry is to let the customs inspector know what you have bought so that, on your departure, the official can ask you to show it to him.

The most popular buys in Japan are cultured pearls, cameras, and transistor radios. Japanese *cameras* vie with those of Germany as the world's best, and many people find them superior. Professional cameramen say that the Japanese lenses surpass those of the German, although German cameras are perhaps mechanically superior. The superiority of Japanese lens-making extends to binoculars, making anything in this line a good buy, from opera glasses to telescopes. Cameras are subject to a tax as high as 18%, and therefore the little piece of paper which you fill out results in a substantial saving. All sorts of cameras are sold, including the very small ones that will take a 36-print roll of film at half-size and produce 72 prints to the roll. In the regular 35 mm. size, you can get a camera practically at any price, depending on your desires.

Cultured pearls are what the women ask for immediately. Japan is the land of cultured pearls. The Pavlov of the cultured-pearl-making industry was Kokichi Mikimoto, the son of a noodle-maker who, after years of patient research, learned how to induce an oyster to make a pearl for him and built up what today is a thriving multimillion-dollar business engaged in by many different pearl dealers. The fact that there are many different pearl dealers should not scare you off. If you are the cautious type, stick to the pearl dealers that you find in your hotel arcade. You can always get the tax off and if you are persuasive enough, probably obtain another 10% as a courtesy. The most famous place to buy pearls is the shop of *K. Mikimoto* (located on the Ginza and with some hotel arcade branches), but his prices are undoubtedly the highest in town. *Yamato Brothers* (a little difficult to find but worth the trouble, at No. 12-12, Ginza 6 Chome, Chuo-ku; tel: 571-2688) is small, very reliable, and much lower in price; the owner is most obliging and his values may be the best in town.

Attention, girls! We're going to discuss pearls, how to buy them, and what they cost. In the first place, good pearls cost money, and if you've got visions of purchasing a good strand for $50, all I can say is forget it. Prices are dependent upon a series of factors—color, shape, size, luster, and also on the demand for certain types of pearls. The matter of color is a personal choice, but should be based upon an individual's skin tone. Obviously what looks good on a woman with an olive complexion will not be nearly so suitable on a woman with a pale, white skin. Pearls come in cream, white, pink, gold, green and black, and variations in between. At the moment, a whitish-pink color is regarded as the best, and naturally prices are higher for this more desirable shade. (Caution: many pearls are being tinted after the holes are drilled. However, the tinting fades after about three years. Your only solution, if you want to be sure that you aren't getting tinted pearls, is to have faith in your source.) Regarding shape, the most desirable (and highest priced) are perfectly rounded pearls; odd-shaped pearls, called baroque, are attractive, but should not be nearly so expensive. If you examine an individual pearl very closely, you will find that there are tiny marks, bumps, or indentations; these tend to detract from the inherent value. The finer the pearl, the fewer imperfections; however, perfect pearls are quite expensive, in addition to being scarce. Unless you're prepared to pay out substantial money, you'll have to compromise on *reasonably* perfect, and comparatively unmarked, pearls. Now as to size, a most important question. Pearls are measured by their diameter in millimeters (remember that there are 25 millimeters to the inch—thus a pearl measuring 8⅓ millimeters is one-third of an inch in diameter). In the 7- to 7½-millimeter category, pearls are quite plentiful, but larger sizes become more expensive and scarcer.

Next comes luster, the glow or reflection that seems to come from inside the pearl—its radiance, for want of a better word. All of these go to make up a pearl—and when assembled, to make up a pearl necklace. The various good features and bad points must be balanced out in making a selection. Pearl dealers love to show their wares on a black background, which is precisely wrong. Always ask for a white background, because defects and off-color will then show up best. Examine the individual pearls slowly and carefully, turning each one over, looking for flaws and imperfections. (If you need glasses for reading, use them!) Also worthy of mention is the fact that some pearls have light or thin coatings, whereas others have thick layers. (As you know, to create a cultured pearl, a small nucleus bead is inserted inside an oyster and the layers develop over the nucleus.) It's no longer possible to quote prices for pearls because they fluctuate from year to year and, unhappily, always seem to go up. The standard size ranges from 7 to 7½ millimeters, and within that size the price may be three times as high for a "gem" quality strand as for an ordinary one. If you look for an 8½-millimeter strand, you can expect the price to be twice as high as for the previously mentioned size. A 9-millimeter strand would be double the price once again, and a 10-millimeter strand would be double that. I'm sorry to be so vague about prices, but on two successive visits to Japan within a 6-month period I found prices up anywhere from 40 to 50% over the previous list. By the time you read this, it could change again, so it is absolutely impossible to quote even a basic price.

Pearl strands (are we still on the same subject?) are classified by length: small ones are 16 inches long, medium size is 17 inches, and large ones are 18 inches in length. There are chokers, which customarily measure about 14 inches, just enough to go around the neck; there are also opera-length strands, usually about 30 inches long. Single strands of pearls are fine, but every red-blooded American girl would rather have two matching strands. Three strands are also not unpopular, as are four-strand necklaces. Five strands (for rich people only) are called a "bib." Should all the pearls be uniform in size, or gradated (with large ones up front tapering down to small ones in back)? It's a matter of taste, of course; at the moment, uniform strands are more in vogue than the gradated ones. How are pearls strung? you ask. Sometimes with knots between each pearl, to separate them slightly, and also to prevent loss in the event the strand breaks. Be sure to have your good pearls restrung every six months, whether you've worn them much or not. When you take the pearls off at night, wipe them dry with a clean cloth; there's always a slight amount of perspiration and perfume on them. Should you wear good pearls every day or just save them for special occasions? There's no agreement on this subject, but who cares? Wear them, I say.

The Japanese also excel in the electronics field and are past masters at making tiny *transistor radios.* They have also produced battery-operated miniature *television sets* which are convenient to take on picnics or other such places. You'll see radios and television sets on sale wherever you turn; prices are very similar in almost all the shops, but be sure the tax is removed. (But see below in this paragraph.) Japanese-made *tape recorders* also are very good. If you are interested in Japanese electronic equipment and if you have a little offbeat curiosity, take a taxi to the Akihabara district, which is on the way to Ueno Park, out on Ginza Street. This is the electronics wholesale area, and the prices are exceedingly low. Here you can buy anything in the radio and TV transistor line, as well as tape recorders and all the equipment needed for a first-rate sound system. Japanese speakers are very good, as are Japanese turntables, pickups, amplifiers, and pre-amps. Any sound enthusiast can save himself a lot of money by browsing around in this area. It is not essential, but helpful, to bring along someone who speaks Japanese. He can buy his system piecemeal; that is, by buying the parts and putting them together. Or he can buy a complete one already put together by experts for about one-third the price of a similar one in the United States.

It may come as a surprise to some, but *watches* are also a good buy in Japan. We are speaking of the Japanese-made watch, like Seiko and Citizen, for there is a heavy tax on foreign watches, which —coupled with transportation costs—makes them very expensive. At any rate you don't want to buy a Swiss watch in Japan. However, the Japanese-made watch is excellent in quality. It rivals the Swiss as far as quality and workmanship are concerned in the lower-priced category, although still far behind in prestige.

Another favorite with the tourists is Japanese *dolls.* The two most famous types include the elaborately costumed art dolls which come in glass cases and depict a Japanese girl, probably a *geisha;* the other popular style is the Hakata doll, a clay doll which is made in the city of Hakata, in Fukuoka. The latter is ingeniously made, and looks very lifelike. Famous characters are depicted, such as a current *sumo,* or Japanese wrestling champion. The first type is very elegant but inconvenient to carry with you unless you have it specially packed. For, obviously, the glass case which protects the doll from dust and dirt is very fragile. The Hakata doll, on the other hand, is much smaller and is packed in a small wooden box that is easy to carry. There are also wooden *kokeshi* dolls; these very tiny dolls make excellent collector's items. The doll departments in the department stores carry the various types of dolls mentioned.

Something colorful to bring home and hang on the wall is a *Noh mask.* These masks are used in the very austere Noh drama and are supposed to depict various emotions and characters. Generally they are made of wood, with excellent craftsmanship. Noh masks also can be bought in department stores, but it is more fun to go out to a district like Asakusa and find a store specializing in masks. There you will be tempted to bring back a whole selection. But just remember the weight if you are traveling by plane. The Noh masks are worn over the faces of the performers in the Noh dance-drama; unlike *Kabuki* actors who depend upon facial makeup, Noh actors never show their faces. They twist their heads in such ways that the mask itself seems to change expression.

For women, *beaded handbags* are an excellent buy. They are well-made and comparatively cheap. The arcade of your hotel should have a shop specializing in these items; but, if not, again try a department store.

Now we get to the *kimono,* the garment that makes young Japanese girls look so feminine, and western girls hope it will. Authentic kimonos, however, are difficult to put on, and they can be so expensive that they are not worth the trouble or money. On the other hand, the *yukata,* a cotton type of kimono worn in the summer, is easily donned, comfortable, and cheap. The difference is this: you don't need an *obi,* that heavy Japanese sash that goes around the waist, with the *yukata.* Any kind of sash that ties around the waist will do. Also, *yukatas* make very good housecoats and dressing gowns for men and women alike. So if you are interested in the kimono line, the *yukata* is preferable.

Another practical buy that is also typical of Japan and can actually be used as clothing, as well as something to remember your travels, is the *happi coat.* This is a short hip-length coat that is the usual wear of workmen, firemen, carpenters, gardeners, and such. Although the real *happi* coat is made of heavy material, because of their popularity with foreigners, *happi* coats are now made out of light fabrics so that they can be used as beach coats, smoking jackets, etc. They are especially colorful because of the large identifying mark which usually appears on the back, and indicates the company which employed the workman. These marks, or *mon,* are copied on the informal adaptations, to the delight of the tourists.

One favorite story told in Tokyo regarding the indiscriminate purchase of *happi* coats, however, must be told. A group of tourists on a shopping spree ran across a set of *happi* coats all with the same *mon* on the back; these were the real workman's coats, not adaptations. The tour members thought it would be a wonderful thing for each to buy a *happi* coat in order to emphasize their togetherness. What they did not realize, however, was that the *mon* was that of a well-known but disreputable Japanese hotel. Though foreigners did not recognize it, Japanese who saw the group of wide-eyed tourists wandering around the Ginza were first shocked and then left hysterical with laughter.

Again, department stores are well-stocked with *kimonos, yukatas,* and *happi* coats. However, you can have some fun bargaining and get some good secondhand garments at the Kimono Mart at 10th Street and T Avenue, about 20 minutes from downtown Tokyo. They also carry a line of new garments at very low prices, all things considered; a little bargaining is in order. The International Arcade, behind the Imperial Hotel, has a large selection of *kimonos.*

A little-known but excellent purchase for men is *menuki* jewelry. *Menuki* are small metal objects generally made in the form of an animal. They were formerly used to decorate the handles of the *samurais'*—the Japanese warriors'—swords. Today, they are made into cuff links for men as well as brooches, rings, and earrings for women. Cuff links, which run from 5,000 *yen* up, are readily available, but articles for women must be made to order. If you have money to spend and have an eye for design, you can invent your own personal *menuki* decorations that will give you the satisfaction of not only having done it yourself but of wearing something nobody else can copy. *Menuki* is definitely one of the most distinctive Japanese products, but it is one item which the department stores do not stock. They are obtainable at the Japan Sword Shop at B Avenue and 12th Street, which also sells *samurai* swords, and good cutlery.

Gold and *silver* jewelry is worthwhile in Japan. Almost all of the silver sold in Japan is a small fraction purer than it is in the United States; however, the lesser amount of alloy used means that Japanese articles are somewhat softer, and tend to scratch more readily. However, it usually sells for slightly over half of American prices, and as you might expect, the more intricate and detailed the handiwork, the better value it represents. Small boxes, cigarette containers, silver plates, and some of the tableware are quite good. (Avoid buying cigarette boxes soldered around a wooden interior; they usually become unsoldered after two years or so.) If you're still taken with charm bracelets, Japan is a great place for them.

Fishing tackle is excellent in quality and represents good value. Probably no other country depends so much upon fish for food as does Japan, and there is ingenious and even elegant fishing gear available. The variety and selection will startle you. The department stores carry tackle, but you might look in the *Tokyo Elite* shop, located in the arcade of the Nikkatsu International Building.

Japan has always been famous for its *porcelain* and *pottery*. The country is rich in the type of kaolin, or clay, required for the industry, and the Japanese have long developed their special skills and technique. Perhaps the best-known of Japanese china is Noritake, if for no other reason than because it was stocked in the post exchanges during the Occupation, and the members of the Armed Forces shipped them home as gifts. There are several other brand names that are about equally good. Whatever the name, the porcelain you buy in Japan will be cheap and probably excellent. Among the most typical and distinctive are Satsuma, Arita, Kutani, Owari, Banko, Bizen, Awaji, and Soma. Satsuma ware is finished with an ivory luster and has fine crackles spreading in a network over the surface. Besides these distinctive features, some Satsuma ware is decorated with elaborate designs, often being garishly decorated with heavy gold. Arita porcelains are noted for their strength and lasting quality. Kutani porcelains are renowned for their elaborate picture decorations in thick gold, red, blue, and other colors. Kutani, two hundred years ago, was one of the greatest types ever produced in Japan; known as *kokutani* or old *kutani,* they are now collector's items and can be found only in antique or curio shops and cost a small fortune. Owari porcelains are of many varieties and are produced around Nagoya in Central Honshu, lying between Tokyo and Osaka. Nagoya, from the point of production volume, is the ceramic center of Japan. Bizen wares are characterized by their peculiarly shaped figures of gods, birds, and animals. Banko porcelains are mostly unglazed; Awaji wares are generally monochromatic with a bright yellow or green glaze; and Soma wares are readily identifiable by the design of the running horse which is commonly used. Most of these types can be found in the department stores and the hotel arcades. If you are interested in porcelain and pottery, you will find many happy hours browsing around the arcade shops and the department stores.

Also, if you are interested in it, a bit of its history won't bore you. The art of pottery-making was inherited from China and Korea, even though the Japanese claim the name "china" comes from Japanese porcelain brought to Europe by Dutch traders in the early 17th century when the art of pottery was at its zenith in Japan. It was introduced in the 12th century by a potter who established his kiln at a place called Seto; hence, the Japanese name for porcelain is *setomono*. The art grew until, by the 17th century, it reached its heights. It had established itself in its own right and was independent of Chinese influence. The best work of that period was the Arita and Kutani ware. With the Meiji Restoration in 1868, western influences crept in, and though Japanese porcelain was still rated highly, it had dropped from its previous peak. Today Japanese porcelain is among the world's best, with designs executed by well-known artists such as Hazan Itaya, Toyozo Arakawa, Munemaro Ishiguro, Toyo Kanashige, Kenkichi Tomimoto, Kanjuro Kawai, and Shoji Hamada. The order of names is at random with no indication of respective merit implied.

Lacquer, too, is one of the best buys in Japan. Like porcelain, it has a long history, though it is much older, and was an art borrowed from China, being imported from that country over 1,300 years ago. By the 11th century, Japanese artisans were producing gold lacquer at the demand of its nobles, and by the 13th century the compounding of lacquer with silver and gold was perfected and a new style of polished lacquerware had been created. By the 15th century the art had reached such a level that Chinese craftsmen and artists were being sent over to learn from the Japanese. Tokyo, Kyoto, and Kanazawa are the centers of the lacquerware industry, as they were in the past. Every department store has a large lacquer section filled with boxes, bowls, and trays of all shapes and sizes. In case you think they are merely decorative, you may discover that lacquered soup bowls are quite useful on a table as well, and likely to bring on a series of ooh's and ah's from the guests. For old lacquerware, try the curio shops; but the gold-and-silver type have a deservedly high price. For excellent lacquerware which will be well worth every yen you pay for it, try the Yamada Heiando, which makes lacquer by appointment to the Imperial Household. It has a shop on the street behind Takashimaya Department Store, a block north of X Avenue.

A word about Japanese *glassware;* it is excellent and rivals the Venetian in quality but not in price, being much cheaper. Especially good is the brand called Iwata, which can be purchased in any department store. It is made by the Iwata family, which is continually striving for new shapes, styles, and color.

There has been enough printed and said about Japanese *silks* to make almost any additional words superfluous. Japan has the highest production of silk in the world, with more than a thousand silk mills. Silk is excellent, of course, for men's suits and women's dresses, and worth buying. Silk ties are plentiful and can be purchased at any department store and generally cost in the neighborhood of $15 to $25. Unfortunately for women, the best silk designs are put on kimono and obi material which are not of the correct width for western clothing unless your dressmaker is a magician. Kimono material comes in rolls about 12 inches wide and roughly 10 yards long, while obi material comes either 9 inches or 21 inches wide, and about 10 feet long. If you're going to Hong Kong, don't have suits or dresses made up in Japan; the Hong Kong tailors are miles better. However, ready-made dresses can be a good buy in boutiques. Hanea Mori is particularly good and has shops in many of the hotels.

If you are looking for silk for dress material, try the Silk Gallery, which is in the *Korin Mansion,* formerly the domicile of Prince Takamatsu, the brother of the emperor, and located off Shiba Street between A and B Avenues. Silks from the leading mills are sold here as well as kimonos, obis, stoles, shirts, blouses, neckties, etc. It is worth a trip to see the silks at the Silk Gallery, for you can also see what a Japanese mansion is like—the long gravel driveway, the garden, the rooms, etc. The Korin Mansion is often the site of important diplomatic cocktail parties, by the way. *Kanebo,* on Ginza and St. Luke's Streets is the Tokyo outlet for Japan's leading silk manufacturer. Material, as well as the finished products, is available here. Oh yes, if you are looking for a suit or dress, Kanebo has a house tailor and a dressmaker who are very good, and are an exception to the general rule. You select the material, and they will make what you want; the finished product usually being a good fit and long-lasting. There are also silk shops in the arcades of the Imperial and Nikkatsu hotels as well as individual stores. You might want to try, also, *Tatsumura Textile* on the second floor of the Mitsui Building on A Avenue near the Imperial Hotel, or *Kogei* on Fifth Street on the same block as the Nikko Hotel.

As can be seen, shopping can be a major activity in Japan. In addition to those already listed, the devoted shopper can find his time well taken-up in any line he is interested in. There are fine *antiques* and *curios;* art galleries where you can buy paintings to gratify your personal desires or as a financial speculation, for art is flourishing in Japan today, with styles ranging from photographic portrait reproductions to abstract calligraphy and over 50 galleries to display and sell them; *cloisonné,* which also is an old art in Japan; *fans,* which, with their delicate designs, are decorative as well as utilitarian; *paper* and *paper products* (Japanese handmade paper has achieved world renown); *stone lanterns* that will grace your garden but cost you a fortune in overweight to lug home (the original price, though, is very reasonable); *toys*—the way the Japanese are turning out toys these days and from the point of view of ingenious design, Santa Claus must be seriously thinking of moving his headquarters here from the North Pole, except that land values in Japan are much higher.

The Japanese still make *woodblock* prints by hand, and they make lovely decorations. Old prints are collector's items and very expensive, but modern prints are reasonable. About the best source is Watanabe Color Prints Company (on the Ginza). Nikko (No. 6, 6-chome, Ginza-nishi) features the traditional Japanese scrolls (*kakemono*). It takes a little effort to find good prints or scrolls, so be patient and look around. (Incidentally, if you're going to Kyto, look in at the shops on Shimonzein Street, which feature prints and *kakemono*.)

Antiques are still available at fair prices. Don't spend serious money unless you know what you're doing; however, if you do see something you like, buy it, provided the price is not out of line. Every Saturday and Sunday, carvings, *kakemono,* art objects, and paintings are exhibited at Yushima-Seido (the Confucian shrine) located at Hijiri Bashi on 10th Street. They are sold on a commission basis on behalf of their owners, and a little petty bargaining (not too much) is permitted. If you are in Tokyo near the end of a month, have your hotel arrange for you to attend the art auctions held around the twenty-sixth of each month; they provide an exceptional opportunity to buy fine pieces at good prices.

Excellent ivory *chess sets* can be purchased at Kita Shoji Company (No. 5, 1-chome, Nihonbashi-dori). *Sandai chests* made with cherry or teak wood, classically made with two drawers, and excellent brass or silver hardware are both useful and handsome; you'll find them at Odawara Shoten (Imperial Hotel Arcade).

Since many of the shopping items can be found in *department stores,* a word about them will not be wasted. The department stores are worth a visit by anyone, including nonshoppers. As a matter of fact, a visit to a Japanese department store by a nonshopper will make a convert of him. The stores are well organized, up to and including store clerks (labeled English-speaking) who speak a brand of English which sometimes makes you question yours if you take the label too seriously. However, understandable English or not, you and the store clerk will understand each other when you are ready to make a purchase. Many times, too, those English-speaking labels correctly describe the wearer.

The stores have art galleries, theaters, and huge food departments. You will be pleased with the demure little misses who stand at the entrance of each escalator and bow their heads with a mur-

mured greeting when you go up and thank you very much, also in a low voice made almost inaudible by the bowed head, for your patronage as you go down. In one store, Takashimaya, there is a purchase system which allows you to shop, make your choice, and finally collect all your bundles and pay the total bill at one time. The following is a list of the department stores in the Ginza area and where they are situated; shopping hours generally are between 10 A.M. and 6 P.M.:

Takashimaya, perhaps the best-known for Americans because of its branch in New York: Ginza Street between X and W Avenues, closed on Mondays.

Mitsukoshi (Nihombashi branch): Ginza Street between W and R Avenues, closed on Mondays.

Mitsukoshi (Ginza branch): Ginza Street and Z Avenue, closed on Mondays.

Matsuya: Ginza and Exchange, closed on Thursdays.

Matsuzakaya: Ginza and Annex, closed on Mondays.

Shirokiya: Ginza and W, closed on Mondays.

Wako: Ginza and Z, closed on Sundays (the only department store which closes on Sundays).

Daimaru: On Fifth next to Tokyo Station, closed on Thursdays.

POINTER:
  If you are a real enthusiast about department stores, by all means visit the Nihombashi branch of Mitsukoshi (the second one listed above). This is the department store to end all department stores, and has a fantastic selection of merchandise. It's readily reached by subway; in fact, it is the only department store with its own subway station. Just wandering about and observing the people shopping, as well as buying anything yourself, is very rewarding and will show you a facet of the Japanese way of life you might not see otherwise. Open daily except Monday from 10–6. The Ginza, Tokyo's main shopping street is closed to auto traffic on Sundays, and most stores are open, making it an ideal day for tourists, who often have little planned for Sundays.

What not to buy. This is simple: Stay away from shoes. Japanese shoes are expensive, lacking in style, and made with inferior leather. Come well stocked with shoes; for if you run out, the recommendation is to buy slippers and pretend you have a foot ailment which forces such wear. As for men's clothing, the ready-made kind is ill-fitting, and even if it weren't, it wouldn't fit you, a Westerner. Most foreigners in Japan have their clothes tailor-made, paying considerable care to the selection of their tailor or dressmaker. Japanese ready-made suits are somewhat peculiar, to say the least. Invariably, there is a dip to the seat of the pants that gives the male Japanese a bottom-heavy appearance. Fortunately, a pair of Japanese slacks probably will not fit you and therefore you will not be tempted.

ENTERTAINMENT Tokyo is a fleshpot. Every kind of gin mill or dive imaginable exists in Tokyo's many entertainment districts, making sin—or near-sin—big business in this, the world's largest metropolis. As a matter of fact, Tokyo gangsters envisioned the prospects a long time ago, and have moved in with all the élan of the old Chicago variety. As a result, Tokyo's entertainment districts have been parceled out and subdivided among the gangs, who collect protection from the establishments within their territories. However, the gangsters leave the tourists and foreign residents strictly alone. They don't want anything to do with international incidents, and therefore the tourist will not notice a thing, but it's there.

Lest the reader think that Tokyo is one big city of sin, it also abounds in more aesthetic entertainment of considerable variety: excellent stage shows that feature traditional Japanese dramas and formal dance-dramas that never fail to appeal to the truly artistic (composers Igor Stravinsky and Benjamin Britten came away from *Kabuki* and *Noh* performances so impressed that Stravinsky announced that his future music would be affected by the rhythms and sounds of Kabuki while Britten's latest work is based on Noh style); first-rate symphonic orchestras; places where you can take in a jam session which is decidedly not superior to what you can hear in the United States; or if you wish, a hectic rockabilly performance (rockabilly is a Japanese word coined from "rock-and-roll" and "hillbilly" and describes a style that is roughly a cross between the two).

But let us start with the less artistic—that is, the more fleshy—spots. There have been various estimates as to the number of bars and cabarets in Tokyo, the guesses running about 12,000 on the average. You may think it is too low. Deep in the heartland of the Ginza you will find areas interlaced with miniature alleys and tiny side streets, some apparently no more than the space between two buildings, but every space fully rented out to tiny bars. If you want to make a tour of these bars, you will find some of them as spacious as a broom closet with about three stools at the bar. But even in such a bar, with its limited space, you will find a hostess. For Japanese men think that drinking without women is as much a sin as drinking alone is to Americans. It is not that they have anything besides drinking in mind, but Japanese say that drinking without a woman (other than one's wife) is a sure sign of incipient alcoholism. The girl's function in these little bars is to laugh at the man's jokes, believe (or make-believe) his tall tales, and in every way give him that feeling of virile, triumphant masculinity which he apparently can get nowhere else, not even in his own home. If he has to buy drinks to get that feeling, well—that's the price he has to pay, and is willing to pay.

At any rate, small bars and bar hostesses are inseparable in Japan. Don't feel sorry for the girls, though. It is an easy way of making a living for them. They need not worry about an education, and they all expect eventually to find a husband. In the meanwhile, all they have to do to make $5 (or more) an hour is to laugh as though they enjoy the customer's jokes and have never heard them before (they have), listen wide-eyed to tales of how he told his boss off, and how he made his wife knuckle under in a tempestuous domestic quarrel, or grow solemn-eyed and sympathetic as the customer recounts a sad story of domestic tyranny in which he is the innocent and abused victim. It beats working in an office and pounding a type-writer, they think.

If you feel you would like to see a bit of this facet of Japanese life, be wary of two things: One, steer clear of those "On Limits-No Cover Charge" clip joints with which the Ginza abounds, and two, be prepared for a polite rejection when you try to go into some bars.

As for the clip-joint signs, they are perfectly truthful it must be admitted. No place on the Ginza is off-limits for our soldiers any more, and so that part of the proud announcement is correct. Also, there is no cover charge; but what they bill you for the plate of peanuts and *osembei* (Japanese crackers) put in front of you is higher than any cover charge would ordinarily be. The polite rejection is the result of the bar being a second home to Japanese men. Some bars have such a steady clientele that they verge on being private clubs. These are the kind that do not like foreigners to intrude themselves upon the members' feeling of relaxed content-ment. Also, they generally have no English-speaking hostess, and the managements have decided that foreigners who speak no Japa-nese are just too much trouble to bother with. It is also a fact that when too many foreigners start going to a small, intimate bar, the Japanese begin to stay away. And the proprietors of some bars have the opinion that the Japanese will, in the long run, be more permanent customers.

You will have to find bars on your own. There is no problem; all you have to do is walk around the Ginza, Shimbashi, Shibuya, Shinjuku districts, etc., observe the previous warnings and cautions, and you will eventually find one to your liking. Once you get in, be pleasant, smile at everybody and don't give the bill a second glance. It is going to be higher than you had anticipated, but no true gentleman, according to Japanese bar standards, ever questions a bill. This is a mistake many foreigners, including long-time residents, make. A tip: To keep your bill within respectable (meaning reasonable) limits, order Japanese beer or Suntory whisky. Scotch, bourbon, and all other imported drinks are subject to a heavy tax which is, of course, passed on to the consumer.

Let us dissect that bill of yours: First, there is that plate of peanuts and *osembei.* Peanuts will have never cost so much in their life, but this plate is the equivalent of a cover charge, and represents the gentle Japanese way of avoiding charging you something for nothing. Now let's consider the drinks. If they're imported scotch, they cost over $5 each (in *yen,* of course). Add your drinks to those of the hostess sitting with you, and the bill can reach astronomical proportions very quickly. Then, consider the hostess charge, which is probably about $5 merely for having the girl sit with you; sometimes it's an hourly charge, whereas in other places, after the first hostess charge, you merely pay for the drinks. When you finally add it up, after an hour, you'll perhaps find that you each had three drinks plus two plates of peanuts and crackers. The chances are the total will be somewhere around $30, or perhaps a trifle more, depending upon whether the bar adds on the service charge of 10% plus the amusement tax of 15%. But it is an interesting experience, and the camaraderie and the opportunity to see another phase of Japanese life may make it all worthwhile to you. Or it may not.

Now as to larger bars, cabarets, and nightclubs: It is easy enough to explain what a bar is. It is a place where drinks and something that passes for food are served, and where there are hostesses who serve the drinks and who will sit down and talk to you. There is theoretically supposed to be no music or dancing. When we get to cabarets, it becomes more difficult, for it is a complicated thing to differentiate between a cabaret and a nightclub. There is a legal distinction, but the tourist who is not a lawyer certainly cannot be expected to cope with it. Therefore, let us (for the purposes of discussion) lump cabarets and nightclubs together, call them places where there are drinks, hostesses, music and dancing, refer to them all as cabarets as a matter of convenience, and let it go at that.

Let us now visit the cabarets, a list of which is appended to this section. Cabarets have either a minimum charge or a cover charge, both names intended to see that your bill is high enough to suit the owner. Cover charges range between 1,200 *yen* and 1,800 in general. Cabarets have a host of hostesses, and sometimes make claims to having even more. But, unlike the bars, the hostesses wait to be called. Then when they sit down with you, every hour costs an extra 1,000 *yen*. It is obvious that cabaret bills can get very high.

Can a wife go to a cabaret with her husband? Of course. If she is really curious about the so-called seamy side of life and can take watching pretty young things making a considerable fuss over her husband, it could be a very interesting experience. The hostesses don't mind the wives at all; they will be polite and probably—if she goes with several couples—won't even know whose wife she is, nor care. Their job is to make men relaxed, happy, and in the mood to buy drinks, although they don't force or press the sale of liquor.

What goes on after the bar or cabaret closes? Who knows? Obviously, girls in the business of making men happy become available sooner or later, usually sooner. The pressure gets too much, and, anyhow, an after-hours spree with a man is part of the job of making him happy, although it has to be considered as overtime—and overtime for cabaret and bar girls is not limited to time and a half. And, just as in the United States, it is a matter of personal choice as to whether the employee wishes to work overtime. The answer to the question is therefore a flat answer—yes and no.

Now we come to a peculiar type of entertainment which is probably found only in Japan. Foreigners call them "coffee shops"; but in Japanese they are known as *kissaten,* which means a place where drinks are served. They differ considerably from the Austrian and English coffee houses, as you will see. These are not bars, although whisky, gin, and beer are sold, because there are no hostesses. All sorts of soft drinks, as well as tea and coffee, are obtainable also. These places are interesting because they provide a variety of vignettes of Japanese life. They range from little holes-in-the-wall where young students (male and female) sit holding hands with empty teacups in front of them, listening to the latest jazz or classical music. There are also loud, jangling places, like the Albion and New Yorker, where the speakers have been turned up so high that music ceases to be that, and becomes noise, and where young G.I.'s and merchant mariners and older businessmen drink and ogle the briefly clad girls.

The following list of cabarets, bars, and "coffee shops" was selected from the point of view of interest and probable longevity (the latter qualification: to be fairly sure that they will be around when you arrive); prices are of course subject to change:

Crown. Ginza-nishi, 6-chome (tel: 572-5511). They charge a stiff cover charge all the time, but usually there's a fairly good show. Foreigners welcome, especially when accompanied by bulging billfolds. Hours: 6–11:45 P.M. Closed Sundays.

Queen Bee, Ginza. 2-chome (tel: 561-8331). Cover charge is substantial. However, no charge at the bar, but you can't talk to the girls who abound there, a management rule to get you to fork over the cover charge. Foreigners welcome. Hours: 6–11:45 P.M. Closed Sundays.

Monte Carlo. Ginza-nishi, 7-chome (tel: 571-5671). Cover charge is substantial. Hostesses plentiful and so are strippers during the Wednesday and Saturday night strip revues. As many as 40 girls in the nude—and nude means more so than in the United States —show off their attributes in front of a huge mirror. Foreigners welcome. Hours: 6–11:45 P.M. Closed Sundays.

Club Marunouchi. Ohtemachi (tel: 231-0622). They have a pretty stiff cover charge starting in the middle of the evening. Hours: 7 P.M. to midnight, but don't be surprised if they don't throw you out after the witching hour and the action keeps on apace. Things like this do happen; and the police might even contribute to your evening by raiding the place. But police raids in Tokyo are not what you think they are. The first sign of a raid is when the band suddenly stops playing and disappears. Old-timers know what this means and stop dancing, go to their tables, and drink and talk. Next, a couple of smiling Japanese men come in; obviously plainclothesmen. They look the place over, know very well what has happened and what has been going on. After a while they leave, having accomplished their purpose: they have stopped the evening's festivities, for the band doesn't come back; and the patrons soon get bored with it all and go themselves. For your information, dancing, not drinking, is the after-hours sin in Japan.

Copacabana. Akasaka, Tamachi (tel: 471-5806). Cover charge is pretty high. Run by the fabulous Madame Cherry who began her career in Kobe with a small bar called the Cherry Club, moved herself and the name to Tokyo, sold out the club and opened the Copacabana. A favorite with foreigners, who find Madame Cherry like a second mother. She attends, though not personally, to all their needs. If the cover is too much, try the bar upstairs. You can drink, and at floor-show time, crowd the rail with the hostesses and other economically minded customers to watch. No regulation against talking to hostesses or inviting them to the bar with you to drink; just cheaper. A convenient and excellent restaurant on third floor, the club Little Copa; try the roast beef.

Pokan. Akasaka, Shinmachi, 5-25 (tel: 481-0235). A bar of the type known as "singing bar." Excellent for husbands and wives. Four cute girls looking as fresh and innocent as all outdoors sing all sorts of songs in any language you may want, except Esperanto. A favorite with Japanese though foreigners are welcome. Keep to Japanese whisky and beer and your bill will be reasonable.

Yie Lai Shian. Shimbashi (tel: 591-4801). Another of those alleged coffee shops. Called the Green Dragon by foreign residents because of its green pagoda-like roof. Features orchestras on a bandstand that goes up and down, stopping at each of the three floors to entertain the guests. Favorite place of Japanese young lovers, who sit on the second floor because they get to see the orchestra twice. Orchestra is always heard, though, because music comes through loudspeakers. This is one place that almost every tourist would enjoy.

Note. All establishments have their telephone numbers listed, for a very good reason: you will rarely find them by the addresses and only with difficulty. It's best to have your hotel phone for directions and write them out, and then you can hand them to the cabdriver.

Now that we have covered the modern night life of Tokyo, it is time to treat that other very interesting subject: *Geisha,* a word sometimes used synonymously (and erroneously) for any Japanese girl in a kimono. In the first place, pronounce it *gay-sha* instead of *gee-sha* to show that you have been around. The term actually means "cultured person," and often used because of the enormous training given the girls.

It used to be that geisha parties were affairs that you had to be invited to. A Japanese arranged it and took you along as a guest—your wife, too, for that matter. Nowadays, however, thanks to travel agencies and especially the Japan Travel Bureau, you can attend a geisha party as part of the JTB's Golden Night Tour, for which a medium-high price is charged. It's worth it, too—if you don't object to being part of a crowd.

If you have been invited to a geisha party, it would be well to go into training by doing some practice knee bends. For you are going to be sitting on the floor a long time; western knees are not equipped with the elastic tendons that Japanese knees seem to have, and the cracking bones that are heard when the westerners begin to arise after a two-hour session at a geisha party sound like firecrackers on the Fourth of July.

A geisha party begins when the guests are all assembled at a long, low table. They sit on *zabuton,* or pillows, with armrests made available to the foreigners. Then the girls come in. They make small, gentle bows and then gracefully seat themselves at the table and proceed to chatter brightly among themselves and with those who speak Japanese, throwing in a bit of broken English to the guests, usually following up this courageous step with hysterical giggles. Meanwhile, they are pouring drinks as fast as your glass empties.

When the dinner is concluded, one or two of the girls sit down in a corner armed with a *samisen,* the Japanese guitar, and strum, singing in a voice that sounds to western ears unpleasantly reminiscent of a barnyard, as two or three other girls dance.

When this phase of the party is over, the girls once more join the guests, this time to play innocent little games with them. Some are quite interesting, like putting some tissue paper over a glass, placing a coin on the paper and then with a cigarette burning the paper until the coin falls in. He who burned the paper last is the loser, and the forfeit generally is drinking a cup of *sake.* Don't worry, though, the cup is only thimble-sized.

Another game consists of filling a *sake* cup drop by drop until the *sake* spills over. The surface tension of the rice wine is quite high and after apparently being filled will take several additional drops until, as you look at it from the side, there seems to be a small mound extending to the height of about a fourth of an inch above the cup. Whoever pours the drop that breaks the surface, causing the *sake* to spill over, has to drink a cup of *sake* as forfeit. There are many other such little games that may seem childish to read about, but with several cups of *sake* influencing your sense of humor, they seem tolerably funny at a geisha party.

The geishas have a history stretching back to the 18th century. At that time they were sort of preliminary entertainers for parties in the Yoshiwara, Tokyo's famous red-light district, where the featured entertainer would be the *oiran,* or trained prostitute. The *oiran* eventually went out of favor, and the geisha replaced her, reaching a peak in social standing during the mid-19th century, when geishas became the favorite companions of some of Japan's leading politicians.

Unfortunately, the geisha sun is setting. Fewer and fewer girls are willing to undergo the strict, long, and expensive training required to become a geisha, preferring instead the easier path to money via the cabaret route. Geishas today belong to unions, and they are registered at an office resembling a central casting agency. Parties are held at Japanese restaurants, whose proprietors call the geishas as needed.

The big question looms. Do they or don't they? (I am not referring to bleaching their hair.) The answer is necessarily vague: Yes and no, or it all depends. Some do and some don't. Let us leave it at that.

To anyone reading this far, Japanese entertainment may seem to consist exclusively of boy meets girl. The following sections will disabuse that thought, for we are now leaving the fleshpots and proceeding into the more artistic form of entertainment, the great formal dramas for which Japan is noted.

First in formality, a formality that approaches austerity, is *Noh.* Noh (pronounced like our word "no") means "performance" and comes from *Sarugaku-no-noh,* or "performance of *sarugaku,*" which was an incidental entertainment performed to musical accompaniment at Shinto festivals. Later, the rest of the word was dropped and only the last part was kept as Noh came to imply a performance of a lyric drama.

The majority of Noh plays are centuries old, and were chiefly written in the 14th and 15th centuries. About 1,000 Noh dramas, which are called dance-dramas because they are basically dramatic presentations in which the action is confined to slow and stately dances, have been written; of these, about 800 survive, of which 242 are still more or less regularly performed.

Noh may also be described as a solemn operatic performance consisting of music and dancing, accompanied by a rhythmic recitation which could perhaps be called singing, although western ears may reject the term. Masks are used by the actors to portray the chief characters. The plays deal mainly with historical subjects, often with a strong Buddhist slant, because of the influence the priests had on their composition. The plays have not been changed over the centuries and everything about Noh is archaic. However, it has its appeal, as witness the effect it had on composer Benjamin Britten when he wrote his recent opus, *Curlew River,* which shows definite Noh tendencies, or so the critics say.

The Noh stage has precise dimensions and all are alike—if you've seen one, you've seen them all. By the rules of Noh, the stage must be 27 feet wide and 18 feet deep, and have a roof like a Shinto shrine supported by four pillars. As you face the stage, on the left is a sort of open corridor, roofed over, which connects the platform with the "green" room, from which the actors enter the stage; it is also used for part of the action. The sides of the stage are open, and the back is painted with a pine tree, symbolic of the times when Noh was performed outdoors before a shrine with pine trees in the background. Pine trees, especially the tall, twisted type, have a special significance for Japanese.

Before the play begins the members of the orchestra seat themselves on the stage floor at the back, facing the audience. The orchestral instruments consist of small hand-drums, larger drums, and flutes. After the orchestra is seated, the chorus file in through a small door at the right and kneel in two rows on the right. Now the actors come out from the room at the left. They enter one by one at a painfully slow pace.

The actors speak their parts in the Japanese language of some 600 years ago, much as though the lines of a Broadway play were spoken in Chaucerian English. The chorus, like a Greek chorus, chant their explanatory parts in unison.

Very little scenery is used. What there is of it consists mainly of a few symbolic objects meant to suggest, rather than to portray. As in Shakespearean drama, much of the scenery is left to the imagination, as stimulated by the actors' descriptions. Noh plays are usually presented on Saturdays and Sundays. There are three Noh stages in Tokyo, two in Kyoto, and one in Osaka. Any travel agency can make arrangements for you, or you can make your own arrangements through your hotel.

Kabuki today is an all-male theater; only men are allowed to perform in it, even with male actors, *onnagata,* taking the female parts. What is not generally known, however, is that Kabuki was originated by a woman. Her name was Okuni, a dancing girl at a Shinto shrine at Izumo who lived in the late 16th and early 17th century. During that period, the only stage performance available to the entertainment-starved populace was Noh, which was too austere for the general public. Okuni saw the need for a popular stage, and sometime between 1596 and 1615, she began to perform sacred dances publicly, clad in clerical robes and to the accompaniment of tinkling bells and singing. With only this and Noh to choose from, the public went wild over her performance and she became an immediate sensation.

Encouraged by the public enthusiam, she joined forces with her sweetheart; their presentations were so successful that other girls began to flatter her sincerely by imitating. Okuni then took her art to old Tokyo where it was enthusiastically received. Soon it became the fashion to go to see a Kabuki performance.

However, something happened. Evil rumor had it that the girls began to give encore performances to special individuals after the theater had closed. At any rate, the authorities forbade women from appearing on the stage because of their effect on public morals (a ban that lasted until the middle of the 19th century). As a result of the edict and the public clamoring for more Kabuki, men took over the shows, even filling the female parts. Thus, we have Kabuki as we find it today.

At first the Kabuki plays were not very good, either being written by the actors themselves, who usually lacked formal education, or being directly stolen from Noh. Later, however, towards the end of the 17th century, playwriting became a special profession with the greatest talents devoting themselves to the Kabuki drama. Ingenious Kabuki playwrights developed the revolving stage where a large circle was cut into the floor and three different scenes fitted within the area. With the beating of wooden clappers and the accompaniment of samisen music, the stage revolved, allowing the scenes to alternate. This bit of stagecraft, which we often regard as a modern technique, was invented about 200 years ago. Another Kabuki innovation was the "elevator" set. It was prepared in the basement with actors in formal poses, plus scenery, and the whole lifted up to the audience level to fit a pre-cut square.

Kabuki will seem more acceptable to westerners than Noh. There are, in general, three types of plays: One category that deals with human nature and feelings; a second with a historical theme; and a third that specializes in fantasy, bombastic dialogue, and grotesque makeup. All these plays are accompanied by song and music, and some of the music is quite pleasant to western ears. So unless you like your drama symbolic and your music a mixture of caterwaulings and squeals, you will probably prefer Kabuki to Noh. If, however, you like Kabuki, why not experiment and see a performance of Noh?

It must be added that Kabuki and Noh are sadly on the wane, so much so that some of the best Kabuki actors are forced to appear on television in order to supplement their incomes. But this does not mean that the Kabuki actors are any less skillful than they were before. If you see a play where Baiko is the *onnagato,* you will be seeing an authentic artist at work; the same holds true for Utaemon, or Kanzaburo, or the up-and-coming young Takenojo, one of the finest dancers on the Kabuki stage today.

Arrangements for Kabuki can also be made through your travel agent or hotel. There are five Kabuki theaters in Tokyo, the most important being the Kabuki-za, the Meiji-za, and the Shimbashi Embujo; one in Kyoto; two in Osaka; and one in Nagoya.

If you don't want to attend a Kabuki or puppet play but are interested in seeing what they're like, read the television pages of Tokyo's two excellent English-language newspapers. They often schedule hour-long shows, particularly on Sunday. It's an easy way to see something of old Japanese culture without getting involved in purchasing tickets, making the trip to the theater, and so forth. Stay with the show for a while; you'll be surprised to see that you'll be able to follow the action without understanding a word of Japanese.

Puppet drama also is a stage art that stems from the 17th century. Imported from China, the puppet show rapidly won public favor and soon many theaters were established in Kyoto, Osaka, and Tokyo. For a short time, the puppets were more popular than Kabuki, but Kabuki soon took over once again. The Kabuki actors took over the puppet plays; and the audience, preferring live actors to dolls, turned away from the puppets and flocked to Kabuki. Today, there is only one puppet theater left, the *Bunraku-za* in Osaka.

The puppets are of two kinds, small and large, the small being not more than a foot high and operated from above with strings. The large ones are two-thirds of life-size and when worked by skillful operators seem like human beings to the audience. Each puppet requires one operator-in-chief and two assistants. The operator-in-chief wears high clogs to give him height over the puppets and wears colorful clothes, while his assistants are garbed in black to be inconspicuous. The large-sized puppets are used at Osaka's Bunraku-za.

Now we come to the *girls' operas,* of which there are two troupes. The *Takarazuka* Girls' Opera Troupe is by far the better known, largely because of James Michener's novel *Sayonara* and the film that was based on it. The other is the *Shochiku* Girls' Opera Company.

In both troupes, girls play both male and female parts. Members of both companies go through long and arduous training before they can become regular members, and then they start in the chorus line. The stagings of both are phenomenal. For the foreigner, however, the pace of the Shochiku group is better appreciated.

The Takarazuka group, although headquartered at Takarazuka Village near Osaka, can be seen at the Takarazuka Theater across from the Imperial Hotel. Their performances generally include a revue or a light opera, sometimes of western origin, like *Rosemarie, New Moon,* and other such favorites.

The Shochiku group is based in Tokyo and can be seen at the Kokusai Gekijo out in the Asakusa district. Theirs is a fast-paced revue with rapid changes of scene. The revue alternates between Japanese and western numbers, with the Japanese numbers being more popular with the foreigners. The entire revue lasts about an hour and a half, letting out in time for a dinner, though rather late by Japanese standards.

Both troupes are noted for their display of stagecraft, which is especially impressive at the very beginning and also at the end. The Shochiku group usually opens with all the girls in a line, cherry blossoms in abundance and lanterns by the gross to make a spectacular first impression. The finales of both theatrical troupes may have water gushing out of stage-made waterfalls or the whole host of girls parading on staircases that seem to stretch endlessly upward. There may be first- or second-act climaxes, such as an earthquake or an out-of-control fire toppling down buildings in a mass of fire and smoke. The Shochiku shows are over in an hour and a half (a Takarazuka show lasts sometimes as long as four hours, divided into two halves with either half being sufficient for the tourist); both should be on the list of the foreign visitor.

Stage shows featuring both sexes and often starring Japanese movie stars and popular singers are given at the *Nichigeki,* a theater in Yurakucho which has five floors and a basement. On the first floor the regular stage show is presented, and this has spectacular openings and finales, too. On the fifth floor, called the Nichigeki Music Hall, is a burlesque show. It features a stage show with acts in which nude-to-the-waist young ladies come out and parade around the platform. Strip shows, too, are a part of the fifth-floor revue, as are some rather raw acts in keeping with the traditions of burlesque.

As long as we are on the subject of *strip shows,* there are a lot of theaters strung along a street in the Asakusa entertainment section which feature only the strip. But even if you find your way out there, they won't let you in, as foreigners are usually barred. Of course, if looking at a naked woman fascinates you, and if you cannot get into the Asakusa theaters, and if the stage shows that interfere with the strips at the Nichigeki Music Hall are too boring, you can always go out to the Papagayo, previously listed among the cabarets, bars, and coffee shops. There they serve strippers with their Mexican food, which is more peppery than their shows. However, you will get your fill of nudity there unless you are insatiable.

To return to a higher level of entertainment, the *music* lover will have ample opportunity to enjoy his favorite indoor entertainment in Japan. There are many first-class symphony orchestras in Japan that have received excellent notices from the most carping of critics. The NHK Symphony, for example, toured Europe a few years back and received outstanding notices from the gimlet-eared continental music authorities. The NHK Symphony is the closest thing to a national symphony orchestra, NHK being the governmental radio and television broadcasting system. Otherwise, there is no government-supported orchestra in Tokyo, which has six major ensembles.

In referring to Japanese orchestras as first-class, there is no implication of drawing a comparison with the top-flight major orchestras of Europe or the United States, those fantastically disciplined groups whose intonation could challenge a tuning fork. However, listening to a good Japanese orchestra, especially to ones like the NHK and the ABC (Asahi Broadcasting Company) is quite satisfying, even though their tempo and approach is reminiscent of the somewhat stolid German school. This is to be expected, since many German conductors have been imported to Japan to lead the local groups.

A fast-rising young conductor is Seiji Ozawa. But you will probably have to go to the United States to hear him. Among other appointments, he is the music director of the Boston Symphony Orchestra and the San Francisco Symphony, and is highly regarded in musical circles. His dynamic approach, though, ran afoul of the staid Germanic NHK Symphony when he was appointed conductor of that group; there was a falling-out and he left. Another first-rate musician is the violinist Toshiya Eto, who has made his mark in the most critical of critical circles in the United States.

Every week there are musical events scheduled in Tokyo, for better or worse. A glance at the Musical Calendar which appears in the English-language *Mainichi,* one of Japan's five English-language dailies, will tell you when, where, and the type of program, the schedule including chamber groups, symphonies, and operas, with programs ranging from the accepted classics to the most advanced and modern.

Movie theaters are plentiful in Tokyo and every major Japanese city. American movies are among the most popular, with Wayne John-san one of the most popular of movie heroes among the Japanese, along with Stewarto Jeemeesan. But the theaters also feature French and Italian movies, and sometimes, German, Swedish, and even Russian products. Of course, Japanese movies are by far in the majority. Major movie stars are Hisaya Morishige, one of Japan's greatest comedians of the human comedy school, whose greatest roles portray an ordinary elderly man; Toshiro Mifune, whose great *samurai* roles have won him fame in the art theaters and film festivals around the world; tough guy Yujiro Ishihara, the idol of the younger set. Among the actresses: Fujiko Yamamoto, considered the most beautiful of all, but whose acting leaves something to be desired; Hideko Takamine, noted for her roles as a poor housewife; and, of course, Machiko Kyo, who should be familiar to

American movie-goers for her role in the *Teahouse of the August Moon.* Then, too, there is Sessue Hayakawa, who is more international than Japanese, competently playing roles in Japanese and American movies. As for directors, Akira Kurosawa naturally heads the list. He has won many prizes for his movies, the best-known of which, among foreigners, is *Rashomon.* Other directors of major standing are Keisuke Kinoshita, Tadashi Imai, Kon Ishikawa, and Shiro Toyoda.

Foreign movies are usually presented in the original language with Japanese subtitles. There is usually no problem for the American, because many of the movies are in the English language. The first-class movie houses are clustered in the Hibiya area in a section directly across from the Imperial Hotel. Others are in the Yur-akucho area close to the Yurakucho Station just off Z Avenue in the Ginza district. The other entertainment districts, like Shi-buya, Shinjuku, and Ikebukuro, all have their clusters of movie houses.

One phenomenon the foreigner will surely notice when he sees a Japanese dramatic movie (and there are many of these because of their great popularity) is the sound of Japanese spectators crying over the most absurd, over-sentimental scenes. He may ask himself: "Are these the stoical, inscrutable Japanese who traditionally smile while experiencing the greatest misfortune?"

Ah, but the explanation is simple. The Japanese have been taught from childhood to withhold a display of emotions when anything personal is involved. So they let out their pent-up, unnaturally repressed emotions at movies, where they can cry to their heart's content in the darkness over some fictitious tragedy without fear of social disapproval. Therefore, just as soon as the hero dies, preferably of some wasting disease which he stoically keeps to himself in the Japanese tradition, out come the handkerchiefs, punctuating a symphony of moans and sobs with trumpet-like nose-blowing. To make the audience happy, some directors find it necessary to kill off someone every few reels.

Before concluding this section on entertainment, let us step gingerly into a field which has wide popularity but whose legitimacy is subject to controversy: the *massage parlor*—the Japanese *toruko,* or turkish bath. (Yes, this comes under the heading of entertainment!) Frankly, there is but one *toruko* in Tokyo whose legitimate activities can be guaranteed, the Tokyo Onsen at 6, 6-chome, Ginza-higashi (tel: 541-3021). Though there may be more strictly legitimate *onsens* (*onsen* meaning "hot springs" and originally applied to the many hot springs that dot volcanic Japan), most of the others have a surface legitimacy, the depth of the legitimacy varying directly with the actual intent of the male customer.

Actually, a *toruko onsen* is quite an experience, and a session at the Tokyo Onsen for husband and wife—or husband alone, for (attention all wives) he will be quite safe—is recommended. The *toruko onsen* may be the only chance you have to take a Japanese bath; and if you don't take a Japanese bath, you will miss an important aspect of Japanese life and the local scene.

The western way of taking a bath is very shocking to the Japanese, who are even critical of showers. To the Japanese, the object of a bath is, first, to get thoroughly clean, and second and more important, to relax and enjoy it. How can you get clean, they ask, when you wash and scrub yourself in the tub? The cleaner you get, they argue, the dirtier the water becomes, and the dirtier the water, the dirtier you become.

The Japanese way? Get in the tub to relax and loosen the dirt. Then get out, sit on a small stool, and wash yourself thoroughly with soap. Next, rinse yourself off until not a particle of dirt or soap remains, using a small wooden pail. Then get back into the tub and relax for as long as you wish in the hottest fresh water you can endure.

The Japanese bath is but one phase of the three-phased *toruko onsen* routine. The steps occur in this order: steam bath, water bath and massage. For all this service the price is usually about 1,000 *yen,* or slightly higher.

The first thing the customer does when he enters the private room is strip himself to the absolute bare skin. Not even a pair of socks is allowed. Shocking? Perhaps to you, but not to the scantily clad girl who is helping you strip. What's it to her? She sees nude men all day long, every hour on the hour, an hour being the normal time a session at a *toruko onsen* takes.

Into the steam bath you go, either lying or sitting, depending on the type of equipment. You remain there as long as you like, and the attendant makes it as hot as you like. Now you get out, and she ushers you into the bathtub, but beware! That water can be very hot, almost boiling. The Japanese seem to have a deficiency of heat-sensitive cells, for they can withstand water that could boil a lobster. And the *onsen* girls never seem to realize that western skin is especially sensitive to heat. At any rate, be sure to test it first. If it seems all right, get in slowly, always prepared to jump out at the first alarm signal sent out by an overanxious nerve. Relax there until you think it is time for the washing. Now you get out, and you will undergo a soaping and scrubbing the likes of which you never had before, not even as a baby. The girl attendant uses a brush, soaping it well before each scrubbing. With the utmost efficiency, she removes every bit of dirt you might have acquired and then rinses you off with the proficiency of the professional that she is. Back into the tub you go.

Now comes the final act of this bathing drama: the massage. You get out of the tub again after a period of relaxation and climb on the massage table. It is covered with foam rubber, from whose clammy coldness your skin is protected by a sheet. She gets to work on your back first, her fingers probing into each vertebra, digging in under the scapulae and kneading the muscles thoroughly. When she is satisfied that she has softened every muscle by apparently pulling the fibers apart and putting them together again, she gets up and *walks* barefoot on your back. This may sound terrible, but it feels very good after you have become accustomed to the weight. Her first step may send your breath out of your lungs as though expelled from a bellows. But after this first moment it is perfectly bearable.

Now she turns you over and begins kneading your chest and abdominal muscles, working down the thighs and calves to the instep. Finished here, she lifts up the legs one at a time and tries to make your toes touch your forehead, a somewhat painful experience. After she has the legs apparently separated from the hips, she proceeds to try to pull your arms out of their sockets. She comes very near to succeeding.

Though this may sound unpleasant, it is almost enjoyable, indicating perhaps that there is a bit of the masochist in all of us. When the massage is finished, you get up feeling as fit as you ever have. She helps you dress and bows you out.

Husbands and wives are welcome at the Tokyo Onsen, or, for that matter, at any of the *onsens*. It is best to go to the Tokyo Onsen, though, as previously mentioned. Married couples can take the same room or go into separate rooms. The latter is preferable, if your faith in your husband permits it.

What happens in the other *onsens*? Your imagination can provide a better description than the written word. Suffice it to say that the Tokyo Metropolitan Government, mindful of Tokyo's reputation during the Olympics, ruled that the doors of all rooms must remain open in *onsens* for the duration. They're closed again.

SPORTS There are only three spectator sports worth mentioning for tourists: *Baseball, sumo* (Japanese wrestling), and *horse racing*.

Japanese *baseball, yakyu*, is an offspring of the American national pastime. And the language used by the child, though heavily accented, is practically the same as that of the American father.

Baseball was introduced into Japan in 1873. It caught on immediately and became the number one sport of the colleges, although professional leagues were not organized until 1936. Even today college baseball enjoys greater popularity than professional baseball. The semiannual Big Six university matches draw huge crowds. To draw a comparison, baseball is to Japanese colleges as football is to American colleges.

There are two professional leagues in Japan, the Central and the Pacific. The season roughly approximates the American, beginning and ending somewhat earlier. At present there are twelve professional teams, six to each league, each team playing from 120 to 130 games a season. American professional baseball men say that Japanese baseball is about the equivalent of Class A baseball in the United States, but not quite of Big League caliber. You will not hear more picturesque names than those which identify the professional teams in Cherry Blossom Land. The Central League teams are the Whales, Tigers, Giants, Carp, Swallows, and Dragons. Those in the Pacific League are the Braves, Hawks, Orions, Lions, Flyers, and Buffaloes. During the season, you may often see Japanese baseball on television. It will be a welcome change from *I Rove Rushi*.

There has been a rumor that Japanese baseball players are very polite, the batter bowing respectfully to the umpire when he calls a strike (though the ball went a mile wide of the plate) and the pitcher taking with equal equanimity a call as unfair for him. Nothing could be further from the truth. Though the Japanese are not as argumentative as American ballplayers, they and their managers have been ejected from games for protesting an umpire's decision too vehemently. Also, Japanese fans more resemble American fans than British. Where the British sports enthusiast reputedly sits quietly at cricket matches doing no more than politely applauding, and accepting calmly any ruling of the umpire, the Japanese baseball fan believes in much more direct action. They have been known to throw pop bottles on the field in the fashion of their American counterparts.

Let's listen to a TV broadcast of a game, bearing in mind that all of the terms have been adapted (and adopted) from English. If you can accustom your ears to the accent, you will have no trouble understanding a Japanese baseball sportscast. Practically the only words in Japanese you need know are *uchimashita*, which means "hit"; and *nagemashita*, which means "pitched."

So the *pitchah nagemashita* perhaps a *cab-vu* or a *do-rop-pu*. Maybe it's a *stro-ri-ku* or a *baw-ru* (the Japanese, as you know, find *l*'s difficult to pronounce). At any rate, when the *battah* gets *sree stro-ri-kus* he is *out-to*. However, *foh baw-rus* and he goes to *fahs-to-bay-su*. Now maybe, with the next *battah* hitting a *shin-gu-ru*, he advances to *second-do bay-su*. If the third *battah* gets on, there is now a *fuh-ru-bay-su* situation; *fuh-ru-bay-su* is Japanese for "bases loaded." Now is the time for the fourth *battah* to get a *home-ran*. Then the stands will go wild. But what a disappointment for them if he gets a mere *bop-pu-fry* (this is Japanese for a pop fly).

Let us go further into Japanese baseballese: A foul is a *fow-ru*; a grounder is now a *go-ro*, which is short for ground. The man behind the plate is the *catchah*. There is the *shaw-to-stop-pu*, the *centah-fee-ru-dah*, and a host of other somewhat familiar names.

Tokyo has four home teams: the Yomiuri Giants, the Kokutetsu (swallows), the Toei Flyers, and the Daiei Orions. The Giants play at Korakuen Stadium in Bunkyo Ward; the Swallows play at the Meiji Shrine Stadium in Shinjuku Ward; the Flyers play at the Komazawa Stadium in Setagaya Ward; and the Orions in Tokyo Stadium in Arakawa Ward. The professional baseball season runs from mid-March to mid-September.

If you are in Japan during the middle two weeks of January, March, May, July, September, or November, you will have an opportunity of seeing what is probably the most popular of all spectator sports in the country—*sumo*, or Japanese wrestling. The tournaments generally begin the second Sunday of the months named, although there are exceptions, and last through the fourth Sunday. In Tokyo the tournaments take place in January, May, and September. In March they are in Osaka, in July in Nagoya, and in November in Fukuoka in Fyushu. However, at all times they are on television.

Sumo is not only popular among the Japanese but also among the foreign residents. It combines technique, speed, strength, and weight with the primary element of personal conflict and the glamour of long tradition to make it a sport unique in the world.

Sumo wrestlers are huge, weighing from 250 to 350 pounds. A wrestler under the lower limit does not have much chance, although, in exceptional cases, some of the small ones do well, even making the highest rank of *yokozuna,* or grand champion. But the undersized ones (puny specimens scaling at say 235) have to make up in speed, skill, and strength what they lack in weight, but this is usually too much of a handicap.

Some foreigners liken *sumo* to *sushi*, the raw fish and rice delicacy. In both cases, once the taste is acquired, the desire for each rises to almost an insatiable peak.

The principle of *sumo* is relatively simple. The two ponderous wrestlers face each other in the center of a ring, hurl themselves at each other and try to throw each other down, or out of the ring. Obviously, there is much more to it than that. There are holds and counterholds; for every offensive thrust there is a defensive counter. Although most of the bouts last only a few seconds, they are a fast and furious few seconds. The most important move is the opening charge, called the *tachiai*. Any football line coach would gaze with admiration and envy at this phase of the match, for the behemoths charge low and fast, the one getting the advantage at this point generally being the winner. The *tachiai* charge is, surprisingly, a thing of beauty to watch; if the wrestler charges too fast, sometimes his opponent will execute a sidestep and, with a push, force him out of the ring.

Each wrestler fights fifteen times, and the one who emerges on the last day with the most wins is the champion of that particular tournament, no matter what his previous rank was. If two are tied, they fight it out because someone has to be crowned champion. The first few days are interesting mainly from a matter of technique and personal attachment to a particular wrestler. After the first week, the contest narrows down to two or three, and the matches become quite exciting. A wrestler may perform well in one tournament and yet be a quick loser in the next. Sometimes wrestling in his home town stimulates a wrestler to better-than-usual efforts, much as our baseball teams seem to do better in their home stadiums. *Sumo* wrestlers are noted for doing poorly immediately after a promotion in rank, and after marriage; draw your own conclusions. In the case of marriage, while the other young bulls are heaving and pushing each other around the training quarters, the young benedict grows soft under the tender ministrations of his bride. Or so they say.

The highest rank attainable is *yokozuna*, or grand champion. They are the heroes of the Japanese, the Rolands, the Beowulfs, and the Siegfrieds of the Cherry Blossom Empire. They are worshiped and acclaimed wherever they go, and in the meanwhile, pile up a considerable fortune. Once a *yokozuna*, a wrestler cannot be demoted no matter how many matches he may subsequently lose. If he does too badly, however, he must retire as a matter of honor, at which time he cuts his long hair—which had been done up in a formal topknot—takes off his kimono and puts on western clothes. A great ceremony accompanies the event.

After him in standing come the *ozekis*, or champions; the *seki-wakes*, or junior champions; next the *komusubis*; and then, lastly in the upper division, or *sumo* big league, the *maegashira*. They fight in reverse order, the *maegashira* wrestling first and the matches involving the *yokozuma* being last.

The matches get very rough, and the wrestlers have to be in top condition to withstand the wear and tear of the 15-day period. An American professional wrestler probably would not be able to stand up too well in the *sumo* ring, because conditioning is such an important factor. This, at least, is the opinion of American trainers who have seen *sumo*. How would an American wrestler do, if trained for *sumo*? Probably not too well, experts say, although some margin for bias must be allowed. However, they insist that the Japanese wrestler is strong from the waist down because the Japanese squat so much in their daily life, while the American wrestler is strong from the waist up. Since the most important part of *sumo* is the initial charge, which involves leg and thigh strength, the American would lose the advantage at the beginning and fare badly.

Sumo is of ancient origin and stems from a religious ceremony. The religious origin is still discernible today in the warmup period that precedes the matches. The most significant of the pre-match ceremonies occurs as follows: there is a clapping of hands, which is intended to call the attention of the gods to the impending match. This hand-clapping phase also takes place at Shinto shrines and Buddhist temples, for the same reason. Then the wrestler cleanses himself by wiping his body, nude except for a loin cloth, with paper and rinsing his mouth with water. Now the ring must be purified. To do this, the wrestler reaches into a box of salt conveniently placed nearby and sprinkles a handful onto the ring. The ring is considered sacred. Where we think of throwing a wrestler down or out, the *sumo*-ist speaks of desecrating the ring. If any part of his body but the soles of his feet touch the ring in combat, he has profaned it and he has lost the bout. If his opponent is able to throw him out of the ring, his strength and skill and spiritual, mental, and physical condition were not sufficient to allow him to remain in the ring, and therefore he is not worthy of this great honor; which is another way of saying he has lost the match. *Sumo* tournaments are held at the Kokugikan in Sumida Ward. It is difficult enough to get tickets during the first week and impossible—unless you know someone—to get them the second, and especially the last, day. But watch it on television, especially from about 4:45 P.M., when the junior champions, champions, and grand champions fight.

Horse racing is sponsored by the national and prefectural governments; betting is allowed. The races are held in the spring, summer, and autumn. There is one race track in Tokyo, the Fuchu, and another, the Nakayama, in neighboring China Prefecture. For every prefecture is allowed to support two tracks. Wherever you go, therefore, you should be able to find one. It's worth a visit, if you like horse racing and want to see the Japanese version.

In the imported class of sports is *ping-pong*, or table tennis. It was imported into Japan about the turn of the century, and the Japanese took to the sport immediately. They soon mastered it and have become champions of the world. Ping-pong does not seem to be a truly American sport, for the American team does not fare too well in the world matches, which the Japanese seem to be able to win with consistent ease. Because of the Japanese interest in table tennis, though, you will find ping-pong parlors in any area. No matter how good you are, however, be careful. That thin, pleasant and smiling young man who agrees to play with you will probably trounce you 21 to 5 or so. And don't bet on the outcome. If you are interested in ping-pong, it may be best just to watch the Japanese play. The average player is exceptional by our standards. To see two Japanese playing is to see speed and skill combined in an assault upon the tiny ping-pong ball.

The number one participant sport in Japan is *golf*, followed by *skiing*. *Swimming* is also very popular. But golf, at least from the standpoint of status and prestige, is tops. If you (as a foreign resident) don't play golf in Japan, you are almost a suspicious character. More business, they say, is now being done on Japanese golf courses than at a geisha party, which traditionally was the place where deals were formerly made. Golf was first introduced into Japan in 1910, and it began to grow in popularity immediately. By 1940 there were 65 courses in Japan. The war, however, did away with most of them. But today golf is more popular than ever, with about 315 golf courses listed by Japan Golf Association.

It received its greatest stimulus in the 1957 Canada Cup international matches, when the Japanese pair not only took the cup but beat Sammy Snead and Jimmy Demaret in so doing; Pete Nakamura walked off with individual honors. From that time, golf, which had been restricted to the wealthy Japanese, spread downward to the middle classes. Memberships in golf clubs went right up to where, at least in one club, what had cost originally $1,500 before 1957, was worth $8,000 in 1958.

Today, the interest in golf is evidenced everywhere, for the Japanese, like the Americans, take their sports seriously. You see amateurs chatting on the street and practicing their golf swings, minus clubs, of course, in the course of conversations. There are driving ranges, protected by nets, on the buildings and even one on both sides of a highway, the cars being protected from the balls by nets which extend over the highway.

With such interest in the sport, obviously there are many golf clubs all over Japan, private and public. You can play at the Kinuta Public Golf Course in Setagaya Ward in Tokyo, or perhaps find a foreign resident to take you to his private club. But the place where most golf bugs go is to Kawana Hotel, at Kawana, Izu Peninsula, in Shizuoka Prefecture, about three hours by train from Tokyo. At the Kawana Hotel there are two 18-hole courses set against a picturesque backdrop of the Pacific Ocean and Oshima Island, which has a volcano that doesn't kick up much of a fuss but is fussing slightly all the time.

Another good course, but with only 9 holes, is in Kyushu in the Unzen National Park. What makes it unique is the flock of blackbirds that make the course its home. If you don't keep a sharp eye open for your ball, the birds swoop in and pick it up; perhaps they think it is an egg. At any rate there is a high rate of incidence of lost balls at Unzen.

Skiing was introduced into Japan, about the same time as golf, by an Austrian army officer, Theodor von Lerch, who taught the Japanese soldiers how to ski. By 1928, Japanese champions were participating in the Winter Olympics. Interest in the sport mounted until more than eight million were crowding the ski resorts before World War II. Today, that number has been far exceeded because of better transportation facilities and the installation of ski lifts, ropeways, and ski tows.

Japan can be called a skier's paradise, for most of the skiing resorts are located at hot springs where the skiers can recover from their fatigue and cold. The skiing season in Japan in general extends from December to March, except in Hokkaido, the northernmost island, and northern Honshu, where it starts earlier and lasts longer.

Here is a list of the principal ski resorts:

Mount Fuji. The slopes of Japan's sacred dormant volcano are for skilled skiers only. Season: mid-December to early March.

Nikko National Park. Extensive skiing grounds on the north shores of Lake Chuzenji and around Mount Shirane and the Konsei Pass. Long downhill runs in a picturesque setting of richly wooded terrain. Season: late December to late March.

Sugadaira. One of Japan's oldest skiing resorts with ski tows operating on the main slope. Sugadaira can be reached by train from Tokyo in 4 hours time. Some 20 Japanese inns in the area offer accommodations. Season: late December to mid-March.

Shiga Heights. One of the most popular spots for Japanese and foreign residents. It lies on a broad, hot-spring-dotted terrain and offers cross-country and slalom skiing with some downhill runs through wooded fields. Ski lifts and a 130-foot takeoff are provided near the Hotel Shiga Heights. To get there you take an electric train to Yudanaka, about 5 hours from Tokyo, and then a bus for 20 minutes to Kambayashi. From Kambayashi, "weasels" operate on schedule to Lake Maruike in the center of Shiga Heights. Season: mid-December to late March.

A sport not discussed much among the foreigners in Japan but which offers excellent opportunities for nimrods is *hunting*. The hunter, however, must be a good walker, for most of the game is found in the mountains where there are no motor roads, and the hunter sometimes must walk about 10 miles in search of quarry. The best game preserves are on Mount Zao, and Kinkasan in Miyagi Prefecture, and Oshima Island in Tokyo Bay. These preserves are maintained by prefectural governments or town and village offices. Japanese game birds include pheasants, copper pheasants, quail, snipe, wild duck, night herons, partridges, wild geese, water hens, and pigeons. Among the game animals are bears, wild boars, foxes, badgers, martens, squirrels, and hares. The hunting season for birds is from October 1 to March 15 except in Hokkaido, where it runs from October 1 to February 15. However, pheasants and copper pheasants can only be hunted from November 1 to January 15 because of the rareness of the bird. It was designated the Japanese national bird in 1948. For animals, the hunting season is from December 15 to the end of February, except in Hokkaido, where the season is from November 15 to January 31.

The Japanese have a special way of hunting wild ducks, a way which extends far back in time. They do not shoot them, asserting that shooting is unfair. For a bullet travels much faster than a duck in flight, and obviously, against a hunter with a keen eye and steady hand, no duck stands much of a chance against a bullet.

The sporting way to hunt ducks (the Japanese sportsman says) is by netting them. In this way the only advantage you have over the duck is a large net. But you have to match your reflexes against the duck's quickness, and the contest therefore is more nearly even. To net a duck, one needs the help of tame, or Judas, ducks. These treacherous fowl swim up little channels set in the shore of a lake and proceed to feed on grain placed there by the professional duck-hunter. He and his amateur hunters hide behind a blind, a wooden wall with a peephole and a chute in it. The peephole is to count the number of wild ducks in the vicinity, and the chute is to send more feed into the channel as a lure. At the given moment, when enough wild ducks have been enticed into the channel by the presence of the tame ducks, and by their own voracity, the professional hunter waves his hand and he and his charges speed silently on sneakers to the sides of the channel with their nets at the ready. Startled by the gathering of the enemy at the sides, the wild ducks attempt to flee. A flick of the wrist if done in time will net a duck or two—if you're quick. Unfortunately, duck clubs where netting wild ducks is practiced are private, except at Kasumigaura near Mito, which charges 3,000 *yen* per person.

Fishing in Japan is a year-round sport. The Japanese are great fishermen and, as mentioned in the section on shopping, make excellent fishing gear. The Japanese waters abound with fish, with the number of species found being more than 1,200. Fishing can be enjoyed in open waters, rivers, streams, lakes, ponds, and practically anywhere there is water in the country.

Of the freshwater fish, trout is the most sought-after by foreigners. Trout fishing can be enjoyed in the lakes, especially Lake Saiko and Lake Motosu at the foot of Mount Fuji, Lake Hakone in Hakone, also in the lakes at Nikko and Lake Haruna near Ikao Spa in Gumma Prefecture.

The most popular spectator fishing for Japanese is *ayu* fishing which is done by cormorants, a type of large bird. The Japanese put a ring around a cormorant's throat to prevent it from swallowing its prey, and then set it out in the river to do the fishing. When it has filled its pouch with small fish, it is brought back and made to disgorge its catch. Fishing with cormorants can be seen on the Nagara River near Nagoya from May to October.

Short Trips from Tokyo

The well-beaten path for day trips from Tokyo goes in two directions, north and south. To the southwest is Kamakura, home of the Great Buddha; and also Hakone, the famous mountain resort with its Lake Ashi, or as it is known to foreigners, Lake Hakone, plus Mount Fuji. To the north is Nikko, a favorite goal for single day trips out of Tokyo. There are other tourist magnets near Tokyo, but Kamakura, Hakone, and Nikko are the most important attractions.

Special Note: The Japanese are great sightseers, and during the summer months on weekends, the traffic can be extremely heavy. This particularly applies to Kamakura, and frankly, I wouldn't head there during the summer months on Saturday or Sunday. Don't forget that it's a very popular weekend destination, and the trains and roads are filled with thousands and thousands of people.

Kamakura

This former *shogunate* capital lies 30 miles from Tokyo. By train, several of which leave daily from Tokyo Station, it can be reached in an hour. By car, you must allow an hour and a half or more, depending upon the traffic. If you want to go to Kamakura on your own, it's really quite simple. Go to Tokyo Station and buy a ticket on the Yokosuka Line train (it's designated clearly by blue marking with white stripes). At the ticket counter, just say "Kamakura" to the ticket agent, and pay for your ticket. Or, you can have a clerk at your hotel write out the information, which you can show to the ticket agent. The trains leave frequently from either Track 9 or 10 (and it's clearly marked).

On the way down you will pass Yokohama, the port city. This is where the passenger liners stop to disgorge their tour groups which immediately head up to Tokyo. Yokohama, being a port city, has its waterfront bars with colorful names like San Francisco, Seattle, Barbary Coast, indicative of the influence that merchant seamen have had upon it. But besides the rugged night life that a waterfront town always has, it is a favorite residence of many foreigners who like to live on the heights that overlook the town.

Yokohama's history is intimately associated with Japanese-U.S. relations. When Townsend Harris, America's first envoy to Japan, finally wheedled an agreement out of the *shogun* (military ruler) in Tokyo, they agreed to open the town of Kanagawa to foreign trade. But when Harris got to Kanagawa, he found that the Japanese were doing some pretty hurried building in some mud flats nearby. A few strategic inquiries brought out the fact that the Japanese had decided that the foreigners would contaminate them and therefore had decided to build a new town on unoccupied land. It turned out this was for the best, for Yokohama, which became the name of the new town, had the better harbor.

The next important town after Yokohama is Zushi, noted for its scenery, good beach and healthful climate. It is dotted with the villas of well-known and prosperous Japanese and has an imperial home not far away at Hayama Beach.

Be sure to watch for the correct stop. Kamakura has three different stations, and the most convenient one is called Hase (called

Kamakura Hase on some signs). Once off the train, take a taxi to see the Great Buddha, the Daibutsu, the renowned statue that sits on a hill overlooking the town, within the confines of the Kotokuin Temple. You can walk, if you wish, but it takes almost a half hour, even after you get the directions (more about the Great Buddha later on).

Kamakura itself is a town full of history. The first *shogunate* (period of military control), which was to set the pattern of Japanese politics for the next several hundred years, was established here in 1192 when Yoritomo Minamoto made Kamakura his capital, after securing the title of shogun from the emperor in Kyoto. The title roughly corresponds to generalissimo, and the hemmed-in emperor had no other recourse but to accede to Minamoto's demands because he had just conquered almost all of Japan, and the emperor, although nominally in control, actually had almost none.

Today, Kamakura is a small community whose population swells extensively when the tourists come to visit its beaches, the Great Buddha, and its Hachiman Shrine, the family shrine of the Minamotos. The whole atmosphere is a far cry from the days when warriors and lords swaggered about and it was the center of the country's life and art of that time (giving its name to a time of Japanese culture, the Kamakura Period).

Its days of glory lasted about 140 years; just as it was originally born as the result of battle and carnage, so did it end its days. The last ruler at Kamakura was a man named Takatoki, a voluptuary and also, surprisingly, a lover of dog fights. He would send his men around the country looking for huge dogs, and they collected some 4,000 to 5,000 of them. Takatoki housed the brutes in kennels richly decorated in gold and silver. Dressing the massive beasts in brocade and tinsel, he made his servants carry them about in palanquins. He was a bit of an eccentric, this Takatoki.

But unrest stirred throughout the land, and the Emperor Go-Daigo, tired of ruling in name only, took advantage of the new spirit and raised an army to restore Imperial power. On July 15, 1333, the emperor's general (who afterwards took the title of shogun and made the emperor a puppet again) hurled three divisions at Kamakura from different directions; Kamakura was doomed. But with defeat inevitable, Takatoki rose to the occasion in true *samurai* fashion and committed suicide by slicing his belly in the approved way. His retainers followed their lord's example, as did over 6,000 other Kamakura residents who feared they were going to be slaughtered anyway by the conquering armies.

The Great Buddha, the major attraction of Kamakura, was built through the efforts of a court lady devoted to Shogun Yoritomo.

How devoted, we don't know, though we only know the wily shogun was a lady's man. She got the idea of erecting the huge statue after Yoritomo, on returning from a visit to Nara in 1195, expressed the wish to have a Buddha of similar proportions built at Kamakura. However, she did nothing about his wish until Yoritomo died in 1199. Then, grief-stricken she obtained permission to leave the court and devote her time and efforts to making the shogun's wish a reality. It took years for her to collect the necessary funds; but finally in 1238, long after all of Yoritomo's immediate family were dead, work began on a huge wooden Buddha. It was completed after five years of continuous labor.

But the wooden Buddha was to be short-lived. In 1248, a terrible storm broke over Kamakura, a tempest so fierce that it carried away the temple and damaged the image. Undaunted, the same court lady went to the shogun of that day and convinced him that another Buddha should be built, but this time of bronze, so that it would be more lasting. On August 12, 1352 the present bronze statue was unveiled. It, too, was housed in a temple, but this and subsequent temples met the same fate as their predecessors, being destroyed by various storms until the Japanese finally gave up. Today, the huge statue is in the open gazing out placidly over the multitudes that come to admire it.

The colossus of Kamakura is considered one of the world's great sculptural masterpieces. Over 42 feet in height, it is about 96 feet in circumference at the base and weighs over 92 tons. The diameter of each of its 656 curls on its head is nine and a half inches. The image itself is a patchwork of pieces of bronze, with the surface being finished off by being filed smooth. Greek elements have been found in the semicircular eyebrows, the horizontal eyes, the fine long mustache, and what is considered the "Ionian smile." Indian influences can be seen in the long ears and the webs between the fingers which symbolize the fulfillment of vows, the meditative posture, the huge curl weighing about 30 pounds which represents the jewel that transmits the light illuminating the universe, and the raised spot on the head which stands for wisdom. Japanese elements are specifically found in the direction of the eyes, which are at right angles to the slightly inclined head and also in the disproportions in size between the head, the upper part of the body, and the lower section.

Among the first foreigners to have seen the colossal Buddha were some English sailors off a ship which anchored in the bay in 1613. They were impressed, according to their captain, John Saris, who wrote about the statue in the typical bad spelling of the day:

"It was in height, as wee ghessed, from the ground about one and twentie foot, in the likeness of a man kneeling upon the ground, with his buttocks resting on his heels, his arms of wonderful largeness, and the whole body proportionable. He is fashioned wearing of a Gowne. The image is much reverenced by Travellers as they pass here."

The worthy Captain Saris, providing evidence that his hearing was as bad as his spelling, wrote that the image "of especiall note" was "called Dabis." Actually, the Japanese call it the "Daibutsu."

Contrary to a popular belief which arises naturally from the English name of the statue, it does not represent the founder of the Buddhist religion, Gautama Buddha, who lived in what is now Nepal (to the north of India) between 566 and 486 B.C. It is the representation, rather, of Amida Buddha, who, according to the beliefs of the sect which worships him, was a king who became a monk, taking the name of Dharmakara. One of his first acts as a monk was to make forty-eight vows to save all living beings. With the fulfillment of the vows, he attained buddhahood and became known as Amida. As such he reigns over the Western Pure Land of the Jodo sect.

The second main attraction in Kamakura is the Hachiman Shrine dedicated to the war god, Hachiman Ojin. It is the family shrine of the Minamotos, and played an important part in the bitter fraternal conflicts that finally saw all the immediate legitimate descendents of Yoritomo Minamoto, the first shogun, wiped out. Founded in 1063 but removed to its present site in 1191 by Yoritomo, the shrine is approached along an avenue of pine and cherry trees and stands at the top of a steep flight of stone stairs.

As you approach it, you will see a hall at the foot of the stairs. This is the site of the famous dance that has become a favorite theme with Japanese drama writers. Here it was that Shizuka, the mistress of Yoritomo's younger brother and a celebrated dancer of her day, sometimes being called the original geisha, danced for the shogun, who was trying to find out the whereabouts of his brother.

The brother, Yoshitsune, is a tragic figure in Japanese history and Kabuki—drama—one of Japan's greatest heroes, young, handsome, brave, and a master of military strategy. It was he who commanded the Minamoto forces which finally exterminated the opposing Taira family forces and won control of Japan for the Minamotos. There is a Robin Hood nature to the tale of Yoshitsune, who was always accompanied by his faithful attendant, Benkei, whom he acquired under circumstances similar to those under which Robin Hood gained Little John as a follower. At any rate, Yoshitsune's great popularity aroused the jealousy of his elder brother, who eventually put a price on his head. In the hunt for Yoshitsune, his mistress, Shizuka, was captured, taken to Yamakura and there given the third degree, but she refused to talk. Finally, the shogun, captivated by the girl's courage and beauty, ordered her to dance for him. In some of the stories there are hints that the shogun had ideas of starting up a relationship a little closer, what would have to be regarded as that of an illegitimate brother-in-law. But Shizuka was faithful to her Yoshitsune. In the hall which stands at the foot of the shrine she danced and accompanied herself with a love song—dedicated to her fleeing warrior-lover. In anger the shogun dismissed her.

On the left side of the stairs stands a huge gingko tree about 70 feet tall and 23 feet in circumference. It was behind this tree that a grandson of Shogun Yoritomo hid, dressed like a woman, as his uncle, the Shogun Sanetomo, second son of Yoritomo, came down the stairs after having performed at an all-night service at the shrine. When his uncle reached the bottom of the stairs, the younger man rushed out and stabbed him crying:

"I am Kugyo. My father's death is avenged!"

This tragic drama had its beginnings several years before when the Hojos, the family of Yoritomo's wife and the mother of his two sons, set out to wrest the power from the Minamotos. First, they killed Yoritomo's immediate successor, his first son, Yoriiye. Then they told Kugyo, Yoriiye's son, that his uncle, Sanetomo, had done the deed so that he could become shogun. Throughout the years they filled the impressionable Kugyo with desires for revenge.

The time for vengeance came in January, 1219, when Shogun Sanetomo was scheduled to worship at the shrine. Sanetomo was twenty-eight at the time, an accomplished poet, gentle by nature, and not at all given to the warlike pursuits of his clan. It is said that he had a premonition of his death; just before setting out for the shrine, he composed the following verse which has since been called his farewell:

> Though I am forth and gone,
> And tenantless my home;
> Forget not thou the spring,
> O plum tree by the eaves.

Against the advice of his counselors, he declined to wear armor under his robes. Although escorted by the usual retinue of state officers and about a thousand horsemen he left them when he reached the shrine, and mounted the broad steps accompanied only by his swordbearer. After the assassination, Kugyo fled. But he was soon caught by the Hojos who executed him as the murderer of the shogun and then took over control.

Within the shrine there is an arrangement of ancient swords, armor, masks, and other paraphernalia of that period, some 600 to 800 years ago. There are also on display the portable shrines, called *mikoshi*, which are carried through the streets during the annual festival held on September 15 and 16. Also during this festival, *yabusame*, or target shooting, by bowmen from horseback is performed. The bowmen are dressed in the costumes of the Kamakura Period and are quite skillful. The giant stone *torii*, or gate, standing 32 feet in height, is designated an "Important Cultural Property" by the Japanese government, denoting its very high value from the standpoint of art and historical significance.

Now that the major attractions of Kamakura are taken care of, there is one other that should not be missed. It is a little-known one, but its lack of fame should not deter the visitor. On a hill not far from the Great Buddha there is a temple within which there is a 30-foot wooden statue of Kwannon, the Goddess of Mercy (it is sometimes also spelled Kannon). This 11-faced gilt image is said to have been carved in 721, by a priest, from half of a large camphor-tree log over 100 feet in length. Two statues were made at the time by the same priest, both of Kwannon. The other is in the Hasedera Temple near Nara, the city that was the capital of Japan before Kyoto.

Tradition has it that the Kamakura Kwannon, after it was carved, was thrown into the sea near Osaka with the prayer that it would save the souls of men from destruction wherever it should wash ashore. In 736, it reached a beach near Kamakura, and the Hasedera, or Hase Kannon, Temple of Kamakura, which houses it now, was erected on the hill to enshrine the statue.

Boasting a population of about 100,000, Kamakura is not only a tourist attraction but a favorite spot for Japanese, who try to escape Tokyo's summer heat at the nearby beaches. It lies on the shores of Sagami Bay in a little valley, enclosed on three sides by evergreen hills, with the beaches on the fourth and south side. Obviously, this geographical setting gave it great strategic value, an important factor in its selection as the shogunate capital.

Because of its long history as a Japanese center of political activity, Kamakura has numerous attractions for the visitors in addition to those listed above. For example, there are 19 Buddhist temples and 19 Shinto shrines at Kamakura or in the immediate area. Its popularity as a tourist attraction as well as resort area is attested to by the fact that in the summer an average of 60,000 persons pass through Kamakura Station every day, most headed for the beaches, but a great many for the shrines, temples, and statues.

The food situation in Kamakura is fair enough. Most of the side streets in the town of Kamakura, which is worth a little exploration, have small restaurants. The leading restaurant in town is surely Oebi, a seafood establishment (incidentally, *oebi* means lobster). The dining room is on the second floor, and the food is excellent. Next best is the Kamakura Inn, located on a hill above the town; it features a barbecue, Japanese style. Most of the tour groups head for Kaseiro, a Chinese restaurant which is fair enough and is conveniently located near the Daibutsu. Then go to the top of the hill, overlooking the bay and Enoshima Island. It is very relaxing here and the scenery is extremely attractive. If you have the time, it would be a good idea to visit the village of Katase, which is located on the shore opposite Enoshima. There is a marine aquarium here patterned after Marineland in Long Beach, California, including the well-trained whales and porpoises. If you have children along, you should not miss Katase.

Katase itself also has played its part in history. In 1270 Kublai Khan sent envoys to Japan to demand tribute (blackmail) and acknowledgement of the Mongolian emperor as sovereign. The enraged Japanese beheaded the envoys at Katase. This undiplomatic action in turn offended the Great Khan, who thereupon outfitted a mighty fleet and army to invade Japan. All seemed lost for the Japanese unless a miracle interposed itself between them and what seemed inevitable destruction. The miracle occurred—in the form of a typhoon which completely destroyed the Mongol fleet.

The grateful Japanese called the typhoon *kamikaze*, or "divine wind," because it seemed heaven-sent in answer to their prayers. Less than 700 years later the Japanese nation again seemed doomed, this time when an American fleet and invasion force was approaching their islands. Again, they prayed for divine intervention, but tried to help it along by making up their own "divine wind" in the form of young suicide pilots whose mission it was to dive their bomb-filled planes onto the decks of the American ships, exploding the bombs and perishing in the attempt. Those unfortunate pilots were also termed *kamikaze*. Today, the word *kamikaze* remains in daily speech to describe Tokyo's taxi-drivers. But the original meaning of a god-sent wind is completely lost; for it has become synonymous with suicide and has been especially applied to the cabdrivers because of their seeming desire to accomplish the destruction of themselves, their cabs, and their passengers.

If you have good legs and would like to exercise them, an excellent walk would be accross the Bentenbashi, or Benten Bridge, 1,335 feet long, from Katase to Enoshima. This beautifully wooded islet is about a mile and a half in circumference and is famous for its "Dragon Cave," which lies on the other side of the hill that crowns the island. Admission is 30 *yen*, and, when you enter, you are given a candle to light your way through the caves, some 360 feet deep. At the far end is an image of Benten, one of the seven Buddhist deities who stand for good luck. Tradition has it that the cave was once the lair of a dragon; hence, its name.

At the top of the hill, which you must climb from the bridge to reach the cave, is the Enoshima Shrine, which originally was a Buddhist temple built at the request of Shogun Yoritomo. During the summer festival held each July 14, boys carry the portable shrines, or *mikoshi*, into the water, wading in up to their shoulders and frolicking around in the waves. From the crest of the hill on a clear day there are magnificent views of Mount Fuji in the distance and of smoking Oshima offshore, the island with the still smoldering volcano.

At the summit, there is an amusement park, an observation tower atop a lighthouse, botanical and zoological gardens, and some amusement facilities for children, including a merry-go-round and musical chairs. If the walk back seems too long, you can hire a boat for the return trip. As you near the shore, you may see floating about in the water various globelike baskets called *ikesu*, and in them the Katase restaurant proprietors keep fish, lobsters, and clams in sea water until a customer orders them.

There are two possible places, should you wish to remain overnight. The best is the Hotel Hayama Marina, which is fairly expensive and excellent; the Zushi Nagisa is more modest and much less expensive.

The Hakone District

Although you can reach Hakone by train, it is better to take an automobile tour that includes Kamakura, with a stopover for one night at Hakone; Hakone is not more than another hour and a half by car from Kamakura. By leaving in the morning, you can see some of Kamakura before lunch, have lunch, and finish up the area, leaving in time to get to Hakone in time for dinner.

Although there is a tendency to refer to Hakone as though it were a particular town, Hakone is actually a district lying within the crater of an extinct volcano, measuring about 25 miles in circumference. There are many hot springs in the area, as well as a mountain lake, Lake Ashi (the Lake of the Reeds), which is often referred to as Lake Hakone.

Because of the volcanic nature of the area, there are numerous active hot springs and no less than 12 hot-spring resorts in the Hakone District. These have been known from olden times as the "Twelve Spas of Hakone." The most popular of these, especially among foreigners, are Gora and Miyanoshita (where there is an excellent western-style hotel).

Miyanoshita is by far the great attraction for the foreigners. It boasts the well-known Fujiya Hotel with its 166 western-style rooms, almost all with bath, as well as community-style baths where you and your family can enjoy a good cleansing together. Miyanoshita stands at an altitude of 1,377 feet, making it cool even in summer and therefore a refuge for the hot and weary. The temperature of the hot spring is 172 degrees, and it is supposed to have excellent therapeutic value because it contains common salt.

Good roads emanate in every direction from Miyanoshita. A ride down to the lake and a boat trip is highly recommended. The village by the lake is filled with souvenir shops, and if you like souvenirs, this is a good place to browse around.

There are also many excellent walking trips. Mount Sengens is in back of the Fujiya Hotel; it is 2,630 feet high and can be climbed in about an hour. From the summit there is a fine view of the Hakone District that will give you a good idea of the topography of the region. The Dogashima Walk is down a path on the side of a ravine which leads in 15 minutes to picturesque cascades and a pinewood park called Matsugaoka Koen. Another favorite stroll is to Kowakidani, noted for its cherry blossoms and azaleas, less than 15 minutes from Miyanoshita; and then on to the Chisuji Waterfall (Waterfall of 1,000 Threads), less than 15 minutes from Kowakidani.

If all these 15-minute strolls seem like child's play to an old walker like you, try this one: Take the electric railway from Miyanoshita to Gora, a 10-minute ride; then go by way of cable car to Sounzan, another ride of about 10 minutes; from Sounzan you walk not quite a mile (but a tough one!) and a half to Owakidani, also called Valley of the Great Boiling. This is a natural wonder which reeks of sulfurous fumes and is constantly covered by clouds of steam being ejected through crevices in the rocks, or from the ground itself. If you thrust a stick into the ground, the earth will seem to try to rid itself of the irritant by ejecting a spurt of steam. When you get to this desolate area, keep to the well-beaten path; there is a very good reason why another name for the region is Ojigoku, or Big Hell.

A last place to be highly recommended for sightseeing is Hakone Shrine, located in a secluded spot on the densely wooded southern slope of Mount Koma, which rises to a height of 4,354 feet. To get to the shrine, take a bus to the village of Moto-Hakone, or go by car. The shrine itself is only 400 yards away from the bus station.

This edifice was supposed to have been erected in 757 A.D. and is one of the largest in Japan. Red *torii*, or gates, rise from the water's edge up to the shrine, which is famous as the place where Yoritomo Minamoto, our old friend and the first of the shoguns, hid when badly defeated by the rival Taira family in 1180.

Although a visit to Hakone Shrine is always interesting, the best time to go is during the festival, which is held on July 31 and August 1 every year. On the evening of the first day, ceremonial rites are observed (aboard boats in the middle of the lake) by priests and parishioners of the shrine, who, along with visitors from neighboring districts, float thousands of lighted lanterns from the shore. The service is offered to the nine-headed dragon which is believed to be the spirit of the lake, a sort of Loch Ness monster with a Japanese touch. The next day the usual portable-shrine-carrying by the young men of the area goes on, to the shouts of *washo, washo*. Although you may have seen many of these before, these shrine processions by the young men, well-fortified by numerous drinks of *sake*, are always interesting sights.

Fuji Lake Area

Perhaps on the beaten but certainly not on the well-beaten tourist path is this area which is a favorite among residents of Japan who know that, if you want to see Mount Fuji (Japan's highest at 12,397 feet and certainly its most beautiful mountain), then the Fuji lake area is the place where you should go. For although at Hakone you might see Fujiyama peeping over the rim of the volcanic cone, the weather has to be clear. At the Fuji lake area, what has been described as the world's most perfectly shaped mountain is visible always, although its top may be covered with clouds. Don't forget it's called either Mount Fuji—or Fujiyama; never Mount Fujiyama, because *yama* means "mount," and you'd be saying Mount Fuji Mount.

You can get to the Fuji lake area from the Hakone district by bus or by car, but this is not a comfortable drive. The recommended way is to make it a separate trip from Tokyo, making the trip by train. The roads are pretty bad.

There are five lakes in the region. Once, over a thousand years ago, the lakes were part of a river that meandered peacefully through the fields at the base of the volcano; and then Fuji blew its top. The lava rolled down the sides, effectively damming the river at various points, and as though a fairy wand had touched it, the river was changed into the five lakes.

From east to west the lakes are: Yamanaka, Kawaguchi, Saiko, Shoji, and Motosu. Each of the lakes claims certain distinctions: Yamanaka is the largest, covering 1,656 acres, and the highest, at 3,220 feet; Kawaguchi has the longest circumference with 12 miles; Shoji is the smallest, covering only 198 acres; Motosu is the deepest with a depth of 433 feet; and Saiko, though having no firsts, has the most seconds—it is the second highest, the second deepest, and the second smallest.

All the lakes are well stocked with trout. Because of their altitude, all being situated at over 2,000 feet, they make excellent summer retreats. The entire region is filled with pheasants, copper pheasants, wild ducks, and doves that attract hunters in season. Like the others, Lake Yamanaka, the largest, is a favorite summer resort. Its shores are dotted with hotels, villas, and clubhouses of various schools and organizations. The Fuji Golf Links of 18 holes is nearby. The district is noted for its many varieties of singing birds, of which at least a hundred are known. The people of the area have placed more than 200 birdhouses in the woods for the convenience of their little feathered friends who sing for their rent. There is an excellent hotel, the Fuji New Grand, which can be recommended.

Eight miles away is the village of Fuji-Yoshida, a starting point for those hardy vacationers who seek to scale Mount Fuji. The Mount Fuji climbing season begins in July, and thousands of amateur Alpinists flock to the village to begin their trek up the dormant volcano and win for themselves a pole with a flag on it that attests to their ruggedness. If you have that kind of blood in you, it is an interesting climb, those who have done it say. (Don't look at me, my knees give way!)

Fuji-Yoshida is noted for its fire festival at the Sengen Shrine, usually held on August 26, when the Fuji climbing season is coming to a close. Towards evening on the festival day, dozens of bonfires are lighted at different places in the city, each of them nearly 20 feet in height. In answer to these, the keepers of mountain huts all along the climbing route also light bonfires. The young men carry a vermilion-colored portable shrine shaped like Mount Fuji through the streets, making a colorful procession. Legend has it that in the old days, when Mount Fuji habitually erupted, it always did so on the side facing Fuji-Yoshida. The bewildered people, wondering why the mountain always picked on them, decided they had better placate whatever god was doing the mischief. Thus, the festival was started.

The favorite lake is probably Kawaguchi because it is one of the most beautiful of the five lakes and provides one of the finest views of Mount Fuji. In the lake itself is a wooded islet, called Unoshima, or Cormorant Isle, on which is a shrine dedicated to the goddess of beauty and music. In autumn, the leaves of the maple and other trees on the islet present a spectacle of marvelous natural color. The view of Mount Fuji from the north shore of Kawaguchi is famous, for it presents not only the mountain in its natural form but also its inverted reflection in the water, which is even lovelier. For good reason the excellent western-style hotel is called the Fuji View Hotel, and it has two view towers from which you can take photographs of the magnificent mountain.

On the southeast shore of the lake is the bustling village of Funatsu, with many hotels, inns, and souvenir shops. On every August 5 the villagers hold a spectacular lantern fete with a fireworks display that draws spectators even from Tokyo. During the festival evening, thousands of lanterns are set afloat on the lake to create a very colorful sight.

Lake Saiko is within walking distance from Lake Kawaguchi, being a little over a half-mile from the latter's northwest shore. Stretching between Saiko and the next lake, Lake Shoji, is a forest, covering about 24 acres, called Jukai, or the Sea of Trees, because of the beautiful shimmering colors the leaves assume in the autumn. Other tourist attractions are Bat Cave, the bats of which are interesting because of the fact that their heads are covered with hair so as to resemble a chrysanthemum (the crest of the Imperial Family); and also Fuji Fuketsu, or Fuji Wind Cave, 600 feet deep and 40 feet wide. The floor is always covered with ice because of its elevation, and the temperature hovers about the freezing point even in summertime.

Lake Shoji's main attraction is Mount Eboshidake, or Panorama Hill, from which a beautiful view of Mount Fuji over the Sea of Trees may be obtained. In the autumn it draws color photographers as honey draws flies.

Lake Motosu, the deepest lake, never freezes over, even in the dead of winter, because of its great depth. Where the other lakes are sending out the siren call for ice skaters, Lake Motosu remains cold and blue, attracting only nature lovers who like to gaze on the placid beauty of its deep blue water. And shiver.

The lakes have excellent trout fishing, and all but Lake Motosu offer *wakasagi* fishing. *Wakasagi* are a species of small smelt which is caught in January and February, when the four lakes have frozen over, by cutting a hole in the ice.

An excellent tour covering 120 miles and taking from 6 to 8 hours is recommended. Start by bus from Lake Yamanaka and go to Funatsu, where a motorboat may be taken across Lake Kawaguchi. Thereafter, you travel by foot for 20 minutes to Lake Saiko, cross it by motorboat, and then resume your journey by bus to Lake Shoji and then to Lake Motosu, continuing on to Kamiide and passing two waterfalls on the way: Otodome (Noiseless Waterfall), and then Shiraito (White Threads Waterfall) which is 87 feet high and 420 feet wide. A short detour to the village of Shiraito is recommended to see the largest white mountain-cherry tree, 28 feet in girth, with the long name of *Yoritomo-nokomadome-no-zakura,* which means "Yoritomo's horse-stopping cherry tree." It received its nonstop name from the tradition that our old friend, Shogun Yoritomo Minamoto, was so struck by the blossoms of the tree that he stopped his horse to look at them in wonder. You can share Yoritomo's admiration for the blooms if you happen to be there about April 10 when the blossoms burst forth.

Beyond Kamiide the road passes the large Buddhist temples of Hommonji and Teisekiji, both founded more than 650 years ago by the priest Nikko, a disciple of Nichiren, founder of the Nichiren sect of Buddhism. After this the tour takes you to Fujinomiya, one of the starting points for a climb up Mount Fuji during the two-month summer climbing season. The village is noted for its paper-making industry. Next comes Yoshiwara, a village not to be mistaken for Tokyo's infamous-until-1958-when-prostitution-was-outlawed red-light district of the same name. This particular Yoshiwara is noted for its famous pine tree immortalized in a woodblock print by Hiroshige (1797–1858), one of Japan's greatest woodblock-print artists, generally called "Yoshiwara." The pine tree itself so attracts the attention of the Japanese, who love the scraggly shaped pines, that they have dubbed it the *Mikaeri-no-matsu,* or Looking-Back Pine Tree, because, they say, you give it one more look over your shoulder as you walk away.

From Yoshiwara the trip goes via the old Tokaido Highway, the main road between Tokyo and the ancient capital of Kyoto. You will know the highway from the giant pine trees bordering each side. The highway runs parallel to the Tokaido Railway Line to Hara, which is famous for the collection of bonsai, or dwarfed trees, owned by Mr. Y. Uematsu. Some of the trees in the collection, though less than two feet in height, are over 500 years old. From

Hara the return trip may be either via Numazu and Gotemba or via Hakone, the Nagao Pass, and Gotemba to Lake Yamanaka.

Now for the main attraction not only of this district but of the districts all around, Japan's majestic sacred mountain, Fujiyama (*yama* means "mountain," as does *san,* so that you will sometimes hear the Japanese refer to it as Fujisan or Fujiyama).

With a height of 12,397 feet, it is the highest in a long chain of volcanoes which starts in the Marianas Group in the South Pacific. Fujiyama is considered one of the two most beautiful conically shaped volcanoes in the world, the other being Mount Cotopaxi in Ecuador if you simply won't sleep tonight without knowing.

It is not even certain what "Fuji" means, although most Japanese will tell you (merely a guess) that it comes from the Ainu word for "fire," the Ainus being the hairy Caucasoid aborigines of Japan now confined to a part of Hokkaido, a northerly island of Japan. Fuji has lain dormant for over 200 years, although there have been 18 different eruptions on record, the worst having occurred in 800, 864, and 1707, which was the last outbreak and lasted intermittently from November 22 until December 4 of that year. It covered Tokyo, then called Edo, with six inches of ashes, although Tokyo is 75 miles away. The people of the then shogunate capital became panic-stricken because of the thundering noises that came from the ash-belching volcano and the darkness caused by the ashes as they fell on the city. Today, only a few wisps of steam rising at one spot of the summit are reminders of the volcano's tempestuous past.

The mountain has been considered sacred by the Japanese from ancient times. Until 1868, when Japan experienced a change of government from the shogunate to the present form, no women were allowed to climb up its sacred slopes. But now, many women are among the more than 100,000 who test their climbing prowess on the mountain annually. Although the climbing season lasts only from July 1 to August 31, hardy and foolhardy climbers try it the year around, and usually regret it.

The crater at the summit is more or less circular in shape and almost 600 yards in diameter. The bottom lies over 730 feet from the highest point on the rim, is level, and has a diameter of 76½ yards. It is possible to descend into the crater, which is regarded with special reverence by the Japanese.

There are eight peaks on the rim, the highest being Ken-ga-mine Peak. From this peak two paths take you along the rim of the crater, one along its edge and the other crossing over the eight peaks. Needless to say, the former is easier, although both take about an hour to cover the mile and a half distance. A shrine is located on one of the other peaks, and near another peak is Sai-no-kawaa, where pious Buddhists have raised heaps of stones to assist the labor of child-spirits, whose task they believe is to pile up stones from the river. It is near this spot that steam with a temperature of about 180° Fahrenheit still rises.

There are 6 popular routes up the mountain with 10 stages separated by varying distances along each. At each stage there generally are huts where accommodations, not to be recommended to those who like the lap of luxury, can be obtained. They also furnish refreshments and a place to rest for the weary, which surely includes you. The reason for the accommodations is because of the popular method of climbing Mount Fuji in two stages. The climbers go about halfway up and then spend the night, awakening early the next morning to make the summit by sunrise in order to view the sun climbing up from the eastern sea (the Pacific).

Nikko

Now we turn northward, leaving from Ueno or Asakusa station for splendid Nikko, about which the Japanese say:

> *Nikko wo miru made*
> *Kekko to yuna.*

Literally translated it means, "Don't say *kekko* until you see 'Nikko.'" This expression seems rather inane to most foreigners when they hear it, even when it is explained that *kekko* means "magnificent." However, the expression in effect means: "See Nikko and die"; for according to the Japanese, nothing more remains in the world to excite your interests.

Actually, the town of Nikko and its surroundings are only one of the local attractions. For Nikko is also a national park whose 206,665 acres stretch over four prefectures and are filled with natural beauty. But let's take each in its turn.

I recommend that you go to Nikko by train, not only because it is faster, but because roads being what they are in Japan, it is more comfortable. The fastest train makes the 90-mile trip from Tokyo in less than 2 hours. Twenty-five miles before the town of Nikko the train goes past an avenue of Japanese cedars which runs all the way to Nikko; they were planted as part of the mausoleum plan built to honor Ieyasu Tokugawa, who made Nikko an important city. The usual tour is a day-long trip, leaving Tokyo about 8 o'clock in the morning and returning at 7 o'clock, in time for a bath and dinner. This tour merely takes in the mausolea (that is, more than one mausoleum) and temples, provides lunch, finishes up in the afternoon, and catches the late afternoon train for Tokyo. This is quite adequate, although it leaves out most of the national park except perhaps for Lake Chuzenji. For those with more time, there are longer itineraries available.

A little history will help to understand the monumental buildings of Nikko. Ieyasu Tokugawa was the third in a succession of great generals who ruled Japan. After defeating the family of his predecessor, he established his capital at Tokyo, then called Edo, in 1603. It is interesting to note that had he lost the struggle, Osaka might have become Japan's capital, since it was the stronghold of Ieyasu's enemies.

Ieyasu died in 1616 at the age of seventy-four; he had directed that he be buried at Nikko. But since there was nothing adequate enough to house so important a corpse, it was temporarily buried elsewhere. Not until 1634 was work on the Nikko mausoleum begun by Ieyasu's grandson, the shogun Iemitsu. Following this example, the next shogun assigned a domain that yielded 50,000 bushels of rice annually for the maintenance of the shrine. At the same time, a prince of the Imperial blood was invited to preside over the shrine, although, for political reasons, he was made to live in Tokyo and had to visit Nikko three times a year to perform his duties.

When Iemitsu began the shrine's construction, no top limit was set on expenditures. The finest artists and the most skillful craftsmen were brought from all over Japan at government expense to do the necessary work. Then they were divided into groups to compete with each other in producing the finest work. An immense amount of gold leaf was used in decorating the mausoleum and shrine, which were completed in 2 years. It is recorded officially that 2,-489,900 sheets of gold leaf were used, an amount that would cover 6 acres. The timber used in the buildings, if placed end to end, would extend for 330 miles, it was even then reported, showing that this method of eyepopping comparison was not the invention of Madison Avenue advertising geniuses. More than 15,000 men, all told, worked on the buildings for the 2 years it took to complete them.

Iemitsu, the obedient grandchild, also lies buried in Nikko, although the buildings and shrines dedicated to him show a different style from that of Ieyasu's, because the younger man was laid to rest at Nikko eighteen years after his grandfather, and styles had changed during the period.

From Nikko, the town, to reach the shrines and mausolea, you cross the Nikko, alongside the Sacred Bridge, or Mihashi, arching over the Daiya River in a graceful curve. The bridge is lacquered a brilliant red with gilt metal ornaments and rests on two huge stone supports shaped like gates at each end. It is supposed to mark the spot where a Buddhist priest crossed the raging river swollen with torrential rains on the backs of two sea serpents. The original bridge was built in 1636, was destroyed by floods in 1902 and rebuilt in 1907. Today, it is used only on ceremonial occasions.

Once across the bridge, you'll see a monument erected by Masatsuna Matsudaira, one of the commissioners charged with the construction of Ieyasu's shrine. On the marker is an inscription dated April 17, 1648, which states that the august commissioner presented to the spirit of Ieyasu the Japanese cedars that line the road to Nikko for 25 miles. The planting of the trees took 20 years, and some 15,000 of them are still standing despite fires that have caused gaps in the arboreal honor guard. A popular story has it that Matsudaira was not as rich as the other *daimyos* (feudal lords) and therefore could not present as expensive an offering to the Ieyasu shrine, so he devised the cheap but more tedious way of planting the trees as his contribution.

Those who find temples fascinating—and this group would seem to be in the minority, for most foreigners have their temple-viewing desires satisfied after seeing two or three—would do well to visit the Rinnoji Temple, which is on the right of the Ote-dori, the avenue which leads to the Toshogu Shrine. To your right as you enter the front gate of the temple is a building called the Hombo, or Abbot's Residence. This is the place where General Grant stayed for eight days when he visited Nikko in July, 1879.

East of the Hombo is the spirit hall, so called because relics of the successive abbot superiors, who were selected only from the Imperial Family, are enshrined. The main attraction here is the hall itself, which is one of the world's finest examples of Buddhist art. A black-lacquered altar fills the entire inner portion of the central chamber. On the alter is a large reliquary, shining with gold foil, its doors embossed with a chrysanthemum, the Imperial Crest.

The main hall, guarded by a cherry tree well over 200 years old, is called the Sambutsudo, or Three Buddhas' Hall, because of three huge images within. One of these is the Thousand-Handed Kwannon (who, we remember, is the Goddess of Mercy). In the center is the statue of Amida Buddha, a few inches shorter than the Kwannon. On the left is the Bato Kwannon, or Horse-Headed Kwannon, the same height as the Amida. The name of this figure comes from the horse's head on its forehead. It is believed to be the incarnation of animal spirits and is worshiped as the deity that protects animals. The Three Buddhas' Hall is the largest structure in Nikko, being over 112 feet long, 70 feet wide and 84 feet high. It was built in the year 848, according to tradition, but the precise date is in some doubt.

From the Rinnoji Temple, the Toshogu Shrine is only a couple of minutes' walk. There is a broad flight of 10 stone steps leading to the shrine, which in olden days was the prescribed limit for the lower classes, since they were not permitted inside. On top of the steps stands a huge granite Shinto gate about 28 feet high. On the left of the gate is a 5-story pagoda. Pagodas, we might point out, always have an odd number of stories, never even. This pagoda dates from 1815, the original one having been destroyed by fire.

The path now leads to another flight of steps on top of which stands a Buddhist gate, 29 feet high. Inside the gate you proceed down the path, and after it bends to the left you'll see (on your left) the Sacred Stable that once housed the Sacred Horse. But the thing that should catch your eye is the familiar sight of three monkeys in the central panel of the building. These monkeys are *the* original of the famous simian trio of "Hear no Evil, Speak no Evil, See no Evil." You can readily identify each one by the position of his hands, as if you didn't already know.

Nearby is the Sacred Library, which contains 700 volumes of Buddhist *sutras* (textbooks) in a revolving bookcase, 20 feet high and 15 feet in diameter, an excellent place in which to browse for those interested in Buddhist *sutras,* but probably willingly passed up by the usual tourist, which includes me. You next approach one of the greatest attractions of the shrine, the Yomeimon, or Gate of Sunlight. This is undoubtedly the most famous and most photographed gate in Japan, and will come as a surprise to those accustomed to the more simple Japanese style of architecture. For this gate, standing about 37 feet high, is a 12-columned, 2-storied structure covered with so much elaborate carving and unnecessary decoration that utter confusion will likely set in when you first see it. The Japanese call this gate Higurashimon, or Twilight Gate, meaning that you will probably want to stay until dusk looking at it. In one respect they may be correct, because it will probably take you that long to figure it out. Carved all over it are giraffes, dragons, children, poets and sages, birds and flowers. It will remind you of some of the excesses of the Baroque Period which coincidentally was simultaneously flourishing in Europe at the time the gate was built.

Whatever your reaction to the Yomeimon, it is one of the main causes for the Japanese saying about Nikko quoted at the beginning of this section. To many, Nikko means the Yomeimon, and you will certainly see it many times, if you have not already, in pictures about

Japan, especially those in color. If you are surprised at the still brilliant color of the Toshogu Shrine after more than three centuries, it is because the paint is renewed about every twenty years and clear lacquer is applied over the gold leaf, so that the color looks today just about as it did when the shrine was first completed.

Within the gate (to the left) is the Mikoshigura, or Sacred Palanquin House, where the portable shrines, so heavy that they take at least fifty men to carry, are kept. They are brought out during the festivals, the main one being on May 17 and 18, and then again on October 17. The major event of the first festival is the procession of *samurai,* priests, and others all attired in the costumes of the Tokugawa Period. This procession brings out swarms of tourists, both Japanese and foreign, and photographers, still and movie.

To the right of the gate is the Kaguraden, or Sacred Dance Stage, a smaller building than the Mikoshigura. It is interesting to note the basket of flowers on the panel at the right-hand corner. Though the flowers are Japanese, the basket is believed to have been copied from the Dutch. If so, it is believed to be the only carving in Nikko which shows occidental influence.

Straight ahead from the gate is another, the Karamon, or Chinese Gate, less than half as high as the Yomeimon. It, too, is garishly carved. It leads to the Haiden, or Oratory, and the Honden, the Main Hall which lies at a lower level from the Oratory.

The Haiden is really just the outer hall of the Honden, which is separated by a small passage chamber. There are three chambers in the Honden, the innermost containing a resplendent gold-lacquered shrine called the Gokuden, or Sacred Palace. Within it are enshrined the three deities of Ieyasu (you remember our old friend), Yoritomo Minamoto, and Hideyoshi Toyotomi. The three warlords were deified after their deaths, and it is to honor these three that the two festivals are held.

To get to the tomb of Ieyasu, you turn left just before the Karamon and proceed along a corridor to another gateway over which a sleeping cat is carved. This is the famous Nemuri-neko, or Sleeping Cat, said to be carved by one of the most famous sculptors of the time. Past this gate you will come to another decorated gate, the Sakashitamon, and going through you will come to a flight of 200 steps. Taking a deep breath and mustering your courage, you ascend the stairs (puffing and huffing all the while) and reach the site where Ieyasu's ashes are buried—but you will have to go through a bronze gate, another entrance hall, and another bronze gate before you get there. The tomb is shaped like a small bronze pagoda, 11 feet high, and surrounded by a stone balustrade. As you stand before the tomb, you might bear in mind that within it are the ashes which represent all that remains of the man for whom this region was constructed.

Now for the natural beauties of Nikko, as opposed to its man-made wonders. Eleven miles from Nikko is Lake Chuzenji. You will have to hire a car with driver for this trip; or, if you are with a tour group, you will undoubtedly be going by bus. Lake Chuzenji is one of the two best-known natural attractions of Nikko, the other being Kegon Falls.

Oval in shape and surrounded by hills, Lake Chuzenji is 15 miles in circumference and has a maximum depth of 528 feet. On its shores are hundreds of cherry trees which blossom in mid-May, about the time of the main Toshogu Shrine festival, not exactly a coincidence since the Japanese authorities moved the festival date up from June so that visitors can see their festival and their cherry blossoms at the same time.

If you are taking one of the longer tours, you will probably stay at the Kanaya Hotel in Nikko, located on a hill; the Lakeside Hotel and the Nikko Kanko Hotel are both on the lake shore, and a little way out.

Nature lovers (the healthy kind) can enjoy themselves with a good, invigorating climb to the top of towering Mount Nantai, which faces Lake Chuzenji. The route to the top is only five miles long and should take a good climber only three hours. On the top there's an extinct volcano's crater, 1,000 feet in diameter; you'll find three shrines, where panting pilgrims make their obeisances. If shrines and craters don't appeal to you, take a look at the surrounding view. It's superb.

For those pilgrims who view with dismay the hike to the top, a shrine is conveniently located on the shore of Lake Chuzenji, where the path to the summit begins. This is Chuzenji Shrine, and a place where purification can be obtained without grunting one's way to the top. Shinto priests of several centuries ago apparently were completely knowledgeable about human weaknesses even then.

About a half-mile away from Lake Chuzenji is Kegon Falls, a 330-foot drop of water which combines its own natural loveliness, if seen at the right time of the year, with the surrounding scenery to make it a touristic destination. Even the Japanese gape and sigh at the wonder of it all, and suicidal romantics (of which the country has more than its share) often decide that the beauty of it all makes this the ideal place to end it all. At any rate, many lovesick Japanese sweethearts have chosen this spot as the place to swear eternal love and then to take the deep dive into eternity.

A little over eight miles from Lake Chuzenji, on a road that skirts the north shore, is Nikko-Yumoto Spa, an attraction because of its hot springs and in addition because it is located beside Lake Yunoko, the Lake of Hot Water, a mile long and a third of a mile wide, where trout fishing is excellent, since the government keeps it well stocked. The summer temperature of the area never goes above 82° Fahrenheit and in winter the lake freezes over to the delight of skaters who enjoy themselves while hordes of skiers thunder down the slopes of neighboring Mount Shirane, the highest peak in the area at 8,507 feet.

The waters of the hot spring, being quite sulfurous, are considered highly therapeutic in effect. (You know the theory—if it smells bad, it's good for you.) There are several public baths at Nikko-Yumoto Spa, where the temperatures of the local waters range from 100° to 149° Fahrenheit.

In addition to the above, there are many other appealing places for the enterprising tourist. The temples and shrines in the lake region are quieter and simpler than those near Nikko, and perhaps as a result more appealing. The drive alone to Lake Chuzenji is a thriller, with many hairpin turns. Besides Kegon Waterfall, there are many other waterfalls of various sizes in the area. The trees and mountain scenery are gorgeous, and the fishing is usually excellent. Many Japanese and foreign residents feel that too much attention is paid to Toshogu Shrine (which is about all that can be seen in a one-day trip to Nikko), and not enough to longer tours that would take in Lake Chuzenji, its waterfalls, its boating and fishing.

Longer Trips from Tokyo

Nagoya

Many trains run daily over the 227 miles from Tokyo to Nagoya en route to Kyoto and Osaka, but the best ones to take are the limited expresses which make the run in a little over 2 hours. The new fast trains on the Tokaido Line are scheduled to make the trip in even faster time in the immediate future.

Because of its industrial and commercial importance and because it lies roughly between Tokyo and Kyoto (East Capital and Capital City), Nagoya is sometimes called Chukyo (Middle Capital). It is Japan's largest city after Tokyo, and Osaka, having a population of about 1,900,000. The city grew up around a number of feudal castles built in the 16th century, but it did not receive much notice until

Ieyasu Tokugawa built a castle there, reputedly one of the three strongest fortresses in Japan, for his son, Yoshinao. This castle, originally one of the main attractions of the city, was destroyed in a bombing raid in 1945 but has recently been rebuilt.

Since the 13th century, Nagoya has been a great pottery- and porcelain-manufacturing center. The art of pottery-making in Japan was started at the village of Seto, 13 miles from Nagoya, by Japan's first potter, Shirozaemon Kato, who lived in the first half of the 13th century. Because of the village's name, porcelain in Japan is known as *setomono*. Seto is still a busy porcelain-manufacturing center, with over 500 factories, and has the National Ceramic Experimental Station located there. In Nagoya itself the famous Noritake brand of china is made by the Japan Pottery Company. About 70% of Japan's total output of chinaware comes from Nagoya and vicinity.

Nagoya is also a textile center, with 85% of the nation's woolen goods made there. It is first in cloisonné production, and specializes also in lacquerware, clocks, toys, lumber and wood articles, musical instruments, and paper products (including fans).

Nagoya also leads in the breeding of *chin,* a type of Japanese spaniel. The chin is a very popular, black-and-white long-haired little dog which is very affectionate and very brave behind windows. They will bark like mad at passing strangers and other dogs as long as there is protection between them and their quarry. Because of this, they make excellent watchdogs and lovable pets. Place them outside, however, and their truculence melts away and is replaced by a pleasant, fawning manner towards humans, and a tendency to run back inside with respect to other dogs.

Nagoya has much of historic and architectural interest to divert the tourist. One of the most important attractions is the Atsuta Shrine. This and Nagoya Castle are the two things for which Nagoya is renowned on the tourist path. A typical village of the Meiji period (1868–1912), a small-scale restoration on the order of Williamsburg is located on Invyama Park, 12 miles north of Nagoya. It's worthwhile and the admission charge is a mere 100 *yen.*

Atsuta Shrine's particular fame rests in the fact that it displays the Sacred Sword, one of the Three Regalia of the emperor. The other two are the Sacred Mirror (at the Ise Shrine), and the Sacred Jewels, kept in the Imperial Palace. The great annual shrine festival is observed on June 21.

How the sword got there is interesting. Back in the early days of Japan, long before anybody could write and everything of importance had to be handed down by word-of-mouth, a certain prince set out to exterminate some rebels in the eastern part of the country.

Before he left, however, he was presented with a gleaming sword while at the Ise Shrine, where he had gone to pay his respects and acquire some good luck for the venture. His mission successfully accomplished, the prince showed a singular lack of appreciation for the sword and left it hanging on a mulberry tree. However, there were others about who did appreciate the sword's value, including a certain princess who stole it. But it was so well polished and shone so brightly, especially when the sun rays hit it, that while the princess was hurrying away, it set fire to a tree which fell burning, giving the field the name Atsuta, or "Burning Field." Apparently, the princess dropped the sword then and there; for the next we hear of it, it was being kept in a sacred storehouse in Atsuta, where it continued to shine with a light so strange that even the king of a Korean kingdom heard about it. Avarice reared its head, and the king decided he simply must obtain possession of the miraculous sword. So a priest went over to Japan, stole the sword and got as far as Kyushu with it before the gods of Atsuta discovered the loss. They were quick to act; emissaries were sent immediately to Kyushu, where they intercepted the robber-priest and killed him. The Korean king did not give up with this little setback but instead sent a general with seven swords over to steal the Sacred Sword. What he was going to do with the seven swords, whether he was to barter them for the one the king wanted or whether he was to use them simultaneously to cut a swath through the Japanese guarding the sword, is not clear. Finally, though, the general reached Atsuta, where the gods, having become cognizant of his plan, killed him. They took the seven swords and had a shrine erected in honor of all eight, including the Sacred Sword. This shrine, the Ya-tsurugi, or Eight-Sword Shrine, still stands today. There are discrepancies in this story which are hard to reconcile, but that is how the Japanese tell it.

Nagoya Castle was built in 1612 for Ieyasu's son, whose descendants lived in it until 1868, when the Tokugawa rule was overthrown. It was completely destroyed by the great American bombing raid of May 14, 1945, but has since been rebuilt. The castle is located in the northwest part of Nagoya and has a 5-story donjon (great tower) standing 144 feet high, mounted with a famous pair of gold dolphins, the symbols of Nagoya. The original of one of these dolphins was lent to the Vienna Exhibition of 1873. On its way back it went down with the steamer *Nile*, which was wrecked off the coast of the Izu Peninsula. It was in the water for six months before being salvaged. The castle was rebuilt at a cost of 600,000,000 *yen* and the ground around the castle is now open to the public as a park.

Other tourist attractions in the city proper include:

Nittaiji Temple, or Japan-Thailand Temple, located on Kakuo-zan Hill in the northeastern part of the city. This temple was built in 1904 as a repository for a relic of Gautama Buddha, and also for a golden image of Buddha presented by the King of Thailand in 1900. It is interesting to note that the Thais, though Buddhists, belong to a different sect, called the *Hinayana,* or Small-Wheel Buddhism, as opposed to the *Mahayana,* or Great-Wheel Buddhism, of Japan, China, and Tibet. The Hinayana believe Buddha is a great teacher and not a god, and do not believe in the multitude of gods which exist in Japanese Buddhism. Therefore, Hinayana images of Buddha are of Buddha himself, unlike the Japanese images (such as the great Buddha of Kamakura) which may represent any one of the several gods in the Japanese religion.

Gohyaku-Rakan, or Five Hundred Rakan, is a temple near the Nittaiji and contains 500 images of Rakan, a Buddhist deity (remember what was said above about Japanese Buddhism); remarkable in their variety of feature, expression, and posture. In a special gallery are 18 Rakan made by Kita Tametaka, a famous carver of figurines of the 18th century.

Higashi-Honganji Temple in Shimo-Chaya-Machi is one of the most important religious centers in the country. It was built in 1692 on the site of a medieval castle and entirely reconstructed in 1836. The premises cover about 12 acres, and if you go there during the middle two weeks of July, you might find a horde of scantily clad athletes pushing, grunting, and jostling each other around. They are *sumo* wrestlers practicing for the tournament that takes place in Nagoya around that time. The *sumo*-ists often stay at temples such as this one to take advantage of the open spaces for their training.

Nagoya has 5 hotels suitable for foreigners, as well as a good selection of inns for those who wish to taste the Japanese way of life. Newest on the scene is the 11-story Hotel Nagoya Castle, located along the western moat of Nagoya Castle. This 300-room hotel has a see-through express elevator which leads to the llth floor sky-lounge restaurant. There are several restaurants, shops, etc. Next in size and scope is the Nagoya Miyako Hotel, only a 5-minute walk from Nagoya Station. It has 294 western-style and 7 Japanese-style rooms. Rates at both hotels are medium priced.

The International Hotel Nagoya with 267 western-style rooms and 5 Japanese-style rooms all with bath is the next largest. It is 10 minutes by car from Nagoya Station and the rates are quite moderate.

The Nagoya Kanko Hotel is 3 minutes from Nagoya Station by car. It has 505 western-style rooms, all with bath. Nineteen stories tall, it has an excellent shopping arcade. Rates are lower than at the other hotels.

Most convenient hotel for those who arrive by train is the Hotel New Nagoya, located atop an office building, right in front of Nagoya Station. It has 89 western-style rooms and 3 Japanese-style, all with bath; the hotel's rates are rather moderate.

Near Nagoya is the Meiji Village, built along lines similar to our own Williamsburg, Virginia. It's very interesting to see, what with reconstructions of Japanese homes, and is located in a park area, together with mementos and souvenirs of the Meiji period.

Nagoya is a good base of operations for trips afield, for example a thrilling ride down the rapids of the Kiso River. For this you take the Nagoya Railway to Imawatari and board a boat for the six-mile, churning, rocking, scudding boat ride. At Inuyama, you'll find a white feudal castle, attractively placed on a hill commanding a view of the rapids you have just traversed. Around Inuyama there is also the famed cormorant fishing for the tiny *ayu,* a troutlike fish. Fishing with cormorants is more a party than a pastime, but it will be described below in the section on Gifu, which is best known for this particular (and peculiar) sport.

An even more popular spot, in fact, one that draws tourists to Nagoya, is the nearby city of Gifu, the capital of Gifu Prefecture, a community of over 300,000 and the site of the famous cormorant fishing. If you want to stay overnight at Gifu, there is a newish hotel, the Grand Hotel Gifu, which is extremely pleasant.

Cormorant fishing is for the birds, not the humans. The cormorants (voracious sea birds resembling pelicans) are caught and trained until they can go out into the river and catch the fish, the tiny troutlike *ayu.* The humans only manipulate the cormorants and later eat the fish.

On moonless nights or after the moon has set the fishermen set out in their boats down the Nagara River with their flocks of cormorants. Each boat has a master and assistant, both of whom handle the birds. A third man handles the tiller and a fourth man attends to the decoy fire which burns in an iron basket in the bow. The fire attracts the *ayu* to their doom. Each cormorant wears a cord around its neck to prevent it from swallowing any but the tiniest of the fish. Thin lines 12 feet long are used to control the birds. The lines are held in the left hands of the master and his assistant, who manipulate the cords with their right. The master works twelve birds; his assistant, four.

When the moon has set or at the appropriate time on a moonless night, the flotilla of five or seven boats, each with its four men, starts out. The birds are gently let into the water; they begin darting about, diving in after the hapless *ayu* until they have filled their beak-pouch, at which time they begin to swim foolishly around in a circle not knowing what to do and are hauled in. The cormorant is made to disgorge its mouth-sized catch of fish, and returned to the water. A cormorant can hold about four good-sized *ayu* in its pouch, and in an evening's work, gather in a total of about fifty fish.

Though cormorant fishing is in fact very interesting to watch, it is the two or three hours beforehand that count with most fish-watchers. For the evening begins when you get into a covered barge and proceed to eat, drink and be merry. A grinning Japanese boatman with a towel wrapped around his head and a blue *happi* coat helps you into the gaily decorated craft. There is a table from which to eat while you sit on the deck, and there is a lot to drink, generally *sake*. A beer boat continually makes the rounds also, to help out if the *sake* fails to quench your thirst or in case you want a Japanese boilermaker—a shot of hot *sake* washed down with the cold, delicious Japanese beer. You can have whisky or any other kind of drink you may want, too, if you make arrangements ahead of time.

Other covered barges are all around you, and the people in them yell unintelligible but obviously good-humored remarks at you. There are many Japanese revelers in these boats, as well as foreign tourists and tour groups. The spirit of conviviality grows to such an extent that you find the occupants on the craft on both sides reaching over to offer you bits of their food with chopsticks. If you have downed enough *sake,* you will probably find yourself accepting— and returning—the compliment. Also cruising about are boats selling fireworks of various kinds. In the spirit of the thing, you might buy some. If you don't know how to work them, your boatman will gladly oblige, and you will find yourself watching as he shoots them off—firecrackers, sky rockets, sizzlers, and all sorts of things that ordinarily belong to a Fourth of July celebration.

You might then perhaps see a large boat with a brilliant red tentlike covering and blue lanterns hanging along the sides. As it passes, you may see dainty little Japanese girls, dressed in white summer kimonos with red sashes, gracefully performing Japanese national dances. This is probably a special party arranged by some organization.

The word eventually comes that the cormorant fishing has started. The noise dies down, and everybody begins to watch expectantly. The first things you see are the flares coming downstream; then the flock of small, brownish cormorants busily swimming around. This is the lead boat; and behind it, four abreast, the barges of the viewers follow. Yours also joins the line, and you watch the birds swim about, get pulled in and put back into the water again. This goes on for about ten minutes. Then the barges of the watchers pull out of line and go their separate ways. What happens to the fish that are caught? They are sold on the market.

Cormorant fishing is of very ancient origin. Perhaps it comes from China, for the Chinese habitually fish with cormorants. The first mention of it in Japan was in a poem in the *Kojiki,* an ancient manuscript compiled in the early 8th century. Our old friend, Shogun Yoritomo, many times enjoyed a meal of *ayu* caught on the Nagara by cormorants. In addition to cormorant fishing, Gifu is famous for its Buddha, a huge figure 45 feet high made of basketwork over which paper, covered with Buddhist scriptures, is pasted and the whole covered with lacquer. It is in the Shohoji Temple near the entrance to Gifu Park.

Gifu Park, laid out in 1888, contains a promenade of about 1,000 feet along the Nagara River and the world-famous Nawa Entomology Institute, which has about 300,000 insect specimens. If you are an entomologist, professional or amateur (or just curious), you will enjoy this museum and probably will be conducted through it by the owner—the son of the founder, Yasushi Nawa. There is also a three-storied pagoda in the park and a bronze statue of Count Itagaki, who might be called a Japanese Patrick Henry. When, in 1885, a would-be assassin wounded him while he was addressing an audience in the park, the count cried: "Itagaki may die, but Liberty never will." Though he failed to succumb (in the heroic tradition) to the attack, the remark so impressed his hearers that they erected the bronze statue anyway. Gifu is a manufacturing center in its own right, producing textiles, paper umbrellas, paper fans, paper lanterns, and just plain ordinary paper. The lanterns are especially in demand and are exported to Europe and the Americas.

Iseshi

A National Railways train leaves Nagoya for Iseshi (71 miles away) several times each day; the trip can also be made in an auto, but the drive is not too comfortable. Iseshi is the location for the Jingu Shrines of Ise, the holiest of holies as far as the Japanese are concerned, for in one of the two shrines is the Sacred Mirror handed down by the Sun Goddess herself to her grandson, Prince Ninigi, when he descended from Heaven to rule on earth. As previously mentioned, the Sacred Sword in Nagoya, the Sacred Jewels in the Imperial Palace, and the Sacred Mirror constitute the Three Imperial Regalia.

The two shrines, one called the Geku, or Outer Shrine, and the other the Naiku, or Inner Shrine, are four miles apart. The Geku, which is dedicated to the Goddess of Farms, Crops, Food, and Silk-weaving, is only a short walk from the railway station.

Both shrines are constructed of Japanese cypress and in a primitive Japanese architectural form which was used before Chinese influences arrived simultaneously with the coming of Buddhism in the 7th century. It has been the prehistoric practice to reconstruct the shrines every twenty years.

The Geku, tradition has it, was constructed in honor of a goddess who came down to earth with Prince Ninigi, on the instructions of the Sun Goddess. At first the shrine was built in Kyoto Prefecture; but later, as a result of a revelation direct from the Sun Goddess herself to the reigning emperor, it was erected at its present site, in 478 A.D. The Geku is set in a magnificent grove of Japanese cedars, and its grounds cover 214 acres. As you cross the bridge and enter the first Shinto gate, you will see on your right the Anzaisho, or Imperial House of Sojourn, where the emperor rests when he visits the shrine; and the Sanshujo, or Place of Assembly, where members of his family rest.

After entering the second gateway, you come to the Kaguraden, where sacred dances are performed. Adjacent to it is a place where religious charms are sold; you'll see several other houses of lesser interest and the Haiden, or Hall of Worship. Next you will come to the Main Hall, enclosed by four fences. The outermost one is called the *itagaki,* and is in the shape of an irregular oblong. This fence is made of unvarnished Japanese cedar; the second fence, or *soto-tamagaki,* is made of alternate long and short logs of Japanese cedar with horizontal rails, and has a thatched gateway at the south entrance closed with a white curtain. This is as far as you can go. Beyond this only the emperor, his family and relatives, and Imperial envoys are allowed.

The shrine itself is within the fourth fence, which, like the third fence, is made of a palisade of plants. The shrine has a thatched roof, is constructed of Japanese cypress, as mentioned earlier, and measures about 33 feet in depth, 19 feet in width, and 21 feet in height.

The Naiku closely resembles the Geku. There is also the Ujibashi Bridge, and beyond it, the *torii,* or Shinto gates. After crossing the bridge and before entering the gates, pilgrims to the shrine first go down to the Isuzu River, where they wash their hands and rinse their mouths, cleanliness not being merely next to godliness to the Japanese, but ranked right along and even with it.

The Sacred Mirror is enshrined in the Naiku, and this is how it came about: The Sun Goddess, in entrusting the Mirror to her grandson, told him to enshrine it in his palace. This was done for many years until the fear arose that the Mirror, being too close to human beings, might become contaminated. So it was moved to a place near Nara. But again the same fear arose, and finally an emperor's daughter was given the assignment to find a new place that would keep the Mirror free from possible desecration. She decided on the present site.

Four miles by auto or streetcar from Iseshi is Futami-ga-ura, famous for its Wedded Rocks. They are supposed to stand for Izanagi and Izanami, the mythical creators of Japan from whom the Sun Goddess descended. The two rocks are joined together by a rope which is replaced each January 5 in a very formal ceremony. The larger one has a Shinto gate on top of it and represents, of course, the male, who always dominates in the Japanese scheme of things.

Less than five miles from Futami-ga-ura is Toba, famous as the place where cultured pearls are produced, as well as for its view, often regarded as among the best in Japan. You can take a drive around for picture-taking or just for plain viewing of the many little islands nearby. There is an excellent hotel in Kashikojima Island called the Shima Kanko Hotel, where the emperor and empress stay when in the neighborhood. If you want something to talk about, ask for the Imperial Suite. Though there is no "the little Emperor slept here" sign, it's a definite fact. You can sleep in the same bed that His Imperial Majesty, with blood made bluer by over 2,000 years of direct transmission, slept in. Kashikojima Island, though over 15 miles and a 55-minute ride from Toba, is a place that should not be missed. For it is situated on Ago Bay where many of the beds of oysters (busily making pearls for the industry) are located.

Now for a little moment of truth regarding the so-called women pearl divers of Toba and vicinity. Many are the pictures that have been printed in promotional folders beckoning the potential tourist to visit the pearl-making center of Toba, of girls in the originals of the topless swimsuit (minus the shoulder straps) facing demurely at three-quarters profile so that the censorable part of the picture is merely suggested. They are beautiful art shots and serve as effective a lure for the potential male traveler as the fire does for the Gifu *ayu*. These girls, the caption says, are the pearl divers of Toba.

However, these girls do not dive for pearls. They dive for seaweed, abalone, and other fruits of the sea. The Japanese like to eat seaweed, which tastes very good and is rich in vitamins. There are similar girl divers all over Japan, not only at Toba. And whether they dive for pearls or for seaweed does not usually matter to the man who buys his ticket to Japan after seeing the pictures.

The oysters in wire cages are suspended on ropes and are pulled up for inspection, or when the experts think their pearls are ready for the market. But, when you tour the pearl beds, there will always be a girl or two ready to illustrate for you how they dive for seaweed. Perhaps their presence at the pearl beds and the diving demonstrations have led to the confusion as to their precise objectives. Sex, apparently, is here to stay.

Cultured pearls were developed by the late Kokichi Mikimoto, called the Pearl King. He found that by putting a piece of the shell of a Mississippi River mussel under the mantel of an oyster, it will obligingly make a pearl. Usually. There is more to it than that, of course; but in essence the oyster regards the piece of mussel shell as something inimical to its well-being and proceeds to encapsulate (all right, surround) the offending substance with what becomes the pearl. As in cormorant fishing, the Japanese are masters of the art of making our dumb friends produce for them.

Kyoto

Of course you can fly from Tokyo to Osaka in less than an hour, and then take a bus to Kyoto, which takes somewhat over an hour. However, this is really the hard way of doing things, and you'll be much better off taking the Shinkansen bullet train, also called the Hikari express. Trains leave Tokyo's Central Station every 20 minutes all through the day and cover the 206 miles to Kyoto in about 3 hours. You have a choice of first and second class. First class is almost twice as expensive and really not necessary because second class is quite adequate. You can have reserved seats, and the Japan Travel Bureau (telephone 274-3921) can arrange for your reservations. They also have offices in some of the chief tourist hotels. The trains are excellent and have a dining car. If you wish, you can buy an all-inclusive tour package for two or three days before you leave Tokyo. Or, alternatively, you can simply take the train to Kyoto and be on your own thereafter.

Kyoto was the Imperial capital of Japan for well over 1,000 years, having become the capital in 794 and so remaining until 1868 when it was moved to Tokyo. Kyoto's original name was Heian-kyo, or Capital of Peace. But, as it became increasingly referred to as the capital city, or Kyoto, it lost its original name (*Kyo* means "capital" in Japanese, as in "Tokyo," or East Capital).

There are well over a thousand temples and shrines in Kyoto, which is considered the cradle of Japanese culture and arts, with Nara, 26 miles away, being the actual birthplace. With so many temples and shrines to choose from, it is impossible to describe them all. What follows here are some of the notable ones which, it can safely be said, you should not miss.

In the northwest district is the famous Golden Pavilion, very frequently illustrated in colored travel folders because of its brilliant gold hue. The Golden Pavilion was built, and the garden around it laid out, in 1394 by the shogun of that period who retired there to live a life of quiet contemplation, free from the cares of the state. The original pavilion was destroyed in July, 1950, by a priest of the temple who set fire to the pavilion. There have been numerous interpretations of this arsonist's act, and a popular Japanese novel made into a film ascribed Freudian motives to the priest. The Japanese have meticulously rebuilt the pavilion precisely as it was when first constructed, including the shining gold exterior. It is the new building which is seen in the tourist folders and in magazines.

In the central district is the headquarters of the Jodo-Shinshu sect of Buddhism, the Nishi Honganji Temple. The Jodo-Shinshu sect probably means nothing to the reader, but it is one of the richest and most powerful of the Buddhist groups in Japan. It was founded centuries ago by a priest named Shinran who took Buddhism away from the ascetics and the intellectuals and gave it back to the common people. He decided Buddhist priests could marry, and to prove his point, did. He also dispensed with the practice of abstaining from meat and with various other ascetic disciplines. Shinran told the people that all they had to do to be saved was to repeat the phrase "Glory to Amida Buddha" several times. (In Japanese, of course.) Is there any wonder the people took to his easily followed, simplified version of Buddhism? (The Jodo-Shinshu sect became so powerful that crafty old Ieyasu Tokugawa encouraged a dissatisfied priest to set up another school, which he did and built the Higashi Honganji Temple in the same district.)

Aside from its position as the main temple of a large sect, the Nishi Honganji Temple is considered one of the finest existing examples of Buddhist architecture and certainly one of the finest in Kyoto. In addition to its splendid architectural design, one of the major attractions of this temple, at least for members of the sect, is the image of Shinran in the Founder's Hall carved by the master himself when he was seventy-one. After his death at the ripe age of eighty-nine, he was cremated; his ashes were mixed with the lacquer with which his followers varnished the image.

In the same area is the Toji, or East Temple. Its full and correct name, Kyo-ogokokuji, is hard to pronounce as well as to remember. It was originally built in 823, but has burnt down to the ground several times and been rebuilt several times. The temple's main attraction is the five-story pagoda which was built by Iemitsu, the third Tokugawa shogun and builder of Nikko's Toshogu Shrine. Reaching a height of 183 feet, it is the highest pagoda in Japan. Another feature is its storehouse constructed of wood without the use of nails and containing an immense collection of ancient works of art unrivaled by any other temple in Kyoto.

In the eastern district is the Silver Pavilion, which the builders intended to, but never actually did, cover with silver. It was originally built by the reigning shogun in 1479 as a villa, but on his death it was made into a temple. There is a classical tearoom in this temple which became the model on which all future tearooms used for the tea ceremony were based. The Silver Pavilion's garden is one of the most attractive in Kyoto, a city of lovely gardens.

In the same district is the Kiyomizu Temple, located in a quiet setting halfway up the Otowayama Hill and surrounded by a background of trees. It was originally constructed in 805 and dedicated to the Eleven-Faced Kwannon, or Goddess of Mercy, but rebuilt in 1633. The particular attraction here is the remarkable setting, for the main temple stands on a cliff. There is wooden platform from which an exciting panoramic view of Kyoto can be seen, looking down into the deep valley below.

Another outstanding temple is the Sanju-sangen-do, or Temple of the Thousand Kwannons, also located in the eastern section. The original temple was built in 1132 and rebuilt again in 1251 after being destroyed by fire. There are three outstanding features to this temple. Firstly, there are two "choirs" of 500 bronze Kwannons, each almost six feet in height, and, positioned on both sides of the Thousand-Handed Kwannon. The overall effect is—well, stupendous is the word. There have been various reactions—some in favor and others opposed—to the overwhelming effect. Igor Stravinsky, the great composer, remarked after seeing the forest of figures that it reminded him of a nightmare. Other viewers have been more charitable, finding in it the beauty of symmetry.

The second attraction is a series of figures of various gods placed in the outside hall. These carved figures are works of art that can compare favorably with the best in the west, especially fine being the figure of the Thunder God.

The third feature is the area situated behind the temple which formerly was used as an archery field. The archers competed regularly in centuries gone by to see how many arrows anyone could shoot from daybreak to sunset. The reputed record is 13,053 shot by a strong-armed *samurai* in the year 1696.

One should not miss the Ryoanji Temple in the western district and its famous rock-and-sand garden. This, too, has been photographed many times and the picture has appeared frequently in magazines and travel folders. The garden is severe in its simplicity, containing only raked sand and fifteen rocks of various sizes, carefully arranged to obtain a desired effect. It is, they say, one of the masterpieces of the great Soami, who was very much influenced by Zen philosophy. You may like it.

Speaking of Zen, you might have a most interesting time if you visit what's popularly called the Zen universe. Take a taxi to the Daitokuji Temple, located in north Kyoto. Daitokuji is a complex consisting of 22 temples, seven of which can be visited. You have to get entrance tickets and leave your shoes outside; the tickets have some information printed in English which you may find helpful. Start with the Daisen-in Temple, with its rock garden, said to be one of the finest examples of Zen gardening in Japan. Other important temples are the Zuiho-in and Sangen-in Temples. If luck is with you, you may be fortunate enough to see priests in distinctive tall hats performing the stylized chanting rites which are part of the ceremonies. You can wander about indefinitely, and perhaps even meditate, Zen style. Anyhow, the trip is interesting if you have any interest in Zen, or if you merely want to see Zen temples as part of your education.

There are really only three shrines that should not be missed out of the hundreds in Kyoto. One is the Yasaka, or Gion, Shrine located in the eastern district. The stone gate on the south side measures 36 feet in height and is one of the largest in Japan. But more important than the shrine is the Gion Festival which is held from July 10 until July 28. Highpoints of the festival are the processions held on July 17 and 24 featuring floats pulled by men, and huge colorful towers standing as high as 130 feet. Don't miss this if you're in the area at that time.

Another major sight is the Heian Shrine in Okazaki Park in the same section of the city. This huge shrine was built in 1895 in commemoration of the 1100th anniversary of the founding of Kyoto. In the movie *Around the World in Eighty Days,* this is the shrine used in the portion devoted to Japan. The annual festival is held on April 15, but the Jidai Matsuri, or Period Festival, held on October 22 features a great procession showing the costumes of the various periods in Japanese history and is even more interesting. The garden of the Heian Shrine is noted for its cherry and iris blossoms, and has a very picturesque setting especially suited for picture-taking, and when the flowers are in bloom, would make a color photographer sprain his trigger finger.

The third recommended shrine is the Inari, or Fox, Shrine in the southeastern section of Kyoto. Though it is listed third, the listing is not necessarily in the order of importance, for the Inari Shrine is one of the most famous in the country. This shrine is frequently used as a color illustration on calendars. The most striking part of the shrine is the Thousand Torii Pathway, and it is this section which is shown in so many calendars. There is a path where reputedly a thousand red *torii*—or it seems at least that many when you first see them—extend as far as the eye can see.

There are also stone figures representing the fox; hence the other name—Fox Shrine. The fox is regarded as the shrine's messenger, and also is believed to bring good luck to the worshippers. At the shrine you will see many people clapping their hands, the way a Japanese customarily calls the attention of the Shinto gods that he is there, so that the deities will hear and heed his prayers. Many of the worshippers are probably planning to open new business ventures, perhaps a new *sushi* restaurant, or a nightclub, or even more ambitious projects, and they desire the blessing of the shrine so as to ensure a successful operation. For the shrine is dedicated to the Goddess of Rice and Food; and, if she gives the new venture her blessing, it will mean more rice and food for them, or in other words, income.

In addition to the above temples and shrines, the visitor should not miss the palaces. The Imperial Palace, though rebuilt many times (the last time being in 1855), occupies the same site the original one did when Emperor Kammu first moved to Kyoto to make it the new capital. Although it is open only twice a year to the general public, foreigners can visit it any day except national holidays by obtaining permission from the Kyoto office of the Imperial Household Agency. (Ask at your hotel desk.)

Although there are many buildings to be visited here, including the Room of Dignitaries (where officials waited), the Ceremonial Hall, and the Minor Palace, to me the most interesting is the Seiryoden, or Cool and Serene Chamber. Here you will see air conditioning as the inventive people of many centuries ago envisioned it.

Not possessing the electrical and mechanical techniques of today, they had to rely on nature. So they diverted a stream of water from Lake Biwa to run under the steps to bring in natural coolness. Everywhere in evidence you will see designs denoting the 16-petaled chrysanthemum which is the Imperial Crest.

Those James Bond fans who have read *You Only Live Twice,* by Ian Fleming, the novel about Japan, will be especially interested in the Nijo Castle. It was built by the wily old Shogun Ieyasu Tokugawa as his personal residence when he came to Kyoto. In the corridors you will see (and hear) the "nightingale floors," cleverly sprung floors that "sing" or squeak when you walk on them. The foxy old shogun had them made that way so that nobody could sneak up on him (with assassination thoughts) in his living quarters unawares. Ironically enough, it was from this palace that the Emperor Meiji issued his edict putting an end to the Tokugawa shogunate. For those interested in art, the paintings on the sliding screens and some of the murals are attributed to Tanyu Kano, who lived from 1602 to 1674 and who is considered one of the greatest artists of the Tokugawa, or Edo, Period.

High on the tourists' just-have-to-see list is the Katsura Imperial Villa, built for an Imperial prince and situated between the Katsura River and the Nishiyama Hills about three miles from Kyoto Station. This villa is famed for its garden, begun in 1590 by one of the greatest of Japan's landscape gardeners, Enshu Kobori, having been commissioned to lay it out by the shogun Hideyoshi Toyotomi. He accepted the commission provided: (1) the shogun set no limit to the costs; (2) set no deadline within which it must be finished; and (3) would not try to see it before it was finished (so that the shogun would not be tempted to make suggestions). So the story goes, believe it or not. The most striking feature about the garden is that wherever you stand, it seems as though you are looking at the garden from the front, for it is constructed so that there is no front or back or side, and no wrong position from which to regard it. Special permission to enter must be obtained from the Imperial Household Agency.

If you truly want to get the flavor of Kyoto life, wear comfortable shoes and take a taxi to Nishiki Market. It consists of a narrow street, about 10 feet wide, which extends for approximately a quarter of a mile. It's lined with shops, most (but not all) selling an unbelievable variety of food. Although the market goes back some 400 years, it's as lively as ever, and you might be surprised to note the large percentage of men shoppers. (And all along, you thought women were subjugated in Japan, didn't you?) The market starts reasonably early in the morning and winds up in the late afternoon. Go—I strongly urge you.

But there is much more to Kyoto than temples, shrines, and palaces. The Kyoto geisha, for example, is much admired throughout Japan, as are the Kyoto girls, for Kyoto is the embodiment of femininity to the Japanese mind. Even Kyoto men tend to talk somewhat softly, as opposed to the hard and almost rough talk of the Tokyo men. There is a saying that the ideal marriage is between a Kyoto girl and the Tokyo man, for then you have the ultimate in femininity and masculinity, from the Japanese point of view, matched. Geishas from other places in Japan, no matter how talented, instinctively feel inferior to the Kyoto geisha.

Night entertainment in Kyoto, however, is much the same as in Tokyo, except that the fleshpots of the latter city are more commercialized. The cabarets and the "turkish baths" also are here.

The nightclubs may be generally described as poor, hardly worth a visit. However, it would definitely be worth your while to spend an hour or two at a very old teahouse, the Ichiriki. Go after dinner; the atmosphere is fascinating.

Gion Corner, Kyoto's amusement center, often schedules various evening programs during the tourist season. It varies a great deal from night to night—sometimes *koto* music, the Bunraku puppets, flower arrangement, and the like. It is run by the Kyoto Tourist Association; it's a good idea to make inquiry or read your hotel's bulletin board.

What may be overlooked in the enthusiasm for the temples and shrines of Kyoto is the city's shopping facilities. Kyoto is a hub of the silk-weaving, porcelain, and lacquer industries. Kyoto is particularly convenient in that most of its fine shops are within walking distance of each other. A shopping stroll could begin at a street called Teramachi, an old and beautiful street where there is an interesting bronze and wrought-iron shop and, a few doors up, a musical instrument shop which has supplied court musicians for generations with Japanese flutes, flageolets (a woodwind), masks, and costumes. Further up is a shop where temple priests buy their specialized garments and other religious paraphernalia. A popular tourist item here is the huge folding fan carried by the priest, which can be used as a wall decoration.

Teramachi Street runs into Shijo, the main shopping district of Kyoto. Here are a number of pottery, bamboo, lacquer, doll, and silk shops. The tourist on a buying spree will find a day well spent in this area. Searchers for authentic antiques might enjoy visiting famous old Shinmonzen Street, which has a score of small shops, many of which look enticing. Gentle, never firm, bargaining is the rule—but speak softly. More expensive, in fact much more so, are the antiques of Yamanaka and Company; this usually involves serious money. In the evening, if you like to wander about, visit the shopping arcade where you can buy slippers, penknives, candy, and various souvenirs—all quite diverting.

One of the best single shopping stops is the Kyoto Handicraft Center (located in the Sakyo-Ku district). It consists of 6 floors of merchandise including silks, radios, cameras, jewelry, screens, etc. If you buy a fair quantity of merchandise, they promise to take you back to your hotel without charge.

HOTELS Of Kyoto's hotels, the Miyako Hotel—completely remodeled—is the one most sought after by tourists because of its excellent position on a hillside overlooking Okazaki Park. It is 10 minutes by car from Kyoto Station, is in the luxury class, and offers 248 western-style rooms and 29 Japanese-style rooms, all with bath, with a wide price range (depending upon size and view) with rates somewhat on the high side, particularly for rooms with views.

Its rival from the standpoint of desirability is the Kyoto Hotel, which is more centrally located, although the same distance in time from Kyoto Station, but lacks the Miyako's view. The Kyoto Hotel has 252 western-style rooms, all with bath, and the price ranges from medium to high.

Newer than those two, and in the same class (deluxe) is the handsome International Kyoto Hotel, which is directly in front of Nijo Castle and also about 10 minutes by car from Kyoto Station. It has 301 western-style rooms and 31 Japanese-style rooms, all with bath; the hotel's rates are in the medium category.

Two new hotels, in which I haven't stayed, are the Kyoto Royal, with 400 rooms, and the 307-room Daini Tower Hotel, located close to the Kyoto railroad station; this last is partly an office building, but it won't affect your visit. Also near the station is the Kyoto Station Hotel, where the prices of rooms run lower than at any of the other places.

Thirty minutes from Kyoto Station and located on Mount Hiei is the Mount Hiei Hotel. Its setting is very pleasant, and even in summer, the rooms are quite cool. It offers 66 western-style rooms and 8 Japanese-style rooms, all with bath; the rates are generally in the medium class.

Kyoto has some excellent Japanese inns especially suited for foreigners. If you're in the mood to try a *ryokan,* Kyoto is an ideal place. Probably the one most frequented by tourists is the Hiiragiya, somewhat on the expensive side but quite accustomed to foreigners and their ways. Also to be recommended is the Tawaraya, with the same advantage as the Hiiragiya. Both these hotels will let you slip into the Japanese way of life pleasantly and painlessly. But if you are one of those who want your Japanese way of life and also the comfort of sleeping in a bed, try the Tozankaku, which has mixed Japanese- and western-style rooms. Here you can live Japanese style and still have your bed.

RESTAURANTS Most people visiting Kyoto tend to eat in the mediocre restaurants of the hotels. However, if you get bored, be forewarned that this lovely town has no really good Western-style restaurant. To sample the Kyoto cuisine, try a dish called *kaiseki,* consisting of an assortment of fish prepared in various styles, and also *shojin ryori,* an incredible variety of Zen-style vegetable dishes. Be sure to have a meal at Hyotei, a 350-year-old teahouse, a sort of rustic inn. Perhaps even more atmospheric is another Kyoto-style restaurant, Kikusui, situated in a beautiful garden. If you don't mind the high prices, head for Kitcho, on a woody hillside, which is truly excellent, even preparing soup and rice individually for each person; Kitcho is regarded as the city's gourmet restaurant. Of course, if you want a steak and a fine one, head for Tsubosaka, which features Kobe beef, and isn't cheap. One of the best of the meat restaurants is Rashomon, on Kawaramachi Street; they are particularly known for their *shabu-shabu,* beef and assorted vegetables cooked at your table. If you want a very good Japanese restaurant which serves many interesting foods (no, not more raw fish or uncooked chicken), try the Nanzenji-no-Yudofu; it's on the grounds of the Nanzenji Temple. You can have *tempura* vegetables (very fresh and fried in a batter), marvelous beer, and try a *tororo,* something like a potato and quite delicious. A house specialty here is a casserole of *yudofu,* which appears on a charcoal fire and is made chiefly of *tofu,* soybean curd. If you enjoy noodles, visit the Kawamichiya, a 400-year-old restaurant; here the specialty is *soba,* buckwheat noodles. Your best bet is a dish called *hokoro soba,* a delightful creation made of chicken, green vegetables, onions, mushrooms, and of course *soba,* served in a special container.

Sidetrips from Kyoto

Nara

A trip to Kyoto should (in fact, "must") include Nara, Japan's first capital (built in 710) until it ceased being the Imperial residence in 784. Before Nara became the capital, it had been the regular custom of the Japanese emperors to change the site of the palace upon their succession to the throne, since it was considered evil luck to continue to reside in a place where an emperor had died. However, under the influence of the Chinese of the Tang Dynasty, these ideas changed, and the value of having a fixed capital was recognized.

Nara can be reached in 50 minutes from Kyoto by the Kinki Nippon Railway or by car, or by bus—the usual way for travelers on a tour—in about an hour. The best-known feature of Nara is its Great Buddha, the one that was responsible indirectly for the construction of the Kamakura Great Buddha, the latter being, by the way, a better work of art. Another feature, well publicized, is Nara's Deer Park, where the antlered animals are so domesticated that they will feed out of your hand. They have become tame, the Japanese say, because they are considered the sacred messengers of the gods and as such are immune from harm by human hands. There are about 800 deer in the park's herds and they roam about in the daytime so unafraid of visitors that they become importunate in their appeals for food, often nuzzling the visitors and licking their hands. Each October their antlers are cut, an occasion for a festival of sorts. With regard to their immunity from harm, Nara residents say this immunity was individually and surreptitiously lifted during the war when food grew scarce. Officials became aware of this lapse when they noticed the deer population shrinking and certain of the citizens beginning to lose that lean and hungry look. Fortunately, the war ended before the dwindling deer population came to nought.

Meanwhile, back to the Great Buddha, said to be the largest bronze statue in the world. Statistics? Here they are: Weight—452 tons; height—58.5 feet; face—16 feet long and 9.5 feet wide; eyes—3.9 feet wide; nose—1.6 feet high; mouth—3.7 feet wide; ears—8.5 feet long; hands—6.8 feet long; and thumbs—4.8 feet long. The pedestal is 10 feet high and 68 feet in circumference. It took 4 years, from 745 to 749, to make the monster statue, taking 8 castings in 3 years before it was accepted as satisfactory by the emperor who authorized its construction. It was dedicated in April, in the year 752, before a gathering of members of the Imperial Family, court dignitaries, and 10,000 priests and nuns. (And that's enough in the way of statistics for the time being.)

The Hall of the Great Buddha was burned in 1180 by the Taira clan, which was then at war with the Minamoto clan for the mastery of Japan. The Minamotos won the struggle, and the shogun, Yoritomo, attended the ceremonies celebrating the restoration of

Weather Strip: Osaka

	Jan.	Feb.	Mar.	Apr.	May	June	July	Aug.	Sept.	Oct.	Nov.	Dec.
Average daily high	47°	48°	54°	65°	73°	80°	87°	90°	83°	72°	62°	52°
Average daily low	32°	33°	37°	47°	55°	64°	73°	74°	67°	55°	44°	37°
Monthly rainfall	1.7	2.3	3.8	5.2	4.9	7.4	5.9	4.4	7.0	5.1	3.0	1.9
Number of days with 0.04 inches of rainfall	6	6	9	10	10	11	9	7	11	9	7	6

the temple in 1195. On this occasion the idea was born to create a huge Buddha at Kamakura. (For the full story, there are more details in the section on the Kamakura Buddha.) Unlike the Kamakura Buddha, which belongs to a different sect, the Nara Buddha actually represents the Buddha we usually think of, Gautama himself. It is located in the Todaiji, or Great East Temple, the headquarters of the Kegon sect of Japanese Buddhism. Although the Todaiji was started in 745 and finished in 752, the present building dates from 1708.

The Deer Park and the Great Buddha are the best known of Nara's attractions, but there are many who prefer the Kasuga Shrine, set in the midst of trees, amid surroundings which emphasize a great feeling of sanctity and tranquility. It was founded in 768 and used to be regularly reconstructed every twenty years like the Ise shrines. Over the years people have been donating lanterns to the shrine, so that there is now a collection of more than 3,000 which line the path between two of the gates. They are lit twice a year, on the nights of February 3 or 4 and August 15, making a spectacle that even Hollywood would be proud of.

For those who like ancient structures, the antiquity of antiquities in Japan and possibly as far as wooden structures are concerned in the world, is located only a little over seven miles from Nara. It is a part of the Horyuji temple complex and is the oldest existing temple in Japan, having been founded in 607. Japanese consider it as one of the Seven Great Temples of the nation, and for some fortunate reason, none of its structures has ever succumbed to a fire, the fate of so many others. This temple area is generally regarded as the fountainhead of all Japanese art and culture. Altogether the temple complex consists of 33 buildings which represent Japanese architectural styles extending from the Asuka Period (552–645) through the Edo Period (1615–1868). The oldest building is the Five-Storied Pagoda, the one that dates from 607 and may well be the oldest wooden structure in the world. During the war, it was dismantled for safe-keeping (the Japanese did not know at the time that American policy was not to bomb the cultural centers of Nara and Kyoto) and then reassembled after peace.

Osaka

And now we come to one of the world's many Venices. This one, Osaka, 25 miles from Kyoto, is called the Venice of Japan because of the many canals it once had, but of which few remain, because of the city's modernization. Slow-moving water traffic has to make way for the faster automobiles if progress is to continue.

Osaka is Japan's number two city in population and number one city in industry. There are just under 3 million people living in the city, and the prefecture (more or less equivalent to our county) has 8.5 million residents. The Osakans are business people, and they look upon those flighty Tokyoites as irresponsible, foolish people who don't know how to save their money. And yet, Osaka probably has as many bars, cabarets, shows, and nightclubs in accordance with its population as does Tokyo, so it is not as if amusements are excluded from their vocabulary. Osakans say that Tokyoites "never have overnight money." They mean that a Tokyoite will drink, dance, and even et cetera with all his money during the night, and have none left to pay for his room for the night nor for breakfast the next day. Tokyoites repay the compliment by saying that Osakans don't know how to enjoy themselves; they are always thinking of the bill and how much things cost, and thus take the joy out of a *donchansawagi,* an all-night carousal. It is definitely true that people in Osaka greet each other by saying "Good morning, how's business?" instead of the more usual "Good morning, how are you?" There's no doubt that Osaka is business-minded, but nevertheless it does have some attractions for tourists.

A different shogun plays the important role in Osaka. Shogun Hideyoshi Toyotomi is to Osaka what Ieyasu Tokugawa is to Tokyo and Yoritomo Minamoto is to Kamakura. Unlike Ieyasu and Yoritomo (the Japanese call them by their given names instead of by their family names—another opposite custom, as is the fact that the family name comes first in Japan), Hideyoshi (to be brief) came from humble origins. Called the Napoleon of Japan, he worked his way up through the ranks of soldiery until he became master of all he surveyed. He succeeded a man named Nobunaga Oda as top military leader of Japan and was in turn succeeded by Ieyasu, if you really want to know.

It is known that two of the emperors built their palaces on the hill where Osaka Castle now stands. During the 4th century, Osaka was called Naniwa, meaning "rapid waves," because of the swift currents in the bay. Its present name, which means "great slope," comes from the hill on which the castle stands.

After the designation of Nara as the permanent capital in the year 710, Naniwa (or present-day Osaka) went into obscurity, from which it did not emerge until near the end of the 16th century when Hideyoshi established it as his base and built the famous castle there. In addition to making it a stronghold, Hideyoshi also encouraged merchants from other areas to settle in the region and set up their businesses. This was the simple beginning of Osaka as a commercial town which ultimately led to its becoming Japan's business and industrial capital. Today, many if not most of Japan's outstanding commercial families are from Osaka.

During the war more than a quarter of Osaka's total area was devastated and well over half of its houses destroyed. At war's end, for one reason or another, less than half of Osaka's prewar population remained. But Osaka has since recovered until it is more robust today than it ever has been, with even more business establishments, shops, cabarets, theaters and other entertainment facilities than before.

This is a great place for shopping, no doubt about it. Because Osaka auto traffic is intense, the shopping has tended to go underground. Even though the number of shops is almost incredible and makes you wonder who does all the buying and how can 2,000 boutiques exist at the same time, it's nevertheless very diverting to wander through the underground rabbit warren of shops. Incidentally, if it should rain, this is the perfect way to spend the time. The biggest and best underground shopping areas are in the vicinity of Osaka Station and southward in the Shinsaibashi area. Shinsaibashi, incidentally, is the main shopping street, and it's filled with theaters, shops, and restaurants; it's great fun to wander along this street on a nice day.

Most visitors go to Osaka as part of a tour to Kyoto or when on business, but not because Osaka attracts them on its own as a tourist center. But just because it is preeminent as Japan's commercial capital does not mean it has little or no appeal for the foreign visitor. It still is a dramatic center of Japan and the home of the famous Bunraku puppets, those life-sized dolls that seem to perform so skillfully on the stage of Osaka's Bunraku-za.

As for tourist sights, however, Osaka, because of its limited historical background in relation to Kyoto and its lack of political standing when compared with Tokyo, has few. Its outstanding attraction is the Osaka Castle, built by Shogun Hideyoshi in 1584 and the seat of his military government until 1596. What remains of the castle today, the 5-story donjon, was rebuilt completely even to the point of installing elevators in 1931. The original walls, however, still survive and contain some enormous rocks, one measuring 47.6 feet in length, 19 feet in height, and 98 square yards in area. In building his castle, Hideyoshi had requisitioned material from his generals, who vied with one another in supplying large stones. The stone described above apparently won the competition and is called the Higo-ishi, or "Higo stone," because it was supplied by the lord of Higo. That's one way of going down in history.

Undoubtedly the most elaborate, expensive, and deluxe hotel in town is the Osaka Royal. It has a beautiful location along a canal in the city center, with a fantastic lobby. It's a giant of a hotel with 1,600 rooms, but the service is just fine, despite its size; there are numerous restaurants on the premises. In the same general area is the Osaka Grand, which is first rate. In the Osaka Station to the north are the Toyo, New Hankyu, the Hanshin, and Plaza Hotels; all are fine. The International Hotel is situated near Osaka Castle. The Dai-Ichi Hotel is round, 30 stories tall, and is in the Shainsaibashi area, which is quite lively. There's also the Osaka Airport Hotel, should you have a connection accompanied by a delay.

Cheaper in price are the Osaka Miyako Hotel; the Toho Hotel; and the International Hotel; these hotels average in the moderate range. For a somewhat American touch, there's a good-sized hotel, the Holiday Inn Nankai.

As I mentioned before, I think you'd enjoy seeing a Bunraku puppet show. The puppets are rather large in size and handled with great skill by people who have learned how to make them seem completely human. In fact, after a matter of minutes, you'll forget they're puppets and think of them as people. The shows go on and on, and people get up and visit the rest rooms and wander out for lunch, then return at their convenience. Generally the shows are matinees, starting at noon and running until 5 P.M. or so. The Bunraku form of performance dates back some three centuries, and it's a definite part of the Japanese cultural heritage; you should try to see it.

Now, as to restaurants. Generally speaking, Osaka hotels serve reasonably good food, but it certainly is far from great. To eat well, you must dine at a specialty restaurant. Kikuya is known for its *tempura* dishes—bits of fish and vegetables, dipped in batter and fried to a lovely golden color. If it's *sukiyaki* you want, it's hard to imagine a better place than Hariju, where the cooking of this dish is a major production. For lunch, you would probably enjoy bits of chicken (and other ingredients) broiled on skewers; about the best place is Gomitori. A well-known chain of restaurants is Shinobu-An, with several different locations. They serve excellent food at moderate prices. Or, if you just want to wander about at random and then dine at the place that appeals to you, head for Dotonbori Street, the one that has the famous Bunraku puppet theater on it; there are at least a dozen appealing restaurants in this area.

Now, a discussion about what most people think is Japan's leading restaurant: the Kitcho. This restaurant is not for everybody for one simple reason—it is one of the most expensive restaurants in the world, and that includes New York and Paris. Prices are so high that it's somewhat difficult to specify, what with inflation and rising prices, but rest assured that the final bill is certain to be VERY high, certainly over $50 each. However, if you don't mind the cost and want to experience the ultimate in Japanese cuisine, read on. Kitcho is beautifully located in a fine old mansion. You'll be received in a reception room and given a strange beginning to a meal (at least in relation to western ideas about food). It consists of a container of toasted chunks of rice in hot water; it's purpose is to clear the palate. There are 7 attractive rooms, and of course, you're seated on the floor. Among the courses served are a series of appetizers, including a number of *sashimi* items (raw fish, shellfish, etc.). But also, they serve something for which they're famous, ground shrimp wrapped in noodles to imitate a bird's nest, then fried; it's marvelous. The crab dishes are superb, should crab be available. Also, there are dishes which you cook yourself at the table, such as beef and mushrooms. In addition, several soups are served. The meal usually ends with melon, and by that time, you should be ready for the bill. Once again, it will be very very high.

Kobe

What it takes to provide a beautiful harbor, Kobe has in full measure.

From the backdrop of its hills, which are dominated by famous Mount Rokko, you can look down upon the sweep of the bay which, in the night, glows from the lights of the harbor.

Kobe is Japan's largest harbor, the favorite jumping-off port for a trip through the Inland Sea because the ship leaves Kobe later than it does from Osaka. Kobe is also the name given to the world-renowned Japanese beef. In fact, so famous has Kobe beef become that you now have to look for it. The best beef in Japan is identified by the small villages, such as Matsuzaka and Omi, where the cattle is slaughtered. This is a defensive measure taken by the cattlemen because of the habit of certain restaurants and meatshops to call all beef "Kobe beef," including that which comes all the way from Australia and New Zealand and is frozen.

Actually, despite all the stories about massaging beef to work in the fat, and giving them beer and *sake,* the tenderness and taste of Japanese beef is probably chiefly due to the excellence of the breed, the Tajima, which is believed to have originated in Hyogo Prefecture where Kobe is situated. The Tajima is a dark-brown variety, quite small when compared to the rugged beef cattle that roam the American rangelands. Perhaps economics are against it, but one must wonder why the United States beef industry does not import some of this superior breed of cattle, because the Tajima produces beef which is superior to any other in the world in the opinion of many gourmets.

Kobe is Japan's sixth largest city with a population of well over a million. It is relatively young. Until opened as a port to foreigners after the Meiji Restoration in 1868, it was only a small fishing village clustered around the Ikuta Shrine. The city is supposed to have obtained its name from the Ikuta Shrine, after several variations, including Kamibe and Koba.

As a port city, it has lively (very lively!) night life centered around its bars and cabarets. Many tired but frolicsome businessmen who come down from Tokyo to Osaka ostensibly for business head for Kobe after the day's work is done to take advantage of its alleged fleshpots and dens of iniquity. You'll note how carefully that last sentence is phrased.

As for the tourist, he should visit the Ikuta Shrine, which is near the Sannomiya Station. It is said to have been founded by the Empress Jingu on her return from a military expedition to Korea in the 3rd century A.D. If you wonder what a warlike empress was doing in Japan, supposedly the Male Paradise, the fact is that Japan in its earliest days was a sort of matriarchy. Early Chinese records concerning Japan tell of queens ruling various parts of the country, women who seemed to have had a substantial touch of the Amazon in them. What makes Japan the happy hunting grounds for men it is today is probably the result of some remarkable social revolution of which little is known today. Historians might do well to probe into the past to find out how the revolution was accomplished so that the same techniques may be used to advantage in other countries, notably the United States.

But we stray. The Ikuta Shrine is consecrated to the Goddess Wakahirume-no-Mikoto, a sister of the Sun Goddess, and she is worshipped as the guardian of all Kobe and its citizens. Its festival, celebrated with considerable ceremony, is held on April 15 and 16. Just south of the shrine is one of the most crowded amusement centers of the city.

The hills of the city, of course, offer the best views of the harbor. North of the harbor Mount Futatabi rises up to 1,535 feet. The precise name, Futatabi-san, means "Mount Twice." It received this name because a certain Japanese monk, founder of a prominent Buddhist sect, visited the hill twice, in 804 and 806, on his way to study Buddhism in China and on his return. Halfway up the wooded slope of the hill is the Dairyuji Temple of the Shingon sect, the one founded by the traveling monk. The chief object of worship in the temple is a lacquered wood statue of the Goddess Kwannon.

The smallest hill is Mount Hachibuse, but it has an excellent view of the Kobe beaches. On the slope of the hill is Sumanoura Park. You can get to the peak of this hill by ropeway, which takes you to an observatory from which you can see a marvelous panorama of sea and mountains, including the peaks of Shikoku Island, smallest of Japan's four major islands.

Second highest peak, standing at 2,293 feet above sea level, is Mount Maya, which is dedicated to Lady Maya, mother of Gautama Buddha. This hill is the site of the Toritenjoji Temple, which is reached after an arduous climb up 398 stone steps, a challenge that can be met only by the vigorous and young. This temple is supposed to have been first established in 646 by an Indian priest.

At 3,057 feet, Mount Rokko, or Rokko-san, in the east is the best known of Kobe's hills and gives its name to the whole range. You can reach its summit by bus or by a one-mile-long cable car line. On the top there is an 18-hole golf course, and the slopes are dotted with the residences of foreigners and Japanese who live there to take advantage of the view and the climate. There are many ponds on the hill that become swimming pools in the summer and skating rinks in the winter, while the slopes provide excellent ski courses, also during the winter. Here is the fine Rokkosan Hotel with 40 western-style rooms. The Rokko Oriental Hotel, with 34 western-style rooms, is another good place to stay.

Forty minutes by train from Kobe is Takarazuka, site of the renowned Takarazuka Girls' Opera Troupe, made world-famous by James Michener's novel *Sayonara* and the movie derived from it. But despite the debt of fame the Takarazuka girls owe Mr. Michener, they don't appreciate the novel, which is an east-west romance between an American Air Force officer and a 'Zuka girl. The girls say they don't like it because they claim such a romance could never happen and they are probably right. So, though *Sayonara* gave the 'Zuka girls a worldwide reputation, they don't enjoy the reputation, and mentioning the name of Michener won't get you any free passes to their show.

The Takarazuka Girls' Opera was started in 1914 by the clever owner of a railway line that ran from Osaka to Takarazuka, which, at that time, was just a hot-spring resort whose "hot" waters were so cold that they had to be heated artificially. So he conceived the idea of forming an all-girl troupe in opposition to the Kabuki tradition, where men play all the roles. He also built the local village up into a substantial amusement center with public and private baths, a library, zoological and botanical gardens, and a children's recreational ground.

But the chief attraction then was, and still is, the 'Zuka girls, who perform at the Recreation and Opera House, which contains—in addition to the legitimate theater—a movie theater and another theater for variety shows. The theater in which the girls give their performances, playing all roles (including the male parts), is one of the largest of its kind in the Orient, with a seating capacity of 4,000. The opera performances themselves vary from copies of western musicals to Japanese dramas similar to the Noh and Kabuki traditions and may be very good or very bad.

The Takarazuka Hotel, with 70 western-style rooms, including 19 with bath, provides adequate (but not luxurious) accommodations. There are also many Japanese inns in the area.

Oh yes, after the establishment of the 'Zuka troupe, the railway line prospered so greatly that now the owner's family owns the leading motion picture company in Japan, a string of department stores, a ranch, a professional baseball team, and a few other profitable enterprises. Just thought you'd want to know.

Back to Kobe, the staging area for these jaunts, hotel accommodations are first-class, although not de luxe. The older Oriental Hotel, offers 204 rooms with bath in the new wing and 86 with bath in the old wing; rates are in the medium class. The newer Kobe

International Hotel is small and is also in the same price category. The New Port Hotel is large, with over 200 rooms, and its rates are medium to high.

Himeji. Thirty-five miles by train from Kobe at the town of Himeji and along the coast of the Inland Sea is one of the finest examples of Japanese castle architecture, the Himeji Castle, sometimes called the Heron Castle because of its white walls and graceful lines. About a half-mile from the railway station, Himeji Castle is a five-story structure perched high above the town of Himeji. Photographers should not overlook this trip.

Hiroshima. If you want to take a six-and-a-half-hour-or-so train ride through mountains and along the coast of the Inland Sea to see the first atomized city in the world, be prepared to enjoy the scenery en route and that is all. For, aside from its historical significance, Hiroshima offers nothing else. Even the cenotaph and marble tomb in the Peace Memorial Park have been consigned to the ruins and the ravages of time. For, as the result of a controversy which not surprisingly has felt the chill of the Cold War, the city administration decided not to maintain the upkeep of the shrines, since it was torn between two groups—one that wanted to pull all reminders of the atom bombing down, and another which wanted to keep its memory forever before the public. The city administration prudently sidestepped the issue and handed the problem over to time and the weather.

Inland Sea

The geological history of Japan apparently consisted of a series of volcanic outbursts one after another, creating in their wake at first devastation, but subsequently beautiful scenic spots, like the Fuji lake area. One of Japan's greatest present-day scenic attractions was created several million years ago by volcanic activity of such gigantic proportions that it split the islands of Shikoku and Kyushu away from Honshu, creating the Inland Sea and dotting its surface with about 3,000 islands varying in size from those large enough to support human habitation to mere rocks jutting out of the water.

The Inland Sea is actually a chain consisting of five separate bodies of water linked together by narrow channels. It is 310 miles long, varies in width from 4 to 40 miles, and covers an area of nearly 4,000,000 (wet) acres. Its waters wash the beaches and coasts of three of Japan's 4 principal islands—Honshu, Kyushu, and Shikoku. In addition to its marvelous scenery, the Inland Sea is noted for the whirlpools at Naruto Straits created by the water from the east and west that meet emotionally and part like violent lovers with the ebb and the flow of the tide. The reason for all this watery passion is the 5-foot difference in level between the Pacific Ocean, which borders the Inland Sea on the east, and the Japan Sea, which is on the west. Four times a day the tides come and go, sometimes rushing in and out with a speed of 14 knots. The channel, which separates Awaji Island, a small island in the Inland Sea, from Shikoku, is only a mile wide and with good reason is popularly called Awano-naruto, or the Roaring Gateway of Awa. Boats are available to view these whirlpools, or you can see them from an observatory located on the tip of a promontory that projects out into the channel.

Ships go westward through the Inland Sea from Osaka then calling at Kobe, to Beppu (located on the island of Kyushu), stopping en route at Takamatsu and Takahana (port of Matsuyama) on Shikoku Island. The trip takes 14 hours and is so scheduled that the passengers can see the wonders of the Inland Sea during daylight hours.

Though there are 7 ships that make the voyage between Osaka and Beppu, the 4 most modern ones are the 3000-tonners, the Koha Ku Maru, the Sumire Maru, the Kurenai Maru and the Murasaki Maru, all of which are quite comfortable and have air conditioning. Ships depart every day from Osaka at 7:20 A.M.; from Kobe, 8:40 A.M., which is the reason most foreigners prefer boarding at the Kobe stop; arrival time at Beppu is 9:50 P.M. On some voyages, which begin at 11 P.M., the ships call at Takamatsu in Shikoku at 8:20 A.M. the next day. (Another group of 3 smaller steamers ply the waters between Osaka, Kobe, and Shikoku, where the Beppu-bound passengers disembark and can stay until the steamer they want comes along. Several other steamers, offering a total of 7 different routes between Honshu and Shikoku and Kyushu, sail the Inland Sea, although the Osaka-Kobe-Beppu route is the most popular with foreigners.)

Traveling through the Inland Sea is a memorable experience for anyone, but especially for the photographer—amateur, professional, or even novice. The islands, small and large, appear one after the other and on both sides, usually verdant with trees, hedges, and other vegetation. On the larger islands farmers can be seen working their rice paddies; the peacefulness and seclusion which seems to emanate from the pastoral scene may stir the back-to-nature feeling dormant in most of us. The trip is very worthwhile, although the boats can get quite crowded during holiday periods, especially in summertime. As previously mentioned, there is a stop at Takamatsu, where it is possible to remain ashore and take a later boat.

Takamatsu is the principal port of call at the island Shikoku, which, fortunately or unfortunately, depending on your point of view, is still woefully underdeveloped from the foreign tourists' standpoint. This lack of development of facilities for foreign tourists is emphasized by the fact that the western-style accommodations are available only at the Hotel Toden Kaikan, in the city of Kochi, which has only four rooms with bath; and at the Takamatsu International Hotel.

Takamatsu is famous for two things—its Ritsurin Park, and for a complicated dish, a culinary specialty that celebrates the final battle of the Minamoto and the Taira clans, generally known by the Chinese reading of their names—Genji and Heike.

Ritsurin Park covers 184 acres and is one of the finest examples of Japanese landscape-gardening technique. On the site of the former villa of the powerful Matsudaira family, it lies at the foot of Mount Shiun and is supposed to have taken more than a century to finish. Harmonizing with the pine forest that provides a background for the garden, it consists of six ponds and thirteen hills divided into a north and south wing. Also in Ritsurin Park is a zoo to beguile animal and bird-lovers.

The dish which commemorates the battle of Dannoura in the Shimonoseki Straits is called *Mukashi-gatari Gempei-nabe,* which, (very) roughly translated, means "long-time-story-of-Genji-Heike stew." It is served at the Kawaroku Hotel in Takamatsu, and the owner is quite proud of it. The story behind the stew: The Battle of Dannoura was fought in 1185 and decided the supremacy of the Minamoto, or Genji, clan. The rival clan of Taira (Heike) was completely defeated in this battle, the survivors fleeing to Kyushu where their descendants can still be found in the same mountain villages where they originally took refuge. Crabs found on the beaches of Shikoku have very strange markings on their backs which the Japanese say are the faces of the Heike warriors drowned in the sea battle. So the crabs are called Heike crabs. In any event, the "long-time-ago-story-of-the-Genji-Heike stew" is prepared in a saucepan something like the one used in making *sukiyaki.* In this culinary reconstruction of the Battle of Dannoura, pigeon meat represents the Genji and chopped Heike crabs denote the Heike clan. Horses are represented by dried wheat figures; the Shimonoseki Straits by fishpaste and Chinese cabbage; and egg rolls are shaped so as to represent war drums. There are many other symbols, some easily recognizable and others you must believe in;

at any rate the dish also includes noodles, gingko nuts, bamboo shoots, bean curd, radishes, lotus roots, turnips, yams, mushrooms, and oysters. Unless you are a trencherman of some experience, you will be fighting a battle of sorts yourself to down it all.

Five miles from Takamatsu and connected by streetcar is Yashima, known for its scenery and a place of last refuge for the Heike warriors. A cable car runs up the hill to the summit where there is the Yashimadera Temple, which contains many relics of the Genji and Heike battles. From this hill, too, a portion of the beautiful Inland Sea with its many verdant islands can be viewed. Around here are the ruins of the residences of the Heike and the infant-emperor Antoku, whom the Heike, fleeing from the Genji, took with them from Kyoto. All of this took place in 1182. Subsequently, the relentless Yoshitsune (the general leading the Genji clan) forced them to flee to Shimonoseki where the final disastrous battle took place.

Aside from Takamatsu, the attractions of the rest of Shikoku Island for the foreigner are few. There are the Kompira Shrines in Kotohira, about an hour's train ride from Takamatsu; the Kompira Shrines are second only to the Ise Grand Shrines in popularity. Tokushima, about 47 miles from Takamatsu, is famous for its Awa Dance in mid-August. At this time the citizens of Tokushima dress in kimonos and rice-straw hats and participate in the annual festival. About 100 miles south of Takamatsu is Kochi, capital of the prefecture of the same name and noted for its roosters with tails sometimes 20 feet long and also for its fighting Tosa dogs. Other than for these attractions, Shikoku Island can be considered as well off even the unbeaten path.

Beppu

When you arrive in Beppu by steamer from Osaka and Kobe, which is the way you should arrive, it will be 9:20 P.M. and time to go to your hotel for a bath and a night's sleep (assuming that you had dinner aboard ship). When you arise the next morning, you will be ready after a good night's rest to visit this mecca for pleasure-bent Japanese. For the foreigner, Beppu is a very little bit off the beaten path, but not so far as to lack the facilities he is accustomed to.

Beppu is noted for its odoriferous hot springs of which it has all sorts—alkaline, sulfur, iron, and carbonated—as well as its great speciality, the sand bath. Because of its many hot springs, or *jigoku* (which means "hell" in Japanese), Beppu can be regarded as a sort of Japanese Yellowstone Park, although in miniature. The Japanese utilize these hot springs in many ways, for pleasure, for cooking, and even for warming hothouses in which tropical fruit are grown.

Regular tours are conducted where all the important *jigoku* of Beppu may be seen, the 15-mile trip in a bus taking about 2 hours and 15 minutes. Largest of the boiling ponds, one that much resembles—in sight and sound—a pot of oatmeal cooking, is the Umi-jigoku. It is about 400 feet deep and constantly maintains a temperature of 191° Fahrenheit. You'll see various hot springs belching forth in all colors of the rainbow—some smelling of sulfur, others not too bad.

In Beppu you will also see the original steam bath, an oven-like contraption which is somewhat disturbingly claustrophobic. There is a community bath where both sexes mingle absolutely nude and think nothing of it; and also Mount Takasaki, or Monkey Mountain, which is self-explanatory and great for the kids. The monkeys are tame to the point of almost being a nuisance, and you can buy peanuts to feed them. Our little simian friends have no fears about going up to you and asking for food, to the delight of the kids. The monkeys are divided into bands, each with its leader.

If you are adventuresome in mind, try the sand bath. This is supposed to cure aches in any bones, and as a result, attracts the lame and the halt from all over Japan. The process of sand-bathing is simple: You lie down on the beach with only a cotton *yukata* (a type of robe) covering you. An attendant shovels sand over you until you are covered to the neck. You soak up the heat from the geological turmoil going on underneath you and, in a half-hour, get uncovered again by the attendant, shower in a room open to view by anyone, and feeling a little parboiled and perhaps like a new man, get into your clothes and go your way.

There are more than 300 hotels and inns in Beppu, so rooms are not a problem. The Kamenoi Hotel is somewhat old-fashioned and has 28 western-style and 42 Japanese-style rooms; its rates are medium. The Suginoi Inn, quite luxurious, is the best and the one most foreigners visit; it is very expensive. Many of the Japanese inns are quite luxurious, catering as they do to wealthy Japanese patrons with large expense accounts.

Fukuoka

Four hours away from Beppu by express train is Fukuoka on the north side of the island of Kyushu. Fukuoka, the most prosperous and modern city in Kyushu, consists of the towns of Hakata and Fukuoka, now joined together, on opposite sides of the Naka River.

With a population pushing three-quarters of a million, Fukuoka is famous as the place where Hakata dolls, those tiny clay representations that look so lifelike, are made. Here is where the best *fugu,* the poisonous blow fish, can be had in the wintertime.

There are four excellent hotels in Fukuoka: the New Otani Hakata, the Hakata Miyako, the Nishitetsu Grand, and the Tokyo Dai-Ichi hotels; all of these are fine. There are also several good Japanese inns. Other than its restaurants, many of which serve the excellent *fugu,* described in the sections on Food Specialties, Fukuoka contains few attractions for the foreigner, but does serve as the jumping-off point for other places because it is a transportation center, being connected by plane and train with Osaka and Tokyo.

To the student of history this area is particularly interesting as the place where the Mongols under Kublai Khan tried to invade Japan. In 1274, on the first attempt, the Japanese drove off the invaders; but in 1281, when Kublai Khan assembled a huge fleet and seemed unstoppable, even despite the 10-foot stone wall constructed by the defenders, it took a typhoon, the original *kamikaze,* to annihilate the invading army and save the day.

Nagasaki

By limited express, Nagasaki, famous as the place where Madame Butterfly waited for her errant lover and where the second atom bomb of World War II dropped, is three hours from Fukuoka.

Historically, Nagasaki is significant in that it was the port where trading ships from Portugal, Spain, and Holland stopped in the 16th century before Japan was closed off from the world by the Tokugawas in the 17th century. When the gates were closed, the only foreigners allowed to remain were the Chinese and the Dutch, who were confined to the island of Dejima in Nagasaki Bay. As a result of the Chinese residents of centuries ago, Nagasaki remains famous for its Chinese food. Many foreign residents claim that the Shikairo Restaurant in Hirobaba-cho offers the finest Chinese food in East Asia. This statement, of course, is open to dispute and probably will excite hot and bitter controversy. The Shikairo specializes in Cantonese and Peking cuisines and is definitely worth a visit.

Glover House, the residence of a foreigner, is often called "Madame Butterfly's house." The reason for this can readily be seen by a visit there. Anyone who has seen the opera will recognize it as the setting upon which poor Cho-Cho-san gazes as she waits for her naval lieutenant. Besides its sentimental appeal to lovers of the opera, Glover House does offer one of the finest views of Nagasaki Bay.

On the hillside in the northeast section of Nagasaki is Suwa Park, which has a library known for its collection of valuable books and documents concerning the history and development of Nagasaki, and also for a banyan tree planted by that indefatigable tree-planter, General Ulysses S. Grant, who seems to have conducted a one-man reforestation program while in Japan. Right next to Suwa Park is Suwa Shrine, noted for its huge bronze *torii,* the largest in Japan, standing 33 feet in height and with a width of 14 feet.

When the atom bomb was dropped on August 9, 1945, it unfortunately exploded near the Catholic Cathedral of Urakami, the section of Nagasaki where numbers of Japanese Christians kept their faith in the face of one-time vigorous persecution by the Tokugawa authorities. The cathedral was dedicated in 1914 after 19 years of construction and was the largest church in Japan, having a seating capacity of 6,000. Destroyed by the bombing, it has now been rebuilt. Near it is Peace Park, where there is a monument to the 75,000 who died as a result of the atom bomb.

Nagasaki has two excellent very modern western-style hotels, the Nagasaki Grand and the New Nagasaki. Each has 67 western-style rooms, and the former has in addition 11 Japanese-style. The rates at both hotels are in the medium category. Undoubtedly, the best Japanese-style inn in the entire island of Kyushu is Nagasaki's Yataro, which perches high on a ledge overlooking Nagasaki. If you ask for a room on the side facing the city, you can see the brilliant sunset light the horizon. A good road rises from the city to the hill where the Yataro is located. Western food is served here for the benefit of those whose palates reject the exotic; most rooms have baths.

We cannot leave Nagasaki without going shopping, since the city has its specialties. The shopping areas are the Hama-michi section, Shin-daiku-dori, and Moto-kagomachi-dori. Here you can buy the usual cultural pearls and delicate porcelains, embroidery, miniature model vessels (which reflect Nagasaki's important seaport past), and also Nagasaki's pride and joys—*kasutera* and tortoise-shell ware. *Kasutera* is a kind of sponge cake. The story goes that many centuries ago Spanish sailors brought some sponge cake made by a bakery in Spain called Castillo. (How it remained fresh, we'll never know.) The Japanese, who have the sweetest tooths in the world, immediately took to the cake and proceeded to make it themselves. Everything was fine; the copied confectionary was just about the same as the original. However, there was only one thing wrong: the Japanese, with their inability to pronounce the letter *l,* could not quite reproduce the name of the Spanish bakery as well as they had copied the product. Hence, the name *kasutera;* if you listen carefully, you will catch the resemblance. The tale, of course, may be apocryphal, but it makes sense.

Nagasaki's tortoise-shell ware is renowned throughout Japan. The Nagasaki artisans make cigarette cases, eyeglass frames, cuff links, small trays, and similar articles from the shell. For some items, sheets of shell are pressed together. But watch out for the imitations, of which there are many! Watch out, for example, for articles made of horn, horse's hoof, and even celluloid instead of the real shell. But if you go to reputable shops, you won't be in any danger.

Unzen National Park

One hour by train and two hours by bus from Nagasaki is Unzen National Park on the Shimabara Peninsula. In the prewar days Unzen was the retreat of many foreign residents of China, who came to the area to take advantage of the scenic splendors, as the guide books like to say, and the many hot baths. The scenic splendors included the azaleas in May, the autumnal rainbow of changing tree leaves, and the so-called "silver thaw" of winter when the trees were coated with snow and ice.

The summer resort that attracted the "Old China Hands," however, was Unzen Spa, the name given to three hamlets known separately as Furu-yu, or Old Spring, Shin-yu, or New Spring, and Kojigoku, or Little Hell. Unzen Spa is situated at 2,400 feet above sea level, and because of its altitude provided kinder weather for those foreigners of the old days who wanted to avoid the sultry summer heat of Shanghai. It provides escape from their sizzling cities for the Japanese who can afford it nowadays. The temperature here never goes beyond 80° Fahrenheit, even in the midsummer; and, if it gets too hot, the thermophobe can head down to the sea and try the surf. The bathing resorts are less than an hour away by car from Unzen Spa.

The area contains more than 30 hot springs which are reputedly good for rheumatism and skin diseases. Perhaps the best inn in the area is the Shin-yu in the little village of the same name. It is quiet, the food is rather good, and it has excellent service. You can have your choice of western-style or Japanese rooms.

A 15-minute walk from Unzen Spa is Unzen Park, which contains about 200 acres and lies in the center of a range of mountains.

On the east side of the park there are many geysers which spew their boiling water high into the air. The park has tennis courts, an archery ground, a swimming pool, a children's playground and a nine-hole golf course that has unwanted caddies in the form of crows who go after the golf balls, thinking they are eggs, pick them up in their beaks and make off with them. Those preparing to play golf at this course always come prepared with many extra balls to take care of the attrition caused to their stock by the egg-hungry, and not very bright, crows. For the walkers there are many interesting strolls: A beautiful, wide-angle view of the coast can be obtained at Nita Pass, a mile and a half below the golf links; and two miles from the park is Fugen Peak, where there is another excellent view, as well as caves for speleologists to explore.

A good highway leads to Shimabara, which looks across Shimabara Bay at Kumamoto. This city is of historical interest in that it was a center of Christianity during the early 17th century. When the Tokugawa shogunate outlawed Christianity, the Christians in this area rebelled. They made their last stand at Shimabara Castle, the ruins of which still remain a few hundred yards from Shimabara Station. About 30,000 Christians lost their lives in the bloody purge that followed the fall of the castle.

Those wishing to continue tracing the historical sequence of Christianity in Japan can take a leisurely ferry ride to Misumi (across the bay on the main part of Kyushu Island) and from there another small boat to the Amakusa Islands, an island group of which the largest are Kami-shima, 90 miles in circumference, and Shimoshima, 185 miles in circumference. After the ban against Christianity was proclaimed in 1637 and the subsequent rebellion failed, Japanese Christians in the Amakusa Islands continued their faith but practiced it in secret. When the ban was lifted after the Meiji Restoration in 1868, many thousands of these Christians appeared, for they had maintained the faith for generations, albeit well-hidden from the jealous eye of shogunate officials. The reason for the strong Christian following in Kyushu lies in the fact that St. Xavier did much of his work here, landing in Kagoshima at the southern end of the island and proceeding up to Nagasaki.

Northern Japan and Hokkaido

Northern Japan and Hokkaido are pretty well off the beaten path for the majority of tourists. Dealing with this area, we must be very selective in our discussion, for it would be foolish to include areas which are unimportant to tourists even though they are important ports of Japan. However, the two cities I have included are significant in that they are on the route to Hokkaido (which a guide book on Japan should include because of its unique quality in the complete Japanese picture), and because in themselves they do have attractions.

Sendai

You catch the train for the 220-mile trip to Sendai at Ueno Station (in Tokyo), which, you may remember, is the station from which all northbound trains leave. We say train because at the present time and undoubtedly for some time to come, automobiles and buses cannot be recommended, the roads being quite bad. You can, of course, take the domestic All-Nippon Airways, which has flights from Tokyo to Sendai.

About 68 miles out of Tokyo, the train stops at Utsunomiya, whose major attraction is a temple established by the founder of the important Shingon sect of Buddhism. This temple is built partly within a huge cavern the walls of which are covered with a maze of Buddhist images, some over 13 feet tall. However, the stop is not long enough to visit this famous temple. (If you wish to see it, be prepared to experience basic Japanese life, because the only accommodations available are Japanese inns, not at all prepared for westerners looking for even the minimum in comfort requirements.)

By express train Sendai is 5 hours and 17 minutes from Tokyo. This "City of Woods" *(Mori no Miyako)* is a haven for those who like to imbibe, having *sake* and beer among its principal products. The Star Festival, or Tanabata Matsuri, from August 6 to 8, which is celebrated throughout Japan, is especially noteworthy in Sendai. The festival itself concerns two stars, Kengyu and Orihime, who are regarded as lovers. During August 6 to 8, they are supposed to meet for their annual rendezvous. This meeting is celebrated by Sendai citizens who decorate their houses with strips of colored paper, paper streamers, and other ornaments. Each street vies with the others to see which can have the most fanciful decorations. If the day is cloudy and the love-rendezvous cannot be seen, the people mourn over the continued separation of the stars and wait patiently for the next year. They figure that the lovers did not meet if the day is cloudy, because the heat of the meeting should have dissipated the mist. I'm serious.

One of the loveliest and quietest places in Sendai is the garden of

Rinnoji, about a 10-minute taxi ride from the center of the city. Its rock formations and dwarf trees, rustic bridges and stone lanterns, lend an atmosphere of the unique natural beauty which seems so typical of Japan. Visit the ruined castle on Aoba Hill, which provides a beautiful panorama of the Hirose River and of the city, with the Pacific beyond and the mountains to the north. The Osaki Hachiman Shrine is one of the national treasures of Japan; built in 1606, it is the site of the Festival of the Burning of New Year Decorations celebrated every January 14.

Several popular hot-spring resorts are situated within easy reach of the city of Sendai. The best of these, the Sakunami Spa, is nestled in the mountains about 1 hour and 22 minutes from the city. Other well-known spas are Narugo, Higashiyama, Nasu, Akayu, and Iizaka.

For eating out in Sendai, try the Ningyo, specializing in Japanese fish dishes, and Robata, which is really a bar constructed in the style of a farmhouse. For western-style food, better stick to the hotels. The best hotels in Sendai are the Grand and the Central; both charge about $12 double.

Matsushima, the pride of Sendai and of the entire Tohoku region, is an archipelago of hundreds of pine-covered islands in the bay to the north of the city. A hasty tour of the most important sights may be made in a day, but most tourists would prefer to stay overnight in the village of Matsushima itself. Most of the hotels are equipped with moon-viewing pavilions which overlook the Matsushima chain. The leading hotel here is the somewhat old-fashioned Matsushima Park Hotel with lovely grounds; a double room and bath averages about $30. When the spring or autumn moons cast a shimmer on the Pacific and outline the grotesque shapes of the pines, the sight is unforgettable. The best way to reach Matsushima is by train to Shiogama, which takes about half an hour, and then on to the islands by steamer, another hour. This sea trip, while short, is perhaps the most beautiful in Japan, more so even than that of the more famous Inland Sea.

Aomori

The Tohoku Express, which takes about 6 hours more from Sendai to Aomori (located on the north end of the island of Honshu), passes through Hanamaki, from which it is possible to take a sidetrip to the Hanamaki Spa (22 minutes by the Hanamaki-Onsen Electric Railway) which is worth the effort. The resort is quite

Weather Strip: Sapporo

	Jan.	Feb.	Mar.	Apr.	May	June	July	Aug.	Sept.	Oct.	Nov.	Dec.
Average daily high	29°	31°	36°	51°	61°	69°	75°	79°	71°	60°	46°	33°
Average daily low	11°	13°	20°	32°	40°	50°	58°	61°	51°	39°	29°	18°
Monthly rainfall	3.5	2.5	2.4	2.2	2.7	2.8	3.3	3.7	5.0	4.6	4.4	4.0
Number of days with 0.04 inches or more	15	12	12	9	9	8	9	9	13	12	15	15

modern with facilities for sports and other less active amusements. Excellent ski slopes are in the vicinity, and there is an unusual collection of alpine plants in the botanical gardens there.

Morioka (332 miles from Tokyo) is a regular train stop, a truly provincial Japanese town which still has its old geisha quarter, and an interesting old temple which has hundreds of gilded Buddhas (and figures of Marco Polo and Erasmus!). Iwate Park in the center of the city is the site of an old ruined castle of the Nanbu clan, which controlled the city during the 14th century. The houses of the town are in the Kyoto style; that is, with long, low wooden fronts and overhanging sweeping roofs.

Aomori is the third largest city in the Tohoku region (over 200,-000) and one of the most modern. Ironically, the war was responsible for this. The city was almost completely rebuilt after the air raids of 1945 practically reduced it to ashes, and its wide streets are a great novelty in Japan. Uto Shrine, dedicated to three Shinto deities, is the most popular, and fairly interesting for a visit. Gappo Park, situated at the eastern coast of the city, affords good swimming in summer. The Nebuta Festival (August 1–7) recalls an incident which is somehow reminiscent of the Trojan Horse story of ancient Greece. According to the Japanese legend, a band of rebels holed up in a northern fortress were enticed outside the walls by a display of large, cleverly constructed dummies *(nebuta)* of *samurai* warriors, horses, and dragons, and were captured by the emperor's troops hiding inside. Nowadays the festivities are marked by replicas of these statues, some 15 feet tall.

Towada-Hachimantai National Park, dominated by Lake Towada, the largest mountain lake in Japan, is easily accessible from Aomori by bus (40 miles). The entire area is steeped in Japanese folklore. It is said that a Paul Bunyan-like woodsman, Hachiro Taro, was transformed into a dragon and created the lake for his own home. The lake is stocked with salmon and trout, and a motorboat service is available; a ride will reveal the lake's peaceful scenery. The park has a wealth of natural beauty, with ever abundant pine trees and striking promontories. You can visit the Tsuta and Sugayu hot springs and spend a night at the local inns there, if you're an offbeat tourist and like to live in the Japanese style, sleep on mats, and eat the local food.

Hokkaido Island

You may of course go by train to Aomori and then cross to Hakodate by ferry service if time is no object. Otherwise, take a plane (Nippon Airways or Japan Air Lines) from Tokyo to Sapporo, the capital city of the island of Hokkaido. By jet, Sapporo is only an hour away from Tokyo.

Hokkaido is the least Japanese part of Japan and seems as remote from such places as Kyoto as does, say, San Antonio from Boston. This region, Japan's northernmost island, will be very familiar to those from the midwestern United States, with its wide open spaces, rolling hills, and sturdy American-style farmhouses. The aboriginal natives of the island, the Ainu, the original primitive inhabitants, complete the parallel to our own American Indians. Hokkaido is not the place for those who want to stay on the beaten tourist path seeking shopping bargains or the night life of the large cities. But those who wish to wander from the tourist trail, and who are interested in majestic untamed scenery and such sports as hunting, climbing, and skiing, may well find Hokkaido the most fascinating part of Japan.

There are five major places of essential interest to the tourist: Hakodate and Sapporo, the two major cities; and the three national parks of Akan, Daisetsuzan, and Shikotsau-Toya. The other cities in Hokkaido, besides the two mentioned, tend to be dull and provincial, and may be disregarded. Sapporo is the largest city on the island and perhaps the most attractive. Snowfall is heavy during the winter, and the city is most beautiful during that season. Its chief celebration is the Snow Festival, held on the first Sunday in February. Highlights of the festivities are the gigantic snow sculptures, displayed in the central square, depicting animals, famous landmarks, and uncomplimentary caricatures of famous people.

Nakajima Park in the southeastern part of the city is a center for recreation, especially ice skating in winter. Mt. Moiwa in the southwest affords an excellent vantage point overlooking the city and the surrounding area. As we know, Japanese beer is excellent, and Sapporo is one of the beer centers of Japan.

The best bet for a hotel is the New Otani, with 348 rooms, which is quite exceptional. Next best is the Washington (where did it get that name?) which is nearly as good. Also completely comfortable are the San-ai and Royal hotels. Rates at all three hotels are moderate. The language barrier is more of a problem here than in other parts of Japan, and this may be especially true in the smaller hotels. After exploring the city itself for a day or two, you may want to use Sapporo as a base of operations for visiting the other areas of Hokkaido.

Daisetsuzan

Daisetsuzan National Park is best described in superlatives. It is the largest such park in Japan proper, and it boasts the highest mountain in Hokkaido, Mt. Asahi (7,560 feet), and has the most extensive zones of alpine flora in the country. The park is relatively poor in lakes, and is most noted for its mountains, cliffs, and gorges. Besides Mt. Asahi, Mts. Kuro, Hokuchin, Hakuun, and Ryoun also provide some spectacular scenery and perhaps the best ski sites in Japan. Sounkyo Gorge has the classic beauty of Japanese *sumie* paintings, with sheer cliff faces cut by towering waterfalls, and faced with tenacious cliff-hanging pine trees. The entire gorge (15 miles) may be explored either by private car or by a local bus.

Shikotsu-Toya

This park, located on the south side of Hokkaido, is a region of lakes, notably Lake Toya on the western side and the larger Lake Shikotsu in the eastern sector. Lake Shikotsu lies on top of a hill and is near Mt. Tarumae, an active volcano. It is well stocked with rainbow trout, salmon, and also is noted for its delicious *zari-gani,* a rare species of crawfish. Shikotsu-Toya National Park is also marked with mountain ranges, the most notable peaks being Yotei, Usu, Showashinzan, Eniwa Mountains. Spas in the area include Toyako on Lake Toya, and Marukoma on Lake Shikotsu. Shiraoi, a small village to the south of Lake Shikotsu, is the largest single settlement of Ainu aborigines to be found on the island.

Akan

This park may be reached by express train from Sapporo to Kushiro (6 hours and 21 minutes), and from there to the Lake Akan or Lake Kutcharo regions by train or bus. In the park, lofty mountains, primeval forests, and crater lakes combine in a purely Japanese manner to make a harmonious whole. The Lake Akan region is the smaller of the two, but is also the richer in scenic attractions. The area is popular throughout the year and has facilities for fishing and hiking in summer, and skating and skiing in winter.

Miscellaneous

LANGUAGE (Many ordinary Japanese terms in regular use are directly taken from English, making the language problem particularly easy in restaurants.)

ENGLISH-JAPANESE

waiter   *waitah*
bill of fare, menu   *menyu*
napkin   *napkeen*
bread and butter   *pan to bata*
orange juice   *orangee joosoo*
boiled egg   *yude tamago*
  soft   *yawarakai*
  medium   *hanjuku*
  hard-boiled   *katai*
  egg cup   *tamago kahppoo*
fried eggs   *medamayaki*
bacon and eggs   *tamago to bacon*
coffee, black   *kohi sato miruku nashi*
coffee with cream and sugar   *kohi sato to miruku*
tea   *ocha* (Japanese green tea) or *kocha* (black tea)
water   *ohiya*
  ice water   *kori mizu*
  mineral water   *mineraru wawtah*
breakfast   *asahan*
lunch   *ohiruhan*
dinner   *bangohan*
haircut   *sampatsu*
manicure   *manicuewa*
How are you?   *Ikaga desu ka?*

Fine, thank you.   *Okagesama de genki desu.*
Please.   *Dozo.*
Thank you very much.   *Domo arigato gozaimasu.*
Good morning.   *Ohayo gozaimasu.*
Good afternoon.   *Konnichi wa.*
Good night.   *Oyasumi nasai.*
yes   *hai* (pronounced "high")
no   *iie*
morning   *asa*
noon   *hiru*
afternoon   *gogo*
evening   *yoru*
night   *ban*
Sunday   *Nichiyobi*
Monday   *Getsuyobi*
Tuesday   *Kayobi*
Wednesday   *Suiyobi*
Thursday   *Mokuyobi*
Friday   *Kinyobi*
Saturday   *Doyobi*
one   *ichi* or *hitotsu*
two   *ni* or *futatsu*
three   *san* or *mittsu*
four   *shi (yon)* or *yottsu*
five   *go* or *itsutsu*
six   *roku* or *muttsu*
seven   *shichi (nana)* or *nanatsu*
eight   *hachi* or *yattsu*
nine   *kyu* or *kokonotsu*
ten   *ju* or *to*
twenty   *ni-ju*
thirty   *san-ju*
forty   *shi-(yon)-ju*
fifty   *go-ju*
one hundred   *hyaku*
one thousand   *sen*

GETTING AROUND IN JAPAN The first-time visitor to Japan should be wary of how he phrases his questions. If he asks a question in the wrong way, he may receive the wrong information, much like the Hollywood producer who recently tried to make a movie on Tokyo's night life. The producer had made arrangements with the manager of a Tokyo nightclub to film some scenes at the latter's place. Everything had been agreed upon except the night. The manager suggested two nights later, but the impatient producer wanted it as soon as possible.

"Can't we film it tomorrow night?" he asked.

"Yes," the manager answered.

The producer thereupon ordered lighting experts and camera crews for the filming. When he arrived at the nightclub the following evening, the equipment truck was there, as were the technicians, all standing outside the club's darkened entrance. To the producer's dismay, he learned that the nightclub was closed that evening. He was another victim of the negative question. That is, yes, you can't.

If you word your questions positively, you should have no trouble. But if you put them in the negative, you are likely to be confused. For the Japanese, "yes" and "no" mean agreement and disagreement. So if you say to a Japanese, "Isn't it a fine day today?" he will express his opinion that it isn't a fine day by answering "yes," or theoretically disagree when he thinks it is a fine day by answering "no." In answering the producer's question, the nightclub manager agreed that filming could not be done the next night. That's what his "yes" meant.

Small differences. Another local custom, differing from ours, could cause a bruise or headache; that involves the *automatic doors.* Be wary when you approach one, for the Japanese automatic door swings *outward* (to you) instead of inward as they usually do in the United States and elsewhere in the western world. Many an unsuspecting tourist has found himself suddenly attacked by an outward-swinging automatic door in Japan by approaching without due caution.

There are many other practices that make the Japanese appear like the mirror-image of the westerners, most of which the tourist will not run across. However, for a better understanding of things Japanese, here are a few illustrative items at random:

The Japanese build the roofs of their houses first on the ground. Then they build the house and lift the roof up and put it on.

The teeth of Japanese saws always angle inward, rather than outward, as do the blades of their planes.

The farewell wave, if done with the arm straight out, is a beckoning gesture to the Japanese. So if you wave good-bye to a Japanese friend, be sure you wave with your arm and hand extended upward, or your friend will be coming back to see what you want.

We write our sentences in horizontal lines from left to right; the Japanese write theirs in vertical lines from right to left. Thus, a Japanese book starts at the end and ends at our beginning; or, more specifically, it opens from left and so their titles are on what we consider the back of the book.

The Japanese say "east-north," "west-south," and "there-here." They have grammatical post-positions instead of prepositions so that you "Toyko to go" instead of "go to Tokyo."

The Japanese use only one hand when they count with their fingers. They start with the fingers closed into a fist and, beginning with the thumb, raise the fingers one at a time until all five are up, and then close them one at a time until all five are down again, and the count of ten has been reached.

They stir their tea and coffee in a counter-clockwise motion, dust the rooms before sweeping, and serve soup for breakfast.

When addressing letters, the Japanese custom is the complete opposite of ours. If they write to Mr. Robert Smith of 24, 1-chome, Azabu, Minato-ku, Tokyo, Japan, they would address it in the following fashion: Japan, Tokyo, Minato-ku, Azabu, 1-chome, 24, Smith Robert Mr. It seems more logical than our system, I must say.

If you happen to see Charlie Chaplin leading a cow down a crowded street in the Ginza, do not clutch your forehead and head for a psychiatrist, thinking the change of water or time has subjected you to hallucinations. He is merely one of those imaginative Japanese sandwichmen, fostered by a breed of advertisers who know how to attract attention in a metropolis accustomed to the unaccustomed. Undoubtedly, Charlie is advertising a *sukiyaki* restaurant, which is why he has the live cow on a rope. You might even see stranger sights, like a couple of *samurai* in full regalia dueling in broad daylight with no one paying any attention to them. Don't worry. They are probably advertising a movie. Or those Japanese gunmen straight from Texas? Probably a John Wayne film. Unfortunately for the sandwichmen, the Tokyo citizenry has become jaded because of their outlandish antics. It takes something more than this to draw the public's attention, something like the brainstorm of the advertising genius who had a sandwichman jump into the Sumida River and thrash about calling for help until a crowd had gathered. Then, as preparations were being made for his rescue, he raised a sign calling attention to a newly opened cabaret. Police marched him off and booked him for disturbing the peace. But he got his message across.

Relatives of the sandwichman are members of the *chindonya group*. They dress in carnival-like costumes, with fanciful wigs, chalked, painted faces, and wander about in groups of three or four with drums, cymbals, and wind instruments. It matters not the key or the harmony so long as they make noise. Their eerie "music" punctuated with drumbeats brings out the dogs and children of the neighborhood, and draws adults to the doors and windows. Advertising signs pinned on various parts of their body do the job for which they were hired.

The sandwichman and the *chindonya* troupe give the crowded streets of Tokyo and other major cities the appearance of a fancy-dress ball. But the Japanese and foreign residents, long accustomed to such antics, don't even raise an eyebrow at a robot plodding down the street; for the tourist, a stroll down a crowded street sometimes will seem like a journey into the land of make-believe.

Ryokans (Japanese-style Hotels). In general, western-style hotels in Japan can compete with the best in western countries in comfort, service and facilities. However, IF you can take sleeping on the floor and IF you like utter seclusion while in your hotel, the *ryokan,* or Japanese inn, is an experience you shouldn't overlook.

The latest list of Japanese hotels and inns registered with their respective associations show 159 western-style hotels and 1,050 Japanese inns. Obviously, the much greater number of inns means that they can be found in more places; thus, if you can take the different mode of living, wider horizons are open to you. But even though there is a western-type hotel in the place where you intend to go, at least *once* during your sojourn in Japan you should try a *ryokan.* Only then can you sample the genuine flavor of Japanese life.

Sleeping on the floor is really not so bad. As a matter of fact, it can be quite comfortable. Cast out of your mind visions of your lying stiffly on a cold, hard wood floor. First, a very soft mattress is placed on the straw mats which cover the floor; it feels spongy and adds to the insulation from the floor. (If you think you need another mattress, the management will gladly oblige.) Thereafter, a sheet is placed over the mattress or the bottom *futon* (the cotton- or down-filled quilt between two of which the Japanese sleeps). The covering *futon* itself is encased in white, sheetlike material. After the bed is made, it looks very comfortable there on the floor with the white-covered top *futon* turned back to show the sparkling white sheet underneath. As for the pillows, they previously used to be a problem when Japanese-type pillows only were furnished. These were minature in size and quite hard, sometimes being crammed full of tea leaves or some other similar substance. Today, however, the better Japanese inns have taken to furnishing foam-rubber pillows, a vast improvement.

Japanese inns are built with a garden and/or wall surrounding them to afford a feeling of seclusion. Even though they may be in the center of a modern, bustling metropolis, as soon as you enter, you feel miles away, as though you were in some remote spot far from the madding crowd. In your room—or rooms, for accommodations in the better inns often take the form of a suite—the feeling of seclusion grows. There generally is a living room, which in the night becomes the sleeping room; a small alcove where you can sit on chairs and have tea or coffee while looking down upon the garden; and the bathroom. All activity takes place in your room (which may even be equipped with a television set), except when you stroll in the garden or leave the hotel for some other business. You eat there, sleep there and bathe there, bathing customarily before dinner.

There is nothing more relaxing than a Japanese inn after a hard day of sightseeing. The hot bath is already prepared and you only have to take off your clothes, sink in until you are covered to the shoulders, and soak. Afterwards, you get out to soap (in the Japanese fashion), scrub and rinse yourself, and then finish it all off with another session of soaking. After you are through, you will find a thin but comfortable *yukata* (a type of robe) waiting for you in the living room. This you don and wait for the maid, or *onesan,* to bring in your food.

This she does after opening the door and making a graceful hands-and-knees bow. She then brings in the food, serves it on the *handai,* or low table, and you and your spouse or whatever guest you might have invited can enjoy the dinner alone, as though in the privacy of your own home. There are no public dining rooms in Japanese inns.

After dinner, you may wish to saunter down to the gameroom and play ping-pong or cards. There is no need to change from the *yukata,* for this is standard wear in a Japanese inn. Or you might wish to sit out on the balcony and take tea there while gazing at the garden, the outlines of which are still barely discernible though night has fallen. The dusk perhaps makes the setting the more romantic—and even more so if a full moon comes up.

At any rate, your game of ping-pong ended (if you have played with a Japanese guest, you probably will have been badly trounced) or your garden- and moon-gazing finished, you return to the living room and find that it has been transformed into a bedroom, with the clean-looking *futon,* the cover, turned back, inviting you to get in. The true voluptuary now will call for an *anmasan,* or a masseuse, for the final relaxing touch before sinking into a deep sleep. Masseurs sometimes are also available, but masseuses are by far the more numerous in *ryokans.*

Japanese inns are accustomed to charge a daily rate for lodging and two meals, dinner and breakfast, which used to be a problem. But you needn't be afraid of the food any more. Before the Japanese inns became tourist-conscious, breakfast used to consist of the usual Japanese morning meal of soybean soup (*omiotsuke*), a bowl of rice, some edible seaweed, Japanese pickles and tea. Today, they will serve you ham and eggs, toast, and coffee, the order for which they take the night before. If you want the Japanese kind of breakfast, however, you can have it. Many foreigners find it not bad at all. You can have lunch there, if you wish, but it will probably cost you 1000 *yen* more.

After breakfast—and you should have eaten it in your *yukata*— you go out to the garden and walk around it, still in a *yukata.* Then, with the little exercise, both physical and esthetic, concluded, you proceed to the business of the day, later returning for the bath and supper, which occasionally will be western-style, served with the Japanese touch, meaning it could consist of lobster, steak, fish with rice, soup, vegetables, and tea or coffee. Desserts are rare, however.

Prices for a stay at a Japanese inn vary according to its class, location, size and decorations of the room. Any travel agent can get you the class of inn and room you want, since a list of the approved *ryokans* is registered with the Japanese Ryokan Association and is readily available.

A word of warning: In the usual moderate-priced *ryokan,* there are common bathroom facilities and rarely are there private baths with each room; the high-priced *ryokans* do have private baths. You are expected to take your bath by yourself, of course, but after waiting your turn. If you want privacy during your bath, just tell the maid. She will keep other maids and other guests, including the ladies, from wandering in to upset your ablutions. Therefore, if you don't want to pay the higher price of a higher-class *ryokan* which furnishes private baths with the rooms or if you really want to feel you are one with the Japanese, tell your agent you don't mind a communal bathroom. Otherwise, to be on the safe side, specify a private bath.

Another suggestion: In your room, you will find an alcove. This is called the *tokonoma,* and in it you will find a hanging scroll, or *kakemono.* This is a place of honor; do not put your baggage in it as some unwarned foreigners have done. Also, you must remove your shoes upon entering a Japanese hotel, wearing slippers on the hardwood floors, and remove even the slippers, wearing stockings only, on the *tatami* (the mat which covers the floor) in your room.

In your inquiries you might hear about the *ryokan* custom of presenting *chadai,* or tea money, on leaving a Japanese hotel. This is a thing of the past in the first-rate inns and is slipping into history in the others due to the efforts of the association and the government. This is a good thing, for *chadai* used to amount to as much as half the daily rate per person for each day at the inn. However, in addition to the 10% service charge, you are expected to tip a little extra for special, personal services.

Japanese and Chinese Usage. Since the visitor to Japan is bound to be confused by the Japanese habit of referring to things and people sometimes by the Japanese and at other times by the Chinese reading of their names, this explanation should help.

The Japanese borrowed their script from the Chinese about the 7th century A.D., about the same time that Buddhism was introduced from China. In borrowing the script, they also borrowed the Chinese readings. For example, the Japanese word for mountain is *yama.* When the Chinese ideograph for mountain was brought into Japan, it retained its Chinese reading, which was *san.* Thus, the ideographs for Mount Fuji, which consists of the symbols for Fuji and the symbol for mountain, is read either *Fujiyama* or *Fujisan,* depending on whether you want to use the Chinese word, which is more formal, or the more ordinary Japanese.

In the same way, Minamoto is the Japanese reading and Genji the Chinese reading for the ideograph standing for that powerful Japanese family; and Taira is the Japanese reading and Heike the Chinese reading for the rival family. Let us hope that this explanatory bit straightens out a little the confusing situation that has developed in the Japanese language over the centuries, where often one ideograph can stand for seven or eight different words.

Pachinko. This Japanese version of the pinball machine is one of the most popular indoor sports in Japan. It is perhaps best described as the hybrid offspring of a marriage between a Nevada slot machine and a pinball machine. Pachinko originally made its advent just after the war ended, and though many persons wise in the ways of the Japanese predicted its early demise because they thought it was just another fad, it's still there.

Wherever you go in Tokyo or Japan, you will hear jangling of pachinko balls. Pachinko parlors are in every neighborhood, rivaling the bars in number. And don't think only the Japanese are pachinko addicts. This is an indoor sport which attracts the foreigners as well.

A pachinko machine is upright, like a slot machine, but it uses little metal balls. You buy a certain quantity and try to get them into the right holes. Every time you score, you get more metal balls. When you are through playing and turn your balls in, you are supposed to receive merchandise, such as candy, cookies, cigarettes, etc., in exchange.

Unique Cultural Activities. Certain Japanese customs, such as the tea ceremony and flower-arranging are difficult for a westerner to understand, or to classify. They are regarded as "cultural" activities by the Japanese themselves.

The *tea ceremony* is a very formal way of drinking tea developed from Zen Buddhist practices and intended to implant a feeling of humility in the individual. It is an esthetic cult and quite popular among certain circles in Japan. The tea cult is sometimes called "the religion of the art of life" which when practiced enables one to appreciate better the finer things of life, as opposed to its crasser aspects.

Although the beginnings of the tea ceremony are obscure, it was already in full flower by the 15th century. By that time tea-drinking had developed beyond the mere taking of refreshment and had become a sort of religion, a philosophy, and an esthetic practice. For the tea ceremony to be performed properly, there must be a suitable teahouse, which is composed of a tearoom, a waiting room, and a garden path leading through a carefully composed garden and connecting the waiting room and the tearoom. However, this is the classical teahouse. The tea ceremony is demonstrated in many places, especially in hotels, where there is only a tearoom.

The tea ceremony is best performed before not more than five guests. The guest entrance to the tearoom is low so that the guests must almost crawl through it, an act intended to bring them in the proper spirit of humility. But we are ahead of ourselves.

First, the guests assemble in the waiting room and then, at a signal and led by the guest-of-honor, they walk down the garden path and crawl into the tearoom. The usual chatting and gaiety of a party is missing from this gathering. Silence is golden, and conversation mere dross.

As they enter the tearoom, they stop before the hanging scroll, or *kakemono,* and audibly admire it, using suitable words, of course. Then, when they have lined up (on their knees), the host enters. He very carefully prepares the tea using powdered tea, two or three teaspoonfuls of which are put in a bowl, hot water poured in, and the beverage whipped up into a froth with a whisk. Each guest, beginning with the guest-of-honor, then drinks the tea as it is handed to him by the host. The green tea is quite bitter, but then, the drink itself is comparatively unimportant. Each one is supposed to admire the bowl in his turn.

The ceremony takes a long time, as all actions are painfully slow. But before it is over, generally a tingling feeling followed by relaxation, much like that experienced by an overtired tense body immersed in a steam bath, comes over the guest. Many foreigners find the tea ceremony not only an interesting but also a refreshing experience. A travel agent can arrange a tea ceremony for you; or, if your hotel has a tea-ceremony room, you can experience it there.

The Japanese take their tea ceremony very seriously; so seriously in fact that various schools have sprung up all differing as to how the ceremony should be performed. It is not the place of this book to go into detail regarding the differences. Suffice to say that much emotion goes into the espousal on behalf of the various methods, emotions which, curiously enough, the tea ceremony is supposed to do away with. However, as an example of the bitterness of the conflict, two brothers, both heads of their own school, no longer speak to each other because of their opposing beliefs on the subject of the humility-inducing tea ceremony.

It may seem odd to Americans that there can be different ways of drinking tea. But to the Japanese, who like to deal in symbols rather than fact, the various branches of the tea ceremony are something to ponder carefully.

Americans also may wonder how an esthetic cult can develop from picking and *arranging flowers.* Leave it to the Japanese, however. They have created a remarkable art form out of it. *Ikebana,* or flower-arranging, they call it, and again they have divided this unique national art into many schools. Today, more than 300 different blooms are flowering in the garden of *ikebama,* to use a Japanese metaphor. The principle lies not in just putting a bunch of flowers together to look nice. That's too easy. You have not mastered your art unless you can take a single blossom and make something that not only looks artistic but has some significant meaning to the Japanese mind.

Now we come to the third cultural achievement unique to the Japanese—*incense-smelling.* Where the tea ceremony appeals to the taste and flower-arranging to the eye, incense-burning and -smelling appeals to the sense of smell. There are formal ceremonies involved, just as in the tea cult. However, one of the more common objectives is to test the individual olfactory sense. The host burns some incense in a censer which is passed around to the guests who sit in a semicircle about him. Each guest writes down his guess as to the identity of the particular scent. At the end, the score is added up and the person with the most correct answers is the winner. In the old days prizes of swords and armor were given. Today, the incense-smelling cult is found only among the upper classes, especially the ex-nobility, who, having lost their former titles, are on the lookout for ways in which to be superior to the ordinary Japanese people.

KOREA

👫 Background

Where did the Koreans come from originally? No one seems sure, but there are points of identification and similarity with both the Chinese and Japanese, and anthropologists can argue backwards or forwards with ease to prove their varying points of view.

A glance at a map illustrates this small country's unfortunate position as a buffer between two powerful giants—China and Japan. Its finger-like peninsula shape, attached to the Asiatic mainland and bordering on China, has caused Korea to be more or less dominated by its enormous neighbor to the north, sometimes friendly, sometimes unfriendly.

It does seem quite clear, however, that beginning almost 2,000 years ago, this country, then called Chosen, was allowed to run itself only under the watchful eye of the Chinese, although sometimes the reins were loosely held, whereas at other periods of history, a strict degree of control was exercised. During the 16th century, the Japanese took a crack at the sitting duck called Chosen, invading the country before the indolent Chinese masters were fully aware of it. Later, the Czarist Russians began meddling in its affairs, and the small country found itself the center of a three-nation power play, and completely unable to make a choice, or have any freedom of action.

Like the philosophical people they were and still are, the Koreans began literally to withdraw from the world, canceling international contacts as much as possible, and refusing to allow nationals of foreign countries to enter their bullied and harassed land. For several centuries Korea became a remote, unknown region, unvisited even by explorers, and began to be called the Hermit Kingdom. Its isolation from the outside world was almost complete, and few Koreans were permitted to leave their homeland, only in the most unusual of circumstances. Its isolation was almost complete; Korean children were taught nothing of the outside world.

The past century has brought many changes, however. In 1895, the Japanese took advantage of the crumbling Chinese national authority, and eliminated them completely from Korea. Japanese imperialism was on the ascendancy and their armed forces were quite strong by Asiatic standards; in 1904, the Japanese went one step further and expelled all Russian influence and then formally annexed Korea in 1910. The Japanese takeover was unwanted, and in fact resented, by the Koreans, but there was, over the years, some economic improvement in the country. On the other hand, the Korean people's desire for freedom never slackened, and there was always a strong undercurrent of national unrest by those who sought independence from Japan.

When the Japanese forces were defeated during World War II, the Allies (meaning the Americans) made Japan release Korea, and the country was given its independence in 1945. But what a half-baked political freedom! It was the kind of freedom dreamed up by politicians, not by people with common sense. The Russians, our allies in the great war, took control of all the land north of the 38th parallel, a purely arbitrary line. Although the Russians had promised, in the Potsdam Declaration, a free and independent Korea, the promise was never kept. The Russians are always reliable about one thing—they never keep their promises. Although the United Nations tried to enforce free elections, the Russians refused to allow their observers to enter the northern half of Korea controlled by them. In 1948, the southern half of the country held free elections and established a republic. Several months later, the Russians established a "Democratic People's Republic," which is a slight misnomer, because it was not democratic, not representative of the people, nor a republic.

Events came to a head on June 25, 1950, when without warning the North Koreans attacked south of the 38th parallel. The United Nations, in a special session, condemned the invasion and asked its members to assist the South Koreans. Over fifty countries offered to come to South Korea's aid, but of course, who do you think (as usual) supplied the vast bulk of men, money, and equipment? Step to the head of the class, you're right, we did. There was a year of serious warfare, and at first the North Koreans were temporarily able to force the line down southwards, but we recovered, and soon pushed the enemy back. Now comes a controversial point. There seems to be little doubt that the efforts of the North Koreans were supported by the Russians, and that perhaps some of their soldiers were involved in the fighting or in support operations and training. Later, when the United Nations forces entered the war, mainland Communist forces joined the North Koreans and actually did a large part of the fighting. When we started to push them back, as you might know we would, our soldiers began to complain that they would suddenly run out of ammunition as the advance rolled relentlessly northwards—and it looked like a great victory for us and a rout for the communists. Foreign correspondents began to report that our soldiers were being deliberately held back as they approached the former line of the 38th parallel. This was vigorously denied in Washington, and thus the controversy. Why, you ask? It seems that the brass in Washington decided that further entry into North Korea could lead to a major conflict, whereas stopping at the line would end in an armistice. Who's right and who's wrong may be known a few decades from now, when the respective military leaders sell their private papers to *Time* and *Newsweek,* or publish their books with huge advances from their publishers, but right now no one seems to know for sure. Or, if they do know, they aren't saying. All that we do know for sure is that the 38th parallel remains a dividing line between North and South Korea, and we seem to have a more or less permanent commitment to maintain it. Armistice talks began on July 10, 1951, and lasted for quite a while, about two years to be exact. The "talks" were held at the tiny village of Panmunjon, and the actual armistice was finally signed on July 27, 1953. Primarily, however, the Armistice established a so-called Demilitarized Zone (about which more later).

Unfortunately for all concerned, during Korea's few years (six, to be exact) of freedom from 1945 to 1951, it had a very stubborn, dictatorial, inflexible leader, Syngman Rhee, whom the United States, with its penchant for always backing the wrong horse, supported to the fullest. Syngman Rhee had delusions of grandeur, and sought to make himself president for life, considered himself a heaven-sent leader, and let the country go to what can only be called pure hell. Everything went wrong, and the young Republic of Korea (popularly called the ROK) went downhill like a steamroller at an unbelievable pace. Unemployment, poverty, and loss of freedom of speech were only the beginning; this was followed by police-state tactics, with considerable rough stuff, unexplained disappearances galore, and even a suppression of the opposition political party. Korean students are always vocal and lively; their demonstrations in 1960 forced the unloved Syngman Rhee out of office, and out of the country, to almost everyone's general delight (except Syngman Rhee, of course).

Since then, there have been upheavals, political shifts, army take-overs, and the like. Korea hasn't yet found itself, politically that is, in all probability. But none of the unrest seems to apply to tourists. On my last visit, I read in English-language papers that demonstrations were going on in Seoul, where I was. But I didn't see them. I wasn't disturbed, however, because the same paper carried an item about the soccer match played in Seoul (the same day as the demonstration) in which the score was Korea 3, Japan 1.

Now let's turn away from politics and world affairs and turn to

Weather Strip: Seoul

	Jan.	Feb.	Mar.	Apr.	May	June	July	Aug.	Sept.	Oct.	Nov.	Dec.
Average daily high	32°	37°	47°	62°	72°	80°	84°	87°	78°	67°	51°	37°
Average daily low	15°	20°	29°	41°	51°	61°	70°	71°	59°	45°	32°	20°
Monthly rainfall	1.2	0.8	1.5	3.0	3.2	5.1	14.8	10.5	4.7	1.6	1.8	1.0
Number of days with 0.04 inches of rainfall	8	6	7	8	10	10	16	13	9	7	9	9

something far more fascinating—the strange customs with respect to names and marriage. In the United States, we have literally tens of thousands of family names, such as Jones, Williams, Smith, and so on. In Korea, there are only 249 family names, and of these, four family names account for slightly over 50% of all names. These are Kim, Lee, Park, and Choi. The Kim name is particularly common, and there are many millions (probably about 6 million) of Kims in the country; it's thought that over 100,000 Kims are born each year. Children of female Kims adopt their father's lineage and leave the Kim clan, but nevertheless the high percentage of Kims still continues. Great problems are caused by the enormous number of the four leading family names, for the simple reason that it is improper for any marriage to take place where there is a common male ancestor, even though he dates back many centuries. The law states that no man and woman with a common ancestor in the male lineage can marry. Only about one half of 1% of Korea's 35 million people have defied this tradition and married illegally. Recently the National Assembly voted a one-time law permitting the 270,000 children produced by these "illegal" marriages to be legitimatized.

🪶 When to Go

Spring starts early, usually towards the end of March, with trees coming into bloom and the countryside looking green and lovely. From late March through late June is an ideal time for a visit with almost perfect weather, as a rule. At the end of June, the rainy season begins, and it continues through August. The damp weather may break up during the end of August, or it may continue a little longer, you never can be sure. From late September through early November, the ideal weather season starts again, with clear days, and dry weather. Forget about the winter months for a visit; it's usually cold and raw. Even during the rainy summer months of July and August, it may rain heavily for an hour or two and then stop. But, of course, you know weather and how difficult it is to predict.

✒ Visa Requirements

Theoretically, no visa is required for a visit of under 72 hours, but I would get a regular 15-day transit visa nevertheless. It can be quickly obtained in the U.S., or in Tokyo (at the Korean Consulate), without charge; no photos required. There is talk that the visa requirements may be modified; be sure to check at the last moment. When applying, have 2 photos and a letter from the airline or travel agent stating that you are a bona fide tourist. The main problem with not obtaining a visa for visits of less than 72 hours, is that the traveler is supposed to have a confirmed transportation onward to a country other than that from which he has just come. Once again, even though you may only be coming to Korea for a 72-hour visit, it's a good idea to get a visa nevertheless.

♨ Customs

They will permit a carton of cigarettes or 25 cigars to be brought in. Cash (not traveler's checks) is to be declared when entering, although this requirement is not strictly enforced. Note: When leaving the country, all baggage must be inspected (the same rule goes even for domestic flights). This takes time; therefore sufficient time should be allowed before airport departure. The airlines generally suggest arriving at the airport two hours before departure time.

⚕ Health

The water in Seoul is perfectly safe, but out of the cities or resort spots a little caution might be in order. Also, the mineral content of the water is different from what we're used to, and it's simply a good idea to go very easy on drinking tap water. Incidentally, beer is the perfect drink with Korean food, and the local beer is excellent. The milk is fine, and of course that means the ice cream is O.K. It's probably safe to eat raw vegetables in the best hotels, including salad, but don't take a chance if you're eating at a regular restaurant or in the dining car of a train. Cholera certificates are listed as a requirement for entry into Korea, but during my last two visits, no one asked to see the certificate; better play safe and get a shot.

⏱ Time

There is a 16-hour time differential between Seoul and California. When it's Tuesday noon in Seoul, it's 8 P.M. Monday in Los Angeles.

💲 Currency

The local currency is the *won,* and the rates fluctuate with some frequency. The hotels offer the poorest exchange rates. The word *won* is pronounced as if it were spelled *wun* or *one,* so when you ask for the price, you'll be told it's 1,000 *won,* for example, which sounds exactly like 1,001. For the first few times, you'll instinctively think it's very peculiar to charge 1,001 for an article instead of a flat 1,000. But you'll get used to it after a while. Remember, currency rates fluctuate.

🌐 Price Level

Of all the countries in the Orient, Korea may be the most moderately priced. Hotels are about two-thirds the price of similar accommodations elsewhere around the world and meal prices may be even lower than that. Sightseeing rates are equally so. One exception: although cab fares are lower than ours, rates for cars hired by the day or half-day are comparatively expensive.

🍎 Tipping

The Koreans rarely tip, but since you're an outsider and a foreigner, you'll require a little special attention, and perhaps a little tipping is in order. At restaurants, leave the waiter no more than 10% of the check, which is inevitably only a small matter, since restaurant checks are usually not too large. The man who carries your baggage should get the equivalent of about 20¢–25¢ a bag. Taxi drivers are not tipped unless they've carried your baggage.

🏃 Transportation

There are thousands of *taxis* in sight, but they're almost always occupied, except during the off hours. Rates have been held to reasonable figures despite a general inflation, so almost everyone seems to have enough money for a taxi. At most places, you're expected to get into a line and await your turn, but it doesn't work just like that when it rains, or during the rush hours, when it's every man for himself. If, as rumored, the government raises the taxi fares, the demand will probably diminish somewhat. If you don't mind paying a little more, there are call-taxi systems, and you can have your hotel or restaurant phone for one. Coming up soon, it is reported, are *drive-yourself cars;* at the moment, Korea doesn't have any, but sooner or later, they will be authorized. However, I don't know if I'd want to drive my own car in Korea, because the road markers aren't usually in English, except on the main roads. The less important highway markers are often only in Korean. Korean Airlines covers the country quite well, but tourists will probably only be interested in flying to Cheju Island or Kyongju (both to be discussed later).

✊ Airport and Tourist Taxes

Kimpo Airport, new and modern, is about 16 miles from the center of Seoul, and a drive of about 40–50 minutes during the daytime, when most of the flights arrive or depart. At night, the trip to the airport takes only about 20–25 minutes. Be sure to arrive at the airport about two hours before departure.

Korean airport security is very tight, and your baggage will have to be opened before it is accepted for a flight, either domestic or foreign. (Remember this when you're packing, so that your suitcases will close readily.) There's a fair amount of red tape, forms to be filled out, and so forth. For your comfort and peace of mind, please follow the advice given above and arrive at the airport about two hours before scheduled departure time. If you wish, you can check in somewhat more conveniently at the Korean Air Lines terminal in downtown Seoul. You'll receive your seat assignment and boarding card at their downtown office, and then ride to the airport on a shuttle bus, with the airline taking charge of your baggage. Don't forget there's an airport departure tax of about $3.00.

▌▌ Communications

Airmail letters to the U.S. take about 5 days, sometimes more. *Aerogram* letters (the self-sealing printed forms usually available at hotel desks) are about half the price of regular airmail letters. Local *telephone* calls are a definite bargain, costing less than 5¢ each; are you listening, American Tel and Tel?

There's an Armed Forces Korean Network, which includes both radio and television. Inasmuch as almost every hotel room has a TV, you might enjoy watching the local AF broadcasts, which do *not* have commercials, a refreshing experience. Also, you can get the news on the hour by listening to the same network on your radio; often there's a sports broadcast of important football and baseball games, plus stock market reports.

POINTER:

In our own country, 13 is regarded as an unlucky number, and you'll find that the majority of American office buildings and apartment houses omit a 13th floor, running from the 12th to the 14th floors. In Korea, 4 is the unlucky number, and therefore it will come as no surprise that the floors often run from the 3rd to the 5th. Sometimes, but not always, they won't even use the number 4 in a hotel room, so that you'll occasionally see room 803, followed by 805. Can you imagine a Korean being asked to check into a hotel room numbered 444?

⚡ Electricity

The local current is 100 volts, which is similar to our 110 volts, but appliances tend to run slowly, or sluggishy on occasion. Otherwise, no problem for American appliances.

✕ Food Specialties and Liquor

Western-style food is available in almost every hotel in Seoul, and many of those in the larger cities, but it isn't terribly good or interesting. On the other hand, it's perfectly edible and wholesome, and no one will ever go hungry here. American breakfasts, with ham and eggs, or hot cakes, are served throughout the country, or in any event, wherever a tourist is likely to go.

Now what about Korean food? Is it wild, exotic, and just too far-out for most Americans? The answer may involve a discussion of your own food habits. If your ordinary diet and food habits consist of eating completely unspiced, plain American food, the answer may well be a loud, clear affirmative—meaning yes, it is too spicy. On the other hand, if you like Chinese food, and enjoy foreign meals (at least while you're traveling), there's every reason to eat Korean food. Incidentally, even the least daring American might enjoy *bul-googi* (about which more later). Let's get the facts out at once, and forthwith; Korean food is fairly spicy, but not unbearably so. Some simple meat dishes are no more exotic or unusual than charcoal-broiled steak strips, and almost anyone would enjoy them. Others are, well, just too spicy for any but the very well-traveled, and those with good stomachs, the kind who like Mexican food. In point of fact, southern Californians, who frequently enjoy Mexican food, will find Korean dishes almost mild.

The easiest Korean specialty on which to take off is undoubtedly *bul-googi.* (You'll see this spelled *pul-googi, bul-kooki, pul-kogi, pul-koki,* and so on. The reason for this is simple, and not because no one knows how to spell. The Korean alphabet is different from ours, and all English-language spellings are merely attempts to imitate the *sound,* not the spelling, of the original Korean.) As I said before, *bul-googi* (my preference) consists of thin slices of beef, pork, or chicken marinated in soy sauce, onions, ginger, and the like, then broiled over a charcoal fire very quickly in front of the diner. It's delicious, I think. *San-juk* consists of beef and vegetables, cooked on skewers. *Jang-po* is made with thin slices of beef marinated in soy sauce with sesame seeds and then broiled; you'll enjoy this too, without being very bold.

Several chicken dishes are likely to please you, such as *tak-chim,* which is really steamed chicken with vegetables; nothing too daring here, unless the chef is overly generous with garlic. The national roast chicken dish, *tongtack juk,* is classic for holidays; it's very tasty, and your only danger lies (as before) in too much garlic. The seafood is quite good, although the Korean cuisine tends to neglect fish, placing most of its emphasis upon meat. The *see-ow chun* is nothing but fried shrimp, prepared in a very good egg batter, and probably better than at home. You'll be lucky indeed if the menu features *tomi-chun,* Korea's tastiest ocean fish (sea bream), which is fried in batter. It's bland and not at all spicy, and may be dipped in soy sauce if you wish, but the freshness of the fish is what makes it desirable. The Koreans also love to eat the edible seaweed *(kim)* which they gather along the shore.

Soups are pretty good here, and the Koreans love them. *Koum-tang* is a rice soup with thin slices of beef; quite good. The fish soup, *jokee-kook,* is delicious if you like fish chowders; but be forewarned, it's made with a little meat and some garlic. The vegetable soups aren't bad, especially those made with scallions *(jukkai-jang-kook);* or spinach soup *(skikoomchi-kook).* A meal-in-one-dish, vaguely resembling a New England Boiled Dinner, is *sin-sullo,* which consists of fish, meat, chestnuts, vegetables, etc., cooked in a broth-like liquid; it is served in a most attractive brass container with charcoal in the center to keep the dish hot during the meal. Even a timid tourist, gastronomically speaking, wouldn't be daring if he tried this.

Now for something a little odd, by American standards. It's *kim-chee,* the national relish, or pickle, or what have you. It appears at every Korean meal, and for most Koreans the meal would be a failure without it. If any dish typifies Korea, it's *kim-chee.* At first you won't like it, because (to be crude) it has a strong odor, somewhat acrid. It smells for the simple reason that it is made with vegetables, to which are added onions, garlic, ginger, red peppers, ground fish, or whatever the cook has on hand. It is then allowed to ferment, and so, quite naturally, it smells. The funny thing is, I hasten to add, that it grows on you. The classic type is made with cabbage, and forms the basis for the most popular type, called winter *kim-chee.* Summer *kim-chee* (intended to be eaten soon after it is made) is prepared with less salt, and is frequently made with white radish, cucumbers or other greens. The closest comparisons, by western standards, are sauerkraut or dill pickles, but they are only slight, distant relatives of the heartier *kim-chee.* To wind up, *kim-chee* came into existence because the Koreans needed a vegetable to carry them through the long winter when no green foods were available.

The favorite local drink is a kind of rice wine, not too strong, called *yakju;* it's passable enough and worth trying if you're a student of national beverage customs. Best of all, I think, is the Korean beer which helps to put out any fires kindled by spicy dishes. Look for the Crown label on beer bottles; about the best.

∞ Time Evaluation

Korea is quite fascinating, and you don't want to miss the opportunity of seeing a truly exotic country. It has a great deal to offer the traveler, and shouldn't be missed. When you come, allow an absolute minimum of three days, which would allow one day for a trip to Panmunjon (about which more later). If you really want to see the lovely countryside, and plan to fly down to Cheju Island, a week would be required.

You can fly to Korea from the west coast of the U.S. on Korean Airlines. Several other airlines have service out of Tokyo, and usually people proceed on to Hong Kong, if making a comprehensive tour of the Orient.

🏛 Capital City: Seoul

Seoul (pronounced as if it were spelled Soul) is now an enormous city, filled with very tall buildings. The main streets look quite a bit like those in downtown Tokyo, but the smaller sidestreets which run in all directions parallel with or at right angles to the main streets are still narrow, loaded with atmosphere, and lined by buildings which are usually only two stories in height. It is extremely diverting to simply wander about at random, up and down the streets, in and out of the numerous department stores, antique dealers, small shops, and coffee houses, just going wherever your feet take you.

You won't believe it at first, but this unusual city has more than six million inhabitants. Will it look more impressive in numerals— 7,000,000? It's busy and trafficky and a trifle noisy, but not more so than many other industrial cities, but don't be discouraged and ask yourself why you came, and why Seoul, Korea, should look so much like Des Moines, or Little Rock, or Scranton. Driving in from the airport, your eyes will wander from the dull architecture and begin to pick out random sights that begin to please. The local food markets are colorful and often fascinating. Then you'll see the people—mostly small and slight of build, quite graceful and pleasant, as you'll later find. (It will be one of the surprises of your life to encounter old-fashioned courtesy and politeness from waiters, drivers, and even porters.) The men dress in somewhat nondescript fashion, half-eastern and half pure Sears-Roebuck. But the women generally wear the colorful and delightful *han-bok,* a national costume which consists of a high full-length skirt worn with a very brief bolero jacket; the fabrics are light and colorful, often with brilliantly contrasting sleeves. Probably these national costumes will disappear for everyday wear, just as the kimono has in Japan. In Seoul, few men wear the full national costume, but in the countryside, the peasant wearing snowy white unusually designed robes, the whole creation topped by a sort of tall, black stovepipe hat (à la Jackie Gleason's Reginald von Gleason), is enough to make anyone take out his camera.

Seoul exerts a strong influence upon the entire nation. For example, it has 20% of the nation's population, who live in about ⅔ of 1% of the total land area. The city has half of the nation's 80 universities, 60% of its hospitals, 45% of its vehicles, a third of the national wealth, 35% of the manufacturing industries and also has 98% of the central government offices. So great has the congestion become in Seoul that the city offers the equivalent of a $200 reward for every household that moves away voluntarily. Despite all of these efforts, the city continues to grow ... and grow. There are some population experts who think that Seoul will surpass Tokyo in size (Tokyo now has about 10 million people, more or less) by 1986.

Sightseeing in Seoul involves no more than two days, at most. There are several palaces definitely worth seeing, but after the first two, perhaps all that will occur is repetition, plus more color pictures. If you are an inveterate sightseer, of course you can go on indefinitely, but I'm assuming that you're like me—a true-blue, red-blooded American who is happy to go sightseeing, but likes to call a halt before exhaustion (and duplication) set in.

Don't miss Chang-dok Palace, originally constructed in 1405 or thereabouts. There are more than 50 separate buildings scattered over some 78 acres of parklike grounds, with streams and ponds meandering at random through the grounds, the whole affair architecturally harmonious, and likely to illustrate the well-known fact that the rich and royal lived very well indeed, even five centuries ago. The various rooms, including the throne room, reception room and bedrooms are filled with much of the original furniture and are quite interesting. The outstanding building is the Puyongjon Palace (or Pavilion), famous because it has 20 sides, and with 2 supporting pillars rising from the water. You'll see the tranquil Secret Gardens, which only royalty was permitted to use; also noteworthy is one building with blue porcelain tiles on the roof, never duplicated because the tile-maker died without revealing the secret.

The second most interesting palace is Kyongbok, constructed in 1554 although since restored. During its heyday, this palace's throneroom was the scene of all coronations, important receptions, and whatever else thronerooms are used for. It has attractive ponds and waterways on the grounds, and it's undoubtedly worth an hour of your time.

By now we get to the law of diminishing returns. So you've seen two palaces. More? There's Dok-so Palace (sometimes spelled

Duck-soo) which is also of the early 15th century, and was often used as a royal residence.

Really devoted sightseers might want to take a cable-car ride up to Nam San, a local mountain peak which offers a view of Seoul. I don't know about that, however. As I mentioned before, Seoul is hardly another Hong Kong, where a tram ride to the mountain's top offers an exciting view. Seoul sprawls and wanders unimpressively in unspectacular fashion for miles in several directions, but so what?

Much more interesting would be a walk through the Myongdong shopping district, looking at the food stalls, fingering and buying fabrics, small souvenirs, and the like. Perhaps you'd like to buy some ginseng tea, sold in cellophane-wrapped individual packets, all very sanitary and American. The Koreans have almost a monopoly on ginseng, a root believed by many orientals to have miraculous and curative properties; it is said to be good for what ails you, and besides will reputedly cure arthritis, falling hair, varicose veins— and bring a healthy glow to the cheeks. If nothing else, it tastes like herb tea. Although some ginseng is produced in communist Manchuria, Korea is its main source, and most orientals believe that it is the most powerful and important of all medicines—a sort of combination of penicillin, aureomycin, and aspirin. Another great Korean cure-all is deerhorn, the bone of which is boiled to produce a health-giving broth. Well, who knows?

One of the most interesting things any visitor can do is visit either of Seoul's two produce markets, the East Gate and South Gate markets. I would suggest that you select the South Gate Market, which is filled with tiny shops selling almost everything edible you can think about, plus a few assorted items you ordinarily wouldn't think of as being suited for eating. It's really diverting to wander about, although the walk may involve wet shoes, because the market is kept clean by washing the ground with water rather frequently. By all means take a look at the famous South Gate, which formerly was one of the four main gates to the city. The gate is quite imposing, and dates back to the late 1300s, as part of the Yi Dynasty. Most Koreans think it is their single greatest architectural and cultural asset, and it is undoubtedly the most photographed place in Seoul.

About 50 minutes by car south of Seoul is the Korean Folk Village, which can be described as a combination of a (serious) Williamsburg with some entertainment thrown in. There are marvelous authentic reproductions of Korean houses of the Yi Dynasty, shops with craftsmen actually reproducing goods of that period, places to rest, and restaurants. Once inside the village itself, transport is by foot, by donkey and cart, or, if you're really up to it, by *palanquin*—being carried by bearers. You can spend hours here; better allow about a half day. The nearest town to the Folk Village is Suwon, a fortress town, which is enclosed by a wall connecting various watchtowers, gates, entrances, etc. Be sure to allow a little time for walking through Suwon; it's what Korea must have been like centuries ago.

At Namsan Hill there's a beautiful new National Theatre, built in the classical Korean style of architecture. There are actually two theaters—one enormous, the other fairly moderate in size. Korean classical music is performed, as are dramas (with instantaneous translations). It makes a worthwhile cultural evening.

ACCOMMODATIONS

Lotte. A 38-story hotel, with over 1,000 rooms. There's a huge lobby with a waterfall. Guest rooms are very attractively furnished and decorated and are of rather good size. There's an indoor swimming pool, a large selection of different restaurants, and many shops. The Lotte is quite outstanding.

Shilla. This is a very luxurious 676-room hotel near Namsan Hill; the Shilla is affiliated with the Okura Hotel in Tokyo. Rooms are larger than usual, and very nicely decorated. There are four different restaurants, many shops, and so forth, excellent service. About 15 minutes from the downtown area.

Hyatt Regency. A 659-room hotel at the foot of Namsan Hill, near the city's largest park. The lobby is enormous and quite spectacular. The rooms are rather attractive and of good size. There are four restaurants, swimming pools, shops, etc. The hotel is 15 minutes from the center of Seoul.

Chosun. A large hotel with rather spacious guest rooms. It has a marvelous location, in the center of town. Spacious and appealing lobby and public areas; several restaurants.

Han Yang. A rather small, elegant hotel, located near the Han River, about 15 minutes from the downtown area. The Han Yang is planning to appeal to the individual traveler who wants quiet, residential accommodations.

Sheraton Walker Hill. This is an entire complex of hotels, villas, casinos, nightclubs, etc. The 535-room addition is the new portion. The complex is located on a 139-acre site that overlooks the Han River. It's about a half-hour ride from central Seoul, but the Walker Hill area has compensating attractions.

Plaza. An outstanding hotel, 22 stories high facing City Hall Plaza and overlooking the rooftops of nearby Toksu Palace. Rooms are of good size, nicely decorated. The public areas are exceptionally attractive. Several restaurants, and all facilities.

Seoul Royal. An exceptionally nice, centrally air-conditioned hotel in a good location; medium-high rates. Several restaurants, night club featuring Korean music and dancing. Architecturally, an interesting structure rising from a 4-story base.

Seoul Tokyu. Together with the two hotels above, this is the third luxury hotel in Seoul. 200 rooms, nicely decorated. Medium-high rates, all facilities, including shopping arcade.

New Korea. Air-conditioned, and very modern, with all of the facilities of a modern hotel. Rooms are only fair in size, but are attractive and comfortable. Choice of restaurant facilities. Generally medium rates. Centrally located.

KAL Hotel. A 165-room hotel on the top 6 floors of the 26-story KAL building. Moderate rates; attractive top floor restaurant serving both western and Chinese food.

Koreana. A 265-room hotel, medium prices. Many of the guests are Japanese, but it also caters to westerners. Several restaurants, shopping arcade, nightclub.

Seoul Garden. In a residential area near the National Assembly and the Han River. Seventeen stories tall, with 410 rooms. Very modern; there is a series of different restaurants. About 20 minutes from the airport.

President. This hotel occupies the top half of a large office building in a downtown location, convenient to shopping. Two restaurants, sky lounge.

Tower. A new, high-rise hotel, with 91 rooms, fairly close to town; centrally air-conditioned. Lovely views from all rooms.

Sejong. A large downtown hotel; 300 rooms, which are large and decorated in the Korean style. Completely air-conditioned and fairly moderate rates. Has some exceptional features, including help in Korean costumes.

RESTAURANTS   Western food may be had at all of the above hotels, as previously mentioned. If you want a western meal, it's best to dine at your hotel, although there are several restaurants in Seoul which claim to serve good foreign-style (western) food. Incidentally, breakfast is usually served between 8 and 9, lunch comes at noon, and dinner is from 7–8. If you tire of western hotel-food, about the best outside places are the Hosu Grill and the Diplomatic Club, which is just a name for a restaurant, not a club. Many people think the Cosmopolitan is the best western-style restaurant in Seoul; believe it or not, it's located in the basement of the YWCA. Don't expect anything too sophisticated, although the food is good.

But you should have Korean food, and the following are recommended:

Keou Ku Jang. Located on a street leading away from the Chosun Hotel, you'll surely enjoy this very large, first-rate restaurant. They have an enormous menu, but also several special dishes, such as one featuring steak cut up in the Japanese style. A most interesting restaurant.

Arirang House. This pleasant restaurant has good Korean dishes, somewhat (very slightly) toned down for western palates. Sometimes there is music and dancing, so inquire when making your reservation.

Korea House. One of Seoul's best restaurants, this interesting spot is suitable for any curious tourist. Don't be afraid to order more than you want, and eat what tastes good to your palate, because it's not too high-priced.

Sam Hee Jong. This is only for the more adventurous, because there are no English menus, although everyone at the restaurant is courteous and helpful. This is a famous *bul-googi* restaurant, and it's probably better here than anywhere else in Korea. If possible, go with another couple, but in any event, ask for a private room; your hotel can phone for the reservation and order your dinner. Don't be discouraged when you walk in, because the ground floor is very unprepossessing; it's nicer upstairs.

Whajung. The most luxurious oriental-style restaurant in the country, and quite appealing to tourists. You'll enjoy a meal here.

SHOPPING The souvenir situation is only fair in Seoul; don't expect to find anything like Tokyo or Hong Kong (with its almost limitless assortment of things to buy). However, there are a few goodies available.

POINTER:
Except in a few department stores, and also in the Tourists' Shopping Center, don't buy anything without bargaining. Prices are inevitably higher than the seller will accept, so spend a few minutes, and get the proper price.

First of all, head for the government-sponsored Tourists' Shopping Center, located near the Chosun Hotel. Here, under one roof, you'll find all of the local handicrafts at fairly reasonable prices, although slightly higher than if you bought them separately in individual stores—but if you want to ship your purchases home, one reliable place is your best bet. Buy here—at least the quality is good. *Lacquerware* articles are a big specialty, and although these are somewhat bulky, the Shopping Center will ship them directly to your home, which is a sensible idea. *Mother-of-pearl* articles are reasonably priced, if you happen to need mother-of-pearl articles, which is sometimes a doubtful proposition. The Koreans make lovely *cotton yard goods,* in a wide variety of colors and textures; these are used to make up into the native costumes, the *han-bok.* The *han-bok,* incidentally, makes an excellent housecoat, for at-home wear. They are very cheap, all things considered, and make a wonderful souvenir of your visit to Korea.

If you have a young girl on your shopping list, Korean *dolls* are exquisitely executed and don't weigh too much. There are much larger dolls, intended for decorative use, but these would positively have to be shipped home. *Brassware* is a great value here; you'll be astonished at the lovely work they do, particularly in relation to the low prices. Candlesticks are handsome, and so are the ashtrays. Brass trivets, for putting under hot dishes at the table, are most appealing and very inexpensive. Consider the *sin-sullo,* the Korean fire-pot described previously in the section on Food Specialties and Liquor; it costs about $25 in a good-sized version and sells in the U.S. for $85 or more. It's not only decorative, but very useful for serving hot food at the table.

Ceramics are a great specialty here; they are low-priced and attractive, but alas, they're too heavy and breakable for taking with you. Be sure to send them home, preferably insured. The Korean *kimchee* ceramic containers are ideal for plants or flowers when you get home. Several Hawaii hotels purchased hundreds of these brown pots and arranged them in their lobbies and rooms, filled with flowers and plants, for decorative effect.

If you know oriental *antiques,* you'll have a marvelous time. Korean antiques and artifacts may be found all over the market district, but these may not be authentic. Best head for what everyone calls "Antique Street" (its correct name is Gwanwoon-Dong, Chong-Ro), about three or four city blocks with antique shops irregularly positioned along both sides of the street. Look for articles from the Silla Dynasty, the most desirable period. If it's just some small souvenir antiques that you want, head for Insadong, popularly known to local residents as Mary's Alley (although taxi-drivers don't know it by this English name). You'll find a wide choice of small items, coins, figurines, etc., none too expensive. If you don't mind a 20-minute ride, head for Itaewon, a district which has some interesting antiques for sale. Wander about the area until you find a shop you like, or articles you're interested in. A reasonable amount of pleasant bargaining is expected, and you shouldn't pay the first price under any circumstances. If you plan to buy something expensive in the antique field, it might be advisable to check on whether or not there will be any difficulty in getting it out. And don't necessarily rely on what the antique dealer tells you, but have your hotel check with Korean customs.

Korean chests, often made of elm wood, are absolutely beautiful. To begin with, antiques are very, very expensive, and then there's the question of whether or not they can be shipped out of the country; inquire closely about this before swinging any deal. The most attractive of these chests are those formerly used by apothecaries, with dozens of small drawers and a Korean symbol on the outside of each section. The other style of chest has heavy brass work. These are reproductions of antiques, very handsome, and far less costly. You can see them in the shopping arcades of your hotel or at one of the department stores in their respective furniture sections, or in the area called Insadong, mentioned before. The best selection of chests, if you're seriously interested, is at a place called Gold House, located at 12, Insadong, Chongro-Ku.

In the *food* line there are two outstanding items. One is pine nuts, which are like what we call Indian nuts, except that Korean pine nuts are far, far larger, absolutely delicious, not inexpensive, and are only sold shelled—which may explain the high price. You can buy them in the food department of the Midopa department store, or for somewhat less money at the Eastgate Market, but remember to do a little bargaining. The other great item is dried mushrooms, which come in a considerable variety of types. They are moderately expensive, but just a few Korean mushrooms added to a casserole will improve the flavor enormously. They keep for years, particularly in a refrigerator. Be sure to wash them carefully before using, then let them soak in warm water for an hour so they can swell up in size.

If you enjoyed *ginseng tea,* why not buy a few packages to take home? They're generally available in groceries and department stores. While on the subject of department stores, you would probably enjoy walking through one or two—may I suggest the Shinsegsye and Midopa department stores. Wander through, and you'll probably buy a few oddities and local souvenirs, ideal for small gifts when you get home.

ENTERTAINMENT *Korea House* is maintained by the government as a hospitality center for foreign visitors. It consists of a number of different structures in traditional style, using old-style construction methods, that is, without nails, etc. There's a lovely garden, and the atmosphere is extremely pleasant. Performances of traditional folk dances and music are scheduled for every Saturday and Sunday afternoon from 3 to 4 P.M. There's no admission charge, and the whole affair is definitely worthwhile. Part of Korea House is a restaurant with a number of private rooms, intended mostly for groups of people. It has rather good food, all in all, graciously served.

The National Theater is sponsored by the government. It has its own cultural center and theater, a complex of 11 buildings southeast of Seoul's downtown area. It presents Korean mask plays, opera, ballet, modern plays, classics, and so forth. Inquire at your hotel and they'll tell you what's playing and usually the concierge can obtain tickets for you.

How about seeing a Korean *movie*? I've seen a few, and they're not too bad, and many are often definitely worthwhile. First of all, ask at your hotel desk if there's anything interesting playing. If the answer is affirmative, have them get you some reserved seats. Despite the language barrier, you'll see something of the life of the average Korean, because that's what most of the movies are all about.

Ask if there's a Korean *opera* playing, as they come and go irregularly. The costumes are absolutely fantastic, the plot confusing and involved, the singing not great—but it's all part of your education, and you owe yourself at least one Korean opera. If you don't like it, leave when you get tired; the investment in tickets is quite modest, so there's no great loss.

For bachelors only—there are numerous *kisaeng* houses; to be brief, the *kisaeng* is something like a *geisha* in Japan, but perhaps, shall we say delicately, more so. The *kisaeng* girls have dinner with their guests, dance for them, and with them. I'm not going to recommend any places, but figure the evening will cost at least $50 and maybe as much as $500 for a group. Inflation has really caught up with the *kisaeng* houses.

SPORTS   The center for all sporting facilities is Walker Hill, which has *tennis, swimming, boating,* and the like. The Seoul Country Club has a rather good *golf* course; ask at your hotel desk for arrangements to be made for you. If you enjoy *deep sea fishing,* it's fairly good off the island of Cheju, all the way south.

Short Trips From Seoul

If you aren't staying at the *Walker Hill* resort group of hotels, I think it would be pleasant to plan on spending an afternoon or evening there, driving out to see this interesting setup. If you wish, go in the late afternoon, and then stay for dinner and a show, either western-style at the Pacific Club or Korean-style at the Korean Restaurant.

However, far and away the most fascinating trip that any American can take is a visit to *Panmunjon,* scene of the border conferences between the United Nations Command and the Chinese and North Korean communists. The easiest way to visit the Panmunjon area is through the Korean Tourist Office, and on one of their official trips. They have desks in some of the tourist hotels, or you can reach them easily by telephone and arrange for the trip, which is moderately priced, and includes transportation and lunch in the price. The drive to Panmunjon takes about an hour plus a little more. However, close to military headquarters, there are many checkpoints where papers and permission will be closely scrutinized (be sure and bring your passport—it may be needed). Before leaving, be sure to ask about lunch, and find out if it will be available—if not, bring a box lunch and something to drink. You'll be shown the borderline, and various buildings occupied by the communists, and also those of the anti-communists, and through part of the demilitarized zone. All in all, for politically aware people, it's an exciting day.

Longer Trips From Seoul

If you really want to see what Korea was like more than 1,000 years ago, a trip to Kyongju is called for. Kyongju is located some 200 miles south of Seoul and can be reached in several ways: by private car; by train to Taegu (and then a bus or taxi to Kyongju); or best of all, by the express bus which makes the trip on the new superhighway from Seoul (continuing on to Pusan), and you can return by plane in the afternoon. I wouldn't recommend going in winter, but it's a marvelously interesting trip the remainder of the year. Kyongju was the capital of a great Korean kingdom which disappeared more than 1,000 years ago. It's basically a sleepy, provincial town, but it's much like an outdoor museum, filled with fantastic temples, tombs, relics, and reminders of the Silla Dynasty, covering the years 57 B.C. up to 935 A.D. Not only the town itself but also the five-mile by seven-mile area surrounding Kyongju was the headquarters for this ancient dynasty. Among the high spots are the famous tombs, some of which are almost 300 feet in diameter and 60 feet in height: the Pulguk-sa Temple, founded in 535 and the oldest Buddhist shrine in Korea; the Chumsungdae, a structure resembling a pagoda, dating back to 647, when it was used as an observatory. Especially interesting are the Silla bells, one of which was cast in 771 and weighs an unbelievable 158,000 pounds.

Kyongju has a most interesting National Museum, the second largest in the country. It's really quite magnificent, considering where it is, and that is said without being patronizing in the slightest degree. Even if you ordinarily avoid museums, you might make an exception and see this one.

Pulguk-sa is a living temple; that is, people come here reverently to pray even though it's also a destination for both Koreans and foreign tourists. Not very far from Pulguk-sa Temple is one of the most exciting attractions in the country—Sokkuram Grotto. It's only 5 miles by auto on a good road (but with a hundred or more curves) to reach Sokkuram, set in a very remote spot almost at the top of a mountain. The grotto, reached by a stone staircase which involves a 10-minute walk, has a fantastic seated Buddha, 11 feet in height. Sokkuram is not a natural grotto so much as a man-made one, consisting of hundreds of granite slabs arranged to form an artificial cave in a recess apparently cut into the mountainside some 1200 years ago.

There are no less than three modern, first-rate hotels at which to stay in the Kyongju area. They are the Kyongju-Bomun, the Cho-sun Bomun, and the Kyongju Tokyu Hotels. (Don't be surprised if they change their names in time; it's much too confusing at present.) Under construction in the area is an 18-hole championship golf course.

Pusan (or is it Busan?) is the second largest city in Korea, located in the southern part of the country. Before you begin to wonder whether or not I don't know how to spell and am confused about Pusan and Busan, just remember that the Korean language is quite different from ours. They have a sound in their language which is similar to, but yet quite different from, our letter "p." To many people the sound is as much like "b" as it is like "p," and as a result, the city's name is actually a cross between Pusan and Busan. However, since our alphabet lacks a sound to duplicate precisely this cross, you can only make a choice of one spelling or the other. For the sake of this discussion, we'll call it Pusan, but don't be surprised if it occasionally appears on maps or elsewhere as Busan.

Anyhow, Pusan (right?) has increased its size by 600 percent within the past 30 years and seems to be growing even more rapidly these days. Pusan means, if you really must know, "cauldron mountain," although exactly what that means I really couldn't say. Anyhow, there are plenty of hot springs in the area, and perhaps the name has reference to those places which might fancifully resemble a cauldron. (Enough of that.) The giant city has slightly more than 2 million inhabitants; since there are comparatively few in the way of high rise buildings around, you might be confused into thinking there are far fewer people living here. It has much milder weather than Seoul, which means the winter months are just lovely (although cool) as a rule, and the summer months are ideal for swimming at one of the many beaches in the general area of Pusan. If you want to stay in Pusan, you have a choice of the Commodore Dynasty, the Pusan Hotel or the Pusan Plaza Hotel, all of which are fairly small, with about 130 rooms each. The Pusan Hotel is better suited for Americans, because the Plaza has rather small rooms. Actually, the ideal place to stay in this area is the Chosun Beach Hotel, with 350 rooms, and related to the Chosun Hotel in Seoul. It's on Haeundae Beach, about a half hour from downtown Seoul, and combines the advantages of a resort with the convenience of being close to Pusan. This is the best place in the Pusan area, without the slightest doubt.

Some of the regular sightseeing includes a visit to a giant observation tower, for which there is an admission charge; from the top there's a spectacular view of the city and surrounding waters. If you don't mind getting up in the early morning, head for the Pusan Fish Market, which extends from City Hall to the Pusan Train Station. The scene is one of great life with plenty of local color as the fish are auctioned off. It's very diverting, but you had better like fish and also not mind the smell or the entire trip will be wasted. In a completely different and very serene vein is a visit to Beomeo-sa Temple located on the slopes of Mount Geumjeong. Beomeo-sa Temple is also called Pomosa Temple and is a complex of buildings going back originally to the 4th century, though the present buildings are only about 350 years old; some people say they were constructed later, but who knows? I should warn you that autos cannot go up the full distance to the Temple, and you must walk for about a half hour. Not far away is a zoo and botanical garden, and from this general area you can take a cable car up some 5,300 feet to the top of Mount Geumjeong; a walk of about 20 minutes takes you to the Castle which has been partly restored and is quite interesting. Also, I should mention that there's a United Nations Memorial Cemetery, about 5 miles to the northeast of Pusan, containing the graves of about 2,000 soldiers who died in the Korean War.

On a more cheerful note, may I suggest that the nicest thing you can do in Pusan is to wander about the downtown area of the city on your own two feet, without a guide, a tour leader, or a car. (If you lose your sense of direction, just hail a cab and ride back to your hotel.) There are several main streets which are quite interesting, and you'll surely enjoy walking in and out of shops, perhaps buying houses, restaurants, and so forth. Have a meal in one of them; you can always order *bul-googi,* a great Korean dish of strips of beef which you personally cook over a charcoal fire. It may be smoky, but the food is delicious and inexpensive.

One final thought: an interesting place to shop is the Gugjae or International market, which is worthwhile even if you don't have any particular items in mind, but just want to look.

Cheju Island is located south of the main portion of South Korea, some 60 or so miles off the mainland. The Korean airline makes the trip daily (about $35 round trip). There's an excellent place to stay called the Cheju KAL Hotel; it has pleasant rooms, some facing the sea, and the food is rather good. Accommodations are good at the Sogwipo Tourist Hotel, well-situated amidst magnificent scenery. Korean Airlines has built an 18-story, 300-room hotel on the north side of the island. It's not precisely a luxury hotel, but the accommodations are just one step below that, say first-class. This is a remote region, about as untouristy as anyone can get, and is recommended only for those who don't mind the simple life, can do without elaborate accommodations, and are quite self-sufficient. I do not mean to imply that you will be living in rough fashion out of tin cans; far from it. The island is partly tropical, with lovely fruit groves and plant life, and very green most of the year. The sightseeing highspots are the scores of women divers who may be seen making dives off various points along the coast in search of shellfish and edible seaweed. There are family groups, sometimes running into three generations and consisting of grandmother, mother, and daughter. The whole island, incidentally, is female-dominated, and there is an apparent surplus of women, men being in the great minority. Cheju Island has good beaches, lots of greenery, plenty of scenery, and women all over the landscape. Bring a good windbreaker or coat—there are lots of offshore winds.

They have a saying here that Cheju is known for three things: rocks, women, and wind. To that trio should be added mushrooms, a great specialty of Cheju. In addition to eating them, you can buy a package of the enormous, dried mushrooms which are a great specialty of the island; they're delicious when used in cooking. Oh yes, about the wind; if you look, you'll probably see any number of thatched-roof houses roped down to keep them from flying away during one of Cheju's regular windstorms.

TAIWAN

👫 Background

Long before recorded time, primitive tribesmen inhabited an island situated to the east of the China coast; it was a lovely, comparatively small stretch of land measuring about 90 miles wide and 230 miles long. The tribal aborigines, many of whom still remain, were a fierce group, but Chinese explorers and settlers finally obtained a foothold several thousand years ago, and became firmly established on the island. The aborigines finally withdrew away from the coast to their own regions in the interior, and the Chinese took over control and government of the island, and that was that.

During the 16th century, the Portuguese (who were everywhere in the Orient during that period) "discovered"—if that is the correct and patronizing word—the island, which they called *Ilha Formosa*, or Beautiful Island. As time went on, it became known simply as Formosa. The Chinese were surprisingly slow to defend their interests, and the Portuguese staked a claim to a portion of the island; they in turn were followed by the Dutch. In 1661, an adventurous Chinese patriot (or pirate, depending upon your point of view) named Koxinga defeated the unwanted foreigners and modestly declared himself king of the island. Shortly thereafter, the Chinese annexed the island as a part of the mainland nation, and it became known once again as Taiwan (meaning Terraced Bay). In 1895, the Japanese defeated the Chinese, annexed Taiwan, and held it until 1945 when the Japanese, in turn, were defeated by the Allies, or was it by the Americans?

In December 1978, the U.S. recognized the People's Republic of China, and in so doing, also severed ties with Taiwan, something the local people resented greatly. They quite logically said that it went back on U.S. commitments to them. But that's the way it is, and Taiwan is in the strange position of being there but not being recognized by the U.S., although trade and educational projects are still continuing.

Although it is possible for Americans to visit mainland China, only a very small number have done so. Taiwan, therefore, offers an excellent chance for curious Americans. This is a rare opportunity to see Chinese culture, Chinese life, Chinese people—all within the scope of the free world. There are good, often excellent hotels, a pleasant atmosphere, and as for the food—if you like Chinese food, you'll be able to experiment with the cuisine of a dozen different provincial styles.

You will enjoy meeting the Taiwan Chinese, there is fair shopping to be had, the scenery is lovely (occasionally exciting), but . . . and now we come to the final point, don't expect to find another Bangkok, Tokyo, or Hong Kong. Taipei, the capital city of Taiwan, just isn't that sort of place, pleasant though it may be. It lacks the modern skyscrapers of Tokyo and Hong Kong, and the shopping bargains are far more limited. Nor will the traveler find the exotic quality of Bangkok, with its distinctive, rather exciting personality. Nonetheless, Taiwan has its charm for those who accept it for what it is—a lovely place with quite a lot to see and do, reasonably colorful, but still best suited for the tourist who can live without nightclubs, not that Taipei doesn't have one.

❧ When to Go

It may come as a surprise, but Taiwan is a subtropical country, with a rather limited winter season, usually brief and quite mild, and a very long summer. The very best months are surely March through May, and also October and November; these spring and fall months are usually beautiful, with clear lovely days. The "rainy" season starts in late November and runs through to part of February. July, August, and September are inevitably quite hot and humid, and furthermore these are the typhoon months, when heavy three- or four-day storms may come out of the south and bring considerable rain. For the winter months, occasional chilly days can be expected, but a light coat should be sufficient.

Weather Strip: Taipei

	Jan.	Feb.	Mar.	Apr.	May	June	July	Aug.	Sept.	Oct.	Nov.	Dec.
Average daily high	66°	65°	70°	77°	83°	89°	92°	91°	88°	81°	75°	69°
Average daily low	54°	53°	57°	63°	69°	73°	76°	75°	73°	67°	62°	57°
Monthly rainfall	3.4	5.3	7.0	6.7	9.1	11.4	9.1	12.0	9.6	4.8	2.6	2.8
Number of days with 0.04 inches of rainfall	9	13	12	14	12	13	10	12	10	9	7	8

♠ Visa Requirements

A visa is required; when issued it's valid for a visit of 30 days and may be used again for up to 4 years from the date of the visa.

♠ Customs

You'll be allowed a carton of cigarettes or 25 cigars for each person. They will probably make you exhibit, and fill out forms about, transistor radios in your possession, and then never ask about them when you leave, but better hold on to the certificate anyhow —you never know. If you have cameras or a typewriter with you, better declare them when entering, because it may facilitate departure.

♥ Health

Don't dare to drink the tap water; that would really be inviting trouble. In turn, that brings up the problem about brushing one's teeth with tap water—yes or no? Use your own judgment, and if you do brush and then rinse with tap water, for heaven's sake, make an effort not to swallow any. Personally, I would suggest some bottled water; since mineral water is rare, you may have to use club soda, Coca-Cola or the like. O.K., so I'm overly cautious, but when I'm on vacation, I don't want to be laid up for even a minute. On the other hand, the milk situation is very good. Milk is usually pasteurized, and is bottled by California's Foremost Dairies. For this reason, their cheese and ice cream are safe to eat. Fresh fruits are all right, providing they have outer skins, like oranges, pineapple, and watermelon. I wouldn't eat raw vegetables except at the Grand Hotel, which is fastidiously careful with them. But remember—don't drink the tap water. That means no water when in a restaurant, so be prepared to drink coffee, tea, soda, rice wine, beer or anything, but not water. The health situation in Taiwan is generally quite good; for entry, you need only the usual smallpox vaccination certificate. Every once in a while, when there is a cholera outbreak in some part of Asia, a cholera shot may be required if you're coming from that general area. Play it safe, I say, and have a cholera shot before you go.

⏲ Time

There is a 16-hour time differential between Taiwan and the west coast of the U.S. When it's 12 noon in Taipei on Monday, it's 8 P.M. on Sunday in Los Angeles. That makes it 11 P.M. in New York, because there's a 3-hour difference between the west and east coasts.

💲 Currency

The local money is called the *Taiwan dollar,* written, for example, $50 NT, meaning New Taiwan. The rates have varied considerably during the past few years, and a currency equivalent is not possible at this time. When entering, the customs will give you a currency slip, on which all transactions exchanging American money into Taiwan money must be recorded; if you have any Taiwan money left over when departing, it can be reconverted into U.S. dollars, but you'll need the currency form.

🌐 Price Level

It is a distinct pleasure to report that prices are in the medium-low category, thus making everything just that more enjoyable. There are exceptions of course. Deluxe hotel rooms, while not so expensive as in some other cities of the Orient, are still not exactly cheap. Meal prices are very fair, all things considered. You shouldn't find food prices high unless you order some very special dishes such as sharks' fin or birds' nest soups, or perhaps camphor-smoked duck. You'll find that you're spending about half or possibly two-thirds of what you would spend in Tokyo. Out in the countryside, prices are even lower.

🍎 Tipping

Every hotel and restaurant adds a 10% service charge, so no additional tipping is necessary, with a few exceptions. The porter who carries your baggage should get the equivalent of 20¢-25¢ a bag. Your roomboy is also entitled to something if he has been particularly helpful; give him the equivalent of about a dollar a day when you leave. Otherwise, the tipping situation here is still quite unspoiled, and tips should only be given for special services, and then with moderation.

🏃 Transportation

Taxis are quite plentiful, and there are always a few around the hotels; rates at present are about as reasonable as you can expect, verging on being an outright bargain. Large taxis are somewhat more expensive. The taxidriver should be given some odd change for a tip, if you wish. Don't worry about the problem of finding transportation back to your hotel after having had dinner out. When your meal is finished, merely tell the waiter that you want a taxi, and he'll get one for you.

The local *railroad* is quite good, providing you ride the express trains; the locals are definitely not recommended. The crack train is air-conditioned, and makes the Taipei-Taichung run of 125 miles in under 3 hours, and the fare is just a matter of a few dollars.

Domestic *airplane* service within Taiwan is completely satisfactory, and the planes operated by the Civil Air Transport (CAT) are pleasant to ride. To give you an idea of the rates, from Taipei to Taichung the fare is very reasonably priced and takes 45 minutes; from Taipei to Hualien, the fare and time are almost identical.

A *private car* may be hired at fairly reasonable rates, including a driver (something that's recommended). There are no *drive-your-self* services available (as yet) in Taiwan, and unless you read Chinese, it would probably be difficult to follow the road signs, although there are occasional ones in English.

✊ Airport and Tourist Taxes

Taipei Taoyuan International Airport is located 18 miles southwest of Taipei; allow about 35 minutes' travel time to reach the airport under normal circumstances. Taoyuan Airport is reached by way of the main north-south freeway that connects Tapei and Kaohsiung; the road is excellent, but can be very busy at certain times of the day.

Sung Shan Airport (used for local flights) is located only 2½ miles from the center of Taipei; allow about 15 minutes travel time.

There is an airport departure tax.

▌▌ Communications

Airmail letters to the U.S. take about 5 days, and not infrequently, a little longer. If you want to use the airmail form, an *aerogram,* which is usually available at the hotel desk, costs about half as much. Don't send cards or letters by surface mail (although much cheaper), unless you don't care if it takes 6 weeks to reach its destination.

Your hotel can place *overseas phone calls* to the States, but remember the time differential when you're placing your call; however, it's not all that simple, because circuits are not always available just when you want to place your call. Figure in the neighborhood of $15 U.S. for a 3-minute call to your home town.

Cable service is first-rate, although expensive. Straight messages, sent without delay, are about 50¢ (U.S.) a word, plus tax; however, delayed messages are considerably less expensive.

⚡ Electricity

The current throughout the island is 100 volts A.C., which is ideal for American appliances. The electric power may fail in the country areas once in a while (for minutes at a time) for unexpected reasons, or it may go off during rainy weather, but this is rare in Taipei. Exception: during the typhoon season, when a real humdinger of a storm is underway, the current may be deliberately turned off all day long (sometimes two days) until the storm has passed. This is precautionary, in order to prevent fires.

✕ Food Specialties and Liquor

If you are an enthusiastic admirer of Chinese cooking, you'll be absolutely delighted in Taiwan. Although you may have thought that you knew something about the range of Chinese dishes, a surprise (very pleasant, indeed) awaits you if you are even slightly curious, culinarily speaking. There are interesting dishes to try, Chinese provincial cuisines to sample, but of course, it's up to you. In a restaurant, explain to the owner or waiter that you want to try some unusual preparations, because otherwise you will get the usual sweet-and-sour pork, egg rolls, and fried rice routine, which you could get back home. This is particularly true in the large tourist hotels, where everything is toned down to satisfy the incurious tourist. Western-style food is served at every large hotel throughout the island, and is certainly passable, if not distinguished. Be sure to order only simple western dishes, because the more complicated preparations are inevitably disappointing.

But why come to Taiwan without sampling the wide range of fine Chinese dishes, almost unbelievable in scope and variety, and just incidentally, at very fair (low) prices? Most Americans are very fond of Chinese food, as indicated by the enormous number of these restaurants to be found in even the smallest towns of our country. In general, however, it must be agreed that except in New York and San Francisco, the selection of Chinese dishes available is quite limited. This has been brought about because almost all of our Chinese restaurants were operated by chefs who came from Canton, a province of southern China. (For comparison, imagine that all of the American restaurants in Taipei were operated by American southerners, and featured only southern specialities like spoon bread, corn pone and pecan pie!) Here is a rarely encountered opportunity to dine upon the tremendous range of dishes from central, northern, and western China. Actually, it is a priceless opportunity for the curious gourmet.

But first, a few words about the difference between western-style food and the Chinese cuisine. China, basically a poor and over-populated country, has had a continuing food problem, and the native cuisine has been built, of necessity, upon large quantities of low cost, satisfying, filling food (such as rice and noodles), flavored with just an ounce or two of meat, poultry or fish. No cook could possibly expect to have an entire roast beef, or a whole chicken with which to prepare a family dinner; a few ounces of meat or poultry would have to serve for an entire family. The necessary bulk, as previously mentioned, had to come from quantities of rice, noodles, or perhaps vegetables. Therefore, no matter what Chinese dish is ordered, it will almost invariably consist chiefly of a satisfying, filling base, plus whatever more expensive ingredients are added for flavoring. But because Chinese chefs are extraordinarily inventive and skillful, the cuisine consists of literally thousands of different dishes, and the food is inevitably delicious.

Also worthy of mention is the Chinese custom of never using knives and forks, their preference being for chopsticks. All food is cut into rather small, bite-sized pieces, small enough to be conveyed to the mouth by means of chopsticks. Generally, meat is cut into small cubes, measuring about a half-inch. The custom is that all dishes ordered are served at the same time, which explains the practice of serving food in covered dishes, to keep them warm. In addition, most Chinese people prefer to eat the best dishes first (why fill up on things you don't like?), followed by the secondary dishes, and then conclude with soup. Desserts are unimportant, and may consist only of a little preserved fruit or a cooky. The only suitable cold beverage with Chinese food is beer, and it may accompany almost any dish. In China, tea is served at the beginning and conclusion of a repast as a rule, although it is frequently served throughout the meal to westerners, who seem to prefer it with the food. Tourists may be interested in sampling some of the Chinese wines; they are almost all slightly sweet and somewhat yellow in color. You might like them, or then again, you might not. Wines are often served hot, but personally, I think most Americans would enjoy them better when chilled. Chinese wines usually are made from rice, but also from grapes.

It seems almost ridiculous to attempt to list the wide range of dishes which the Taipei restaurants serve. Many of them have menus the size of a small book, listing many hundreds of different dishes. Some are the kind anyone might enjoy (like chicken prepared with mushrooms in parchment paper), and range all the way down the scale to such exotic dishes as pig's liver with bamboo shoots (which most Americans would automatically shy away from).

Don't, please, order the first group of dishes that sound slightly familiar. Take the trouble to read through the menu, and then make your selections. If you need additional time, order a few appetizers and then spend the next five minutes in perusing the menu carefully. Order some dishes you have never tried before that sound interesting but not necessarily outlandish. Inasmuch as Taiwan food is so good, you will invariably be served with something enjoyable. It is best to have at least four people along, because the proper way to sample the seemingly limitless range of Chinese food is by ordering a wide variety of different dishes. However, even two people should order at least three or four main courses, and share them.

While in Taipei, try some of the other regional culinary styles. For example, if you like spicy food, try a Szechuan restaurant. Peking-style restaurants feature duck dishes, fish in sweet-and-sour sauce, and spring rolls (which we sometimes call egg rolls). Shanghai food is noted for its excellent preparations of shellfish and noodles. (You might also read the section on Food Specialities in the Hong Kong section for more details.)

If you have a real curiosity about the local food and the cooking style, head for Nanking Road, where there's a "food circle." Here you'll find about 50 small restaurants doing business under one roof. To eat or not to eat? That is the question, and I think perhaps not, although sometimes the temptation is nearly irresistible. Even though I rarely eat anything here, I can watch with fascination for quite long periods, the range and skill of the various chefs, and the dishes requested by their patrons.

∞ Time Evaluation

If you come for only 2 days, you'll be quite rushed and be able to spend 1 day around Taipei, and the other flying down to see the Taroko Gorge. However, this assumes 2 full and complete days; for example, arriving Wednesday morning and departing Friday evening. It would be much better to plan on a minimum of 3 days, if you want to relax and enjoy this lovely island. For those who want to spend a day or so at the Sun-Moon Lake, an additional 2 or 3 days would have to be included.

🏛 Capital City: Taipei

Taipei (pronounced Tie-pay), the capital of Taiwan (pronounced Tie-one), is not a charming, lovely, or handsome city to wander through, if you are looking for natural beauty or a lovely setting. The capital is situtated on flat ground, there is a paucity of important buildings or striking architectural treats, and even the temples are few and far between. Street scenes are lively, and there is considerable color in the marketplace, but Taipei is disappointing, and there can be no denying that simple fact. The city is set up on a simple grid pattern, with most streets crossing each other at right angles, and the overall effect is somewhat less than exhilarating; if the signs were not in Chinese, with some English ones intermixed, it would rather closely resemble a town in the mid-west. Most buildings are two and three stories tall, with shops on the ground floor, and offices above, the whole affair hardly conducive to much that will excite the tourist's mind. Of course, there are more and more tall buildings being constructed, making the city look even more Western.

And yet, although difficult to relate, Taipei has a certain elusive something, rather difficult to put into words, but quite perceptible to the senses, at least to a sixth sense. Although mainland China is now open to American visitors, this is actually China, wide open to view, for the vast majority of American tourists. Or is it, purely and simply, the friendly feeling all around him, the unspoken but obvious atmosphere of welcome, a place where Americans are really liked? Whatever the reason, Taipei is a pleasant place, definitely worthy of a visit, with the understanding that the city in and of itself will not charm or beguile the eye and mind of the beholder.

Allow about a half-day for Taipei sightseeing. The travel agencies and hotels have trips arranged around the town on both a half-day and all-day basis; figure about $5 for the half-day and about $8 for the entire day, but personally, I think a half-day is sufficient for Taipei itself: make it a full day, if you want to spend several hours at the National Palace Museum. Here are the highspots:

The *National Palace Museum* is something bordering on the unbelievable, and may, in and of itself, constitute a very good reason for visiting Taipei in the first place. It houses the fantastic Palace Collection, consisting of major Chinese antiquities, displayed in eye-catching and, indeed, fantastic fashion. Even for those to whom museums are ordinarily a bore, I have no hesitation in recommending this marvelous museum. Most of the nation's national treasures are displayed here at one time or another, although the collection is so vast that only a portion can be shown at any one time. The collection is changed from time to time, so that a dozen visits, over a period of several years, would be required to see it all.

The museum, which opened in 1965, combines Chinese palace architecture with more modern design. It is built against a forested area of a suburb of north Taipei called Waishuanghsi (sorry, that's the name). The museum can only display about 3,000 exhibits at a time, but the total collection (held in storage) amounts to a staggering 300,000 art objects, believe it or not! There are rooms devoted to prehistoric stone objects, religious implements, jade and bronze art items, paintings, pottery, and so on, representing a collection put together by various Chinese emperors over a period of many centuries. The Palace Museum is open daily from 9 A.M. to 5 P.M. (although no one is admitted after 4:30) and there's a small admission charge. There are guided tours in English at 10 A.M. and 3 P.M. (but verify, because these may be changed). Incidentally, cameras are not permitted within the museum; refreshments and lunch are available.

Lung Shan Temple is believed to be the oldest Buddhist temple in the city, although it has been rebuilt a few times since its original construction in 1738. It is an attractive building, well-executed, and warrants a half-hour of wandering about, picture-taking and the like. Allow a little extra time when planning to visit the Temple, because there is a rather interesting marketplace across the street, an intricate maze of tiny shops.

The *Grand Hotel,* if you aren't staying there, is a prime sightseeing highlight, believe it or not. If you're stopping at the hotel, be sure to take a little time and wander through its three sections, beginning with the Golden Dragon, and then to the Jade Phoenix, and finally, the newer Unicorn section. In its own parklike district, the Grand Hotel is situated on a small hill that was formerly a Japanese Shinto shrine.

The fourth sightseeing "must" is the *Confucian Shrine;* this is an interesting building, which looks like, but is not, a temple. The reason: Confucianism is not precisely a religion, but a way of life. When you drive up to the shrine, don't be surprised if the main gate is closed; it always is, except on September 28 (Confucius' birthday). The side gate is open, however. If you can manage to get to Taipei on September 27, your hotel or travel agency can make special arrangements for you to see the elaborate, very exciting ceremony to honor the great philosopher. BUT, and we warn you, the ceremony starts at 4:30 A.M. Nevertheless, you will see something unique in your lifetime, and to be in Taipei on September 27 and not attend the birthday ceremonies would be a serious mistake. Even if you like to sleep late, it would be a mistake.

If you go on an organized tour, you (probably) will also be shown several more temples, which is all right if you want to see several more temples, but rather repetitious and not worth getting out to visit. You'll also be shown the Government Guest House (who cares?), the Presidential Palace (which looks like a large, dull building, and is), several mediocre statues, the National Science Hall, and various other sightseeing fillers. There is a very good Botanical Garden, however, which will be interesting to amateur gardeners, and the local zoo isn't too bad either, if you're staying a week or so; otherwise, devote your time to more serious activities, like shopping or especially eating and drinking. There is even a live-snake place, the Saimentin Snake Shop, if you don't automatically shudder at the sight of them. (I know, I know, they're immaculately clean and many of them are man's best friend, and they eat the local pests and help farmers, and all of that. I still can work up no enthusiasm whatsoever for them.)

After dinner, you will certainly find it amusing and worth your while to head for a place called The Circle, located at the far end of Nan King West Road. Here is Taipei's leading night market, with hundreds of small stalls selling food and merchandise. In the general area, there are any number of bars, theatres, nightclubs, and small shops. It's always lively and stimulating in The Circle area. You also might want to visit one of the famous theatre-restaurants, where you dine while watching a very good, long show. Usually, there's an early evening show at about 6:30 or 7 P.M., and then another somewhat shorter show starting at either 9 or 10 P.M., depending upon the starting time of the first show.

ACCOMMODATIONS   The choice of hotels is nothing short of excellent, and that's more than you can say for many places. To begin with, the Grand Hotel is something unique, more or less in a class by itself for local atmosphere and architecture. The Hilton is top-notch in the same way that Hiltons are all over the world. The President and Ambassador Hotels are completely first-class, and tend to be slightly less expensive than the first two hotels. Incidentally, rates in Taipei, on the average, are somewhat lower than in Tokyo or Hong Kong.

Grand Hotel. This is truly a unique hotel. The older portion has some old-fashioned but modernized rooms, although one section, the Unicorn, is particularly fine. There's also a 12-story, 500-room extension to the older portion of the hotel. The high-rise section includes the famous red columns, gold trim, and upswept roof style of palace architecture. The Grand has an assortment of restaurants, a nightclub, tennis courts, a fantastic pool, and a large shopping arcade. It is on a hill, somewhat outside of downtown Taipei.

Hilton International Taipei. A large, attractive hotel with 525 well-decorated rooms, in a particularly convenient location, ideal for shopping and walking. Rates are medium-high. There are numerous restaurants featuring Chinese, Japanese and international food, a Chinese night club, a health club with Japanese bath, sauna, etc. An excellent Hilton in a fine location.

Taipei Regency. An architecturally remarkable hotel, with a 15-story high atrium lobby. There are 450 rooms, furnished well, with refrigerator and color TV. Quite a few different restaurants, many shops. A little bit out of the main part of town, but not too far.

Ritz. A 283-room hotel, with pleasant rooms. There are many foreign restaurants, numerous shops. The hotel's decor is quite interesting and rather attractive.

Lai Lai Shangri-La. An 800-room hotel located in downtown Taipei. Rather nice, medium-sized rooms, all with color TV. Many restaurants, large shopping arcade.

Century Plaza Hotel. A Del Webb operation, this is an 11-story hotel, with 250 rooms. The guest rooms are somewhat on the small side, although reasonably attractive in appearance. There are numerous restaurants, a sauna, rooftop garden, meeting halls, and so forth, making it suitable for groups. The rates tend to be much more moderate than at the hotels listed above.

President Hotel. A large (400-room) hotel located on a side street a few minutes away from the central business area, and not too inconveniently located. The rooms are fair in size, although not too large, and everything is quite modern; centrally air-conditioned.

Taipei Miramar. An absolutely first-class hotel with 584 rooms, in a rather good location. The lobby is well decorated, as are the rooms. There are a number of restaurants, plenty of shops, and the hotel is well run.

Ambassador. A 500-room hotel situated on a busy, heavily trafficked main street; however, because of the central air conditioning, this problem is minimized. Rooms are rather pleasant, and it's an extremely convenient hotel.

San Polo. In a convenient location, this 456-room hotel is surrounded by office buildings and department stores. Moderate rates.

Mandarin. A new, quite large hotel not too far from the airport, but some distance from downtown Taipei. Good rooms, several restaurants, Chinese entertainment at night, swimming pool. In a residential area.

Shih-men Sesame. This is Taiwan's leading resort hotel, located 33 miles southwest of Taipei, and not far from the airport. It is adjacent to the Shih-men Reservoir, is 8 stories high with 235 rooms, and has a giant swimming pool area. Numerous restaurants. Fishing in the reservoir is permitted.

POINTER:
For some reason, restaurants come and go faster in Taiwan than almost anywhere else in the world. On one visit a particular restaurant may be jammed with patrons and a year later may have disappeared and be completely out of business. For this reason, it is always advisable to check and see if the particular place is still operating.

RESTAURANTS As mentioned in the section on Food Specialties and Liquor, the western food in Taiwan is certainly adequate, wholesome, and unimaginative in the style of hotels around the world. So, if you insist on eating the same food you do at home, rest assured that you will never go hungry. There is no point in listing western-style restaurants, inasmuch as none of them is better than the other to any noticeable extent. The regular restaurants at the Grand, Hilton, Ambassador, and President hotels are quite similar, and it might be interesting to try them all on successive occasions.

But the curious gourmet will have the time of his life in Taipei. Here, in one city, are gathered the culinary artists, the great chefs, and food in abundance, and what a marvelous opportunity to eat the many delicious specialties of the provinces of China! To say the opportunity is unparalleled is to say the obvious; on top of everything, prices are quite moderate, and the food is superb. If you have never eaten real Chinese food (and I am skipping for the moment such routine clichés of ordinary Chinese restaurants as chow mein, egg drop soup, and egg rolls), you will be astonished, perhaps even floored, by the variety, the scope, and the imagination of Chinese cookery as practiced in Taipei.

SHANGHAI-STYLE: These restaurants feature well-seasoned dishes with emphasis on seafood, meat, and poultry preparations.

January. Located on the second floor, this large restaurant has many excellent dishes on its large menu; many seafood specialties.

NORTH CHINA: A novelty to most Americans, for there are very few of them to be found in the United States. The cuisine of North China features noodles, chicken, and eel.

Shan Si. Situated at 83 Yengping South Road, an unassuming restaurant but one that specializes in excellent food as its main attraction. Order their noodles, in four different styles; or the eel, served in four different fashions. Don't overlook their chicken with green peas, or their mushrooms and boneless fish.

Tung Sheng Lou. At 79 Chung Hsiao West Road, this is a popular, down-to-earth place, with little in the way of decor. The food is fantastically good however, with excellent crab preparations, fish dishes, etc. Not too expensive, and don't order before you study their long menu.

SZECHUAN-STYLE: A cuisine of China which has become very popular in some cities of the U.S. but which most Americans hardly know. The method of preparing duck is perhaps their culinary highpoint. Many dishes are rather spicy, but not unbearably so; if in doubt, ask them to tone down the hot peppers.

Rong Shing. Most people regard this as the best Szechuan restaurant in town; I agree. The great specialty here is smoked duck, absolutely delicious; the smoking is done with tea leaves, camphor wood, and spices. Dried beef with peppers is worth trying, too.

Omei. Almost on a par with Rong Shing, this very good restaurant has excellent food, often somewhat spicy. Ask if they have Royal Princess chicken on the menu; highly recommended.

Szechuan Restaurant. On the 12th floor of the Ambassador Hotel, this restaurant features mostly spicy dishes. The food is generally quite good on all counts.

Taton Restaurant. Located at 2 Nanking E Road, Sec 3, of Taipei, this has become recognized as another outstanding Szechuan restaurant, with a most interesting menu.

HUNAN-STYLE: Mix together the styles of many provinces, add a touch of spice (as they do in Szechuan) and come up with an excellent provincial cuisine, one of the most interesting of all.

Golden China. On the 3rd floor of the Taipei Hilton Hotel, this is almost certainly the best Hunan-style restaurant in Taipei. An enormous choice, with everything ordered almost certain to be first class.

A great many comparatively new restaurants have come to the fore and are highly regarded on the local restaurant scene. I should like to call your attention to the following:

Apollo Revolving Lounge. On the 14th floor of the Central Hotel, the Apollo features Cantonese cooking; it's particularly interesting at lunchtime when the restaurant serves *dim sum.*

Golden Palace. On the 2nd floor of the Sesame Hotel, this is an excellent place for Cantonese food.

Hoover Theater Restaurant. For those who want a rather elaborate show combined with a Cantonese-style meal, the Hoover is worth a trip. The show usually starts at 7:30 PM.

Roma Steak House. In the Roma Hotel, this restaurant specializes in steaks, which are quite good. They feature a double chateaubriand, which is fine for two people.

Trader's Grill. Situated on the 2nd floor of the Taipei Hilton, this has become a leading Continental restaurant; the cuisine features mostly French food, and is rather good.

SHOPPING   In all likelihood, before coming to Taiwan you've been to either Hong Kong or Tokyo and shopped quite a bit. However, Taiwan is fast becoming an excellent place to buy manufactured goods, such as radios, computers, etc. The three leading shops are government-approved department stores—Far Eastern, Shin Shin, and Today's. Prices are definitely fixed, the stores are reliable, and you can count on getting anything they ship. Stores generally remain open until 10 P.M.

What about bargaining? In the Chinese Handicraft Mart (government operated), the answer is a simple no; elsewhere, in general, a slight amount of reasonable, gentle bargaining is in order, with a saving of about 10% or so, seldom more. Don't be too adamant, too firm, or too decisive in your bargaining, and don't say "take it or leave it," because most shopkeepers aren't equipped to receive an ultimatum and will merely look surprised, unless they're out to unload a piece of junk on you, in which case they'll accept your final offer. Be gentle and discuss the price softly and with a smile; it usually works. Now, an exception: when buying antiques or articles without a usual, or standard, price, some firm bargaining (with a smile or two) is in order. This is one type of purchase in which a good deal of (good-natured) bargaining is definitely in order, and you should get about a third off from the original asking price.

Taiwan does good work in *brassware;* there are candlesticks, ashtrays, trivets, dinner bells, cigarette boxes, and the like, and I would say that prices are about 40% of what they are in the U.S. But, of course, brassware is heavy, so if you buy a good deal, have it sent to you. *Lacquerware* is excellent; there are low-priced bowls, boxes, and miscellaneous articles. Just the opposite of brassware, lacquerware is very light, but bulky, so use your own judgment. The *embroidery* was well made in Taiwan, what I saw of it, but I didn't buy any because the designs looked old-fashioned; perhaps they'll improve. There's *bambooware* all over the place, but the handsomest bamboo articles in sight, in my opinion, are the ladies' handbags; very, very reasonably priced. *Wood carvings,* skillfully executed, make excellent souvenirs; the small ones are easily portable, but larger carvings would have to be shipped home. The *dolls,* in native costumes, are ideal gifts for any little girls on your list; older girls like them, too, if you know what we mean by older. *Decorative screens* are very attractive, oriental-style of course, and are unexcelled for covering or blocking the view of your kitchen door back home, or serving as a room divider. Last on this list is *ramie fiber rugs,* which are exceptionally beautiful and may be purchased in a wide variety of colors and patterns; no use going into prices for these, because they vary greatly according to dimensions, design, etc.

All of the above articles are best purchased at either the Handicraft Promotion Center (run by the government) or—a private enterprise—the Taipei Handicraft Center. Prices are similar in both establishments, but may vary slightly from one to the other depending upon the particular item involved. I can only suggest that, if in doubt, you shop both stores.

You might find it very interesting to do some shopping at the Chunghua Emporium, consisting of 8 buildings in downtown Taipei joined together to form the longest bazaar in the Orient. You'll find an absolutely fascinating assortment of junk and treasures, and offhand it's difficult to think of a place with more local color.

Did you know that until recently Taiwan did not have a real copyright law, and that *books and phonograph records* were copied here, without paying any royalties to the author or publishers involved? Well, sir, this led to some interesting situations. Various reference books, popular novels, and the like were pirated by photographing the pages, blocking out the publisher's name, and selling them at a mere fraction of their American prices. Recently published novels, retailing at $6 a copy in New York, were selling for $1.25 in the pirated edition. The large Columbia Encyclopedia was selling at a list price of $11 in Taiwan, a small fraction of its American price. Many dictionaries, including the Webster, were less than a third of the U.S. price. Some of these books are still around, if you look for them. However, and this is the problem with big books, you'll have to take them out of Taiwan with you, because the postal authorities (at the request of the U.S. Government) do not accept shipments of books. If you take them on the plane with you, they can be mailed from Tokyo or Hong Kong.

Phonograph records were pirated, too, and there is a large selection of monaural and stereo records. These make excellent gifts, because they are flat and don't weigh too much, and the prices cannot be criticized. If you like Chinese music, phonograph records (not pirated) sell at very low prices.

Antiques may be found on Haggler's Alley (so-called by all foreign residents in Taipei) on Chung-Hua Road, situated across the street from the Shin Shen Theater; you shouldn't have any trouble finding it. The tiny shops are located in a three-story building. Walk to the top, wander about, and gradually work your way downstairs. You'll find old china, small curios, scrolls, decorative screens, and the like. Junk is intermingled with rarities, but you're strictly on your own. To repeat what was said before, this is the place for some serious bargaining. Try to get your antiques for half the original price, but certainly not less than a third off.

If you're really serious about *important antiques,* you might pay a visit to Chou Me-Nan, a dealer in more important antiquities, with prices to match. He's located at 123 Chung King Road, and has an unpretentious place on the second floor. Talk to him gently and he may bring out some of his better antiquities.

Taiwan's greatest *artist,* in the opinion of many experts, is a man named Ran In Ting, whose excellent watercolors usually sell in the neighborhood of $350. Your hotel or travel agent can phone and make the necessary appointment if you wish to see his work.

ENTERTAINMENT Not too much here, except for nightclub-type entertainment in the important hotels. The Grand has a dinner show almost every night, but it really isn't too good. They regularly schedule dinner shows at the President and Ambassador hotels, so drop by their bulletin boards and see what's scheduled.

The only *nightclub,* strictly speaking, is the Central Theater Restaurant, which features Cantonese food (only so-so, I regretfully report) and a 2½-hour show which starts at 9:30. The entertainment is a peculiar hodge-podge of Chinese or Oriental acts and spectacles, depending upon how the management feels at the particular time. Originally, the shows were supposed to be completely Oriental, on behalf of western tourists, but since Taiwan is low on tourists during much of the year, the local people wanted to see something foreign and exotic, you know, like a western nightclub show. Therefore, the show may be Oriental, or western, or most likely, a combination. An evening for two people, consisting of dinner and a drink or two, should cost about $30 or only very slightly more.

Chinese opera is an experience which you owe yourself, at least once. Performances are given almost every day at either the Ming Hsing Theater or the Ta Chung Hua Theater; afternoon and evening performances are usually scheduled. Tickets are not expensive, and if the whole thing gets to be too much for you, you can always leave without any great financial loss. Opera, in the Chinese fashion, is not realistic, the costumes are fantastic, the scenery is rather limited, and the singing is keyed in with drums and gongs. The stories are romantic, the endings are usually happy, and it's not difficult to tell the hero from the villain, even if you can't speak a word of Taiwanese. If you don't want to go to a regular opera performance, ask your local travel agent if you can attend a performance at the Fu Hsin Opera School; as a rule, these are only arranged for groups, but perhaps when you ask, a performance may be on the schedule.

Sports There's *tennis* and *swimming* (in a pool) at the Grand Hotel. There are additional tennis courts at the Cosmo Club, and your hotel desk can phone for permission to play if you're interested. The local course for *golf* addicts is the Taipei Course, situated on the Tamsui River. However, I strongly recommend that you go out to the Tamsui Golf Course, about an hour's drive away; this is an excellent course, one of the prettiest and best in Asia. Good *boating,* but mediocre swimming, is available at Green Lake, about 15 minutes (6 miles) from Taipei.

Short Trips From Taipei

Grass Mountain

More correctly called Yang-ming-shan, Grass Mountain is only 8 miles north of town. It's a parklike area, filled with beautiful shrubbery, greenery, and if you're there during the right season— late February through the middle of March—a marvelous floral display. Then the azaleas, peaches, cherries, and plums are all in bloom, there are wild flowers galore and the whole place is magnificent. The rest of the year, alas, it's just another park, known for its hot springs. So, if you're not in Taipei during the flower season, should you visit Grass Mountain? Probably not.

Green Lake

Green Lake (Pitan is its formal name) is about 8 miles south of Taipei. The lake is really beautiful, and the name results from the greenish color of the water caused by the reflection from the foliage which borders it. The best thing to do is rent a boat (which is propelled like an Italian gondola) by the hour, and eat the lunch you have thoughtfully taken with you from the hotel. Not bad, on a beautiful day, but don't go unless the weather is fine. There are seagoing refreshment stands which sell drinks, coming directly to your boat.

Wulai

Wulai can be seen by driving farther along from Green Lake about another half-hour; the round trip from Taipei and back takes about 5 hours. Wulai, a rustic community, has aborigines (who were here before the Chinese came some 3,000 years ago); they will pose for you (for money), and even put on a dance for you (for more money). The village is worth wandering about, particularly if you're not going on any excursions to the rest of the island. You can hire a carriage and pony and drive about. However, the classic ride, and kind of fun at that, is the pushcar ride which runs from the village to the local waterfalls, via the railroad tracks (otherwise used for hauling lumber). At the end of the ride, the aborigines will obligingly pose with you near the waterfalls (for some money).

Longer Trips From Taipei

The Taroko Gorge

In my opinion, the Taroko Gorge is the principal sightseeing attraction in Taiwan, and definitely worth a day of your time. The only convenient way to make the trip is to fly (via CAT) down to Hualien; flying time is about 45 minutes, and it's a comfortable trip. Hualien has two good hotels, the Astar, which overlooks the ocean, and the much larger Marshal Hotel, in a parklike area. At Hualien, you can sometimes hire a local taxi to drive you through the gorge, wait for you while you have lunch, and then return you to the Hualien Airport in time to return via the afternoon CAT flight back to Taipei. However, since travel agents are quite reasonable in Taiwan, it might not be a bad idea to book your tour through them, in which case all transportation can be arranged in advance.

From the Hualien Airport, there's a drive of about 20 miles northward to the Taroko Gorge, which is the eastern end of the Cross-Island Highway (more about this later). It's difficult to describe the beauty of Taroko Gorge, because, you know, one picture is worth ten thousand words (old Chinese proverb). However, the gorge is something like a smaller Grand Canyon, but the fabulous road is cut out of the solid rock, not at the top, but down near the bottom of the gorge. There are suspension bridges, roads cut out of the cliffs, waterfalls, tunnels, and it's an exciting 12-mile ride. Traffic is one-way, and there are convenient rest houses all along the route. At the end of Taroko Gorge, there's a small hotel, the Tien Hsiang Lodge, which greatly resembles a small motel in California or Florida. If you'd like a quiet, restful night (there's absolutely nothing to do in the evening but eat dinner), the rooms are perfectly satisfactory and there's good Chinese food. After lunch, drive back through the gorge, and if your travel agent has been successful, you'll be taken to see a local tribe of Ami aborigines perform some dances for you; quite diverting.

The Taipei travel agents offer a return trip back via the new Cross-Island Highway. An exciting road has been hacked out of rock, but the ride is not too bad, and anyone can make the trip who isn't disturbed by winding roads. There is an overnight stop at a hostel at Li Shan, a rather pleasant place with comfortable rooms and fair enough food. It isn't absolutely luxurious, but for a small mountain-resort, it's quite good. The scenery all along the Dragon Road, as it is popularly called, is quite exciting, and you should have an enjoyable trip, particularly if the weather is good. (Be sure to take a sweater and a raincoat, because you never know in the mountains.) The road goes on to Tai-chung, and then northward along the west side of the island to Taipei (or you could fly back, if you wish to).

Sun-Moon Lake

This visit requires a minimum of 2 full days. Although I enjoyed visiting the lake, which is praised as Taiwan's beauty spot, you may find it just another lake.

There are three ways to start out for the lake. There is a daily express train, a daily flight by CAT, or you can drive down to Tai-chung. The train takes about 3 hours, the airplane requires less than an hour, and the automobile takes about 3 hours to negotiate the 125 miles. Tai-chung is a noisy, rather nondescript town. You can have lunch at the Railway Hotel, or stay overnight if you wish to do a thorough job on the National Museum.

From Tai-chung, the 50 miles or so to the Sun-Moon Lake takes about 1½-2 hours through pleasant countryside. Most people will head for the Sun-Moon Lake Tourist Hotel, which is an astonishingly modern building extending along the lake shore. They have several dining rooms, shopping arcades, and boats for hire. Rates are medium, not high. The other possibility is the Evergreen Hostel, which is not nearly so modern in appearance, but has been redecorated. Rates are about the same as those at the Lake Tourist Hotel. There's no swimming in the lake because of dangerous currents. Sightseeing boats take you to an aborigine village across the lake, which features a sign in English inviting everyone to talk to the chief and his daughter; it's all very commercial and not terribly exciting. You'll also be shown a shrine honoring a monk who first brought Buddhist sacred writings from India to China. Nuns honor the long-departed monk by ringing bells 360 times, and beating a drum 4,000 times, each morning at 4:30.

Orchid Island

Orchid Island, also known as Lan Yu, is situated in the Pacific Ocean less than 50 miles south of Taitung. This interesting island is about 10 square miles in size, with rocky beaches. Some of the

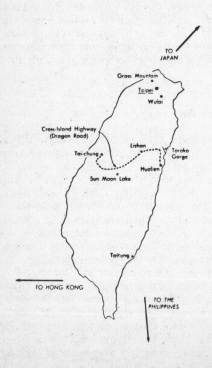

travel agents in Taipei will arrange package tours, including the round trip flight to Orchid Island, plus local sightseeing and a stop for lunch. The main reason for going to the small island is a group of approximately 1,600 aborigines, called *Yami*. These primitive people apparently prefer to live in the old style, farming and fishing from their brilliantly colored boats carved from tree trunks; the bows and sterns are raised to sharp points. The Yami are good woodcarvers and sell some of their work, especially miniatures of the fishing boats. There's a passable road around the island running through the various villages; en route, you'll be able to see 250 or more tiny rocky islands. Also worth noting are the native orchids and (usually) the enormous numbers of butterflies. A stop for lunch is made at the Orchid Island Guest House, which is rather pleasant. The flight (which departs from Kaohsiung) takes just under an hour each way, and the trip to Orchid Island requires a full day. It is sometimes combined with a visit to the gardens described below.

Kaohsiung

Taiwan's port city Kaohsiung is in the southwestern part of the country. Once a rather inconvenient place to reach, it's now connected to Taipei by a branch road, leading to a remarkable expressway, which links the north coast city of Keelung with Kaohsiung. The highway varies from 4 to 8 lanes, with toll stations about 22 miles apart; exit signs are in both Chinese and English. You can make the trip in a drive-yourself car, but it would be somewhat expensive. By all means take the very comfortable bus service which operates over this route, leaving Taipei Bus Station every 15 minutes from 7 A.M. to 7 P.M., making the trip in somewhat over 4 hours. The buses are air-conditioned and bear a striking resemblance to Greyhound buses in the U.S.

Kenting Tropical Botanical Garden is all the way south of Kaohsiung, close to the extreme southern end of Taiwan. It consists of a natural park measuring about 100 acres, and includes hundreds of varieties of trees, shrubs, and an experimental forest. In addition, it features a cave and an observation tower, so you get both extremes, high and low. Inside the garden is a 3-story hotel called Kenting House, overlooking a beach (although you have to walk to reach it); the rooms are O.K. and the food is fair enough. This trip is also arranged by some travel agents, and includes a flight from (and returning to) Kaohsiung. It's a worthwhile trip only if you have a special interest in gardening or horticulture, otherwise it's fairly expensive for what it offers.

HONG KONG AND MACAO

👫 Background

Imagine, if you will, a group of small rocky islands off the coast of Asia near the city of Canton, China. Imagine further that it is the year 1841, and that sailing ships take a year (or longer) to reach here from their mother country, England. These small islands are being used as the base of operations for pirates and smugglers of opium, and anyone setting foot on them is in imminent danger of almost certain death, by violence, or from malaria, and a few other diseases. Under these circumstances, a British naval officer, Captain Charles Elliot, took possession of these islands from China as a prize of war. When the news reached England, the pink-cheeked English squires guffawed wildly. "Elliot must be out of his head!" "Dashed cheek!" "Run this man out of the British Navy!" and many other (and worse) things were said about the loyal naval Captain. Others laughed loudly and long, and the British newspapers were filled with cartoons of the simple-minded naval officer who had accepted a pile of rocks as a prize of war. Well, sir, I'm sorry that Captain Elliot isn't alive today to see just how right he really was.

Hong Kong is unbelievable. Here is a ridiculous piece of real estate, consisting of merely 29 square miles for the island of Hong Kong, although now somewhat increased by annexations to be discussed shortly, right off the coast of the People's Republic of China. The Chinese could move in almost any time they wish to and take over this indefensible island. But they don't. And life goes on. It's impossible, but not by the weird calculations in this, our twentieth century of peace, understanding, and enlightenment.

I have been to over eighty different countries around the world. It is my considered opinion that Hong Kong is probably the most fascinating and exciting spot in the world, all things considered. Here, in one compact area, are magnificent scenery, good climate, marvelous shopping, superb food, excellent accommodations, sightseeing galore, and such a colorful population that even a walk along the streets is a full-scale tourist treat. It is a remarkable and stimulating collision of the East and the West, all the more exciting subconsciously because of the ever present knowledge that the People's Republic of China is just a few short miles away. The harbor alone, filled with tramp steamers, luxury liners, junks, and sampans, seen at any hour of the day or night, is a fabulous sight. It has been said that there are three great harbors of the world—Naples, Rio de Janeiro, and Hong Kong. In my opinion, Hong Kong is easily the most beautiful and fascinating of these.

Let's fill in a little on our history. From 1839 to 1841, the British fought the so-called First Opium War. During this period, the war was called by many laudatory names, and the British press was filled with self-praise about how their government was performing a noble service. But, of course, wars weren't fought for noble reasons; the main point was that the British were expanding their overseas territories, and this was a convenient point to step in, and also to take over, which they did. But the British Admiralty realized that Hong Kong Island was almost indefensible, and could easily be conquered, and so, after waiting a while, they fought the Second Opium War, from 1856 to 1858; this ended, as planned, with the British receiving the Kowloon peninsula (to the north of Hong Kong) and an island. Later, as the population began to grow, it was obvious that adjacent farmlands would be needed for the production of foodstuffs. Instead of using a new war as an excuse, the British entered into a lease in 1898 with the Chinese for what is called the New Territories (north of Kowloon), an area of about 365 square miles; the lease runs out in 1997, and what happens after that is anyone's guess.

You should have bought real estate in Hong Kong in 1924. In that year, the population was about 800,000; it is now about 4.7 million and growing steadily. With the increase in population and business, land values have multiplied in what can only be called a fantastic rate of progression. Great fortunes have been made here in real estate within a comparatively short period of time.

Hong Kong is a British Crown Colony, and that's its postal address—Hong Kong, B.C.C., and never Hong Kong, China. It is regularly referred to as "The Colony," and the capital C is deliberate, not accidental. It is one of the few remaining places in the world where the word "colony" does not have an insulting connotation. Everyone seems quite satisfied with its status. Although the island is not a paradise—what place is?—for many thousands of poor refugee laborers, others have done well. The Chinese are satisfied with the Colony because the People's Republic banks provide the mainland government with the hard cash—dollars and pounds sterling—which they desperately need. Britain is happy with Hong Kong, because it is a good source of revenue. Southeast Asia regards Hong Kong as a reliable, stable pivot point, where British financial integrity permits money to be invested with safety.

From the tourists' point of view, Hong Kong has everything. The world of Suzie Wong (the oriental beauty with the high split skirt called the *cheong-sam*), the west's listening post on China, a bargain basement shopping center for luxury merchandise, the Chinese listening post on the west, a flourishing, ingenious industrial oasis off the coast of China. You name it—Hong Kong is it, has it, or soon will have it.

When to Go

This will take a little explaining, because if I were asked when to go to Hong Kong, I'd say anytime. But of course, some times are better than others. First, the absolutely ideal period is from the middle of September through March, with lovely weather and little rain. During that period, the "idealest" months of all are September, October, November, February, and March. December and January are fine, but some nippy days can come; however, with a topcoat along, the weather is no great problem. The rains begin in April and last through June, but when it precisely begins and ends varies from year to year. It is impossible to say that there won't be much rain until say April 10, because one year will be perfect, while the next will be rainy. During the rainy season, however, the weather is very unpredictable, because there may be torrential downpours, or just a series of showers. July and August have rain two days out of three, which can be rather tiresome, but sometimes it rains at night leaving clear days—all very chancy. The big problem with the rainy seasons is the possibility of typhoons, those tropical Asiatic storms which bring very heavy rains for two or three days at a time. Airline flights in and out of Hong Kong can be canceled, and your schedule completely disrupted. In that case, there's nothing to do but hole

Weather Strip: Hong Kong

	Jan.	Feb.	Mar.	Apr.	May	June	July	Aug.	Sept.	Oct.	Nov.	Dec.
Average daily high	64°	63°	67°	75°	82°	85°	87°	87°	85°	81°	74°	68°
Average daily low	56°	55°	60°	67°	74°	78°	78°	78°	77°	73°	65°	59°
Monthly rainfall	1.3	1.8	2.9	5.4	11.5	15.5	15.0	14.2	10.1	4.5	1.7	1.2
Number of days with 0.04 inches rainfall	4	5	7	8	13	18	17	15	12	6	2	3

up in your hotel with a good supply of paperback novels, and wait it out. There's always plenty of food on hand, but the power often goes off, taking with it the radio and television stations.

🖊 Visa Requirements

You can stay in Hong Kong for 1 month without obtaining a visa—provided of course you have a valid passport, adequate funds, and tickets onward to some other place.

♨ Customs

Hong Kong customs officials are very pleasant, and outside of asking you about tobacco, aren't likely to be more than cursory. The tobacco allowance is one carton of cigarettes or 25 cigars per person. Also, only 1 bottle of liquor, but what of it?—liquor is cheap here. Speaking of liquor, as we were, don't forget that if you buy any hard liquor in Macao (discussed at the end of this chapter), it will be subject to duty when you return, so the bargain may be pretty well dissipated. Hong Kong is one of the world's great currency exchange centers, and there are absolutely no restrictions on bringing in money of any country; in fact, the currency situation permits you to buy and sell money of all countries, and sometimes it's possible to buy many currencies at far better than the regular rate.

⚕ Health

The water that comes from your hotel room tap originates in mainland China, where the health standards are something of an unknown quantity. Many people drink it without bad effects, others have been disturbed by drinking quantities of it. Unless your hotel has a notice indicating that the water is filtered, go very easy on tap water. If you have a sensitive stomach, stick to bottled water, soft drinks, beer, tea, or coffee. Avoid green salads, raw vegetables, and fruits, unless you can peel them yourself; of course, melons are O.K. You'll need smallpox and cholera certificates (if coming from an affected area) to enter Hong Kong. Also, if you've come from what the local authorities call a yellow fever area, that inoculation may be required. What is a yellow fever area? Usually Southeast Asia, India, Africa, or wherever there has been an outbreak of yellow fever. If convenient, play it safe and get a yellow fever shot before you leave if you're visiting those parts of the world. Health certificates should be stamped by your local health authority, because a doctor's signature alone is not enough.

⏲ Time

It is 16 hours later in Hong Kong than in Los Angeles. For example, when it is noon in Hong Kong on Monday, it is 8 P.M. on Sunday on the U.S. west coast, and 11 P.M. Sunday in New York City.

💲 Currency

The local money is the Hong Kong dollar, usually written HK$. The HK$ has 100 cents, by the way. You can use American dollars wherever you go, in most shops, and the majority of restaurants. However, it is advisable to change some money into Hong Kong dollars, in order to avoid confusion. It is comforting to know that, in an emergency, American dollars are acceptable. Of course, don't expect a cab driver to be prepared to accept American money.

🌐 Price Level

There was a time when Hong Kong was possibly the greatest single place in the entire world for bargains. It was possible to have a man's suit made to order for $40 and a woman's dress made for even less; forget those bargain days, which probably will never return again. Prices now represent good values, but are far from being outstanding bargains. Hotel rates are fairly high, and are only somewhat lower than in New York, Paris or London, for example. But you can have marvelous Chinese dinners at moderate prices even now. Often, you can buy Japanese merchandise such as tape recorders, radios, and cameras for less than in Japan. Sightseeing remains very reasonably priced, and inasmuch as the distances aren't great, prices tend to be moderate. A trip to Macao is worthwhile and not too costly—unless of course, you lose money at the gambling casinos.

🍎 Tipping

At your hotel, a 10% service charge is added to your bill, and this, in general, covers most hotel tipping with a few exceptions.

Give the baggage porter who carries your luggage HK$1 for each bag. Taxi-drivers are only given 10% of the meter, except for special services, like carrying baggage, etc.; the tip is therefore a small amount, rarely over 10¢ U.S. The hotel cars which pick you up at the airport include a tip in their transportation charge, but you could give the driver an extra HK$2–3, if you wished. If you have breakfast, or any other meal in your hotel room, tipping is not necessary, because meals also are subject to the 10% service charge; of course, if you send the waiter back to get you something extra, another HK$1 would be appropriate. At the beauty parlor or barber shop, the general custom is to tip 15% of the bill. Don't go overboard with tipping in Hong Kong; in restaurants a flat 10% is expected even though there's a service charge. Moderation is the word.

🏃 Transportation

Taxi fares are moderate, at least when compared with those of America or Europe. All cabs have meters, and don't let anyone tell you that you must pay more than the meter, unless you go through the tunnel that connects Hong Kong and Kowloon. In that case you must pay double the tunnel toll, in addition to the meter reading.

Hong Kong has a *subway*, called the Mass Transit Railway, usually abbreviated MTR. It has air-conditioned stations located near the major hotels in the Central District on Hong Kong Island, and it goes to various points in Kowloon.

Now, what about *rickshaws*, those hand-drawn conveyances which are so atmospheric but controversial. If you do take one, make it at night, after dinner, when the auto traffic is lighter; you'll enjoy it much more. Be sure to settle the rate in advance before you go; otherwise you might find yourself being held up for an extortionate amount.

There are two *ferries* which make the 7-minute crossing from Kowloon to Hong Kong with a high frequency schedule; the operation is smoothly run, and the ferries depart every few minutes. The whole ride is a delight, and constitutes a sightseeing "must" which should not be overlooked. Be sure to go First Class.

Nowadays, there's a *tunnel* which goes under Hong Kong Harbor, and you can ride across in a bus or taxi, rather than taking the ferry. It also cuts down the travel time to and from the airport, if your hotel is on the Hong Kong (rather than the Kowloon) side.

The local *bus* service may often be crowded, but it can be ideal for a low-priced do-it-yourself sightseeing tour. Go at either 10 A.M. or 3 P.M. and head for the bus' upper deck; you can leave anytime you wish; merely get off and take another bus, or jump into a taxi and head back towards your hotel. Try a bus ride along Nathan Road or to Aberdeen and Repulse Bay.

Although there are many organized tours of the New Territories (more about this later), you can take the *railroad* and see quite a good deal for very little money. Buy a First Class ticket (they're quite inexpensive) to Sheung Shui; the station is located in an area called Hung Hom. Sheung Shui is the last stop on the British side, and the trip is quite diverting, but I personally would recommend the automobile trip because you'll see much more. Incidentally, they're planning to move the railroad station in the near future to a new location.

Drive-yourself cars are plentiful. They may be rented at reasonable rates from Hertz (on the Kowloon side) and the Far East Self Drive Ltd. (on the Hong Kong side); new agencies are always springing up, and every hotel porter can arrange for a car. They are not necessary within Kowloon or Hong Kong because taxis are so cheap and numerous; however, you might want to use one to drive around Hong Kong Island, or to make a trip to the New Territories.

✊ Airport and Tourist Taxes

Kai Tak Airport, very modern and efficient, is only about 4 miles from the harbor. If your hotel is on the Kowloon side, you need allow about 25–30 minutes (except during rush hours) to reach the airport. Using the new tunnel which runs under the harbor, if you're staying on the Hong Kong side, you should allow about 30 minutes to reach the airport unless it's during the rush hour periods, in which case additional time should be allowed. Don't forget that, in addition to travel time, you're supposed to be at the airport 60 minutes before departure. At the moment, there's a departure tax of HK$15.

▌▐ Communications

Airmail service to the U.S. is very good, and takes about 3 days (sometimes 4 days) on the average; the rate is equivalent to 31¢ U.S., but an airletter form is much less. A *telephone* call to your home town costs about $15 for 3 minutes. Much less expensive is a fast *cablegram,* costing about $5 for 10 words.

⚡ Electricity

The standard voltage is 200-volt 50-cycle A.C., which means your ordinary appliances won't work without a transformer. Many of the newer hotels, however, have special standard voltage outlets for electric shavers in the bathroom. If in doubt, ask, otherwise your appliance can be damaged.

✗ Food Specialties and Liquor

If you think you've eaten Chinese food in your home town, wait 'till you come here! The scope and variety will amaze you, and it's inevitably delicious. Of course, there are western-style restaurants all over, and in general it may be said that the western food is generally better in Hong Kong than elsewhere in the orient. Insofar as western food goes, I don't mean to imply that you'll be able to get a marvelous steak, but it won't be too bad. The French food is fairly good, too, but to compare it to Paris would be somewhat ridiculous. In addition, there are Malayan, Japanese, Indian, and Mongolian restaurants. The problem here is inevitably one of choice, more than of finding any place worth eating at.

Back to Chinese food, and the many provincial styles. Chinese food is not all the same, as many people think, and there may well be almost a hundred complete culinary styles. For our purposes, however, Chinese cookery may be divided into five principal types: Shanghai, Peking, Cantonese, Hunan, and Szechuan. To begin with, Shanghai does remarkably well with fish dishes of all types, especially shellfish. There are also excellent small dumplings, usually filled with a meat mixture, which can be ordered boiled or fried and which are delicious when eaten with a little sharp mustard and sweet plum sauce. The Peking culinary style is quite different from the usual type of Chinese cooking found in the United States; many of the dishes will sound somewhat strange, but rest assured, they are inevitably well-prepared and very tasty. Of course, no one needs to be prepared for the succulence of crisp-skinned, mouth-watering roast duck, prepared in the Peking style.

Cantonese cookery is the best known of all cooking styles to Americans, because the vast majority of Chinese restaurants in our country are run by people who are descendants of emigrants from Canton, China. Cantonese cookery is very varied, and is generally prepared with what is called the "stir-fry" method of quick cookery; this preserves the crispness and succulence of the vegetables used. Because the meat is usually cut into thin slices or slivers, it must all be prepared and served quickly, otherwise everything will be overcooked. An interesting novelty, and one that tourists should not overlook, is the opportunity to have a marvelous lunch of Cantonese *dimsum*. The diner is merely served with tea and a plate. Young girls, wheeling trays of various small foods, such as miniature dumplings filled with shrimp, or small balls of dough filled with a delicious pork mixture, pass by. Each person selects what he likes, and the moderate bill is totalled by adding up the number of plates remaining on the table. As many as forty different dishes may go by in the course of an hour. Loads of fun, and not at all expensive.

Hunan food emphasizes dishes highly spiced; the cuisine is extremely imaginative, and although the combinations may, on occasion, sound exotic, they are really not in most cases. It is true, however, that Hunan food often is somewhat spicy, so ask before ordering, if in doubt. Szechuan food is definitely likely to have red pepper used in its preparation, and is at least full-flavored, rather than mild, as is true with most of Cantonese cookery. But there are many mild dishes in the Szechuan repertoire. The restaurants of Hong Kong are mostly in the Cantonese, Shanghai, or Peking traditions, but many of them will serve dishes from the Hunan or Szechuan cuisine if you ask; sometimes they appear on the menu with the words "Szechuan style," or the like, following the name of the dish.

Incidentally, almost every restaurant has an English-language menu, and it will be handed to you automatically in 9 restaurants out of 10. There's nothing dangerous, or even vaguely risky about dining out in a Chinese restaurant. Transportation is very simple because cabs are cheap and plentiful.

∞ Time Evaluation

Hong Kong deserves as much time as you can possibly spare, no matter how pressed for time you may be. I would say that the absolute, barest minimum would be 5 days, and you'd be bound to leave with a feeling of not having been there long enough. According to government statistics, the average tourist stays about 8 days. To allow for sufficient time for shopping, for a trip around the island, for a visit to the New Territories, for a boat ride to one of the outer islands, and a visit to Macao, better make it a full week. Or more.

The Crown Colony: Hong Kong

Hong Kong is the name of the small island off the China mainland's coast; its chief city is Victoria. Probably because the name Hong Kong rings like the sound of a Chinese temple bell, and

the word Victoria brings to mind the dullness of England of a
century ago, the choice has fallen upon Hong Kong, and the name
is used to encompass the entire region. Hong Kong actually means
Fragrant Harbor.

To begin with, imagine a finger pointing downward from southern China into the sea; this is the mainland portion, most of which
is called the New Territories (the 365 square miles leased from the
Chinese), consisting mostly of bucolic countryside. At the tip end
of the finger is the city of Kowloon, a lively bustling city. The vast
majority of tourists arrive by plane at Kai Tak Airport, at the
northeastern outskirts of Kowloon. Most of the hotels, restaurants,
and shops are also located in Kowloon. Across from Kowloon, and
separated by Victoria Harbour (as the British spell it), is the city of
Victoria, although the name has been all but swallowed up in the
more generic term of Hong Kong.

Both Hong Kong and Kowloon have their own merits, like two
talented sisters. There are more good shops and restaurants in
Kowloon than in Hong Kong, but Hong Kong has its fair share. It's
a rare tourist who doesn't make one round trip daily on the ferries,
but inasmuch as the trip is delightful, no one cares. One side is not
necessarily "better" or more interesting than the other, and it is
difficult to make a choice between the two; in actual fact, a choice
need never be made, except to select a hotel on either the Kowloon
or Hong Kong side. Whichever side is selected, you may be sure that
each day, some shop, restaurant, or sightseeing attraction will draw
you to the opposite shore. But that's part of the undeniable charm
of Hong Kong (and Kowloon).

Hong Kong Island

Known as Hong Kong Island, as Victoria, but (by residents)
more often just the Island, this part of the Colony is home to about
1.5 million people—most of them crowded into the houses of Ken-
nedy Town (named for a former governor), Causeway Bay, Happy
Valley, and North Point, or more comfortably spaced in the new
high-rise apartments of the mid-level (that's between the Central
District and the Peak). The old-money people live in mansions on
the Peak, where they can enjoy the best views—except for about two
months a year when there's a heavy mist. All major business houses,
banks, airlines and shipping companies have offices in the Central District around Queen's and Des Voeux Roads and Pedder
Street.

A large part of the island's 29 square miles consists of green hillside, sandy beaches, coastline, and quiet rolling valleys. You can ride, if you wish, through the center of the island; or you can drive all the way around (and include a brief stop for lunch) in about 3½ hours.

In Hong Kong all roads lead to the ferries that crisscross the harbor. The best known is the Star Ferry; they carry passengers between the island and Kowloon over the narrowest part of the harbor. There's a tunnel under the harbor which is quick and efficient, but denies one the great pleasure of riding on the ferries which shuttle back and forth across the harbor. By all means, be sure to take a few rides, for the cost is infinitesimal, the trip takes about 6 minutes, and there's constant service until 1:00 A.M.

On the Hong Kong side, the ferry maneuvers alongside the terminal in the shadow of the high, white Mandarin Hotel and the glass-fronted City Hall. Between the two is Statue Square with its green lawn, War Memorial, and the Victorian bronze figure of Sir Thomas Jackson, manager of the Hong Kong & Shanghai Bank from 1876–1902. The three most important banks—Hong Kong & Shanghai, the Chartered Bank, and the Bank of China—stand solemnly around Sir Thomas. The high-domed Supreme Court and the white stone turrets and balconies of the very dignified Hong Kong Club on another side of the square face the new Prince's Building, behind the Mandarin Hotel. Next door to the Hong Kong Club is the telegraph office and the studios of Radio Hong Kong. Rising behind and a little above the Bank of China is the Hilton Hotel with its stylized double *H* purposely designed to look like a Chinese character.

Behind the Hilton, up steep Garden Road is the U.S. Consulate —not Embassy, because Hong Kong is not a capital city. However, it is larger than the majority of our embassies due to Bamboo Curtain snooping and peeking—that is, in more dignified language, the compiling of statistics on mainland China. Opposite the Consulate is the Peak Tram terminus. A ride, or rather two rides (if you're planning to return!) on the Peak Tram should be made by all visitors. I know it's touristy, but that doesn't make it less impressive or exciting. The tram consists of a cable car that travels the 13,000 feet at about a 45° angle, although at times almost vertically, in about 10 minutes. It may look dangerous, but a set of complicated brakes minimizes any possibility of danger. If you think the harbor looks fabulous you should see it at an angle of 45°! There's an assortment of restaurants at the top, consisting of a regular restaurant and an informal coffee shop. The view is particularly spectacular from the top of the structure, which offers a 360° panoramic view of the entire Crown Colony. In addition, there are shops, a post office, bank, and heaven knows whatever else may occur to the owners. You can also take a footpath around the Peak and see the harbor from a hundred different angles if you have the time and inclination for an hour's walk. The tram usually leaves every 15 minutes until late at night. The fare is quite nominal, and the trip would be worth even three times as much.

Let's go back to the Star Ferry for the purpose of our discussion. Facing the island from the Star Ferry pier, the City Hall is to your left. It consists in part of a tall rectangular building which houses an art gallery, museum, lecture halls, a marriage registry, and even lending and reference libraries. Between this and a nearby smaller building is a colorful garden arranged around a small Hall of Memory which contains the book of names of those residents of Hong Kong who died in the two world wars. The low building is spacious and attractive, and is the heart of the Colony's cultural life. Internationally known symphonic orchestras and popular entertainers perform in its Concert Hall; the local drama societies—both English and Chinese—schedule plays in the theater. The huge restaurant has a glass front along its length to provide diners with a fascinating view of the harbor and the ferries.

City Hall backs onto Connaught Road, which extends along the waterfront and runs eastward into Wanchai and Causeway Bay. Wanchai is the rough-and-ready saloon area because of the dozens of navy ships—American, British, Australian, and New Zealand—which regularly anchor off this part of the island. The sailors come ashore at Fenwick Pier, opposite the China Fleet Club which, together with the bars, the Luk Kwok Hotel (where the *Suzie Wong* saga was written), and the innumerable restaurants and tailor shops, is built on land reclaimed from the sea during the 1930's. It really isn't very sinful, although the usual port-city professionals can easily be found along the narrow streets or in some of the bars. However, all bar girls are not necessarily prostitutes. They are hired to provide female companionship and dancing partners for the thousands of very lonely sailors who come ashore. The bars are rather stereotyped: neon names like "Suzy Wong," "Diamond Horseshoe," "Ocean Bar," etc.; uncomfortable table booths and long bar counters; juke boxes with the latest rock-and-roll hits; the widest variety of drinks at lower prices than in the States. The girls are neat and slim, often quite young, and sometimes pretty. The atmosphere is noisy, but good for a diverting hour, if you like that sort of thing, but not recommended for everyone.

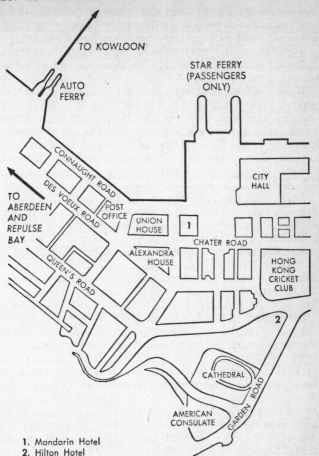

TO KOWLOON

AUTO FERRY

STAR FERRY (PASSENGERS ONLY)

CONNAUGHT ROAD

CITY HALL

DES VOEUX ROAD

TO ABERDEEN AND REPULSE BAY

POST OFFICE

UNION HOUSE

1

CHATER ROAD

QUEEN'S ROAD

ALEXANDRA HOUSE

HONG KONG CRICKET CLUB

2

CATHEDRAL

GARDEN ROAD

AMERICAN CONSULATE

1. Mandarin Hotel
2. Hilton Hotel

At the far eastern end of Connaught Road (where it turns into Gloucester Road) is the Royal Hong Kong Yacht Club, located at the edge of Causeway Bay. Stately yachts moor in the typhoon shelter, a small body of water protected by a long breakwater, which is also home to thousands of people who live on the junks and sampans. The club house has a restaurant and bar, and during the season there are yacht races every weekend, usually from the Yacht Club out to Waglan Island at the mouth of the estuary that leads into the harbor. Yacht owners and those with powered pleasure boats take off each weekend for the bays and beaches around the island and along the ragged coastline of the New Territories.

The Causeway Bay area is quite built up now with shops, restaurants and apartment houses. It's an interesting area to wander around.

If you ride farther eastward around the island, you pass the new gigantic housing region of Sai Wan Ho, home of 40,000 resettled refugees. Then suddenly you are out of the urban areas into the rural. Gently undulating hills, covered with pine, banyan and camphor trees, lead to Big Wave Bay and the Shek-O Beach and Country Club. Some of the Colony's most beautiful homes are located in this area. More low hills are passed, and you can look down to your left on the fishing boats clustered about the village of Tai Tam.

Next comes Stanley, simultaneously the name of the island's prison (where, during the war, Europeans were kept), the pleasant fishing village and the upper class residential district. Its neighbor is Repulse Bay, just a few minutes away, where 25-storied apartment buildings are rising up out of the foothills above the attractive, curved bay. The most popular beach in Hong Kong, it also has the Repulse Bay Hotel, a traditional ceiling-fans and cocktails-on-the-terrace establishment—and perfect for lunch, dinner, or afternoon tea.

It's impossible not to visit Aberdeen, even if you've been told that the floating restaurants charge too much for inferior food, or that the smell is sometimes unpleasant. Both statements are true, but more important, this colorful village on the water, with its thousands of inhabitants who are born, live, work, marry, and die on board the junks and sampans that cram into the bay, is quite unique. You could literally spend hours watching the small boats rocking to and fro, propelled by the women of the family by means of one long oar at the back of the boat. Some of the sampans have been designated to carry diners to the Sea Palace and Tai Pak, the two-storied floating restaurants with tanks of live fish and seafood attached to the sides. The newest and most elaborate of all the floating restaurants is the Jumbo Floating Restaurant, which is 3 stories high and can accommodate 2,500 diners at one time; it's not intimate, but it is amusing and quite an experience. (There are plans to move the floating restaurants to a new location, so it's best to inquire.) The most intriguing feature of Aberdeen is the way in which people live aboard boats in such restricted surroundings. A sampan is not a very large boat, yet a woman and her four or five children somehow manage to sleep, eat, and move around on it.

(The man of the family will probably be out on one of the ocean-going junks—huge wooden craft that have been successfully used for fishing over the centuries, with no change in their construction except for the addition of motors.) An added point of interest here is the large Chinese cemetery that covers the whole of one hillside.

If you're on the Victoria side, you would surely enjoy a visit to the Open Air Night Market, located in front of the Macau Ferry Pier. Take a taxi there, anytime from 8 P.M. to midnight. During the day it's a parking lot, but at night the cars are gone and the area is turned into a very typical, Chinese-style outdoor marketplace. You'll find food stalls, fortune tellers, musicians, story tellers (in Chinese, of course), and lots of entertainment. Bring along a handful of coins, you'll need them, although there is no admission charge. After having dinner, assuming you're on the Victoria side, head for the Macau Ferry Pier, and you'll be able to pass a pleasant hour or so. I don't mean to imply that you can't go there if you're on the Kowloon side, but of course this involves a longer trip (going through the tunnel).

A rather interesting place for a visit is a replica of what a Sung Dynasty village once looked like; it's quite appropriately called the Sung Dynasty Village and is located at Laichikok, not too far from the principal hotels, say, about 30 minutes by car or bus. There are group tours during the week, which sometimes include lunch. (Avoid, if at all possible, eating here because the food is poor.) The village itself is a remarkable reproduction of the way of life during the Sung Dynasty, which ran from A.D. 960 to 1179. There are some remarkable buildings to see, shops, an opera house, musicians, other forms of entertainment, and everyone is dressed appropriately in costumes of the period. It's rather pleasant, not at all vital to a visit to Hong Kong but harmless, and quite touristy.

Kowloon

Kowloon means "Nine Dragons," and consists of 3½ square miles of British territory sliced from the southern tip of the China mainland. To the north of Kowloon are the 370 square miles of New Territories, leased from China for 99 years in 1898, and mostly agricultural. Within the small area of Kowloon city are most of the tourist hotels, a large proportion of the tourist stores, some of the best restaurants and many of the nightclubs.

Before the building of the Mandarin and Hilton Hotels on the island, almost all tourists stayed in Kowloon, particularly at the

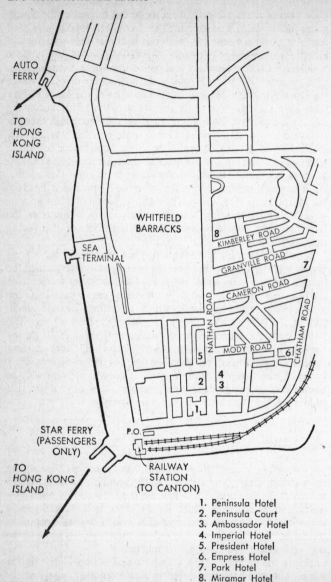

AUTO
FERRY

TO
HONG
KONG
ISLAND

WHITFIELD
BARRACKS

SEA
TERMINAL

KIMBERLEY ROAD

GRANVILLE ROAD

CAMERON ROAD

NATHAN ROAD

MODY ROAD

CHATHAM ROAD

8

7

5

6

2

4

3

1

P.O.

STAR FERRY
(PASSENGERS
ONLY)

TO
HONG KONG
ISLAND

RAILWAY
STATION
(TO CANTON)

1. Peninsula Hotel
2. Peninsula Court
3. Ambassador Hotel
4. Imperial Hotel
5. President Hotel
6. Empress Hotel
7. Park Hotel
8. Miramar Hotel

venerable Peninsula with its huge, leisurely lobby where ceiling fans whirred, waiters in soft-soled slippers moved around with coffee or cocktails, and you could meet everyone you knew in the Far East. Kowloon's main street, Nathan Road, used to be lined with very old-fashioned buildings, out of which hung wash, and from which exuded the delicious aromas of home-style Chinese cooking. Now new hotels have sprung up where Edwardian tenements used to be. The Hyatt Regency Hotel has 830 rooms and a dozen exotically named public rooms, such as the Hall of Nine Dragons Restaurant and the Fire Cracker Bar. Behind the Ambassador is the Empress Hotel, financed by Hawaiian-Chinese millionaires.

Kowloon is so conditioned to catering to tourists that it has gradually grown into a compact arrangement, with almost all the stores packed into a small triangle, bounded by Nathan, Chatham, and Kimberley Roads. Within this area you can buy tailor-made clothes, custom-made furniture and jewelry, made-to-order table linen, and cameras, carpets, and China dolls, and just about anything else anyone can dream up. Along the various streets of this small district you can buy, at among the world's lowest prices, German cameras, Thai silk, English wool, Japanese lacquer, Filipino wood carvings, Swiss watches, French perfume, Burmese sapphires, African diamonds, Indian sculptures, and the thousand and one delightful products of local craftsmen in ivory, jade, bronze, wood, silver, gold, rattan, and brocade. Also, a few other substances which elude me at the moment.

On the opposite side of Nathan Road from the previously described shopping triangle but further north are alleys like Shanghai Street with crowded tenements and tiny stores, loaded with local color. At night the pavements are covered with food stalls, and the wares of thousands of vendors who spread their goods along the sidewalks. Usually the whole family is present, calling out encouragement to passers-by to purchase their kitchen utensils, cotton clothing, and patent medicines. This is an intriguing place to walk about in the evening and completely safe. Most Chinese who live in the confines of tiny apartments apparently enjoy the spaciousness of outdoor life, and like to walk around the streets at night, window-shopping and talking with friends, or gathering for noisy mah-jonggsessions. One block from a sophisticated nightclub with a French menu, an American jazz orchestra, and an Australian floor show is this other world of China—Cantonese opera, snake dinners, and the rattle of mah-jongg tiles.

The big wharfs of Hong Kong are on the Kowloon side. Great liners tie up alongside the Ocean Terminal, which is located two blocks to the west of the Star Ferry. In the Terminal are shops, restaurants, and all in all it's one of the high spots of a visit to Hong Kong. If you run into an inclement day, you can wander about the Ocean Terminal for hours, and there is a wide assortment of places at which to have a cup of coffee or a complete meal.

Along northern Nathan Road, beyond the regular tourist area, are the small shops and factories of many of the Colony's skilled craftsmen. By walking around these streets you can watch people weaving rattan, carving ivory, building camphor-wood chests, or sewing the suits and dresses sold in the downtown stores. Also easily visible to the passer-by are the joss-stick makers, the boat builders, the metalware molders and hundreds of other trades being followed in the open-doored workshops or on the sidewalks. It's all fascinating to a curious sightseer, and the only prerequisite to an hour of informal enjoyment is a pair of very comfortable shoes.

New Territories: Sidetrip from Kowloon

Assuming it's not raining, a trip around the New Territories is a wonderful way to spend a long morning or even the whole day. One road runs more or less around the countryside, which provides Hong Kong with much of its fresh vegetables, poultry and meat. The inhabitants of this region are either Cantonese or Hakka, the latter believed to have come from Northern China a century ago. They speak their own dialect, and wear distinctive clothes, such as the wide-brimmed rattan hats with black fringe that protects them from the sun when working in the rice paddies.

Leaving Kowloon by auto and following the western coast road, you drive via the new industrial town of Tsuen Wan, with its textile mills, past the beaches and summer homes to Castle Peak. From there you go inland into what is exactly like your mental picture of traditional China. Water buffalo pull the simple wooden ploughs across the black, rich earth. Tiny villages, curly-cornered roofs on the houses, and colorful Buddhist temples are much as they have been for hundreds of years. The whole atmosphere is tranquil and quiet, and the pace unhurried.

Turning north and eastwards you reach Yuen Long, another village that is being developed in order to expand Hong Kong's new industries. Most of the factories in the Colony are post-1949. Before the Chinese Revolution, Hong Kong prospered from the "entrepot" trade. (The entrepot trade was a term given to the use of Hong Kong for the temporary storage of goods in transshipment to or from China, or other Asiatic destinations.) When China cut herself off from most of the world's international trade, the Colony had to diversify her interests. Success was immediate and fantastic, and today her major source of income is the textile trade. With almost no natural resources, most raw materials must be imported, but the finished goods can still undersell and compete in quality with any other country in the world. In towns like Yuen Long, Tai Po, Tsuen Wan, and Kwun Tong, there are factories that make plastic items and cheap clothes, transistor radios and semi-conductors, electrical goods and machinery, rubber footwear and cigarettes, and many, many more articles, actually too numerous to mention.

Two of the most interesting places in the New Territories are Kam Tin and Lok Ma Chau. Kam Tin is a small walled city, all of whose inhabitants are members of the same clan, or family. They live in a huddled group of stone houses and work in the fields outside the village walls. Villages such as this used to be the rule in China during the last century, when warlords were in the habit of attacking unprotected communities, or even other warlords if they ran out of unprotected communities. Nowadays, Kam Tin is rather dirty and shabby, but very photogenic.

Lok Ma Chau is interesting for a very political reason. From this hill you can see the People's Republic of China, an eighth of a mile away on the other side of the Shaum Chun river, which is the frontier. Located in Lok Ma Chau is a British police station and border post; on the other side of the "Bamboo Curtain" are the communist police posts and a small commune. With good binoculars, you can see the workers in their blue pyjamas marching to or from the fields, and sometimes gun-toting guards are visible. The purpose: to prevent disgruntled Chinese from escaping across the border. Between these two worlds are the ever present rice paddies of eternal China, and on the British side are huts where farmers work right on the banks of the river.

The actual frontier crossing point is at Lo Wu, a few miles further along the road, but this is a closed area to all but the border police and those with visas for China. Every day, fifty legal immigrants enter Hong Kong over the bridge at Lo Wu, and every night an unknown number of illegal immigrants somehow cross the border. Some escape by junks, or swim the river at night, others arrive the longer and safer way via Macao. All risk death at the hands of the communist guards, who shoot at anyone seen trying to cross. They also risk being caught by the Hong Kong police and returned to the border. At the same time, peaceful commerce is carried on across the bridge and a dozen trains a day cross from one side to the other, usually carrying vegetables, chickens, and pigs. Alongside the railroad track is the pipeline which brings water from China at the rate of 5,000 million gallons a year (at a very reasonable price). On occasion, the Chinese have offered to furnish the water without charge, but Hong Kong prefers to pay.

The road away from the border leads to the small village of Fan-ling, the favorite destination for the Colony's golfers, because it has two good 18-hole courses. The club house is traditionally British, and the atmosphere is old-world British, that is, somewhat stuffy. Visitors who want to play can usually get a guest card by requesting it from the club manager.

From Fanling the main road returns to the coast, this time to the eastern side of the peninsula. Tai Po, a flourishing market town with bordering industries, looks out over Tolo Harbor, a section of which, called Plover Cove, is dammed to create a huge new reservoir. The road and the railway both run along the pleasant coast, with its beaches and junk-filled bays, to Shatin. This pleasant green valley of Shatin is one of the most fertile in the whole of South China. Beside two rice crops, the local farmers grow many kinds of vegetables, and farm animals flourish.

On the hill which looks down upon the valley is the Shatin Heights Hotel, a pleasant retreat from the city, and with a large terrace, ideal for a tour break. While sipping tea or martinis, you can gaze into the green valley, watch the trains go by, or study the Amah Rock. This last is a strangely formed pile of stone which looks exactly like a Chinese woman with a baby on her back. Legend has it that (a long time ago) a wife would regularly stand on the hill with her baby and wait for the fishing boats to return with her husband. Some say she died there and became petrified in stone, others that the gods erected the statue in honor of her loyalty. Draw your own morals from this fable.

Between Shatin and downtown Kowloon are a string of hills. On one of these is the Carlton Hotel, which would be a number one choice for dinner just for the fantastic view of the island, the harbor, and most of Kowloon. By a happy chance the food is excellent. Best go there on a clear night and sit out on the terrace.

Other of the hills in this general area have been leveled to make flat ground for construction sites. The airport runway was built by dumping the earth from the excavated hills into the harbor, and reclamation of land is still continuing. A great deal of the building is being undertaken by the government on behalf of the under-privileged people of Hong Kong, many of whom recently fled from China. One outstanding example of how the problem of overpopulation is being solved are the resettlement estates. The largest one to date is the Choi Hung Estate on Clear Water Bay Road, just beyond the airport. The 50,000 inhabitants of the 20-storied blocks pay the equivalent of $10 to $30 U.S. for their apartments. The estate has its own schools, shops, and post office. Right now, due to resettlement, the government is landlord to 604,754 people, that is, about 17% of the total population. New blocks of apartments capable of accommodating thousands of people are being built at an extremely rapid rate. Many of these apartment blocks use the roofs for playgrounds or schools. In Hong Kong every inch of level ground is important, and space is at a great premium. In addition to the government, several voluntary organizations have helped put a roof over the heads of the poorer members of the community. The largest of these, the Hong Kong Housing Society, has provided accommodations for over 45,000 people at rents similar to those in the resettlement estates.

When you look at some of the older resettlement estates, you may be horrified at the smallness of the rooms, which often house a family of 7 or 8. It will undoubtedly make you feel better if you compare these noisy, crowded, but seemingly happy blocks of apartments with the miserable cardboard and packing-case shacks on some of the hillsides, where those unfortunate residents exist without sewage facilities, and must walk 500 yards or more for water at the public faucet. (Don't, for heaven's sake, start giving money to the children. If you want to donate money, do it through one of the welfare societies.) With a population increasing at the rate of 14 every hour, with a greater life expectancy and a constant flow of illegal immigrants, this "problem of people" as Hong Kong calls it, is going to be around for a long time. From 1950 to 1963, the total of refugees from China to Hong Kong was a staggering 1,160,000. The local authorities deserve all possible praise for their tremendous efforts to house the refugees in apartment houses with modern conveniences at moderate rentals.

On the southwestern side of Kowloon peninsula, not terribly far from the main shopping area (allow about 1 hour travel time each way), is a fantastic reconstruction of a Sung dynasty community, called, quite naturally, the Sung Dynasty Village. The "Village" extends over a fair amount of ground and re-creates the main street of the town of Hangchou, one of the capitals of the Sung dynasty, which covered the period from 960 to 1273 A.D. It's something like returning to the twelfth century, with shops staffed by clerks in costumes of the Sung period. There is a late afternoon mock wedding ceremony, which reproduces the customs of that period in Chinese history. It's perhaps best to plan on having lunch in the excellent two-story Restaurant of Plentiful Joy, which features Sung dishes. You can buy package tours from many of the hotels which include transportation, lunch, and coupons that can be exchanged for candy, tea and so on.

Hong Kong's Other Islands

Of the 236 islands included in Hong Kong waters, most are small, dry, and uninhabited, but the exceptions are truly exceptional. Lantau, the biggest island—almost twice as large as Hong Kong Island —is the mountainous green home of Trappist and Buddhist monks, farmers and fishermen, and, during the summer, the weekend resort of many Hong Kong residents. Lantau is an hour's ferry ride away from the downtown business district. The ferry boats charge low fares, are quite comfortable and are a good way of seeing the harbor, the outlying islands, and the junks that dot these waters. You know, sometimes the pleasantest of trips cost just a few cents and this is the case here. The views of the harbor are absolutely delightful.

At Lantau you'll find a comparatively rural island, roughly twice the size of Hong Kong Island. Be sure to visit the Temple of the Precious Lotus (also called Po Lin Tse), which is a destination for devout Buddhists during certain Chinese holidays. The monks at Po Lin serve vegetarian food only, Chinese-style of course, in the restaurant beneath the temple. I should warn you, however, not to visit Lantau on Chinese festival days, because the crowds are absolutely overwhelming. It is delightful, otherwise, to wander about and observe the life of the people at Silvermine Bay, where the ferry comes in.

To the southeast of Lantau, there is the charming and colorful island of Cheung Chau. Shaped something like a dumbbell, this island has no vehicles. It is very small, and anyone who takes the trouble to walk about the narrow streets, or along the roads that lead to the hills at either end of the island, will feel as though he were in old China. A third of the population lives on the water and fishing is the major industry. One long bay is usually crowded with sampans and junks and ferries from Hong Kong. The other long bay has bathing beaches. The atmosphere of Cheung Chau is generally quiet and rural, except on weekends. Well-fed dogs, pigs, chickens, and ducks walk around the streets in a state of organized confusion. Most of the pigs and poultry end their days in the crowded market where housewives come to fill the twin baskets hung on bamboo poles and balanced horizontally over their shoulders. And when not working, the men of the village sit in the high-ceilinged cafes open to the streets and drink tea, play *mah-jongg* or discuss the day's catch around huge round tables covered with bowls of rice and fish. Needless to say, this somnolent island is a photographer's dream.

The sleepy existence of Cheung Chau is shattered every year during a week in May when the Bun Festival is held. Then the entire population is occupied in building the huge towers of bamboo on which they fasten doughy white and pink buns, and in preparing their floats. The festival is held to placate the spirits of those who, in times past, were killed by the pirates who once used Cheung Chau as headquarters. It is also a Buddhist and Taoist celebration during which the gods are honored in the hope that the fishing will prosper. For three days no meat or fish is eaten, and nonstop, screeching Cantonese opera is performed. On the last day, the floats of the different families, groups, and trades are paraded through the streets led by drummers and strenuous, gyrating lion dancers. The Governor of Hong Kong and thousands of others travel to Cheung Chau for this parade; some stay on until midnight, when the people of the village gather around the bun towers and the young men, on a given signal, scramble up them to snatch the highest bun they can. It's good luck. For the ferry schedule, which changes frequently, contact the Hongkong Yaumati Ferry Company. (Round-trip fares to Lantau and Cheung Chau are very low.)

Macao. For those with an extra day or two, an excursion to Macao makes an extremely pleasant trip. For details, see the material at the end of this section.

ORGANIZED TOURS   It's worthwhile to drive *around the island;* you can hire a taxi (be sure to get an English-speaking driver and prearrange the price) or you can take one of the organized tours which are offered. Although it's possible to hire a drive-yourself car, I wouldn't recommend it because the roads aren't too well marked, and besides you won't see very much if you're driving. Figure about a half day.

Kowloon and the New Territories tours usually take a half day, although the time required is longer if it includes lunch. Some of the trips begin with a railroad trip into the New Territories, followed by a boat ride, lunch at a local restaurant, and then the return trip.

Numerous *water tours* can be taken. These are highly recommended because seeing Hong Kong by water is probably the most pleasant and the most informative way. There are harbor tours, trips around the island, evening sails and, probably best of all, a trip to Aberdeen, lunch on a floating restaurant, plus a return.

The most exciting craft, in my opinion, for water tours is the brigantine *Wan Fu* (which means "10,000 Blessings"). This stately boat makes trips in the mornings and each evening around the harbor and out to Aberdeen for lunch or dinner. The office is situated in the Hilton Hotel lobby.

ACCOMMODATIONS   The luxury hotels in Hong Kong are indeed luxurious, and not many cities in the world can match them for rooms, decor, facilities, and service. The three leading hotels—the Peninsula, Mandarin and Hilton—are really extraordinary hotels, and would be so considered anywhere in the world. Naturally enough, not every room can face the harbor with its fabulous view, but all rooms are modern, good-sized, and somewhat more expensive than those in other hotels.

At one time Hong Kong had a water shortage, and permanent residents remember it distinctly. Since those days, the local government has signed an agreement with the Chinese mainland government, which supplies vast quantities of water, so the shortage is now gone and (hopefully) forgotten.

VICTORIA (HONG KONG ISLAND) HOTELS:

Mandarin. One of the really beautiful hotels in the world, very attractively decorated. Public rooms are extremely nice, as are the bedrooms. Each room has a balcony, many of which look out over the harbor. The location is absolutely perfect and extraordinarily convenient, just opposite the Star Ferry. There are several restaurants, all quite good; the Lookout Lounge on the roof has an absolutely breathtaking view of the surrounding region. The rates are fairly high.

Hilton. With 828 rooms, this is the largest, and perhaps the best-looking hotel in the entire Hilton chain. The location is good, but slightly less convenient than that of the Mandarin, being a few blocks further away and slightly elevated above the harbor. The rooms are attractive and good-sized, much as Hilton hotels are all over the world. My criticism of this otherwise admirable hotel is the location of its lobby, on the third floor, the first two floors being devoted to shops. Rates are medium-high.

Furama Inter-Continental. An elaborate 32-story hotel with revolving restaurant on an upper floor. A deluxe hotel with medium-sized rooms. Several restaurants, shops, and all facilities. Caters to groups.

Lee Gardens. A very large hotel in the Causeway Bay region, quite a bit away from the main part of town. It's in an atmospheric area but not very convenient for most tourists. The lobby is fine, the restaurants are excellent, but the rooms are mediocre, to say the least, and the furnishings not well chosen. Rates are lower than at most Hong Kong hotels.

Repulse Bay. For those who want to combine resort living with a visit to Hong Kong, this pleasant old-world hotel features large rooms, very good service, and a terrace that is famous for its view, combined with good meals. A huge new wing is due to open any day now, and this will change the image of old-fashioned grandeur. It has a minibus which takes guests to and from the Central District of Victoria in 20 minutes. Rates are in the moderate class.

Excelsior. A very large, busy hotel, with remarkable convention facilities. It has 986 rooms, pleasantly decorated, and there are specialty restaurants, cocktail lounges, shops—the Excelsior is almost like a small city. Located in Causeway Bay area. Medium rates.

Plaza. Also in the Causeway Bay district, this popular hotel has 850 rooms. It is ideal for tour groups and conventions. Moderate rates.

KOWLOON (MAINLAND) HOTELS:

Peninsula. As long as anyone can remember, the Peninsula has been one of the world's great hotels, with a worldwide reputation. Although the structure is somewhat old, the hotel has generally been very well maintained, and the rooms are large, with high ceilings and lots of atmosphere; the service is topnotch and there is also a new wing. My main complaint is with the lobby; it has a very commercial look, being filled with small tearoom-style tables and chairs. But it's still a fine hotel.

Sheraton Hong-Kong. An enormous, rather impressive hotel in a key location, convenient to almost everything on the mainland side. It has 865 rooms, nicely decorated. There are dozens and dozens of shops, a large assortment of restaurants, and it is particularly convenient for tourists. The service is excellent and concerned. The hotel is almost a self-contained city.

Regent. A very large hotel with a marvelous view of the harbor, about 5 minutes walking distance from Nathan Road. Rooms are good sized and attractively decorated. The Regent is operated as a luxury hotel, with fine service. There is a good choice of restaurants and shops.

Shangri-La. A giant 720-room deluxe hotel with an excellent location facing the harbor. Rooms are pleasant, large in size, and attractive, and all have refrigerators and color TV. Next to two large shopping complexes. A Westin International hotel.

Royal Garden. Almost adjacent to the Shangri-La, a 16-story hotel
with many restaurants and shops. Very nice rooms, all with color
TV and refrigerator. Excellent management; one of the Mandarin
hotels.

Holiday Inn Harbour View. A 19-story, 600-room hotel facing the
harbor (harbour, British style). All rooms have double or king-
size beds, refrigerator and color TV.

Regal Palace. A 625-room hotel, with many shops and restaurants.
Fairly good rooms, somewhat less expensive than most other
hotels in Kowloon; all rooms with color TV and refrigerator.

Marco Polo. Located in west Tsimshatsui, on Canton Road, near
the Ocean Centre shopping complex. Rooms have queen-size
beds in double rooms, two double beds in twin doubles, all with
color TV and refrigerator.

Regal Airport. As the name indicates, it's opposite Kai Tak Airport, on Prince Edward Road; particularly convenient for those
with overnight airport connections.

Hong Kong Hyatt Regency. An exceptionally large, 800-room hotel, on Nathan Road, convenient to shopping. Rooms are medium
in size, pleasantly decorated. The lobby is lively and busy, many
shops and restaurants. Rates are medium, edging toward being
somewhat high.

New World. An absolutely enormous complex of a large hotel and
shops, plus a residential complex, right at the waterfront. Rooms
vary greatly, depending upon price—some are good-sized, others
less so. Rates range from inexpensive to moderate, depending
upon the category selected. Many shops and a good selection of
restaurants.

Ambassador. A smart modern hotel, financed in the Philippines,
but American-managed. Good location, fairly good rooms, but
too many shops interfere with access to the lobby. Rather good
restaurants and room service.

Empress. This is a very pleasant, somewhat small hotel, handsomely
set up in a tall building. The rooms are medium in size and nicely
decorated; even the rates are medium, not high. About 5 minutes
from the Star Ferry on Chatham Road, with excellent views of
the harbor. Two restaurants.

Holiday Inn-Hong Kong. A 19-story, 593-room hotel situated conveniently on Nathan Road. Like all Holiday Inns, the rooms are
of rather good size and fairly well decorated. All sorts of facilities,
including several restaurants, bars, pool, sauna, steambath, etc.
Rates are lower than at many other Hong Kong hotels in this
location.

Park. A little farther along Chatham Road from the Empress is this comparatively large, very pleasant hotel facing the harbor. The Park has some of the largest guestrooms in Hong Kong, and is very nice, although just slightly inconvenient for the Star Ferry, but extra convenient for shopping.

Hong Kong. An enormous hotel, very conveniently located near the Star Ferry. Rooms facing the harbor have a fabulous view, but those in the rear may have an unattractive outlook. The hotel has several restaurants, not that Kowloon is lacking in choice. Rooms range in size from smaller than average to quite large, depending upon the price category selected.

Imperial. Next-door to the Ambassador on busy Nathan Road, this is quite good, although some rooms tend to be smallish. There's a top-floor restaurant featuring western food; also a Japanese restaurant, most attractive.

Miramar. This hotel consists of two parts; the original section and a new Miramar Princess Wing, making a total of 1300 rooms. It has a large shopping complex, numerous restaurants, and a convention hall. The rooms are fair in size, and the hotel is ideal for tour groups. Moderate rates.

RESTAURANTS   If you like Chinese food, by all means try several of the restaurants listed below. Sanitation is good, service pleasant, and prices aren't high. You'll usually find any number of local western residents in these restaurants, so that's a pretty good indication of how they're regarded locally.

Now, I realize that making a choice from the places listed below isn't easy. So, if I may, I'd like to suggest my own personal choices. If you want to dine on the Victoria side, visit the Yung Kee Restaurant, at 32 Wellington Street. It's not an elaborate place, but the food is generally excellent. If you like Cantonese food, visit the Jade Garden, on the fourth floor of Star House, just a few minutes walk from the Kowloon ferry terminus. Most of the diners here are Chinese, but there's an English menu and the food is topnotch.

For those who want to sample the high points of Chinese cuisine, I would suggest dining at the Peking Gardens Restaurant, located in the Excelsior Hotel, in the Causeway Bay district. Their menus feature all the great dishes, and it may be the best single restaurant in Hong Kong to try dishes which are ordinarily only available on special order.

If you like spicy food, you'd surely enjoy a Szechuan (pronounced setch-wan) meal. I don't suppose that there's a better place for this interesting style of cooking than a small, unassuming restaurant called the Red Pepper. It's located behind the Lee Gardens Hotel; take a cab there and ask the doorman or anyone else to direct you around the corner to the restaurant. The food is delicious, prices moderate, and it's loads of fun—but you must like spicy food.

May I urge you strongly to try a dim-sum lunch. It consists of small snacks, which you select from carts pushed by waitresses who wander about the dining room. It's lots of fun, and very inexpensive. I suggest you try the lunchtime dim-sum served at the Sheraton Hotel in the spacious dining room that is on the right and to the rear as you enter the hotel. It's a delicious, not very costly lunch, and you'll enjoy trying the various small items as the girls wander about the room, offering them on trays or carts. If you're more in the mood for privacy, go up to the second floor, where the restaurant is broken into a series of medium-sized rooms, and the food is perhaps even better. The entrance to the second floor restaurant bears the somewhat cryptic name of "Chinese Restaurant and Night Club," which it isn't, of course. In any event, don't leave Hong Kong without having at least one dim-sum lunch.

If you really like seafood, I'd definitely suggest Siu Lam Kung, on Hanoi Road in Kowloon. It's an attractive place with excellent seafood preparations and is one of the few comparatively expensive restaurants you'll encounter. For those who regard themselves as experts in Chinese food, I would also suggest a visit to the Spring Deer Restaurant, at the far end of Mody Road; the food is truly exceptional and they have a fascinating menu.

Surprisingly enough, elegant dining is uncommon, for the Chinese believe in putting all of their money into food and little into decoration. Two exceptions to this rule come to mind. The Chinese restaurant atop the Mandarin Hotel combines good food and elegance. If you don't mind a 15-minute taxi ride, another choice would be the Mayflower Restaurant, located in Wanchai on Tonnochy Street; the food at both places is generally excellent.

Turning to western food, I think the best single place in all of Hong Kong is on the Victoria side. It's the Rotisserie, located on the third floor of the Furama Hotel. The atmosphere is very pleasant, the food first class, and the service borders on the elegant. Just a personal suggestion: If you like fish, and they happen to have fresh Macao sole, be sure to order it. To my way of thinking, it's even better than Dover sole.

In Kowloon, the best continental restaurant is the Marco Polo, especially for beef and pork dishes and very fancy desserts (Baked Alaska and very alcoholic Cherries Jubilee). Hugo's, in the Hyatt, is a favorite with locals for Western food. The Pink Giraffe, in the

Sheraton, is very elegant, and there's also a floor show. The Royal Hawaiian Room (Empress Hotel) is very good for thick sirloin steaks. The Carlton restaurant serves good steak and chicken. Gaddi's (in the Peninsula Hotel) is fairly good and quite expensive; they also serve Chinese and international specialties. Also good is the Starlight Room at the President where the surroundings are very pleasant.

One of the most diverting places for those interested in food, and particularly suitable for lunch or even an informal dinner, is a complex of some 24 restaurants on Food Street, an indoor arrangement under one roof. It's located in the Causeway Bay District, opposite the entrance to the Cross-Harbour Tunnel. You'll find a *dim sum* place, noodle restaurant, Japanese barbecued steak, curry specialist, pizza house, coffeehouse, and more. It's lots of fun, but it can be quite busy at lunchtime.

A really great novelty, but best in the early morning, is the famous "bird restaurant" Hing Wan, at 119 Queens Road Central, in the main business area of Hong Kong. Breakfast consists of small snack foods called *dim sum* (mentioned previously), plus tea. There are bird cages hung overhead, and the atmosphere is extemely pleasant. Another famous *dim sum* restaurant in the Central District is the Luk Yu Teahouse, situated at 24 Stanley Street. It is famous for its remarkable teas, said to be placed in storage for one year in order to ferment before being used.

A most interesting restaurant is the Vegi Food Kitchen, on Cleveland Street in Causeway Bay. The food, as you can tell from the name, is strictly vegetarian, but wait! It doesn't consist of boiled string beans cooked in bicarbonate of soda or soggy boiled potatoes. It has a marvelous reputation with local people, and the food is admirable, being imaginative and carefully prepared. You won't be sorry you went. Particularly good are the deep-fried taro rolls and silver frills, a dish made from mushrooms, bamboo shoots, and bean sprouts.

SHOPPING Without very much doubt, Hong Kong is the greatest shopping spot in the entire world. Paris and Rome may lead in fashion design, England may do the finest work with woolens, Germany may be best with cutlery, and Japan may be the leader in cameras, binoculars and transistor radios. But Hong Kong often undercuts the original price in the country of origin, so that Japanese cameras (for example) may often sell for less than in Japan. The reason is not too complex: prices are generally fixed in the country where the goods originated, but in Hong Kong a merchant may go below the suggested retail price in order to make a sale. In addition, Hong Kong is a "free port," so that merchandise is sold practically duty-free.

Shopping in Hong Kong is a full-time occupation for many Americans. There is quite a bit of sightseeing in the area, but it's a rare tourist who fails to succumb to the siren call of bargain prices combined with excellent merchandise. The woman who comes here with dress designs or sketches from *Harper's Bazaar* or *Vogue* will be ahead of the game, and save a great deal of time if she plans to buy custom-made clothing. My recommendation, if you're planning to order clothes, is to start having them made *before* sightseeing is commenced. Don't start your sightseeing, then expect to have your tailor whip up dresses and suits in the last minute or so; you'll be disappointed. The very same logic goes for men, because good tailoring takes time. I know, you've heard that a Hong Kong tailor can make up a suit in 24 hours. He can, but it won't be very good, and you won't be pleased.

Any Chinese mainland merchandise is without any restrictions other than those applying to regular foreign purchases; that is, you are only permitted $300 worth of merchandise, which must be taken with you, free of duty. Anything above that amount, or merchandise which is sent, is dutiable. This, of course, means that you can now go to mainland Chinese-operated stores in Hong Kong and Kowloon where a very large selection of every type of merchandise is available.

Women will be delighted because there are exceptional values in jade which heretofore was not permitted to be brought into the U.S. Jade prices vary from a few dollars to several thousand, according to the color and quality. The Chinese have always had a great devotion to jade and, in addition to admiring its beauty, believe that it will assure the wearer of good health. Many people always wear a piece, generally hidden from view. The color of jade ranges from the deepest emerald green all the way to almost pure white. The Hong Kong jewelry stores are always stocked with a good supply of jade, generally made into jewelry. A popular place to buy jade, and enjoy the experience, is the Jade Market. This takes place outdoors from 10 A.M. to about noon along Canton Road in the Kowloon area. You can buy some serious (that means expensive) jade pieces here, but I wouldn't advise it; however, if you see a bit of jade that pleases you and it's only a matter of a few dollars, there's no reason why you shouldn't buy what you want. Bargaining is imperative; the seller would be startled if you paid his first price. Don't forget that jade varies in color, and you'll see some articles in yellow, pink, red, brown, and blue. For serious jewelry shopping, Falconers, in the Peninsula Hotel, has a good selection.

Women's clothes. As previously mentioned, start your visit to Hong Kong by placing your orders for custom-made garments; know what you want when you go, if possible, and bring sketches or photographs to show the tailor. It will help a great deal, but of course, you can make up your mind when you get there, if you wish. Every woman in the world knows of Hong Kong's bargain prices, which have become almost a legend, but like all touristic legends, there are always a few exceptions and details. The legend that every Chinese tailor could put the Paris fashion houses out of business if only he could get a French visa can definitely be classified as nonsense. Chinese tailors, and there are literally thousands of them in Hong Kong, are generally good, but the truly gifted ones are pretty rare. Also, as mentioned before, any suit or dress whipped up with excessive speed and at ridiculously low prices will look it. You should have an absolute minimum of two fittings, and three would be better. If you pay the absolute bottom price for tailoring, you'll be able to amaze your neighbors and friends with your skill in bargaining, but you won't come back with something you'll really enjoy. If you are at all seriously style-conscious, I think in all sincerity it will be better to spend just a little more and order something you'll get pleasure out of for years, rather than a bargain-basement garment, for which you pay a minimum price, and which will look—alas—just as though you bought it in a bargain basement. When you're ordering a dress or suit, be very specific about linings, buttons, seam widths, in fact every possible detail, and make sure that the tailor understands what you're saying. Make him repeat the details. As to prices, don't compare a custom-made dress or suit with ready-to-wear clothes. For example, an outfit of wool with a silk lining and hand detail will cost about five times as much in the U.S. as it will in Hong Kong.

Just about every store in Hong Kong that displays fabrics has a resident tailor, who may be talented or may not be. In addition, every hotel has at least several shops prepared to whip up any desired creation, particularly in the Hilton, Peninsula, Ambassador, and President hotels. To my way of thinking, the best and most reliable place to have clothes made, although certainly not the lowest-priced, is the shop of Celia Chien, which is located in the Peninsula Hotel.

The next group are a long step away (meaning less expensive) in both workmanship and price. Although prices vary and depend upon the material selected and the amount of handwork required, expect to pay a medium price for a dress at the following: William Loo and Betty Clemo (both in the Peninsula) are quite good, and can turn out a well-designed garment for you, and have been doing so for quite a long time, which is inevitably a good sign. The Star of Siam (again, the Peninsula) makes up western-style clothing out of Thai silks, which are really beautiful; there is also some ready-to-wear merchandise on hand. If you like to deal in a department store, Lane Crawford's (in Hong Kong, and in the Miramar Arcade, Kowloon) is very reliable, although slightly less style-conscious than the others, which is perhaps suitable for someone with a mature figure. If you don't want to bother, wander about the shops in your hotel and make your selection after a little preliminary comparison, and use your own judgment.

Men's clothes. Everything that has been said about women's clothing goes equally for men's suits and coats. Although on first blush, men's tailoring would appear to be a simpler job than comparable work for women, the opposite seems true, for a good man's tailor is often more difficult to locate. Almost every man who comes to Hong Kong has heard about the marvelous opportunity to stock up on enough suits for several years for a matter of just a few dollars, with just one fitting. Forget it! Good tailoring (this is getting repetitious but it's true) takes time, and two fittings are an absolute minimum, and three would be far better. It may be possible to find a tailor who will make a suit for $50 but please don't, or you'll waste your time and money. A good suit in Hong Kong, tailor-made, should cost about $150 U.S. or so on the average, and it will be equal to one costing two or three times as much in the U.S., if all things work out right. Don't forget that the man who takes your measurements and smiles and is so understanding and considerate, merely writes down your measurements on a piece of paper. Those measurements then go to a tailor, and how closely he follows them is the crux of the matter. If the tailoring work is actually done on the premises, that should offer some clue as to the likelihood of obtaining a satisfactory fit. But if the work is executed away from the shop by some Chinese tailor sitting on the floor in a cluttered back alley tenement, with children running about, and paid piece-work according to his individual speed, you may be sure that a good many of the carefully taken measurements will be overlooked or even disregarded. As the British tailors say, a man's suit must be "built," not just sewn together. Occasionally, inner seams are not carefully sewn and because they are not visible to the eye, often lead to problems several weeks later after the suit is worn a few times. Don't try and find the cheapest tailor in Hong Kong, just to brag to friends at home about the low price you paid. I'd much rather you paid the higher price, and then lied to your friends. In point of fact, I think many men do just that and I think that is how the rumors originated about $35 suits made to order in Hong Kong. Don't accept the suit unless it fits to your satisfaction, and insist on as many fittings without additional charge as it takes to get the suit tailored as you think it should be. Also, don't waste your time in getting wash-and-wear or similar lightweight summer suits made up to your order; the American fabrics and mass production know-how make regular American summer suits a better value all around.

Now, where to go. First of all, every hotel has a number of men's tailoring shops. These are bound to be fairly reliable, because otherwise the hotel management would evict them after a few complaints, and this offers you a good degree of assurance. On the other hand, hotel shops are inevitably a little more expensive than outside shops, but there is a great deal of personal convenience in being able to drop into the shop for a fitting on your way in (or out) of the hotel. If you want some specific recommendations, William Yu (Kimberly Road, Kowloon) has been very well known for many years; the same goes for George Chen in the Peninsula Hotel.

If you like custom-made shirts, Hong Kong is a marvelous place to get them made up with precisely the collar, material, sleeve length, buttons, monogram, etc., that please you. Again, the price paid is important. Shirts can be ordered for only a few dollars, but for a dollar or so more, well-fitting shirts will probably be the result. S. L. Wang and Company in Kowloon is here highly regarded as an excellent shirtmaker, although slightly more expensive than most. Most of the hotel tailoring shops also make shirts which will prove an excellent value, and can usually be ordered from the same tailor who makes your suits. In a class by itself is the shop of Ascot Chang, located on Kimberley Road in Kowloon. Their work is excellent but not inexpensive.

Women's shoes. Most women like to have matching shoes to complement a suit or dress, and these can be made up, if you wish, while here. Furthermore, a handbag to match an outfit is also easily to be had. The shoes can be made in brocade, embroidered satin, jewel-encrusted silk, or even alligator. The prices are reasonable, although the finished shoes do not wear so well as one might wish. However, and this is a very big however, the shoes do not fit too well, as a rule. Nine times out of ten they will be uncomfortable or require repeated visits to correct the defects; often the tourist will have to leave the shoes behind to be mailed home. But occasionally they do fit right off the bat; so use your own judgment. On the other hand, golf shoes and riding boots usually come out quite satisfactorily.

Cameras, radios and binoculars. All of these precision items, although made in Japan, are for sale in Hong Kong at prices similar to those of Tokyo. Sometimes the sales tags are slightly higher or slightly lower, depending upon local conditions, but as often as not, cameras and radios can be purchased for slightly less than in Japan. You'll find virtually every make of camera or radio in the various shops; it may be necessary to visit several shops to locate a particular model, although the largest shops have just about every make. Even though the prices are marked, you can generally ask for and expect to receive a 10% discount. Inasmuch as the marked price is almost identical to that in Japan, it is often possible to buy for 10% less than the country of origin. You'll find camera stores wherever you turn. Developing service for black and white and Kodacolor is very good and fast. They can also process Ektachrome, but not Kodachrome.

Pearls and jewelry. With the same logic (small profit, high volume of sales), the Hong Kong shopkeepers often sell pearls at better prices than Japan. Pearls cost anything you have to spend, from a few dollars to many thousands, and that's U.S. dollars, not Hong Kong dollars. (For a discussion of pearls, please see the appropriate section in Japan.) Unlike cameras (which are all identical in the same model number), pearls are very variable, and no strands, nor even two pearls, are exactly alike. A little bargaining goes a long way in the smaller pearl and jewelry shops. Although many Americans hesitate to bargain, please remember that there are a half-dozen shops in the same block, all trying to sell pearls. The storekeeper knows this, too, so just ask the price, look unimpressed, say it's too much, and head for the door. Slowly, however. You do want him to have a chance to lower his price. In this highly competitive free market, it's only by keeping prices low that Hong Kong attracts visitors and maintains its fantastic rate of growth and prosperity. Don't be won over to the asking price by sad stories and believe that the article is being sold to you at a loss, etc.; it's just part of the local scene.

Hong Kong is truly like the oriental treasurehouse of myth and legend when it comes to *jewelry,* particularly jade. In a hundred (or more) stores, you'll be tempted by jade, or what looks like jade. The hardest kind of jade, the best, is called jadeite; soft jade is used in making decorative objects. Jadeite comes in three gradings of color, but the most desirable (called Imperial Jade) is median in color between very light and very dark green, almost an emerald shade. Formerly jade was not permitted to be brought into the U.S. from China. The only rough and ready test for good jade is that it does not scratch readily, but it often takes an expert to know the real thing from an imitation. Don't invest any substantial sums of money in jade without having it first appraised by an expert; certainly don't spend a great deal in a tiny shop in a fast transaction. A small jade stone which is translucent, brilliantly green, and with an emerald color, sells for at least $1,000 and frequently much more. But you can also buy something for a modest price as well. Gold and diamonds are available, but prices are similar to those all over the world; only in the cheaper labor required for settings can a substantial saving be anticipated. Gold jewelry is very good, and the low labor cost makes rings, bracelets, pins, etc., all worthwhile purchases. There are so many jewelry stores that it's impossible to make any recommendations.

Beaded sweaters. This is inevitably a good, standard purchase and solves a great number of gift problems. They are elaborate or simple, as you wish. Sweaters are available in heavy beading, beaded patterns, with sequins, etc. According to the state of contemporary fashion (in vogue or out), the range of choice will be limitless or limited.

Furniture. Camphor wood (pleasantly aromatic) made up into chests and carved furniture is a Hong Kong specialty. If you're interested, take a stroll down Canton Road in Kowloon when you're looking for bargains. Slightly higher in price is a reliable shop in the Miramar Arcade (Kowloon); also highly regarded is the store operated by S. Y. Ma (Ichang Street in Kowloon). You need a good shipper to send anything in the way of furniture. I wish I could tell you whether this furniture will (or will not) warp when you get it home; I've heard varying reports, some complaining, others saying the furniture stood up well. The wood tends to dry out when removed from Hong Kong and taken to less humid climates, but a system of doweling and tongue-and-groove construction has been devised which minimizes warpage.

Leather goods. If your luggage is starting to give way, it can be replaced at very reasonable prices, but pick and choose carefully and don't buy the very cheapest. It may look good, but it won't stand up in the long run. Nylon luggage in Hong Kong seems well-designed and light-weight, but make sure the locks are imported, for the local ones are definitely poor. The Himalaya Leather Shop in the Ocean Terminal has very good luggage and handbags. Aluminum luggage is available, but it dents quickly, and even when covered with slip cases, doesn't stand up too well. Kam Lung (in Kowloon) is about the best shop on the mainland for luggage.

Carpets. With the reopening of mainland China to western trade, and the embargo on imports lifted from that country, the famous Tientsin carpets are now available. Remarkable carpets are to be had at the Hong Kong Carpet Manufacturers, who have a showroom in the Peninsula Court. They can follow any design you have in mind, so bring measurements with you, and have it made up here.

Linens, handkerchiefs. Tablecloths, placemats, napkins and handkerchiefs are among the best buys here, and as usual, the more you spend, the more you save. To paraphrase, the cheaper linens with little handwork are excellent values, but the magnificent examples of linen and handkerchiefs are fabulous buys, a fraction of their stateside prices. I know you'll find this hard to believe, but a handkerchief purchased for $3 here could retail for $15 back home.

Antiquities and art objects. Let's begin by restating what has already become the obvious: You must be very careful when buying Chinese merchandise. On small inexpensive articles, there isn't too much problem, but be careful when spending a good deal of money. For screens, decorative scrolls, and a wide variety of ornaments, recommended shops include Ada Lum (in the Mandarin Hotel), Lien Hing Ivory Factory (in the Chung King Arcade), Eileen Kershaw (Peninsula Hotel), the Temple Bell (in the Mirador Mansion), and Hong Kong Old Mary (Chung King Arcade). In the Ocean Terminal (Kowloon), there is a store which sells handicrafts from every oriental country. This American-owned shop has a great array of unusual and exotic goods, ranging from Bombay taxi horns to Taiwanese statues; definitely worth a visit, the next time you're near the Star Ferry Terminal in Kowloon.

For many years there was a prohibition against bringing ivory products into the United States in an effort to stop the killing of elephants. It has been determined that this ruling was not necessary nor helpful, and, as a result, you can now bring home with you ivory purchases from Asia. You must carry the ivory products as accompanying baggage for personal noncommercial use. This procedure covers all souvenirs that you might want to buy: You must take them with you. If you want to ship them, the dealer must obtain Certificates of Origin for them. Don't pay for the ivory products until the dealer shows you he has the Certificates of Origin.

Many people like to do all of their shopping under one roof, and this is a particularly good idea if the weather is less than perfect. One place to accomplish this is the Ocean Terminal (mentioned below).

Another good spot is the Sheraton Hotel, where the shops are located on the lower level and on the second and third floors; the escalators take you directly to and from the shopping areas. A third excellent place for shopping under one roof is the New World Shopping Centre; it is diverting merely to walk about here, much less to shop. On the street level there's a mainland Chinese store, but that's only the beginning.

Chances are that you've heard about Hong Kong's famous Cat Street or visited it, if you've been here on a previous trip. It was an area extending along Upper Lascar Road, lined with antique shops that sold a great collection of junk intermixed with an occasional authentic bargain. The shops bulged with gilt carvings, lacquerware, ceramics, Ming-type copies of the classic horses, ancient opium pipes, statuettes, figurines, china bowls, gongs, copper articles, brassware, scrolls, paintings, etc., etc., and even etc. Now all of that is gone, for Cat Street has been replaced with a housing development and the shopkeepers have scattered.

If you're looking for the finest of *antiques,* including those of India and Thailand, be sure to visit the shop of Charlotte Horstmann, located in the Ocean Terminal, Kowloon. She also has a large selection of fabrics and gift items, and anything bought at her shop is bound to be of the highest quality.

Don't buy anything expensive in the way of antiques elsewhere, unless you know what you're doing, or can get expert advice. There will also be a shipping problem if the antique you bought is too large or cumbersome to carry. The Ocean Terminal is a fascinating place for shopping. There are literally hundreds of different types of shops where everything from a handkerchief to a priceless gem necklace can be bought.

Chinese antiques. China has set up several stores to display the merchandise it is producing, and of course, to garner some hard currency for itself. Obviously, these stores sell "Chinese-type" merchandise, which is quite unusual. Two shops are on the Victoria side; the Chinese Arts and Crafts, located on Wyndham Street, right off Queen's Road in Hong Kong; the other is the China Products Company, in Wanchai, just a few minutes from downtown Hong Kong. There are new articles (such as high-fi sets) and well-carved chests, and a few authentic antiques, plus many copies (but the clerks will tell you which are genuine). You can buy, or merely browse around, then leave without buying.

The Chinese also have an elaborate shop in Kowloon, between the Star Ferry and the Peninsula Hotel. They have all sorts of merchandise, including fancy handkerchiefs, art objects, antiques, silks, and jewelry. It's fascinating to wander about, and to talk to the sales help, and remember, it's no longer against the law to bring any of this merchandise into the United States. If you're really interested in what the mainland Chinese are producing in the way of consumer goods, take a taxi (or walk if you're in the mood) to the corner of Jordan and Nathan Roads, Kowloon, to a large shop called Yue Hwa, and wander through the food section (the candied ginger is absolutely delicious), look at the Chinese medicines, and go upstairs into the china and kitchen equipment section. I almost always buy some table mats, which are exceptionally attractive and low in price.

ENTERTAINMENT If you like music with dinner, plus dancing, all of the hotels have a room or two. In your bedroom, the hotel will usually have a card announcing this fact. Gaddi's and Marco Polo have pleasant dance music with your dinner, but no floor show. In addition, almost every hotel has a small bar, or *boîte* if you prefer, where you can listen to music while thoughtfully drinking some liquid refreshment. At the Ambassador Hotel in Kowloon, there's string music, but no dancing. The Sheraton has live entertainment, which is generally very good. Don't forget the Chinese floor show at the Hotel Miramar's nightclub.

UNDERSTANDING THE LOCAL TALK There are certain words and phrases used in Hong Kong which form a part of the local scene. It's nice to know what they mean:

Amah. A Chinese maid or nurse.

Central District. The business and commercial center of Hong Kong Island.

Cross-Harbour Tunnel. The tunnel which connects Hong Kong and Kowloon.

Government House. Situated between Lower and Upper Albert Road.

Gwai-lo. Literally, "foreign devil," the Chinese term for all foreigners.

I.D. Card. A card which must be carried by all residents.

Junk. The classic Chinese vessel, with a high, flat stern and a low bow; may be operated only by sails, but nowadays most have motors.

Ladder Streets. Streets with many high steps.

Mah–Jongg. A game played with ivory or plastic tiles; may typically be seen in certain restaurants following the dinner hour.

Nullah. One of the man-made canals provided to take care of excessive rainfall.

Peak. Used generally to cover a fair-sized residential area high above the main portion of sea-level Victoria, on Hong Kong Island.

Picul. Chinese measurement of weight, about 133 pounds.

Tael. A Chinese weight amounting to 1⅓ ounces.

Tai Tai. A Chinese housewife.

Sampan. Small boats intended for close-in waterfront operations, controlled by a single oar at the boat's stern.

Star Ferry. The ferry service that operates between Hong Kong and Kowloon.

Victoria. A generic name intended to cover both the residential area and the Central District on Hong Kong Island.

Macao

❧ When To Go

As far as weather goes, it usually matches the local conditions in Hong Kong, and similar weather can be anticipated. Of course, it's rather discouraging to make the trip on a poor day, but what can you do, if you're only going to be here for a few days? It'll still be a worthwhile trip, short of a monsoon.

✒ Visa Requirements

Getting from Hong Kong to this tiny bit of Portugal is not terribly complicated but takes just a little effort. First of all, you'll need a visa, and this may be obtained from a Portuguese Consulate in the United States when you're obtaining your other visas; there is a fee of $5.85. If you've come to Hong Kong without obtaining the necessary visa, merely take your passport to the Portuguese Consulate located on the 14th floor of the Central Building in Hong Kong, and they'll issue the visa while you wait. (Sometimes the travel agents who sell organized tours will relieve you of this requirement and obtain the visa for you.)

You can even obtain your visa when you arrive in Macao, but there's usually a little delay. However, it takes time to get your visa in Hong Kong, so it all comes out even.

$ Currency

The local money is called the *pataca,* and the rate of exchange is almost identical to that of the Hong Kong dollar, although it may fluctuate occasionally, but even the fluctuations are quite slight. It really isn't necessary to convert your money because Hong Kong dollars or U.S. dollars are acceptable almost everywhere. When paying for anything, ask for your change in Hong Kong dollars, because *patacas* are worth much less in Hong Kong, and you'll lose quite a bit reconverting them when you leave.

Accommodations

Truly outstanding, and really an exceptional hotel, is the Lisboa, which has more than 300 rooms and suites plus some apartments. On the second floor, there's an elaborate casino, so you don't even have to go outdoors to lose your money. There are, in addition, nightclubs, another less grand casino, 2 Chinese restaurants, a Portuguese restaurant, a 24-hour coffee shop, 2 grills, 5 bars, a bowling alley, sauna, steam bath, shopping arcade—well, you certainly get the idea. Room rates are, by American standards, nothing short of bargains. Indeed, if you like luxury, you can have a beautiful suite for 2 people at the cost of an ordinary, mediocre hotel room elsewhere in the Orient. However, the Lisboa is so very busy and frenetic, what with scores of shops, a dozen restaurants, and gambling rooms, that it isn't everyone's cup of tea. If you're looking for something quieter, I would recommend the Hotel Sintra, which is much (much) quieter, and is also deluxe on all counts. The Hotel President, with 340 rooms, is also a worthwhile place at which to stay. For something different, there's the Pousada de Santiago, a Portuguese-style inn built within the walls of a 16th-century fortress; the Pousada is small and compact, and quite charming, with excellent food. If you really want peace and quiet, the Pousada de Coloane, on Coloane Island, is on a beach surrounded by a pine forest. This is really a very quiet place and is ideal if you want to break up your trip with a few days of rest. Because it's small, the Pousada is booked well in advance, so it's difficult to obtain a reservation at the last minute. The point that should be remembered about Macao is that the hotels are always jammed during the weekends but far less busy Monday through Thursday. Bear this in mind when making reservations and also remember the hydrofoil transportation to and from Macao.

Health, Customs, Etc.

You'll need certificates for smallpox and cholera. Bring your passport and visa. The customs inspection is largely theoretical, because no one cares. However, when you're returning to Hong Kong, please remember that each person can bring back only a bottle of Portuguese wine duty-free; brandy and other purchases are subject to Hong Kong duty, if the inspector is in the mood to make the levy, and he often is.

How to Get There

There are three ways of going from Hong Kong to Macao. You can go by ferry (slow but restful), hydrofoil (the boats that lift out of the water and move quite swiftly), or jetfoil (even a bit faster than the hydrofoils). Don't—repeat *don't*—go to Macao without confirmed space back, no matter what anyone tells you. Space can become *very* scarce, particularly on weekends.

There are several *ferry* services leaving at various times of the day; the schedules change rather frequently. In general, the ferries make the 40-mile trip in anywhere from 2½ to 3 hours or so. They all have staterooms, should you wish to take one, but it's really not necessary unless you take one of the night ferries. All of them serve meals, but the food is hardly distinguished, and you'd do well to just have a snack and save yourself for the Macao food, which is far, far better. Your hotel can make the ferry reservations, obtain tickets, etc.

Hydrofoil service is an excellent way to make the trip to Macao. These hydrofoils, which rise out of the water, move at a good clip, and make the crossing in about 1¼ hours each way. The *jetfoils* make the trip in 45 minutes, and almost everyone wants to travel on these much faster boats. The hall porter at your hotel can obtain your tickets. There is little sensation of motion aboard either the hydrofoils or the jetfoils, seats are booked in advance when making the reservation, and the trip is quite comfortable. The time passes very quickly, what with getting settled, watching the scenery, and perhaps buying some refreshment. You can expect a little confusion on the pier in Macao, because you have to clear through their immigration procedures (arriving and departing), but it doesn't take more than ten minutes or so (unless you haven't obtained your visa for Macao; in that case it might take a half hour).

Restaurants, Food Specialties and Liquor

If you feel like having Chinese food, the best is probably Long Kei, conveniently located near the Post Office. A great reputation has been developed by the Fat Sui Lau Restaurant, located at 65 Rua da Felicidade, particularly for its roast pigeon. For Portuguese atmosphere, head for the Pousada de Macau, next door to the Governor's Palace. Although their fish dishes are excellent (no matter what you select), the great specialty of the restaurant is called African chicken—chicken sauteed with garlic, lots of it. If they happen to have Macao sole, it's absolutely fantastic, light and delicate. If you're near the Lisboa Hotel, that beehive of life and activity, there's a basement restaurant called A Galera, which has both Continental and Portuguese food; it's generally excellent. However, although it's quiet at lunchtime, at night there's a combo. If you've been yearning for some good wine, which many people find they miss when on a trip through the Orient, Macao features reasonably priced Portuguese imports, and in the usually warm weather of this province, I think the Mateus *rosé* would be a good choice; it's light and pleasant. Portuguese brandies are rougher than cognacs, but still good.

If you don't mind venturing where few tourists have gone, and want to have the best of *dim-sum,* those marvelous small bits of Chinese food, head for a restaurant called Loc Koc, located at Rua 5 de Octubro, just a brief walk from the main street called Avenida Almeida Ribeiro. You have to climb two flights to reach this sky-light-lit place, which has a most remarkable ceiling. You may find the young waiters staring at you, because they seldom see western-ers; there's no English menu, and you'll have a little difficulty in placing an order. Your best bet will be to merely stop one of the waiters who bring around trays filled with small bits of food—buns filled with meat, fish balls, rice mixtures, shrimp, and so forth. It's a lot of fun, and very offbeat. Your check will be computed by counting the number of plates on your table when you've finished.

MACAO SIGHTSEEING To me, there is something quite amusing about the travel agencies' method of promoting business for Macao. They talk of its historical importance, about the number of churches, the old buildings, and the Portuguese atmosphere. Buried in their literature are some discreet references about visiting the gambling casinos. In actual fact, it is the gambling which draws the crowds to Macao, and why be devious? Not that Macao isn't very pleasing and worth a trip on its own; in my opinion, it is a diverting excursion. But it's the gambling that constitutes the big tourist attraction. Nevertheless, what is Macao really like?

The six square miles of Portugal's "overseas province" at the mouth of the Pearl River estuary that leads to Canton in mainland China is unique in many ways. For one thing this is just about the easiest entry into China, with numerous trips offered directly out of Macao. For another, this oldest European settlement in Asia is simultaneously known as a "City of God" and also as the "Monte Carlo of the Far East," and has a reputation for more vice per capita than any other spot in the world. If you watch television movies on the Late Late Show, you would expect to find opium-smoking in the streets, skulduggery in the alleys, and heads being conked wth blackjacks at every turn. Well, that's not Macao today.

Macao has for a long time managed to reconcile all kinds of paradoxes. When you approach it from your ferry or hydrofoil, the white buildings, the cathedral on the hill, and the sleepy atmosphere all point to a small Mediterranean town. But soon the bay filled with junks and the swarming Chinese tenements correct the image, and the unlikely (and successful) marriage of old Europe and old China is apparent. The whole effect is similar to Hong Kong, yet different. It is Portuguese-Chinese, not British-Chinese.

The mainland part of Macao is only 2 square miles in size, but it contains an amazing array of attractions. With the addition of its 2 islands of Taipa and Coloane, the grand total is all of 6 square miles. The cathedral on the hill, the burnt-out church of Sao Paulo built by Japanese Christians and symbolizing a meeting of Eastern and Western thought, and the many monuments to ancient battles all give Macao the feeling of recent history. Wide avenues and tree-shaded mansions are home to the Portuguese civil servants and army officers assigned here. And simple stone houses stand, within sight of the Barrier Gate into China, as housing for the many refugees who somehow escape. One of the exciting things about Macao is that China can be seen across the harbor, and also at the border crossing, the Portas do Cerco.

Macao has in the past achieved an importance quite disproportionate to its size. Camoëns, the most famous of all Portuguese poets, lived here for a time during the 16th century, and a garden built around his statue celebrates his visit and the "Lusiadas," a part of the famous poem he wrote here. Nearby is the Kam Yung Temple courtyard with the round stone table on which was signed, in 1844, the first commercial treaty between the U.S. and China (by Caleb

Cushing and Viceroy Yi and it shouldn't be difficult to tell who represented which country). During the last century Macao was the summer base for the opium-trading British companies, who afterwards moved on to Hong Kong. It was also in the first decade of the 20th century the home of Sun Yat-sen, the author of the 1911 revolution in China against the Manchu emperors, and regarded as the George Washington of the Chinese Republic. Unfortunately, the inescapable fact appears to be that Sun Yat-sen never lived here himself, but his family did.

Even more than Hong Kong, Macao reflects the traditional way of life of the Chinese at rest, at work, and at play. The difference between the two places is that the signs above the Chinese herbalist's store or the Chinese bingo parlor are in Chinese and Portuguese in Macao, rather than Chinese and English. But the sounds are the same. The mah-jong tiles clatter throughout the day, Cantonese opera bursts from hundreds of transistor radios, and the plastic slippers of coolies flip-flop along the streets.

Macao is a great gambling town. The place with most of the action is at the Hotel Lisboa, but there are quite a few casinos. In them, locals and visitors try their luck at Chinese gambling games such as *fan-tan,* or at the roulette wheels, the dice tables, or the black-jack boards. Gambling tables are in operation 24 hours a day and many thousands of dollars exchange hands every hour. How do you play *fan-tan?* No game could be simpler, because the bettor selects 1, 2, 3, or 4 as his choice. The house operator places a group of counters or buttons upon the table, then gradually removes 4 at a time. The winning number is the remainder, which must be 1 to 4. Don't bring your camera to the gambling casinos; they don't allow pictures. Another form of gambling is the new greyhound racetrack. There are meetings almost every weekend, when Macao is generally packed with people from Hong Kong.

You really don't need an organized excursion when you go sightseeing in Macao. The area is so small that it can be covered on foot, if you're not lazy (like me). Probably the best way is to hire a taxi by the hour, and make sure the driver speaks fair, or at least understandable, English. Be sure to bargain—they almost always ask for more than they're willing to accept; 2 or 3 hours should be sufficient to sightsee quite thoroughly.

Here are the things you should see in Macao, and it should take about two or three hours to cover all the ground (after that you can have a great lunch). The Temple of Kun Iam (this last word is pronounced eye-am), on the Avenida do Coronel Mesquita, goes back about 400 years, and may be even older. It's like entering another world to wander through the temple; you can buy some incense and make a wish (who knows?). In any event, take a little time to absorb some of the atmosphere of this Buddhist retreat. (If you really like temples, there's another one to the Goddess A-Ma, but you don't have to go unless you really enjoy temples.) Then head for the ruins of St. Paul, all that remains of a church dating back to 1602, according to the cornerstone. In 1835, the church burned to the ground, having caught fire during a typhoon, leaving only the facade and a few additional bits and pieces, most of which have since been removed. At the foot of the small square below the church is the best antique shop in Macao, which has some interesting items for sale, plus a good deal of tourist nonsense. Next on the sightseeing "must" list is the Portas do Cerco, the famous Barrier Gate, which is Macao's only official crossing point into China. It's possible to approach only within 100 yards (more or less) of the Chinese frontier and look out onto Chinese soil. In the general area are stalls and small shops selling authentic Chinese merchandise, such as beads, jewelry, small decorative objects, etc. All of these have been imported from China, which only proves that they make a great deal of souvenir junk. After this, you can see the Guia Fortress (if you insist), but I think you might do better to walk through the center of town and just look at the shops and the people. Or, you might want to try your luck at one of the casinos.

Incidentally, if you have the time, a visit to the islands of Taipa and Coloane is most interesting. There is a rehabilitation center for drug addicts on Taipa. Coloane is a green and pleasant rural island, with beautiful summer mansions dotted along its beach-lined coast. Don't expect to do any ocean swimming at Macao itself, for the water is muddy and not at all appealing; it's excellent at Coloane, however. You can drive to the islands over a bridge, and stay at the Pousada de Coloane, which is informal, unprepossessing, and quite pleasant. A new luxury hotel is under construction but was unnamed at the time this book went to press.

Plans are now underway for a river trip to Canton from Macao —that is, when the Chinese grant permission. Check on it, if you're interested.

CHINA

👫 Background

This giant among nations has an obscure origin, extending back for several thousands of years. The earliest, and somewhat vague beginnings probably started with the first dynasty, the Hsia, which lasted from 2205 to 1766 B.C. After this came the Shang dynasty, followed by the Chou dynasty, which ran from 1122 to 256 B.C. Although the empire appeared to expand in size, it simultaneously began to fragment into numerous feudal states. Chaos followed, and the winning group was the state of Chin, which is probably the origin of the word China.

Ever since that time, and until the previous century, China had various great periods, during which powerful rulers controlled the nation, literature and the arts flourished, and great commercial progress was made. However, much of the time there was confusion, minor and major skirmishes and numerous wars, and the general population suffered greatly from famine. Commercial relations with the western nations were limited, and as recently as 1834, only Canton was open for restricted trade. In that year, however, the British managed to have some of the restrictions lifted, and they also demanded that the entire nation be opened to foreign trade. The Chinese refusal led to the Anglo-Chinese War which ran from 1839 to 1842, often called the Opium War because the Chinese wished to end the traffic in this drug, whereas the British, alert to the profits involved, wanted to continue the trade. It was the British who won the war and had their way, leading to the Treaty of Nanking, in which various ports on the coast were opened to traffic. (It was at this time that Britain gained Hong Kong, a fabulous bit of territory.)

Because of the loss of several wars, the Manchu dynasty lost much of its authority, while foreign influence and power increased. During the years from 1861 to 1908, the true ruler of the country was the dowager empress, Tzu Hsi; this behind-the-scenes power was retained during the rule of three emperors of China. Although she was vicious, unyielding, and unscrupulous, it is nevertheless a fact that the dowager empress took steps to cut down gradually on the opium trade, abolished the binding of women's feet, and created the first public school system. However, she was also contemptuous of the public needs and spent money at a great rate to satisfy her own personal whims.

In 1894 and 1895, the Sino-Japanese War over Korea took place; the Chinese were defeated. In 1900, there was the Boxer Rebellion, a step encouraged by the dowager empress as a form of reaction to progressive steps. Then came Sun Yat-sen, a political leader who prepared the way for the revolution which took place in 1911, an event that ended the rule of the Manchus forever.

From 1919 to 1927 the times were turbulent, and there were sporadic revolts and revolutions, mostly of a local nature. The great political event of this period was the rise of the Kuomintang (or Nationalists) headed by Chiang Kai-shek, who set up his government at Nanking in 1928. Within the country confusion, anarchy, and utter chaos was the general situation. Chiang Kai-shek's government was a failure, and ultimately it was found to be corrupt and riddled with graft and extortion. On October 1, 1949, the People's Republic of China (PRC) was founded, and Chiang Kai-shek fled with some of his followers to Taiwan. The head of the new government was Mao Tse-tung, chairman of the Chinese Communist Party from 1949 until his death in 1976. He was followed by Hua Kuo-feng as the party chairman.

After Mao died, there was a period of some turmoil and confusion, during which a small group of radicals, which included Chiang Ch'ing, the widow of Mao, tried to take control. They were designated as the "Gang of Four" (there were three other important politicians implicated), and the term is a shorthand method of referring to that period of temporary political disturbance. Within a year, however, the political situation had stabilized.

It is also important to mention the visit of President Nixon to China in 1972; it was this visit that constituted the beginnings of the reopening of the political relationship between China and the U.S. which led to the exchange of ambassadors and the opening of consulates.

Ever since 1949, the People's Republic of China (incidentally, it is not considered proper to refer to the country as Mainland China, although the word China itself is satisfactory) has made enormous strides on behalf of its citizenry. It is an undoubted fact that prior to the PRC, literally hundreds of thousands of people starved to death during periods of political unrest and extreme weather when the crops failed; this has now been much alleviated. The diet of the average Chinese is somewhat limited in scope by our standards, but it is certainly adequate—as can be noted from the healthy appearance of the majority of people. Rice remains the staple food, eaten as a breakfast cereal, and also combined with meat and fish during the day.

The overall health of the public has taken giant steps forward, and Chinese medicine is innovative, sometimes daring, and occasionally backward; there is local medical service in the smallest of communities. In the open countryside there are "barefoot doctors," that is, people who have been trained to attend to general health, and recognize conditions (for referral to hospitals) which they are not equipped to treat. Side by side, Chinese herbal cures and western medicine are routine. It is not unusual for a patient to be receiving a modern antibiotic and at the same time to have herbs applied to a particular area of the body. The Chinese are great believers in acupuncture for a wide variety of cures, and also as an anesthetic.

The entire agricultural land area of the nation was declared to be the property of the citizens of a particular commune, owned as a group. Each adult receives a certain specified amount of land in addition, and even a child receives a tiny plot. Commune land is planted and cultivated by a vote of the group ownership, but the small, privately owned plot of land may be planted with whatever the owner wishes. The produce may, after certain conditions are met, be sold at what amounts to a "free market," held on specified days.

POINTER:
For centuries, westerners had become accustomed to spelling Chinese names and places in a certain way. The Chinese, as we know, use "pictures" or ideograms, instead of an alphabet; therefore, phonetic spelling merely represented the sounds implied in the characters. The Chinese have decided to use what's called Pinyin, a somewhat different way of reproducing the ideograms. For example, the name of Mao Tse-tung, with which we are familiar, has been changed to Mao Zedong in Pinyin. In this book, the Pinyin system has not been used, because it is unfamiliar to readers. There has been considerable opposition from librarians to switching to Pinyin, and it remains to be seen which system will prevail.

 When to Go

China is an enormous country, with a tremendous range of temperatures, much like the U.S. Just as Minnesota winters are bitter cold, whereas those in Florida are mild and pleasant, similar conditions prevail in China. The northeast portion of the country, with Harbin as its chief city, is extraordinarily cold during the winter, and a trip there during that season is only for the hardy. Summer months, on the other hand, are rather pleasant. The north central portion of the nation, typified by Peking is usually very cold in winter and reasonably hot during the summer; Peking itself can be very dusty during the warm-weather months. Eastern China, with Shanghai as its most important city, has medium-cold winters, much like New York, for example, whereas summers are fairly hot. South China, including Kwangchow (once called Canton), is not far from Hong Kong and has similar weather. Winters are quite mild, with hot, wet summer months.

There can be no question but that spring and fall seasons are undoubtedly the best for travel to China.

Visa Requirements

This is required before entry into the People's Republic of China. The PRC has shown signs of easing the application process; the travel agency or other organization sponsoring the trip will give you the necessary forms to fill out. Passport photographs are required, and at the moment there is a $6 fee for the visa, although this may (or may not) be included in the price the visitor will pay for the trip. Some people are under the impression that there is a U.S. governmental restriction against travel to China, but there is none.

For anyone who has visited Taiwan, a stamp in the passport indicating a stop in that country will (sometimes) prevent a visit to the PRC. Therefore, if your passport does show a Taiwan stamp, it may be best to obtain a new passport. It is possible, when the appropriate explanation is made to the U.S. State Department, to have a special passport issued solely for a visit to China.

Incidentally, once in China, your passport will be retained until the day of departure; there is no cause for concern in this regard. Although smallpox has all but been eradicated around the world, at present you MUST have a smallpox vaccination certificate with you on entry.

Customs

The Chinese are surprisingly easygoing and relaxed about their customs rulings and inspection, as a rule. Visitors are permitted to bring with them 4 bottles of liquor, 3 cartons of cigarettes, an unlimited (more or less) amount of American currency, and all the film you wish. Professional film equipment requires special permission, however. Before entering China, you will receive a customs declaration form, which requires an itemization of cameras, jewelry, money, and so on. Because you may be required, at the time of departure, to exhibit all of the items involved (and account for the money), be sure not to give away any articles (but more about this later on). Whenever changing money, be sure to save the exchange slips because they may be requested when leaving the country.

A Special Note About Traveling in China:

Conditions and opportunities for tourists in mainland China are changing constantly, mostly for the better. Generalizations are possible, though always subject to the chance of error. At the moment, however, the general situation is as follows: Hotels are controlled by the government, and it's not ordinarily possible to specify at which hotel you wish to stay. The rooms are seldom luxurious, with just one or two possible exceptions, but they are usually comfortable, with private baths. The sanitation is passable but could be improved. Beds—mostly twins—are sometimes comfortable, sometimes hard as boards. Each room is usually supplied with boiled water for drinking, hot water for making tea, and fruit. Traveling about the country is variable—sometimes good, sometimes a little rough. Airplanes are mostly Russian, although the supply is becoming more American; they are almost always very crowded. The trains are fairly good, and overnight trains have either two or four berths in each compartment. Trains move quite slowly, but this is good for sleeping.

♪ The Actual Entry

Occasionally, American travelers on a charter or group flight are permitted to enter China by a direct flight. However, at the present time, the vast majority of American visitors fly to Hong Kong and take the train to Kwangchow, also called Canton. In general, most visitors take the morning train from Hong Kong and reach the border an hour and 15 minutes later. While the train is en route to the Chinese border, various forms will be distributed, including a currency declaration, baggage declaration, and health report. The baggage and health forms are turned in, but the currency slip must be carefully retained until departure from the country, as mentioned in the previous section.

Once at the border, everyone disembarks from the train and walks across a railroad bridge to the Shumchun area, where passports are handed over to the Chinese border personnel. Any baggage that has been checked through will routinely be transferred across the border, but don't forget to carry your hand luggage with you.

After crossing the bridge, passengers are taken into waiting rooms while the passports are processed. Customs and health procedures are conducted, although these are typically rather routine in nature. This is the time when money can conveniently be changed. A lunch will then be served. There's a delay of a couple of hours, and finally the train will leave for Canton. It takes about two hours to cover the 90 miles to that city, and the ride is most comfortable, the diesel train being air-conditioned and quiet. At the Canton end of the trip, a representative of the China tourist department will oversee the arrival as well as the transfer of passengers and their baggage.

℞ Health

Sanitary conditions in China are only fair, sometimes poor. Because dishes are washed by hand and not sterilized in a machine with high temperatures, it is customary for colds to go from one person to another in a group; the same applies to coughs. Many people experience mild diarrhea from eating vegetables (raw ones, mostly) which have been grown with what used to be called "night soil," that rather euphemistic way of referring to human waste. Nowadays, most travelers take Lomotil or a similar remedy with them, as a precaution against extended periods of diarrhea. Most important of all—and absolutely essential—is to remember never to drink tap water, even in the largest cities, much less the countryside. In every hotel room there will be a thermos bottle or carafe of boiled water which can be used for brushing teeth and so forth. Even so, it's best not to drink large quantities of the boiled water, but rather to have tea, coffee, beer, etc. Ice, on the other hand, is reasonably safe, having been made with boiled water. Even so, don't take too many beverages (even in the hot summertime) with ice, because it may affect you. In Peking, where it can be very dusty, many people experience bronchial problems, and if you are sensitive to swirling dust, it may be a good idea to tie a large handkerchief or scarf around the face in order to cover the nose and mouth.

Be sure to take along all the medication you normally use; it will rarely be available. Also, don't forget to take Lomotil, an antihistamine to minimize allergies or other minor reactions, and perhaps something for a cold or cough.

The Chinese are absolutely marvelous about anyone who becomes ill or even gives any indication of being sick, and travelers will be taken, perhaps by the guide for your group, to a local hospital for treatment. The Chinese hospitals represent a sort of compromise between traditional herbal medicine and western treatment. However, all in all, by not drinking the water, avoiding raw vegetables, and exercising a reasonable amount of care, there is no reason to expect any medical problem while visiting China.

⏱ Time

Eastern China is in the same GMT zone, that is +8, as is Hong Kong. For this reason, most of the year, China has the same time as Hong Kong. During the summer months, however, Hong Kong advances its time by one hour, and there is a difference of one hour between Eastern China and Hong Kong. When it's 1 P.M. in Hong Kong during the summer, it's noon in eastern China.

💲 Currency

The money in the PRC is called by the generic name of *renminbi,* that is "people's currency" or "people's money." However, the unit of money is the *yuan,* which appear as paper money in denominations of 1, 2, 5, and 10 *yuan.* At the moment, although always subject to change, the *yuan* is worth about 58¢ U.S. If you cash $100 into Chinese money, you will receive about 170 *yuan,* but remember that rates may change. The *yuan* divides into hundredths, and one hundredth of a *yuan* is called a *fen.* 10 *fen,* one tenth of a *yuan,* is called a *chiao.* There is rather small paper money issued for *chiao,* such as 5 *chiao.* Very light coins, made apparently of aluminum, are to be had, but only in denominations of 1, 2, and 5 *fen.*

You may bring travelers' checks or American currency with you when entering China; it is usually not possible to buy Chinese currency outside of the country, and in any event, it would be illegal to bring it in. There is usually a slightly better rate for travelers' checks. Don't arrange for a letter of credit from your local bank, unless you want to spend hours in a branch of the Bank of China. You will find facilities for cashing travelers' checks or currency at the Friendship Stores (more about these later), at your hotel, or at the Bank of China. The rates are identical and the hotels may be the easiest of all places to change money. Don't cash too much money, and always save the receipts. At the moment, credit cards are not accepted, but it seems likely, as time goes by, that they will be recognized. However, don't count on it, and bring sufficient travelers' checks or cash. American Express has arranged with the Bank of China for American tourists with American Express credit cards to cash personal checks. The card is still (at the moment, at least) not valid for purchases made in China. But the situation is very changeable, and it may be that in the future credit cards will be accepted, but not yet.

At one time, when tourists changed their money at their hotels, they received *renminbi*, the Chinese currency. However, a local black market developed, with offers of more *renminbi* for the U.S. dollar than the legal rate. In order to control this, the government now issues scrip (which is a piece of paper) but not currency; it's redeemable in most shops.

⊕ Price Level

The vast majority of travelers will be on all-inclusive tours which cover hotels, meals, and sightseeing, so that the price level will not be of primary concern except when shopping. It is a fact that China is moderately priced for almost everything, with a very few exceptions. Hotel meals are included in the cost of the trip, as mentioned before, but it is possible to have more interesting dinners at restaurants on your own. You'll be asked, when making the reservation, exactly how much you wish to spend, and your answer should depend upon whether or not you regard yourself as a gourmet and expert in the Chinese cuisine; you can select a meal for as little as 10 *yuan*, about $6, but you can also order a banquet for as much as $30 per person.

With regard to shopping at the various stores, many articles are no cheaper than for the identical merchandise available in Hong Kong, and may even be a little more. Before leaving for the PRC, it might be a good idea to check out prices in the several stores of the China Arts and Crafts, just to get an idea.

Tipping

This question can be answered very quickly with an absolutely flat statement. There is no tipping whatsoever in China, and attempts to do so will often be refused with embarrassment. This also means that tour guides, for example, will not welcome such gifts as cosmetics, small articles of clothing, and so forth. The correct gesture is to thank the person involved, with appropriate expressions of warmth and friendliness. In some cases, particularly those involving special interests (professional or educational groups for example) the classic method of saying "thank you" is to arrange for a special banquet. One exception to the above rule: if you have a Polaroid or the new instant Kodak with you, a picture of the people you meet will be very welcome; this should not be presented so as to be a "reward" or tip, and merely given as a friendly gesture.

ﾠ Transportation

Train tickets are rarely purchased by individuals, but instead are controlled by the appropriate division of the PRC. Almost all trains have what are called "hard" and "soft" seats; obviously foreigners will get the more comfortable accommodations. First class trains are somewhat small by American standards, and typically hold only 32 passengers; long-distance trains usually have 8 compartments, each accommodating 4 passengers. There are dining cars on most of these trains, serving western breakfasts, but Chinese food only for the other meals; the food is fair enough.

Air travel tickets are also supplied to visitors, and it is not necessary to become involved in the process of buying tickets or making reservations. The Chinese airline is known as the CAAC and uses a very wide assortment of aircraft gathered from all over the world, including American 707s. The baggage allowance is 44 pounds per person for checked luggage plus 11 pounds of hand luggage; there is a charge for excess baggage. By all means see that your baggage fits within these limits to avoid delays and minor problems on flights. Generally speaking, only box lunches will be served on flights, with hot meals being made available on the ground; on short flights, only light refreshment will be served. Very often, small souvenirs of the flight will be distributed, including lapel pins, address books, etc.

Taxis are almost always available for foreigners; this includes at hotels, many tourist stores, and some restaurants. If dining at a restaurant, a request at the conclusion of a meal for a taxi will bring one within a reasonable time. At the hotels, there is often a desk where the person desiring a taxi can specify where he wishes to go, and how long he expects to be using the taxi; the rate will then be fixed, depending upon the distance and time involved.

▐▌ Communications

Air mail letters to and from the PRC take anywhere from 5 to 10 days; it is often difficult to arrange to receive mail. If anyone is writing to you, be sure to tell them to address the letters to the People's Republic of China. Letters addressed to Mainland China or Communist China may never be delivered.

Telephone calls to the U.S. go through with reasonable speed, although the rates are fairly high. It's best to write out the name of the person you wish to speak to on a piece of paper, together with the area code and local telephone number and hand it in at the hotel desk or other designated bureau. There is a service charge which will be made even if the call does not go through for any reason. Don't forget the time difference between China and the U.S.

Cables can be sent with no difficulty from the hotel; they can also be received in the regular course of business.

⚡ Electricity

The current is 220 volt AC throughout most of the country. On the other hand, Shanghai, in some areas, has 110 volts. In addition, most outlets require two round prongs, or sometimes 3 flat ones. If you have an appliance with you, ask at the hotel desk for an adapter; they may have an extra one or two around. Some of the new hotels, it is reported, will have special 110 volt AC outlets, suitable for electric razors in the bathrooms.

✗ Food Specialties and Liquor

For a discussion of the various styles of Chinese cooking, please turn to the appropriate section in Hong Kong.

It seems more appropriate here to talk about the meals which are available through the PRC. To begin with, most meals will be taken at the hotels, except for a banquet or other special meal which may be arranged at a particular restaurant. Breakfast typically is western style, including fruit juice, eggs, toast, a pastry, and coffee (this last is fair, not great). For those who want to sample a Chinese breakfast, it can usually be arranged, particularly if a group of people request it. Chinese breakfasts vary a bit but usually include some rice porridge, which contains an assortment of vegetables, meats, or nuts. Noodles in chicken soup or pork broth are also routine, but the tastiest of all is a scallion pancake. Also, sweet pastries and cakes are served, together with tea. It's quite good, if you're slightly adventurous.

You'll probably, at some stage of the trip, be invited to a Chinese banquet, which consists of many courses. If you eat everything that's served, you'll never make it to the end, being filled to capacity by the fifth or sixth course. It is considered good manners, however, to at least taste every course that's placed before you. If you've never used chopsticks, it's a good idea to make an effort to learn to use them; it comes easy for some people, not quite so easy for others; on request a fork will usually be supplied. One word of caution: it is considered extremely bad manners to play with the chopsticks, or point them at people, or in fact, do anything but eat with them in decorous fashion.

Although the food in the hotels is good, much more interesting and exciting food can be had at the various restaurants in the large cities. If you merely walk along the street and decide to walk into the first restaurant that appeals to you, an embarrassing situation may occur. The management of the restaurant may order all the diners at a particular table to get up and move elsewhere, even during the middle of their meal. Also, the menu will be only in Chinese, not English, making it difficult to order. Much of the problem can be avoided by arranging, at your hotel desk, for a meal at a particular restaurant, and tell them just how much you wish to pay; a meal commensurate with the figure you mention will be served when you reach the restaurant. Unless you are a gourmet, it is not necessary to pay the highest amount suggested, because the middle range of prices is sufficient for the majority of people. If you do arrange to dine out, be sure to tell the hotel restaurant, so they won't wait for you to appear.

The classic strong drink in China is *mao-t'ai*, and it's surprisingly strong. Also popular is a kind of warm rice wine called *shao-hsing chiu,* which tastes like sherry; it's OK, no more. Best of all, most visitors think, is the local beer. It's customary not to drink alone. Instead, turn to a neighbor or person opposite you, and propose a toast. Once a banquet is finished, everyone leaves without further ado, and there is little or no standing about and chatting; everyone departs almost swiftly.

📖 What to Wear

China is very conservative about clothing; almost everyone,

man or woman, will be wearing simple, rather nondescript clothing of a solid color. For this reason, flamboyant, bright, or revealing clothes should never by worn by women and low-cut dresses are completely out of place. Simple dresses or pant suits are ideal, bearing in mind the season of the year in which you are traveling, and whether your trip goes to the north, where it can be very cold anywhere from October through April. Men, equally, should not wear bright colors, such as Hawaiian-style shirts, Bermuda shorts, and so forth. The best bet for men, all around, is solid color slacks to be worn with a plain shirt during the summer months, and a sport jacket during the remainder of the year. Women should take one dressy, but still conservative, dress for the almost inevitable banquet, and men can get along with one business suit. On one occasion, the girl guide commented in absolute amazement that a certain woman kept changing her clothes from one day to another, remarking that the Chinese have only one or two outfits in their wardrobe.

Little in the way of jewelry should be worn by women, except perhaps for a watch, ring and earrings, and make-up should be applied with great moderation. Bear in mind that in China lipstick is generally regarded as the only cosmetic for even modern women, and that the overwhelming majority of Chinese women wear absolutely no makeup. Don't worry about laundry; the hotel services are excellent, and can generally be done on an overnight basis, or certainly within a day.

📖 What to Take Along

By all means, Kleenex or other tissues; these are scarce in China. Also, your usual toilet articles, although toothpaste and brushes can be purchased at the local department stores. If you like to read before going to sleep, take whatever reading material you need, because none is to be had in the PRC. If you're a photographer, take more film than you think you need; sometimes western-style film is available, but mostly not. A Polaroid or other instant camera will be very handy as an ice-breaker with strange people. A transistor radio, with fresh batteries, will be worthwhile.

Don't forget any medication you customarily take, plus a few precautionary ones, such as Lomotil, which is excellent for possible diarrhea. If you wish, take along your favorite liquor; it will seldom be available even at tourist hotels. Although the coffee served is fairly good, if you're in doubt, bring along some instant coffee.

A Few Thoughts on Behavior in China

Every country has its own customs, and in the PRC, this is particularly true. Don't seek to understand why the Chinese don't do things just like the Americans, for example; they simply don't, and they are entitled to do things in their own fashion. Group travel is always conducted at a somewhat slower pace than individual travel, and it's best to put yourself in a relaxed, easygoing mood and play along with whatever delays may be experienced. There are frequent conferences and meetings, presenting the Chinese point of view; because of the translations to and from Chinese, the meetings may run a little long. It's best not to become impatient.

Also, the Chinese are rather conservative in behavior. When meeting someone, a polite handshake and smile is considered proper, but it is not advisable to go further than this. Remarks about a person's appearance are not welcome, and it's best not to tell a girl guide that she is attractive, as it may be taken in a wrong context, inasmuch as the Chinese are very prim and proper about sex. In this respect, anything that even vaguely resembles a sexual innuendo should be avoided.

Punctuality is one of the great virtues in this country. If the departure for a trip is scheduled, for example, for 8:45 A.M., it is considered to be in extremely bad taste to arrive even minutes late. Indeed, it's best to be ready some five or ten minutes before the scheduled departure. The same applies to all meals, conferences, or sightseeing.

The Chinese are great believers in what is called "face." That is, the person's dignity and right to respect. For this reason, if anyone has a complaint, it should not be made in the presence of a group of people; it's best to speak to the tour group leader privately, and quietly state the grounds for the complaint. If the tour leader says that—for one reason or another—a certain scheduled event cannot take place or must be postponed, it should be taken without comment. There is little point in discussing the delay or cancellation of a particular trip or event, or arguing as to the merits of the reason for the delay or cancellation. Even such a transparent reason as "inconvenient at this time" should be taken at face value and not discussed further. It is the Chinese way of saying that the event is cancelled (perhaps for the time being), and the word "inconvenient" is merely a polite way of phrasing it.

Don't worry about leaving articles about in your hotel room.

Nothing will be taken, and anything left behind accidentally will be returned. In this regard, those who might compare the Chinese way of doing something when compared to the American way, might do well to remember that crime is a great problem at home, and an almost nonexistent one in China.

At meetings or group discussions, it's best to take a positive view of Chinese-American relations, and mention the hope that both political and economic ties between the two nations will continue to improve. Don't criticize the Chinese leaders; you wouldn't want the Chinese criticizing the American leaders.

Hotels

In the vast majority of cases, at least at present, all hotel assignments are made by the governmental organization, and it is rarely possible to request particular hotels in various cities. Of course, foreigners will almost automatically be assigned to one of the hotels reserved for them in any city; these are inevitably the best available. New hotels are under construction in the major tourist areas, and the situation will surely change from year to year.

Except in the newest and best hotels, rooms can sometimes be somewhat spartan, with simple but reasonable comfortable furnishings which would not excite an interior decorator to whimpers of ecstacy, but are certainly OK for the one or two nights that will be passed in them. One of the great conveniences to be found in many hotels (not all, however) is a sort of buffet on each floor where it's possible to buy simple requirements, such as bottled water, cigarettes, and an assortment of refreshments. Some hotels—again not all—place some conveniences in the room without charge, such as cigarettes, fruit (in season), small candies, etc.

The laundry is good and fairly priced; service usually is extremely quick as mentioned previously. However, avoid the dry cleaning unless absolutely necessary.

Shopping

The United States is a country built upon products designed to tempt the consumer-oriented society. If a person wants to buy a bathrobe, for instance, there is literally a choice of hundreds of styles, models, fabrics, and sizes. Anyone interested in hi-fi can choose from dozens of different models, many made in the U.S., others imported. The Chinese society is not built up along those lines. The governmental authorities decree what clothing shall be manufactured and in precisely what sizes and (usually) just one fabric. Most of the articles offered for sale—there are some few exceptions intended exclusively for foreigners—are primarily intended to be sold to the Chinese public. The exceptions are items sold in what are called Friendship Stores, located in almost all cities, which feature merchandise of primary interest to foreigners. Only dollars or other foreign currency are accepted in these stores.

Strangely enough, as mentioned before, on the average the prices charged are about the same (or even slightly higher) than in Hong Kong; for this reason, if you are returning home via Hong Kong, it might be best to delay purchases until that time, to avoid the necessity of crowding your suitcases with bulky articles. On the other hand, if you see precisely what you want, don't hesitate to buy it; after all, you may never see it again. Some of the largest Friendship Stores, such as in Peking, have a section where arrangements can be made for shipping large purchases to your home; they are completely reliable.

If you're looking for Chinese antiques, you're probably in for a disappointment, because these have largely disappeared from the market. The earliest visitors to China were the lucky ones; since that time, the government has stepped in and almost completely blocked the sale of important antiques. Anything over 150 years old cannot be purchased. However, there are numerous antique stores scattered about, and with patience and a little knowledge of Chinese antiquities, you may uncover something worthwhile.

POINTER:

At the present time, most travel to China is on a group basis, with no individual trips permitted. The entire group will be assigned to a hotel, depending chiefly upon the availability of rooms in the city at a given moment. One luxurious exception is the Jianquo Hotel in Peking under the management of the Peninsula Hotel in Hong Kong; the Jianguo may be requested.

The Principal Cities and Tourist Areas

Kwangchow (Canton)

A rather strange-looking city to most foreign visitors, Kwangchow is an industrial area and seems to have grown up with little advance planning. It is a combination of a busy commercial city, but there are also any number of streets lined with trees, and several large parks; the overall effect is not unpleasant. The main thoroughfare is Chung Shan Road, which cuts through the city. There are three railroad stations—the Canton, the South, and East Stations. Bai Yun Airport is in the general direction of the Canton Railway Station but farther out from the city, of course.

The local people are extremely proud of Yue Hsi Park, which goes back to the year 1380 during the Ming Dynasty. If you're here about November, there's a marvelous Chrysanthemum Festival, which is breathtakingly beautiful. You'll also be shown the Mausoleum of the 72 Martyrs, the National Peasant Movement Institute, plus several temples and a mosque. Try to get to the Kwangchow Zoo, if for no other reason than to see the pandas. Just 10 miles from Kwangchow is Foshan City, which visitors usually see on a day's excursion. Once a religious center, it's now famous for its pottery.

Although there are hotels galore in the city, most visitors will be assigned to one of the following: The Tun Fang, which is pretty good on most counts, although not precisely a deluxe hotel. The old wing has been remodeled, whereas the new wing is quite modern by Chinese hotel standards. It has a very good dining room on the 8th floor, although it's often reserved completely for special delegations. Another good hotel, much newer, is the Bai Yun, 33 stories high; it is, however, located somewhat out of the center of town.

If you want to dine out on your own, you might consider the Ta Tung, which has a top floor section reserved for foreigners; it's moderately expensive. Even better, I think, is the Pei Yuan, which

Weather Strip: Kwangchow (Canton)

	Jan.	Feb.	Mar.	Apr.	May	June	July	Aug.	Sept.	Oct.	Nov.	Dec.
Average daily high	63°	63°	69°	77°	86°	88°	91°	91°	89°	83°	77°	69°
Average daily low	49°	52°	55°	66°	74°	76°	78°	78°	76°	67°	60°	54°
Monthly rainfall	1.8	2.7	3.6	5.9	9.9	10.6	9.9	9.6	5.4	2.3	1.6	1.4
Number of days with 0.04 inches or more	5	8	11	12	15	17	16	13	10	4	3	5

is unimposing from the exterior, being located in a former private house, in picturesque surroundings facing a garden. Another good choice is the Pan Hsi, a large, beautiful restaurant; it's famous for its many different styles of dumplings.

Nanking

About 185 miles from Shanghai is this most attractive city, which has an extraordinary backdrop of mountains and is situated in a sort of natural valley area between the mountains and the Yangtze River. For the Chinese people, the bridge over the Yangtze River is of paramount importance, and has great symbolic meaning to them. Of course, it has great economic value to the country, because prior to its completion in 1968, the Yangtze River constituted an impasse, hindering the flow of traffic from the local valley to Peking. Several decades before its construction, western engineers had attempted to build the bridge, but unsuccessfully; then the Russian engineers tried, and also failed. The main reason for the difficulty involved the depth of the river, typically about 65 feet and rather fast moving. Finally the Chinese, acting completely without assistance from any other country, built the bridge. For this reason, there is a symbolic importance to the bridge, because it indicated to them that their bridge-building skills were perhaps even greater than those of the western world, at least in respect to this particular bridge. There can be no doubt that it represents a spectacular achievement, and a great success for the PRC.

Weather Strip: Nanking

	Jan.	Feb.	Mar.	Apr.	May	June	July	Aug.	Sept.	Oct.	Nov.	Dec.
Average daily high	43°	46°	55°	66°	78°	83°	88°	88°	80°	71°	59°	48°
Average daily low	29°	32°	40°	50°	59°	69°	75°	74°	66°	55°	43°	32°
Monthly rainfall	1.6	2.0	3.0	4.0	3.2	7.2	8.1	4.6	3.7	2.0	1.6	1.2
Number of days with 0.04 inches or more	8	7	6	9	7	8	8	8	5	3	4	8

The weather in Nanking leaves something to be desired. The summers are quite hot, the fall season is good, the winter bearable, but there is some rain in the late spring. However, don't be put off by the weather.

Among the other sights of Nanking which tourists usually visit is the Sun Yat-sen Mausoleum. The leader of the 1911 revolution was also the founder of the first national government of China, an event that took place in Nanking in 1912. By all means visit the Ming Tomb, built in 1381 for the founder of the important Ming Dynasty. There are parks and lakes galore, including Ling Ku Park, not far from the Sun Yat-sen Mausoleum. There are also the Mo Chou Lake and Hsuan Wu Lake; they are quite pleasing, although low key. Another worthwhile sight is Shan Hsi Lu Square, within reasonable walking distance of the Nanking Hotel; the Square has a lively market, a department store, and so forth.

At the moment, the only hotel for foreigners is the Nanking Hotel, which is enclosed with gardens and has a wall separating it from the main road, Sun Yat-sen Boulevard. The rooms are indeed mediocre, although not unbearable. A new hotel is scheduled to open very soon. Strangely enough, Nanking has little in the way of good restaurants; it's best to dine at the hotels.

Shanghai

During the years before the revolution, Shanghai was the most popular and important of all Chinese cities with foreigners. As a result, it remains today the most sophisticated and cosmopolitan of

Weather Strip: Shanghai

	Jan.	Feb.	Mar.	Apr.	May	June	July	Aug.	Sept.	Oct.	Nov.	Dec.
Average daily high	46°	47°	55°	66°	77°	82°	90°	90°	82°	74°	63°	53°
Average daily low	33°	34°	40°	50°	59°	67°	74°	74°	66°	57°	45°	36°
Monthly rainfall	1.9	2.3	3.3	3.7	3.7	7.1	5.8	5.6	5.1	2.8	2.0	1.4
Number of days with 0.04 inches or more	6	9	9	9	9	11	9	9	11	4	6	6

all the cities in the nation. It seems to be growing steadily; at the present time, the best estimate is that about 11 million people make it their home. It also covers an enormous area, something like Los Angeles, consisting of over 2300 square miles. The city looks more western than any other in China, with tall buildings and rather fewer structures in what we think of as the Chinese style. Of course, this applies to the main part of Shanghai, not to the old section, south of the main shopping area.

Three main roads cut across Shanghai—they are Peking, Nanking, and Yenan roads. Another important street, Chungshan Road, more or less follows the contours of the Whangpoo River. It's a busy commercial city but should prove fascinating to the tourist because it offers an excellent opportunity to see the millions of people living their daily life in an enormous city. Shanghai lacks any important great ruins or archaeology; there are comparatively few temples, but there are a great many parks. Surely the most important of these is People's Park, alongside People's Square. In addition, there is Fu Hsing Park and a small zoo; Hsi Chao Park is interesting and it has the city's largest zoo; also worthwhile is Lu Hsun Memorial Park, named for one of the country's greatest writers.

In the old quarter of Shanghai is the Garden of the Mandarin Yu, sometimes called Yu Yuan; there's a very pleasant teahouse, just right for a refreshment stop. You'll probably also be shown Futan University, mostly involved with the various sciences.

As to hotels, the best bet at present is the Peace Hotel, 14 stories tall, but not very large. There's a large and rather good dining room on the top floor, with a fine view of the river. Other hotels are the Ching An; the International Hotel, 18 stories high, has a rather convenient location; the Shanghai Mansions, which has some good and some ordinary rooms, has a theoretically pleasing location between two waterways, but on some nights the foghorns can be somewhat disturbing to light sleepers; the Chin Chiang Hotel is inconveniently situated, a fair ride from the center of town, but it is perhaps one of the best places to stay in Shanghai at the moment.

Although the Shanghai cuisine is a most interesting one, there are comparatively few restaurants suitable for foreigners who wish to dine out away from their hotel. The two best of these restaurants, neither spectacular, include the Yang Cho and the Sin Ya.

Kweilin

This is surely one of the great beauty spots of the entire nation. It's located northwest of Hong Kong (and also Kwangchow) and

Weather Strip: Kweilin

	Jan.	Feb.	Mar.	Apr.	May	June	July	Aug.	Sept.	Oct.	Nov.	Dec.
Average daily high	53°	56°	65°	74°	80°	88°	91°	91°	89°	78°	68°	60°
Average daily low	40°	44°	51°	60°	66°	75°	77°	75°	72°	62°	53°	44°
Number of days with 0.04 inches or more	9	12	14	17	17	18	14	13	7	7	7	8

is therefore in an area of reasonably mild winter weather and warm, indeed hot, summers. Kweilin itself is only a moderate-sized community of about 350,000 people, not much as Chinese cities go, and it's an exceptionally compact place, ideal for walking about.

The scenery here is spectacular, with mountains and rivers of unsurpassed beauty. For example, visitors are taken to see Fu Po Hill, within the city limits of Kweilin; there is an interesting walk that passes many temples and a cave. Another great sightseeing spot is Banyan Lake, also called Jung Hu; it has lovely gardens, walks, pavilions, and teahouses. Seven Star Park (Chi Hsing Shan) has Seven Star Hill, where the peaks of the hills approximately represent the shape of the Big Dipper. In addition, there are numerous caves of moderate interest. The best cave in this area is the Reed Flute Cave, the Luti Cave; the reeds are found near the cave's entrance.

Everyone who comes here, in all likelihood, will take the much heralded trip on the Li River. It takes about 6 hours to cover the 50 miles or so down the Li River, ending up at Yangshou. It's a wonderful way to see the life on the river, and also the people who live alongside its banks. At the other end, there's a bus ride back, taking about 2 hours, and there's almost no time to view Yangshou, a rather interesting town in its own right.

As to accommodations, the leading hotel here without a doubt is the Kweilin Hotel, 12 stories high. The higher floors of the hotel have glorious views of the mountains in the general area. Sometimes people are put up in the Banyan Tree Lake Hotel, a much smaller place; its dining room is noted for serving local specialties and is worth a visit for a meal if you're staying at the Kweilin Hotel.

Peking (Beijing)

This remarkable city is the capital of the People's Republic of China, and as a result, the center of its political life. In addition, much of the nation's culture, entertainment, and business is located in and around the capital city. Peking's history is somewhat difficult to trace prior to the 10th century, but then it became associated with the Liao Dynasty and subsequently was the capital of several succeeding dynasties, such as Jin, Yuan, Ming, and Quing.

Sightseeing here is quite extensive. To begin with, the center of the town and the best place to begin sightseeing is surely T'ien-an-men Square. It was here in T'ien-an-men Square that Chairman Mao first raised the flag of the People's Republic of China, to start the new country on its way. All around the square will be found museums, monuments, and memorabilia of those hectic days when the country came into being. It is also a square that is visited by literally thousands and thousands of people, and during the day it is truly a sight to see the Chinese either marching or strolling through the square. But of course there are other places to see: the Summer Palace, the Palace Museum, the Temple of Heaven, the various Ming tombs, and Beihai Park.

The outstanding single sightseeing attraction of all is surely the Great Wall. It takes about 2 hours from Peking to reach the rolling mountains that were formerly the nation's northern frontier. At Pataling Pass, you'll be able to see a restored section of the wall, extending for about 1500 feet. At one time, the Great Wall extended for over 3000 miles, being built from 480–422 B.C. It was constructed so that six horses could run abreast in most sections. There are "towers" built at intervals of about 450 feet. Most impressive of all is the knowledge that from the moon, American astronauts reported that the only man-made object to be seen was the Great Wall.

Kunming

This city is located in Yunnan, the southernmost province of the People's Republic of China. The weather here, as might be expected, is much milder during much of the year than in the more northern provinces and cities. During World War II, Kunming was the eastern end of the famous "Burma Road." Records indicate that this city and its surrounding area were settled more than 2,000 years ago, although today it is primarily noted for mining and chemical production. It has many sightseeing attractions, particularly parks, fine old temples, lakes, and also an important university.

Hangchow (Hangzhou)

Hangchow is mostly an industrial area and—from the tourists' point of view—the place where silks and other fine fabrics are manufactured. While you're in Hangchow be sure to have some of its famous Langjing tea; if you like it, buy some to take home. However, the great single attraction here is the renowned West Lake. It is particularly beautiful because of its unique location, surrounded by hills on three sides, thus setting off its natural beauty all the more. There is a causeway that divides the lake into three chief parts, called Back Lake, Inner Lake, and Outer Lake. Two places you shouldn't miss (indeed it would be difficult not to see them) are Liuhue Pagoda and Lingyin Temple. The market area of Hangchow is particularly interesting, and if time permits, it is rather diverting to wander about and see the great variety of fruits and vegetables offered for sale, plus the many herbs and spices which apparently are unique to China.

Wuhan

At one time, the city of Wuhan consisted of three separate towns called Hangyang, Wuchang, and Hankou. As can be noted, the new name is more or less taken from the three older place names. In 1957, the great bridge across the Yangtze River was completed, and the three cities became one vitally important center of transportation for this part of China. In addition, Wuhan is the capital of Hupei Province and is so large that it extends across both sides of the Yangtze and Hangshui rivers. Of all the cities of the PRC, Wuhan has more natural charm than almost any other place, in the opinion of many artists and photographers. The great sightseeing attraction in this area, without any doubt, is the East Lake, a scenic area of considerable interest. There are any number of tombs, pagodas, monuments, and temples in the vicinity of the lake, all worth a visit. On any tour of this area, you'll be shown the Children's Library, the People's Theater, Chang Ma Cavern, Yu Huang Palace, Yellow Crane Court, and Snake Mountain.

Sian

Marco Polo put this place on the map of the western world when he came here during his visit to China. Its history goes back to when it was known as Hsien-yang and was the capital under an emperor, Shi Huang Ti (247–210 BC), and also under later dynasties. Because of its important location on trade routes, Marco Polo made it a point to come here during the 13th century. During the Boxer Rebellion (1900–1902), the Empress Dowager and the Emperor Kuang Hsu made this city their place of refuge until things calmed down a bit.

Sian has, in its surrounding industrial complex, a great number of steel and iron plants, and also produces cement, chemicals, and so on. A great sight here is the series of famous old city walls, some of which are about 30 feet high, and an ideal place at which to have your picture taken. In addition, visitors will surely be shown the various colleges and universities, the many notable temples and tombs, as well as the ancient fortified points intended to protect the old city. At Peilin, south of the city, there is a remarkable collection of more than 1,000 historical stone tablets, discovered in the year 1625; it's an impressive sight.

Shenyang

The capital of Liaoning Province, once called Mukden, is the largest city in the northeastern part of the People's Republic of China. With a population of more than 3 million, the city is still growing, mostly because it is highly industrialized and offers employment to hundreds of thousands of people. Shenyang specializes in transport manufacture, including aircraft, autos and trucks. Although the new portion of the city has its points of interest, visitors will particularly be drawn to its old quarter, which was originally a walled city measuring some 4 miles in circumference. The great sight in Shenyang is probably the Imperial Palace, as well as the North and East Tombs, all of which will be high points of your visit to the PRC.

THAILAND

👫 Background

Understanding Thailand (or Siam as it was formerly called) is not easy, for it presents a somewhat complicated picture, the complexities being beneath the surface. As a tourist spot it ranks very high, and the country overflows with a variety of touristic attractions, but that has nothing whatsoever to do with its political and international situation. First of all, direct your eyes towards a map of Southeast Asia (a very hot spot indeed) and note Thailand's neighbors—Laos, Cambodia, Burma, and Malaysia—all of which have their own problems, to say the very least. So far, Thailand has maintained its firm front against encroachments from the communist world, and is today one of the United States' best friends in Asia.

It is believed, although not with absolute certainty, that the Thais established themselves at some point in southeast China about thirteen centuries ago. When Kublai Khan, the leader of a wild horde of savage conquerors, attacked their homeland in the year 1253, the people migrated southward into an area called Siam, taking several years in the process. They settled at Sukothai, where they founded their first capital city. In 1350, for various reasons, the capital moved to Ayudhya. Times were not peaceful then, any more than they are now. There were invasions, alarums, battles, and not a few wars, chiefly with Burma and Cambodia. The Portuguese traders arrived at the beginning of the 16th century, then came the British and the French, in the classic pattern. In 1767, the Burmese attacked once again and just about destroyed the capital city of Ayudhya, whereupon the capital was moved to its present site, Bangkok. If you remember *Anna and the King of Siam,* you'll recall that Siam was a monarchy in the strict sense of the word, the king having absolute powers of life and death over his subjects. In 1932, there was a general "protest" led by the political leaders, the Army and the Navy, and the king relinquished many of his powers, and agreed upon a limitation of his absolute authority by consenting to an elected senate, general education for the masses, and many other reforms which changed the general nature of the kingdom. Thailand was supposed to become a democracy, but this has not worked out in practice precisely as planned; as a rule, there is a dictator or strong man, or *somebody* who actually runs the country. The people today have a good deal of personal freedom, there is criticism of the government in the press, but nobody is allowed to vote for the candidate of his choice (that would be going too far!). For about 40 years, Thailand was governed by one army group or another, without much opposition from the public. During October 1973, there was a student uprising which resulted in a democratic form of government. Whether or not the army will limit itself to exerting some degree of control over the civilian government remains to be seen. However, it should be remembered that Thailand is a monarchy and that a king sits upon the throne. Although the king's powers are limited and although he apparently leads only a ceremonial life (dedicating monuments, receiving diplomats, etc.), actually he does have a degree of power, sometimes only moral, sometimes by the force of his personality. The king is very popular in his own country, and made a great hit in the U.S. when he said, while addressing Congress, that he was looking forward to the day when Thailand might be independent of American aid. For this, he received a standing ovation, that is, after the Congressmen got over the initial shock that his words first produced.

While on the subject of the king, it should be remembered that he is the titular head of the Buddhist religion, which is the one practiced by about 90% of the population. However, all faiths are permitted freedom of religion, including the sizeable Moslem and Christian minorities. If one stands on a certain bridge spanning the broad Chao Phya River in Bangkok, it is possible to see in one panoramic view a Thai Buddhist temple, a Chinese Buddhist temple, a Muslim mosque, and two Christian churches.

If you ever take the trouble to read tourist folders, it is almost impossible to avoid running across the word "smiling" in discussing the people of Thailand. Peculiarly enough, although most tourist folders are pure nonsense, this happens to be an absolutely true statement. The Thais smile a great deal, rarely lose their good nature, and are truly very friendly. This friendly feeling seems to be directed especially towards Americans, whose aid and assistance has been greatly appreciated, unlike some of our old friends in Europe who only complain as to the meagerness of the billions of dollars poured into their economies.

There is a long tradition of aid and friendship between Thailand and the U.S., going back about a century. King Mongkut, great-grandfather of the present monarch, once wrote to President Lincoln offering him some work elephants. President Lincoln replied courteously, declining the offer, and the obvious fact remains that it was the Thais who made the first offer of mutual aid. Incidentally, the Thais place an enormous degree of emphasis upon good manners and courtesy, and have nothing but contempt for a person whose breeding is so low that he shouts, raises his voice, or loses his temper. There is a saying in Thailand that one should "keep a cool heart," which simply means not allowing yourself to get upset or violently annoyed. In any event, most of the time it's too hot to become cross, whatever the reason, including the weather.

The Thais are almost insatiably interested in American life, customs, and family matters. They may ask you a lot of questions—some very personal—about your income, social standing, and the like. None of these is intended to be rude or impertinent; it's merely that the Thais themselves ask each other a lot of personal questions, so it's hardly surprising when they ask us. In fact, you may be sure you're being subtly flattered when someone asks you how old you are, strange as that may seem.

 ## When to Go

Tourists seem to come to Thailand in all seasons, of which there are three. Winter, if you can call it that, extends from December through February; the hot season runs from March through May, and you can definitely call it hot; and the rainy season extends from June through November, and that too, is positively rainy. Of course, the actual dates vary somewhat from year to year, and you might not encounter a drop of rain in November, or it might be very hot in February during what should be the winter season. Don't blame us; that's the way with the weather in Thailand. Variable is the word.

To be more specific, needless to say the best season and the coolest one is from December through February. However, if your time only permits you to travel during July for example, don't let the prospects of the rainy, or monsoon, season keep you away. The word monsoon, incidentally, should not be confused with typhoon, a type of storm which Thailand never gets. The rain can be very sporadic, and you should trust to luck. The lucky Thais are rarely troubled by earthquakes, dust storms, volcanos, or even blizzards (but surely you guessed that?). If you're coming during the cool season, doublecheck to make sure your hotel reservations are in order; this is a very popular time for visitors. During the hot season, it really does get torridly hot. Daytime temperatures are in the mid-90's as a rule, but the humidity makes them seem hotter. However, hotel rooms, dining rooms, bars, etc., are all air-conditioned. During the day, women should carry parasols or wear broad-

Weather Strip: Bangkok

	Jan.	Feb.	Mar.	Apr.	May	June	July	Aug.	Sept.	Oct.	Nov.	Dec.
Average daily high	89°	91°	93°	95°	93°	91°	90°	90°	89°	88°	87°	87°
Average daily low	68°	72°	75°	77°	77°	76°	76°	76°	76°	75°	72°	68°
Monthly rainfall	0.3	0.8	1.4	2.3	7.8	6.3	6.3	6.9	12.0	8.1	2.6	0.2
Number of days with 0.04 inches or more	1	1	3	3	9	10	11	13	15	14	5	1

brimmed hats. Men can wear shirts and slacks (no ties or jackets) during the days; only a few hotels request a jacket and tie for dinnertime. Thailand is worthwhile at any time of the year, but expect it to be warm whenever you go.

Visa Requirements

No visa is required of U.S. citizens for visits of up to 15 days. However, this can usually be extended for an additional number of weeks with little or no problem.

Customs

You're allowed 200 cigarettes (1 carton) per person, and 1 liter (about a quart) of liquor. According to the regulations, 1 still and 1 movie camera may be brought in, but most of the time, they won't bother you if you have more. You're permitted 5 rolls of still camera film and 3 rolls of movie film, but again, they're inclined to be liberal about this.

Health

Health hazards in Thailand are about the same as in any tropical country, but you can feel reasonably safe if your shots are up to date (smallpox, cholera, typhoid), and if you observe normal precautions. It is best (to say the least!) to stay away from raw vegetables, raw seafood, etc., except in the first-class hotels and leading restaurants, where a shellfish cocktail or a lettuce salad is probably safe enough. (If you're in doubt, just don't eat uncooked foods.) Foremost Dairies set up a plant in Bangkok a few years ago, and you can get their fresh milk and excellent ice cream in most of the better hotels and western-style restaurants.

If you wander off the beaten path to small restaurants and coffee shops—stick to the freshly cooked dishes and bottled soft drinks, Polaris water soda, or beer, all of which are safe. The water served in the hotels and best restaurants (and which you will find in your hotel room) is all right. Avoid ice in drinks except in the best hotels.

The sunlight in Thailand is intense, and it's just as well to wear a hat or carry a parasol. Dark glasses also are a big help. If the ladies can be so persuaded, it is best to wear flats or low-heeled shoes for sightseeing, especially for the boat trips on the *klongs* (canals). Also ladies, a lightweight blouse is better than bare shoulders, as the sun can burn before you know it. Men should wear loose, cool cotton clothes (no synthetics)—because cotton is much cooler.

Bangkok's greatest nuisance in all seasons is its mosquitoes. If you find them in your room, ring for the boy who will spray for you. For evenings out of doors, cover your ankles and forearms with repellents which come in a variety of scents. Sketolene, a local product (obtainable in both liquid form or spray in just about any grocery shop) is good for short times, whereas 612, the American product, is long-lasting. Don't be afraid of the little lizards sometimes seen scuttling on walls and ceilings. These *chinchucks* are entirely harmless, except to mosquitoes and other bugs on which they feed.

Bangkok has good medical facilities, should they be needed. The two best hospitals, are the Seventh-Day Adventist (often called the "Mission" hospital) and the Bangkok Nursing Home. There are any number of well-trained doctors, Thai, European, and American. In a real quandary or emergency, you always can call the American Embassy. On holidays, evenings, and weekends you always will find a U.S. Marine Guard on duty who can put you in touch with a doctor or the American Duty Officer. Although always glad to help in time of trouble, the Embassy people understandably do take rather a dim view of those who call to ask where's the best place to buy a princess ring.

⏱ Time

There is a 12-hour time difference between Standard Time on the east coast of the U.S. and Bangkok, bearing in mind the fact that it is a day later in Bangkok than in New York. Thus, when it's 8 P.M. in New York on Wednesday, it's 8 A.M. in Bangkok on Thursday.

💲 Currency

Thai currency is one of the most stable in the world, scarcely varying from year to year. The basic monetary unit is the *baht* (sometimes called a *tical*).

The largest-denomination bill is the red 100 *baht* note. Going downwards: 20 *baht* (green), 10 *baht* (brown), 5 *baht,* (purple), 1 *baht* (blue). Using the other word for *baht,* one can remember its worth with a jingle—"a *tical* is a nickel." The one *baht* notes are gradually being replaced by half-dollar-sized nickel alloy coins. Below one *baht,* the coinage runs: 50 *satangs,* 25 *satangs,* and 10 *satangs* (with which you can buy very little indeed).

All the better hotels will change greenbacks for *baht* at the going rate, sometimes giving a slightly better rate for bills or traveler's checks of $20-to-$100 denomination than for the smaller bills. Generally the hotel cashier has a typed-up list of exchange rates at the counter. Shopping around for *baht* may get you very slightly better rates, but the difference is so small as not to be worth the time. Greenbacks and traveler's checks are acceptable, but not personal checks. In fact, it is theoretically against Thai law to accept personal dollar checks. Some shops do accept them, however.

Tourists sometimes are approached in shops and in the street by those who would buy dollars, but be sure of your exchange rate before you bargain with these. In general it's better to stick to the hotel or to authorized money changers, whose shops are numerous in the main shopping areas.

Tourists are only supposed to bring in $500 (U.S.) in *cash* per person, but there is no limit on the amount of traveler's checks. If you have more than $500 in cash, the Customs Superintendent will have to give specific permission, and this is time-consuming. Also, don't bring in or take out more than 500 *baht* in currency.

🌐 Price Level

At one time, Bangkok was a very modestly-priced city for tourists. Now it's higher, but still represents a rather good value in today's inflated scale of prices. Let's call it medium-expensive. Hotel rates at the best hotels are generally much lower than they are at similar establishments in the western world, certainly far less, for example, than in New York or Paris. Meal prices are generally much more reasonable than elsewhere, if comparing equivalent types of restaurants. Sightseeing tours, on the other hand, for reasons unknown, tend to be higher than you might expect—of course, gas is extremely expensive in Thailand, making auto travel fairly costly. In any event, Bangkok should not be shockingly expensive.

Tipping

In general, it may be said that light tipping is the rule in Thailand. Many of the employees in tourist hotels and restaurants have been spoiled by American tourists and have begun to expect tips; however, rarely if ever will anyone stand about waiting for a tip. But what can you do? The previous situation has been altered, and some tipping is probably in order. Hotels usually add a 10% service charge, so remember that theoretically you've already paid for service. However, the baggage porter should get the equivalent of about 25¢ a bag; a bell boy perhaps should be given the equivalent of 25¢ for a typical service. In dining rooms, tip 10% to the waiter, also in bars. In beauty parlors and barber shops, just a few *baht,* say 5–10, are all that is expected. At the international airport, the porterage charge amounts to about 25¢ for each piece of luggage.

A guide or tour conductor may or may not be tipped, as you wish. Taxi-drivers do not ordinarily receive tips, unless he's carried your luggage; in that case, give him 3–5 *bahts.*

🏃 Transportation

Taxis are everywhere, and even at rush hours it's usually not difficult to find one. However, it's not just a matter of jumping into a taxi and telling the driver where you want to go. To begin with, many of them speak very little English, and unless you're heading for one of the hotels, they may not know where you wish to go. Also, although the cabs have meters, they're all out of order and you must bargain. Don't get into the cab until you agree on the price. No matter what the driver asks (they speak enough English for that), it's too much, so offer him about one-third less. And don't get into the cab until you've both agreed on a price.

The easiest way to get about is by using the special cars which almost all of the hotels make available. There's a transportation desk, usually in front of the hotel, where you tell your destination, they quote the price, and you pay for it on the spot and receive a slip to give to the driver. It includes his tip, by the way, although taxi drivers are not usually tipped.

There's good *train* service if you travel first class; don't go second class. Fares are comparatively cheap, but the trains don't exactly rush to their destination, and most tourists prefer planes. The *domestic airline* is pretty good. They have frequent flights to Chiengmai, for example, and to all the typical tourist destinations. Fares are medium, neither high nor low by world standards. *Drive-yourself cars* are available, but I wouldn't attempt to drive in Bangkok on a bet; the traffic is very heavy. Once you get to Chiengmai or Phuket, however, there's no reason for not driving about on your own, except that you might get lost. But everyone is so friendly and helpful that the local people will see that you reach your destination.

 Airport and Tourist Taxes

Bangkok's very modern new airport is called Don Muang, and is located 18 miles out of town. Travel time is approximately one hour, and you should be at the airport 1 hour before departure on international flights. Bangkok has some incredible traffic jams, so if you're traveling to the airport during the morning rush or anywhere from 4:00 P.M. to 8:00 P.M., better allow plenty of time to reach the airport. It's not at all unusual for the trip to take 1½ hours, sometimes even longer. There is an airport "service charge" of about $3 per person for all outgoing passengers leaving on international flights; no service charge is imposed on domestic flights.

Communications

Airmail letters to the U.S. cost the equivalent of about 31¢, but they must weigh less than 5 grams (equivalent to one sheet of airmail paper enclosed in an airmail envelope); each additional 5 grams costs about 13¢. It takes 4–5 days for airmail letters to reach the states, and vice versa. Surface mail takes a minimum of 5 weeks and may take 2 months. A long-distance *phone call* to your home town is usually accomplished with a fair degree of speed (but don't forget about the time differential when calling); it costs about $13.50 for 3 minutes. *Cablegrams* go through with speed; the cost is typically about $3 for 10 words to the U.S. The easiest way to send a cable is to write it out at your hotel, and have the hotel desk send it for you.

Now what about *local telephone calls?* Of all the cities of the entire world, Bangkok probably (undoubtedly is a better word) has the worst telephone system. It's nothing short of a disaster area insofar as telephone calls are concerned. It doesn't always happen that you get a wrong number, but let's say that you will 2 out of 3 times. It's far easier to reach the U.S. than it is to make a call to someone living a few streets away. If you really are anxious to put the call through, it can result in high blood pressure, red spots on the cheeks, a sense of total frustration, and, of course, not reaching the party you wish. Many years ago, the Telephone Organization of Thailand (the equivalent of our own AT & T) stopped replacing broken or inoperative phones and told their customers to buy their own telephones in a shop. More recently, in a vain effort to improve its service, the telephone company issued new telephone directories with big changes in them. Every telephone number was new. All of the old numbers were cancelled. That meant that every single telephone number in your personal file was wrong, and you had to learn the new number—for your home or office, for example—and also to notify everyone you knew. Instead of the former 5- and 6-digit numbers, every single telephone number was replaced by a 7-digit set of numbers, as in most western countries. But it was all a dream, and no new exchange centers have been installed, despite the notice. It's not all the telephone company's fault, however. Because of the humid, tropical climate and high humidity, telephone wires tend to corrode, become flooded by heavy rains, and act in strange fashions.

So you see that getting a local number in Bangkok requires skill, patience, total self-control, and, most important of all, a great deal of luck.

⚡ Electricity

Some places have 110 volts A.C., but others have 220; you'll have to inquire before using any American appliances, because obviously the 220-volt current cannot be used without a transformer. Furthermore, some hotels use British-style plugs (those with round prongs). The newer hotels usually have special outlets for electric shavers, etc., with the appropriate current indicated.

✗ Food Specialties and Liquor

Thai food and the traditional ways of serving it are interesting and worth experiencing if you have the inclination. Some of the dishes are very peppery, though Americans from the southwest whose tongues have been leathered by Mexican food will not be fazed. The villain here, as in Mexico, is the tiny red or green chili pepper. Look sharp before you take a mouthful, testing it with the tip of your tongue as you would a bath with your toe.

There are several delicious Thai specialties quite free of the chili's incandescence, such as chicken stewed in coconut milk (*gai tomeka*); or bits of beef or pork skewered on thin bamboo sticks and served with a mild peppery sauce into which you dunk it (*nua-a sat-teh,* if beef; *moo sat-teh,* if pork). One of the best and fairly bland curries is made with beef and peanuts, served rather like a stew over rice (*musoomahn*); another, usually quite mild, is a yellow curry usually made with chicken (*gang curee*); and a somewhat hotter one which can be made with beef, fish, or pork mixed with vegetables (*gang ped* —*ped* means "hot" in Thai). A good side dish with curries, or by itself, is a fried sweetish noodle, with bean sprouts (*mee krop*). A simple, popular, and filling Thai favorite is fried rice mixed either with shrimp, pork, fish, or beef (*kow-paht*). Bangkok abounds in seafood—try fried pomfret, fried or steamed shrimp, fried or steamed crab claws, and mussels. These are good and always fresh.

Don't expect to find steak, lamb chops, veal chops, or roast beef, except in European-style hotel restaurants. The Thais just don't cook food in that fashion. They prefer to cut it into pieces, and prepare it as a form of curry. Bland foods simply do not have any regular place in the Thai cuisine.

With every main course comes some of the local rice, *khao suay,* and it's very good indeed. If you find Thai food very spicy (as you probably will), learn to take small quantities, transfer it to the rice, and eat the hot food with plenty of rice, which will neutralize the spiciness. If any dish is burning to the taste, don't drink water; cool beer is more refreshing to the sizzling palate.

In most Thailand restaurants catering to westerners, food is served course by course. By local custom, however, all dishes are brought to the table at the same time, except for the dessert. When the main part of the meal is finished, there may be a pudding-like dessert, or another kind of sweet dish made from fruits, tapioca, or the like. As a rule, the Thais like to end their meals with fruit, which seems a good idea in view of the spiciness of the dishes. The mangos, pineapple, papaya, guava, and custard apples are all worth tasting. Some local fruits worth asking for include the *mangosteen,* which has a snowy-white interior and a purple-red exterior; the tangerine-like sections have an interesting taste. The *durian* is something else; it has a superb taste, but when the skin is cut, the odor is repellent —you're on your own with this item. *Pomelos,* something like our grapefruit, are good, and you might ask for *saton,* the wood apple, often made into a sweet drink and served at the end of a meal as a sort of liquid dessert.

In most Thai restaurants, at least those accustomed to serving foreigners, there will be an English version of the menu and usually a waiter or waitress who can speak at least a little English. They also will temper hot dishes for the tender tongue on request. Do just that.

There are innumerable Chinese restaurants in Thailand, some of them very good, though the standard falls below the best Chinese cuisine of Hong Kong or Taiwan. There also are Japanese, French, American—and even a Korean—restaurants. Prices generally are very moderate, though imported whisky runs high because of the import duty.

All the usual foreign liquors and mixed drinks are available at the hotels, big restaurants, and nightclubs, the prices are medium to high. If you want to try it, the local rice whiskey, *mekong,* is not bad, is only 70 proof, and costs comparatively little for a large bottle. Other good local whiskeys: Marshall, and White Cock, both Scotch-ish in flavor and only slightly more expensive than *mekong.* Soda, ice cold, is always available, as is the excellent Thai Beer, Singha. There is a wide variety of soft drinks, including Coca-Cola, Pepsi-Cola, Seven-Up, Bireley's (orange), and others—all safely bottled at modern plants in Bangkok.

The hotels all serve western-style food, sometimes fairly good, sometimes not. But no one need go hungry.

∞ Time Evaluation

Because Bangkok is such an interesting city, I'd allow an absolute minimum of 4 days for pure local sightseeing; of course, this makes no allowance for sitting around your hotel's swimming pool, or any time for shopping. You'll surely make at least one daytrip out of Bangkok, so that means a minimum of 5 days. However, a week is not a bad guess as to what you'll really need. For more distant sightseeing, say to Chiengmai, an additional 2–3 days should be allowed.

Some Local Customs

The Thais are very special people, and quite different from their neighbors to the east and west. To begin with, Thais rarely, if ever, raise their voice, and they regard anyone who gets angry or shouts as having poor manners. Please remember this: no matter what the situation, speak quietly and calmly. Also, as mentioned previously, the Thais smile a good deal and appreciate people who smile in return.

Another important point: it is regarded as extremely insulting to touch the head of another person; avoid doing this under any circumstances. For this reason, if you ever want to have your picture taken with a statue of Buddha, be sure not to put your hands on his head.

The Thais are, as you might expect, very sensitive about Buddhas, which may be seen in various parts of Bangkok. Therefore, the law in the country prohibits the export of any reproductions of Buddha figures or statues. Also, if you visit a temple, you'll be required to remove your shoes before entering (it's a good idea to save those airline socks which some companies distribute to their passengers). Be sure to be soberly dressed when you visit a temple. Women should not wear shorts or slacks, and men should not roll up their sleeves, although short-sleeve shirts are suitable.

Don't be surprised if some Thais are hesitant about shaking hands, although many sophisticated, westernized Thais do so. It's simply not the custom, and it's much more customary for Thais who meet to make a *wai,* which consists of putting the tips of the fingers together, upraised, so as to form a miniature temple.

🏛 Capital City: Bangkok

Every city that has a mud puddle is called the Venice of some-place-or-another, to my intense annoyance. Bangkok, wouldn't you know it, is called the "Venice of the East"; well, for once the term is deserved, because this exotic city is filled with meandering canals, which lead off from the main river, the Chao Phraya. The canals, especially in the early morning hours, are bustling with activity, and constitute one of Bangkok's outstanding (and deservedly so) sightseeing attractions.

Bangkok rarely disappoints the tourist. I'd make a rough calculation and guess that nine out of ten visitors think that it is one of the most interesting cities in Asia. That may well be so, and it certainly is an unusual place, well worth the days you allot to it on your trip. However, and this is one warning I'd give to anyone before seeing Bangkok, don't think that it has nothing but royal palaces, colorful temples, exotic dancers, and the whole color-poster or airline-calendar bit. It has all of those, but not all of the time nor every place. What I'm hinting at, somewhat delicately, is that Bangkok is a very large city of over 4.8 million people, doing a considerable amount of trade and commercial business, manufacturing a variety of goods, and very well-aware that this is the 20th century. Thus, the city has modern shops, air-conditioned office buildings, fine homes, and plenty of automobile traffic, and guess what, a parking problem. Not too exotic, this showcase of the Orient, you mutter to yourself. Well, surprisingly enough, it still is exotic, to stay with that word. You'll see a mixture of Southeast Asia and the 20th century when you get there, but somehow Bangkok is still Bangkok, in its own peculiar way. The contrasts are often astonishing, sometimes absolutely startling, and occasionally laughable. Impressive temples, shimmering with gold and green, the roofs extending downward at steep angles only to turn up gracefully at the corners, stand alongside of twenty-storied office buildings. Along the street, a monk, wearing his traditional saffron-colored robes, rides on a motorcycle, darting in and out of the traffic lanes like a Connecticut hot-rodder. Along the canals (here called *klongs*), houses are built upon stilts, and young children jump into the water all day long, regarding it as an extension of their houses. It seems trite to say it, but almost unavoidable, that Bangkok is a city of contrasts. It is also a very, very interesting place to visit.

Bangkok is growing at a rapid pace; there is new construction everywhere, and detours are not only common-place but routine. As it has grown, the new structures have the international appearance of new buildings everywhere in the world, whether in New York, Hong Kong, or Bangkok. But somehow, and one hopes it will continue, the city seems to retain its distinctive Thai flavor and atmosphere. Perhaps this is because of the great number of pagodas and temples, palaces and monasteries. But perhaps, more than the physical surroundings, it may be that the Thai themselves create their own mood and atmosphere. (Nine-tenths of the population is Thai, the balance being made up chiefly of Chinese, Malays, Indians, and Europeans.) The people themselves are graceful, slight, not too tall, and very soft-spoken. A Thai who raises his voice and shouts is considered extremely crude, and hardly worthy to associate with decent people. The women frequently wear the national costume, the *pa sin,* a full-length skirt customarily worn with a brief jacket; the men (at least in Bangkok) seem to prefer western clothes. Try to strike up conversations with the Thais, especially if they look educated. English is the second language (after Thai) in the local schools, and not a few people speak it reasonably well.

There is no business or downtown area in Bangkok, but rather six different concentrations—Patpong, Gaysorn, Ploenchit, Oriental, Sukumvit, and Siam Square. This last, adjacent to the Siam Inter-Continental Hotel, is convenient for shopping and general tourist activity.

Now, what about Bangkok sightseeing? How to allot the all-too-elusive days that will slip out of your hands if you don't make a few plans. Assuming 5 days for Bangkok, here is a suggestion on how to spend your time.

First day. City tour in the morning; afternoon free for shopping. See some classical Thai dancing in the evening.

Second day. Early morning boat trip along the *klongs;* see the royal barges, and visit the Temple of the Dawn. In the afternoon, visit the zoo, or the snake farm.

Third day. An all-day trip to Ayudhya; or, a half-day trip to Nakorn Pathom.

Fourth day. Morning free for shopping, or see the various temples and the museum, or visit Jim Thompson's house. In the afternoon, the Grand Palace (on Tuesdays and Thursdays) and the Temple of the Emerald Buddha. Evening, see Thai boxing.

Fifth day. A river trip to see the famous bird sanctuary at Wat Phai Lom, or in the alternative, to the fishing village called Maha Chai.

At one time, there was a fascinating floating market which operated more or less in front of the Oriental Hotel, starting at about dawn. It became so popular and the traffic was so intense that regular river traffic was unable to get by the small boats in the floating market. As a result, the city authorities decided to close down the floating market and move it upriver. A trip through the *klongs* (that is, the canals) was once something unique and fascinating. The people who lived along the *klongs* in their stilt-supported houses jumped into the river each morning and washed and brushed their teeth, and even etcetera (if you know what I mean), in the same water. It wasn't at all sanitary, but everyone seemed to thrive. The children seemed to spend the entire day in the river splashing about, the housewives bought their food and household supplies from passing small craft that offered medicine, brooms, and even furniture.

Nowadays, in order to see this unique sight, you must head for the Damnoen Sauak floating market, located about an hour and a half from Bangkok. It's much more relaxed and much more sanitary than the original floating market. A boat ride through the canals is truly worthwhile, and you'll enjoy it. Be sure to bring along a sunhat and sunglasses, and because of its distance from Bangkok, it might be best to take a package tour and avoid all the problems of transportation.

The Grand Palace is actually a small self-contained community, completely enclosed by walls. The grounds are attractive, the buildings represent the best in Thai architecture, and there are fantastically-designed figures of gods and demons scattered all over the palace grounds. The trip through the palace and its grounds is quite fascinating, but don't take movie cameras, as only still cameras are allowed. (Men may wear short-sleeve shirts and slacks, but not shorts. Women should not wear slacks or shirts, dresses only.) In the compound adjacent to the palace is the Temple of the Emerald Buddha, a really beautiful *wat,* as the temples are called. Inside, you'll see the famous Emerald Buddha, a 31-inch figure carved out of a remarkable piece of green jasper; no picture (not even still) may be taken *inside* the Temple of the Emerald Buddha. While you're in the mood for Buddhas, close to the Grand Palace, you'll find the Temple of the Reclining Buddha, one that is merely 160 feet long. Inside the chapel, there are almost 400 more Buddhas; the whole affair is more than merely impressive, it is almost overwhelming.

If you're really fond of Thai artifacts, visit the National Museum, which is open daily except Saturday and Monday. If you don't particularly care for Thai art, don't go. However, even if the Thai figures don't carry any special message for you, a visit to Jim Thompson's house (a donation for maintenance is required) is definitely in order. Mr. Thompson, who started the silk business in Thailand, disappeared a number of years ago; however, you may visit his magnificent house built in the Thai style, filled with valuable works of art. For the typical tourist who otherwise would have no opportunity to see the interior of a fine Siamese house, this is a priceless opportunity.

You might spend a few hours exploring "Chinatown." It's an intriguing area to wander through, with narrow streets and lanes, marvelous displays of food, clothing, and so forth. Be sure to look into the nearby Chinese "gold stores." Two or three hours of Chinatown sightseeing is fascinating.

By all means pay a visit to the Muang Boran, the Ancient City. Despite its name this is a semicommercial venture, and there's an admission charge, but it's most definitely worthwhile. The Ancient City is actually an outdoor museum of Thai temples and monuments that is situated on an area of over 200 acres. It's located at Sukumvit Highway, about 20 miles southeast of Bangkok, and takes about 40 minutes to reach. It should take about 2–3 hours to wander, preferably by car or bus, through the grounds, and the buildings of ancient Thailand have been meticulously reconstructed in breathtaking fashion. I was astonished at the scope and magnificence of the buildings. If you go in the morning, an ideal time, see if you can't stop at 199 Sukumvit Road, just a few minutes from the Ancient City, and have a delicious seafood lunch at the Bangpoo Restaurant, on the road leading back to Bangkok.

Many tourists are interested in seeing what really goes on inside a shrine. In most temples there is very little to be seen, unless a festival is in progress. One exception is Lak Muang, a temple which is sometimes called the City Post Shrine. However, if you take a cab from your hotel—it isn't more than 15 minutes from any of them —tell the driver you want Lak Muang, rather than the English name, which wouldn't mean too much to him. It's best to go as early in the morning as possible, certainly not later than 9 A.M. I suggest if you're making the excursion on a weekend that you go to Lak Muang first, and then walk over to the nearby Weekend Market, which takes place outdoors on Phramane grounds and is really quite fascinating.

ACCOMMODATIONS The hotel situation in Bangkok is quite good, with plenty of good fairly expensive rooms available most of the year, although they can become scarce on occasion. Bangkok is a great convention center for Southeast Asia, and the hotel situation can sometimes become extremely tight; it's best to have confirmed reservations. There are three luxury hotels here, the Oriental, the Siam Inter-Continental, and the Montien.

Siam Inter-Continental. An extraordinarily attractive resortlike hotel, with plenty of open area, large swimming pool, and outdoor areas. Architecture is fascinating, the rooms are quite attractive. Several restaurants, numerous shops, and tennis courts.

Oriental. This famous hotel has been completely rebuilt and has a new wing. Fantastic location at the river's edge. Outdoor terrace dining and rooftop restaurant. Elegant and luxurious.

Montien. A large, luxurious hotel with 600 rooms, conveniently located in the center of activity. Rooms are almost lavish, with individual refrigerators, private balconies, and marble-trimmed baths. The Montien has regular and tower wings. Excellent choice of restaurants; the Chinese one is first rate.

Ambassador. A very large hotel with a fine circular tower wing. Located slightly away from the city's center, it offers large enclosed areas and a feeling of spaciousness. An enormous assortment of restaurants from which to choose.

Hyatt Rama. On Silom Road, in a convenient location, in the downtown area. The new Tower Building is very modern, has a swimming pool and numerous restaurants. A good hotel.

Narai. A centrally located hotel, with 519 rooms of moderate size, nicely decorated. The hotel has several restaurants and all facilities. First class but not deluxe.

Indra Regent. An 18-story, 500 room hotel; specializes in tours and groups. Rooms are somewhat small but more modestly priced than those listed above. Very large shopping arcade.

Dusit Thani. An extremely large and rather good hotel in a central area. An excellent assortment of restaurants and shops. Like the Narai, it's a first-class hotel, but doesn't make the luxury class.

Erawan. An older, but fairly good hotel; all rooms are air-conditioned. Swimming pool, many shops, several restaurants. Near extensive shopping area.

Sheraton Bangkok. As in all hotels of this chain, the rooms are nice and the hotel has all facilities. Busy location.

New Imperial. In the Embassy area, this "garden" hotel has spacious grounds; it's large and rather lively. Rooms are fairly nice, numerous restaurants and shops.

President. Close to the Erawan, this is a rather good, moderate-priced hotel that caters to tour groups. In two sections, connected by a long passageway. Rooms are of surprisingly good size, pleasantly decorated. A good value for the budget-conscious.

RESTAURANTS   Every hotel has its western-style restaurant, and in general, the food is fair enough. Rarely however, is it really excellent—the kind of meal you might want to exclaim about. The steaks, which used to be poor, are now imported, and are rather good, although not great. Fish is more likely to be good than meat (which is usually frozen) because at least it has the virtue of being fresh. If you grow bored with hotel food, or in the alternative, if you don't even want to bother with it, by all means try some of the Thai, Chinese, or other national restaurants in Bangkok, many of which are quite good. As a rule, except in hotel dining rooms, meals are moderately priced, sometimes even bargains. Of course, drinking imported liquor, like scotch, will send your final check up very quickly. Let's just review some of the better western-style restaurants, including some of those in the hotels.

Vendome. An attractive French restaurant, in its own small house, close to the Erawan Hotel. The ambience is pleasant, the service gracious, and the food rather good. Moderately expensive.

Le Chalet. A small place, located in the Erawan Hotel. A rather interesting selection of European dishes, including cheese fondue, etc. Moderately expensive.

Chez Suzanne. French provincial food, rather well-prepared, and nicely served. Pleasant atmosphere. Located on Silom Road, a brief ride from the center of town. Medium-high.

Normandy Grill. Situated beautifully atop the Oriental Hotel tower, with a fabulous view of the river. Good European dishes, calm, friendly atmosphere. Fairly expensive and probably the only restaurant in Thailand that requires a jacket and tie.

Two Vikings. As a change of pace, you might like to visit this pleasant Scandinavian-style restaurant, which features a special buffet on Wednesday. Good food, medium to high prices.

Nick's No. 1 Hungarian Inn. This may be one of the best-known places in town, and serves a wide variety of dishes, including steaks and seafood.

Inter-Continental. The seafood restaurant is excellent and very attractive.

Now, as you know, Thai food is fairly spicy. All right, we'll agree on that. But you owe yourself a visit to a Thai restaurant, and as a rule, there are so many dishes that you'll be able to pick and choose and surely not go hungry. All of the restaurants mentioned below are primarily concerned with group tours. If you go as a party of two, they will often become confused unless you phone for a reservation; be sure to ask when the show starts and arrive early enough to have dinner before the show.

Baan Thai. I would classify this attractive, air-conditioned place as a "must" for tourists. To begin with, they know you're not used to highly spiced foods, and most of their dishes have been toned down. There are pretty waitresses, and the whole mood is pleasant and charming. Located just behind the Rex Hotel. Medium-high. The show here is about the best in the city.

Chit Pochana. This interesting Thai restaurant has both an open-air and an air-conditioned section. Good food, Thai dancing. Medium prices. On Petchburi Road.

Piman. This is extremely popular with tourists, because the food, atmosphere, and service are excellent. There's a pleasant short program of Thai dancing.

The restaurants above are mostly for tourists and are very pleasant, but the food is not distinguished nor completely authentic. It is toned down a great deal and takes into consideration the fact that most visitors are unacquainted with Thai food. However, if you are a serious gourmet and are interested in fine food, visit one or all of the restaurants listed below:

Rang Toa (Tollgate). If you are really serious in learning something about Thai food, this is surely the best and most beautiful place. The restaurant is at 245/2 Soi 31, Sukumvit Road, and they're open every day but Sunday for lunch and dinner. The Tollgate is part of a private home with limited seating. The food is outstandingly good; be sure to phone early in the day for a reservation, telephone 391-3947. Medium prices.

Sea Food Market. There are several branches of this interesting operation serving seafood only. In one section you personally select your fish; the restaurant then cooks it in any of a variety of styles. Amusing, diverting, and not expensive.

Apichart. In the Thonburi residential area, this restaurant has a country atmosphere and is mostly outdoors. The specialty here is seafood, with particular emphasis upon prawns and crab, both of which are delicious. Inexpensive, but very worthwhile and completely authentic.

The Chinese food in Bangkok is very good indeed, and the variety of dishes available will astonish an American, used to the limited menus in our local Chinese restaurants. Figure about $3 or so per person, or more if you order a large selection.

Golden Dragon. An exceptionally popular, and deservedly so, Chinese restaurant. Almost anything you order will be delicious, but be sure not to overlook the seafood, especially crab dishes. If you like Chinese food, don't overlook the Golden Dragon. It's on Sukumvit Road.

Shangarila. A small air-conditioned place located on Silom Road; Shanghai-style cooking is the specialty. I recommend their fish and prawn dishes, also chicken with walnuts.

Miramar. On Rajdamri Road, near the Erawan Hotel; this place features Peking-style cookery. Many interesting dishes, but especially the duck preparations.

SHOPPING To begin with the easiest and most expensive shopping, most hotels have an arcade, or at least a cluster of shops.

These all carry the better type of locally produced merchandise, and obviously they satisfy the needs of their customers, for otherwise, the hotel's manager would have evicted them a long time ago. But bear in mind that prices will usually be higher, but not always; so shop around locally before deciding. At one time, it seemed to me that the prices in hotel shops were always higher than elsewhere, but now this does not always hold true.

There are four principal shopping areas. First, the hotels, which we've just mentioned. There are also a good number of shops on New Road (in the vicinity of the Oriental and Rama hotels); this is really the main area for buyers, and also extends off in both directions on some of the side streets leading away from New Road. Then there is the Sampeng district, also called Chinatown, where you can do a little more bargaining on the prices and perhaps get better values. Don't worry about the language problem—almost every shopkeeper speaks English, and the exceptions are comparatively rare. On Saturdays and Sundays, you might enjoy visiting the famous weekend market, conducted on the Phramane Ground.

There are two easy ways—and cool ones—to shop under one roof. There's a large complex of shops selling clothing, fabrics, art objects, antiques, jewelry, etc. very close to the Siam Inter-Continental Hotel; it's called the Siam Shopping Centre, and it's just 2 minutes' walk from the hotel. Another complex of shops, not quite so extensive perhaps, but nevertheless worthwile, is just behind the Oriental Hotel, and this one is called the Oriental Plaza. If you're staying at either of these hotels, the shops within these complexes offer a pleasant way to take care of a large amount of your personal and gift shopping.

POINTER:
   This should not be forgotten, don't buy too hastily. In Bangkok, prices are always subject to offers. In other words, do some serious bargaining before spending any real money. Don't buy too quickly, and courteously ask the proprietor to lower his price a few times. Don't issue any ultimatums, but talk it over. I know most Americans think bargaining is beneath them, but as a rule, prices are set too high. Of course, there is no bargaining at government shops, or at the best shops.

Before you begin your buying, it might be a good idea to pay a visit to the government's Shopping Center which displays all of the locally produced arts and crafts. Prices are fixed, and are slightly higher than at many of the privately owned shops; however, at least you'll know what the typical prices are before you start. Furthermore, all of the goods have been carefully checked as to quality. Now, out with the traveler's checks, and with pen poised in midair, ready to sign your name, here are the most worthwhile buys:

Thai silk is among the finest in the world. Although prices vary from store to store, and according to quality, figure about $8–$12 a yard as a basic figure. In New York, the same merchandise can cost five times as much! (That's what I call a good value; none of this nonsense about half the price, etc.) Seriously, Thai silk is of excellent quality, handwoven and handspun in small quantities, and especially renowned for its lustrous, rich colors. Before you leave home, if you're really foresighted, you'll measure out carefully any pieces of furniture that need recovering, potential drapes, or the like; for the price of ordinary fabrics back home, you can acquire some remarkable silk material, because Thai silk is ideal not only for clothing, but also for household use. Of course, many of the shops have ready-made blouses, dresses, coats, stoles, men's ties, shirts, place mats, scarves, and dozens of other articles. In general, however, most of the Thai silk is to be had as yard goods, usually in 40-inch widths. The colors are fast, so no worry need be expended on that score. The best known shop of all is that started by Jim Thompson, the Thai Silk Company, 9 Surawongse Road. The prices are perhaps somewhat higher than most, but he does have a large selection. Also very good is the Bangkok Silk Co., at 92 Patpong Road, and the Star of Siam, across from the Erawan Hotel. Design Thai, opposite the President Hotel, has an excellent selection of ready-made silk and cotton garments.

While on the subject of fabrics, and although the silks outshine them, the local *cotton fabrics* are outstanding and unwarrantedly neglected. The colors and textures are similar to those used in the silks, and prices are lower. About the best are Kohmapastr; also Scandia, in the Gaysorn Shopping Center, across the road from the Erawan Hotel.

Thailand's jungles are the home of a remarkable wood, *teakwood,* which as used here represents a good value for trays, boxes, carvings, etc. They can make up articles to order, too, if you wish. Perhaps the best place for teakwood is Design Thai Showroom, near the Erawan Hotel. Teak furniture, at exceptionally low prices, including desks, may be purchased in this area, at a furniture company called, believe it or not, Sweet Home. They're reliable and will ship to your home, if you allow about three to four months.

The locally produced *jewelry,* chiefly made of semiprecious stones, is fairly interesting, but the designs tend to be mediocre. The best buy in jewelry, in my opinion is the Princess Ring, shaped like a high crown, and also called the Nine Precious Gem Ring, because it is made with zircon or diamond (depending on price), moonstone, sapphire, ruby, cat's-eye, emerald, garnet, and topaz. Exotic Siam (in the President Hotel) has a very good selection of Thai jewelry, which is probably the best in town.

Nielloware, an unusual and distinctive amalgam of silver, copper, sulfur, and lead, is used for making flatware, cigarette boxes and the like. Silversmiths make *silver* articles in both the Bangkok and Chiengmai patterns; bowls, tea sets, jewelry, etc. Prices aren't too high. You'll see these articles for sale every place, so there's no use making recommendations. However, if in doubt, check the Shopping Center, previously mentioned.

Gold jewelry may be seen in great profusion on Yaowaraj Road in the heart of Bangkok's teeming and exciting Chinatown district. (Incidentally, I am sorry about that name, Yaowaraj, but that's what it's called.) In any event, gold is available as necklaces, rings, and bracelets, as well as gold units of weight, which people buy as a hedge against inflation. Prices tend to follow the price of gold on international markets, and generally speaking, there are no great bargains to be had, only small ones, because the price of the jewelry is based strictly upon the weight of the gold used, plus a small charge for workmanship. No bargaining is permitted, and prices are definitely fixed. You can only bargain on the workmanship, not on the weight of the gold. You should always remember that gold has a changing but high price throughout the world. However, in Thailand, skilled craftsmen work for rather little money, and that's where the bargains (theoretically) come in. In general, the gold is plain, simple 24-karat gold. Each day the prices change for necklaces or other jewelry based upon the day's quotation for gold received from Hong Kong, plus say $5 for the workmanship—and that's the price. Even if you don't buy anything, it's interesting to see the street that isn't paved with gold, but lined with it, on both sides.

If you're interested in *Thai figures, heads,* and authentic *antiques,* you may be disappointed to find the selection somewhat limited. That is, if you're interested in original Thai art. Most of the merchandise on sale is from Burma. Naturally, it depends on what you select, but good pieces are becoming scarcer all the time, and the government has clamped restrictions on certain shipments, so you may expect to spend anywhere from $50 to $10,000, which is a pretty wide range, but is just intended to show you that prices depend upon what is selected. Incidentally, this shop also carries marvelous *temple rubbings* (which are handsome when framed). The very best rubbings are made on rice paper rather than on cloth; some of them are comparatively inexpensive, and they look marvelous when framed. In my opinion, this is the best shop, by far, for antiques. An antique may be taken out of Thailand only if it carries a Fine Arts Department permit, and a lead seal. Don't buy an image of Buddha and put it in your luggage. If you do, and your luggage is opened, it may be confiscated by the customs officials. It's much safer to buy it at a shop that can arrange for the legalities of shipping a Buddha image out of the country. (Of course, this restriction does not apply if the antique you buy does not represent an image of Buddha.) Furthermore, this restriction applies even to *copies* of Buddha images and is not limited to originals.

If you're a real *antique-hunter,* or bargain-finder, perhaps a visit to the Thieves' Market, Nakorn Kasem, might be enjoyable. Take a taxi over, and then wander about at random, walking in and out of the many small shops. Sometimes you'll encounter a bargain, sometimes not, but in any event, it is very diverting. And you're perfectly safe, so have no fears on that score. When finished, take a taxi back to your hotel (with your bargains?).

Celadon, lacquerware, rattan and *bamboo articles* and *Bangkok dolls* just about wrap up the shopping picture in Thailand. One word of warning: don't forget that Chinese antiques cannot be brought into the U.S., for all practical purposes.

POINTER:
  Be very careful never to touch a Thai on the head. This restriction applies even though it may be intended as a pat or a friendly gesture. To the Thais, the head represents the dwelling place of the human spirit, and there is nothing that will be resented so much as touching a person's head. It is a very serious social error.

ENTERTAINMENT At one time, Bangkok was a quiet town at night, but all of that is in the past. Nowadays, there's plenty of night life, of all sorts, ranging from the most sedate spots for late dinner dancing, which most of the hotels offer, all the way down to sailors' hangouts, rough and ready.

If you want to attend a full performance of Thai classical dancing (a little too much, in my opinion), you might inquire at your hotel. Take my suggestion, and see a brief program at one of the restaurants, listed in the Thai restaurant section, which offer a half hour, or so, of dancing. It's enough. If you're a student of drama, perhaps a performance might be seen at the Silpakorn Theater, from November through May. It's really not possible to list the nightclubs in Bangkok, because they change so quickly, coming and going from one season to another. Just inquire locally, if you're interested.

The seamy (but interesting) side of much of the local life may be seen at night on Patpong Road. Here there are massage parlors, nudie shows, bar hostesses, etc. Be quite careful and watch your wallet. It can sometimes be dangerous.

SPORTS Thailand has many unique sports, all of which are worth seeing, if only for their novelty value. First of all, there is *takraw,* a game played with a woven rattan ball. The point of the game is keeping the ball in motion, the players being allowed to use any part of the body. You can see pickup games in open areas, but the scheduled contests are held at Phramane Ground from March to May.

Kite-fighting, which doesn't sound exciting, really is. There are large *chula* kites, denoting the male, and smaller *pakpao* kites, representing the female. *Chulas* are star-shaped, and *pakpaos* are diamond-shaped. The idea is to knock down your opponent's kite, and it's fascinating to watch, especially in high winds. The way the Thais fly kites, it is definitely not a child's game. There are special tournaments held at Phramane Ground from February through May.

Thai boxing, previously mentioned, is most unusual. Before each bout, the contestants do a sort of shadow-boxing exhibition, representing homage to their instructors. The boxers use fists, of course, but also knees, feet, elbows, and it's really wild. There is music during the bouts, intended to give the boxers a sense of rhythm.

There is also *cock-fighting,* and *fish-fighting,* the first being the usual sport seen in the Caribbean; it is enormously popular in rural areas. In fish-fighting contests, two male fish are placed in a bowl, and I must say, this is an acquired taste.

If you want to play *golf,* there are six courses in Thailand, three of which are in Bangkok—Royal Bangkok Sports Club, Royal Dusit Golf Club, and the Royal Thai and the Royal Thai Air Force Golf Club. However, guest privileges require an introduction; if you don't know anyone, call the club's secretary and ask for permission.

All of the principal hotels have *swimming pools,* so that should present no problem; it is warm enough in Bangkok for swimming most of the year, although occasional cool days do come along— now and then. There are *horse races* every Saturday at either the Turf Club or the Royal Bangkok Sports Club; but how the horses race in that temperature, I'll never know. If I were a horse, I'd walk.

Short Trips from Bangkok

Tourists to Japan rarely limit themselves to Tokyo; trips from that capital city to Nikko, Kyoto, and Nara are the regular custom. In India, everyone goes outside of Calcutta or New Delhi to see the countryside. For some unknown reason, the vast majority of tourists limit themselves to Bangkok, and rarely get out of town. Why? Is it the shopping? The local sightseeing? Or is it merely that few tourists allow sufficient time for Thailand? Whatever the reason, it would be very wrong not to go outside of Bangkok, because there's so much to see. Take at least *one* trip, and two if at all possible.

Rose Gardens

Within an hour or so from downtown Bangkok is this tourist-oriented area which is really worthwhile. Of course, it's an expensive trip if you hire a private car, so it might be better to buy a package tour. Rose Gardens covers a fair amount of acreage and includes both an outdoor and also an air-conditioned restaurant along the banks of a canal; the food is surprisingly good and not all that expensive (that is, if your package trip doesn't include lunch). Afterwards you can see a very pleasant show, including some Thai dancing and music, all quite authentic. You can wander about and watch artisans weaving silk or making handicrafts, and it's all rather diverting. There are various shops where you can buy things, and the whole of Rose Gardens, although totally commercial, is nevertheless low-keyed and a trip here makes a soothing, enjoyable outing. They even have a modern hotel on the grounds should you wish to spend a few days away from the excitement of Bangkok.

Ayudhya

One of the most interesting places to visit is *Ayudhya,* situated 53 miles north of Bangkok. Ayudhya was the capital of the country

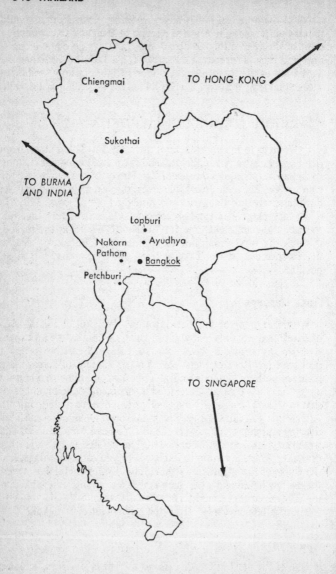

from 1350 to 1767. It makes a pleasant day's trip, and you'll definitely enjoy it. Go by automobile, because although a train can be taken, you won't see the countryside nearly so well. You can hire a car and driver on your own, or you can arrange for a package tour; prices are therefore very variable. It's a very long day, somewhat tiresome in hot weather, but worthwhile nevertheless.

The trip upcountry is very pleasant, although not wildly thrilling. En route, you'll see the people at work on their agricultural projects, the water buffalos, the rice paddies, the sleepy villages, and you'll learn something of the daily lives of the Thais. About 40 miles out from Bangkok, you can visit the former Royal Summer Palace, at the tiny hamlet called Bang Pa-In. They used to know how to live in those days, for the king built his summer home on a small island, surrounded by water so as to have the most scenic and coolest location. You'll see temples, a church (yes, that's right), water towers, and numerous palace buildings, including many excellent examples of Thai architecture.

When you reach Ayudhya, at first you'll be disappointed. The little village itself has nothing to recommend it, but the ruins (and that's just what they are) of the old capital city are tremendously interesting. It was once a great city, as you'll see from what is left of the place after the Burmese attacked and conquered it in 1767. There are reservoirs, ruined buildings, standing arches, bronze images, monasteries, temples, and palaces. It is a scene of some desolation, and somehow, strangely moving. The Royal Palace itself consists of five principal buildings, some of which have been partially restored. You'll undoubtedly want to see the Elephant Kraal, a very large enclosure (using teak logs as a fence), once used to contain wild elephants. The government has constructed a museum, the Ayudhya National Museum, which houses many of the most interesting archeological finds.

A few points about making a trip to Ayudhya. If you take a guided tour, ask if you can't return to Bangkok by motorboat, which will not only add variety to the trip but also permit you to see some of the upcountry river life. (If you hire your own car, this will be impractical.) If you wish, take a picnic lunch along from your hotel; there really isn't anyplace too good en route to Ayudhya. There are a couple of barely passable, but not terribly good, hotels at the old capital. In Ayudhya, you'll be offered small heads for sale, but most of them are not genuine, particularly those sold in the streets; if you want something authentic, buy at a good shop.

Nakorn Pathom

Nakorn Pathom is only 35 miles to the west of Bangkok, and is another suggestion for a day trip. It's possible to remain overnight, if you wish, but I would advise you to return the same day. No one knows when this ancient city was first founded, although various guesses place it as early as the 3rd century B.C. It was from Nakorn Pathom that Buddhism was first introduced to the Thais, and the city reached its height of importance when it became the capital of the Dvaravati Empire (10th–15th centuries). It subsequently became abandoned until 1853, when King Mongkut (the actual king who was portrayed in *Anna and The King of Siam*) began its restoration. The outstanding single sight of Nakorn Pathom is the enormous Phra Pathom Chedi, a spire rising 380 feet, which can be seen from many miles away.

If you can see both Ayudhya and Nakorn Pathom, by all means do so. If you have to make a choice, I think perhaps Ayudhya might be the more interesting of the two.

Longer Trips from Bangkok

Pattaya

About 100 miles southeast of Bangkok is the resort area of Pattaya, which has witnessed a really stupendous boom in the past few years. It still has lovely white beaches, backed by coconut palms, lovely views, and marvelous seafood, but it's changed. At one time, only Thais knew of the area, now American tourists are visiting Pattaya in increasing numbers because there are several good hotels on the scene, particularly the Regent Pattaya and the Hyatt Pattaya; both are excellent. There is a very large (370 rooms) Holiday Inn Sands Hotel, which, like all Holiday Inns, has pretty-good-sized rooms, plus swimming pools, tennis courts, shops, and even a tiny zoo. Another good place to stay is the Royal Cliff Beach Hotel, the largest in Pattaya, with several restaurants, a night club, convention hall, movie theatre, two swimming pools, tennis, and a shopping arcade. There's also the very good Nipa Lodge in its own lovely gardens. The water here is ideal for swimming, scuba diving, and boating; the deep sea fishing is exceptional, and there are several charter boats for hire. The beach resort features interesting shopping, a number of excellent restaurants on the beach, night spots, and even a supermarket.

Several years ago, Pattaya was a placid, semi-deserted beach resort lined by waving palm trees with long stretches of almost empty beaches. It was a quiet, tropical spot, ideal for a brief vacation. But all of that has changed, and for the worse unfortunately. Along the water's edge are cheap, unsanitary restaurants; the pure waters of the Gulf of Siam are said to be polluted, and the surf may be filled with floating garbage. If you stay at one of the better hotels, it's still a nice place to visit, but unless the local authorities do something very quickly, Pattaya will surely deteriorate into a very undesirable, noisy, unpleasant place, guaranteed to go in only one direction—downhill.

En route to Pattaya, 20 miles south of Bangkok, you'll encounter the marvelous reconstruction of old Siam, on a 216-acre site, called Ancient City. It has exact reproductions of innumerable Thai buildings, and is definitely worth a visit.

Lopburi

Lopburi is about 95 miles north of Bangkok by road, and slightly less by railroad train. The trip can be made in one (very) long day, but you might come back exhausted; don't forget that it's pretty hot in Thailand most of the year. It may have been founded as early as the 5th century A.D. (the precise date is subject to conjecture), but it was politically most important during the later Dvaravati period, although many of its best buildings were constructed later on. However, it had one interesting and rather fantastic interlude during the 17th century. A Greek adventurer (or confidence man if you prefer that word) came to Thailand and was able to gain the personal friendship of the king. Constantine Phaulkon, for that was his name, became the king's minister and wielded enormous influence. During this period, he built many of Lopburi's buildings, including the ramparts, forts, the Royal Reception House, and the palaces. However, Phaulkon came to an unfortunate end, for in the process of rising to the top he made many powerful enemies. After a little governmental flare-up, the opposition came into power and he was executed. One of the sights of Lopburi is the house where Phaulkon lived with his wife, believed to have been Japanese.

I don't know how to rate Lopburi as a tourist attraction. It would be definitely worthwhile except for its distance from Bangkok. During the hot or rainy season, it might be just a little too difficult to manage; the trip takes about 3 hours each way, plus time for sightseeing and lunch. In the cooler season, the trip is more easily managed.

Surin

If you happen to be in Thailand during the end of November, you might consider a trip to Surin, to see the famous Elephant Round-Up, which takes place during the third weekend of the month. The Tourist Organization of Thailand has arranged a prepackaged tour at a rather moderate rate, and if you want to make the trip, it's best to get in touch with one of their offices in the U.S. before departure. As a rule, you leave Bangkok by sleeper train, with supper served on the train; the sleepers consist of upper and lower berths and are moderately comfortable. In the morning breakfast is served at a local high school. Then from about 8:00 A.M. to noon, there is a program involving about 200 elephants of all ages, showing how they are rounded up in the jungle and trained; all in all, it's quite spectacular and rather worthwhile. In the afternoon, you have a choice of seeing some ruins of ancient temples or of wandering about in the town of Surin; lunch and dinner are also served in the high school. Then back to the train, and the following morning you arrive in Bangkok station.

Phuket

A delightful island in southern Thailand is called Phuket, but pronounced poo-ket. Although the island is connected to the mainland by a causeway, and can therefore be reached by train or bus, it's best to fly down; the flight takes from one to two hours, depending upon the type of plane used. Once there, you have a choice of three hotels. Most likely you'll choose the Phuket Island Resort, which has a series of small bungalows set among the palms, with marvelous views; there's a swimming pool, and the hotel has its own transportation to a nearby beach. The next best hotel for tourists is the Pearl, which is located in the main part of Phuket town; it also has a swimming pool. Actually the Pearl Hotel is the best on the island, but it is in town, which involves transportation to and from a beach, should you wish to swim. Third best is the Patong Beach Hotel, which is definitely not luxurious, but nevertheless passable enough; it caters to European tour groups. As to dining, you'll probably eat in your hotel most of the time, and the Chinese restaurant atop the Pearl Hotel is quite good. The seafood is exceptional here, as you might expect, and the lobster and crabs extraordinarily good, as well as inexpensive. To sample the local cuisine, the Lai-An Restaurant is your best bet; it's in town, not far from the Pearl Hotel. If you're moderately brave, try the sea grasshoppers (which taste like crab) and the turtle eggs. For sightseeing, it's necessary to take one or two boat trips. You can visit the Moslem stilt-village on Pannyi Island, and also see the rock islands in the area, mostly uninhabited. And of course, the bathing and scuba diving are superb.

Chiengmai

The only convenient way to reach Thailand's largest northern city is by air; the distance is 469 miles. The plane is not expensive; flights usually leave Bangkok early in the morning and take about 2 hours. The return trip leaves Chiengmai about noon. In contrast, the train trip requires 17 hours each way.

Chiengmai is in a valley surrounded by mountains, and is much cooler than Bangkok. It is an extremely attractive city, scenically lovely, with lots of flowers, many colorful festivals, and an attractively garbed population. The best place to stay in Chiengmai in town is the Chiang Hotel, large and surprisingly good. It has 160 nicely furnished rooms, a swimming pool, several restaurants, and a shopping arcade. The Hyatt, slightly out of town, is exceptionally good, with large rooms, good service and food. Next best is the Chiang Mai Orchid, which is about midway between the airport and the downtown area; it's exceptionally nice, and the hotel maintains a complimentary shuttle service between the hotel and the downtown district. The Rincome Hotel is closer to town, and it's a very satisfactory place at which to stay. The Poy Luang Hotel is close to Chiengmai's edge; it's large and the rooms are fair enough.

This region is, in many ways, more interesting than the Bangkok area, although for different reasons. You'll see the hill people in their unusual costumes, you'll shop at the various small areas, each of which makes a special product. For example, there's a Silver Village, a Cotton Weaving Village, a Pottery Village, and so on. Chiengmai is famous for its handicrafts, and prices are far lower than in the capital (incidentally, Chiengmai is frequently called the Northern Capital). The sightseeing is interesting: be sure to see the Wat Phra Dhat Doi Sutep (no, I did not make up that name) built in 1383; the Poo-Ping Rajinives Palace (no, I did not make up this name either); Wat Phra Singh, the largest monastery of Chiengmai, built in 1345; and lots more *wats,* as the temples are called by the Thais. If you can manage to arise early in the morning, say 6:30 or so, there's a fascinating food market which remains in operation until 8 A.M. Varorot Market has an interesting display of local food

Weather Strip: Chiengmai

	Jan.	Feb.	Mar.	Apr.	May	June	July	Aug.	Sept.	Oct.	Nov.	Dec.
Average daily high	84°	89°	94°	97°	94°	90°	88°	88°	88°	87°	86°	83°
Average daily low	56°	58°	63°	71°	73°	74°	74°	74°	73°	70°	66°	59°
Monthly rainfall	0.1	0.4	0.3	1.4	4.8	4.4	8.4	7.6	9.8	3.7	1.2	0.5
Number of days with 0.04 inches or more	1	1	2	5	12	15	21	20	17	8	4	2

on sale, but from the tourist's point of view, the handicrafts are even more interesting. You'll see wood carvings, handwoven cotton fabrics, pottery, lacquerware, silver, silks, etc. Be sure to pay a visit to the private museum in the home of Mr. and Mrs. Kraisri Nimmanhamindr; their house is a model of a 150-year-old Thai house and is filled with antiques.

BURMA

👫 Background

Only a comparative handful of American tourists visit Burma, perhaps because the Burmese government makes it difficult to enter it. It is also very true that Burma has few important tourist attractions as such, certainly when compared with the scope and variety of Thailand. Unless pressed for time, this small, charming country is definitely worth a visit, providing you know what to expect, and what you'll find when you get there. (If you can get in.)

The Burmese people are small and extremely attractive in appearance, they are graceful and agreeable to be with, and extremely hospitable to foreigners. If the foregoing sounds as though it were copied from a travel folder issued by the government's tourist office, that is pure coincidence. Burma's people actually smile and seem quite contented, which is a statement that cannot be made about many other countries around the world. They come, according to anthropologists, from Tibeto-Mongolian stock, having emigrated southward from Tibet about the year 1000 A.D., probably looking for a region with a milder climate, and better land on which to grow their rice. Originally, they probably settled in the northern portion of the country, around Pagan, building an important and advanced type of civilization founded upon Buddhism. Some two and a half centuries later, with everything seemingly going right, along came the savage army of Kublai Khan (grandson of Genghis Khan), coming out of southern China and looking for new lands to conquer. This 13th-century Hitler ravaged Pagan, and destroyed much of the region. In the early 16th century, the adventurous Portuguese came as traders, but they failed; they were followed by the more systematic British. It is difficult now, in the 20th century, to comprehend the English mentality of several centuries ago. In all honesty, on rereading British authors and politicians of that period, it seems in retrospect as though they regarded themselves as a sort of chosen people to lead underdeveloped and primitive nations out of their backward state for the greater glory and profit of the tight little island, that little Eden, England. The fact that the primitive people rarely wanted to be developed interested them not at all. The English definitely had a knack for running Asiatic countries, for development of the country's natural resources, and in seeing that all rebellions were swiftly and courteously crushed. The slight detail that vast sums of money which belonged to the undeveloped country were being systematically drained out of the land that produced them, had no effect upon the British. In general, they ran Burma quite well, constructed harbors, managed rubber and rice plantations, and built and maintained railroads. But at the same time, no Burmese were permitted in their organizations or clubs, nor were they educated to take over positions of responsibility, nor treated as equals. When World War II came along, the British were pushed out of Burma in 1942. If you saw that very good motion picture, *The Bridge on the River Kwai,* you'll recall the odd British mentality of that period. In fact, when the Japanese originally took over Burma with the British gone, at first the local people weren't a bit depressed, and were not at all unhappy about the British departure. But shortly thereafter, they couldn't wait to get rid of the Japanese, which probably proves a point. Since then, Burma acquired independence, along with not a few troubles, and then the Burmese Army took over. But even now, local uprisings and rebellions occur sporadically, and before visiting certain rural parts of the country, local inquiry should be made for last minute developments.

Religion is tremendously important to the Burmese, and controls most of everyday life. When girls reach puberty, they go through a formal celebration, called an "ear-piercing" ceremony. This permits the young girls to wear earrings, regarded in Burma as a sign of womanhood, or to be crude, ready for marriage. Young boys also have their heads shaved at a special religious ceremony, and every young Burmese male must live the life of a Buddhist monk at least for a brief period, although a very large proportion (say 10%) ultimately do become priests. Everywhere one goes there are pagodas, religious monuments, and other evidence of the Burmese' inherently religious nature. Without this in the back of your mind, an understanding of the culture and people of this smiling land will be impossible.

Burma is in that stage of its new life when it is trying desperately to return its life and activities to its own people, and is forcing out resident foreigners by economic pressure. Psychologists refer to this phase as xenophobia, a fear of foreigners. Only Burmese citizens are permitted to have licenses to conduct a wide variety of everyday businesses—physicians, lawyers, shopkeepers, travel agents, banking, export-import, and the like. The next result has been that foreigners, especially Indians, have left Burma for purely economic reasons, having been squeezed out by the loss of their livelihood. Flights on planes out of Rangoon and into Calcutta are often booked for a month ahead with Indian nationals, whereas flights into Burma are largely empty. Tourists are welcome—for short visits—in groups, usually out of Bangkok.

 When to Go

It is *very* hot (yes, *very* hot) between late March and late May. It isn't impossible to visit during that period, but you'll have to adjust to the weather, doing your sightseeing early in the morning and quitting at about noon; have a cool lunch and take a rest until late in the afternoon when the temperature breaks, and then continue until dark. The evenings aren't too bad, but daytime temperatures running 95°–100° are not conducive to intensive sightseeing. It's very hot, but there's rarely any rain. Then towards the end of May, there comes the rainy season which runs until the end of October. It rains about two days out of three, but don't visualize a light, misty rain. It pours cats and dogs, something like solid water, often for an hour or two at a time, or sometimes a few days in succession. The humidity is the big problem during the rainy season, averaging about 98%. Clothes have to be changed at least twice daily, and although the temperatures drop off somewhat, it's quite uncomfortable. But maybe you'll have a break, and get some good dry weather even during this period. But then comes Burma's cool season, the country's best period, running from November through early March, when the air is fairly dry and the temperatures run in the 80's. During January and February, I regret to say, there are

Weather Strip: Rangoon

	Jan.	Feb.	Mar.	Apr.	May	June	July	Aug.	Sept.	Oct.	Nov.	Dec.
Average daily high	89°	92°	96°	97°	92°	86°	85°	85°	86°	88°	88°	88°
Average daily low	65°	67°	71°	76°	77°	76°	76°	76°	76°	76°	73°	67°
Monthly rainfall	0.1	0.2	0.3	2.0	12.1	18.9	22.9	20.8	15.5	7.1	2.7	0.4
Number of days with 0.1 inches or more	0	0	1	2	14	23	26	25	20	10	3	1

often cloudy, misty mornings with 99%–100% humidity. I'm sorry to give you the hard, inescapable facts, but there you are. On the other hand, I once visited Burma during April, presumably the hot season, and the weather was lovely, dry and in the 80's during the day, in the 70's at night. But I can't promise you good weather during the rainy season—that would be pure luck.

Visa Requirements

Until recently, it was nearly impossible to get a visa for Burma. Now things are relaxed, and you can obtain a visa valid for 7 days. There's a fee of $6.30, and 4 pictures are required for the visa. It's hoped that pretty soon Burma will loosen up even further and issue visas valid for longer than 7 days, but when, no one knows.

♟ Customs

You're not supposed to have more than 200 cigarettes with you (1 carton), a ruling sometimes overlooked by the authorities, sometimes not; in the alternative, 50 cigars. It has been my personal experience that if you arrive on a plane whose passenger list is composed principally of tourists, the customs inspection is rather cursory and theoretical. On the other hand, sometimes the inspectors do a very thorough job on everyone (tourists, residents, etc.) so that they cannot be accused of preference. One bottle of liquor is O.K., also 1 bottle of perfume. They sometimes make you register your cameras, and count your rolls of film, but not always, and the same goes for portable radios. You never know for sure. Important: because Burmese currency usually is sold at better rates outside of the country than inside, you are not allowed to bring any Burmese currency with you. Getting caught with Burmese currency when you arrive can be quite serious, and at the very minimum, a big pain in the neck and cause much delay. Of course, unlimited amounts of traveler's checks and foreign currency may be brought in, but you'll have to declare it on arrival. When you leave, you can reconvert back into dollars any unused Burmese money up to 25% of what you have cashed. Therefore, don't cash too much of your money into Burmese money while you're there.

✹ Health

Be somewhat careful here. To begin with, I don't care what anyone says, don't drink tap water, and to carry it a step further, make sure you drink only bottled water or soft drinks from recognized, well-established bottlers. Make the waiter open the bottle in front of you; yes, that's how careful I would be. (All joking aside, it isn't very amusing to feel poorly for even one day when you're on a vacation and trying to make the most of every minute.) Milk and ice cream are definitely out of the question. The same goes for green salads and uncooked vegetables. Coffee and tea are all right, because the water has been boiled. Incidentally, some hotels say that their water has been boiled or filtered, but I wouldn't rely on it. Stay with cooked foods at all times; better safe than sorry, as they say. Because it's warm, you'll be tempted to have cold drinks frequently. Be sure not to have any ice cubes placed directly in the glass. Also, avoid too much in the way of iced drinks in hot weather; that can cause problems, too. Only a cholera shot is required; yellow fever if coming from an infected area.

◔ Time

When it's noon in Rangoon (that's real poetry for you), it's 12:30 A.M. in New York, on the same day of the week. But bear in mind, however, that it will be 9:30 P.M. in San Francisco the day before. To restate, when it's noon on Tuesday in Rangoon, it will be 9:30 P.M. on Monday on the west coast of the United States.

💲 Currency

The unit of local money is the *kyat,* which is pronounced as if it were spelled *jutt;* no use asking why they don't spell it jutt, they jutt don't. The *kyat* subdivides into *pyas,* of which there are 100 to the *kyat.* On the black market (or in free markets in Hong Kong and Singapore) you can get two or three times the official rate, but it's dangerous if you get caught. So don't.

A Special Note About Traveling in Burma

Obviously, conditions can and will change, but at the moment of going to press, this is the situation about travel in Burma. Almost everything of interest to tourists is under the control of Tourist Burma, a state agency. It's best to make arrangements in advance, however, to avoid wasting time, because visas are currently limited to 7 days. Most of the tourist traffic to and from Burma is operated by Diethelm Travel, a travel agency based in Bangkok. When you reach Burma, your visit will be handled by Tourist Burma. Be sure to bring along all the color film you'll need, as this is rarely found in Burma. The same goes for cigarettes and toiletries which may sometimes be purchased, but only at very high prices. When you arrive in Burma, you can expect to fill out a form listing your jewelry, camera, and so forth, and you must have them with you upon departure. Foreign currency must be declared upon arrival, and all money exchanges must be recorded on the special form which you'll receive. Note: Don't mail any postcards from Burma. Write them if you wish, but mail them from the next country, that is, if you want your friends to receive them. And one final thought: Don't expect to have a luxurious trip. Accommodations are in adequate hotels, which are generally somewhat run-down; bus rides are in passable, but far from luxurious un-air-conditioned buses. The food is fair enough.

⊕ Price Level

At the present time, individual tourist travel through Burma is discouraged, to say the least. Because everyone, without exception, travels in a group tour, the individual cost of hotel rooms and meals is not apparent to the individual traveler. However, on your own, when there is free time, you'll find that taxis are inexpensive (comparatively speaking of course) and that prices for local merchandise are generally low.

Important: Imported items—Kleenex, toothpaste, and razor blades, for example—are astronomically costly. Be forewarned, and before leaving on a trip to Burma, check and see that you have all your toilet articles, a good bar of bath soap, and all the film you'll need. Don't forget your sunglasses.

🍎 Tipping

In general, the great menace of tips has not reached Burma. To begin with, taxi-drivers need not be tipped, but if you have hired a car for the entire day and the driver has been accommodating and pleasant, a tip of 2 *kyats* or even 3 will never be refused. When your luggage is carried for you, that is not so much a tip as payment for a specific service, and 1 *kyat* (or 2 *kyats* if you have many pieces of luggage) is expected. At your hotel, a service charge is included in your hotel bill amounting to 10% of your meals and room charge, so it is not really necessary to tip the waiter, although if he has been very helpful in getting you special dishes, a *kyat* each meal would not be amiss. For small errands, such as bellboys getting your laundry, a small tip of 50 *pyas* is plenty. To sum up, go easy on tips, and when in doubt, a small tip should be sufficient. But be reasonable; if you have put someone to a great deal of trouble, and he has served you well and cheerfully, a tip might be in order.

🏃 Transportation

The city has *taxis,* antiquated and battered, converted jeeps, three-wheeled affairs, and even regular cars. All are required to have meters (which don't necessarily work), except that occasionally an unmetered car will hang around a hotel, hoping someone will hail him and forget to set a price in advance. Because local rates are generally reasonable (no use quoting them, they've probably changed again by now), expect to pay about 2 *kyats* for a local run within Rangoon. If you're using a car by the hour, don't offer to pay more than 5 *kyats* per hour. Incidentally, if you want to do some all-day sightseeing on your own, hire it at a flat price for the day's run (but first be sure the driver speaks a *little* English), and agree on an all-inclusive rate; it won't be terribly expensive for a day, gasoline included or not, depending on how good a bargainer you are. *"Jeep"* taxis are informal, somewhat uncomfortable, and not suited for long sightseeing, but perfectly all right for a run around town, to a restaurant, etc.; they are cheaper than regular taxis, but since regular taxis are pretty cheap, the saving is not great. The point is that if you're in a hurry, what's the difference (unless it rains)? The three wheelers, *trishaws,* come with motors or cycles attached; lots of fun.

Trains run frequently, and the service is not bad, but please don't go by train; not now, anyhow. The countryside is unsettled, and while train after train may go through unmolested, one never knows, so forget the trains. Trips by *automobile* are surely safe around the Rangoon region, but driving to Mandalay would be foolhardy and a nervous ride, under the best of conditions. Fly, we say.

The *plane service* within Burma is good, and is flown by the Union of Burma Airways. The trip from Rangoon to Mandalay takes 2 hours, but before you go, have confirmed space back, because there are no alternative methods of transportation. The flight from Rangoon to Pagan takes about the same length of time; same advice (about return booking) also in order.

No *drive-yourself* automobile service is available in Burma, and I'd be just as happy if you don't drive out into the country on your own, in any event.

Airport and Tourist Taxes

Mingaladon Airport is 12 miles from Rangoon, and free transportation into Rangoon and its leading hotels is usually provided. It takes about 30–40 minutes to drive to the airport, and you should arrive at least 45 minutes before departure for checking-in. There is a departure tax of approximately $1.50.

▮▮ Communications

Cables from and to the U.S. are fairly expensive; best ask for the delayed rate unless your message is urgent. *Airmail* letters cost about 35¢, but postcards are less. Allow at least 4 days for a letter to reach the United States. The *airletter* form, usually available at the hotel desk, is slightly over 10¢. Surface mail to the United States can take 2 months.

⚡ Electricity

The local current is 220 volts, 50 cycles A.C., so your regular appliances won't work. Some hotels have special outlets with notices indicating that they may be used for electric razors; if not, inquire at the hotel desk if they have transformers. In any event, don't be surprised if at any time the lights flicker, or go out for a few minutes. That's par for the course in Rangoon and most of Burma, particularly as it begins to get dark, and lights are turned on. But don't worry, the power will come again soon (except that sometimes in the heavy rainy season, they might stay out longer). And if your electric razor seems to drag, and doesn't shave you as well as usual—it's only a local power fluctuation.

✖ Food Specialties and Liquor

The Burmese have somewhat different food customs from the western world, although tourists staying at a hotel would hardly notice. Burmese hotels, as hotels do all over the world, cater to their guests, and the three-meal-a-day pattern will be followed. The delightful people (and they are!) of this small country usually have two meals a day, although they usually have coffee and some form of bread upon arising. In Rangoon and other cities, there may be a morning meal and it is eaten between 9 and 11 A.M., and then an evening repast between 5 and 6 P.M. The reason for this custom is probably based upon the local climatic conditions, which omits meals during the warmer part of the day.

To a Burmese, a meal has three main parts—a curried food, boiled rice, and a salad. If the family has any means whatsoever, there will be at least several different curries, possibly made with fish, meat, and poultry. All dishes are usually placed upon the table at the same time, in small covered dishes similar to those used in China. Appetizers or hors d'oeuvres are rarely served, the exception being reserved for special occasions. Soups are popular, although they do not appear at every meal; these come in two principal categories—the regular, or *hingyo* type, and the acid soup, called *chin-ye-hin,* which is really a little too much for the average tourist. However, the main part of the meal is the curried foods; although similar to those made in India, the Burmese curry is distinguished by its use of coconut and coconut milk, which add an interesting, smooth texture.

A salad in Burma looks like a salad in California or New York, on first appearance. However, appearances are often deceiving, and this is one time to proceed with caution. The favorite salad dressing is called *nga-pi-yet,* a concoction of garlic, onions, chili peppers, and dried fish. The taste may reasonably be described as noxious to begin with, and then you can proceed from there, depending upon the scope of your vocabulary. Peculiarly enough, on second or third tasting (if you get that far!), it becomes tolerable enough.

Although this is primarily a tea-growing and -drinking country, coffee is well liked. The Burmese have a custom of adding grains or cereals to the tea, until they attain a thick, gumbo-like consistency, although this practice is largely confined to rural areas. Chinese food is very popular in Burma, and the Chinese cooking style has had a strong influence upon the Burmese, so that the two cuisines have many overlapping dishes and methods of preparation. It is not unusual to find Chinese-style curries on the menu of certain restaurants.

∞ Time Evaluation

From what I gather, in former times, 9 out of 10 tourists only spent about 3 days on their visit. This would be sufficient for Rangoon and an excursion to Pegu (discussed later). If you could manage a week's stay, a trip to Mandalay or Pagan (or both) would definitely be worthwhile. (All of this assumes that the Burmese are granting visas good for more than 24 hours.)

🏛 Capital City: Rangoon

Unlike most other Asiatic cities, much of Rangoon is laid out on the grid plan, like the majority of American cities. That is, streets are of similar length and width, and cross each other at right angles, not wandering about at random, as is the situation in very old Asiatic communities which just grew up. It's a good-sized town, with about 850,000 people, mostly living in small houses, many with dirt floors and often without running water. Rangoon is on the Rangoon River, approximately 21 miles from the sea, and (forgive me, Chamber of Commerce!) is not an impressive or particularly handsome city. There are few great sights, little in the way of imposing buildings or monuments (except for a few to be mentioned), and no grand boulevards. No one should reasonably expect grand Parisian boulevards in Southeast Asia. However, Rangoon lacks the regional charm of Bangkok or Singapore, nor is it rural or tropical-looking, if that is what the visitor is seeking. But it is not the fault of the Burmese, for the city and its unimposing public buildings were designed and built by the British. The result—Rangoon has all of the physical atmosphere and lack of charm of a middle-class industrial city in the heart of England, and it was further damaged during the course of World War II. Added to all of their other problems, most homes are built of wood, and fires frequently wipe out whole regions of the city.

Now, we've said it and we're glad. Next, we'll tell you why Rangoon is still very interesting, and in fact, fascinating. It's so simple, you'll be floored. It's the people.

First off, the Burmese are very appealing to the eye, being most attractive, with very good, regular features. If you ask them a question, or become involved in a conversation (assuming they know some English), it won't be more than a matter of a minute before you receive a smile. Burmese men and women have pleasant expressions, as a rule, but in addition, they dearly love to smile. I don't know about you, but that makes a very strong impression on me, and sometimes the memory of a pleasant conversation with a Burmese will be remembered better than the largest or tallest Buddhist shrine in all of Rangoon.

With the whole world, Asians included, wearing routine, run-of-the-mill, nondescript western clothing, it's very refreshing to see almost everyone dressed in the graceful classic costume of the country. The standard article of clothing is the *longyi,* a length of fabric wrapped about the hips of both men and women, usually reaching to the ankles. Men wear solid colors or simple designs on their *longyis,* but the women go in for bright colors or elaborate workmanship. Above the waist, women like short, sheer blouses of a light color; men wear quiet, subdued short jackets. The men often wrap turban-like cloths around the head, but the women rarely do. All in all, they look most attractive in this becoming national dress. Just in passing, it might be mentioned that of all Asiatic countries, Burmese women are the only females regarded as equal to their menfolk. In China, Japan, Korea, etc., women are usually accorded a type of second-class citizenship, and, not often, it is more like third-class.

When your plane approaches Rangoon, be sure to keep watching just outside the center of town; you'll probably be able to see the city's leading sight—the Shwe Dagon Pagoda. (It's pronounced Schweh-de-GONE.) The Shwe Dagon is a most impressive affair, 326 feet high, and situated on a hillside at that. At one time, it was necessary to climb laboriously to the top, but progress has been made; one can now ride to the shrine in modern elevators. This is one of the most important Buddhist shrines in the world, and certainly the leading one in Burma. The central spire (to use a nontechnical term) is covered with gold leaf, but the top "bud" has gold plates, valued at well over $3,000,000. Besides that, there are hundreds of diamonds, and thousands of semiprecious stones which may be seen, but not touched. Surrounding the central spire are about seventy-five smaller pagodas, and it is extremely diverting to make a complete circuit. Don't forget that shoes may not be worn, so take along slippers, or heavy socks; also, don't go during the middle of the day—it's too hot.

Also of importance is the Sule Pagoda, in the heart of town. It would otherwise be a prime sightseeing spot, except for the fact that Rangoon has its Shwe Dagon. If you're staying at the Inya Lake Hotel, it would also be interesting to visit the nearby Kaba Aye Pagoda, also called the World Peace Pagoda, built in 1953–54. Adjacent is the Great Cave, the one in which the sixth Buddhist Synod was held; the Great Cave is really a huge auditorium. Inya Lake itself is quite pleasant, and has boating facilities. For a touch of local life, wander about the park on weekends.

Bogyoke Market (on Park Road and just a few minutes from the center of town) is a permanently-covered walk with a wide variety of shops, and has most of the best spots for local handicrafts. At night, this market is replaced by the Night Bazaar, which runs from just before 6 P.M. to midnight. Although this constitutes a shopping area, it is also part of the standard sightseeing of Rangoon.

Anything more? Rangoon University (also on the way to Inya Lake) is quite handsome, and worth seeing. Otherwise, not much else, although the zoo is interesting. If you happen to be in Burma during a holiday or festival, by all means visit Bogyoke Gardens, along the Royal Lakes; it comes alive with lots of stalls and amusements, and the fashionable ladies wear their very best.

ACCOMMODATIONS The hotel situation is poor, inasmuch as all of the hotels are run-down. Expect to find spots on the carpet, worn upholstered furniture, and a shortage of good towels and sheets. This is due to the fact that Burma is short of the necessary hard currency to import these needed foreign goods that are not produced in Burma.

Inya Lake Hotel. This sprawling hotel is located between Mingaladon Airport and downtown Rangoon. The rooms are fairly nice, although a trifle seedy. The food served here is erratic—sometimes good, sometimes poor. There's a swimming pool, spacious grounds, and central air conditioning, and it's well located on the shores of Inya Lake.

Strand. In town, and very convenient, but shabby and rundown. Some rooms are attractive, but most are rather seedy-looking, although comfortably air-conditioned (although not *all* rooms are). The food at the Strand is just so-so, but you'll never starve. Rates are about $22 double for a room, including continental breakfast.

Kanbawza Palace. In a pleasant setting, halfway between the airport and Rangoon, this sort of vaguely ramshackle building is quite pleasant but rather outdated. Prices are about the same as at the Strand, and is under the same management. The food is passable, but no more.

The *Railway Hotel* in an emergency is not bad, averaging about $10 double including continental breakfast; the *Tourist Tavern* is also perfectly all right, with prices running about $12 double. Beyond that, I wouldn't care to recommend any other hotels in Rangoon.

RESTAURANTS The *Inya Lake Hotel* has a good restaurant and may well be the best western-style restaurant in Burma. Although that is not great praise, for western food is not terribly good here, the hotel restaurant is a real haven.

Airport Restaurant. Quite good, with an interesting menu featuring western, Chinese, and Indonesian food, and possibly a few Burmese dishes too. Moderate-priced.

Continental. Open for lunch, closed in the evening. A pretty good meal, with little choice, but rather good. No liquor; moderate prices.

Envoy. An attractive spot, featuring European food with some Italian and Burmese dishes. Moderate-priced.

CHINESE RESTAURANTS:

Kwan Lock. One of the better Chinese restaurants in Rangoon. For a good meal, phone in advance and tell them how much you want to spend, and leave it to them. Generally moderate-priced.

Mya Nanda. Chinese dishes, but also some Indian and Burmese specialties. Attractively located near the river. Quite moderate.

New Oi Hkun. Very good Chinese food, with quite a good variety of dishes from which to choose. Moderate prices.

Bankok and Namsin. Both of these Chinese restaurants are informal places, located in the suburbs about 10 minutes from downtown Rangoon. Both good, but not expensive.

SHOPPING   For general shopping, it might be best to head for a "department store," set forth in quotes because they really aren't that elaborate nor do they have many departments. Because they carry a varied line of merchandise, it's possible to buy *handwoven silks, carvings of wood and ivory, textiles, woven reed baskets, lacquerware, silverware,* and the like. A-La-Mode, Lekhraj & Sons, and Sein Brothers are about the best all-purpose "department stores," the words again appearing in quotation marks.

Most people would have a great time shopping in the Bogyoke Market (previously mentioned), the covered pavilion where many Burmese handmade or, in any event, *handicrafted articles* are offered for sale. In most cases, you'll be able to do all of your souvenir shopping at the Bogyoke Market, except for precious stones. At night, the Night Bazaar is open from about 6:30 P.M. until midnight, on Anawrahta Street; it's not quite so good a shopping area as the Bogyoke Market, but otherwise very satisfactory.

Burma produces many fine *gem stones,* including rubies, sapphires, moonstones and jade, but of course, the rubies are best. The Burmese sell most of the stones unmounted; those that are mounted have an old-fashioned, heavy appearance. But wait! Before buying rubies, for example, stop and think. Do you know *anything* at all about rubies? I don't mean to imply that the shopkeepers are dishonest, but getting a good value depends on having something in the way of expert knowledge, or in the alternative, expert advice on what to buy and how much to pay for it. So go easy. Burmese pearls are fantastically beautiful, and fantastically expensive. The leading places for precious stones are Ceylon Trading, Khin Mya and Company, and Burma Gem House.

Before buying *anything,* and no matter where you're doing the buying, ask for a better price, and bargain a little, or better yet, a lot. It's a national custom, and first prices are set higher than the merchant expects to finally receive.

ENTERTAINMENT Night life, as we understand it, is practically nonexistent. At the Inya Lake Hotel, there will probably be dinner dancing, or dinner with music, on most evenings. There are no quiet places, with music and dancing, candlelights and romantic atmosphere, anywhere in Burma.

If you happen to be here when there's a festival (and this happens *very* frequently during the year), there's dancing outdoors, fireworks, marionette shows, and most interesting of all, the famous *pwe* shows, consisting of legendary stories set to music. Ask at your hotel desk if there is a festival going on, or in the offing.

SPORTS Be sure to see a local *boxing* match; they're quite colorful and fascinating to watch, because the boxers are permitted to use their feet, knees, etc. Ask at your hotel desk where you can see *chin-lon,* a type of ball game—well, it's not like baseball, and it's not like football, it's really like . . . *chin-lon,* I guess. The most I can tell you is that the ball is not supposed to touch the ground. The truly favorite spectator sport, without exception, is *soccer football.* There are two *golf courses* near Rangoon, the Burma Golf Club and the Rangoon, both of which permit nonmembers to play if your hotel phones and asks for permission, which is usually granted.

Pegu

The outstanding single trip from Rangoon is to Pegu, about 55 miles away. It can be reached by car in just under 2 hours one way, and makes a good all-day trip. Better bring your own food and—especially—something to drink. The countryside is rich and green, and the drive is pleasant, but food and drink are hard to locate. Pegu has some interesting pagodas, and the highspot is a reclining Buddha measuring 180 feet in length. If you take a picture, be sure a person appears in the foreground, or no one at home will realize its great size. There is also an Ordination Hall, etc., etc.

Pagan

If time permits, a flight to Pagan, about 300 miles north of Rangoon makes an exciting 2- or 3-day excursion. By all odds, Pagan is the most interesting tourist sight in the entire country, and should not be missed if time permits. You can remain overnight at the Government Guest House for a very modest charge; very comfortable and informal. Pagan is largely a deserted city, and there are (no exaggeration) thousands and thousands of pagodas stretching across the landscape. It is definitely exciting, and will move the most pagoda-weary tourist. I promise!

The other worthwhile trip in Burma is to Mandalay (where the flying fishes play, if you remember your Kipling). This also makes a good 2- or 3-day excursion from Rangoon, and if you wish, it can be combined with a trip to Pagan by adding on an extra couple of days. Mandalay is the second largest city in the country, and is filled with monasteries, markets, and pagodas, and is regarded as the most Burmese city of the country, in the sense that things have changed least of all over the centuries. In Mandalay, the Tun Hla is probably the best place to stay; in any event, it has a swimming pool.

INDIA

👫 Background

Let's try to imagine a big switch. If an Indian swami, sitting on top of Mt. Kanchenjunga, suddenly decided to move India to the United States, Denver would become a seaport called Calcutta, and Colorado a flat estuary named West Bengal. The decendants of rugged miners would be transformed into rather lazy, soft-spoken intellectuals wearing once-white bedsheets. San Francisco would feel quite at home as a port called Bombay, and its cosmopolitan tone would be little altered by the sophisticated, affluent, western-ized Parsees. Getting a drink is no longer a major problem in India, for the country has decided to forget about Prohibition. Except for one state, liquor is available, although at very high prices.

Alaska would come out ahead, thanks to the holy man, for it would be Kashmir, a lush Garden of Eden. Tall, bearded Sikhs would roam Washington state, addressing one another as Mr. Lion. Oregon, alas, would lose its forests and become a semidesert called Rajasthan. Finally, a line would be drawn between Denver and Los Angeles, cutting through Colorado, Nevada, and Arizona to southern California. Tigers would prowl the streets of Las Vegas, just as they apparently do today; while the south would be the home of the dark-skinned original inhabitants, the true Indians. And things might seem a bit crowded, for the population of this area would increase twentyfold, to 450,000,000 people. The west, where American English is spoken with accentless purity, would become a babel of 14 languages and 250 dialects. Half the population would understand Hindi; however, English, as taught at Oxford, would be the common speech of the upper class.

A traveler in this transplanted land would stay at hotels very much like the Brown Palace in Denver and the Sheraton Palace in San Francisco; ornate, old, high-ceilinged and big-bathroomed. He could fly at reasonable rates from city to city in Caravelles, Viscounts, Fokker Friendships, and trusty DC-3's (which he'd call Dakotas), but only on one airline—IAC, the state-owned Indian Airlines Corporation. Passenger trains would prove comfortable enough in first or air-conditioned class, and their on-time performance would be excellent, but their style would be European, with compartments along one side and a corridor along the other. The passenger would search in vain for the club car or diner. If you want a meal aboard a train, they wire ahead to the next station and put your meal aboard; it's not bad at all, and quite inexpensive.

The steak-eating Westerner would be lost in a land where a cow may be somebody's reincarnated grandmother, to be treated with grandfilial reverence and never, never—well, hardly ever!—to be broiled. He'd find the water buffalo on a Delhi menu, a distant cousin indeed to a Texas steer. But the Arizonan, bred on tortillas and enchiladas from neighboring Mexico, would smack his lips over the hotly spiced curries. And "Chicken Tandoori" might almost make up for the loss of the southern fried version.

After dinner and a drink, what? Bed. No scantily-clad chorus line waiting in the wings. The traveler might watch the odd acrobat in Calcutta, listen to a local imitation of Ella Fitzgerald, but that would be it. Suppose the traveler boarded an airplane and struck up a conversation with the Indian sitting next to him. Would they understand each other? Almost certainly, because the Indian who is able (financially and mentally) to fly is virtually sure to speak English. After all, English was the language of the people who ran India for 200 years, and generations of Indians who wanted to do business with their British masters found it prudent to learn their language.

What might his seatmate look like? If he's a northerner, he may be light-skinned, approaching blond; his ancestors may well include among them Macedonian soldiers of Alexander the Great. Or they may have been Chinese mandarins, thus explaining his Mongoloid features. If he wears a beard and a turban, has soft brown eyes and a massive frame, he's a Sikh from the Punjab. If he's brown, medium in height, and draped loosely in white cotton cloth called a *dhoti,* he's from Bengal. And if he's small, very dark, and cheerful, he's a southerner, one of the Dravidians who were driven further and further south by successive waves of foreign invaders. The chances are almost 9 in 10 that he's Hindu in religion. If not, he's most probably a Muslim—or Mohammedan—who coexists somewhat uneasily with his Hindu brethren. He could be a Buddhist or a Christian, but the odds are much against it: 30 to 1. If he's Hindu, he's probably a vegetarian, though not in the absolute sense, because he may well accept fish. If he's westernized by education or environment he may eat meat and even beef, though not in front of his grandfather.

Although 9 out of 10 Indians are villagers, the traveler's seatmate is likely to be a city man, because he has the money or the position which enables him to fly. Economically, he's middle or upper class, but socially—beware! He may be high-class Brahmin or low-class Harijan, a so-called "untouchable." In democratic (?) India it's hard to know. Professionally, he may be a doctor, lawyer, engineer, or teacher; a civil servant, businessman, or industrialist; hardly ever a farmer, for most are poor, with a few barren acres each. But perhaps he's one of the leisured class, maybe even a *maharajah,* of whom there are hundreds. His politics are likely to be leftist-socialist, following the Congress Party of Gandhi and Nehru, unless he supports the right-wing, free-enterprise Swatantra Party—or unless he's a socialist or communist. If he's in business, it may be in business for himself or with an Indian firm; but he could very likely work for one of the many British—or the growing number of American—companies incorporated in India. Whatever his position, though, he's likely to gross about $300 a month, about 50 times the per capita income of his countrymen as a whole.

If the conversation turns to politics, the businessman will be right of, and the civil servant left of, the official Congress Party line, but one thing they almost all have maddeningly (and irritatingly to an American) in common: neutralism. Nehru set the style which most Indians follow. As a result, the "plague on both your houses" philosophy prevails. Very frustrating to an American who has no doubts as to the evils of the Russian way of life. It is important to note that the average Indian doesn't feel too strongly about either America or Russia. However, that's certainly not true of the Indian government, which, when it is neutral, seems to be neutral against the United States and in favor of Russia. It seems clear that at the moment of writing, India and the U.S. aren't getting along too well with each other, but perhaps the situation will improve.

As the jet plane speeds toward Bombay, the typical Indian will talk. That at least is predictable, for most Indians love to talk! As he talks, gestures, and sometimes even listens, his personality will emerge. And what will that be? Only a fool would attempt to characterize nearly half a billion people, so exceptions *do* exist to the general rule that an Indian is: friendly, sociable, inconsistent, hospitable, argumentative, defensive, opinionated, excitable, generous, chauvinistic, curious, and kindly. And how he loves to talk!

One subject he may not wish to discuss is the weather, for in India it is usually unspeakable. Since India lies wholly within the temperate zone, it is difficult to understand why most of the country should be so infernally hot most of the time. The reason is the Himalaya range, which blocks the cool southbound Siberian winds that would otherwise air-condition the subcontinent. As a result, Calcutta and Delhi are almost unbearable from March to mid-June, after which the monsoon drops the temperature to a mere 90°. Bombay is hot the year round, but never seems quite so sizzling, because of the ocean breezes. On the other hand, Delhi temperatures can plummet to the mid-forties in the winter, and Calcutta becomes positively Hawaiian. It can and does snow in Kashmir, while some of South India, hilly and forested, is pleasant in all seasons. The center? Jungly and steaming.

This, then, our swami has done: transformed the western third of America into a teeming cauldron of half a billion "socialists." He has traded the Rockies for the Himalayas, substituted the Ellora and Ajanta Caves for the Grand Canyon, Los Angeles for Benares, and San Francisco's Golden Gate for Bombay's Gateway to India. Instead of cattle they raise tea. Cowboys become Sikhs. Plains and deserts are jungles. Three hundred years of history become six thousand. But planes fly, trains chuff, the hotels are generally agreeable, the restaurants passable, the sightseeing magnificently incredible.

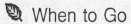 When to Go

By all means in the winter, because of the weather factor. Never in the late spring, unless you must. A compromise might be during the monsoon, from June to October, for it isn't really as wet as Louis Bromfield made it sound in *The Rains Came,* and the temperatures do drop to 80° on some days. Kashmir, of course, is at its loveliest in summer and fall, and Delhi can be chilly in winter. But, as the Bengalis say, "What to do?" You must go sometime, for India should not be missed. The weather situation in India is no joke, because the weather there is no joke either. When we talk about rain, we mean solid water falling torrentially, not the kind of misty rain experienced in your home town. India, being an enormous country with lowlands and mountains, has a wide range of temperature. However, as previously mentioned, the best weather comes in wintertime, say from November through February (the exception is Kashmir, discussed later). For particulars on each region, see the Weather Strips in the appropriate sections, which will give you a good *general* idea. However, here are a few specifics: *Calcutta* is at its very best during the December-February period; very, very hot the rest of the year, except that during July-September you can expect occasional monsoons, loads of rain, but slightly cooler temperatures, although accompanied by plenty of humidity. No, Calcutta does not have ideal weather, we agree. But the rainy season is very erratic—sometimes it just rains for an hour, sometimes for days on end. *Delhi* has marvelous, sometimes crisp weather from November through February, making it the ideal season for a visit. From April through June, intense heat is the rule; you'll have to sightsee during the early morning and late afternoon to avoid the over 100° temperatures. Starting in July, the temperatures ease off into the 90's, but it begins to rain (off and on, sporadically). October is a changeable month, sometimes good, sometimes bad. *Kashmir,* as previously mentioned has completely different weather. The good weather starts in April, and May is absolutely lovely; the summer months are quite good, in fact, almost as good as the two preceding months; the real enthusiasts, however, claim September as the best of all. October is all right, but chilly, and from then on, it's definitely cold. *Bombay* is like most of India—best during the winter months, but hot the remainder of the year, although slightly cooler during the monsoon season from June through early October. However, Bombay has a good sea breeze, and temperatures are pleasanter (or seem pleasanter). *Madras* is something like Bombay, except that the monsoon season extends from June all the way through to December (but you never know, it may rain for days, or for only an hour).

✒ Visa Requirements

India has recently decided to loosen up its old, stiff visa requirements. Now you don't need a visa if you're a tourist and intend to stay in India for 21 days or less. That's pretty simple.

However, if you plan to enter then leave and re-enter the country (as for example, if you make side trips to Nepal or Ceylon, returning to India), you would need a visa that would be valid for 3 entries within a period of 6 months from the date of issue. You can then, with this visa, stay for a total of 3 months. For the visa there's a fee of several dollars and 1 picture is required, plus proof of onward transportation.

⚕ Health

Well, sir (or ma'am as the case may be), we now come to a knotty problem. No, that's not true, it's not a knotty problem, it's a simple one. India is going to require constant vigilance and thoughtfulness on your part, because the general health situation is, well, precarious. I've been looking over all of the tourist literature about India, and not once does the colorful literature issued by the government say one word about being careful about what you eat and drink. However, someone must acquaint you with the facts of Indian life, and regretfully, it's going to be me. (Now, let's not panic —it's not all that bad. Just stay with me). All should be well.

India has a long long (yes long) way to go before it becomes sanitary, at least to an American's way of thinking. Let's start with the most obvious question of all, is the water safe to drink? The answer is No for almost the entire country, and don't (please) ever forget it. I'll make only one exception: if you're staying in a hotel where the management says the water is filtered, you may use it sparingly, however, for brushing your teeth, etc. Even if the management guarantees it, don't drink it as a beverage, because even pure, the mineral content tends to throw off delicate American tummies. When you get in your hotel, order a large bottle of mineral water, beer, etc., or what have you, and drink that. Otherwise, stick to tea and coffee, which must of necessity be boiled. There's no point in ordering iced tea or coffee—the ice is made with the local water. Far better to let the tea or coffee cool (if the weather is hot) than to use ice.

In large cities, boiled milk for your coffee is all right. Be careful about ice cream, cheese, custard desserts, mayonnaise, and other natural breeders of bacteria. Salad greens and raw vegetables are out —out—out! (You get the idea now, don't you?) Fresh fruit is all right, just so long as *you* personally cut them open, and providing you peel off the skin yourself. If you're eating a banana, cut away the tip too. If you stay with cooked foods and boiled liquids, all should be well.

Tourists are subject to a form of intestinal disturbance popularly known as Delhi Belly; it's the same as Montezuma's Revenge in Mexico, and the Tokyo Trots. In any event, it's unquestionably annoying to be laid up in your hotel room, and my best advice is not to eat or drink anything without thinking first. If you do feel any stomach rumblings, or have a queasy feeling, or have diarrhea, by all means take a Lomotil, which is a prescription pill which almost always arrests the worst symptoms. Although the local drugstores in India usually have the pill available without prescription, by all means have your doctor write out a prescription at home and take it with you. Just in case. Even if you don't need it, it's still worth the investment.

Before you go to India, be sure you have a reasonably fresh vaccination for smallpox (not too old), and then get cholera, typhoid and paratyphoid shots. Yellow fever shots are required if you're coming from infected areas—generally regarded as Southeast Asia, parts of Africa, and Latin America.

Don't worry unnecessarily. Go easy at first with the spicy food. Use care with regard to water, milk, and raw vegetables. I've been there many times and have never gotten sick.

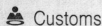 Customs

Somewhat improved from what used to be one of the world's worst and most tedious customs examinations. Even today, Indian Customs views suspiciously every camera and transistor radio you happen to have. Reason: such goods are greatly in demand in luxury-starved India, and you *could* double your money, and more, if you bought a camera in Hong Kong and sold it in Calcutta. So it's best to declare such goodies and make out a form, which you present on leaving the country. If you don't have the item on leaving, you'll have to pay the duty on it. Otherwise, a tourist is permitted 1 bottle of liquor, 1 of wine, 200 cigarettes, 2 cameras plus 25 rolls of film for each, and any amount of jewelry, etc., you are willing to declare. At the insistence of the hard-pressed Indian Tourist Office, Customs recently agreed to adopt the "1 in 10" rule in inspecting tourist luggage. That means they'll ask to poke through 1 bag out of every 10 on the counter. These are pretty good odds, but it's still best to declare doubtful items. If you're carrying medicines, have the prescription with you or they may be confiscated as drugs are a big problem in India.

You may bring any amount of foreign currency into India, but no more than 75 *rupees*. For the reason, see "Currency." You'll be required to set forth your dollars and traveler's checks on a declaration, and every time you change them for *rupees* the transaction will be noted in your passport. On leaving, you've got to "balance out."

💲 Currency

The local currency is known as the *rupee*. Each *rupee* subdivides, on the decimal system, into 100 *naye Paise* (abbreviated as nP).

A word about the black market: we don't recommend you dabble in it, but it does exist. Since the war, many local people have made fortunes in India, all in *rupees*. Since the Exchange Control Authorities are understandably stingy about granting foreign exchange for Indians to travel abroad, many people are dying to trade in their *rupees* for a wad of dollars. Also, too many *rupees* are seeking to purchase too few goods in inflation-ridden India. Result, you'll be approached many times to change your dollars "on the black," and the rates are tempting.

Tourists frequently succumb to these get-rich-quick schemes because they make the trip through India so much cheaper. Some even buy *rupees* in Beirut or Hong Kong, both free money markets, and get even better rates than they can in India. But any way you do it, it's a crime in India.

You're supposed to fill out a detailed currency declaration form listing all of the different types of money you hold—dollars and travelers checks, etc. That's the theory; but the practice is somewhat different, because the forms aren't always distributed, aren't always collected on departure and so forth.

At the moment, the very best place to cash your dollars is at the American Embassy's West Building. Before you go, phone them and check on what hours they're open, rates of exchange, and so forth. Of course, if you're just cashing a few dollars, it probably isn't worth the trip, but it certainly is if you're planning to spend a substantial amount. Be sure to take your passport along.

🌐 Price Level

Western-style "luxury hotels" are comparative bargains now. But remember, there's a 12% to 15% service charge added to the price of the room. Western food is not unreasonably high, averaging about $6 to $8 for an elaborate dinner. Air travel and train fares are cheaper than in most countries. The shopping can be what you make it, but handmade goods and textiles are great bargains. All in all, you won't save money but you shouldn't spend too much, except for the inflation now creeping over India.

Now, another special note about prices. Although the Indian economy is very spotty, prices are steadily advancing, and some hotels and restaurants have not been slow to take advantage of the situation. So don't rely on posted room rates—sometimes they'll be higher than the listed price. When checking in, better confirm your hotel rate in advance, with service charge included.

🍎 Tipping

Virtually all hotels add a service charge, and then display large signs which proclaim "Tipping forbidden. Staff members who accept tips are liable to dismissal." Of course it's not true, and a little modest tipping is still in order. Just don't overdo it.

Best to bow to the inevitable, even though it costs the poor fellow his job (an unlikely story if I ever heard one). But remember the average basic wage for unskilled labor is 3 *rupees* a day. If you go around strewing 5- and 10-*rupee* notes you'll spoil the situation for future tourists. So: tip a maximum of 1 *rupee* for any given service, unless it's exceptional (i.e., one porter, 5 steamer trunks!). At the end of your stay, figure 1 *rupee* for each day the room bearer has served you. He'll be unhappy, of course, but he'll respect you, probably think you were born British. If your hotel does not have a 10% service charge, tip the room bearer 2 *rupees* a day. The baggage porter who carries your luggage should be given a *rupee*.

Incidentally, taxi-drivers are *never* tipped. It's simply the custom. Waiters theoretically shouldn't be tipped, because the restaurant adds a service charge, but they are: give them 1 *rupee* or 10%, whichever is more. Theater ushers and others who perform routine services expect nothing, and that's what they usually get. On a day's sightseeing trip by car, tip the driver 5 *rupees* if he's been pleasant and helpful.

Moral: do not confuse India with America. The per capita income difference is at least 50 to 1!

🏃 Transportation

Getting About In India On Your Own As any reader can tell, I am a great believer in independent travel. However, and this is a big however, it's somewhat difficult in India. For example, airline tickets must be constantly checked and reconfirmed; flights are often delayed without any announcement; hotel reservations must be double-checked. As a result, the independent traveler may find that he is devoting a disproportionately large amount of time to merely working out the mechanics of the trip, rather than spending every single moment enjoying the great wonders of this truly remarkable country.

Therefore, may I suggest that you work with a travel organization with dozens of branch offices scattered throughout India. In this way, you'll be met at the airport, with transportation provided, and instead of looking for porters, everything will be taken care of. Further, they will previously have checked on your hotel space, and will attend to taking care of local sightseeing, and onward transportation, which has to be confirmed and often reconfirmed. About the largest and best of these firms specializing in Indian travel is Travel Corporation of India, with its principal office at Chander Mukhi,

Nariman Point, Bombay, just behind the Sheraton Oberoi Hotel. They have an office in New York at 20 East 53rd Street.

A choice of *airlines* there is not: just one, the state-owned Indian Airlines Corporation (IAC). They are surprisingly good in the air, but somewhat lackadaisical on the ground. Their food is pretty awful, but their pilots are excellent. These days you'll find good-sized jet planes most of the time, although smaller planes are occasionally used. Reservations are not easy to make. Best to have them before you leave home. Be sure to reconfirm local flights in each city. And plan to get to bed early: the IAC flights seem to depart at dawn! (They all don't, really; merely most of them.) Fares—which are usually included in your round-the-world or round-trip ticket—are about 6¢ a mile, which is quite reasonable by world standards. Everything is Tourist Class, with side-by-side 2- and 2-seating. Warning: IAC is quite stiff about late cancellations, can and does charge anything up to 100% for a "no-show." There can be little doubt that airplane travel is the best way of getting around in India.

India now charges a whopping 100 *rupees* as a departure tax, and that amounts to about $12.50. It applies to all flights with international destinations, except those bound for Pakistan, Afghanistan, Nepal, Bhutan, Bangladesh, Sri Lanka, and the Maldive Islands; for these destinations the departure tax is $6.25.

Trains are numerous and quite good, but rather a slow way to travel if you're in a hurry, as most tourists seem to be. Americans tend to insist on the air-conditioned class, which costs only a shade less than air travel; but in the comparatively cool wintertime, ordinary unairconditioned First Class is a bargain, less than half the air fare. Berths are standard in air-conditioned and First Class, but meals, as noted before, are ordered in advance from station restaurants, as all trains do not have diners. Incidentally, the rails are state-owned, too, so if something goes wrong, don't bother to write a letter of complaint to them—write to the Tourist Department!

A rail bargain is the 30-day "Travel As You Like" tourist scheme, which offers unlimited, air-conditioned rail travel throughout the country for somewhat over $100 per person. If time is not a factor, this is a leisurely way to get around and see a lot. But, frankly, there are so many problems connected with rail travel—getting to the station, crowds, no dining cars, red tape, bugs, etc.—I don't recommend it as a steady diet.

Buses, as we know them, don't exist in regular service. Nor are they recommended to the foreigner, because even to get aboard is an achievement, and you won't stand a chance against the locals. Same goes for streetcars, or trams, as they're called. What's left are *taxis* and *rented cars.* Taxi fares are very reasonable: although rates vary from city to city, it's very hard to clock up a dollar unless you leave the city limits. The charge for a *hired car* and driver (don't try it yourself!) varies, of course, depending on the vehicle, the season, and the operator. In fact, if you rented a car for long tourist trips, you'd actually be living like a maharajah, because you'd be paying his prices. Sometimes, by inquiring around, a car and driver can be hired at lower rates. If so, *inspect* the car first, and talk to the driver, to see if he knows where he's going and what he's doing.

▌▌ Communications

Telephone service certainly isn't up to U.S. standards—you can't dial another city—but it's not bad. Operators understand English, and a long-distance call will be handled with reasonable efficiency if you're patient. Don't look for phone booths except in hotel lobbies; and don't expect good telephone service in outlying areas. But in the larger centers you'll be speedily connected.

Cables are handled by the post office, but most hotel desks will take care of them for you. They don't always arrive, and they're not awfully fast.

Airmail service on the other hand is reasonably good. Do *not* send checks through the mail: they have an odd way of vanishing and then showing up in your account stamped "paid"—to the wrong party. *Airmail letters* back home cost about 30¢ and about 20¢ for an *airmail postcard,* It takes about 5 days to reach the U.S. by airmail. Surface mail takes months. When shipping parcels out of India, make sure they're insured.

⚡ Electricity

The current is 220 A.C., but may go up or down. In power-short India it can fluctuate alarmingly. You'll need a transformer and also an adapter plug for your electric razor, but even then, some hotels have the two-prong socket, some the three. Ask at your hotel desk for a transformer. Best to take a safety razor along and play it safe. Don't use an electric appliance without asking about it *first.*

✕ Food Specialties and Liquor

Western-style hotels, where you'll almost certainly stay, serve European food, and it's average, just average. At hotels, meal prices are the highest of all of India, but still well below comparable prices at home; moderate might be the word to describe meal prices in India. If you eat in city restaurants which are not part of a hotel, you'll find them considerably lower-priced than hotel restaurants. And one word of advice: if you are accustomed to particular cuts of meat, you're not going to find them in India. Getting a steak, for example, is possible, but only barely so. And another point, if it isn't on the menu, don't ask for it.

There's no young lamb in India; it's all heavily flavored mutton. Pork varies, but is apt to be more fat than meat. Oddly enough, beef isn't bad at all in Calcutta, where it finds its way to your table from black-market Muslim butchers, but you won't find much of it in Delhi, while Bombay is in the middle, sometimes yes and sometimes no. Many times what you think is beef is really buffalo; beef is considered to be sacred in some areas of India. In smaller places, forget it, because the beef will be stringy and tough. Chicken is plentiful: a bit stringy, but familiar-tasting. Along the coasts, fish is often excellent. The *bekti* in Calcutta, a kind of white perch, is marvelous. Plenty of seafood in Bombay, too, and of surprising variety.

If you like Chinese food, several hotels and restaurants in India specialize in it, and it's the real thing. You can find good Italian food at Firpo's in Calcutta. But, by and large, there are few specialty restaurants in India. The demand for Hungarian food, or for bagels and lox, just doesn't exist.

But—if you like curry, you'll never leave! It would take an IBM computer to calculate the variations of curry dishes served throughout India, and most would merit three stars. Curry—rice with sauces, herbs, vegetables, and frequently meat or fish—is the national dish of India. You can order it mild, medium, or hot, but watch out! Mild to them may be hot to you!

The reason Indian curry is so much better than what you'd get at home is twofold: first, the rice is wonderful—as far a cry from the "minute" variety as can be imagined, and Indian rice has a distinctive nutty flavor. Second, the herbs and spices are fresh, ground and pounded daily by the cook in his own bowl. The pre-packaged curry powder you buy at home just doesn't exist here. That's why. Curry, you see, is not a single spice but a blend of ingredients.

To illustrate, there's an amusing story—quite true—about a British woman who was born in India, spent most of her life there, and became Lady M. when her husband was knighted for services to the British business community in India. Not long ago she found herself in New York, guest of honor at a dinner given at a fashionable Fifth Avenue hotel which prides itself on its Indian cuisine. Curry was the main dish, of course, and after dinner the hotel manager was anxious to know what Lady M. had thought of it. Very good, she said, with true British tact. But how did it compare with what she was used to? Quite well, she assured him. No, really—he persisted —was it as good as what she had at home? He'd gone too far. Lady M. looked at him sweetly and said, "If my cook served me the curry I had tonight, I'd sack him!"

Aside from curry, *kababs* (meat on a skewer) is excellent, *tandoori* (barbecued) chicken is a Delhi specialty you shouldn't overlook, and some of the Indian desserts are exotically delicious. Bombay duck, as gourmets know, isn't duck at all, but a small dried fish, usually eaten with curries. All in all, if you're not the steak-and-potatoes type, you won't go hungry! If you are, better eat the second-class European-style food.

The word "curry" itself is derived from the Indian word *turcarri.* A basic curry is made from meat, fish, vegetables or eggs, a few spices, and has a rather thin, unthickened gravy. It may, as previously mentioned, be mild, medium, or very hot. Somewhat richer, but with less gravy, are the various *korma dishes,* which often are served almost dry. A *do-peeazah* is a type of dry curry made with lots of sautéed onions, usually both ground and sliced. *Bhoona* meat dishes are first fried, then subsequently steamed in their own natural juices. *Tandoor* dishes are cooked in clay ovens, as a rule, and may often be only mildly flavored. *Koftas* are meat balls or croquettes, and are very popular in India.

Rice forms the basis of Indian cookery, and it's very good. A *pellao* is rice prepared with butter, spices, and any desired ingredient. A *kitcheri* is rice and lentils; and so forth. Indian food, to be perfectly frank, is quite unlike anything you've eaten in the U.S. On first tasting, it will be quite strange. Be a little patient, and give it a try. Within a day, you'll probably learn to like it, or you never will.

Everyone, however, could like the local breads. *Chapatis* are a sort of wholewheat pancake, *parathas* are a kind of wholewheat bread; *puri* is crisp, deep-fried bread. An interesting appetizer of curried meat or fish, wrapped in pastry, is *samosas,* you'll enjoy these. The desserts are good, although a little unusual. *Halwa* is a sweet dessert, often made with carrots and very good, too; it can also be prepared with pumpkin, rice, nuts, bananas, etc. Don't leave India without trying *jalebi,* a sort of thin cruller or doughnut. Very often, you'll find what looks like gold or silver leaf on your desserts. Guess what it is? Gold or silver leaf, that's right. It's definitely edible, and completely harmless, but you don't have to eat it if you don't want to, although it does make an attractive decoration.

As noted, scotch whisky is ruinously expensive, and there's no point in looking for rye or bourbon. (Better bring your own bottle). The locally made scotch has a strong molasses flavor and costs about $5 a bottle. Indian gin isn't bad, nor is the rum, but both are a lighter proof than you're used to, and at $8-plus a bottle, hardly a bargain. Beer is pretty good and much stronger than ours, but costs 80¢ a quart in stores, $1 and up in bars.

SPECIAL NOTE:
India keeps changing its rules about drinking alcoholic beverages. It seems impossible to predict in which direction the prohibition of sales of liquor will go. Some Indian states are more liberal than others. Inquire locally.

Language

Most everywhere you go in India, you'll find someone who speaks English. But if you want to make like a *burra sahib,* you may find that a bit of simplified Hindi comes in handy. Here are a few words and phrases, most of them intentionally (slightly) misspelled so that you may pronounce them phonetically.

ENGLISH-HINDI

one	*eck*
two	*dough*
three	*teen*
four	*char*
five	*pahntch*
six	*chay*
seven	*saht*
eight	*aht*
nine	*now*
ten	*dass*
yes, okay	*teek high*
no	*nay*
sir	*sahb*
madam	*memsahb*
big	*buhra*

small	*choata*
tea	*char*
tip, money	*bahksheesh*
how much?	*ketna high?*
where is?	*kidduh high?*
food, meal	*kahna*
want, need	*mahnta*

As in any language, gestures often take the place of words. Among most people, a nod means Yes, a headshake No. But not in India! Yes—without words—is a peculiar gesture: the chin bobs up in the direction of the ear and slowly comes back to rest. To the undiscerning foreigner it looks like someone who is trying to say no, but is too tired to turn his head the full 180°. Take care: avoid the example of the tourist couple, hot and weary after a hard day's sightseeing, who decided to have dinner in their room. The room bearer was summoned.

"Have you any soup?" A mute headshake.

"Any eggs?" A twitch of the chin toward the ear.

"Well, for heaven sakes, what *do* you have to eat?" the frustrated man asked, unaware that the bearer had been saying yes every time.

Approaching India and Its Cities

Perhaps you're an amateur archeologist ... a collector of Asian art ... a student of Sanskrit. If so, you're not at all typical, by no means the garden variety of tourist. But if—when India is mentioned—snake charmers and the Taj Mahal flash through your mind, read on.

At a guess, only one tourist in fifty goes to India *before* he's done Europe. If that's true, then the average tourist expects to find in India the same descending priority of tourist attractions he's used to in Europe: monuments—nature—people. By "monuments" I mean the usual sights—castles, cathedrals, ancient cities, and museums ... all the tangible glories of the past. By "nature" I am thinking of the Alps, the Italian Lakes, the Norwegian *fjords*, the English countryside, the French Riviera. By "people" I mean the local people, who, in Europe at least, tend to dress like you, speak English as a second language, watch television, and like Coca-Cola. But these priorities must be *reversed* when you come to India. Not that India lacks monuments. The Taj Mahal refutes that statement, and so do the temples, scores of them, some dating back thousands of years. But because our knowledge of Indian history is so scanty, and Indian architecture so foreign in style to our own, most Indian temples seem to our uneducated glance like crenelated piles of masonry thickly covered with carvings. We look in vain for the soaring grandeur of the Cologne Cathedral and the magnificence of St. Peter's or the Parthenon.

India has its palaces, many of them now converted into luxurious hotels. And forts. And museums. But, here again, knowledge plays its part. Can you name *one* Indian artist? Can you visualize any Indian painting or sculpture as well as you can—say—the Mona Lisa or the Venus de Milo? There's the difference: when you go to Europe, you're seeing art and architecture you've known about and become familiar with all your life. But when you go to India, everything seems alien except the Taj. And the unfamiliar takes a bit of knowing!

That's why monuments should not be your prime objective in visiting India. But nature, as in Europe, seems to hold its middle position as an attraction. You'll certainly not be disappointed in Kanchenjunga Mountain, seen on a clear day from Darjeeling . . . the fabled Vale of Kashmir . . . or the browns and greens and oranges of an Indian forest, so artfully masking a tiger behind each bush. No, India is full of natural beauty. So far, nature is second, monuments are third. First? People. The astonishing diversity of appearance, color, costume, and speech. The lovely houses and the miserable hovels they live in. The splendor and squalor of their lives. Their sheer numbers on a street, in a park, at a stadium. The shattering contrast between their way of life and your own. Yes, people are the prime attraction in India.

SUGGESTED ITINERARIES   Seeing India in a week is impossible, but that's what most people do. When they've come so far, it seems a shame to miss so much. Still, the world's a big place full of fascinating wonders, and provision must be made for people who have to be back at work on the twenty-third at 9 A.M. So we'll start with the least time you could possibly devote to India, and work up. We'll assume you travel by air.

3 Days: Delhi-Agra.
5 Days: Delhi-Agra-Jaipur.
7 Days: Madras-Benaras-Agra-Jaipur-Delhi.
10 Days: Madras-Goa-Agra-Jaipur-Delhi plus Kashmir or Udaipur or Bombay.

14 Days: Madras-Kathmandu-Benaras-Agra-Jaipur-Udaipur-Delhi plus Kashmir or Bombay.

21 Days: Calcutta-Kathmandu-Benaras-Agra-Jaipur-Udaipur-Del-hi,Bombay and nta.

30 Days: Calcutta-Bhubaneswar-Benaras-Agra-Jaipur-Udaipur-Delhi-Kashmir-Boay-Ellora and Ajanta-South India.

You've probably noticed that Kashmir, Bhubaneswar, Ellora and Ajanta, and South India seem like afterthoughts, while Darjeeling, isn't mentioned at all. To take the last first, Darjeeling is omitted simply because it's a sidetrip by virtue of its location. Tack it on whenever you have 2–3 extra days. As for the others, they are off the beaten path too; But that doesn't mean you couldn't substitute Bhubaneswar for Bombay in the 10-day itinerary. Except for South India, which is a time-consuming luxury addition, because of its size, all of these places are "musts." If you can, see them! Traveling by train? Add half again the time to each itinerary.

SPECIAL NOTE:
   The material on the regions of India has been arranged in a somewhat different style than that used in the other countries in this book. Instead of starting with the capital, the first city which appears is Calcutta on the eastern edge of India.

Calcutta

Calcutta is the capital of West Bengal and the fourth or fifth largest city in the world. Nobody is sure just what the population really is. The last census estimated 10,000,000, but how do you count people who live on the sidewalks? What address do you give for refugees who poured in daily from what used to be Muslim-dominated East Pakistan? One thing is sure: after the 12-mile ride in from Calcutta's Dum Dum airport, you'll think Times Square on New Year's Eve a rather lonely place!

What's most remarkable about Calcutta's size is that the city didn't even exist before 1690, when a British merchant named Job Charnock decided it would make a convenient trading center. Why he picked that site, Kali (a Hindu goddess) alone knows! The settlement was and is almost 100 miles from the sea, down the twisting, treacherous Hooghly River (the comically named tributary of the

Weather Strip: Calcutta

	Jan.	Feb.	Mar.	Apr.	May	June	July	Aug.	Sept.	Oct.	Nov.	Dec.
Average daily high	80°	84°	93°	97°	96°	92°	89°	89°	90°	89°	84°	79°
Average daily low	55°	59°	69°	75°	77°	79°	79°	78°	78°	74°	64°	55°
Monthly rainfall	0.4	1.2	1.4	1.7	5.5	11.7	12.8	12.9	9.9	4.5	0.8	0.2
Number of days with 0.1 inches or more	1	2	2	3	7	13	18	18	13	6	1	0

sacred Ganges River). Actually a delta, the region is more water than land. The climate is atrocious. The Park Street Burying Ground, Calcutta's oldest cemetery, testifies to its rigors. Again and again you see this: "Here lieth William Patterson. Merchant, The Honourable East India Company, Who died in His 28th Year." Next to William, "Sarah, aged 24, Beloved Wife of William Patterson." And of course, "John Patterson, aged 5," "Mary Patterson, aged 3," and pathetically, "Barbara Patterson, Whose Tiny Tenure were as but a Dream from which She Wakened not." A hard life in those days, but a blessedly brief one.

The British put up with Calcutta for 120 years and made it the capital of the Raj, but in 1911 finally transferred the seat of government to Delhi. The major reason for the shift was the cross-grained nature of Calcutta's inhabitants, the Bengalis, a volatile, tempestuous, talented, freedom-minded people who resent authority in any form. Ironically, it is Bengal which today leads all Indian states in workdays lost through strikes against its own leaders. And it is Bengal which furnishes many of the country's communists. Any connection? Incidentally the term "Raj" refers to the period of the British rule of India.

Because the British ruled Calcutta for so long, reaching the pinnacle of their power in the 19th century, the city is Victorian in architecture and atmosphere. Behind the gingerbread facades of Clive Row and Dalhousie Square, still citadels of British commerce, thousands of Bengali clerks enjoy their "elevenses" the traditional late-morning tea break. It is an extraordinary sight to see them swarm out at 5, descend on the trams like ants on a green leaf, cling to impossible holds on the outside, and then hop off, the fare still clutched in their moist hands.

The British themselves do not wear heavy black suits any longer or carry tightly furled unbrellas, and they no longer sport "solar topees," the tropical sunhelmets of Kipling's days. They go hatless now, these former rulers, as they settle back in their chauffered cars for the ride to Ballygunge or Alipore, the town's fashionable suburbs. On the way, they are bound to pass the Victoria Memorial, a marble monument that was thought to surpass the Taj Mahal in beauty when it was dedicated by the Prince of Wales in 1921. (It doesn't.) It houses the Queen-Empress' piano and other relics, and dominates the south end of the Maidan (My-don), Calcutta's Central Park. If you stood on the Memorial dome you'd see the vast sweep of the park before you, stretching two miles north to the stately Raj Bhavan, once the residence of the Viceroy of India. A bit south of the Memorial is St. Paul's Cathedral, neo-Gothic but still very English. Fort William, built in the late 18th century to defend Calcutta, still stands nearby. British accents once rang through the officers' mess, but the men with the pips on their shoulders are now Indian.

From the dome you'd also have an excellent view of the finish post of Calcutta's race course, which gave the famous Calcutta Sweep to the world of racing silks. The winter races are still a gay occasion: ladies wearing elaborate hats and long gloves mingle with maharajahs in the Owners' Enclosure. *Saris,* spanning the entire color spectrum, shimmer in the bright Indian sunlight; and a vast sea of brown heads above white *dhotis* fills the stands. A stone's throw away lies the polo field, scene of possibly the best polo in the world during the December holiday season.

All along the Maidan runs fashionable Chowringhee Road, studded with posh clubs, airline offices, and the Grand Hotel. At the Bengal Club, the oldest British one in the world outside of the United Kingdom, sahibs sip pink gins and play rowly-bowly. Only recently, after bitter acrimony, Indian members were admitted, but only the "right" type, mind you: Oxford and Cambridge men. Below the club's windows, trams and buses, black with humanity, ply toward unfashionable North Calcutta, some of the most densely populated square miles on this earth. Here stands Calcutta University, which grants somewhat dubious degrees to thousands of students every year, turning them out into a world which has one job for each ten applicants. Here, too, is Calcutta's port, one of Asia's busiest, dominated by the vast cantilevered span of the Howrah

Bridge. Ships from every nation lie in the Hooghly's deep basin, slowly settling with their cargos of jute and tea, ready for the 85-mile haul to the Bay of Bengal. As you stand amid this scene of swarming activity, it's hard to imagine that only a few miles away leopards prowl; and tigers, in the marshy Sunderbans, wait for woodchoppers, the prey they prefer.

Calcutta is a "people" town, not a "monument" town and nowhere in India will you find less to inspect and more to see. It *is* true that cows saunter down main thoroughfares, unhindered, tying up traffic for blocks. They settle on sidewalks, too, and pedestrians circle round them unconcerned. A short time back the police launched "Operation Bull," on the premise that if you round up and deport enough males, the cattle population of the city will dwindle predictably. Off to the city limits the Brahmas were carted, but no barriers were erected to keep them out, and no Hindu would lift a hand to block their return. So back they plodded, to the despair of all motorists but to the delight of the tourist officials, who rightly regard the sacred cow as one of Calcutta's great attractions.

You will probably notice that there are far more men than women on the streets of Calcutta. At the moment, it's believed that there are approximately 600 women in Calcutta for every 1,000 men. The reason is that hundreds of thousands of men come from rural areas to find work here, leaving their wives and families behind because of the lack of money. Each week, millions of dollars are sent by postal service to the lonely wives in their villages.

Something you should see—if you can take it— is the *bustee*. This is the term used for a *registered* slum area, mind you, not just a slum, but an acknowledged one, involving a complex system of rents, registered with the municipal Corporation of Calcutta. You will see, if your stomach is strong, poverty beyond belief. But don't think Calcutta is a poor city only; it is the wealthiest city of India, and has more rich people than any other city in the country.

It may be that very small boys—say from 5 to 13 years of age—will offer to render various services for you, run errands, and so forth. These *kangalis* almost never have any parents, perhaps having been born upon the sidewalk and deserted immediately afterwards. They are not beggars, but want to earn small change for small services—carrying parcels, finding you a taxi, and so on. Just remember that they will almost certainly sleep upon the sidewalk that night, even though your first thought will be that they are nothing but pests or beggars. Sympathetic though you should be, that doesn't necessarily mean giving them a package to deliver to your hotel, for the temptation may be too great.

No one knows the actual population of Calcutta, but it is probably about 10,000,000, and looks even more crowded. The city is a complete mess, insofar as housing is concerned. There are perhaps a million (yes, that's right) people who have no place to lay their heads at night except on the city streets; many of them have no other assets in the world than the clothes on their back and the few precious possessions they cling to, tied up in a soiled handkerchief. It's all rather pathetic, and many sensitive tourists find it not a little depressing. Those on an all-expense tour, staying at luxury hotels, may hardly notice the extreme poverty, being well insulated from contact with the masses. But the ruggedly individualistic tourist who walks about the local streets will often shudder in dismay, and turn his head away at other times. But somehow, miraculously, Calcutta is so alive, so vital and trying so hard, that you want to hope that things will get better. They can hardly get worse. Many people, reading this, will say to themselves, why not omit Calcutta? Please don't—it's very definitely India as it is today. Besides, there's so much in the way of sightseeing in the vicinity of Calcutta, you really couldn't skip it.

When you arrive, as you probably will, at Calcutta's Dum Dum Airport, you'll probably be taken aback by the confusion, masses of people, and seeming lack of order. Don't worry, your baggage will safely appear. (If you are only making an overnight transit stop in order to catch another flight the following day, you might consider staying at the Hotel Airport Ashok, which is only about a mile from the airport itself. The Hotel Airport Ashok, is excellent, almost luxurious, and highly recommended, and there are 2 restaurants with fairly good food; the coffee shop is open 24 hours a day, in recognition of the fact that air travelers arrive and depart at rather odd hours.) As you drive from the airport, the highway passes alongside a canal, usually covered with water hyacinths. Many people are more or less astonished as they drive in by the teeming humanity, the wandering cows, the homeless young children, and the extreme poverty which is apparent even to the most casual spectator. You'll see people washing in the open canals or under street hydrants and living their lives outdoors in full view. May I suggest that you respect their privacy and limit your picture-taking to a discreet number. The local residents, poorer than any western church mouse, are somewhat reluctant to pose, and are quite sensitive, as most Indians are, about the city's poverty. Please use your best judgment.

Rickshaw *wallahs,* too, lend an exotic air to the city. Like the gondoliers of Venice, their numbers are shrinking, for unlike their brethren in other cities they have resisted the introduction of the bicycle rickshaw, now so prevalent in Delhi and Bombay. Fortunately for them, Calcutta is flat, and during the monsoon, Calcutta streets always flood; it is then that the rickshaw comes into its own. Rates soar inversely to the depth of the water. From one corner to the next may cost a *rupee*. Ah, how the rickshaw *wallahs* pray for rain!

There are only three outstanding hotel possibilities in Calcutta. These are the Grand, the Great Eastern, and the Hindustan International. Let's consider them thoughtfully. The Hindustan International is the newest and is so modern that it even has a coffee shop, something quite rare in India. The Great Eastern is the oldest, and while it's good, it has a poor location, being in the business part of town, which is noisy and of no particular interest to the tourist. The Grand unquestionably has the best location, being almost adjacent to the New Market and very convenient for most tourist destinations. The Grand doesn't look like much from the outside, but it's very well maintained and most comfortable. All in all, I imagine the Grand is the best place for a stay. Rates are rather moderately priced, European plan at all the hotels, although quite naturally they have less and more expensive accommodations available. But not every one wishes to travel the luxury route, and I should mention the new Park Hotel, which is pleasant enough; both the 110-room Ritz Continental, and the 77-room Rutdeen are also fair enough and somewhat less expensive than the three leading hotels. You may be surprised to find that Calcutta hotels seem overstaffed by western standards, for they average about two employees per hotel room.

Places to eat are plentiful in Calcutta. Many people think the Ali Baba is the single most interesting restaurant in town, and if you like fine food, and have a culinary curiosity, don't pass up the Ali Baba. Prince's at the Grand Hotel and Maxim's at the Great Eastern Hotel are popular, but not quite up to Firpo's, a restaurant owned for generations by an Italian family of the same name. Their western and especially Italian dishes are quite good. The Nanking is the best for Chinese food, with the Waldorf a little behind. The Skyroom is pleasant and inexpensive and so is Trinca's. There are hundreds of Bengali restaurants, but few foreigners go to them since all western-style places serve Indian food too.

By far the best "nightclub"—really a restaurant with small band, girl vocalist, and dance floor—is the Blue Fox, which wouldn't seem out of place in New York City. Prince's, Firpo's, and Maxim's also have bands, dancing and rather uninspired floor shows, and are called in British parlance "cabarets." Mocambo's is another imitation of the Blue Fox, but not in the same league.

In general the hotel food may kindly be dismissed as very routine, and that goes for all the hotels in Calcutta—without exception, I regret to say. The places mentioned above wouldn't make any gourmet shout aloud with joy, but at least they're better than the hotels. Don't worry about transportation to and from the restaurants, because taxis are always available. At the restaurant when you're ready to leave, merely tell the waiter you want a taxi, and he'll get one for you; they're very inexpensive. But none of this answers the question of the tourist who really wants to sample Indian food and isn't satisfied with the mediocre stuff served in the hotels.

Calcutta's a fine place for shopping. Wander through the New Market, a huge bazaar behind the Grand Hotel, and you'll find something of everything made in India. But bargain firmly and hard! Brass trays, rectangular or round, some a full 48 inches in diameter, cost about a fifth of their U.S. price and aren't expensive to ship. Textiles, too, are marvelous. If you have the time, buy some of the gorgeous *sari* material, perhaps Benares brocade, and have it made into an elegant sheath or a jacket for women. Raw silk or madras (here it's pronounced mad-*rahss*) make superb sports jackets for men. Constantine's in the Great Eastern Hotel arcade offers a wide selection of material and will do the tailoring for no more than you'd pay in Hong Kong. And just about as good. Other cloth marts include the Bengal Home Industries and the various government stores which display goods for West Bengal, Kashmir, and Assam. Handicraft of all kinds abounds, too; and jewelers, the best and starchiest of whom is Hamilton's. But don't buy gold, at twice the world price!

Some standard sightseeing: Calcutta has a first-rate museum of Indian art and antiquities; the Kali and Jain temples are well worth seeing; the Botanical Gardens contain the biggest and possibly the oldest banyan tree in the world; the Zoo is interesting, especially the white tigers; and the Ramakrishna Mission is a magnet for those interested in the noted home of nondenominational religious faith. But there's nothing to compare with Delhi's Red Fort, Jaipur's pink palace or the Taj Mahal. Calcutta is people, and uniquely so, as I've said to the point of repetition.

One of the most interesting—indeed "weird" might be a more precise word—sights of Calcutta is its famous Marble Palace. In the midst of a slum area stands what resembles a Roman mansion, complete with statuary, fountains, and pools. The interior contains many wonders, marvels, and curiosities definitely worth your time, including a rather remarkable garden, complete with macaws, peacocks, and mynah birds. The entire Marble Palace is filled to the brim with objects, worthwhile and banal, from all corners of the globe, including a great number of priceless art objects, world famous paintings, and not a little bric-a-brac. However, bear in mind that although open to the public, this is not truly a museum, it is occupied by the renowned Mullick family who make it their home. But you are definitely welcome during the day.

Andaman Islands

A Side Trip From Calcutta For The Exceptional Traveler. Just south of Calcutta are the Andaman Islands, a rarely visited spot and a most interesting destination, but not necessarily for everyone. To begin with, at the moment of writing, special permission to visit the Andamans is required, although this can usually be obtained with only a little advance planning. There are twice-weekly flights from Calcutta to Port Blair, the chief city and center for the various islands, using large, comfortable jet planes; the trip takes about 2 hours. There's only one suitable place to stay, Corbyn's Cove Hotel, a small modern structure located on an excellent beach. Of course, at the hotel you'll find all of the resort amusements that you might expect, although there's no golf. Be sure to hire a boat and make a tour of the harbor, which is absolutely enormous and quite fascinating; the boat can make a stop at one of the plantations, where you might drink the delicious water from a green coconut. The Indians are always anxious for visitors to see their infamous Cellular Jail, where the British imprisoned (among others) those who were agitating for independence. The islands are lush and tropical, the local people extremely friendly and anxious to be of help, and all in all, the Andamans would make a very nice place for a break in a long trip. However, because of the complexities in obtaining permission to visit the islands, being sure of hotel space, and so on, it might be best to get in touch with Travel Corporation of India (which owns the hotel) and arrange the details; they're at 20 East 53rd Street, in New York.

Darjeeling

Darjeeling is India's best-known "hill station," one of many cool, lofty towns to which British *memsahibs* and their children used to retreat during the torrid spring. To see it, you must leave from and return to Calcutta, usually by air. Never mind, as the Anglo-Indians

Weather Strip: Darjeeling

	Jan.	Feb.	Mar.	Apr.	May	June	July	Aug.	Sept.	Oct.	Nov.	Dec.
Average daily high	47°	48°	57°	62°	64°	65°	66°	65°	64°	61°	54°	49°
Average daily low	35°	36°	42°	49°	53°	56°	58°	57°	55°	50°	42°	37°
Monthly rainfall	0.5	1.1	1.7	4.1	8.5	23.2	31.4	25.1	17.6	5.1	0.9	0.3
Number of days with 0.1 inches or more	1	3	4	7	14	21	26	24	17	5	1	1

say, because Calcutta is the gateway to your next stops: Bhubaneswar and Benares. Darjeeling is a disappointment in summer, because it rains a good deal and monsoon clouds generally hide the mountains. But in the winter it's glorious, although chilly. Watch out, though, for accommodations during April and May, when the visibility's fine and the town is packed with residents escaping the heat of the plains; and also in October, when many people flee the last of the rains during the month-long Hindu religious festivals, the Pujas.

An hour and a half directly to the north by an Indian Airline's aircraft, Darjeeling is partly reached by an airport located at the town called Bagdogra. Here you board a miniature train at nearby Siliguri and travel a few hours up and up and up until you reach Darjeeling. There are other ways, of course, such as taxi or rented car; but if you want the mighty spectacle of Kanchenjunga (28,208 feet high, a mere 800 below Everest) to astonish you as you round a bend, take the train. It's so leisurely that you may be able to pluck a white orchid as you pass through the orchid village of Kurseong. Incidentally, this toy train was featured in a Cinerama production.

Darjeeling is a series of stepladder streets. Make the going easy, unless you're a mountaineer, for the altitude is 7,000 feet, and the air is pure, champagne-cool, and light-headedly thin. The view is absolutely incredible: there is nothing to match it anywhere, if you have a feeling for mountains. Tiger Hill at sunrise, when the weather's fine, offers the vast sweep of the Himalayas, Everest being just visible because it's so far away (140 miles), but compensated for by the stupendous sight of Kanchenjunga. You don't have to take a taxi seven miles to Tiger Hill to see the mountains. Observatory Hill, in town, is an excellent spot to photograph Kanchenjunga. Besides peaks, Darjeeling has plenty of shrines and Buddhist monasteries, the most interesting of which is in a village named Ghoom, halfway between Tiger Hill and town.

Rai Bahadur Oberoi is the Conrad Hilton of India. His Oberoi Grand is the "best" hotel in Calcutta, and in Darjeeling you meet him (or rather his hotel) again at the Oberoi Mount Everest. Most tourists go there, but interestingly enough most residents don't, for they prefer the smaller, less pretentious Windamere.

The shopping in Darjeeling is exotic: Tibetan devil masks, carvings of all sorts, caps of fur, bizarre jewelry, colorful cloth—just the kind of souvenirs the folks back home would appreciate. Okay, so much of it's junk. Can you buy it in Kansas?

The people of Darjeeling are of the Tibetan type, or they are Nepalese with high cheekbones, slanted eyes, and broad, cheerful grins. This is the breed that hauls the packs up glamorous peaks. Here lives Tenzing Norkay, the Sherpa guide who may or may not have been the first man on Everest. Ask him: "Was it Hillary—or you?" and watch him smile. But don't wait around for an answer.

Bhubaneswar

Bhubaneswar (Boo-ban-esh-war), 1 hour and 40 minutes southwest of Calcutta by plane, is the hub of one of India's most compact and fascinating tourist areas. Within a small circumference are the city itself, one of the great temple towns of India, Puri, with a 12th-century temple of Jagannath; and Konarak, with its Black Pagoda, which ranks just behind the Taj Mahal as a unique sight.

Five hundred temples still stand in Bhubaneswar, capital of the ancient state of Orissa, most of which were erected between the 8th and 13th centuries. You may not fathom them as architectural masterpieces, but their sheer number is overwhelming. The Lingaraj is the largest and finest; its erotic carvings are merely a hint of what you'll view at Konarak.

Forty miles to the south from Calcutta, Konarak faces the Bay of Bengal. Its great temple, called the Black Pagoda because time has darkly weathered the stone, is a vast edifice covered with many thousands of carved figures, some miniscule, some larger than life. Most of them glorify the act of love in all its infinite variations. Gods and goddesses, youths and maidens, birds and beasts sing a frozen hymn to Eros. The effect is stupefying and yet somehow not offensive because it seems so artless, so unapologetic. Fertility, of course, was its object; and its basic premise goes far to explain India's 450,000,000 population. There is nothing else like it in the world, and even this suggestive description won't prepare you for the real thing. I do hope you don't blush readily. If you want to remain overnight at Konarak, there is a very nice government-owned Tourist Bungalow. The only satisfactory place at which to stay—and it's more than satisfactory—is the Hotel Bhubaneswar Ashok. It's a moderate-sized attractive structure, with fair-sized rooms, all pleasantly decorated. The food is rather good, and the atmosphere is pleasant.

After Konarak, the Temple of Jagannath at Puri, 40 road miles south of Bhubaneswar, seems slightly tame. (You can make a triangular trip from Bhubaneswar visiting both Konarak and Puri.) Still, it's a tremendous structure which even today requires 6,000 men to serve its daily needs. We've corrupted its name into "Juggernaut," for it is here that the rite of ceremoniously hauling the great chariot has taken place since time immemorial. Pulled through the streets of Puri by thousands of the devout, the chariot of Lord Jagannath, with 16 wheels each 7 feet high, used to dismember fanatic pilgrims who threw themselves under it as sacrifices to the god.

Puri, and its neighbor Gopalpur-on-sea, are delightful beach resorts, very popular with Calcutta residents. If you've time for a swim, Puri's best hotel is the Southeastern Railways; at Gopalpur's, the Oberoi Palm Beach is quite satisfactory.

Benaras (Varanasi)

Benaras, the sacred city of India, is now linked by air with Calcutta (1 hour and 40 minutes by Viscount). It's a controversial city among tourists: some find it revolting, others fascinating. But if people interest you (and you have a strong stomach), the great Hindu shrine on the Ganges is a must.

About halfway between Calcutta and Delhi, Benaras—which the Hindus call "Varanasi"—is holy not only to them but to Buddhists, for only 6 miles outside the city is the place called Sarnath, where the great Buddha preached his first sermon and enunciated his cardinal precept, the famous Middle Way. The sites where these events took place are marked by *stupas,* or mounds.

Benaras is old, perhaps one of the oldest cities in the world. It is to the devout Hindu what Mecca is to the Mohammedan: a holy place of pilgrimage. The Ganges River on whose banks it stands is itself holy, and immersion in its sacred water speeds the devout on their way to salvation. To facilitate bathing for the hundreds of thousands who come as pilgrims each year, broad steps—or *ghats* —are built down the steep banks to the river itself. Over three miles in length, they are literally crawling (and that is the only possible word) with humanity during the October Pujas, the most important of Hindu religious festivals. *Sadhus,* holy men, sit meditating; children sport noisily up and down the steps; young men gather in groups and chatter vivaciously; beggars are everywhere, pleading, importuning; and in a never ending procession from dawn to sunset, come the pilgrims to stand, waisthigh, in the sacred water. It is a fantastic scene, best observed from a sightseeing launch in the middle of the river.

Squeamish stomachs ought to avoid the burning *ghats,* where the dead are cremated. It is this clean and altogether logical rite which puts off so many tourists and leaves them with a distaste for Benaras. Seriously, be forewarned and stay away from the burning *ghats* if you're queasy, or don't feel up to it. If you decide to go, the very early morning is the best time. You'll be asked (very politely of course) not to take pictures here.

Shrines crowd the city, of which the holiest, Viswanatha, is closed to the nonbeliever but can be viewed well enough from a house across the street. The Durga Temple numbers even more monkeys than people, and that's a lot of monkeys! Streets are narrow, crowded, often filthy, but emblazoned with color by the Benaras brocades and silks. Everywhere there are people. People. People. Until the mind reels. Keep in mind that many have traveled hundreds of miles on foot to reach this place, and their predecessors have been doing so since recorded time. Then, perhaps, Benaras won't seem just another dirty, rather smelly alien city, but the Indian equivalent of Jerusalem.

If you take one of the regular tours of this fascinating and yet repellant city, here's the way the day will probably go. There's an early morning start, followed by a visit to the bathing ghats, where you'll see men and women bathing (very modestly) in the Ganges. Then, perhaps, a boat ride on the river, which is usually alive with boats; this trip on the water presents a more interesting view of the temples, the city, and the ghats than that seen from land. Afterwards, a visit to the chief temples, such as the Vishwanath or Golden Temple. If you're not a Hindu (and the chances are reasonably strong that you're not) you will be requested to view everything from a special vantage point and also to stay away from certain holy places. If time permits, you will probably be taken to the Hindu University, which is particularly proud of its marble Shiva temple and has a remarkable collection of Indian miniatures. On some trips, a visit to Sarnath, where Buddha preached his first sermon, may be included. In addition, stops may be made at various weaving centers and also at silk stores; here you can buy yard goods, saris, etc., at prices which are sometimes outstanding bargains and at other times not at all cheap. It's just that certain handwoven fabrics may contain gold or silver threads, and these are naturally quite costly; to outfit a Hindu bride involves a wedding ensemble which may cost quite a few hundred dollars.

The best place to stay in Benaras is the Hotel Varanasi Ashok, each room of which has a balcony overlooking the Varuna River. Situated on an 8-acre site, it offers a swimming pool, two restaurants, and shops. The decor of the hotel is quite interesting and modern. Much older, but still suitable for a stay is Clark's Hotel, which is somewhat old-fashioned, but has the advantage of having a lobby-long cloth market, with excellent values—particularly in brocades and silks. There is also the Hotel de Paris, which isn't too bad for an overnight stop. Of course, the Hotel Varanasi Ashok is the best place to stay, no doubt about it.

(Note: Although tourists often visit nearby Lucknow and Allahabad, as far as I am concerned, they can readily be omitted.)

Delhi

Delhi looks new but is old, as Indian cities go. People lived there 5,000 years ago, although they left few traces. It was only when the Muslims came to conquer, almost a thousand years ago, that monuments were erected, many of which still stand today. Delhi, then, is a monument town, and for that reason peculiarly one of the less interesting in India.

This may sound odd until you recall the priorities we discussed earlier—people, nature, and monuments. Somehow Delhi people don't measure up to Calcutta's as an attraction. Most of them are clerks (pronounced clarks) in government offices. As they swarm down the Rajpath on their bicycles, they have the look of civil servants everywhere: soft, smug, and secure. A far cry from the Bengali refugees of Calcutta huddled on a sidewalk!

Weather Strip: Delhi

	Jan.	Feb.	Mar.	Apr.	May	June	July	Aug.	Sept.	Oct.	Nov.	Dec.
Average daily high	70°	75°	87°	97°	105°	102°	96°	93°	93°	93°	84°	73°
Average daily low	44°	49°	58°	68°	79°	83°	81°	79°	75°	65°	52°	46°
Monthly rainfall	0.9	0.7	0.5	0.3	0.5	2.9	7.1	6.8	4.6	0.4	0.1	0.4
Number of days with 0.1 inches or more	2	2	1	1	2	4	8	8	4	1	0	1

For all its history, Delhi is two cities today: Old Delhi and New Delhi. New Delhi is a latter-day Washington, D.C., planned and constructed less than half a century ago. The result is stately and impressive, if a little dull, much as Washington is basically dull. Broad avenues, tremendous lawns, large-scale buildings, expensive homes and Cadillacs (the government ministers of poverty-ridden India dearly love Cadillacs, the larger the better).

If New Delhi is spacious and antiseptic, Old Delhi is the opposite: narrow, crooked, crowded streets, tiny shops, hawkers, the inevitable cows, aromatic and sometimes unpleasant odors . . . a little like the Casbah without its menacing reputation. Most of Delhi's 3,000,000 people live here, Hindus and Muslims together, sometimes amicably, sometimes not.

Dominating this maze is Delhi's outstanding relic: the Red Fort. As forts go, this one is truly a whopper. The busy Moghuls built it in 1648 out of red sandstone, and it covers several city blocks. Except for their glorious interlude in Agra, all of the Moghul emperors lived here. They lived well. Marble—which must have been the equivalent of concrete in those days!—is the interior wall decoration. Probably the most expensive room on earth was the Private Audience Chamber, where the emperor received ambassadors and important dignitaries. You'll have to use your imagination as you stand there. Picture its marble walls topped by a ceiling of solid silver. Dominating the room was the Peacock Throne, which must have been ablaze with gold and precious stones, for even in those days it was valued at twelve million British pounds—sixty million dollars! An Afghan invader finally carried it off—surely one of the biggest hauls in history!

It was this fort which refused to surrender one burning hot summer against a tradition-ridden British army during the Indian Mutiny of 1857. Its fall marked the end of Moghul power forever. Akbar's imperial line was finished, and with it one of the world's greatest architectural epochs was ended.

The unpronounceable Qutb Minar is Delhi's next most impressive monument. Started by a Muslim sultan in 1200, it was finally completed in the middle of the 14th century. Some say it was a minaret from which the faithful were called to prayer by the *muezzin*. Others think it was simply a victory tower. Whatever its purpose, it still stands, the top an impressive 234 feet above the ground. Climb the steps if you can, for the tower provides a stunning view of the Delhi plains. (But I won't blame you if you don't feel up to it, with the temperature in the 90's.) Humayan was an important emperor during the middle of the 16th century, and his grieving widow erected a stately tomb which, in the shape of its dome, seems the precursor of the Taj Mahal. It would appear that royal couples in those days were all quite devoted to one another. Smaller mausolea may be seen scattered round Humayan's Tomb.

There are dozens of other relics in and around Delhi, most of them dating from the Muslim era. A dramatic contrast would be to switch from tomb-touring to embassy-examining. The Diplomatic Enclave is a battleground of embassy architectural styles. You'll be happy to observe that Edward Stone's American effort leads all the rest, or so the vast majority of observers think.

All Delhi meets at Connaught Circus, a colonnaded circle lined with shops, banks, and travel agencies. This is the hub of the wheel, from which broad avenues terminate in great buildings like the President's Palace and various legislative buildings. Not far from here is an interesting observatory built long ago by a Maharajah of Jaipur. Huge slabs of stone, cunningly placed, formed sundials and starsights, and most of their observations are reasonably accurate today.

If you're lucky enough to be in Delhi in late January, you'll see the Republic Day parade on the twenty-sixth, surely one of the world's most colorful pageants. But book *now,* because hotel space is very, very tight!

The city's newest and most revered shrine is the Rajghat, near the Yamuna River, where Gandhi (and most recently Nehru) were cremated. Visiting heads of state invariably lay wreaths at their pyre (it's not a grave), while Indians come to pay homage to their two greatest leaders.

It's easy to overlook seeing one of the city's many excellent museums, mostly because there's so much to see in the way of outdoor sightseeing. Perhaps the leading Indian art exhibit may be viewed at the National Museum; it is said to have over 500,000 individual exhibits. There are also the following: a Crafts Museum; Gallery of Modern Art; Tibet House (small but very interesting); Rail Transport Museum (fascinating old Indian trains); and even an International Doll Museum.

ACCOMMODATIONS

Oberoi Inter-Continental. This hotel is a sort of marriage between the Oberoi hotel chain and Pan American's Inter-Continental Hotel Corporation. A 600-room structure, something like a resort hotel, with a swimming pool and other facilities, adjacent to a golf course. Rooms are fair in size and face either the pool area or the parking section.

Maurya Sheraton. A really impressive hotel, exceptionally well run and with a personality all its own; situated in the lovely diplomatic part of town. The rooms are somewhat small, although the lobby is large and imposing. The restaurants are quite exceptional, and the Maurya has the best hotel food in New Delhi.

Taj Hotel. Located on Mansigh Road, this is a fine hotel with 350 rooms, quite attractively decorated. It is skillfully run by the Taj Group of hotels. There are a fair number of restaurants, ranging from informal to gourmet dining.

Ashok Hotel. Government operated and absolutely enormous, with corridors that seem to go on forever. Not quite so luxurious as the hotels mentioned above, but totally comfortable and pleasant for a stay. The elevator service is often erratic. Excellent Indian restaurant with delightful music on the lower level. Good swimming pool area.

Imperial Hotel. An old hotel, completely remodeled. The rooms are spacious and pleasant. The Imperial has the great advantage of being rather close to the shopping area.

Claridge's, Ambassador, and *Janpath.* All these hotels are one step below those described above, but completely comfortable and suitable for a stay.

Akbar. An excellant small hotel, somewhat removed from the center of shopping and sightseeing. It has a large, imposing lobby and is known for its spectacular dining room, serving fine food and adorned with what appear to be millions of bangles suspended from the ceiling. This is a good hotel, if, for one reason or another, you wish to be close to the airport.

Maiden's. Another Oberoi hotel, located in Old Delhi (the others are in New Delhi). It's a very nice hotel, and has an attractive garden and nice rooms. For those who seek Old Delhi atmosphere, this hotel is known for its fine service.

Delhi doesn't offer much in the way of dining places outside of the hotels, but the hotel food is generally good, so don't worry. Moti Mahal's is a restaurant which specializes in Moghul food (*Mughlai* in the vernacular). *Tandoori* chicken is the great specialty. A *tandoor* is a slow-heat oven, and the barbecued chicken it cooks is reddish in color, tender and mouth-watering. With the chicken, they serve *nan,* a delicious type of soft bread. All of the Embassy set can be seen at Moti Mahal's, eating chicken with their fingers. Moti Mahal's is open from 10 A.M. to 1 A.M., and has lovely Indian music in the evening. During the winter, there's an awning overhead, but you sit outdoors during the summertime. When you go, be sure to order the *tandoori* chicken, some kababs and, if they're in season, the *pomfret,* a small but excellent fish. Speaking of *tandoori* chicken, another place for this is the President Hotel, in Old Delhi, with candlelight and quite an atmosphere. Their homemade breads are absolutely delicious. If you want to be formal, the Mughal Room (at the Oberoi-Inter-Continental) is excellent, and the room is quite attractive. If you want to sample authentic Madras-style vegetarian cooking, try the Woodlands restaurant, at the Lodhi Hotel. The best dish is the *thali,* in which the dinner is served with a series of small dishes, each containing a delicious, differently prepared vegetable.

If you want to combine atmosphere and Indian food, by all means visit the Gufa Restaurant, which is rather interesting. It's been decorated to look like a cave, with carved figures, atmospheric lighting, and waiters in special costumes. The food is strictly Indian, but there's a large variety, including *tandoori* chickens, and everything is attractively served. Not very expensive.

If you like golf, Delhi boasts one of India's best courses, and although it's actually private, guest facilities can generally be arranged and clubs rented on the spot for practically nothing. The going rate for caddies is quite modest. Ask at your hotel, and they can generally arrange permission.

Shopping in Delhi doesn't have Bombay's range, but the jewelry is better, and handicraft in ivory is a local specialty. Brassware is excellent too. If you're not headed for Kashmir (which is slightly cheaper), Delhi is the place to buy their exquisite woolens, or perhaps a lovely carpet. Again, the government emporia are your best places to shop, but if you're in a hurry you need never leave your hotel, for the lobby arcades offer a bit of everything—at elevated prices. In front of the Imperial Hotel, there's an outdoor market featuring carvings and curios at rather low prices. The Nepalese and Tibetan are worth seeing in any event. The government maintains an interesting shop featuring a good selection of handicrafts—it's located close to the Imperial Hotel. Now—how fixed are prices? At the government shop, they're fixed. At hotel shops, prices are pretty stable, except on antiquities. Elsewhere, bargain. When buying from outdoor stalls or the like, bargain *very* firmly.

Enough of generalizations, how about some particular shopping information? I would definitely make my first stop the Central Cottage Industries Emporium (now that's a name!), which is generally shortened to the Cottage Industries. This shop, located on Janpath, is known by every cabdriver. It's run by the government, and the merchandise inside has been controlled as to quality. Of course, there's absolutely no bargaining. You'll find a wide assortment of just about everything made in India, and it may be that your shopping can begin and end here. If not, there are other places to visit. Many of the states that make up India have shops on Irwin Road, fairly close to Connaught Place; it really pays to wander from one state shop to another and see what they have to offer. In the Kashmir store, upstairs, they have a selection of those famous Kashmiri scarfs or shawls, which may be the softest and most delicate fabrics produced anywhere on the globe; prices are not low for merchandise of this quality, I may add.

If you're wondering when you'll see a snake charmer, it's in Delhi. It seems as if almost every street corner of the native quarter has one. Don't be afraid to go too near: most, if not all, of the cobras have been discreetly defanged. At least they haven't lost a tourist yet! Sometimes the local lads will stage a "fight" between a mongoose and a cobra, but the actors rarely take their roles seriously because they know that their master, in order to protect the continuity of his merchandise, won't let the battle proceed to its inevitable conclusion.

If you really want to see the true nature of India, and particularly if you wish to get away from the streamlined atmosphere of luxury hotels, I have a walking trip for you that's really worthwhile. Wear very ordinary clothes—ladies in particular should avoid slacks or shorts—and take a taxi to Dariba Kalan, and ask to be dropped at the Chadni Chowk entrance. You will then be able to walk through the moderately wide street, which encompasses all of the local color you probably visualized when reading the travel folders about India. You'll pass by all manners of shops and crafts—candlemakers, jewelers, silversmiths, slipper merchants, vendors of snacks and goodies, fabrics, and so forth. It's an exciting walk, one of the most interesting of your life, you'll probably think. It takes a little over an hour, and then you'll find yourself at the south gate of Jama Masjid, where you can take another taxi back to your hotel.

Agra

Home of the Taj Mahal, Agra is 125 miles from Delhi by automobile, but it's a great ride and one that can be recommended. Figure the drive will take 4 hours each way, so if you plan to drive, stay overnight. Of course, there is also good plane service. If you want to go by train, there is a special Taj Express, permitting a one-day excursion from Delhi to Agra. The train leaves New Delhi at 7:15 A.M. and reaches Agra at 10:15. The return trip leaves Agra at 7 P.M. and reaches New Delhi at 10:05 P.M. There is one First Class air-conditioned coach, and also a dining car; if you wish, they'll serve you meals at your seat. There is also an air-conditioned bus service leaving Delhi at about 7 A.M., returning at 9 P.M. Better check the times; train schedules often change.

Agra represents another civilization, that of the Moghuls, the Muslim conquerors of northern India who became the great warriors and builders of the 16th, 17th, and 18th centuries. Agra holds two attractions: the Taj itself, and the Fort. Saving the best for the last, you ought to visit the Fort first, catching a tantalizing glimpse of the Taj as its builder, Shahjahan, saw it from his prison cell (more about this later on). Then go to see it at sunrise, sunset, or best of all, by moonlight.

Akbar the Great, founder of the Moghul empire, began the construction of the powerful fortress which stands on a bluff overlooking the Jumna River. His son Jahangir continued it, and *his* son Shahjahan completed it. The outside is in red sandstone, but much of the remaining interior is pear-white marble. Its original purpose was defense, of course, but as the empire became more and more secure, the Fort was gradually transformed into a palace, or set of palaces; for as each ruler died, his son evidently decided his father's home was much too modest for him, and proceeded to

Weather Strip: Agra

	Jan.	Feb.	Mar.	Apr.	May	June	July	Aug.	Sept.	Oct.	Nov.	Dec.
Average daily high	73°	78°	89°	101°	107°	105°	94°	91°	93°	92°	85°	76°
Average daily low	43°	46°	55°	67°	67°	83°	80°	79°	75°	61°	48°	43°
Monthly rainfall	0.5	0.5	0.3	0.2	0.5	2.3	9.1	8.1	4.1	0.8	0.1	0.3
Number of days with 0.1 inches or more	1	1	1	1	1	4	11	10	5	1	1	1

build a more lavish one. Some of the original splendor is still intact. This fort, visualizing it as it must have appeared in Moghul days, makes Buckingham Palace seem like a class-B hotel. In a small town.

But the splendor of the Fort lies much in the mind's eye. Not so Shahjahan's masterpiece of masterpieces, the Taj Mahal. The Taj still stands by the banks of the Jumna in all its original, untouched glory.

The majority of viewers find it staggering. In fact, it almost cannot be oversold, say what you like about it. Part of the reason for the stupefying impression of beauty is the way it's presented: there's a large gate, a sizeable courtyard with a high wall blocking the view, and in the wall a rather small door. You walk through the door, and there at the end of a lovely long lagoon stands the Taj. The effect is overwhelming, even when one of the minarets which flank the tomb is covered with scaffolding, as one always seems to be!

As most people vaguely remember, Shahjahan, Emperor of the Moghuls in the early 17th century, built the Taj Mahal as a tomb for his beloved wife Mumtaz Mahal. Deeply affected by her death in 1630 (she bore him fourteen children, one of whom later proved to be his father's undoing), the emperor summoned the finest of craftsmen from Europe and the Middle East to build a sublime memorial as her final resting place. Nobody is quite sure who the architect was: generally he is thought to have been a Persian named Ustad Isa, but it's probable that Shahjahan himself played an important part in the design and construction, for he was so completely absorbed in the project that he allowed his kingdom to slip from his hands.

After two decades of work carried on at enormous expense, the mausoleum was finished. During that time, Shahjahan—who never thought small—conceived of a twin structure to be built in *black* marble directly across the river from his wife's tomb, to serve as his final resting place. But Shahjahan's son and heir, who obviously did think small, deposed and imprisoned his own father in the Fort, and ultimately buried him beside his mother in the one and only Taj Mahal. (That wasn't a bit nice of his son, was it?) This leaves us with the question: would *two* Taj Mahals, like *two* perfect roses, have been one too many? We shall never know ... fortunately, perhaps.

There is rather little point in describing the Taj. You've seen it too often on calendars or on boxes of chocolates. But no picture can capture the pure beauty of the Taj. No doubt you'll want to have a picture of yourself taken in front of it. As you sit on a marble bench by the lagoon, with the tomb in the background, here's an idle thought for you: since the invention of the daguerreotype, every crowned head, every dignitary—and every tourist—to visit Agra has sat where you are sitting. Except the comparatively few misanthropes who found the Taj disappointing. They belong in the same lost company as the Noel Coward character from *Private Lives* who found China "large" and Japan "small."

Turning to the question of accommodations, you have two excellent, topnotch hotels at which to stay. There's Clark's-Shiraz, which has nice, attractive, air-conditioned rooms, and the food served in the hotel is fair enough. They have a swimming pool; on the top floor of the hotel is the Mogul Restaurant, which usually features classical Indian music and dancing. The very best place, and very luxurious indeed, is the lovely Mughal Sheraton (incidentally, don't be disturbed by the different spellings, for it appears as Mogul, Mughal, and Moghul). It's a garden-style, resort-type hotel, with unexpected nooks and crannies, changes in level, and passageways and balconies. It has 200 good-sized rooms in a low-rise construction and is quite outstanding. The Mugahl has an observation deck from which it's possible to view the Taj Mahal. It's within walking distance of the Taj Mahal, if you don't mind walking 10 minutes in the heat of the day or in the cool of the evening. If you're lucky and are there when the moon is full, you'll see the Taj as it should be seen. A third suitable place to stay is the Holiday Inn Agra, which isn't luxurious, but is completely comfortable. Of course, the Holiday Inn is somewhat out of the main part of town, but still perfectly OK for a stay. The fourth possibility is completely outclassed by the first three hotels; it's the venerable old Laurie's Hotel, which is passable but has somewhat depressingly old plumbing, and the food is nothing less than dreadful. But, I hasten to add, not impossible for an overnight stay, providing you dine at one of the other hotels. Restaurants? None that I can recommend, and I suggest you eat at your hotel unless you're staying at Laurie's.

If time permits, and it usually does (because sufficient time is permitted on either train or airline schedules), hire a car at your hotel, and make the round-trip drive to Fatehpur Sikri. You can swing a fixed-price deal at the hotels for a driver and an air-conditioned car.

An hour's drive from Agra are the remains of India's ghost town, Fatehpur Sikri. It is worth the sidetrip. Less than 400 years ago it was Akbar's capital, the greatest city in his considerable empire. But a scant 14 years after it was completed, the emperor and his court left the city forever, probably because of a water shortage. Taking the hint, everybody else left too, and the great city was soon deserted. Now it stands, crumbling, uninhabited, merely a relic of a remarkable civilization. It's most impressive and you won't want to miss it.

The Agra region is full of ancient cities, temples, and palaces. Eighty miles south of Agra is another great fort at Gwalior, far older than Agra's; and 100 miles farther south, at Khajuraho, stand the remains of 85 1000-year-old temples, with erotic carvings that rival Konarak's (which we mentioned previously). If you have the time, see them. If not, don't worry. If there's one thing India has, it's old temples. There's plane service from New Delhi to and from Khajuraho, which, by the way, is pronounced ka-jure-ah-ho. There are various package tours which include air fare, transportation to and from the airport, sightseeing with a guide, and lunch at one of the two good hotels in the area. The temples at Khajuraho are absolute marvels of three-dimensional sculpture, showing erotic activities involving a wide assortment of people. For example, there are two men and one woman, two women and one man, one with about six women and one man, and so on, endlessly. It is wildly fanciful and shows that many centuries ago sex was as prevalent as it is now, if not more so. As one person said while inspecting the temples and the many ingenious positions assumed by the participants, "Didn't they ever hear about a bed?" A guide once remarked to me, somewhat apologetically, "You must remember that in those days they had no radio or television or movies and had to divert themselves somehow." In any event, after a few hours of examining the erotic three-dimensional sculptures, you'll be happy to head for either of the two excellent hotels. The original hotel, very good by the way, is the Chandela, which is most attractive. The newer hotel is the Jass Oberoi, part of that enormous chain, and it's excellent. Some of the tours stay overnight at either of the hotels, and it's all very pleasant and most comfortable. Should you go at all? It's hard for me to answer, because some people think the ruins are nothing but a bunch of three-dimensional French postcards, and others find them tremendously interesting and artistic. If you can make the time for Khajuraho, fine; if you don't, don't fret. But we were talking about Agra, weren't we? Of course we were, so let's continue:

Jaipur

One hundred and fifty miles west of Agra by road (or 55 minutes from Delhi by air) is Jaipur, capital of the desert state of Rajasthan. Many people like to do the Delhi-Agra-Jaipur triangle by private car rather than air, but much less expensive (less private, too) is the India Tourist Department's air-conditioned bus tour of the golden triangle. There's a good bargain value in the air-conditioned bus service between Delhi and Jaipur, taking 5 hours.

Jaipur is a princely city built of pink stone, and the effect, particu-

Weather Strip: Jaipur

	Jan.	Feb.	Mar.	Apr.	May	June	July	Aug.	Sept.	Oct.	Nov.	Dec.
Average daily high	74°	78°	89°	99°	105°	103°	94°	90°	93°	94°	85°	76°
Average daily low	47°	51°	60°	70°	78°	81°	78°	76°	73°	65°	54°	48°
Monthly rainfall	0.4	0.3	0.3	0.2	0.6	2.2	7.7	8.1	3.2	0.5	0.1	0.3
Number of days with 0.1 inches or more	1	1	1	1	2	4	10	10	5	1	1	1

larly at sunset, is very beautiful. A walled city, it was the home of the Rajputs, a fierce race of warriors who apparently fought with one hand and painted with the other. (No, not at the same time.) They are the creators of the Rajput school of painting: those marvelous miniatures, filled with sloe-eyed maidens in stylized and sometimes seductive poses. Nobody has the skill or patience to paint like this any more, so pick up a Rajput if you want to invest in something that's bound to go up in value.

In Jaipur you'll see several palaces and probably live in one, for the Maharajah converted a former residence, the Rambagh Palace, into a very good luxury hotel. Next best is the Welcomhotel Mansingh, which is conveniently located just off the main road, near the downtown market area. If that's full, there's also (although definitely not in the same class) the Jaimahal Palace, Khetri House, or the Rajasthan State Hotel. All of these three are all right, but not every room is air-conditioned.

Part of the city's charm is its feudal character. It's easy to imagine the mighty maharajah and his horde of devoted (they had no choice —they had to be devoted) slaves. Crocodiles in the palace pool and elephants nibbling the foliage complete the illusion. In fact, if you'd like to ride on one of the brutes (elephants, not crocodiles!) take the 7-mile ride to Amber, the hauntingly named former ruling seat of the state of Rajasthan. The palace stands on a hill beneath a grim fort, and it's up those slopes you can advance on elephant back. Kind of fun.

The people of Jaipur dress in a blaze of color. The men wear turbans, no two alike, and the women stride gracefully in long skirts, tight blouses, stoles, and a vast profusion of silver bangles. Needless to say, everything you see them wearing is on sale in Jaipur, where the dyed textiles are wonderful. So are the enamel work and the elaborately set precious stones. Ivory and filigree are excellent, too, for the Rajasthanis are, by tradition, great craftsmen. The state government has several excellent shops which display (and sell) the locally produced goods. Tourists like to buy the pink wedding turbans of this region because they make up very well as evening dresses—they're so large!

Jaipur is definitely worthwhile, but there's something even better only a short ride away.

Udaipur

Udaipur is India's most neglected wonder, for it is off the beaten path. The majority have never even heard of the place. An hour and a half to the southwest from Jaipur by plane, Udaipur is pure romance, a city built on the shores of a lovely man-made lake. In its sapphire-blue water stands the island palace of Jag Nivas, a gossamer structure which today—by a stroke of genius—has been converted into a luxurious hotel. And what a hotel! It is a former residence of the Maharanah, who alone in India bears this strange title (all of his fellow princes are maharajahs). The Udaipur Lake Palace is straight out of the Arabian Nights; it is actually a series of apartments, exquisitely furnished and decorated with colored-glass, amber, and jade. Fountains sparkle over green gardens, and the view from the terrace is magical. You owe it to yourself to stay here so that you can store up memories to draw from when you're in bed with the grippe, or other depressing times like that. There is also a new modern wing but to capture the sheer romance of the place, stay in the old wing.

There's another most interesting place to stay, for those who enjoy country-like surrounding. It's the Oberoi Shikarbadi, a re-modeled hotel that was once the hunting lodge of the royal family. The hotel is surrounded by many acres of forest filled with wild game and colorful birds. The Shikarbadi has spacious gardens and a swimming pool; it's much like a resort hotel. Obviously, staying at the Shikarbadi is nothing like being at one of the large chain hotels, but it is a marvelous experience and offers a chance to rest for a few days in the middle of an arduous trip. The Laxmi Vilas Palace Hotel (now there's a mouthful!) is rather pleasant, but be sure to get a room with air-conditioning.

The town complements the palace wonderfully. Built against a background of green hills, and fronting on Lake Pichola, it is encir-cled by defensive walls and dominated by the Maharanah's city palace, the largest in Rajasthan. The people are as colorfully dressed as Jaipur's, with an exotic difference: in Udaipur there's the scent of sandalwood coming from the women's *saris*.

The environs of Udaipur might be called India's "Lake District," for everywhere you find artificial lakes (don't forget, Rajasthan is mainly desert). The largest is Lake Dhebar, 32 miles away. It was created by means of a dam 100 feet high and a quarter of a mile across, no mean engineering feat hundreds of years ago. A striking temple to the Hindu goddess Siva stands on its shore. Every lake seems to have its temple, the most renowned at Nathdwara, 25 miles to the north. Dedicated to the god Krishna, it is one of Hinduism's holiest sites. On the way back to Udaipur there's the white-marble temple of Mewar situated at Eklingji, with its black-marble statue of Siva. And Ajmer, 82 miles from Udaipur, is still another city of palaces built on an artificial lake. Ajmer is ancient and holy to the Muslims. It was built by Akbar, founder of the Moghul empire, as a base from which to subdue the Hindu Rajputs (he finally did). The town is filled with marble mosques and temples.

In short, Udaipur is a gem which sparkles in a wonderful setting of lakes, temples, and ancient cities. Use it as a base to explore the country, and keep returning to its marvelous Lake Palace Hotel or, if that's full, to the Lakshmi (Laxmi) Vilas Palace in town. Spend as long as you can in Udaipur, for it's a place to compare with Venice for sheer romanticism as something straight out of Keats, magic casements and all! I don't know why, but you'll feel like reading poetry when in Udaipur.

Kashmir

Like the Taj Mahal, Kashmir lives up to its reputation. No wonder Pakistan wants it so badly! No wonder India swears never to give it up! This is one of the loveliest spots on earth. The Vale of Kashmir is 80 miles long and 25 miles wide, and those are the exact dimensions of the nearest thing to heaven on earth.

Srinagar (pronounced Sri-*nug*-ger) is the capital of Kashmir, and is 1¼ hours from Delhi by airplane. It stands at the head of the Valley, on the Jhelum River beside the sparkling blue of Dal Lake. Snow-covered mountains surround it, all over 20,000 feet high. The meadows are filled with flowers and the air is soft and gently cool. Those Moghuls (again!) planted *chenar* (plane) trees and laid out lovely gardens around the lake with marble terraces and fountains in pleasant profusion. The effect cannot be lost even on the most jaded and sophisticated.

Problems should have no place in such a paradise, but in Srinagar you do have a difficult choice: whether to stay at the splendid Oberoi Palace Hotel, or on a houseboat. It's hard to decide. The hotel, a little outside the town, is truly first-class, with a rolling terrace offering remarkable views. On the other hand, some of the houseboats are positively imperial, with 3 bedrooms, baths, hot and cold running water, electricity, a garden patio, 4 servants including a cook, and 3 sumptuous meals a day . . . all for about $15 a day per person! Personally, and again this is purely personal—I would select the houseboat. You can always stay at a hotel. If you want to reserve one in advance, write to the Director of Tourism, Srina-

Weather Strip: Srinagar

	Jan.	Feb.	Mar.	Apr.	May	June	July	Aug.	Sept.	Oct.	Nov.	Dec.
Average daily high	41°	45°	57°	66°	76°	85°	88°	87°	82°	72°	60°	48°
Average daily low	28°	30°	38°	45°	52°	58°	65°	44°	54°	41°	31°	28°
Monthly rainfall	2.9	2.8	3.6	3.7	2.4	1.4	2.3	2.4	1.5	1.2	0.4	1.3
Number of days with 0.1 inches or more	6	6	7	8	5	3	5	5	3	3	1	3

gar, Kashmir, India; tell him exactly what you have in mind, and he'll take care of reserving your houseboat.

The houseboats are scattered about in an assortment of locations and are permanently moored to land of one sort or another on the opposite side of the lake from the road; they can only be reached by what are really water taxis, called *shikaras*. These are very comfortable long, narrow boats, with one or two paddlers. Each houseboat comes with its own *shikara* and it is yours for the duration of your stay. If you're in the houseboat, the *shikara* will be available at a moment's notice on your side of the lake; if you cross over to the mainland, it will be waiting for you there. It's not necessary to pay separately for each ride, and the cost of the *shikara* is generally included in the price of the houseboat; inquire about this when renting. As you ride from the mainland to your houseboat, small floating sellers of just about anything you can think of will pull alongside and gently offer their merchandise. If you want to see it, that's fine; if you're not in the mood, just tell them politely, and they'll pull away. If you sit on your front porch, very often merchants floating on their boats will approach you. There's certainly no obligation to buy anything.

The food on the houseboats is generally pretty good, and they'll cook as you wish, either European-style or Kashmiri, which is somewhat spicy; or you can have a mixture of the two styles. Although three meals a day, plus tea, are included in the price, you owe it to yourself to have the great Kashmiri feast, called a *wazwan*, consisting of about 36 courses, which is a great experience. Call or visit the Broadway Hotel, and ask what nights they have a *wazwan*. Oh yes, I certainly wouldn't drink the water in Kashmir under any circumstances. Stay with bottled water, tea, coffee or beer.

Srinagar itself is unlike any other town in all of India. Because the winters here are quite extreme, with plenty of snow and ice, the buildings are far more substantial, rising several stories in height. The streets of Srinagar are narrow and winding, lively and noisy, and very exciting for photographers. The shopping is excellent, notably for rugs, shawls and embroideries, which are available all over the area. However, there are almost no shops at which to buy quality merchandise, except at the Kashmir Art Emporium, which has a good selection of all sorts of local specialties. Another good area for shopping, although spread out along a considerable distance, is on the opposite side of the street from the landings where the *shikaras* take their passengers. Most of these shops are located in small buildings some slight distance off the main road. They have far better merchandise than that to be found in what might be called downtown Srinagar.

When you're through shopping, there's lots to keep you busy. If you fish, Kashmiri trout are big and obliging, and you can rent all the tackle you need on the spot. The golf is superb. The hiking's free, and so are the swimming and sunbathing. And just sitting around luxuriously in the sun on your houseboat is the best of all ways to pass the time. The only flaw to a houseboat in Kashmir, insofar as I can see, is that if you sit on deck, the vendors of assorted merchandise, fruits, and flowers on their small boats can become a bit of a nuisance. If you buy anything, your houseboat may become surrounded by what looks like the Fifth Fleet. While on the subject of shopping, may I add that you should not have anything sent from Kashmir. If you see what you want, buy it. However, do not order anything made up for you and then have it shipped by parcel post —years may go by before you see the merchandise. Take it with you, or don't buy it.

If you can tear yourself away from Srinagar, take the short trip to Gulmarg, the "Meadow of Flowers," 40 miles to the west. Cars cannot go all the way, and it's necessary to walk the last half mile or so to the hotels. The walk up is somewhat steep, but certainly not all that difficult, although some people have trouble because of the altitude, which is over 8,000 feet. If you walk slowly, you should have no trouble, unless you have a history of cardiac problems. Even then, you'll be followed by men leading ponies, who will let you ride to the top on their rather undersized beasts; be sure to strike a bargain before getting on. Finally you'll reach the local summit.

From here you can see the whole tremendous sweep of the glorious valley. Nanga Parbat, a 26,000-foot giant of a mountain, looms in the near distance. If you like golf, the town has the world's highest course. The best place to stay is the 24-room Tourist Bungalow. It's quite attractive and has central heating, which is no small matter, because it's often quite chilly in the evenings, even during the summer months. The rates are quite moderate, to say the least, and the food is fair enough. Next best is the Highlands Park Hotel, which might be described as comfortable, although not luxurious. Accommodations are in simple cottage-like building scattered about the grounds.

On the way back to Srinagar, take the brief detour to Lake Wular, Kashmir's largest. Do it at sunset and you'll never forget it. In fact, the entire valley is full of unforgettable sights. An outstanding one is Sonomarg, the "Meadow of Gold," 50 miles from Srinagar. Not far from there is the massive Kolhoi Glacier, with Kashmir's most spectacular views. Everywhere in the Vale there are lakes, streams, fragrant fields, and always the great peaks.

Most Kashmiris are Muslim, and the veil of purdah sometimes hides the women's faces. But the people are friendly and engaging, as well they can afford to be, when they can call this earthly paradise their home.

April and May are wonderful months to visit Kashmir. June, July, and August are not far behind; and some maintain that September is the best of all. Why not remain all summer and see?

From Srinagar, you can make a fascinating trip to an unspoiled and extremely interesting area of India, rarely if ever seen by tourists. Indian Airlines has regular jet service to Ladakh, the capital of Leh, in far northern India, landing at one of the highest airports in the country. The trip is a short one, taking just over a half hour, and is far better than the old way to reach Ladakh, which took 2 days of bouncing in a 4-wheel drive jeep, assuming the road was passable. There are reasonably comfortable, but not luxurious, accommodations in Ladakh, and it has some marvelous temples, ruins, and sights. Not everyone is comfortable in Ladakh, because of the extreme altitude, over 10,000 feet. If you're in normal health, there shouldn't be any problem, but it's not recommended for anyone with a health problem.

Bombay

Bombay, often called the Gateway to India, is somewhat over an hour from Delhi by airplane. A major port on the Arabian Sea,

Weather Strip: Bombay

	Jan.	Feb.	Mar.	Apr.	May	June	July	Aug.	Sept.	Oct.	Nov.	Dec.
Average daily high	83°	83°	86°	89°	91°	89°	85°	85°	85°	89°	89°	87°
Average daily low	67°	67°	72°	76°	80°	79°	77°	76°	76°	76°	73°	69°
Monthly rainfall	0.1	0.1	0.1	0.1	0.7	19.1	24.3	13.4	10.4	2.5	0.5	0.1
Number of days with 0.1 inches or more	0	0	0	0	1	14	21	19	13	3	1	0

Bombay is actually an island, separated from the mainland of India by an unpretentious little creek. Perhaps this explains the feeling of separateness the Bombayite displays toward other Indian cities. He is convinced that his town is more sophisticated, forward-looking, and beautiful than Calcutta and Delhi combined. He has a point there.

Bombay's airport is called Santa Cruz and it's a pretty fair distance from the tourist hotels, say 45 minutes. There's an airport bus to town, but unless you are a masochist, you should take a taxi. It doesn't make any difference about the fact that the taxi is twice as expensive; please listen to me and take the taxi. Close to the airport is the Centaur, a very nice airport hotel; it is run by the Air India Hotel Corporation, and the rooms are quite nice. I would particularly recommend staying here if you have a very early morning flight out of the airport; to make things even better, passengers flying on Air India may check in at a special Air India counter, and that's no small advantage. The Centaur Hotel is circular, has 300 rooms and 4 restaurants; the food is pretty good, too. Fairly close in to the airport, along the coast at Bandra, is the Welcomhotel Searock, which is quite nice, and very convenient.

The long sweep of Bombay's waterfront, backed by hills crowned with high-rise, high-rent apartments, is a bit reminiscent of Rio de Janeiro's Copacabana Beach. And for a good reason. The Portuguese "discovered" both cities. The port isn't quite so busy as Calcutta's, but the city throbs with industry and gives the impression of affluence, even though most of its 4,000,000 people exist at the subsistence level on the inevitable *rupee* a day. You forget this, though, as you stand in the lobby of the Taj Mahal Hotel and watch the sleek Parsees saunter to their business lunch. Somehow, Bombay is smart and wide-awake and doesn't hesitate to admit it. Perhaps it's the cosmopolitanism of a great seaside city, or maybe it's because Bombay has always been the first port of call from Europe.

Or perhaps it's the relationship with royalty. After all, Bombay is a jewel, given as part of her dowry to Charles II of England by the Portuguese Catherine of Braganza in the 17th century. It was the Portuguese who were the first European power to control Bombay, and until recently held the dubious distinction of being the last colonial power in India, until Nehru's army forced them to relinquish Goa, not far north of Bombay.

The city was already a thousand years old when the foreigners arrived. The original inhabitants, the Maratha, may have carved the mighty cave temples of Elephanta, on a nearby island. In any event a civilized and flourishing dynasty existed when the Portuguese appeared, only to be supplanted by the British through Catherine's generosity. Today there are few signs of Portuguese rule, but the British have left their mark with a stone arch, dominating the harbor, which they called the Gateway to India.

Nowadays, Bombay and Maharashtra State are wholly Indian. The city is a melting pot of Maharashtrians, Gujeratis (who have had some very nasty battles about whose language would prevail in the state), Parsees, Goans, and settlers from north and south. You see few Bengalis, however, for they transplant poorly.

Of these, the Parsees are (from the tourist's point of view) the most interesting people, and are not really and truly Indians, but Persians. They migrated a long time ago, but still tend to intermarry and worship Zoroaster, who, long before Christ, was said to have been born of a virgin and died to redeem men's sins. A place you are not permitted to see (thank heaven!) is the Parsee "Tower of Silence," where their dead are laid atop high pillars to be stripped to the bone by vultures. In spite of this alien practice, Parsees are otherwise the most westernized of Indian citizens in their dress, speech, and general air of sophistication. They are also outstanding businessmen, controlling a large share of the commercial activity.

Here's the hotel situation in the proverbial nutshell. To start with, the grand old hotel here is the Taj Mahal Inter-Continental, which has a long record of fine food and service. It occupies a remarkable location on the waterfront, with marvelous views. The hotel is in two parts—the older section dates back about 70 years, but has been extensively remodeled, and the rooms are quite large and attractively decorated. The newer portion has much smaller rooms, but this 22-story building constitutes a connected annex with 300 rooms. The Taj (as everyone calls it) has excellent Indian food.

Then there's the very impressive Oberoi Towers, which also has an excellent waterfront location and marvelous views. The 462 rooms are large and very pleasant on all counts. The lobby is most unusual, and there are many shops and a series of different restaurants throughout the hotel. All in all, Bombay has two truly excellent hotels, and picking at which one to stay is somewhat difficult. Try them both, particularly if you're returning. Rates are moderate by American standards and very reasonable when compared to those in Paris and London. Now, of the other hotels, I would mention the Hotel Nataraj, the Shalimar, and the President. Here you can have a satisfactory room, not deluxe but still passable, if you want a lower priced accommodation. If you feel like relaxing for a day or two before plunging into the tourist whirl again, try the new Sun-n-Sand Hotel at Juhu Beach, 12 miles outside Bombay. It's deluxe, air-conditioned, complete with swimming pool and Arabian Sea. For those who want to have the feeling that they're at an American-operated hotel, there's a Holiday Inn at Juhu Beach which is quite nice on all counts. Juhu Beach is rather nice for people who want to combine a little sightseeing with a little vacation time on the beach, picking up a sunburn, and having a nice rest. It's quite true, of course, that in the middle of any fairly long trip, it's nice to break up the sightseeing with a few days spent relaxing and resting at a resort-type place. The Holiday Inn is 7 stories high and has 140 rooms, pleasantly decorated, although not overly large. The food is just so-so, but there are quite a few places in the Juhu Beach region for dining, if you're in the mood.

If you have an interest in food, be sure to pay a visit to the city's famous Crawford Market, which dates back a century or so. You can wander through the market, which mostly features fruits and vegetables, many of which you won't recognize. There's a spice section, and may I recommend that you buy some whole peppercorns, at bargain prices, for grinding at home.

If you're not adventurous, you'll probably do well dining at your hotel. But try some local restaurants too. Because of sanitary conditions, be careful at which restaurants you eat. The Khyber has an interesting, large selection. Fish dishes are excellent here. For *tan-*

doori (clay oven) dishes, Sher-E-Punjas is recommended. If you really want to have an excellent and traditional Indian-style vegetarian meal (and it is definitely delicious, I assure you) head for Purohit's Restaurant on Vir Nariman Road, in the Churchgate district. My suggestion is to order the thali, which includes an assortment of preparations, skillfully prepared. If you are fond of ice cream, be sure to have at least one fling at the Princess Kulfi House, on Princess Street, which has some of the best ice cream you ever ate; my favorite is the mango, but the pistachio is a close second. All the hotels serve European (in particular, French) food, and it's all right, but nothing like Paris, I can assure you.

Pearl-encrusted evening bags are a Bombay specialty somehow unobtainable anywhere else in India; buy them here, because you may perhaps not see them again on your trip. Textiles are plentiful, a best buy being the Cambay silks bordered in gold. The government's Handloom House (excellent for shopping) and Pearl's Palace (privately owned) are good places to buy those bags. Hotel arcades, particularly that at the Taj Mahal and Oberoi, are crammed with shops. The antique district may be found along Vir Nariman Road.

Bombay is not a "monument" town like Delhi, but you definitely won't want to miss the Elephanta Caves, on an island 6 miles from the city. Not only do you see magnificent carving, but the view of Bombay is marvelous. A leisurely launch takes you across to the tiny island, called Gharapuri. This is an ancient Hindu shrine, created perhaps 1,500 years ago in honor of the god-goddess Siva (pronounced Sheeva). The "caves" aren't really caves at all, but sculptures and carvings in the hollowed rock. Much of the tremendous sweep of Hindu mythology is portrayed in exquisite workmanship. They are not at all lascivious, like the erotic masterpieces at Konarak and Khajuraho, but are pure, stylized and beautiful in concept. Not to be missed, we think.

Bombay has a rather interesting red-light district called Cages. It gets its name from the fact that the women sit behind railings while waiting for patrons. The area extends over Foras Road and also into the Gol Pitha region. Just tell your taxi driver where you want to go, because they know just how to drive through this area. Incidentally, I wouldn't recommend walking through the district, and a slow taxi ride will be more than adventurous. Watch out for eunuchs putting on one of their dances; they're very colorful and it's worth watching. Also, the eunuchs aren't a bit shy about having their pictures taken, so you might remember that. Obviously, the Cages area is far more interesting after 6 P.M. than during the middle of the day.

There is daily boat service, departing from a pier opposite the Taj Mahal Hotel; be sure to check with your hotel about departure times. As a rule, there's always a morning boat except during the monsoon months from June to September, when the entire trip is more or less inadvisable. The reason is simple: chances are you'll get caught in a very heavy rain. When you arrive at the landing, there's a half-mile walk, climbing a kind of stone staircase. On hot days, it's pretty warm, so be sure to wear a hat; if it looks like rain, be prepared to get wet. But all in all, the excursion is worthwhile.

Also outside Bombay, but rather a chore to reach, is the ancient ruin of Cheul, said to be 3,000 years old. It's an archeologist's delight, with various civilizations superimposed and merged together, but there is actually nothing memorable in itself to see. Don't bother, we think. Besides, it's a 3-hour trip each way. Far better to spend your time visiting the Elephanta Caves, and wandering through Bombay, seeing the lovely, long sweep of the Marine Drive, swank Malabar Hill with its mansions, apartment houses, and fine views, the Crawford Market, Bombay's bazaar, the Colaba fish market and village, Chowpatty Beach, where all Bombay seems to congregate on holidays, not to swim, but to meet, talk, argue, harangue, and have a good time.

The Ellora and Ajanta Caves

Let's state a few plain facts: not many tourists visit these caves, because they're rather inaccessible, and doing them means you've had the time and money to see the more obvious attractions *plus* the caves. But this much is true: if you're the least bit interested in art or religion, the type who is impressed by Delphi in Greece, or Luxor in Egypt, you ought to see these caves.

You'll stay in Aurangabad, where the hotel situation is fairly good. Here, you have the Rama-International, which is completely air-conditioned (and that's most important here for much of the year) and has quite nice rooms, plus cocktail lounges, several restaurants, swimming pool, tennis courts, etc. It's surprisingly nice, considering the remoteness of its location. Also first rate is the Aurangabad Hotel, not too large, and very cheerful and pleasant for a stay. The rooms aren't lavishly decorated, but they're perfectly acceptable for an overnight stay.

Aurangabad itself has a rather poor mausoleum built by Aurangzeb, whose father, Shahjahan, used up all the local talent in creating the Taj Mahal. There are caves here too, with ancient Buddhist sculpture, but they're merely a prelude to the great art of Ajanta.

Ellora and Ajanta are in the middle of nowhere, which explains why it took more than 2,000 years to rediscover them, a happy event which took place in the 19th century. It is a 17-mile bus ride from Aurangabad to Ellora, and 66 miles to Ajanta. You simply cannot visit them during the summer, for the roads are impassable. I won't even mention the unbearable heat.

Ellora's caves, 34 in all, were dug from a hill 1,300 years ago, and are almost a thousand years "newer" than Ajanta's. Because of this, the earlier carvings are Buddhist and the later, by far the majority, are Hindu and Jain (an austere offshoot of Hinduism). They were carved out of the naked rock by monks and craftsmen, and some are about three stories high. Images of Lord Buddha dominate the first works, but his serenity is shattered in the later Hindu carvings, where a tremendous pantheon of gods and goddesses is displayed. Kailasa Cave, a vast excavation dedicated to Siva, is great art in stone, too varied and stupendous in concept and execution to be described by mere words. This cave alone could justify the trip to Ellora. Ellora is an emotional experience for most people, but even if you're not interested in art, it may just be impressive for its sheer splendor and size. At the caves, the government has stationed guides who'll take you through the caves, lighting your way with torches. The guide's rates are fixed, and quite reasonable.

The Ajanta Caves are pure Buddhist, and offer not only carvings but wall paintings. Unfortunately the colors have faded and some are badly damaged, but the best preserved can be ranked as masterpieces along with Michelangelo's "Creation" on the ceiling of the Sistine Chapel, and other classic examples of European art.

To describe what you'll see here, and in Ellora, is a little like trying to explain the Louvre. It's enough to say that if you travel so far to see India, you ought not to miss one of her greatest treasures.

It is perfectly possible to see both caves in one hurried, slightly frenzied day, but it would be best to divide the trip into two days. After all, if you've come this far, why knock yourself out with hasty, unsatisfying sightseeing? There are government State Guest Houses not too far from each of the caves where you can have lunch or dinner, remain overnight if you wish, and especially, use the ladies' and gentlemen's rooms. Reservations for the Ellora and Ajanta Guest Houses should be made at the National Tourist Office in Aurangabad.

POINTER:
If you book a flight on Indian Airlines (the domestic carrier) bear in mind that they have very stiff penalties for late cancellations, going all the way up to 50% of the cost of the ticket if the cancellation is made less than 12 hours before departure. Furthermore, you can't plan on getting a ticket at the last moment, because the airline's flights are booked heavily in advance.

Goa

Roughly halfway in flying time between Bombay (250 miles away) and Madras is one of the most interesting of all destinations in India. It's called Goa, and it consists of a considerable number of islands, most connected by bridges; it was Portuguese territory for hundreds of years, ever since 1510. When the Portuguese weren't looking, or were otherwise preoccupied, the Indians took it back in 1962, and now the area is a marvelous combination of Portuguese and Indian cultures, making it just that much more interesting to tourists and visitors. The older part of Goa has a convent and cathedral and is called Old Goa. New Goa—or Panaji—is more or less a suburb of the old city and is filled with rows of shops, small dwellings, and the like. The total territory involved in all of what is generically called Goa is 1404 square miles, and there are 62 miles of coastline. However, statistics are seldom interesting, and I am only quoting them so you'll have an idea of the size of the area involved. The landscape is green and luxuriant, quite tropical in appearance and restful to the eye. Minerals are found here, but most people live by raising rice and various fruit crops.

The main reason for coming here is to stay at one of the resort hotels, which combine the pleasures of sightseeing and the luxuriousness of sitting around a pool or at the water's edge, resting up in the middle of a trip. To begin with, there's the Hotel Fort Aguada (A-gwada), built, as you can tell from the name, alongside the site of an old Portuguese fort. The hotel is very nice, with adequate rooms, all facing the sea. The food is fair enough, but the main problem with this otherwise nice hotel is that it simply doesn't have enough seats in the dining room for all of its guests. As a result, at dinnertime, long waits for a table can sometimes be expected. The management has promised to do something about this situation, but so far, nothing appears to have been accomplished.

The Oberoi Bagmalo Beach resort has a wide range of facilities and is good for a stay of several days, in the middle of a rigorous sightseeing schedule. I should also mention that the Oberoi Bagmalo is only about 10 or 15 minutes from the airport, and this is no small matter, because the Fort Aguada is well over an hour away, involving considerable transfer time in each direction. In Panaji, the chief town, there's an extremely pleasant hotel, the Mandovi, which has excellent food in its second floor restaurant. If you're sightseeing, it makes an excellent lunchtime stop.

The South

Not many tourists visit South India either, and in a way that's a pity, because the South *is* India at its purest. Nobody ever invaded the South, and that is where the Dravidians fled to escape the invading Greeks, the Persians, the Aryans, and the Moghuls. These earliest of India's people still inhabit the South, and thus are a living representation of over 5,000 years of history.

Madras, somewhat over an hour's flying time from Bombay, is the jumping-off place for excursions to Mahabalipuram and Kanchipuram (the place names are inevitably long in South India), the former 37 road miles to the south and the latter 40 miles inland. Mahabalipuram, the "place of the seven pagodas," has huge sculptures based upon the Hindu beliefs as to the origin of the universe, carved out of cliffs on the seashore. A group of cottages, intended for tourists, has been opened in a beach resort set-up by the Tamil Nadu Tourism Development Corporation. The cottages face the sea, have excellent bathing, and are reasonably well decorated, but not air-conditioned. The bedrooms are on a sort of mezzanine, with a lower floor sitting-room arrangement, and a sunbathing terrace. There's a restaurant in the cottage complex which offers an offbeat place to stay for a night or two, not very far from the sightseeing at Mahabalipuram. Kanchipuram, one of India's holy spots, is a city of countless shrines and temples, and ranks with Benaras as a place of pilgrimage. The unquestioned leading hotel of Madras is the Taj Coromandel, which has a good location for most things that interest tourists, particularly sightseeing and shopping. (Incidentally, the hotel has a very good shopping arcade of its own.) By Indian standards, the charges are high. However, the hotel is top-notch and if I may be a trifle patronizing, surprisingly luxurious for Madras,

Weather Strip: Madras

	Jan.	Feb.	Mar.	Apr.	May	June	July	Aug.	Sept.	Oct.	Nov.	Dec.
Average daily high	85°	88°	91°	95°	101°	100°	96°	95°	94°	90°	85°	84°
Average daily low	67°	68°	72°	78°	82°	81°	79°	78°	77°	75°	72°	69°
Monthly rainfall	1.4	0.4	0.3	0.6	1.0	1.9	3.6	4.6	4.7	12.0	14.0	5.5
Number of days with 0.1 inches or more	2	0.7	0.4	0.9	1	4	7	8	7	11	11	5

which never before had a deluxe hotel. There's another good hotel here, the Hotel Chola Sheraton, located near Marina Beach. It's centrally air-conditioned and has good restaurant facilities; the rooms are OK, and there's a swimming pool. Another good possibility is the Holiday Inn which, as does almost all hotels in the chain, offers medium-sized, pleasant rooms at moderate rates, with far from thrilling food. If you can't get into one of these, there's still the Connemara, which is older but has added a new wing; it's perfectly fine for a stay of one or two nights. In general, eat at your hotel unless you want to sample some Madras cooking, quite spicy by the way, on the roof garden restaurant of the Hotel Dasaprakash. Their curries are famous, but hot, hot! About 20 miles to the south of Madras is an exceptionally nice place called Fisherman's Cove. About half the accommodations are in a main building, and the other half in cottages overlooking the sea. In addition, there's a swimming pool and a choice of restaurants; it's an ideal place to make a break in your trip and yet be fairly close to a good deal of local sightseeing.

An hour from Madras by air is Trichinopoly (some call it Tiruchirapalli, but they're just being difficult). It boasts a mighty rock fort. Fifty minutes farther on is Madurai, the cathedral city of India. Here, the Meeakshi Temple with its Hall of a Thousand Pillars is the attraction. A hundred miles south, India ends at Cape Cormorin, where the Bay of Bengal meets the Indian Ocean and the Arabian Sea. One hundred and fifty miles north of the Cape is one of the South's resort hill stations, Kodaikanal, 7,000 feet high, green and verdant the year round. A hundred miles to the northeast, its rival, Ootacamund ("Ooty"), recalls the finest days of the British Raj, for in architecture and landscaping it is more like England than England itself.

Bangalore is beginning to see some American tourists in recent years, and the simple reason is that it now has a first-rate hotel, the Ashoka. As to sightseeing, the local Parliament Building looks just like a wedding cake, and it's sufficient to see it from the outside, because there's nothing of great interest within the structure. You might enjoy taking a look at the Lal Bagh, a rock estimated to be 3 billion years old (not by me, I may add); it seems clear that this is one of the oldest rocks in the world, if that's of any interest to you. Also, visit the Ganesh Temple, sometimes called the Bull Temple; it's not thrilling, but pleasant enough for a visit. For shopping, the Karnataka State Arts and Crafts Emporium, at 23 Mahatma Gandhi Road, is the place to go; the merchandise available is exceptionally good.

While in Bangalore, you may give some thought to hiring a car and driving over to Mysore; it takes about three hours, and just remember there are no toilet facilities en route, so don't drink too much coffee in the morning if you go. It's an interesting drive, and when you get there, the outstanding sight is the famous palace, definitely worth exploring. Mysore has a marvelous place for lunch, the Lalitha Mahal Palace Hotel, on the outskirts of the city; it is a masterpiece of its kind, the sort of "palace hotel" building constructed during the days of the British Raj.

South India is not a place to visit if you're in a hurry. It's too big, too hard to get around. There's no one place to head for, but many —most of them well worth visiting—if you have loads of time. It's an area in which to relax. Some day, after everyone has compared snapshots of the Taj Mahal, South India may become *the* place to go. If you can, why not go now?

Nepal

Sidetrip from New Delhi (Allow an extra 3 days or so.) Nepal is a sovereign country ruled by a proud young king who expects aid from everyone and pays homage to none. Until recently, India was the only gateway to Kathmandu, the Nepalese capital. Now you can also fly in from Dacca, East Pakistan, but few tourists do because (absolutely) Dacca has nothing to offer.

Kathmandu (which also appears frequently as Katmandu) can be reached from either New Delhi or Calcutta; according to the route taken, the flying time varies from a little over an hour up to 2 hours. When you arrive in Kathmandu you'll be absolutely astonished to learn that you must advance your watches by 10 minutes from Indian time—10 minutes! That will give you just a little idea of how different Nepal is from the rest of the world.

Part of Nepal's fascination is its centuries-old inaccessibility. Not until 1950, when the ruling Rana dynasty was overthrown, could a foreigner enter the kingdom without special, Rana-approved permission, which was rarely given. No tourist could, certainly, so that even today you feel one of the first. You will be, too, but only if you hurry—for an American hotel chain is negotiating to build a luxury hotel in Kathmandu, and when that happens Nepal will be very much *on* the beaten track.

Just a few tips about a visit here: don't come during July or August, because the weather is almost impossibly bad, with heavy monsoon rains. Another thing: don't arrange to have your mail sent to Nepal, the mail delivery system isn't all that it should be. The best season for a visit is unquestionably October through March, although April is usually fine, when it's dry and cool. Incidentally, if you come during December and January, bring warm clothes, because they'll surely be needed, although the days are usually sunny and pleasant.

Kathmandu is in a fertile valley ringed by Himalayan foothills (the flight in through the pass, with the peaks *above* the wingtips, is quite an experience). This must be the place James Hilton had in mind when he created Shangri-La. The city is full of colorful pagodas, and lively market places, and palaces. Its inhabitants are the hill-types you see in Darjeeling. They look Tibetan, broad of cheek, slant-eyed and swarthy, and many of them are, for the town is full of traders who plod over high mountain passes with heavy loads on their backs, simply to sell their wares in a market better than Chinese-dominated Lhasa, the Tibetan capital. This region is the home of the Gurkhas, those fierce little warriors who even today are "leased" to the British Army. Note the curved knives at their belts: called *kukris,* they are deadly weapons.

Kathmandu is a rather interesting city, with a few sights, especially the Pasupathinath Temple. Be sure to ask to see the "Living Goddess," a young girl chosen to symbolize the reincarnation of a goddess and worshipped by the populace. When she matures, another young girl is chosen, and the previous one is given a dowry and married off to an eligible young man.

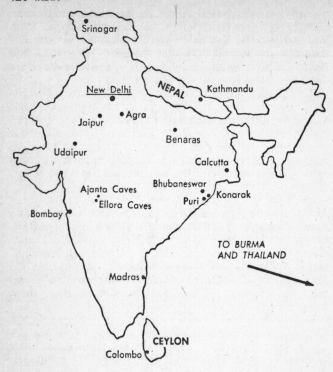

The natural center of town is called Durbar Square; take a taxi there from your hotel and wander about on your own. Durbar Square is an area of temples and palaces, dozens of them, and you should allow about 2 hours for local sightseeing. Walk into as many as possible of them, and you'll be absolutely astonished at the great variety of what can be seen and at how different they are from India. If there is one problem with Kathmandu, it's that young children and beggars tend to cluster about and beg for money. My advice, and very firm advice is: don't give them any, because it merely brings on more beggars and only encourages them to bother the next batch of tourists. From Durbar Square you can see a busy street, narrow and atmospheric, leading away from the Square; walk through this street, and you'll be in the middle of Kathmandu's liveliest part of town. If you have the opportunity, look for what the local people call Freak Street; it's where all the hippies, gathered

Weather Strip: Kathmandu

	Jan.	Feb.	Mar.	Apr.	May	June	July	Aug.	Sept.	Oct.	Nov.	Dec.
Average daily high	65°	67°	77°	83°	86°	85°	84°	83°	83°	80°	74°	67°
Average daily low	35°	39°	45°	53°	61°	67°	68°	68°	66°	56°	45°	37°
Monthly rainfall	0.6	1.6	0.9	2.3	4.8	9.7	14.7	13.6	6.1	1.5	0.3	0.1
Number of days with 0.01 inches or more	1	5	2	6	10	15	21	20	12	4	1	1

from all over the world, assemble; dope is sold casually on the street, even to passers-by.

After you've roamed through the temple area of Kathmandu, take the jeep or Land Rover ride a few miles to Pathan, a small place literally full of temples, some of them covered with the erotic Hindu carvings that typify Konarak (discussed in the Calcutta section). Also worth visiting is Bhatagaon, with some fascinating old buildings, wonderfully decorated temples, and very active market places.

From Kathmandu you have a breathtaking view of the Himalayan range, and if you take the daily airplane flight to Pokhra, you'll be *in* it. There's a modern place to stay, the Fish Tail Lodge, consisting of two circular buildings, in ideal surroundings. This is an unusual and offbeat spot for the tourist who enjoys outdoor life and is self-sufficient. Great for hikers and mountaineers.

The Hotel Soaltee Oberoi is the only 5-star hotel in the country, quite large, modern, with nicely furnished rooms, and medium-high. It's about a mile and a half from the center of town, in an interesting countryish location. They have several restaurants, including one that serves Nepalese food, for those who are gastronomically curious. The next best hotel, and indeed almost precisely as nice, is the four-star Hotel de l'Annapurna, which is air-conditioned and quite luxurious, surprisingly so. It's in town, between the Royal Palace and the Old City. Across the road from the Annapurna is the Yak and Yeti Hotel, which is extremely nice on all counts; however, on foot it can only be reached by a somewhat dusty walk. The Shanker Hotel is first rate, and the same can be said for the Malla Hotel; these both have all that you would expect of a fine hotel anywhere—coffee shop, restaurant, shopping arcade and so forth. Close to the embassy area, opposite the state guest house, is the medium-size Hotel Kathmandu; it has a 4-story atrium in the lobby, which is quite attractive. By all means, have your meals at the hotels and don't try any of the local restaurants; their lack of sanitation is notorious, and you'll be taking a chance if you eat at one of them. Finding Nepalese food (and music) is not easy; my suggestion is to head for the Himalchuli Restaurant in the Soaltee Hotel (which incidentally is pronounced Salty). If you're interested in wild game, there's the Tiger Tops Hotel, in Rapti Valley within a national game reserve, and reached by connecting flight from Kathmandu airport. Rates are quite high, but they include the use of a Land Rover, and boat trips are included in the rates. It's a unique experience, but once again, remember that the charges are quite high.

This may be the only opportunity of your lifetime to view Mount Everest, which is located precisely 97 miles to the east of Kathmandu. You have a choice: a rough 1½ hour ride on a terrible road to Nagarkot, or a much more comfortable ride on a good highway for 70 miles leading directly to the Tibetan border, followed by a half-hour climb on your own two feet. (Incidentally, you might be interested to learn that this road was built by the Chinese, or more precisely with Chinese money.) Actually, the second choice is preferable, all things considered. The excursions start at 5 A.M. so that you can see the dawn, which is spectacular if clear, but the chances are almost 50-50 that you'll see nothing but clouds, loads of them. The weather is best for viewing from October through March, but even then there's no guarantee.

SRI LANKA (CEYLON)

👫 Background

In the Mohammedan religion, it is a tenet of the faith, a basic principle, that the first human beings were Adam and Eve. After being evicted from Paradise, they were allowed to meet once again on earth, that is, Paradise on Earth, or Sri Lanka. Sri Lanka may well be Paradise on Earth, or, in any event, it could be.

This lovely island has had a lively history, and it has always been a crossroads for traders, marauders, adventurers, fortune-hunters, and explorers, probably even before recorded time. The chauvinistic people of Sri Lanka believe that the island was formerly called Lanka, but all of that goes back to a period when fact and mythology were inextricably intertwined; to this day, the word Lanka means a great deal politically, and the ancient name appears frequently in the public print. Buddhism came to Sri Lanka in the 5th century A.D. and had an enormous influence on the lives of the people. Shortly thereafter, Sri Lanka entered into a period of power, with great dynasties of kings, who built important cities and lived on a grand scale. Polonnaruwa, Anuradhapura, and Sigiriya still remain, although in ruins, to show what life must have been like. Sri Lanka's population in those days may have been ten times what it is today, according to historians and researchers. During the 11th century, the Tamils (from India) came to Sri Lanka, and their numbers have been increased over the past centuries by the additional immigration required to work the plantations. The need for Tamil workers is quite simple; the Sinhalese (the majority of Sri Lankans) do not like to work regularly in the fields, whereas the Indians have no such objection. The Sinhalese are not necessarily lazy, but seem to have a different set of values, which attach a high degree of importance to the benefits of leisure. But the Tamils (who are of the Hindu religion) and the Sinhalese (who are Buddhists) do not get along too well with one another, because of the religious problems, because of the difference in character, and also because of the fact that this is Sri Lanka.

At one time the Portuguese and Dutch forcibly took over parts of the island, but they were followed by the British, who colonized more thoroughly, building railroads, setting up enormous tea and rubber plantations, and getting things going in a hot climate, more suitable to a feeling of lethargy and indolence than of work. In 1948, there came independence from Great Britain. Now in office is a very pro-Western government, which seems to be going quite slowly insofar as finding its way in the complex modern world is concerned.

Sri Lanka has ended its old ties with Great Britain, although it remains (at the moment) a member of the British Commonwealth. It has changed its name from Ceylon, but the national tourist office is still called Ceylon Tourist Board.

Sri Lanka, through its Tourist Board, has a home visit program which should not be overlooked. Large numbers of volunteers, mostly residing in the Colombo area, welcome overseas visitors to their homes for a no-cost chance to meet someone like yourself. For example, if you're a professional man, a doctor, dentist, lawyer, architect, businessman, artist, writer, etc., the Tourist Board will arrange for your visit to the home of someone with whom you're almost certain to have something in common. This could be a priceless opportunity to get below the surface and really learn something about Sri Lanka.

When to Go

The weather situation is not consistent all over the island, with the Colombo area (where tourists arrive) getting a great deal of rain from May through much of September. The ideal time for a visit to Sri Lanka is undoubtedly November through April, and this is when the days are lovely, the skies are clear, and the nights are refreshingly cool. If you can't visit the island during that idyllic period, it's best to plan on arriving between July and September when the "second season" comes. It's always warm along the seacoast at any time of the year, but up in the hills during the winter months, it can be mighty chilly at night. How about the so-called second season, from July through September? It rains heavily, but often briefly, and although you may be slightly inconvenienced, it should not really interfere with your trip. Actually, and in all honesty, you could come any time of the year and still enjoy your trip, although naturally, the November–April period is best of all.

Visa Requirements

American citizens need no visa for a 1-month visit. All that is required on entering is proof that you have a paid ticket out of Sri Lanka, or have sufficient money on hand to buy one.

Customs

You can bring in 200 cigarettes or 50 cigars per person, a bottle of wine, but only ½-pint of hard liquor. Cameras and radios are admitted with little delay, although occasionally you may be asked to fill out a form. The tourist may bring in only 40 English pounds, and 75 Indian or Pakistani *rupees,* for Sri Lanka has a theoretically tight control on money. On arriving, declare all traveler's checks, cash, etc., on their Form D, which is stamped by Customs on arrival. All exchanges of money must be entered on Form D during your stay, and then surrendered on departure. Whereupon they probably throw it away.

❡ Health

Be very careful, and don't drink water unless you know it's been boiled and filtered, and of course, milk is always suspect unless boiled. When thirsty, you'll do better with bottled beer, soft drinks, tea or coffee, pineapple juice or the like. Avoid green salads, raw vegetables; however, fruits are safe, if you peel them yourself. Cooked foods are inevitably safe. I wouldn't eat raw shellfish, but there should be no problem if it is cooked. The general health

Weather Strip: Colombo

	Jan.	Feb.	Mar.	Apr.	May	June	July	Aug.	Sept.	Oct.	Nov.	Dec.
Average daily high	86°	87°	88°	88°	87°	85°	85°	85°	85°	85°	85°	85°
Average daily low	72°	72°	74°	76°	78°	77°	77°	77°	77°	75°	73°	72°
Monthly rainfall	3.5	2.7	5.8	9.1	14.6	8.8	5.3	4.3	6.3	13.7	12.4	5.8
Number of days with 0.04 inches or more	7	6	8	14	19	18	12	11	13	19	16	10

situation is satisfactory, and only a smallpox vaccination is required on entry, unless coming from a yellow fever or cholera region.

○ Time

When it's 12 noon in Colombo, it's 1:30 A.M. in New York on the same day. However, in San Francisco, it's 10:30 P.M. on the evening before.

$ Currency

The *rupee* is the local currency. Each rupee has 100 Sri Lankan *cents*. Be sure not to confuse American cents with Ceylonese *cents,* although it's easy to become mixed up; Sri Lankan *cents* are worth much less than American *cents.* There is a black market in the local currency, but it's best avoided.

⊕ Price Level

In general, Sri Lanka is extremely moderate, even low for most tourist expenditures. The only exceptions are the leading hotels, where the charges are moderately high. Meals are moderately priced and, by American standards, are downright bargains outside of Colombo, except at resort hotels. During the period from May to October, many outlying hotels reduce their rates by about 20%.

○ Tipping

At the airport, give the porter who carries your luggage about half a rupee for each bag. The same rule applies at your hotel for porters, except that a limit of 2–3 *rupees* is enough for even 3 or 4 pieces. Inasmuch as the hotels include a 10% service charge (except at the Galle Face Hotel), no additional tips are required, except for special personal services. At the Galle Face, moderate tipping is in order. At the resthouses, no tipping is really required, but a spare *rupee* or two might be given if you are well satisfied with the service. Taxi-drivers can be given, if you wish, the odd change. Sightseeing guides should receive a moderate tip, say 3 or 4 *rupees* for a day's outing.

👟 Transportation

Taxis are all over the place and charge modest rates, all things considered, depending upon the newness, size, etc.; rates somewhat higher late at night. Incidentally, you can tell a taxi by its license plates (red numerals on a white background), because many of them have no other sign. Warning: avoid taxis without meters. Stay off the public *buses,* as they're very overcrowded. Plenty of local *train* service throughout the country, but only First Class can be recommended; rates are reasonable. *Airplane* service, operated by Air Ceylon, is mostly by means of somewhat elderly DC-3's but perhaps some will be replaced soon. Ask about 1-day excursions to some of the principal places of tourist interest, such as Anuradhapura and the like. Actually, the best way to see the country is by *automobile;* roads are good, but a trifle narrow, so don't count on making fast time, but then, who would want to in Sri Lanka? *Self-drive* cars are available for quite reasonable rates. If you read the signs, you can go anywhere in the country and never get lost. If driving on the left bothers you—it probably won't after a half-hour—get a chauffeur for a few dollars a day extra. If you go on a trip around the country, the chauffeur makes his own arrangements about sleeping accommodations, and you're not expected to pay for them. All in all, you might really be better off if you hired a driver to take you on a trip because he'll know all of the more interesting places to see and the best places for lunch, etc.

✊ Airport and Tourist Taxes

Katunyake Airport involves a long ride from Colombo, being about 23 miles away; allow not less than an hour's travel time because it's not a fast ride except during off-hours. Arrive at the airport no less than 1 hour before departure time to allow for the usual formalities. There's an airport departure tax of about $3.50.

▌▌ Communications

An *airmail* letter to the U.S. takes about 7–8 days. The *telephone* service is just passable, and it's quite difficult to get a phone call through to the U.S., although perhaps you'll be lucky. *Cable* rates to the U.S. are high, but fast and reliable; there are special lower rates for delayed messages.

⚡ Electricity

All of Sri Lanka has 230-volt 50-cycle A.C., which is unsuitable for American appliances. Don't try your electric shaver, and have it burn out—ask at the desk first! Sometimes they have a transformer.

✗ Food Specialties and Liquor

Much of the Sinhalese cuisine closely follows that of India, with emphasis upon curried foods, usually well-flavored, but often rather highly seasoned. Not all of the local dishes are necessarily spicy, but a good many are. Since the choice, for most tourists, is eating imitation British food, a little understanding of Sinhalese food is definitely worth the effort. British food is dull enough to begin with, but the native imitations of English dishes are usually very poor indeed. Horrible, in fact.

Needless to say (so we'll say it), rice is the mainstay. Rice appears at almost every meal, and why we said "almost" is hard to understand; it appears at *every* Sinhalese meal. Curried dishes are made of just about every conceivable ingredient, but especially seafood, poultry, meat, and vegetables. (Even egg and lentil curries are prepared.) These are often made with coconut milk or *ghee* (clarified butter), and scores of other ingredients, but especially hot chili peppers. Some dishes, like chicken curry, are the kind that any but the fainthearted would enjoy at once. At the other extreme are curries made of dried fish and garlic that would repel Richard the Lion-Hearted. Inasmuch as almost every meal features a choice of many dishes, the tourist might do well to take a little of each dish offered, make a simple taste test, and then call for a larger quantity of the dishes that appeal to him. With every meal, there is inevitably a selection of *sambols* and *chutneys,* which are relishes or pickles and go well with curried dishes. *Sambols* are made from onions, cucumbers, fish, shrimp, coconut, and even from the lovely red shocflowers. *Chutneys* are prepared from fruits, such as apricots, dates, tamarinds, but particularly from mangos, the best of all.

If you get to Kandy (and you should), look for some specialties of that region. Ask for *kos ambul,* a curry made with jak-fruit; an omelet from katurumurunga flowers; or perhaps a *potato badun,* that is if you like potatoes with a little garlic. The Tamils, an important segment of the population, have their own specialties; you might well be tempted by a white curry made with lamb, *kuruma iraichchi;* perhaps a *mulligatawny,* a really delicious chicken curry made with coconut milk (but ask them to go easy on the garlic and ginger); or perhaps a *prawn vadai,* made with prawns and onions.

The Sinhalese are mad for sweet dishes, and there is almost no end to their variety. First of all, there are *appas* (popularly called Hoppers), which might roughly be described as a baked coconut-flavored thin pancake. Then there are *seenakku, pasong, pittu, konda kavum, wandu appa* ... but surely you get the idea.

After a spicy meal, may I suggest having some of the local fresh fruits, which are plentiful, delicious, and sometimes even luscious. They cool the palate, and prevent waking up in the middle of the night with an overpowering thirst.

There is plenty of imported liquor around, particularly scotch; in fact, much of Sri Lanka's upper crust is so snobbish that they drink expensive imported liquor and eat horrible imitation British food in preference to their own. Sinhalese beer is excellent, by the way, and goes very well with the local food. The favorite drink of the people is *arrak,* made from coconut flowers, and it's strong. In fact, very.

∞ Time Evaluation

Sri Lanka is not on the regular tourist route, being somewhat south of the regular route for round-the-world travelers, who usually go through from New Delhi to Bangkok, or vice versa. Anyone who does get to Sri Lanka, and has to go out of his way to get here, should certainly not spend only a day or two, and then take off. Allow an absolute minimum of 5 days, or why spend all that time and plane fare? Naturally, cruise ships will make their scheduled stops, and the passengers will have to be satisfied with whatever time is allotted, but that is hardly the way to see Sri Lanka. Although you can see the touristic highlights in a day or so, that's not necessarily the point with this lovely island. It's the mood that counts, and you'll never be able to capture it by tearing around the island, sightseeing at a breakneck pace, and then racing back to board the ship. If time permits, a 2-week visit would be lovely, particularly if you can come during the winter months when the weather is almost ideal.

🏛 Capital City: Colombo

With about 700,000 inhabitants, Colombo is not a tremendous city and is not very impressive physically. The buildings are mostly Victorian, never a very impressive or memorable style of architecture under the best of circumstances, and this is not the best. There are no skyscrapers, and the majority of buildings are only a few stories high; in the suburbs, the private homes are pleasant, with lovely lawns and lush plantings. Looking in the opposite direction, towards the sea, the view is ravishingly beautiful.

There are quite a few interesting sights to see in Colombo, although in strict truth, there are no specific monuments, buildings, or sightseeing attractions that cry out to be visited. Without a doubt, the most important sightseeing will be done on foot, walking through the lively, bustling, commercial heart of town, the fort region (centered about Prince, York, and Chatham Streets), which has some good shops, from the tourist's point of view. It's all somewhat British, but colonial British, and quite diverting. Next, head for the noisy, frenetic, vibrating, exciting, steaming, teeming (all right, we all get the idea) *pettah,* the bazaar section of Colombo. Don't buy a thing at the *pettah* without doing a little (I mean considerable) bargaining, or you'll overpay. It's fascinating and loads of fun, even if you don't really need anything, for who can resist getting into the excitement of trading?

Scattered about the city are the mosques of the Moslems, and the Buddhist and Hindu temples, and the various religious markers and monuments, but none of them is actually important or outstanding, although worth visiting, if you're in the mood. On the other hand, if you don't visit any of them, you won't be missing a great deal. I don't think, however, that anyone who likes animals and birds would want to miss the unusual Dehiwela Zoo, and especially the elephant show given in the late afternoon, shortly after 5 P.M., say 5:15. The Cinnamon Gardens district of Colombo is the best residential neighborhood, filled with lovely, gracious houses on wide, green avenues—all denoting a way of life once pictured by Somerset Maugham which is now disappearing swiftly all over the world, but remnants still remain in Colombo. But for how long?

Beyond that, the charm of Colombo lies in its street scenes—the life of the city inherent in its people, colorfully dressed, slight of build and quite slim. The women are dressed in *saris,* plain or colorful according to their means or the particular occasion. The men wear western dress if they wish, but the majority still cling to the long white cheesecloth *verti,* a most distinctive costume indeed.

ACCOMMODATIONS   Until recently, there wasn't a single new skyscraper type of hotel to be found in the entire country, which may or may not have been a good thing. Now things are changing, but not very swiftly, so there's no cause for alarm for those who yearn for the good old days. The Inter-Continental and Lanka Oberoi hotels are modern and luxurious; however, if you long for the days of Somerset Maugham, you'll find hotels loaded with atmosphere and featuring old fashioned plumbing which doesn't always work too well. The Galle Face, Mount Lavinia, and Taprobane are all old world to one degree or another, although they are all trying valiantly to meet the new competition. Outside of Colombo, the "resthouses" are generally the best places to stay in Sri Lanka, in order to combine the maximum amount of atmosphere with a reasonable degree of comfort. I might make a comparison between the Sinhalese resthouse and the Japanese inn, called the *ryokan.* However, in Sri Lanka, you'll sleep on a bed, rather than on the floor. Some resthouses are fairly old, some are quite new, but although rarely luxurious, they are inevitably comfortable and friendly. And certainly very inexpensive.

Lanka Oberoi.   Sri Lanka's best and most elaborate hotel, located about ten minutes from downtown Colombo. The lobby is absolutely spectacular, being open and airy with hanging banners. Rooms are of very good size, well-decorated. Centrally air-conditioned. Several excellent restaurants.

Inter-Continental.   An excellent place to stay, just at the edge of Colombo. Marvelous location, facing the waterfront. Rooms are cheerful and of rather good size. Centrally air-conditioned.

Holiday Inn.   A 10-story hotel located in the Galle Face area. Centrally air-conditioned, with pleasant, medium-sized rooms. The hotel's restaurant features Sri Lankan food, plus western dishes.

Pegasus Reef.   A somewhat smaller hotel located about 7 miles from Colombo. Occupies a large area with a long beach; swimming pool. This 3-story hotel is quite attractive, but guests are required to dine at their hotel; rates include meals. Rooms are air-conditioned and have balconies.

Galle Face—The Regent of Colombo.   This is an old Colombo hotel (and to get it over with, the name is pronounced Gawl-fayze). A rather large, completely remodeled British-style hotel facing the sea. Rooms are good-sized and comfortable; there is a swimming pool. The location is good, although about a mile from the center of town. Rates are not too high and include so-so meals. The Galle Face has a sedate, sober, proper atmosphere; food rather routine, often dull, for western dishes; the occasional Sinhalese dishes which appear are much better.

Mount Lavinia Hotel. Located in a beautiful spot some 7 miles south of Colombo, on the sea, with its own beach, surrounded by gardens, palm trees, etc. Mount Lavinia is really a resort, but it's very suitable for tourists, as taxis into town are cheap and plentiful. About the same price, or slightly less, than the Galle Face.

Taprobane. Central location in the downtown section of Colombo, very handy for business and shopping. Rather small, with remodeled rooms and a rather good restaurant.

RESTAURANTS   The western-style food in Colombo is disappointing as a rule. Nothing like a steak or lamb chops or roast beef can be found; even though it may appear on the menu, it's inevitably poor. The Sinhalese food is quite good, if you like the curried flavor. If not, try the Chinese food which is really very good. The hotel food at the Galle Face and Mount Lavinia leans towards western dishes, unimaginatively prepared, but if you don't want any surprises, by all means stay with the hotels. When traveling through the island, eat at the resthouses, and be careful to avoid local "restaurants," which are very chancy. For offbeat Colombo dining, try:

Chinese Dragon. Unpretentious, but with an interesting Chinese menu; all in all, pretty good food. Inexpensive.

Modern Chinese Cafe. Very good Chinese dishes, especially if you call them before coming and ask for a special dinner. Not expensive.

Green Cabin Cafe. This is about the best place in town for sampling the Sinhalese cuisine, short of a visit to someone's home. Lots of curries and other local specialties. Inexpensive.

SHOPPING   Disappointingly, the shopping here is not too good. Of course, there are many things to buy, but values are not outstanding, nor is the workmanship all that good. *Fabrics,* although attractive, are usually made in India; if you're going to have some time in India for shopping, chances are you could do better there. *Inlaid brass* and *silver work* are quite good, but these are heavy and not suitable for air travelers; when bought, better arrange for shipment by sea. You'll find *lace* made in Kalutara is attractive, if you like lace. The *lacquerware* made in Sri Lanka is outstanding, and does represent a good value, although the colors are somewhat lively.

The big shopping specialty of Sri Lanka is undoubtedly its *gem stones:* topazes, sapphires, rubies, moonstones, amethysts, and many more. Your best place for fixed prices is the government-controlled main shop, on York Street; here you can rely on the quality of the merchandise you select. They have a very large selection, and you can pay almost anything that your budget permits. Incidentally, yellow sapphires (as well as those in various other shades including white and pink) have become increasingly popular; as you can see, sapphires come in colors other than the usual blue. In addition to the principal shop, there are branch shops at the Inter-Continental and Lanka Oberoi hotels, but the selection is somewhat smaller than that at the main, downtown, government shop.

For small items, don't fail to wander through the bazaar, the *pettah.* Here you'll find attractive, inexpensive items that make very good, though low priced, presents for the family back home.

Remember—bargain, bargain, bargain. Except in the best shops in the Fort area, be prepared to spend a few minutes of cheerful haggling to get the right price.

ENTERTAINMENT   The Inter-Continental Hotel has a night-club, which is quite pleasant. The Lanka Oberoi has several rooms where there is music and entertainment. At the Galle Face Hotel, there is the Mascarilla, a sort of *nightclub;* the Little Hut is a similar type of dignified spot at the Mount Lavinia Hotel. The Tropicana is at Horton Place, and is not too bad for a visit when you feel like going someplace after dinner. Otherwise, a quiet after-dinner drink, or a little time spent gazing thoughtfully at the moonlit waters, is about all there is to do in Colombo after dark. Once out of Colombo, there's even less to do after dinner. (How can there be less than nothing?)

SPORTS   The Sinhalese (and the British residents) are mad for *horse racing,* but racing events are scheduled at odd times, so follow the local announcements in the newspapers. Lots of *tennis* (anyone?), on courts at the various hotels, almost wherever you go. There is a good *golf* course near town, the Royal Colombo; the best one in the country, however, is at Nuwara Eliyah, and it may be one of the best in Asia, if not the most beautiful. This is a great region for *hunting,* permitted from November through April; write for details to the Warden, Dept. of Wild Life, Colombo. Marvelous *bathing* on the wonderful beaches which ring all of Sri Lanka. *Deep-sea fishing* can often be superb, although it's likely to be poor during the rainy months. *Freshwater fishing* is fairly good, but inclined to be best at Horton Plains, an hour from Nuwara Eliyah.

SHORT TRIPS FROM COLOMBO   About the best short automobile excursion out of town is to *Kelaniya* and *Negombo,* a run of only about an hour. First, head for Kelaniya, only 6 miles north of town; the Raja Maha Vihara (a temple) is famous for its murals, and also for a well-executed figure of Buddha. Then on to Negombo, a colorful fishing port about 15 miles farther along. The small harbor is quaint (please forgive us for using that overworked word), and while there is nothing particularly exciting to see or do, it's all very pleasant. You might want to visit the old Dutch fort, a reminder of the days when Holland controlled part of the island. Negombo has two fine small hotels, Brown's Beach and the Blue Lagoon. Brown's Beach is located on a lagoon, ideal for swimming. At the Blue Lagoon, accommodations are mostly in cottage and cabana. Both hotels are fine if you want to enjoy some resort life and don't mind being away from Colombo.

If you can spare an entire day, and I urge you to do so, the outstanding trip is surely a visit to *Kandy,* the medieval city of Sri Lanka. If you possibly can, stay overnight. Although Kandy has two large hotels, they are both old and somewhat uncomfortable, though not impossibly so for overnight; they are the Suisse and Queens hotels. The Topaz is a new hotel, not deluxe, but first class, with a fairly nice atmosphere. But I'd much rather you stay overnight at one of the tiny guest houses in the area, such as the Castle Hill, the Graylands, or the Sunray Inn. There's also a good medium-sized place, with about 23 rooms, called The Chalet. Any of these places are preferable to the Suisse and Queens, but if you're part of a large group, obviously they have to put up the group at one of the two large hotels. The Frangipani Hotel has nice rooms, too; in any event, may I suggest you have one meal there, if at all possible. Another interesting small hotel is the Dehigama, which is quite nice for a stay.

It's only 72 miles from Colombo to Kandy and the easiest ways to go are by private auto or by the Sri Lanka Rail Tours. If you go by train, the morning air-conditioned train leaves at 8:50 A.M. and returns in the late afternoon. Be sure to sit on the right-hand side of the train for the best views. Once in Kandy, the great attraction is the Temple of the Tooth, said to have an authentic tooth of Buddha, who originated the religion. The Temple itself is not too prepossessing, but it's worth visiting to see how the prayers are conducted and learn something about Buddhism. (If you're very lucky, you'll be here in late July or early August, when the annual Perahera, a giant and colorful procession, takes place.) In the general area, there are numerous other temples, all worth visiting if time permits.

Even more interesting than the Temple of the Tooth to many visitors is the opportunity to see elephants taking baths and performing on the river at Katugastota. It's customary to tip the trainers of the elephants the equivalent of about 50¢ in rupees if you ask them to pose or do tricks. The shopping situation is fairly good here if you want articles that are typically Sri Lankan. The shops are located in a number of small, unimpressive buildings in the general area of the Queens Hotel; you can buy articles made of brass, copper, silver, wood carvings, etc. Of particular interest are articles made of lacquerware produced in Ukkuwella, just a few miles from Kandy. Before you leave the Kandy area, by all means visit their world-famous Botanic Gardens at Peradeniya. It's very pleasant to drive through the park area slowly (it has about 150 acres) and see examples of Asiatic trees and shrubs. However, the orchid collection is the highpoint, and it is nothing short of breathtaking.

Another good trip is a 38-mile journey southward to the Bentota Beach Hotel, 3 stories high and very attractive. It's built around a decorative inner pool, on the site of an old Dutch fortress. The hotel's granite base follows the outlines of the old fort, if that interests you. However, it's a great spot for an excursion (don't forget your bathing suit), and you can have lunch at the hotel. Across the river lagoon from the main part of Bentota is the Ceysands Hotel. It's a low-rise affair, with guaranteed privacy, because the only way to reach the hotel is by boat. Of course, the Ceysands Hotel is on the water, and although getting to and from by boat may be a novelty, it might become tiresome for those who plan to use it as a base of operations and go sightseeing every day. On the other hand, it's very nice if you intend to stay put most of the time. Roughly 2 miles from Bentota, at Beruwela, there's the Neptune Hotel which has some pleasant beachside rooms, most of them (not all) are air-conditioned.

In the opposite direction, and on another day, there is a slightly more ambitious all-day excursion to *Hikkaduwa,* about 60 miles (2 hours of driving) in each direction over good roads. This is going to be an important resort spot some day, because Hikkaduwa has everything—not to mention a new hotel and beach resort called the Coral Gardens, with an excellent view. The region around here has been proclaimed an ocean sanctuary because of the amazing undersea life and fabulous coral formations, much of which can be seen in glass-bottom boats. If you wish to, you can remain overnight at the resthouse, or merely have lunch and return to Colombo later in the afternoon. Be sure to see the Sinhalese fishermen who stand on stiltlike arrangements; really fascinating, and just the sort of thing on which to use up a roll (or three) of color film. I'm not at all sure that I can recommend the accommodations at Hikkaduwa, because they certainly could be improved.

A Tour of Sri Lanka

If you can manage about a week or so in Sri Lanka, there's a very rewarding week of sightseeing to be had, in comfort and at very low cost. All in all, it can be a most delightful week which you'll thoroughly enjoy. As a 5-day outline (which can take a week —by remaining an additional day or so at places that please you), here is a suggested route:

FIRST DAY

Drive from Colombo along the west coast through Negombo, Chilaw, Puttalam, and then cut inland to Anuradhapura; the total run involves about 130 miles. Stay at the very good Anuradhapura Resthouse. At one time, it is believed that Anuradhapura had 3,-000,000 inhabitants, and in any event it must have been a great city. Anuradhapura (if only there were an abbreviation!) is the greatest of the lost cities of Sri Lanka, and may have reached its height of power and importance about the 1st century A.D. You'll see the *pokunas,* the stone baths, used for religious bathing. There are many *dagobas,* the Sinhalese term equivalent to "pagodas" in other Southeast Asian countries; it is said that the word *dagoba* is actually a corruption or variation upon the word pagoda. Of great importance to the Sinhalese is the Sacred Bo Tree, thought to have been planted more than 2,000 years ago. The region covers about 14 square miles of ruins, and all in all, it's a very impressive region, well worth a complete day's sightseeing. It's worth more, if you like antiquities and ruins.

SECOND DAY

Drive from Anuradhapura to Mihintale and Polonnaruwa, a trip of about 85 miles. Probably the best place to stay here is the air-conditioned Seruwa Hotel, situated beautifully on a lake; it also has a swimming pool. The accommodations are really pretty good, all around. Up the hill is the Giritale Hotel, which is rather nice, and it's a pleasant place to stay overnight. The traditional and picturesque place to stay is the Polonnaruwa Resthouse, which was the only place to stay in years gone by. The Resthouse is old, but rather friendly and informal. Although most people claim that Anuradhapura is the more important ruin (and of course, it is older and larger), I personally like the Polonnaruwa region somewhat more. The city was at its height of importance during the 10th and 11th centuries, and it is most impressive even today. The outstanding single building here is the Lankatilaka, with its enormous statue, unfortunately headless, of Buddha. But this is only the beginning, for there is a Lotus Bath; the Gal Vihare, a shrine with three Buddhas; and especially the classic Milk Dagoba, so called because of its whitish color.

THIRD DAY

Drive from Polonnaruwa to Sigiriya, a matter of 45 miles. After about an hour's drive from Polonnaruwa, you'll see a hotel called The Village, set up as bungalows, and really quite attractive. There's no air-conditioning, but the rooms are cooled by fans. If you're not staying at The Village, the trip from here to Sigiriya is only about 20 minutes' driving time. At our destination, there's a choice of the Hotel Sigiriya, which is just fine, or the older and most picturesque Sigiriya Resthouse. This is an incredible place, a stone fortress, very romantic, and completely unbelievable. There are the ruins of a palace atop an enormous rock, complete with baths, terraces, and famous murals. There is something vaguely sinister, however, about Sigiriya, and the natives think the place haunted, and often avoid it. It should be pointed out that Sigiriya hardly belongs in the same class of ruined cities as do the two preceding ones, yet it nevertheless is definitely worth a half-day's sightseeing.

FOURTH DAY

Drive from Sigiriya to Kandy, a run of 55 miles. If you're lucky, you might manage to get into one of the four rooms at the Castle Hill Hotel; it's absolutely delightful, although expensive by local standards. In the alternative, you could remain overnight at the Chalet Guest House, almost as good. If you don't mind staying out of the Kandy area, perhaps your best bet might be the very modern Hunas Falls Hotel, located 17 miles from Kandy. On a 3,000-foot mountain, the Hunas Falls has marvelous views, and its own lake for swimming and boating; it's an ideal place to stay. The town of Kandy is famous for its Botanical Gardens, which are magnificent and should not be missed even if your only crop each year at home is crabgrass. As a rule, there are elephants wandering about in the vicinity of Kandy, at the lake, or along the roads; this is always diverting to watch. The outstanding tourist attraction here is the famous Temple of the Tooth; it gets its name because it is said to have a tooth from Buddha; there are great festivities here lasting for 10 days during July and August, varying each year.

FIFTH DAY

Drive from Kandy to Nuwara Eliya, a run of about 50 miles. You can stay overnight here at either the government Resthouse Ella, with lovely views of the countryside, or at the ancient Grand Hotel, which is not known for its good food, to say the least. This hill station has an altitude of about 3,600 feet and is quite cool, which may be just what you want during a hot spell. Nuwara Eliya (pronounced Nur-eh-lia) is a resort town, with golfing, fishing, etc. If you're not in the mood to remain, continue on to Colombo, a distance of 132 miles.

Of course, the above schedule is merely bare bones, and allows for very little sightseeing at the three great ruins of Anuradhapura, Polonnaruwa and Sigiriya. If any of these places excites your imagination, the probabilities are that you'll want to remain over for an extra day or two. While the trip covers only 5 days, it can easily take twice that time if you become fascinated with Sri Lanka's magnificent ruined cities.

Trips to the Seychelle Islands

The Seychelle Islands, in the middle of the Indian Ocean, more or less between Nairobi and Bombay, are among the most fascinating places in the world. British Airways has direct service from Colombo to these lovely, unspoiled islands, and you're strongly urged to include them on a round-the-world trip. The islands (there are about 98 of them) are lush and delightful, and there's a great deal to see and do. The best hotels on the principal island, Mahé, are the Coral Strand, The Reef, and especially Fisherman's Cove. There are fabulous islands with bird refuges, places where you'll have the beach completely to yourself, and Praslin, the island where the coco-de-mer, the world's largest coconut, grows. While there, tours can be arranged through Lindblad Travel Services Ltd., which has its own fleet of boats. When will you ever again have a chance to visit the Seychelles? Don't pass up this opportunity.

SINGAPORE AND MALAYSIA

👫 Background

At one time British, a new nation called Malaya came peaceably into existence in 1957; it changed its name to Malaysia in 1963. Singapore, nowadays, is completely independent of Malaysia, and has its own government and money. They are combined in this section purely for convenience, since the two countries are adjacent and most tourists arrive at Singapore and then continue on to Malaysia. Malaysia consists of what were formerly the separate entities of Malaya, Sarawak, and Sabah (which was formerly called North Borneo).

Before going any further, perhaps a few words about Malaysia's past history might be in order, because otherwise the complications of the 20th century might be difficult to follow. Malaya (as it was then called) had, and still has, a commanding situation in Southeast Asia, as can be seen from a map. No one knows where or when the Malays came into existence as a race, but they probably originated on the central Asian continent, and moved into the region several thousand years ago. The land was extremely rich in natural resources, and about the year 1500 the Chinese also began to drift southward into Malaya, trying to find a new home away from their own overpopulated and hungry country. Then came the Europeans, seeking new lands and wealth, chiefly in the form of the mines and rubber plantations. The Portuguese and Dutch took control at various times, and starting in 1824 the British took over, under the command of Sir Thomas Raffles, a name you'll frequently see while in Singapore.

Then came World War II, and the invasion of Malaya by the Japanese, who confounded the British naval authorities in Singapore by having the audacity to attack by land, instead of by sea, when all the defenses of the city were trained to repel invaders from the sea! Dashed unsporting! After all, every British expert had said that the "impenetrable" jungle would prevent an overland invasion and any attack would have to come from the sea. (Perhaps the Japanese army never read the report.) With the end of the war, the bid for independence began, and the new nation was soon off to a flying start. Indonesia, another merger of territories to the south, has opposed Malaysia and relations between the two new nations are often touchy (or sticky), but otherwise Malaysia seems to be making a go of it.

Now, with the background material out of the way, the peculiarly complex, diversified population of Malaysia can be understood. At present, it is estimated that it consists of 45% Malayans, and about 36% Chinese; the balance consists of Indians, various regional tribes, and Europeans. From the Malay point of view, the disastrous fact is that the Chinese are engaged in a population explosion, and are likely to outnumber them in a matter of ten years or so, and end up by controlling the vote. A new development, which may perhaps alter the picture, is now taking place in Singapore. The local government has been deeply concerned about the loyalty of the majority of Singapore Chinese residents to their homeland, now communist China. (The point often made is that the Chinese are loyal to China, regardless of its form of government, even though it is now communistic.) Until recently, the school curriculum had been taught in English, Malay, Chinese, and Tamil (an Indian dialect). The local government has been pressing for the use of English in schools, as a method of lessening China's political hold and influence among the Chinese residents of Singapore. A great measure of success appears in the offing, for 55% of the children are now taking their regular courses in English, an indication that the Singapore Chinese do not wish their children taught in Chinese, and therefore a step forward has been made in promoting a feeling of Malaysian identity among the Chinese.

Consider this remarkable small country called Singapore. It consists of a rather small island and one very large city; it does not have fisheries, timber, mines, or other natural resources found in almost all other countries. It has one important resource and that consists solely of its resourceful people. With a total population in the general neighborhood of 2 million people, about half of them are engaged in retail trade. Thus, this country manages to stay afloat financially in a difficult world of trade and commerce by selling goods—to themselves and to foreign visitors.

The basic language of the country is Malay, but this is a country of linguists. English is also spoken and understood almost everywhere (not surprising after more than a century of British rule), plus Chinese and Tamil (Indian). This does not mean that every single plantation worker in Sarawak speaks unaccented English, but it does mean that the tourist will have little or no trouble in making himself understood wherever he goes.

Singapore itself is an exceptionally interesting city, but the countryside of Malaysia cries out for a visit if you're at all interested in seeing a lush, inviting tropical region. The roads are very good, the people are extremely pleasant, tourists are very welcome, so what more could anyone want?

Malaysia has a problem, a very big problem. Its population is a combination of Malays and Chinese, and the two parts don't mix too well. It's something like oil and water; no matter how the mixture is shaken, the two parts separate afterward. The government is controlled by Malays, and they have put into effect a controversial program called the New Economic Policy, sometimes called the Bumiputra Program. Bumiputra is Malay for "sons of the soil." The Chinese say that the Bumiputra policy is simply a means for reconstructing Malaysian life in favor of the Malays. The Chinese account for 38 percent of the population and the Malays 48 percent. (The balance is made up of other small groups.) The Chinese are particularly annoyed at what they call discrimination in education, and education is almost sacred to the Chinese. They claim that enrollment in the country's five universities is heavily stacked in favor of the Malays.

The material which follows applies more or less equally to both Singapore and Malaysia. Sightseeing information about Malaysia appears at the end of the chapter.

🍃 When to Go

The temperature varies but little all through the year, with an *average* of 80° at its coolest, and 82° at its warmest, so the average of averages is very average indeed. During the day, the thermometer usually goes up to 90° or so (from noon to 4 P.M.) and during the night it may drop into the low 70's, but there it is—warm, mostly humid, and very tropical in feeling. The city of Singapore is situated only 80 miles north of the equator, and there are no seasons as we know them. This is one spot that can be visited all year round without worrying about the weather, and that is a rather startling fact, as any traveler will admit. It rains every second or third day, but as a rule, the rains come in heavy, brief and sudden showers, get it over with, and leave the remainder of the day clear. There is no distinct rainy period as such, nor is there a dry period. Because of the generally warm weather, only light, tropical clothes need be worn. During the day, informal clothes are the rule—conservative sport shirts and slacks for men, a cool cotton dress for women; at night, however, men wear a jacket and tie to restaurants or in hotels. Women might take a very light wrap for evening wear, because a cool, damp breeze is usually blowing outdoors, and many restaurants are overly air-conditioned.

Weather Strip: Singapore

	Jan.	Feb.	Mar.	Apr.	May	June	July	Aug.	Sept.	Oct.	Nov.	Dec.
Average daily high	86°	88°	88°	88°	89°	88°	88°	87°	87°	87°	87°	87°
Average daily low	73°	73°	75°	75°	75°	75°	75°	75°	75°	74°	74°	74°
Monthly rainfall	9.9	6.8	7.6	7.4	6.8	6.8	6.7	7.7	7.0	8.2	10.0	10.1
Number of days with 0.01 inches or more	17	11	14	15	15	13	13	14	14	16	18	19

 # Visa Requirements

You'll need your passport of course, but no visa is required for a visit of up to 3 months.

 # Customs

When you arrive, you're allowed to bring in 200 cigarettes (that's a carton) or 50 cigars (a large box); 1 bottle of liquor per person also permitted, but this is hardly of interest to the tourist, because if there's anything Singapore has, it's liquor. Might bring bourbon or rye, if you wish, because those are sometimes in short supply. The currency regulations permit you to bring in 500 dollars in Malaysian currency, but why bother? Malaysian money is sound, and there could be no possible advantage in bringing in local currency purchased abroad, except for a little small change for tips and transportation to your hotel. (Not that U.S. money isn't completely acceptable most of the time.) Theoretically, but only theoretically in my experience, you may be asked to record your cameras, binoculars, etc., on a form—but usually this requirement is skipped.

Health

If you're coming from a cholera or yellow fever area (meaning parts of Africa or India), an international certificate covering inoculations against both is required. The tap water is safe to drink in the leading Singapore hotels and better restaurants; once out of Singapore or other large cities, better stick to bottled soft drinks, beer, coffee or tea. Milk may be pasteurized, or it may not; usually safe in Singapore, however, at the leading hotels. Otherwise, nothing to worry about in the way of special precautions, except perhaps to avoid green salads in rural areas.

⏱ Time

This is going to be a little complicated, because Malaysia is 15 ½ hours *later* than Pacific Standard Time in the U.S. For example, when it's 12 noon on Saturday in Singapore, it's 8:30 P.M. Friday on the west coast of the U.S., 11:30 P.M. Friday on the east coast. If you're planning to telephone home, just remember the difference of time and date, or you'll find your family sleeping, or out for a Sunday drive.

💲 Currency

The local money is the Malaysian *dollar*. Singapore also has its own currency. There are 100 *cents* to the Malaysian dollar.

🌐 Price Level

Hotel rates here, once moderate, are now fairly high, and you'll probably pay as much for your room as in Tokyo or Hong Kong. Outside of your hotel bill, most other expenses are not too great, for taxis are cheap, and shopping is a great bargain, perhaps second only to Hong Kong. On second thought, although both Singapore and Malaysia are moderately priced, you might well end up spending more than you thought, because it's difficult to resist all of the bargains available.

🍎 Tipping

Here we find a quandary. The local residents are trying to discourage the American habit of tipping, except for baggage porters. However, even the local people are beginning to tip a little. Of course, in a luxury hotel, the waiter might well receive a tip, but in no event more than 10% of the check; in local Chinese restaurants, perhaps somewhat less. For carrying your luggage, tip the equivalent of 20¢ U.S. for each bag, or perhaps 50¢ U.S. for three suitcases. Most hotels do not tack on a service charge, so a few Malaysian dollars might be spread around at departure time if your room service has been exceptionally good.

☀ Transportation

Taxis are easily obtained in Singapore and Kuala Lumpur, and are quite reasonable. The *trishaw,* a touristic carry-over, is disappearing at a swift pace, and the equivalent of 25¢ or 30¢ U.S. is plenty for a brief ride.

Trains are operated by the Malayan Railways and are excellent —air-conditioned, private compartments, dining cars, etc. Prices are low, but as is the case with trains all over the world, you won't see much. The run from Singapore to Kuala Lumpur is quite slow. The best way of all to see the country is by auto, if time permits. *Cars* may be hired with driver, or self-drive if you wish, at fair prices. Drive-yourself cars have moderate daily rents, but gas is extra. You'll need an International Driving License, however; it can be obtained here if you bring your regular state driver's license. A drive-yourself car can be highly recommended because the local roads are excellent, well-marked, and there are good accommodations scattered about the countryside. A trip from Singapore to Kuala Lumpur is a pleasure and can be made in one day, then a day's sightseeing at K.L., and another day back to Singapore. You won't regret it.

If you want to fly in Malaysia, Malaysia-Singapore Airlines has good, frequent service to various parts of the country, but especially to Kuala Lumpur and Malacca. It's possible to leave Singapore early in the morning, sightsee in Kuala Lumpur or Malacca, and return in the evening. It's a very worthwhile but slightly tiring one-day excursion.

✊ Airport and Tourist Taxes

Changi International Airport is connected to Singapore by a 4-lane highway. Another, older airport, Paya Lebar, is chiefly used for shorter flights. Although bus service is provided from the airport to the city's chief hotels, by all means take a taxi because rates are comparatively inexpensive, and you'll avoid waiting for the bus to load. On departure from Singapore, you'll have to pay a departure tax, currently about $3.

Passengers arrive and depart from KL's Subang International Airport. The departure tax is roughly $3.50 U.S.

▮▮ Communications

A *phone* call back to the United States is not inexpensive, costing $14 U.S. However, be sure that you're calling at a reasonable hour back home, because of the great time differential. As previously mentioned, a call made at noon in Singapore will reach your party at 8:30 P.M. on the U.S. west coast, and 11:30 P.M. in New York, both the evening before. *Cables* are fairly high-priced, a 10-word message costing about $3.25, but there are a few types of delayed service which allow for many more words. Be sure to use airmail paper so that the envelope and letter do not weigh more than ½ ounce; allow not less than 5–6 days for the letter to arrive at its destination in the U.S.

⚡ Electricity

Hold it! Before using any electrical appliance, best make sure of the local current. As a rule, the Malaysian current varies from 230–250 volts A.C. and is absolutely no good for electric razors and the like. The newer hotels have special outlets marked "For Electric Shavers Only," but if not, be sure to ask if they can lend you an adaptor. Those small "immersion heaters" which boil water will probably not work, unless you've bought the so-called international type.

Public Holidays

SINGAPORE: New Year's (January 1), Hari Raga Haji, Chinese New Year, Good Friday, Labor Day (May 1), Vesak Day (May 17), National Day (August 9), Deepavali, Hari Raya Pussa, Christmas Day (December 25).

MALAYSIA: Hari Raya Haji, Chinese New Year, Good Friday, Wesak Day, Birthday of Supreme Head of State, Malaysia Day (August 31), Christmas Day (December 25).

✗ Food Specialties and Liquor

Western-style food in Singapore is fairly good, but seldom distinguished. It is rare indeed to have anything exciting, or for that matter very satisfying, except in a few leading restaurants. Good steaks are almost never seen, although passable roast beef is not an impossibility. The British, as we all know, may have some remarkable talents and traits, but good cookery is not among them. The British are not a nation of chefs, and the British public is so conditioned and apathetic that the poorest, almost inedible food causes no comment. If you wish to eat European food while in Singapore, do the best you can by eating at the hotel restaurants. As for me, I always have at least one Chinese meal a day, because it can always be relied upon.

In Malaysia, the local cuisine is far, far removed from the British cookery style. Never, in Malaysia, does one encounter a plain boiled, broiled, or roasted meat dish. Foods are rarely served whole, but are cut up into pieces, well-flavored with spices and served with boiled rice, as a rule. What we call curried foods are the standard, classic manner of preparing food in Malaysia. Almost every meat, poultry, fish, or vegetable dish has a curried taste. Incidentally, this may be a good time to clear up the confusion about the term "curry" itself. In Malaysian usage, there is no such thing as a curry powder. Every housewife buys the various flavoring ingredients which she grinds and combines, to her individual discretion, to flavor dishes. There is no single spice called curry, for the term actually denotes a combination of various spices used in cookery. A mixture of spices and flavoring ingredients suitable for making a curry might include black pepper, coriander, star anise, mustard seeds, cardamom, dried chilis, turmeric, cumin, and many others. Malaysian food is quite good, once the palate has become accustomed to the somewhat unorthodox use of spices. Many foreigners take to it immediately; others require a few sessions. You owe it to yourself, in the interests of keeping an open mind, to try at least one Malayan meal. Begin, perhaps with chicken soup, *boerboe ayam,* which is hardly exotic. If you enjoy fish, don't miss *otak otak,* fillets of fish baked with coconut and coconut milk in parchment papers—it's absolutely delicious. *Moolie,* another fish dish, made with cashew nuts and onions is also very worthwhile. Singapore is famous for its lobster curry, although perhaps it might be advisable to specify one that is not too spicy. The shrimp in Malaysia is superb, and *laksa,* shrimp with thin noodles, is one of my favorites.

There are dozens of chicken preparations; I should not want to miss trying *opor,* a sort of chicken fricassee, and *rendan santan,* a coconut-flavored chicken dish. I'm not so sure about the local duck, which has a stronger flavor than we're used to: if you don't think it will bother you, try *pangang golek,* a rather interesting way of roasting duck. The meat curries are always good, and you could hardly go wrong. *Satay,* of course, is an enormous favorite in Malaysia; it consists of squares or cubes of meat broiled on skewers and usually served with a spicy peanut or almond sauce. Satay is so popular that it's almost difficult to avoid. A local novelty is the "steamboat," which is occasionally available, if you ask. The steamboat consists of a buffet table filled with an assortment of food (meat, poultry, fish, etc.) which the diner himself cooks in hot broth, and then eats with boiled rice, hot sauces, and condiments.

In Singapore, a *stengah* is a half-drink of scotch whisky; if you've read the stories of Somerset Maugham about Malaysia you may have thought it was a large drink. It isn't, for it contains only about ½-ounce of liquor, and is served with soda at room temperature in the British style. In the tourist hotels, however, ice is not regarded as sacrilegious. It was in Singapore that the famous "gin sling" was invented. It is a rather good cool drink, made with cherry brandy, gin, a twist of lemon peel, and club soda. (Sometimes a little Benedictine is added.)

The Malaysians do not like alcoholic drinks, and seldom bother with them. However, the beer is very good indeed and is excellent with spicy foods; Anchor and Tiger are about the most popular brands. An interesting novelty is *samsu,* a beer prepared from rice. Malaysia is a tea-drinking country, but the local coffee is very good.

∞ Time Evaluation

On the fastest of all trips, surely two days in Singapore would be a minimum. On this limited amount of time, you would have a chance to see the island, and also to drive over to Johore Bahru and see a tiny bit of Malaysia. If your schedule permitted, 3 or 4 days would be much better, and you would enjoy it. If you can spare a week, by all means plan to fly (or drive) up to Kuala Lumpur or Malacca.

Singapore

This famous crossroads of the world is a lively, exciting city, loaded with natural color, having over 2,000,000 people living and bumping into one another on one corner of an island measuring 27 miles long and 14 miles wide. The Chinese are the majority group here, constituting four-fifths of the population, many of whom still have strong ties with their homeland. Peculiarly, however, the city's flavor is not basically Chinese, nor is it British (although you might think so in certain parts of town), and it most certainly does not have a Malaysian atmosphere.

Centuries ago, the Malays called it Tumasik, meaning Sea Town; then it was renamed Singa Pura, meaning Lion City. When Thomas Stamford Raffles set foot here in 1819, it was just a swampy, malarial island with a few hundred fishermen as its only inhabitants. Raffles came to set up a trading center for the ambitious British East India Company, and was he successful! (Everyone should have bought stock in that company, a better deal than buying I.B.M. at $10 a share.) Raffles wouldn't recognize the place now, for it's grown enormously—into a modern free port (which he visualized) and the center of all ship traffic in the Orient (which he also anticipated). He may be gone now, but Raffles is not forgotten and there are statues, parks, places and what-have-you with his name attached. Whenever the city fathers are in doubt about a school or a park, they name it after him.

The first thing you'll notice about Singapore is that the traffic keeps to the left, which supplies a certain superficial British atmosphere, but this feeling is soon dissipated by the mixed Malay-Chinese-Indian mood of the city. Our friend Raffles went to considerable trouble (and profit) to see that Singapore became a great commercial center, and that's what it is today—all of which adds up to the simple fact that it has few touristic attractions, as such. But hastily, however, I want to add that this doesn't mean that Singapore isn't fascinating to see, it's merely that no one of the various monuments or specific sights is that important. There are loads of conducted tours, usually of the half-day variety, which take you around to see the local sights. I would recommend them as offering good value; a 3-hour bus tour is moderately priced and hits all of Singapore's highspots, such as they are. (I would not, however, take a 7-day bus tour covering the entire country under any circumstances; too long, and not enough break from the monotony of riding in a bus.) It's really the people, sounds, and the general atmosphere that make Singapore so interesting.

The center of town is called (guess what?) Raffles Place, the heart of Singapore. This is the British part, and it does look a good deal like London. Raffles Place is not bad for walking around, because there are several good department stores, handy for shopping, but more about that later. Running from Raffles Place toward the waterfront, look for Change Alley, the most interesting single street in Singapore, and to me, one of the very few real sightseeing attractions of the Lion City. Change Alley is full of lively trade, and is more illustrative of the local way of life than hours of sightseeing from a tourist bus. You can buy hundreds of things you may or may not need, and in any event, it's loads of good clean fun. Change Alley is hard to explain, for one tourist can walk through and not buy a thing, whereas another will take an hour and end up with arms full of bargains and have to take a taxi to his hotel. For heaven's sake, don't pay the first price asked for *anything;* offer about half of the asking price, then settle for two-thirds. If you're still bargain-hunting, look for the Arcade, after you leave Change Alley; it faces the waterfront. The Arcade sells literally everything, and it's also amusing to wander through, in its own special way.

At the far end of Change Alley is Collyer Quay, and pointing a finger into the harbor is Clifford Pier. Walk out onto the pier and you'll see Singapore Harbor (pardon, Harbour, in the British fashion) at its liveliest. Perhaps of all of Singapore, the heavily trafficked harbor is the most exciting place of all. You'll see small sampans, the tiny boats which wander about the harbor. Want to do something off the beaten path? Hire a sampan at Clifford Pier, and make an hour's circuit of the harbor. The cost should be rather modest —in fact, a bargain. Those with outboard motors may be slightly more expensive, so agree on the price before you go. For tourists who prefer a larger, standardized sightseeing boat, there are regular tours of the harbor from Clifford Pier (but usually only on weekends) which are inexpensive and worthwhile. As a rule, your hotel will have a notice posted, or you can ask at the desk when the harbor cruises operate. One trip goes to Balakan and Pulau Brani, rural islands, and probably worth a visit if you have extra time.

For those who love temples and mosques, there are a few that warrant a visit. Close to the Raffles Hotel is the famous Sultan Mosque, the center for Mohammedans; you can hear the morning and evening calls to prayer. If you plan to go inside, you *may* (not always) be asked to remove your shoes and stockings, hold your feet under running water, and then enter. (Ninety per cent of the time, you can enter by merely washing your hands and removing your shoes.) Another interesting sight is the Sakya Muni Gaya Temple, located on Race Course Road, which houses a 50-foot Buddha said to weigh over 300 tons. (But don't look at me, I always take someone's word about anything that weighs over 300 tons.) The best marble and wood carvings of all, however, may be found in the Sian Lim Sian Si Temple, located on Kim Keat Road, which is also Buddhist.

Roughly 5 minutes by taxi (about 1 mile) from downtown Singapore is Chinatown, liveliest after 4 P.M. or preferably in the evening. The best starting point for a Chinatown walking tour is around New Bridge and Tanjong Pagar Roads. Of course, why this region is called Chinatown, when in fact the entire city is 80% Chinese is difficult to understand; it's just that the Chinese local color reaches its peak here. The district is overcrowded, stimulating, busy, has wash hanging from the windows, people sitting outdoors, food being eaten from food stalls (don't be tempted, no matter how delicious, and save your appetite for the government-licensed stalls located along the river between Raffles Place and Collyer Quay), lots of noise, the clanging of cymbals, the reverberations of gongs, music coming from radios, and even from local theaters. Over all, there is the skin-tingling excitement of being in a very foreign place, the smell of joss sticks from a local temple, and also the ever present odor of cooking. You can wander about freely, and no one will bother you, nor will you be made to feel unwelcome, but do use a bit of common sense. Dress simply, and don't point out (in a loud clear voice) the fact that your way of life is different from theirs, nor that their living standards are lower than ours. There are theatres featuring Chinese opera, and it's an excellent opportunity to wander into one and spend a half-hour bemused by the costumes, high-pitched voices, and odd music. The cost is quite low, and even if you only spend a little while in the theatre, it's all part of your education. While here, if it suits your temperament and personality, you could visit Sago Lane, a rather small street which has a Chinese House of Death; sick old people come here to die, on the theory that those who are about to leave this world wish peace and quiet and an opportunity to reminisce with their contemporaries, and thus spare their families the pain and anguish of the last few weeks of life. While on this morbid subject, you may perhaps encounter a Chinese funeral on the local streets. Instead of a sad occasion, the Chinese regard funerals as a party or celebration, with lots of lively brass-band music. Behind the cortege are the official mourners, usually paid for the occasion, and they can be identified by their bare feet.

It isn't often that a guidebook recommends a funeral as a sightseeing attraction, but this is an exception.

Most tourists head back to their hotels in the late afternoon, for a little rest, a bath, and then dinner. However, they often miss some of the authentic excitement of a visit to the night market—*pasar malam*. These informal markets get started at about 6 P.M. and continue on until midnight or later, and each different market has its own personality. Small merchants, with their wares on pushcarts, fill up the streets, offering a wide selection of goods for office workers and others who cannot find the time to shop during working hours at regular stores. You'll find clothing and food, of course, but also leather, brass, perfume, stamps, woodcarvings, kitchen equipment, jewelry—in fact, anything and everything. The most famous night market of all is held on Wednesday evening on tree-lined Tanglin Road not far from most hotels. There are other markets in different locations every night of the week; check these out at your hotel desk. Rather similar to the *pasar malam* is the Thieves' Market, which is open during the day as well as at night. It's located alongside the Rochore Canal (which doesn't exactly smell like Chanel #5). Don't believe everything the vendors tell you, but there are occasional bargains to be found here, including some excellent values in antiques. But be cautious!

The impressive Singapore Botanical Gardens are very pleasant indeed for a visit, particularly if you like orchids, which grow here in profusion. Buy some peanuts when you enter, and feed the monkeys who wander about freely, and frequently pull at visitors, asking for nuts. The collection of plants, shrubs, and flowers will delight any home gardener, but the problem in Singapore is only that of cutting away excess foliage, for *everything* grows here. To anyone who has nursed a temperamental philodendron through a steam-heated winter, the sight of similar leaves measuring two feet across is always somewhat disturbing.

If you have any interest in orchids and tropical gardening, take a taxi out to the Mandai Orchid Gardens. They're located on Mandai Lake Road, and the trip takes about 20 to 25 minutes, but it's truly worthwhile. There is a moderate admission charge, but inside you'll find literally millions of orchids growing amid lovely surroundings. The Gardens extend from a valley all the way up the hillside nearby, and the experience is exciting, particularly if you enjoy gardening.

Just outside of town is Haw Par Villa, also called Tiger Balm Garden. (If you're going to make a trip to Johore Bahru, to be discussed later under Short Trips from Singapore, this can be seen en route.) The Villa itself is pure nonsense, consisting of fanciful plaster figures, mostly of mythological characters, brilliantly colored, absolutely and utterly ridiculous. It was created (if that is the word) by a Chinese millionaire, Aw Boon Haw, who made a fortune in patent medicines. If you saw the gardens of the same name in Hong Kong, don't bother about this one. Inside the house, however, is a truly priceless collection of jade; also there is a fine selection of other forms of Chinese art, particularly scroll paintings.

I don't care what anyone says, that just about concludes the sightseeing attractions of Singapore. Anyone who wishes to vist the Assembly House, Fort Canning Hill, City Hall, the Supreme Court, or Victoria Theatre has my permission to go—just so long as I don't have to. Is there anything else to do, say, on a quiet Sunday? Of course, don't overlook a day's outing to Johore Bahru, which is discussed later. Well, there is a pleasant drive which heads eastward out of downtown Singapore along Mountbatten Road. The road passes through a good residential area, Dunman Estate, and then into East Coast Road, which faces the sea. It's all very pleasant and attractive, and you can see the *kelongs,* the fish trap fastened to poles; the poles direct the fish towards the trap, then at night a lamp attracts the fish into the net. Finally, one reaches Changi Point, which has a good bathing beach; boats can be rented here, if you're in the mood. Although the trip can be made by taxi, there is frequent service to Changi Beach by bus for a few cents. The buses may be crowded on weekends, but ordinarily it's not bad at all. En route to the beach, sit on the right-hand side, and returning, take the left-hand side, for best views of the water.

If you like birds, there's the Jurong Bird Park, which is an exceptionally interesting place to see tropical birds of Asia under the most ideal conditions. In an area of about 50 acres, and for a modest admission charge, you can view birds in a fashion not duplicated elsewhere in the world. There are walk-in aviaries, waterfalls, lagoons, and you will be astonished at the clever fashion in which the birds are displayed. It's most unusual and very worthwhile—but you have to be interested in tropical birds as a starting point.

Also in Jurong Park is Seiwaen, a Japanese garden, probably the largest garden of its type outside of Japan, covering 32 acres. Many of the gardens follow designs originally executed between the 14th and 16th centuries when, experts believe, Japanese gardening reached its heights. There are ponds, waterfalls, islands, traditional bridges, stone lanterns, and, of course, lovely plantings.

In Old Chinatown there's an absolutely enormous shopping area located in the People's Park Complex. It's a fascinating place to visit, with more than 350 different shops in one high-rise structure. The selection of merchandise is overwhelming and fascinating, and there is a great deal of excitement and local color. It's really an old-fashioned bazaar in modern surroundings.

ACCOMMODATIONS For some reason, Singapore has far too many hotels, and most of the year rooms are readily available. There are several categories: the most luxurious have high daily rates; the moderate hotels have a range of rates; and there is a group that is very reasonably priced. It's still advisable to have a reservation, although the chances of not finding a hotel room is not very likely at the moment. Many hotels are located on Orchard Road, constituting a sort of "Hotel Row."

THE LEADING HOTELS:

Shangri-La. Most people think this is Singapore's leading hotel, and they're probably right. Located in its own 12 acres of private grounds, it has much of the atmosphere of a resort in a big city. Attractive rooms (520), each with a balcony; lovely gardens, numerous restaurants and shops. Large, gracious lobby and plenty of elevators. The Chinese restaurant is surely one of the best in Singapore.

Mandarin Singapore. This 1200-room hotel on Orchard Road is perhaps the most elaborate in town. The lobby and all public areas are nothing short of theatrical in decor and effect. Rooms are exceptional, and every bathroom has twin basins, bidet. More restaurants than any other hotel in Singapore.

Singapore Hilton. Also on Orchard Road, this is surely one of the city's leading hotels. It is, perhaps, more American than the two hotels listed above. Nice rooms, convenient location.

MORE MODERATELY PRICED:

Goodwood Park. An older but well-maintained suburban hotel with spacious gardens and grounds, making it ideal for a longer stay. The older wing is adequate, but the rooms are nicer in the new wing of the hotel. Sunday lunch here is a Singapore tradition; the hotel has a British atmosphere.

Hyatt Singapore. An absolutely enormous hotel, with 900 rooms 21 stories tall, just off Orchard Road. Rooms are fairly nice, and each has a refrigerator. Several restaurants. Criticism: a comparatively small staff, which often causes slow room service.

Oberoi Imperial. Converted from a former apartment house; the 600 guest rooms are satisfactory although the ceilings are too low.

Although in central Singapore, it is actually isolated from tourist interests such as shops, restaurants, amusements, by a 15-minute taxi ride.

Dynasty Hotel. A 30-story tower building, also on Orchard Road. It has a spectacular 3-story lobby, several restaurants, and quite a few shops. Rooms are quite pleasant, and double-glazed for soundproofing to reduce street noise.

Ming Court. Also on Orchard Road, this hotel has 350 rooms, which make it pleasant for tourists not willing to pay top rates. Each room is fair-sized and has its own balcony. Several undistinguished restaurants.

Marco Polo. Excellent location at the beginning of Orchard Road, a main shopping area. Three hundred rooms, nicely decorated, with pleasant views of the surrounding area. Several restaurants, shops, etc.

SOMEWHAT DIFFERENT:

Raffles. There had been rumors that Raffles, the most famous hotel in Singapore, was closing. It's still here, and retains some (not all) of its once glamorous atmosphere. Most rooms are cooled by air-conditioners, many quite noisy. Faded, remodeled elegance is the standard here, but if you dream of the days of Somerset Maugham, this is it. The suites are exceptionally nice.

Summit. A very small hotel, with only 61 accommodations, all suites. Even so, the rates are lower than for ordinary rooms at the luxury hotels. Located about 5 minutes from Orchard Road, in a quiet, isolated setting. Ideal for longer stays.

ECONOMY ACCOMMODATIONS:

Singapura Forum. A surprisingly nice hotel considering its modest rates. Rooms (195) aren't large, but are completely adequate. On Orchard Road, and very convenient to almost everything. Swimming pool, shops, restaurants.

Equatorial. Somewhat away from the main hotel area. It has 225 rooms, passable but not great. Lobby isn't well-decorated, but the staff seems friendly and willing. Large selection of restaurants, many quite good.

RESTAURANTS   All of the hotels listed above serve good western-style "hotel" food, which may be praise indeed (or not) depending upon the particular person. There are many people who are delighted with familiar items on a hotel menu, and nothing makes them happier on a trip than the opportunity of ordering chicken soup, roast beef, and baked potatoes, and ice cream for dessert, even though they're in Singapore. Many others can't wait to try the local restaurants, and wouldn't consider having any meal but breakfast at their hotel. It would seem that part of traveling, part of having an open mind, and part of your sightseeing would consist of dining out, and seeing what the world eats. *Hotels* generally have several restaurants serving cuisines of different nationalities. In Singapore, the Chinese food is superb, and the Malayan food is quite interesting, and both are definitely worth sampling. If you're tempted to eat from some of the outdoor stalls, be sure they have signs indicating that they are approved by the government as to sanitation. Tourists interested in sampling the local cuisine in Singapore style should head for the Rasa Singapura Food Centre, located next to the Handicraft Centre. All under one roof, this outdoor dining area has been selected by the local authorities as the best place of all and a Singapore tasting committee recommended Rasa Singapura as outstanding. You can wander along the stalls and see the specialties of particular places, such as oyster omelets, roast pork, Hokkien noodles, Indian pancakes, curries, and so forth. Diners select a table (shielded from the sunshine by umbrellas during the daytime) and wait for the orders to be brought to the table. Payment is made when the food is brought to the table. It's lot of fun, and besides, you'll try dishes you never saw before, much less knew about. The complex is open daily from midmorning to 11 P.M.. It's worth a visit, and the sanitation has been watched by local authorities.

WESTERN FOOD: The hotels all serve Western food. *Prince's:* European specialties are featured here, and fairly well prepared. Pleasant surroundings, and worth a visit. Just a little short of being fairly expensive.

CHINESE FOOD:

Peking. An elaborate place, with dancing; also an outdoor dining room. The specialties are those from north China, and if you can manage to go with a party of about six people, it will be a most interesting experience. Moderate.

Chew Kee. A very authentic Cantonese restaurant in the center of Chinatown. Atmospheric, interesting, and moderate-priced.

Capitol Chinese Restaurant. Entered through the Capitol Theatre, this Szechuan-style restaurant features spicy dishes. Be sure to try the Szechuan Chicken, and the roast sucking-pig (not suckling, in Singapore). Moderate in price; dancing.

Tai Seng. A real novelty, a Teochew restaurant, with a menu listing dishes rarely seen outside of China. I think their Rolled Duck is an extraordinarily good dish; this restaurant also features fish dishes, almost all of which are exceptional.

Wyman's Haven. Nine miles from town is this pleasant spot; featuring Chinese cuisine, served on a terrace overlooking the water; dinners only. Their specialties include chicken stuffed with yam, and roast pigeon.

Great Shanghai. Very good Shanghai-style cooking is served here. The decor is rather mediocre, but the food is definitely authentic. Moderate.

Cathay. This busy spot also has very good food, and take your time in ordering, because the menu has many seldom-encountered dishes. There is a floor show of sorts. Medium to high in price.

Almost all the hotels also have good Chinese restaurants. To my way of thinking, the Chinese restaurant in the Shangri-La Hotel is easily the best of these, with a most interesting menu and excellent food.

Singapore Food Stalls. One of the most interesting dining adventures in this colorful city was informal food eaten at the Old Orchard Car Park food stalls. But nowadays it's even better at the Rasa Singapura Food Center, which is a complex of food stalls under one roof, located behind Tudor Court on Tanglin Road, next to the Singapore Handicraft Center. It's half indoors and half outdoors, and you can sample a great variety of oriental foods, such as chili prawns, satay, Chinese and Malayan food, and even *nonya* dishes (which are Chinese dishes adapted to Malay style). Prices are moderate, it's all very informal and diverting, and the entire operation is closely supervised as to health standards by the Singapore authorities. The Center is open from 11:00 to 2:30, and again in the evening from 6:30 to 11:00.

INDONESIAN FOOD:

Cockpit. If you aren't going to Indonesia, and you happen to be in Singapore on Saturday or Sunday, by all means pay a visit to this pleasant restaurant for lunch. They serve a good *rijsttafel* (a Javanese rice table), more fully described in the Indonesian section. The Cockpit also has pretty good charcoal-broiled steaks. Medium-high prices.

MALAYSIAN FOOD:

Islamic. A very atmospheric place, colorful and interesting. A good place to sample Malaysian dishes and Indian curries. The dining room is on the second floor. Moderate.

SHOPPING   In Paris, the music suggests the can-can; in New Orleans, it's jazz; in Brazil, they like the mambo rhythms; but in Singapore, the prettiest music this side of heaven to the local residents is the clinking of coins in the city's enormous business and commercial trade.

But first, as they say in the television commercials, a word, not from the sponsor, but from me. Chinese-type merchandise is available in Singapore. The merchandise regarded as Chinese-type includes antiques, jade, jade figurines, stones, many fabrics, and, in fact, a whole list of goods.

To reiterate, as I have said in other sections, be very careful what you buy. There are many copies of antiques and many dealers will say they are authentic. Don't spend any large sums of money without having the item authenticated.

Antiques of 130 years of age or older are not subject to duty, so that you can buy as many articles as you like if they are that old. However, be sure that you have proper authentication attesting to the age of each article, so that the U.S. Customs will not charge duty.

In this small country and city of Singapore, trade is everything; the nation has almost no other asset than the retail business ability and trading skills of its people. Shops are open 7 days a week, from 9 to 6, except Sunday when they close at 5 P.M. Department stores are frequently open at night, until as late as 10 P.M. In addition, some of the small shops are open just as long as there are customers around, and, of course, the Thieves' Market and the *Pasar Malam* (the night market which moves to a different location each night) have their own hours.

Although Singapore merchandise is generally free of import duties and represents great values all around, there are certain things that should not be bought in Singapore stores. They are liquor, perfume, and tobacco. These are subject to duty and do not represent a bargain when purchased in shops in town. They are a good value, however, when bought at the Singapore airport's duty-free shop.

Now, back to the pleasures of spending money in Singapore. This is a free port, and prices are low on almost all imported goods. Let's get the number one question over with immediately—is Singapore cheaper than Hong Kong, or vice versa? About the same, I would say, although there is bound to be a certain amount of variation on individual items, but it should not exceed more than 5% (higher or lower) at the very most. There can be no denying the much larger stock of merchandise, and the greater choice available to the purchaser in Hong Kong, but if you find what you want, it's likely to be just as cheap here as in Hong Kong. If you are a good trader, or bargainer (all right, haggler), it is possible to buy at even lower prices than Hong Kong, because there isn't too much bargaining or price-reduction to be obtained there on standardized merchandise like cameras and transistor radios. (When it comes to antiques, curios, and the like, anyone who doesn't bargain is completely out of his head in any oriental country.)

I would start shopping, if I were you, right at Collyer Quay, on the waterfront, and nearby where you'll see many of the more interesting shops in town. Little's Arcade has some of the best and most expensive shops. Walk into Clifford Arcade, which is lined with stores, stores, and more of the same. Almost anything you can possibly expect to buy may be found here—Swiss watches, fine imported fabrics, transistor radios, German and Japanese cameras, French cosmetics and perfumes, oriental jewels, and even pink Kleenex. There are two particularly good shops in the Arcade—the Malaysia Arts and Crafts (which features carvings and examples of Indonesian crafts), and the National Watch Company (for watches, of course).

Step out of Clifford Arcade and into Change Alley (which has been previously discussed as part of the almost compulsory sightseeing for Singapore). Change Alley, to me, is fascinating. It has small shops of almost every conceivable type, but don't ever pay the first price they ask. Or the second. Or the third for that matter. By the time they get around to the fourth price, you might possibly give in—don't be overanxious or you won't get any bargains. It is very possible that you could buy everything you want in Singapore right here in Change Alley, but then again, not always.

If you want to just wander about and walk into shops as you wish, the best general area is the Orchard Road and Tanglin area. Orchard Road is lined with shops, boutiques, and complexes of stores. Here you'll find air-conditioned, smart shops offering very good quality merchandise. On the way, you'll pass the interesting shop, easily recognized by its Chinese-style architecture, called C. K. Tang which has an enormous selection of merchandise under one roof, thus simplifying shopping for anyone with limited time (another suggestion follows later on). Tang's has lots of handmade merchandise, lots of absolute junk, but some occasional good values. (No bargaining is permitted here anymore than at Robinson's, for example. Save your bargaining for Change Alley or the People's Park Complex, to be mentioned later.)

The Communist government of the People's Republic of China, that is, the mainland Chinese, have a number of shops scattered about Singapore which sell a good deal of assorted merchandise manufactured in China. There are many interesting food items, clothing of all sorts, toys, souvenirs, and what-have-you. It's quite diverting to wander through one or two of them, and you can spot them by their name, the Chinese Emporium. Yu Yi is the most convenient; it's at the corner of Orchard Road and Grange Road. The Chinese aren't strong on fashion, but you might like to buy small bowls, ivory chopsticks, or other small items for gifts.

If your plans do not include a visit to Japan, it's worthwhile going over to Isetan, on Havelock Road adjoining the Apollo Hotel; it's a branch of the department store chain in Japan, and they have an excellent range of top-quality merchandise. Another good Japanese store is Yaohans, located in the Plaza Singapura, on Orchard Road; in general, the store has excellent goods.

If you aren't going to India, and you do want to buy some Indian sari fabrics, there's Gian Singh's, also on Raffles Place. Don't forget that sari fabric makes up beautifully into a long evening dress, especially the light colors. Speaking of fabric, Siamese silks are absolutely superb and are ideal for dresses, shirts, blouses and the like, and also may be used for curtains and drapes. All I can tell you is that Thai silk purchased in Singapore at about $6 a yard was selling on my return to New York City for $45 a yard—and if that isn't a bargain, I can't imagine what is. You'll find Thai-Craft, a shop specializing in Siamese fabrics at No. 11 in the Arcade leading off Raffles Place.

For your own amusement and entertainment, as well as the opportunity to buy a great value, visit the Thieves' Market. It gets underway in the late afternoon, about 4 P.M. and runs on indefinitely. There are stalls and carts extending along Rochore Canal all the way from Sungei to Kelantan Lane, so take a taxi to the general area and wander about at random. You'll see anything and everything for sale at this market, and it's great fun. (Put wallets in inside pockets, but the entire area is generally quite safe.) If you do see something you really want to buy, be certain not to act excited or particularly interested, or you'll never get a bargain. They watch your face and are experts at reading your intentions. On the average, bid about half of the asked price, and then settle for about two-thirds of the original price.

Similar to the Thieves' Market, but smaller, is the *Pasar Malam*, that street night-market which is in a different location every night. The local publication, *Singapore This Week*, issued free at all hotels, lists the location of each night's market. Even as interesting as the merchandise offered for sale, and the possible bargains to be had, are the people themselves—the sellers and the buyers. They are simply marvelous to watch, and you'll surely get a great kick out of watching them, even if you don't buy anything. But that's not too likely.

If you really want to simplify your shopping, head for a remarkable building called People's Park. It's very modern in appearance and looks like a department store, but the interior contains about 350 different shops, and it's more like a bazaar than you might think. Incidentally, the reason for this is not difficult to understand; it originated as a bazaar over a century ago and grew into these modern quarters only within recent memory. So, at heart, it's just a series of 350 different shops and 350 different shopkeepers, and you bargain just as if you were buying something at an outdoor stall. You'll find everything here, making it ideal for one-stop shopping.

For those who want to shop without traveling to all of the countries of Asia, visit the Singapore Handicraft Center, set up in 26 different structures at one location. Here, craftsmen and artisans make a wide variety of articles, such as batik paintings, jade carvings, opal and diamond cutting, weaving, copper and brass items, Thai silk, and lots more. The handicrafts represent a selection from Australia, Bangladesh, Hong Kong, Indonesia, India, Japan, Malaysia, Pakistan, the Philippines, Sri Lanka, Taiwan, and Thailand. The Center is open from 10 A.M. to 9:30 P.M.

If you want to have a suit or dress made, my suggestion is to use the tailor shop or dressmaker located in your hotel. Why am I so arbitrary, when your third cousin's friend who came through Singapore twelve years ago had a marvelous suit made for $12 with only one fitting in 24 hours? I'll tell you why. Calmly. It's because no one, repeat, no one can make a decent suit with only one fitting in 24 hours. And forget about that nonsense about $12. It will more likely cost in the neighborhood of $100 (or more) to come up with anything worthwhile. If you are going to be in Singapore for not less than three days (and don't necessarily count Sundays in the three days), it is possible to have a good suit or dress made. If you have it made in your hotel, your fittings can take place in the mornings before you begin sightseeing, or later in the day when you return perhaps to wash up for lunch, or in the early evening. If you have it made in downtown Singapore, that involves separate trips to and fro, at least several times. Then again, if it doesn't fit satisfactorily, it's better to have it under your hotel's roof so that a word to the desk clerk or manager will help the situation along. I have spoken, and you are now on your own. (But have it made at your hotel tailoring or dressmaking shop. Be reasonable; do it my way.)

How about more bargains? Lanka Jewellers is the place to buy gems and the like. (But do you really know values?) If you plan on buying Malayan arts or crafts, what could be better than visiting the Malayan Arts and Crafts Society Store, located on the other side of Singapore River, near the government offices. They have batik fabrics, jewelry, basketware, and interesting silver made in Kelantan.

When completely loaded down with your purchases, and if they seem to be too many for you to carry back to St. Louis, ask your hotel clerk to suggest a nearby shipping company that specializes in small shipments. If he can't, there's always the Singapore Baggage Transport Agency located in the Asia Insurance Building (telephone: 23011), who will undertake the job. When parcels are shipped out of Singapore unaccompanied (by the passenger), a special export permit is usually required. Be sure to inquire about this.

POINTER:

Department stores are open from 9 a.m. to 5 p.m. Smaller shops open a little earlier, and some close at about 5, but others remain open until about 8 p.m. Some small merchants remain open to midnight, particularly in Chinatown. The more important shops are closed from 1 p.m. on Saturday until Monday morning, but smaller shops never seem to close at all.

ENTERTAINMENT   Of course, all of the leading hotels have dining and dancing, and many have special shows (which are inevitably announced in the hotel lobby). However, all dancing ceases at midnight on weekdays, and 1 A.M. on Saturday. With the opening of the Shangri-La and Mandarin hotels, they have become the leading nightspots in town. A late night drink may be in order at the Coconut Grove. The Arundel Room (at the Goodwood Park Hotel) is also very popular with the local residents for dinner-dancing.

Singapore has two outdoor amusement parks (wait, please don't say it isn't for you), both of which are called "Worlds," because they are named the Happy World and Great World. They are fairly similar, and are entertaining places to wander about to absorb some of the local color. Sometimes there are performances of Chinese opera, sometimes of the Malaysian *joget* or *ronggeng* dancing, and there are always small bazaars, sideshows, restaurants, games of chance, and dance halls with hostesses, and lots of people wandering about. I'd say yes, at least one visit is in order, preferably on a Friday or Saturday night when the Worlds are at their liveliest; on weekdays, best go between 8 and 10 P.M. Which World is the best World? Probably the Great World, because it's the oldest and largest.

If you're in Singapore on a Sunday evening, inquire about the People's Variety Concert (more correctly called *Aneka Ragam Rakyat*), which is presented on alternate weeks. It features Malayan dancing, and performances are given from 7 to 10 P.M. Worthwhile, if you're interested in the art of the dance.

If you're at loose ends after dinner, take a taxi to Chinatown, say to Burgis Street, and just wander about. Most interesting, we think.

SPORTS Two *golf courses,* both pretty good, are the Royal Singapore and the Royal Island Clubs. Frequent *horse racing,* which may be followed by checking announcements in the local newspapers; these are often quite a social event. *Swimming* at the hotel swimming pools, particularly at the Singapura and Goodwood Park; also in the sea at Changi (previously mentioned), but it is only good when the tide is high. There is *big game hunting* in parts of Malaysia, especially tiger and leopard. The Game Department can give details, price of licenses, and additional suggestions as to time of year, equipment, etc.

SHORT TRIPS FROM SINGAPORE The classic one-day excursion out of Singapore is to Johore Bahru in Malaysia. It isn't that Johore Bahru is the wildest, most exciting place in the world, but if you've never been to Malaysia, it's an experience that you owe yourself, and all joking aside, it's a pleasant, diverting day, although not absolutely thrilling. You should allow about 6-7 hours for the round trip, computed as 1 hour for travel time each way, plus 1½ hours for lunch, plus 2½-3½ hours for sight-seeing. The trip can be made by railroad, but I think this is the wrong way to go. By all means, hire a car, or drive yourself in a rented car; either way, no problem is presented. There are road signs, and anyhow, everyone knows the way to Johore Bahru via the Causeway which joins Singapore and the mainland of Malaysia, a run of only 16 miles. Be sure to take along your passport, for it will probably be asked for at the Singapore-Malaysia border.

J. B. (to be brief) has an interesting native market, and there are two Sultan's Palaces (if you plan to visit them, ask at your hotel desk in advance for permission, which may be granted unless the Sultan is expecting company for dinner, or the like). In any event, you can always visit the beautiful gardens of the Sultan of Johore. Drive up to the hill where the local government has its offices; there is a very good view of the area. If you enjoy mosques, there is an interesting one here, the Abu Baker Mosque. Along the Strait of Johore there are attractive homes, and if you wish, there is a place nearby to have lunch—the Hotel Straits View at Jalan Scudai. (In Johore Bahru, you could also have lunch at the Government Rest House.) Incidentally, there's a rather small zoo in Johore Bahru which is worth visiting, but be warned, it's crowded on Sundays. Less than a mile from the border with Singapore is a medium-size hotel, the Merlin Towers, which has a pleasant restaurant.

If you wish to, drive farther out into the countryside and see the pineapple and rubber plantations. If time permits, drive 35 miles to Lombong and view the attractive waterfalls near Kota Tinggi, but alas, there's no place to have lunch there, so take it along with you.

Malaysia

A TOUR OF THE COUNTRY   I don't imagine that more than one tourist in ten makes a visit outside of Singapore and into the true back country of Malaysia, which is a shame, because few nations have such magnificent scenery, good roads, and good climate. A trip to Kuala Lumpur (the capital city) may be made by train, bus, air, or best of all (if you are even slightly adventurous) by self-drive auto, or by chauffeur-driven car. Buses leave at 8 A.M. every morning, and the charge is modest. If you drive, the route goes from Singapore to Johore Bahru, then to Malacca (overnight stop at the Government Rest House), and finally into Kuala Lumpur. K.L. (as everyone calls it) is distinguished by its interesting streets, the unusual combination of modern skyscrapers side by side with Moorish-style buildings and mosques, and the colorful Chinese quarter.

Most people arrive in Kuala Lumpur by plane. When you arrive at Subang International Airport, and have rescued your baggage, you'll find a booth where taxi coupons are sold. Tell the person where you wish to go, and he'll tell you what the fare is to your destination—your hotel in the vast majority of cases. In return you receive a coupon which is to be turned over to the driver at the end of the trip. This system has been instituted to prevent overcharging and arbitrary fares, and it works marvelously. Don't give the taxi driver any money at all, except for a small tip, if you wish, and only at the end of the journey.

There are many hotels from which to choose for a stay in Kuala Lumpur. The best bet is the Hilton, which has about everything going for it, including nice rooms and plenty of resort facilities. The Regent of Kuala Lumpur is really an elegant hotel, and perhaps may appear to be better than the Hilton; unfortunately, its rooms are a little too small (and not very well decorated) to make it qualify as a luxury hotel in my opinion, but it's still very nice. Next best is probably the Holiday Inn, a 14-story structure with 192 rooms, which is somewhat less expensive. Then I would rate as a tie the Federal and the Merlin Hotels, both of which are fine, and perhaps have more local atmosphere than either the Hilton or the Holiday Inn. There's a Travel Inn Kuala Lumpur, located above a public transport terminal, in the heart of the city; it's busy and bustling and bearable for an overnight stay. But it's hardly a luxury tourist hotel. Standard sightseeing includes the Chinese Goddess of Mercy Temple (Kwan Yin) in Ampang Road; the Hindu Mariamman Temple, located on High Street, and the Sultan Suleiman Mosque (more popularly called Majid Jame), which is somewhat off Mountbatten Road. Only seven miles from K.L. are the Batu Caves (2), with a miniature temple inside; I think this is a pleasant short excursion. If you want to take a somewhat longer outing that day, head toward Templer Park, a game reserve (but more like a jungle), which is worth walking through. En route, you'll see tin mines, rubber plantations, and lots of local life. Golf enthusiasts would enjoy playing at the Selangor Golf Club, about 3 miles from K.L. It's a championship course, and clubs can be rented from the club's pro. Just outside of K.L. is a commercial complex intended for tourists called Mimaland. It has a good deal of junk, but some very interesting exhibits, and there's a rest area, a restaurant, shops, etc. It's moderately interesting, but don't worry if you don't visit it.

On the chance that you might be fond of museums, may I suggest a visit to the country's National Museum, called the Muzium Negara, located on Jalan Bungsar. It's housed in a particularly attractive structure and is open 364 days a year (it is closed on a Muslim holy day). On display are examples of arts and crafts from Malaysia's rich cultural heritage, examples of the animal and bird life of the nation, aboriginal art and, indeed, almost anything to do with Malaysia and its life, people, and activities.

At night, you would probably enjoy seeing a little of Chinatown, if you haven't already seen it. If you like, have a good Chinese dinner at any one of the restaurants in that district. Then head for Petaling Street, the center of Chinatown, which is blocked off to traffic at night. This street becomes a pedestrian mall and is simply packed with people wandering about, gossiping, shopping, and just enjoying the evening. There are small shops and stalls where you can buy just about everything, and you might want to try some of the strange-looking fruit that's offered for sale. Another outdoor bazaar is held on Saturday night and is called (believe it or not) the Sunday market. This is a Malay market, and it's surely worth a visit if you happen to find yourself in K.L. on a Saturday.

Now, let's turn to shopping. My suggestion is to visit Pineapple Hill, whose more precise name is Bukit Nanas. After a brief cable car ride you'll reach the TDC Handicraft Center, a complex of small, attractive shops selling just about everything in the way of local arts and crafts. The shops are open every day, by the way. The hill is close to two hotels, the Hilton and the Equatorial, actually within walking distance.

What to buy: The great specialties of the country include batik, that is, fabrics printed with the use of wax, but actually, batik is not native to this part of the world. Silverware is good, as is what's called Selangor pewterware, made from refined tin, to which certain hardening agents (antimony and copper) are added. Also of interest is Songket fabric weaving. This type of cloth has silver and gold threads woven into the fabric and is made by hand. It is not inexpensive, because of the metal threads, as you might guess. Ceramics is another national handicraft, and the most famous type is called labu, or water vessel, pottery. Cane (or rattan, another name for it) is a very strong vine found in the jungle and is useful for making baskets, furniture, and so forth. A tree known as the screwpine (mengkuang in Malay) produces a type of leaf that is soaked in water for a few days, then sun-dried. It can then be used for weaving, mostly for place mats, floor coverings, and so forth.

On every long trip, there comes a time when it's a good idea to have a few days of pure rest, as a respite from an excess of sightseeing and solid days of activity. From Kuala Lumpur there are three very nice places to visit, all quite easily reached and quite inexpensive by our standards. These are all in Malaysia's Highlands, and quite worthwhile. To begin with, there's Genting Highlands, which is the closest of the three resort areas. It's at 5,600 feet elevation, and the views from Genting are nothing less than fantastic; all right, let's make that impressively beautiful. The trip takes about an hour by car, although you can also go by helicopter in a matter of only 10 minutes. The leading place to stay is the Genting Highlands Hotel which is good-sized and has a wide range of facilities. Much less expensive hotels include the Genting Ria, Genting Pelangi, and Sri Layang, all of which are less elaborate but still comfortable. Of course, the Genting Highlands Hotel is the most luxurious and elaborate, with any number of different types of restaurants. The big attraction here is legalized gambling, if that's of any interest to you. A second possibility for a mountain vacation is at Fraser's Hill, which is 63 miles northeast of Kuala Lumpur. On the average, a trip here should take about 2 hours by private car. The ideal place for a stay is Fraser's Hill's Merlin Hotel, which has complete resort facilities and is quite attractive on all counts. The gardens and plantings in the area are truly remarkable, and you'll see an enormous range of flowers, plants, and shrubs. The third possibility for a mountain vacation is Cameron Highlands, but it is located a fair distance away—140 miles northeast of Kuala Lumpur. Strangely enough, although the days are mild, the evenings can be quite chilly, so bring along a sweater if you plan to go outdoors at night. The trip takes half a day by car. The leading hotel is Cameron Highlands Merlin, but the strangely-named Foster's Smokehouse House is loaded with Olde Englishe charm.

OTHER INTERESTING SIDETRIPS

Penang is one of the thirteen states that make up Malaysia, that is, if you include Province Wellesley. There are about a half-million people living here. The Chinese, as usual, run the downtown businesses, whereas the Malays live in the countryside surrounding the city, called Georgetown. The most interesting places to visit for shopping include Penang Road and also Campbell Street which lead off Penang Road. Rope Walk is another good shopping street. In all of these places, a little gentle, low-voiced bargaining is expected and enjoyed. Penang has a subtitle, "The Isle of Temples," and needless to say, the title is well deserved. The most interesting one of all is a Clan House, built by the Khoo Kongsi (the mutual benefit society of the Khoo clan); it's a sort of imperial palace and there's also a seven-tiered pavilion. Not too far away from the Clan House is the Kapitan Ling Mosque. Also worth seeing is the Goddess of Mercy Temple—but prhaps you've seen all the temples you care to see on one trip.

Penang is easily reached by plane in about an hour or so. The fine new airport is called Bayan Lepas International. It's located 11 miles from Georgetown, the capital; if you're heading for the marvelous beach area in the north, it's 15 miles away. Georgetown was founded by a British sea captain in 1786, and he named the capital after the reigning monarch, George III. Not far away is the port city of Butterworth. During the years of British rule, fine old mansions were built in the Colonial style; you'll enjoy seeing these stately structures with their columns and arches, in varying stages of decay and semi-maintenance.

The island itself is a melting pot, with 450,000 Chinese, 100,000 Indians, 250,000 Malays, and only about 13,000 Europeans. This makeup produces colorful scenes and a fascinating population. The weather, as you might expect, is completely tropical. There are two so-called rainy seasons, one in April-May, and the other running from September through November. The main problem in Penang is high humidity.

Now, where to stay? Just remember that the months of peak occupancy are December, February, and April; during the remainder of the year, obtaining rooms should not be too difficult. On Farquhar Street, the main street of Georgetown, are two quite dissimilar hotels. One is very modern, the high-rise Merlin, which even has a revolving rooftop restaurant. The other possibility is the renowned and venerable Eastern & Oriental (popularly called the E & O), and it's built in the old style, with lots of space around, and what's sometimes called Old World charm. The Hotel Mandarin is fair enough.

If you want to stay at one of the beach resorts at Batu Ferringhi Beach, there's a rather good choice. Perhaps the most important (and the largest) is the Rasa Sayang Hotel, which is quite elaborate, with attractive gardens, and noted for its Malay designs. Much smaller and quite informal, is the high-rise Casuarina Hotel, surrounded by lovely trees. In addition, there's a Holiday Inn and a Penang Hyatt (those American chains get in everywhere, it would seem!).

Many people think that simply walking around Georgetown is all that needs to be done in the way of local sightseeing, but you can ride about in one of the trishaws, which is loads of fun. The shopping can sometimes be worthwhile, mostly for native crafts. At the beach resorts at Batu Ferringhi Beach, I don't have to tell you what it's like. Days are spent leisurely, on the beach or around the pool. Most people stay in their bathing suits for lunch and then in the afternoon, wander about the beach area. In the evening, usually somewhat late, there's a delicious dinner of seafood, which is superb here and includes some Malay or Chinese specialties. It's not exciting, but it is lazy and luxurious.

MISCELLANEOUS NOTES ABOUT MALAYSIA AND SINGAPORE

By this time, you're beginning to get a little confused about Malay, Malayan, Malaysia, etc., and even etc. To begin with, a Malay is a person who is a member of the Malay race. Malaya is a geographic region which includes such cities as Malacca and Kuala Lumpur. The entire grouping of Malaya, Sarawak, and Sabah is now called Malaysia. Thus, a Malaysian is a person who is a citizen of Malaysia. So far, so good? A Malayan lives in Malaya, but he can also call himself a Malaysian, because he is a citizen of Malaysia. Pan-Malayan (where did that come from?) is used by various government departments to cover affairs which are of national scope.

The language is Malay (are we back to that again?), but English is spoken all over the country, although naturally enough, not every person actually does. Little difficulty should be experienced, however.

If, in your wanderings about the country, you encounter any fresh *lichees,* you'll find them to be one of the most luscious fruits in the world. Ask for them, and if you're lucky enough to be there when in season, you're in for a treat.

No American newspapers are generally available.

This is a hot and steamy country most of the year, and men can wear shirtsleeves only during the day; it's all right at night, too, except that jackets and ties are required on weekends at the better hotels.

Orchids grow profusely here and the prices are low; treat yourself to a large bowl of them. The cost should be about $2–$3 here and it would be worth $50 back home.

INDONESIA

👫 Background

These fertile, beautiful islands were always of great interest to international traders and merchants from Europe, who sailed here and began to trade during the 15th century and even earlier. Beginning in 1509, the Portuguese came upon the scene, followed by the Dutch, then the British, and ultimately the Dutch once again, who controlled the region from 1814 until the Japanese invasion during World War II. The Dutch were never the greatest of colonists, and their rule tended toward the heavy-handed and autocratic. Whatever profit the colony made (usually more than substantial) was drained out of these lovely islands year after year for the enrichment of the small mother country back home. The only word that can be used to describe the Dutch rule in Java and Bali is exploitation, and it was colonialism at its worst. The country was literally stripped of its resources, and although railroads were built, and roads were constructed, and the islands were built up to a certain limited extent, whatever was done was undertaken primarily to make even more money for Holland.

The end of the war brought a violent revolutionary movement to the forefront in the country, and to be very brief, the Dutch were forced to leave. In 1949, Indonesia became independent; the new nation includes Sumatra, Java, Bali, Timor, part of Borneo, and many other comparatively unimportant islands. From a touristic point of view, Java and Bali are the islands of greatest interest and concern, and are about all that can be conveniently seen. Since its inception the country has found the going somewhat rough, and has been roundly criticized in the western world for seizing the assets of many foreign firms, for waging a sort of undeclared war against its neighbor to the north, Malaysia, and also for its attitude toward the western world. Although, at the moment, it is not strictly speaking in the communist camp, somehow it always seems to have the communist approach toward most world problems.

There is, perhaps, a reason for this attitude. Of all liberated colonial countries in the entire world, in no other new nation of the world is there such an intense dislike of their former rulers. When the British and French have gone, the populace has usually applauded, but it has seldom gone past that stage; on the other hand, the Indonesians actively dislike and distrust their former Dutch rulers, not that it has affected their recent willingness to do business with Holland. Nevertheless, more than a century of Dutch rule has inbred a distrust and antagonism in the populace toward all things Dutch, and for that matter, all things western. An American or European can usually tell a Frenchman from an Englishman on sight, but not always. To an Indonesian, such fine points are rarely within his ken; to him, all white-skinned people are Dutch, and he still doesn't like the Dutch.

Sukarno was in power for a number of years, but was thrown out of power by a violent revolution; since that time he has died. The country is now run by the army, and the government seems to be at last trying to make things work. Everything has returned to what is considered "normal" in Indonesia, and foreign investments in this lovely country may see a more stable situation. But the tourist should remember that tourism is something quite new, and schedules are not necessarily sure to be kept. Sometimes a local flight will be canceled, or a sightseeing car may fail to appear on time; all of these things are a part of the local touristic scene. If you go, be prepared to maintain a good-humored approach toward all of the petty problems that may arise. Don't arrange too complicated an itinerary, because you're sure to have something changed, switched, or even canceled. Don't fret, don't be annoyed by brief delays, and you'll have a good time in this physically glorious country.

Changes are coming to Indonesia, indeed, many have arrived; this remarkable nation is moving gradually into the present century while still retaining its remarkable, offbeat, and rather fey qualities. Nowadays, it's possible to say with complete assurance that the tourist, concerned with creature comforts (private bathrooms, air-conditioning, luxury travel, and excellent service) can unhesitatingly travel to Indonesia. But it should be remembered that Indonesia is the fifth most populous country in the world. And, in addition, about two-thirds of its enormous population live on a single island, Java. This can present some problems, or rather some slight inconveniences or delays, because of excessive traffic on the streets and roads, and so forth.

🌿 When to Go

Being very close to the equator, the temperatures are similar during most of the year, varying only by a degree or two. It is always warm, or perhaps hot would be the preferable word; however, it is seldom unbearable. Even at its warmest (or hottest) there is always a breeze, and quick showers tend to cool the air. June through

Weather Strip: Jakarta

	Jan.	Feb.	Mar.	Apr.	May	June	July	Aug.	Sept.	Oct.	Nov.	Dec.
Average daily high	84°	84°	86°	87°	87°	87°	87°	87°	88°	87°	86°	85°
Average daily low	74°	74°	74°	75°	75°	74°	73°	73°	74°	74°	74°	74°
Monthly rainfall	11.8	11.8	8.3	5.8	4.5	3.8	2.5	1.7	2.6	4.4	5.6	8.0
Number of days with 0.04 inches of rain	18	17	15	11	9	7	5	4	5	8	12	14

September are the very best months, and especially from late July onwards. It begins to rain somewhat in late October and November, but it is slightly cooler in compensation. The monsoon (rainy) season gets underway toward the end of November and continues on until April; but don't worry, you can come anyhow, for the rainstorms just last an hour or two at a time. Usually, that is. Evenings are always quite pleasant. If the temperature bothers you, head for one of the mountain resorts, where it can actually be quite cool.

✒ Visa Requirements

A tourist visa, valid for 30 days (it changes), must be obtained from the Indonesian consulate. You must fill out a special application form, 2 pictures are required, and you must present a letter from your travel agency or transportation company stating that you are a bona fide tourist. The charge is $3.50 per passport, plus $2.20 per person. Visas are generally issued in 24 hours; be sure they fasten a special visa card in your passport, which is necessary in order to obtain the special rate of exchange (see also Currency).

♟ Customs

Be careful at the customs inspection when entering Indonesia. If you have any cameras, typewriters, binoculars, electric razors, transistor radios, or the like, be absolutely sure you have these items noted in your passport. You are permitted to bring in 200 cigarettes (1 carton) or 50 cigars. The big problem is with Indonesian *rupiahs,* the local currency. You could easily land in jail, and Indonesian jails are not terribly luxurious, if you know what I mean. When you cash any money, be sure to have it noted in your money declaration, a form which will be given you on entry (more about this later under Currency). Bear in mind that you must logically have cashed a reasonable amount or the customs officials will become suspicious when you depart Indonesia.

♥ Health

Don't drink any water in Indonesia unless it has been boiled; better stick to coffee or tea, which must of necessity be boiled. They'll tell you the milk is safe; I wouldn't drink it myself, and I would advise you not to. Don't eat any raw vegetables, and only fruits that you peel yourself; cut fruits or melons are definitely taboo. Don't be tempted, and limit yourself strictly to cooked foods, and all should be well. Smallpox and cholera shots are necessary, but I wouldn't go to Indonesia without also having typhoid and paratyphoid shots. Please read this paragraph over once again.

☉ Time

There is a 12-hour time differential between most of Indonesia and the eastern seaboard of the U.S., but of course, bear in mind that when it is 3 A.M. on Wednesday in Jakarta, it is 3 P.M. on Tuesday in New York. When it is 8 P.M. in Los Angeles on Friday, it is 11 A.M. in Jakarta on Saturday.

＄ Currency

The currency of Indonesia is called the *rupiah,* and is now floating after it was devalued recently. Beware the black market; that's really looking for danger. Also, don't bring in any *rupiahs* when you come to Indonesia; unless they change the rules, it's against the law.

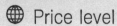 # Price level

Hotel rates at the luxury American hotels in Jakarta and Bali are medium high. Meal prices are fair enough, as are taxis. However, tours, controlled by the government tourist office, are surprisingly high.

🍎 Tipping

Light tipping is the general rule in Indonesia, and I mean light. For example, porters receive the equivalent of 25¢ U.S. for each suitcase. Taxi-drivers need not be tipped unless they have been particularly pleasant and helpful. It's also not necessary to tip guides, beauty shop personnel, or barbers, but everyone gives them a little something. At a hotel, you'll find a service charge added to the cost of your room. Nevertheless it's customary to give your room servant the equivalent of 25¢ a day, but not more than $1, even if you stay for a week. At the end of your meal, leave the waiter some very small change, say the equivalent of 25¢, even though it's in addition to the service charge.

🏃 Transportation

Taxis are difficult to locate when you want them, and charge rather moderate rates if you are lucky enough to locate one; cars are quite scarce for tours, most of them having been requisitioned by Nitour, Inc., the official government tourist office. It may be best to make sightseeing tour arrangements through their office; the address is Djalan Madjapahit Nr. 2, Jakarta. There are no *self-drive cars* available—guess why? The local chauffeurs' union objects to them. If you're pressed for transportation, take a bicycle-powered rickshaw; it's kind of fun, and the rates are really modest. There's *railroad* service on the island of Java only, none in Bali; very good train service between Jakarta and Jogjakarta, and also to Surabaya. The more adventurous might want to take the train to Surabaya, cross over to Bali on the boat, and then continue on (via bus) to Denpasar, in Bali. Almost every tourist who comes to Indonesia does so in order to visit Bali, which shows good judgment on their part. The simplest way (if everything works out right) is to *fly* via Garuda Indonesian Airways, from Jakarta to Denpasar. There is frequent service throughout the day from Jakarta to Denpasar, although it's not at all unusual for flights to be delayed; you'll get there sooner or later.

Airport and Tourist Taxes

Halim International Airport is located about 10 miles southwest of the center of the city; travel time takes anywhere from 20 to 30 minutes under ordinary circumstances, but can take an additional 15 minutes if you happen to hit holiday or rush-hour traffic. The airport is quite modern and can accommodate the wide-bodied jets. Sometimes, for domestic flights, departures will be made from Kemajoran Airport, which is only about 3 miles and 10 to 15 minutes travel time from the downtown area. On overseas flights, arrive at the airport at least an hour ahead of time, maybe even a trifle more than that. There is a departure tax of a couple of dollars. If you think I'm being vague, I am; it's because the *rupiah* keeps fluctuating in value, and they keep changing the departure tax.

Communications

It's easy to send off *cables,* and *phone calls* are put through to the U.S. within a reasonable length of time. It's difficult however, to quote the rates, because of currency problems with regard to the *rupiah.* Allow about 5 days for an *airmail* letter to reach the U.S.; it may even take 6 days occasionally.

Public Holidays

Galuggan (Bali) a New Year holiday lasting 10 days (April 26), Hari Maulud Nabi (April 26), Waicak Day (May 25), Sekaten (June 13–19), Independence Day (August 17), Balinese New Year (August 31), Idhul Fitr (November 8).

Electricity

Throughout most of the country, there is 110-volt A.C. current, which is good news. In some areas, it may be 127 volts, which means that your appliances won't work, or erratically at best. Better inquire.

✕ Food Specialties and Liquor

The classic dish of Indonesia is the famous *rijsttafel* (which may be pronounced rice-tafel), or "rice-table," in English. Each person is given a large soup plate which he fills with a generous portion of boiled rice. A number of waiters then offer the diner a choice of various dishes, which are individually placed upon the rice, and then upon a second plate when the first is completely covered. In the old days, a Sunday *rijsttafel* often consisted of forty or more different dishes, but in these more restrained times, as few as four or five dishes may be served. Some of the items are hot and spicy, quite a few are bland, certain foods are crunchy, whereas others are soft in texture. The chief idea behind a successful *rijsttafel* is a contrast in flavors and textures, one food being crunchy and sweet, another sharp but soft. Encouraged by the bright colors and the exciting array, the diner inevitably selects more than he can eat —but then, who cares? Be sure to select some cooling items, such as sliced bananas or cucumbers, in case one bites into a very spicy food. Incidentally, nothing is good to drink with *rijsttafel* except chilled beer; before the meal, dry gin is the classic drink.

If you do not wish to have a complete rice table, perhaps a simpler rice dish will do. The Indonesian cusine, like others in Southeast Asia, is built solidly on a firm foundation of rice, here called *nasi.* A famous dish is *nasi goreng,* fried rice, and has nothing whatsoever to do with the air force general of similar name in Hitler's Germany; this dish is like a miniature *rijsttafel,* and may be ordered if you don't wish to eat too much. *Nasi uduk,* made similarly, but with coconut milk, is delicious, as is yellow rice, *nasi kuning.* Having much the taste of *nasi goreng,* but made with noodles in place of rice, is *bahmi goreng,* which is really delicious.

In fact, noodles are among the best things in Indonesian cookery. *Mie goreng* is literally fried noodles (but with a dozen delicious ingredients); *ifu mie tjha* is a dish of crisply fried noodles with ham, shrimp, pork, and chicken, and if encountered on a menu, should not be overlooked. An interesting novelty is *bihun,* rice sticks, prepared from boiled rice, molded into shape and then air-dried. *Bihun* are used as the basis for making *laksa,* rice sticks served with chicken, shrimp, and chopped hard-cooked eggs.

The Indonesians love all seafoods, but none more than shrimp, which they call *udang*. Since *goreng* means fried, naturally *udang goreng* is fried shrimp. Shrimp and almonds are *udang masak amandel,* and curried shrimp is *udang kerie.* But best of all shrimp dishes, I think, is *bakso udang goreng,* fried shrimp balls. There are also numerous good dishes made with chicken, pork, and beef; however, try to have some barbecued pork *(babi panggang),* barbecued spareribs *(tulang babi panggang),* and steak prepared in the Javanese manner *(bifstik Djawa).* A favorite appetizer preparation is cubes of meat or poultry on tiny skewers, the food being first rubbed with spices and then usually served with a spicy soy or peanut sauce; these are *sate,* pronounced sat-ay. *Sates* make excellent first courses, and are very good with drinks.

Indonesians are extraordinarily fond of relishes, which they serve at every meal. The sweeter types, made with pineapple or other fruits, are called *petjilis.* The very hot kind are called *sambalans,* and these (made with burning-hot red peppers) are to be used with great caution. There are also pickled vegetables *(atjars),* the most interesting of which is made with radishes.

In the morning, the Indonesian custom is to have coffee, plus an egg or two, or sometimes boiled bananas. Both the midday and evening meal are quite similar, consisting of several different rice dishes. The Indonesians are also very fond of having their excellent Java tea in the late afternoon, together with the famous tea specialties, but don't think in terms of pastries or cakes; at teatime, the favorite is likely something on the order of *lumpia goreng,* a type of fried egg roll filled with shrimp or meat.

As previously mentioned, the tea is excellent in Indonesia. Don't forget, too, that the very word Java is synonymous with coffee in the English language, and the local coffee can be very good indeed (when it's made properly). The prepared desserts are generally unimportant, except possibly for some fruit fritters made of pineapple *(nanas goreng)* or banana (*pisang goreng).* By far the best dessert, especially after a spicy meal, are the local fruits; probably never again will you have the opportunity to sample so many different and fascinating luscious fresh fruits. In addition to the usual citrus fruits, there are mangos, which come in a dozen different types, some having a vague pineapple taste, while others seem flavored with strawberries. The pineapples are mellow and sweet, and you will see a score of different kinds of bananas. However, this is just the beginning; ask for *dukus, sawos, nangkas,* and *rambutans.* The *durian* has a marvelous taste, but I wouldn't blame you if you didn't eat it, because the odor is not only unappealing—it's devastating!

Although alcoholic beverages are available in most of the regions tourists visit, the Indonesians rarely if ever drink them.

∞ Time Evaluation

Inasmuch as it's so difficult to get to Indonesia, why not allow enough time to see things properly? To begin with, Jakarta is worth a couple of days. Also, because of the way local flight connections work out, you'll usually have to stay overnight in Jakarta after flying in from another country, and leave for Bali or whatever other destination you have in mind. Bali deserves a minimum of 3 full days and that should not include the day you arrive, but 4 or 5 would be better. Then 1 day back to Jakarta. Thus, the absolute minimum would have to be 5–6 days, but a week would be more enjoyable. More time would be needed for a visit to Jogjakarta, etc.

🏛 Capital City: Jakarta

Jakarta is an enormous city, having almost 7,000,000 by last count, and apparently growing all the time. The central "downtown" area looks fairly prosperous, with business offices, banks, and the like. However, the old canals (another inheritance from the Dutch) are slow-moving, almost stagnant open ditches which run malodorously through parts of the city. Perhaps they were appropriate in Amsterdam, but in this hot tropical climate, they tended to breed disease; although the disease phase of the canals is now apparently under control, the insect life attendant thereto is not.

Jakarta is a confusing, stimulating, exasperating, exciting, disoriented, humid city, with modern, glass-fronted structures alongside wooden shacks. The traffic is nothing short of bedlam, with some of the strangest types of conveyances you'll ever see in the entire world. In addition to normal automobiles and trucks, there are motor scooters and *becaks,* which are three-wheeled pedicabs. *Bemos,* three-wheeled trucks, dart in and out of traffic. Always there is noise—bells, horns, whistles. Soon the mind adjusts, shutting out the traffic sounds, which may soon be abated when the new system of roads in Jakarta is opened. It's not easy to become completely acclimated to this sprawling city, for it has a dozen suburbs and perhaps two score villages within its borders.

As far as I am concerned (as the perspicacious reader has undoubtedly guessed), regular sightseeing could easily be omitted in Jakarta. Yet this, in reverse, is somewhat of an exaggeration. To start off your day, pay a visit to the Gedung Artja Museum; it has a really fabulous collection of Indonesian artifacts, and is a good place in which to begin your understanding of the country. Another touristic sight here is the President's Palace, which isn't too bad; there is a very large garden. If you like local color, visit the harbor, which is loaded with potential Kodachrome shots. More than any of the above (except for the museum), I think you might enjoy an early morning visit to the Pasar Ikan, the fish market, which is quite stimulating to the eye and the mind, and needless to say, the nose.

Yet another sight is a restoration project called *Old Batavia*. Beginning with the 17th century, the original name for this giant city was Batavia, when it was controlled by the Dutch East Indies Company. The city grew up, despite the differences in climate, to resemble a Dutch city such as Amsterdam, featuring canals, small bridges, tile-roof buildings, etc. Many of the best of these older buildings are being restored. Most of the work has been done around lovely old Fatahillah Square, restoring (and in some cases, imitating) the architecture of several centuries ago. When everything is completed, there will be small shops, restaurants, and a sailor's tavern. It's worth seeing.

Two more (somewhat commercial) possibilities include *Indonesia in Miniature* and the *Jaya Ancol Dreamland* complex. Indonesia in Miniature is close to the airport and covers about 100 acres. You'll see representations of craft workshops, traditional homes from various parts of the country, and demonstrations of how wood carvings, batik, etc., are done. It's all quite nice and pleasant, and you can have a meal or refreshment if you wish. The Jaya Ancol Dreamland complex covers an enormous area, about 1,400 acres, and includes an exceptionally large number of amusement attractions including restaurants, jai-alai matches, a casino, swimming pool, and even an oceanarium with performances by trained dolphins. It may or may not be your cup of tea, but it does show you what the local people are like when they go off for an evening's entertainment.

Actually, the best thing about Jakarta is driving or walking about and looking at the people in the pursuit of their everyday lives. It's diverting to stroll through the food markets, to see the vendors of outdoor meals (which I wouldn't advise you to eat), to walk through the handicraft shops, and in general to absorb the local way of life.

There will be places where you'll laugh in sheer pleasure, and others where you'll shrink back in some disgust, but it's Indonesia, and unless you like to see a country on the luxury, assembly-line tourist belt, this is the way to learn about this enormous city.

The hotel situation is excellent here, and there is really an embarrassment of riches, as the French say. That is, you can hardly go wrong staying at any of the city's very good hotels. The largest of all is the Borobodur Inter-Continental, with a giant total of 866 rooms, all quite attractively decorated. It has any number of restaurants—Chinese, Indonesian, western, and Japanese—also a shopping arcade, swimming pool, tennis courts, etc. In the same luxury category is the Jakarta Hilton, located in a 32-acre garden complex. It's about half the size of the Borobodur and offers exotic dining amid lovely surroundings; the grounds are truly beautiful. As in all Hilton hotels, the rooms are of good size and nicely decorated. Most interestingly, they have an outdoor bazaar with a large number of shops featuring craftsmen at work, handicraft displays, and so forth. It's a delightful place to stay. Another interesting hotel is the Hyatt Aryaduta Jakarta, which has about 270 rooms, making it the smallest of the three. It is in a residential area, rather than the business section, and has a swimming pool, shopping arcades, restaurants, etc. Rates are somewhat lower at the Hyatt than at the first two hotels mentioned. The President Hotel is quite nice, too. It has some 350 rooms, nicely furnished, plus the usual assortment of restaurants, shops, etc. The President is operated by a subsidiary of Japan Air Lines. Much older than any of these is the Hotel Indonesia, with a total of 666 rooms. It has fairly spacious rooms and almost everything that the other hotels have in the way of facilities, although it is not as fresh looking as it might be. Nevertheless, it is a completely suitable place at which to stay.

The Indonesia Sheraton, a branch of that chain, is an enormous hotel, in two sections, with 666 rooms. The hotel is known for its personalized service, and is rather conveniently located, whereas most of the other good hotels in Jakarta are rather far out of town. It has restaurants galore, and everyone in town comes to the Sunday Indonesian *rijsttafel* dinner and cultural shows. Rates are comparatively moderate for a hotel of this standing. An interesting and offbeat hotel, but not for everyone, is the Horison, the only beachfront hotel in Jakarta. It has 331 rooms in a high-rise structure, and is located within the Jaya Ancol Dreamland, a sort of amusement park and sports facility. Most of its patrons are Indonesian, although a moderate percentage are European and American. There's an adjacent casino.

A very deluxe hotel, the Jakarta Mandarin, is 29 stories high, with over 500 rooms. It's a quite elaborate place and is located in the financial center of the city. Also very nice is the Holiday Inn, located in its own extremely spacious grounds, even including a small lake; the hotel's rooms are very large in size, all things considered. For those who like a quieter, less active atmosphere, the Sahid Jaya Boulevard Hotel, with 500 rooms, has more Indonesian mood about it than most other hotels in town. A comparatively small hotel, with 175 rooms, is the Kartika Chandra, located on the highway leading to the airport; the food here is generally recognized as well above average.

SHORT TRIPS FROM JAKARTA   In most cases, tourists will arrive in Jakarta on one afternoon, and leave the following morning for Denpasar, in Bali. Perhaps this is the way most tourists do it, but if you can spare an extra day, a visit to *Bogor* is definitely worthwhile. There are packed half-trips to Bogor by private car or bus. Or, if you wish, two people can usually hire a taxi, if they can find one, and make the trip on their own initiative.

It's about 38 miles from Jakarta to what may well be the world's most magnificent gardens, in Bogor. To get the statistical details over with, there are 275 acres, with 10,000 species of trees, and 500,000 plants, not to mention a fantastic collection of orchids—over 8,000 *varieties,* and well over 100,000 orchid plants. Even if you don't think you'd be interested, please go—it's a lovely ride through the countryside in any event, and you'll enjoy it. This trip can also be turned into an all-day excursion, by continuing on to *Puntjak,* which is a charmingly situated resort located above Bogor amidst tea plantations, waving palm fronds, and rice paddies. When it's hot in Jakarta (when isn't it?) the weather is cooler in Puntjak, which has almost magnificent scenery, plus a restful air. Near Puntjak, you'll find the government-owned Puntjak Pass Restaurant-Inn, which serves very good Indonesian-style food, one of the few places in the country that does, surprising as that fact may at first appear.

Not too many people get to *Bandung,* with its population of over a million. Too bad, for it's a colorful city, with pleasant-looking, gaily-dressed people. The food here is far above average for the country, which is never unpleasant news for the tourist. The big sightseeing attraction is the Tankuban Prahu Crater, which is still smoldering. The only hotel worth mentioning is the Savoy-Homann; fair enough, but not luxurious.

Even fewer tourists visit *Jogjakarta* (also spelled Yogyakarta and usually called Jogja), although it does have a topnotch first-class hotel, the Sheraton Ambarrukmo Palace. Foreign visitors come here from June through October for the fabulous Ramayana Ballet Festival; if you're here during that period, be sure to allow for an extra day or so. Nitour can make all of your arrangements, and let you know when the performances are scheduled during these months. The ballets are usually scheduled during weeks with a full moon. The dances are given in 10th-century Roro Djonggrang Temple, about 10 miles from Jogja. A group of over 500 dancers and musicians take part, and the whole proceeding is of epic proportions, and not to be missed—a great experience, we think. Besides the Ballet Festival, Jogja is famous for its *batik* work, and also for its silverware. Drive out to Borobudur, 24 miles away, scene of one of the world's most important Buddhist sanctuaries. Another 2 miles from Borobudur is the Mendut temple, which is known for its remarkable statue of the seated Buddha. The Indonesian government has been urging everyone to call Jogjakarta by a new and preferred name—Yogyakarta. Whether the new name sticks remains to be seen.

If you're an art lover, why not acquire a painting by Indonesia's leading artist, Affandi (he uses no first name). Affandi usually works in oils, with heavy bright colors, having strong hues in yellow, red, green, and blue. The results are lively (to say the very minimum), quite vivid, and definitely expressionistic. Although prices may change, a typical canvas might go for $1500 U.S. In any event, he's the best, and it seems likely that his works will increase in value. Affandi's works may be seen and purchased at his small bamboo house in Jogjakarta.

Bali

The vast majority of tourists coming to Indonesia are more interested in seeing Bali than any other place in the country. They show good judgment in doing so, because it's surely the high spot of any trip to this part of the world.

Flights arrive at the modern airport near Denpasar, and from there, it's only a 20-minute ride to most of the hotels. One leading place to stay is the Hotel Bali Beach (an Inter-Continental hotel) which is in two sections. The first and older part is a 10-story structure with 300 rooms, all attractively decorated and rather elaborate in scope. (You might be interested to know that the late

President, Sukarno, insisted on this high-rise over the objections of almost everyone else.) The new wing consists of a garden section, low in height, with 208 rooms. The Hotel Bali Beach Inter–Continental has just about everything—swimming pool, outdoor dining, and just about every facility of a luxury resort hotel. Several nights a week, there are Bali Beach Nights, held outdoors, while diners eat local specialties and watch spectacular Indonesian dancing. If I have any criticism of the hotel, it's that the entire operation is too smooth and sophisticated for Bali.

For those who don't wish to stay in the high-rise section, there are 111 rooms in seaside cottages, obviously in low-rise accommodations which are perhaps more suited to this charming area than are the Miami-style rooms in the tall building. The duplex cottages have red tile roofs, the rooms are most attractively decorated in authentic Balinese style, and are delightful.

Across the road from the cottages is the Hotel Segara Village, with accommodations in 2-story bungalows; the most attractive feature here is an outdoor dining room in a large garden area. There are numerous other small hotels and bungalow colonies in the general area, including the Gazebo, Irama, Tandjung Sari, and the Santrian. Perhaps the most impressive of these is the Tandjung Sari, which is beautifully decorated with carved wood doors, classic lamps, thatched roof ceilings. Accommodations are offered in twin cottages (not all of which are air-conditioned, incidentally), located in lovely garden areas.

On a rather large scale, the Bali Hyatt has 400 rooms, constructed in 4-story buildings around a central courtyard in such a fashion that each room has a good view. This hotel chain has done a good job creating a Balinese sense of design, including the famous terraced landscape so typical of this steeply inclined island where every bit of land must be used. The rooms are simply decorated—perhaps too simply—using Indonesian carvings, rattan, and batiks. The Bali Hyatt is further out than most hotels, about 30 minutes from the airport. Also worthy of mention is the Sanur Beach Hotel, about 7 miles from the airport, and with 300 rooms. This hotel is appealing for those interested in bargain prices—they are lower than elsewhere in Bali—but the rooms are very compact—indeed, they are small.

At nearby Kuta, the classiest of all the hotels (on the entire island) is the Hotel Bali-Oberoi, a part of that fine chain of hotels. It has both lanai units and individual "villas" which seek to duplicate features of the local architecture. Also very good, and also at

Kuta, is the Pertamina Cottages. Fairly close to the airport at Jimbaran Bay is the Regent of Bali, which has some cottages as well as a main building. The architecture is most attractive, being typically Balinese.

Bali! It's truly a fabulous—though surprisingly small—island in view of the enormous reputation it has developed. For some reason, the world (although writing it up) has pretty much left it alone, which explains why Bali has developed its own pattern of culture, and still retains much of its original charm and continuing attraction for western tourists. When the Moslems brought their religious fervor to the island of Java, they converted most of that large island's inhabitants; for some reason, they practically neglected Bali, so that the island still remains basically Hindu. You might anticipate that an artistic people, with a high degree of expressiveness and sensitivity would tend to modify even an adopted religion, and this was precisely what happened. The Balinese became Hindus, but with their own special variations and modifications, so that it is officially called the Bali-Hindu religion. During the centuries when the Dutch controlled these islands, they paid little or no attention to Bali, because most of the potential income from plantations was best developed and controlled in Java, rather than on this tiny island. The people continued in their own fashion, first under the Dutch and now under their own government, which still seems to neglect Bali in preference to developing Java. Whatever the various reasons may be, or the series of coincidences that occurred, the fact remains that Bali is still lovely, largely unspoiled by ugly (although perhaps necessary) factories, billboards, superhighways, commerce, and other requisites of our modern times, but hardly calculated to invite tourism.

How can anyone explain Bali in words? Of course, surely it can be said that the island is gloriously green and verdant, with lush countryside, rice paddies, palms, terraced landscapes, ponds, and other tropical ravishments. Premier Nehru of India once called Bali the "Morning of the World," and perhaps he fairly encompassed in a phrase the budding young loveliness of the island. Even in the few minutes it takes to drive from Tuban Airport, where air travelers land near Denpasar, one is engulfed by the pure physical loveliness of the landscape, but more than that, there is a feeling of peace, of quiet enjoyment, and of tranquillity. Not that Bali is paradise; far from it. There is desperate poverty, sometimes even starvation when the crops are insufficient; the people need many things in the line of material, worldly goods, but in the matter of inner resources, it is not impossible that the Balinese are rich.

Bali is a place with quite a few touristic attractions, and Nitour can arrange 3 or 4 different tours of the island, and perhaps this is the easiest way to get about, for taxis (especially with English-speaking drivers) are hard to come by. These tours can be arranged in Jakarta, or subsequently when you arrive in Bali, at the tour desk in your hotel. A typical 3-day tour goes along the following lines: Morning flight from Jakarta to Denpasar. After lunch, a visit to local art galleries, shops, etc. In the late afternoon, drive to the village of Bona to see a *ketjak* dance performance. After dinner, a *legong* performance at your hotel. The next day is taken up with drives through the countryside, first visiting Tjeluk to see the silver-smiths at work; then on to Mas, home of the wood carving craft of Bali. By far, this is the best place to buy fine wood carvings. The Balinese have always been highly skilled in this fine art, but tourism has caught the carvers' attention, and they are turning out many inferior pieces, with a thought to securing the visitor's dollar. Prices are quite fair—from about $6 for a small piece to perhaps $40 for a large one, to give you a very rough idea. However, pick and choose carefully, avoiding the stereotyped identical carvings that look al-most machine-made. Keep your eye on the lookout for unique, imaginative, well-conceived carvings and you'll do well. The most distinguished, although unorthodox wood-carver in Mas is a mid-dle-aged artisan named Ida Bagus Njana, whose pieces look as modern as something produced by a Paris sculptor, perhaps on the order of an Epstein sculpture. Njana's work sells for much more than the average, perhaps running from $50 to $200, although these figures are only generalizations.

After the wood carving town of Mas, the trip goes to Kintamani, located about 5,000 feet above sea level. On another day, the tour takes you to the Sacred Forest, where the tame monkeys can be fed, then on to the temple near Sangeh, and also to the water-surrounded temple at Sangeh. The hotels send along picnic lunches, and it's all quite pleasant and the countryside is lovely.

The 3-day Bali tour can be extended into a 6-day trip with a visit to Jogjakarta or Yogyakarta, if you prefer. On the fourth day, fly from Denpasar to Jogja; in the afternoon, visit Borobudur, a famed Buddhist temple. The next day, visit the silversmiths' shops, other temples, the Surakarta Palace, and also a demonstration of *batik* making, a most complicated art. On the sixth day, fly back to Jakarta.

But more than the actual sightseeing, you are likely to be beguiled by the people themselves—small, swarthy, slight of build and with charming manners. There is a Bali-Hindu festival almost every week, so with any reasonable luck at all, you should see at least one of these colorful affairs. Besides this, the Balinese enjoy holidays and time off, and there are festivals for almost everything—births, tooth-fillings, birthdays, weddings, and especially cremations (which although slightly chilling to the ears of Americans, is nonetheless a very exciting religious ceremony, and you'll be fortunate if you encounter one). The Balinese regard the cremation ceremony as a very happy event, because then the soul is liberated from earthly bondage. You would have to close your eyes, or never leave your hotel room, in order to spend three days in Bali without seeing some sort of special ceremony, or a festival or a dance program. And this is what everyone comes to Bali to see. Oh yes, bare-bosomed girls, they do come to see them, too. The central government in Jakarta, like all young governments unduly concerned with its dignity, issued an order (several years ago) that no women were to go about without covering above the waist. This has been largely disregarded in Bali, and outside of Denpasar many women wear nothing to cover their breasts. Tourists may take pictures, if they wish, but in a courteous fashion, first requesting permission by sign language, or through an interpreter. It will rarely be refused, if the permission is gently and softly requested.

If you have a free afternoon, why not hire a small boat, a *djukung*, which generally holds three people; take a sail along the coastline and admire the lovely views of the island of Bali, a sort of never-never land. The cost is not too great, but best do a little bargaining and agree on the price in advance.

If you're staying at the Bali Beach Hotel and want to dine out, there are two interesting places within walking distance from the hotel. One is Las Barracudas Restaurant, and it features continental food with loads of romantic atmosphere; fish, especially barracuda, as you might guess from the name, is the restaurant's feature. If you want to dine on excellent Indonesian food, call Madame Ni Pollock, who lives adjacent to the hotel in a Balinese-style home and will cook dinner, if you give her some advance notice. At both places, the charges are very moderate indeed, and the food well above average.

Some Other Islands of Indonesia

Sumatra. Most tourists don't venture off the beaten track, which consists of Jakarta and Bali. For those who do so, however, there are rewards and actually almost no inconveniences. There's plane service from Jakarta to Medan, the chief city, several times daily, and the flight takes from 1½ to 2 hours, depending upon the stops. In Medan, the outstanding place to stay is the Danau Toba International; it's really a rather good hotel. You can take a package tour, but it's perfectly possible to wander about on your own, hiring a car in Medan. The island is very large, and there are almost 100 volcanos, fortunately all quiet at the moment. Most tourists will agree that Lake Toba is the most interesting sight in Sumatra, and it can be reached by car using either of two roads. The more interesting road goes through a dense tropical forest, in which you can see traditional Batak communal houses built on stilts and covered with extraordinarily high roofs of semi-waterproof thatch. Lake Toba is a remarkably beautiful place, filled with twists and turns of exceptional charm. Around the lake are villages and settlements, but the most interesting ones are on Samosir Island. Although almost all have fantastic houses and marvelous community buildings; those in Simanindo village are the most remarkable of all.

Sulawesi. There is daily plane service from both Jakarta (about 2 hours) and Bali (70 minutes). In Ujung Pandang the best hotels are the Grand and the Pasanggrahan Beach. The town itself is moderately interesting, and the usual sightseeing includes the native market, colorful and lively, and the 16th-century Dutch fort. The roads are not great, and getting about calls for a jeep (or other four-wheeled drive) or the public buses. It takes anywhere from 6 to 7 hours to drive the 185 miles from Ujung Pandang north to Toraja, including a lunch-hour break during the trip. Toraja is unquestionably one of the most beautiful areas in all of Indonesia, green beyond belief and extremely fertile. The chief communities, Makale and Rantepao, are government and commercial centers. Within a day's driving are a number of lovely villages.

SHOPPING Anyone who comes to Indonesia and stays only in Jakarta would be unfortunate on two counts—Jakarta is a large city, and secondly, most of the shopping bargains are to be had in Bali, that land of sensitive, natural-born craftsmen. One might think that prices within a given country would be quite similar; for example, in the U.S. a typewriter costs the same in New York or California. Indonesia, as might be expected, has its own way of doing things, and prices in Jakarta are far, far more expensive than in Bali; this holds particularly true with regard to anything made in Bali. If you're going to Bali, do most of your shopping there no matter how tempting anything in Jakarta may seem at first glance. If you arrive in Jakarta late at night, and are departing early the next morning (a frequent itinerary in view of the airlines' schedules), the only place for shopping would probably be the arcades of the various hotels. If you have some free time, on the other hand, some of the city's shopping areas are probably worth a visit; in view of the paucity of sightseeing attractions in Jakarta, perhaps some comparative shopping is the only attraction here. But try to limit your purchases only to Javanese-made articles; wait for Bali for Balinese merchandise. In Jakarta, head for the Pasar Baru-Pos, Utara-Pintu Air, the central shopping area of the city, particularly if you're looking for souvenirs, and examples of local arts and crafts. The Djalan Nusantara is the best area for more expensive merchandise a step or two above the souvenir level, such as elaborate fabrics, jewelry, wearing apparel, and the like.

In Bali, the hotels all have their arcades, but prices tend to be somewhat higher than other sources, and the selection may be limited. The single best place for Balinese arts and crafts is the Bali Art Foundation, operated by the government; it is located in the middle of Denpasar, the handicrafts must pass a test for excellence before being sold, and everything is strictly one price, no bargaining allowed. To be precise, it's the Sanggraha Kriya Asta, Tohpati, in Denpasar.

Now what to buy? To start off the list, *wood carving* is a great specialty, and it may well be that the Indonesians are the most talented nation in the world in this field. They carve heroes, demons, mythological creatures, gods and goddesses, men and women, birds, and in fact, almost anything they can see, feel, or imagine. Some (a moderate percentage) of the work is talentless, turned out along the road by commercial "art shops" or "studios," almost all of the figures in a particular shop being identical. The more imaginative carvers seldom repeat themselves, turning out something different almost every time; these are the carvings to buy. It takes a little looking, but if you have a degree of patience and refuse the first carvings shown, you may often get them to bring out the better pieces; of course, in the mass-production "art shops" they won't bring anything else out, because there's nothing better in the entire shop. If you're really serious about wood carving, don't forget to visit the studio of Ida Bagus Njana, the leading artist in his field; his studio is in the village of Mas, in Bali.

Paintings are worth looking at, if you're a collector. Indonesian artists are presently in a state of flux; they seem torn between the marvels of western techniques and an inbred desire to express themselves in a more nationalistic style. A truly Indonesian style has not been found, although the local artists are pressing in that direction. You'll find cubism, expressionism, realism, and abstract art, all expressed on canvas here; prices are quite moderate, all things considered. As previously mentioned, the leading artist is a man named Affandi who has no first name; his studio is in Jogjakarta, and prices are moderately high.

Antiques are quite hard to locate. Most of the good pieces had previously been shipped out of the country by the Dutch during their occupation of the country, and most of the balance placed in national museums by the Indonesian government. If you have a few extra days, by dint of careful inquiry, it may be possible to run across some genuine antiques; by and large, they are rarely seen.

One of the most representative of the local arts and crafts is *batik.* The term actually refers both to a kind of fabric, and also to a method of decorating fabric. The procedure consists in placing melted wax over portions of a design on cloth, and then dipping the material into a vegetable dye, the portions covered by the wax "resisting" the dye. When the wax is removed, the design appears to stand out against the background of the dyed fabric. As a rule, the women draw the patterns, and the men do the dyeing. This quick, oversimplified description cannot begin to explain the highly skilled, tedious processes involved; when you see *batik* actually being made, you'll be greatly impressed by the craftsmanship displayed. *Batik* is suitable for clothing, for upholstering furniture and for draperies. Be forewarned, however, that real, authentically made *batik* is moderately expensive; the very cheap copies are of inferior quality, usually mass-produced.

Puppets of all sorts are part of the religion and artistic life of the country. Wooden puppets make interesting souvenirs, and are very decorative. There are also leather "shadow" puppets which look very well when artistically arranged on a wall. In addition, you'll probably see some doll-sized three-dimensional puppets, which run into more money.

Both Bali and Java produce *masks,* used in the various dances and religious ceremonials, a group of which would make an interesting decoration for a wall in your home. Some of them are quite grotesque and may scare the devil out of you (or your guests) in a dimly lit room.

Silverware is good, particularly around Jogjakarta; sometimes the designs are too elaborate, so pick and choose carefully. I thought that the *handbags* were quite interesting, some of them made with conventional leather but others ingeniously produced from bamboo (ideal for summer use), and also some types made of pandanus, a variety of dried leaf. Articles made of *crocodile* are only fair, the finished articles seem to lack the usual Indonesian skill; be sure to use care in making a selection, checking the seams where the crocodile is joined. *Cigarette cases* and *boxes* are very attractive; they come in gold, silver, tinware covered with a silver alloy, unfinished wood, and even novelty boxes made of orchid fiber and horsehair.

Shipping articles home has always been a problem in Indonesia. Several of the more important shops have received permission from the government to package and ship your purchases; charges are somewhat steep, and don't expect them to show up at your home in less than three months. Shipping charges are frequently in excess of the original costs. If humanly possible, carry them along to your next stop (probably Singapore in the majority of cases) and ship from there. If the articles are too cumbersome, visit Nitour in Jakarta and make inquiry, because the situation is fluid and may improve.

ENTERTAINMENT AND RESTAURANTS There's very little in the way of scheduled night life, although *dance recitals* and *concerts* of Indonesian music are frequently given. The hotels in Jakarta and Bali usually have notices posted concerning any planned entertainments, and these should never be missed. (More about the local music and dance later in this section.)

The Hotel Indonesia in Jakarta has *dancing* and *entertainment* in its rooftop garden restaurant with a marvelous view of the harbor; prices are moderately high, but not excessive. The other good spot for an evening's entertainment is the Wisma Nusantara, an outdoor garden restaurant, which features dancing under the stars. The food is both western and Indonesian, the entertainment is both western and Indonesian, but the prices are more western than Indonesian. For a taste of Indonesian life, it might be more interesting than the Hotel Indonesia's rooftop restaurant, particularly for those who are curious. The resident foreigners are fond of another spot, the Ambassador (located next-door to the Hotel Dharma Nirmala), which has western music, food and atmosphere; I would imagine that most American tourists would also enjoy the nightclubs in the Borobudur and Hilton Hotels.

If you're looking for something more cultural, there are Indonesian puppet shows scheduled at the Tji Tjih Hall; better ask at the Nitour office in your hotel. If you really like the local music, ask if there's a concert scheduled; there are irregular performances given during the early afternoon at the Wisma Nusantara restaurant.

Another interesting Indonesian entertainment is a *wajang* performance; for this, better check at your hotel or with Nitour. *Wajangs* are of various types, one style has wooden puppets, another is a sort of shadow dance, and still another with live actors. It is difficult to describe, but an hour's visit to a *wajang* (no matter what style) will be a delightful experience.

Many tourists consider a fine dinner in the nature of a complete evening's entertainment; certainly this is true in France, where dining out is all that a great many people plan for an evening. Peculiarly enough, the Indonesian food here is inferior to that which may be had in Burma or Singapore, for example. Of course the leading hotels serve just-fair western food, and somewhat better Indonesian meals. There are only about two restaurants in Jakarta (apart from the hotels) that can be recommended. One is the Jawa Restaurant (telephone: Gambi 4151); this is not a beautiful gourmet's palace, to say the very least. The atmosphere is nonexistent, the decor hasn't even been considered, but for the curious student of gastronomy, a visit here might be in order. Phone ahead (they speak English) and ask for a special Indonesian meal. As far as I could see, this was the only place serving authentic local food. But don't go if you object to informal, friendly service, and very undistinguished surroundings. The other good restaurant is Kadipolo, with two branches, one located only ten minutes from the Hotel Indonesia. It features Javanese and Madurese culinary specialties and is recommended for the curious gourmet. I would order *sate kambing,* charcoal-broiled cubes of lamb, perhaps one of their rice dishes, and then have *gudeg Jogjakarta,* made with chicken, eggs and jackfruit. To my mind, you might be just as well off dining at your hotel, because at least the sanitation is better. If you want to try some good Indonesian dishes, just ask the restaurant manager to prepare some, giving him a day's advance notice.

Indonesian *dancing* is world famous, and every tourist is bound to be exposed to it at various times. A little understanding may go a long way towards further enjoyment of this unique art form; students of the subject say there are really three principal dance forms. The most famous one, the most highly publicized version, is the type which might be called classical dance-drama. These are ancient dances, many of which are centuries old; they are usually based upon classic Indonesian tales of mythology, or upon the nation's epic stories, such as the Mahabharata or the Ramayana. In the classic dance, every movement is stylized and requires years of study, customarily beginning in early childhood; some of the leading dancers are actually hardly more than children. The dance form most commonly scheduled is called the *legong,* usually performed by several young girls in the stylized classical manner. The *legong* is composed of several parts—an introduction, the main story itself, and the conclusion. While the dance is being performed, a narrator recites the story line. The *ketchak,* or monkey dance, is also performed with some regularity.

The second dance category consists of the modern school, which tends towards the abstract, and places considerably less emphasis upon the stylized movements so characteristic of the classic dance-drama. Some performances given in the hotels are combinations of these two styles (the classical and the modern), but the emphasis is usually placed upon the classical form. The third category is that of folk dancing, far less skillful and stylized, but very amusing to watch. This is the dance form which tourists occasionally see, and its themes are similar—superstition, symbolic fights, religion, the supernatural.

Indonesian *music* appeals to many tourists, but not all. For one thing, the music lacks modulation; western orchestras play in various keys within one particular composition; this is not the situation with *gamelan* music. The word *gamelan* itself has several meanings in Indonesia—orchestra, a matched group of instruments, and other similar meanings. The word is believed to be derived from the Indonesian word *gamel,* or "hammer," in English. The *gamelan* instruments are generally struck with small percussive hammers, which may in turn induce a slight headachy feeling in some tourists; many of them do learn to enjoy it, and not a few become quite enthusiastic. A rough comparison might be made between the *gamelan* and our own xylophone, to give you an idea. *Gamelan* music is closely associated with Indonesian dancing, and the two are often considered as inseparable. It should also be understood that just as the dancing varies from one region to another, so do the *gamelan* orchestras vary in style, technique, and scope. When the orchestra is made up only of bamboo instruments, it is called a *bumbung.*

Bridging the not inconsiderable gap between *gamelan* and western music, is a unique type of Indonesian music called *kerjontjong.* The Portuguese traders in Java some 400 years ago introduced certain western-style musical instruments and also European popular musical forms; thus, the surprised (sometimes startled) tourist may see a local orchestra featuring the cello, violin, guitar (but no saxophone, insofar as I know, because it hadn't been invented when the Portuguese brought their music here). The *kerjontjong* is easy to listen to, quite similar to western musical forms, and no one will find it too exotic.

INDEX

Aberdeen, Hong Kong, 268–269
Agra, India, 404–408
  weather, 405
Ainu aborigines (Hokkaido Island, Japan), 195, 196
Air India, 4, 415
Air travel, 2–7
  advantages and disadvantages of, 1–2
  cost of, 5–7
  jet lag and, 22, 44–45
  selecting airline, 3–5
  selecting class, 5–7
  See also under names of countries
Ajanta Caves (India), 419–420
Akan National Park (Japan), 197
Alcoholic beverages. *See* Liquor
All-Nippon Airways, 192
Amakusa Islands (Japan), 191
American Express Company, visa department of, 19
Amethysts, buying (Sri Lanka), 439
Andaman Islands (India), 393
Antiques
  China, 314
  duty-free status of, 48
  Hong Kong, 48, 290–291
  India, 418
  Indonesia, 495
  Japan, 109–110
  Korea, 223–224
  Singapore, 460
  Taiwan, 248
  Thailand, 345
Anuradhapura, Sri Lanka, 442
Aomori, Japan, 193–194
Art objects, buying
  Hong Kong, 48, 290–291
  Japan, 109–110
  Taiwan, 247–248
Aurangabad, India, 419–420
Ayudhya, Thailand, 347–349

Bagdogra, India, 394
Bags. *See* Handbags
Bali, 480, 484, 488–492
  air travel to, 481–488
  entertainment, 496
  hotels, 488–490, 496
  people, 491–492
  restaurants, 492, 496
  shopping, 493–495
  tours of, 491–492
  transportation in, 490, 491, 492
Bamboo articles, buying
  Taiwan, 246
  Thailand, 345
Bandung, Indonesia, 487
Bangalore, India, 424
Bangkok, Thailand, 334–347
  airport in, 330
  entertainment, 345–346
  hotels, 338–339
  long trips from, 350–354
  medical facilities, 327
  mosquitoes in, 327
  price level, 328–329
  restaurants, 339–341
  shopping, 341–345
  short trips from, 347, 349–350
  sightseeing, 336–338
  sports, 346–347
  telephone system, 331
  time differential, 327–328
  time evaluation, 333
  transportation in, 329–330
  weather, 325–326
Basketware, buying
  Burma, 367
  Singapore, 467
Batik, buying
  Indonesia, 488, 495
  Malaysia, 472
  Singapore, 467, 468
Benaras, India, 396–398

Bentota, Sri Lanka, 441
Beppu, Japan, 186–187
Beruwela, Sri Lanka, 441
Bhatgaon, Nepal, 427
Bhubaneswar, India, 395–396
Binoculars, buying
  Hong Kong, 288
  Japan, 101
BOAC. *See* British Airways
Bogor, Indonesia, 487
Bombay, India, 414–419
  airport, 415
  hotels, 416–417
  restaurants, 417–418
  shopping, 418
  sightseeing, 418–419
  weather, 373–374, 415
Bona, Bali, 491
Books, buying (Taiwan), 247
Borobudur, Indonesia, 488
Brass articles, buying
  India, 392, 402
  Korea, 224
  Singapore, 458, 467
  Sri Lanka, 438, 441
  Taiwan, 246
British Airways, 4, 444
Bunraku puppets, 122, 178–179
Burma, 355–369
  air travel in, 361–362
  airport and tourist taxes, 362
  background, 355–356
  communications, 362
  currency, 16, 359
  customs, 358
  duty-free merchandise, 45–46
  electricity, 362
  entrance papers, 16
  food specialties, 362–363
  health, 358–359
  longyi (costume), 365
  medical requirements, 16, 359
  price level, 360
  time differential, 359
  time evaluation, 363–364
  tipping, 360–361
  tobacco regulations, 16, 358
  transportation, 361–362
  traveling in, 359–360
  visas, 16, 358
  when to go, 357
  See also Rangoon, Burma

Calcutta, India, 386–393
  entertainment, 391–392
  hotels, 391
  restaurants, 391–392
  shopping, 392
  sidetrip from, 393
  sightseeing, 388–389, 393
  weather, 373–374, 387
Cameras, buying
  Hong Kong, 288
  Japan, 101
  Singapore, 465
Cameron Highlands, Malaysia, 473
Carpets. *See* Rugs
Celadon articles, buying (Thailand), 345
Ceramics, buying
  Korea, 224
  Malaysia, 472
Certificate of Origin (Form A), 45–46
Ceylon. *See* Sri Lanka
Cheju Island, Korea, 230
Chess set, buying (Japan), 110
Cheul, India, 419
Cheung Chau, Hong Kong, 276–277
Chiengmai, Thailand, 353–354
Chin (dogs), 157
China, 300–322
  actual entry, 304–305
  background, 300–302
  behavior in, 312–313
  communications, 309
  currency, 16, 306–307
  customs, 303–304
  electricity, 309
  entrance papers, 16

food specialties, 309–310
health, 301–302, 303, 305–306
hotels, 313
language, American spelling of, 302
liquor, 311
medical requirements, 16, 303
price level, 307
shopping, 313–314
time differential, 306
tipping, 307–308
tobacco regulations, 16, 303
transportation, 308
visas, 16, 303
what to take, 311
what to wear, 310–311
when to go, 302–303
See also names of cities
China Airlines, 3
Cholera vaccination, 40, 41, 42
Cigarette boxes and cases
Indonesia, 496
Japan, 106
Taiwan, 246
Thailand, 344
Cigarettes. *See* Tobacco
Cloisonné, buying (Japan), 109
Clothing
buying
Hong Kong, 284, 285–287
Indonesia, 494
Japan, 105–106
Singapore, 467–468
for travel, 22–27
men's, 23, 25–27
packing, 26–27
shoes, 23
women's, 24–25
Coloane (island), 299
Colombo, Sri Lanka, 436–442
entertainment, 439
hotels, 437–438
restaurants, 438
shopping, 438–439

short trips from, 440–442
sightseeing, 436–437
sports, 439–440
weather, 430
Conducted tours, 7–10
Cormorant fishing (Japan), 135, 160–161
Cosmetics, buying (Singapore), 465
Cotton fabrics, buying
Korea, 224
Thailand, 343
Crocodile articles, buying (Indonesia), 496
Curios, buying
India, 403
Japan, 109
Singapore, 465
Currency, 38–40
regulation checklist, 16–18
See also under names of countries
Customs
foreign. *See* under names of countries
U.S., 45–49

Dacca, East Pakistan, 424
Daisetsuzan National Park (Japan), 196
Darjeeling, India, 386, 393–395
weather, 394
Delhi, India, 398–404
hotels, 401–402
restaurants, 402
shopping, 402–403
weather, 373–374, 399
Denpasar, Bali, 490, 491
Diamonds, buying
Hong Kong, 289
Singapore, 467
Diarrhea, 28, 42–44
Djakarta, Indonesia. *See* Jakarta
Dolls, buying
Japan, 104–105
Korea, 224
Taiwan, 246

Thailand, 345
Doxycycline, 43
Drinking water, 28, 42, 43
    See also under names of countries,
        health
Duty-free articles
    gifts, 48
    under Generalized System of
        Preferences (GSP), 46

East Pakistan, 424
Eklingji, India, 410
Electricity. *See* under names of
    countries
Ellora Caves (India),
    419–420
Embroidery, buying
    India, 413
    Taiwan, 246
Enamel work, buying (India),
    409
Enoshima (Japanese islet), 143
Entertainment. *See* under names of
    countries and cities
Entrance papers. *See* under names of
    countries
Everest, Mount, 428

Fabrics, buying. *See* Cotton Fabrics;
    Silks; Textiles
Fanling, Hong Kong, 274
Fans, Japanese, 109
Fatehpur Sikri, India, 407
Filigree, buying (India), 409
Fishing tackle, buying (Japan),
    106–107
Flower arranging (Japan), 206
Food
    health and, 43–44
    U.S. Customs requirements,
        48
    See also under names of countries
Foreign Independent Travel (F.I.T.),
    10–11
Fraser's Hill, Malaysia, 473
Fuji Lake area (Japan), 57,
    145–150
Fujinomiya, Japan, 148

Fujiyama (Japan), 57, 133,
    145–148, 149, 150
Fuji-Yoshida, Japan, 146
Fukuoka, Japan, 187–188
Funatsu, Japan, 148
Furniture, buying
    Hong Kong, 289
Futami-ga-ura, Japan, 164

Garuda Indonesian Airways,
    480–481
Geishas (Japan), 96, 117–119, 171
Gem stones, buying
    Burma, 367–368
    India, 409
    Singapore, 464, 467, 468
    Sri Lanka, 439
Generalized System of Preferences
    (GSP), 46
Genting Highlands, Malaysia,
    472–473
Georgetown (Malaysia),
    474–475
Gifts, duty-free, 48
Gifu, Japan, 160–162
Ginseng tea (Korea), 220, 225
Glassware, buying (Japan), 108
Goa, India, 421–422
Gold articles, buying
    Hong Kong, 289
    India, 392
    Japan, 106
    Thailand, 344
Gopalpur, India, 396
Gora, Japan, 144
Grass Mountain, Taiwan, 249
Green Lake, Taiwan, 249
Gulmarg, India, 413
Gwalior, India, 407

Hakodate, Japan, 195
Hakone District (Japan), 143–145
Hanamaki Spa, Japan, 193–194
Han-bok (Korean costume), 218,
    224
Handbags, buying
    India, 418

Indonesia, 495–496
Japan, 105
Handkerchiefs, buying (Hong Kong), 290
Hangchow, China, 321
Happi coats, buying (Japan), 105–106
Health, 40–45
    diarrhea, 28, 42–43
    diet, 43–44
    time change and, 44–45
    vaccinations, 40–43
    See also under names of countries
Hikkaduwa, Sri Lanka, 442
Himeji, Japan, 183
Hiroshima, Japan, 183
Hokkaido Island (Japan), 195–196
Hong Kong, 255–293
    airport and tourist taxes, 261
    art objects, 48
    background, 255–257
    communications, 261
    currency, 16, 259
    customs, 47, 258
    electricity, 262
    entertainment, 292
    entrance papers, 16
    ferries, 264, 265, 266
    food specialties, 262–263
    health, 258–259
    hotels, 270, 271, 274, 278–281
    islands of, 276–277
    Kowloon, 261, 264, 269–271, 277
    medical requirements, 16
    New Territories, 261, 272–276, 277
    Peak tram, 265–266
    price level, 259
    refugees from China, 274–275
    resettlement estates, 275
    restaurants, 265, 267, 268, 281–283
    shopping, 271–272, 283–292
    time differential, 259
    time evaluation, 75, 263
    tipping, 259–260
    tobacco regulations, 16, 258
    tours, 277–278
    transportation, 260–261
    Victoria, 264–272
    visas, 16, 20, 258
    weather, 257
    when to go, 257–258
Honshu (island), Japan, 183
Hotels
    making reservations, 13–14
    See also under names of cities and countries

Incense-smelling (Japan), 206–207
India, 370–428
    air travel in, 379
    Ajanta Caves, 419–420
    approach to, 384–385
    background, 370–373
    communications, 380
    currency, 16, 376–377
    customs, 376
    duty-free merchandise, 46
    electricity, 380
    Ellora Caves, 419–420
    entrance papers, 16
    food specialties, 380–383
    health, 374–376
    itineraries, 385–386
    language, 383–384
    liquor, 383
    medical requirements, 16, 375
    price level, 377
    South, 422–424
    Taj Mahal, 404–407
    tipping, 377–378
    tobacco regulations, 16, 376
    transportation, 378–380
    travel organizations, 378–379
    visas, 16, 374
    weather, 372–374
    when to go, 373–374
    words and phrases, 383–384
    See also names of cities
Indian Airlines Corporations (IAC), 379, 414, 421

Indonesia, 476–498
  airport and tourist taxes, 481
  background, 476–477
  communications, 481
  currency, 16, 479
  customs, 478–479
  dancing, 497–498
  electricity, 481–482
  entertainment, 496–498
  entrance papers, 16
  food specialties, 482–484
  health, 479
  liquor, 484
  medical requirements, 16, 479
  music, 498
  price level, 480
  time differential, 479
  tipping, 480
  tobacco regulations, 16, 479
  transportation, 480–481
  visas, 478
  weather, 478
  when to go, 477–478
  See also names of cities
Inland Sea, traveling through, 65,
  183–186
Inoculations, 16–18, 40–42
International Date Line, 29–33
Iseshi, Japan, 162–165
Itineraries, 12–13
Ivory articles, buying
  Burma, 367
  India, 402, 409
  Singapore, 466

Jade, buying
  Burma, 367–368
  Hong Kong, 284–285, 288
  Singapore, 464, 467
Jaipur, India, 408–409
  weather, 408
Jakarta, Indonesia, 484–488
  hotels, 486–487, 496
  restaurants, 496
  shopping, 493–496
  short trips from, 487–488
  sightseeing, 485–486
  weather, 478

Japan, 50–207
  address system in, 62–64
  air travel in, 65
  airports, 66–67
  background, 50, 52–56
  Bunraku puppets, 178
  cherry trees, 56–57, 89, 148
  communications, 67–68
  currency, 17, 60
  customs, 58–59
  economy, 55–56
  electricity, 68
  entrance papers, 17, 58
  etiquette, 54, 55
  flower arranging, 206
  food specialties, 68–75
  Fuji Lake area, 57, 145–150
  geishas, 96, 117–119, 171
  getting around in, 198–207
  health, 59–60
  hotels and inns, 61, 201–204
  incense-smelling in, 206–207
  Inland Sea, 65, 183–186
  Kabuki plays, 120–122
  language, 197–198, 204
  liquor, 59, 74–75
  map, 51
  medical requirements, 17, 58,
    59–60
  Noh plays, 119–120
  Northern, 191–197
  pachinko (pinball machines),
    204
  price level, 60–61
  restaurants, 60–61
  sports, 127–135
  steamer and steamship service, 65
  tea ceremony, 205–206
  time differential, 60
  time evaluation, 75
  tipping, 61–62
  tobacco regulations, 17, 58–59
  train service in, 65
  transportation in, 62–65
  unique cultural activities, 205–207
  visas, 17, 20, 58
  weather, 57–58
  when to go, 56–58

words and phrases, 197–200
See also names of cities
Japan Airlines, 4–5
Japan National Tourist Organization, 82, 84
Java, 476, 481
Jet lag, adjustment to, 22, 44–45
Jewelry, buying
Hong Kong, 284–285, 288–289
India, 392, 395, 402
Japan, 101–103, 106
menuki, 106
Singapore, 464, 467, 468
Sri Lanka, 439
Thailand, 344
See also Gem stones
Jogjakarta, Indonesia, 487–488
Johore Bahru, Malaysia, 469–470
Juhu Beach (India), 417

Kabuki plays (Japan), 120–122
Kam Tin, Hong Kong, 273
Kamakura, Japan, 136–143
Great Buddha of, 137–139
history, 137
restaurants, 142
shrines and temples, 139–142
transportation to, 136
Kamiide, Japan, 148
Kanchipuram, India, 422
Kandy, Sri Lanka, 440–441
food specialties, 434–435
Kaohsiung (Taiwan), 254
Kashikojima Island, 164
Kashmir, 385, 386, 411–414
weather, 373, 374
Katase, Japan, 142
Kathmandu, Nepal, 424–428
weather, 425
Kelaniya, Sri Lanka, 440
Khajuraho, India, 407, 408
Kimchee (Korean ceramic containers), 224
Kimonos, buying (Japan), 105, 106
Kintamani, Bali, 491
Kobe, Japan, 179–183
Kochi, Japan, 186

Kodaikanal, India, 423
Konarak, India, 395, 396, 427
Korea, 208–230
air travel to, 218
airport and tourist taxes, 214
background, 208–211
Cheju Island, 230
communications, 215
currency, 17, 213
customs, 212
duty-free merchandise, 46
electricity, 215
entrance papers, 17, 21
Folk Village, 220–221
food specialties, 72, 215–217, 225
health, 212–213
liquor, 217
medical requirements, 17
price level, 213
shopping, 223–225
time differential, 213
time evaluation, 217–218
tipping, 213
tobacco regulations, 17
transportation in, 214
visas, 17, 20, 212
when to go, 211–212
See also names of cities
Korean Airlines, 214, 230
Kowloon, Hong Kong, 261, 264, 269–271, 277, 282
hotels, 270, 271, 278–281
Kuala Lumpur, Malaysia, 470–473
Kunming, China, 320
Kurseong, India, 394
Kwangchow (Canton), China, 314–316
Kweilin, China, 318–319
Kwun Tong, Hong Kong, 273
Kyongju, Korea, 227–228
Kyoto, Japan, 165–173
entertainment, 171
geishas, 171
hotels, 172–173
palaces, 169–170
restaurants, 173
shopping, 110, 171–172
shrines and temples, 166–169

sidetrips from, 173–191
transportation to, 165
Kyushu, Japan, 183, 184, 185, 187

Lace, buying (Sri Lanka), 439
Lacquerware, buying
  Burma, 367
  Japan, 108
  Korea, 224
  Sri Lanka, 439, 441
  Taiwan, 246
  Thailand, 345
Ladakh, India, 414
Lantau, Hong Kong, 276
Lanterns, buying (Japan), 109
Leather goods, buying (Hong Kong),
  289–290
Linens, buying (Hong Kong),
  290
Liquor
  taking your own, 27
  U.S. customs regulations, 46
  See also under names of countries
Lok Ma Chau, Hong Kong, 273
Lombong, Malaysia, 470
Lomotil, 28
Lopburi, Thailand, 351

Macao, 258, 259, 293–299
  currency, 17, 294
  customs, 295
  entrance papers, 17
  health, 295
  hotels, 294
  liquor, 258
  medical requirements, 17
  restaurants, 296
  sightseeing, 296–299
  tobacco regulations, 17
  transportation to, 295
  visas, 17, 21, 293
  when to go, 293
Madras, buying (India), 392
Madras, India, 422–424
  weather, 374, 423
Madurai, India, 423
Mahabalipuram, India, 422
Malacca, Malaysia, 470

Malaysia, 446–448, 470–475
  air travel in, 451
  airport and tourist taxes,
    451–452
  background, 446–448
  communications, 452
  currency, 17, 450
  customs, 449
  electricity, 452
  entrance papers, 17
  food specialties, 453–454
  health, 449–450
  holidays, 453
  language, 447
  liquor, 454
  medical requirements, 17
  price level, 450
  time differential, 450
  time evaluation, 454
  tipping, 450–451
  tobacco regulations, 17
  tours, 470–473
  transportation in, 451
  visas, 17, 21, 449
  weather, 448–449
  when to go, 448
  See also names of cities
Malaysia-Singapore Airlines, 451
Mandalay, Burma, 369
Mas, Bali, 491
Masks, buying
  India, 395
  Indonesia, 495
  Japan, 105
Matsushima, Japan, 193
Medical kits, 28
Medical requirements, 16–18,
    40–43
  See also under names of countries
Menuki jewelry, buying, 106
Mihintale, Sri Lanka, 443
Misumi, Japan, 191
Miyanoshita, Japan, 144
Money. See Currency
Moonstones, buying
  Burma, 367–368
  Sri Lanka, 439
Morioka, Japan, 194

Mother-of-pearl articles (Korea), 224
Mount Everest, 428
Mount Fuji (Japan), 57, 133, 145–148, 149, 150
Mysore, India, 424

Nagasaki, Japan, 188–190
Nagoya, Japan, 156–162
Nakorn Pathom, Thailand, 350
Nanking, China, 315–316
Nara, Japan, 173, 176
Negombo, Sri Lanka, 440, 441
Nepal, 424–428
  currency, 17
  duty-free merchandise, 46
  entrance papers, 17
  medical requirements, 17
  tobacco regulations, 17
  See also names of cities
New Delhi. *See* Delhi, India
New Territories (Hong Kong), 261, 272–276, 277
Nielloware, buying (Thailand), 344
Nightclubs. *See* entertainment under names of countries and cities
Nikko, Japan, 150–156
  history, 151–152
  hotels, 155
  natural beauties of, 155–156
  shrines, 151–155
  sports, 135
  transportation to, 150–151
Noh masks, buying (Japan), 105
Noh plays (Japan), 119–120
Northwest Orient Airlines, 4
Nuwara Eliya, Sri Lanka, 444

Old Delhi. *See* Delhi, India
Ootacamund, India, 424
Opals, buying (Singapore), 467
Orchid Island (Taiwan), 252–253
Osaka, Japan, 176–179
  Bunraku puppets, 178–179
  hotels, 178
  restaurants, 179
  shopping, 177
  weather, 175

Pachinko (Japanese pinball machines), 204
Pacific Area Travel Association (PATA), 49
Packing, 26–28
Pagan, Burma, 369
Paintings, buying
  India, 409
  Indonesia, 494–495
  Japan, 110
  Taiwan, 248
Pakistan, East, 424
Pan American World Airways, 3
Panmunjon, Korea, 227
Paper products, buying (Japan), 109
Paratyphoid vaccinations, 40–42
Parcel post, shipping packages by, 48
Passports, 14–15
  See also entrance papers, visas, under names of countries
Pathan, Nepal, 427
Pattaya, Thailand, 350–351
Pearls
  Burma, 368
  cultured, 101–104, 164–165
  Hong Kong, 288
  Japan, 101–102
Pegu, Burma, 368–369
Peking, China, 320
  health, 305
  weather, 303
Penang (Malaysia), 473
Perfumes, buying (Singapore), 465
Pewterware (Malaysia), 472
Phonograph records, buying (Taiwan), 247
Phuket, Thailand, 352–353
Pokhra, Nepal, 427
Polonnaruwa, Sri Lanka, 443
Porcelain articles, buying (Japan), 107–108, 157
Postage. *See* communications under names of countries
Pottery (Japan), 107–108, 157
  See also Ceramics
Precious stones, buying
  Burma, 367–368
  India, 409

Singapore, 464, 467, 468
Sri Lanka, 439
Prints, buying (Japan), 110
Puntjak, Indonesia, 487
Puppet drama (Japan), 122, 178–179
Puppets, buying (Indonesia), 495
Puri, India, 395, 396
Pusan, Korea, 228–230

Radios, buying
Hong Kong, 288
Japan, 104
Singapore, 465
Railway Express Agency, shipping
packages by, 48
Rangoon, Burma, 364–369
entertainment, 368
hotels, 366
restaurants, 366–367
shopping, 365–366, 367–368
sightseeing, 364–366
sports, 368
time differential, 359
transportation in, 361–362
weather, 357–358
Rattan articles, buying
Malaysia, 472
Thailand, 345
Records. See Phonograph records
Repulse Bay (Hong Kong), 268
Rubbings, buying (Thailand), 345
Rubies, buying
Burma, 367–368
Sri Lanka, 439
Rugs, buying
Hong Kong, 290
India, 403, 413
Taiwan, 246–247

Sabah. See Malaysia
Sangeh, Bali, 491
Sapphires, buying
Burma, 367
Sri Lanka, 439
Sapporo, Japan, 194, 195–196
Sarawak. See Malaysia

Screens, buying
Hong Kong, 290
Taiwan, 246
Scrolls, buying
Hong Kong, 290, 291
Japan, 110
Sendai, Japan, 192–193
Seoul, Korea, 218–226
entertainment, 225–226
hotels, 221–222
long trips from, 227–230
restaurants, 222–223
shopping, 220, 223–225
short trips from, 226–227
sightseeing, 218–220
sports, 226
weather, 211–212
Seto, Japan, 157
Seychelle Islands, 444–445
Shanghai, China, 317–318
weather, 303
Shatin Valley (Hong Kong), 274
Shawls, buying (India), 403, 413
Shenyang, China, 322
Shikoku (island), 183, 184, 185–186
Shikotsau-Toya National Park (Japan), 196
Shimbara, Japan, 191
Ship travel
advantages and disadvantages of, 1–2
extra costs in, 2
Shiraito, Japan, 148
Shopping. See under names of cities
and countries
Siam. See Thailand
Sian, China, 321–322
Sightseeing. See under names of cities
and countries
Sigiriya, Sri Lanka, 443, 444
Silks, buying
Burma, 367
India, 392, 398, 418
Japan, 108–109
Singapore, 466
Thailand, 343
Silver articles, buying
Burma, 367

India, 404, 409
Indonesia, 488, 495–496
Japan, 106
Malaysia, 472
Singapore, 468, 472
Sri Lanka, 438–439
Thailand, 344
Singapore, 446–470, 475
    airport and tourist taxes,
        451–452
    communications, 452
    currency, 450
    duty-free merchandise, 46
    electricity, 452
    entertainment, 468–469
    food specialties, 453–454
    health, 449–450
    holidays, 452
    hotels, 460–461
    liquor, 449, 454
    medical requirements, 17
    price level, 450
    restaurants, 461–464
    shopping, 456, 458, 459–460,
        464–468
    short trips from, 469–470
    sightseeing, 455–459
    sports, 469
    time differential, 450
    time evaluation, 454
    tipping, 450–451
    tobacco regulations, 17
    transportation in, 451
    visas, 17, 449
    weather, 448–449
    when to go, 448
    See also Malaysia
Smallpox vaccinations, 40–41
Snake charmers (India), 403
Sound systems, buying (Japan), 104
Sri Lanka (Ceylon), 429–445
    airport and tourist taxes, 433
    background, 429–430
    communications, 433
    currency, 17, 432
    customs, 431
    duty-free merchandise, 46

electricity, 434
entrance papers, 17
food specialties, 434–435
health, 431–432
liquor, 435
medical requirements, 17
price level, 432
time differential, 432
time evaluation, 435
tipping, 432
tobacco regulations, 17, 431
tour of, 442–444
transportation in, 433
visas, 17, 21, 430–431
when to go, 430
See also names of cities
Srinagar, India, 411–414
    weather, 412
Stanley, Hong Kong, 268
Stone lanterns, buying (Japan), 109
Sulawesi (Indonesia), 493
Sumatra (Indonesia), 492–493
Sun-Moon Lake (Taiwan),
    251–252
Surin, Thailand, 352
Suwon, Korea, 221
Sweaters, buying (Hong Kong), 289

Tai-chung, Taiwan, 251
Taipa (island), 299
Taipei, Taiwan, 232, 239–249
    entertainment, 248–249
    hotels, 241, 242–243
    long trips from, 250–254
    restaurants, 238, 243–245
    shopping, 241, 246–248
    short trips from, 249–250
    sightseeing, 239–242
    sports, 249
    weather, 232
Tai Po, Hong Kong, 273, 274
Taiwan, 231–254
    air travel in, 235
    airport and tourist taxes, 235
    background, 231–232
    communications, 235–236
    currency, 18, 234

customs, 233
electricity, 236
entrance papers, 18, 233
food specialties, 236–238
health, 233
liquor, 238
Kenting Tropical Botanical Garden, 253–254
medical requirements, 18
price level, 234
sightseeing, 249–254
sports, 249
time differential, 234
time evaluation, 239
tipping, 234
tobacco regulations, 18
transportation in, 235
visas, 18, 21, 233
when to go, 232
See also names of cities
Taj Mahal (India), 404–407
Takamatsu, Japan, 185–186
Takarazuka Girls' Opera, 86, 122, 182
Taroko Gorge (Taiwan), 250–251
Tea ceremony (Japan), 205–206
Teakwood articles, buying (Thailand), 343
Television sets, buying (Japan), 104
Tetanus vaccination, 40, 42
Textiles, buying
    Burma, 367
    India, 392, 395, 398, 409, 418
    Malaysia, 472
    Singapore, 464, 465, 466, 472
    Sri Lanka, 438
    See also Cotton fabrics; Silks; Woolens
Thailand, 323–354
    airport and tourist taxes, 330
    background, 323–325
    communications, 330–331
    currency, 18, 328
    customs, 326
    electricity, 331
    entrance papers, 18
    food specialties, 332–333
    health, 326–327

hotels, 338–339
    liquor, 333
    local customs, 334
    medical requirements, 18
    price level, 328–329
    restaurants, 332–333, 339–341
    shopping, 341–345
    sightseeing, 336–338
    sports, 346–347
    time differential, 327–328
    time evaluation, 333
    tipping, 329
    tobacco regulations, 18, 326
    transportation in, 329–330
    visas, 18, 21, 326
    when to go, 325–326
    See also names of cities
Time change, 29–33
    adjustment to, 22, 44–45
    See also under names of countries
Tipping. See under names of countries
Tjeluk, Bali, 491
Toba, Japan, 164
Tobacco
    regulation checklist, 16–18
    taking your own, 27
    U.S. Customs requirement, 47
    See also under names of countries
Tokushima, Japan, 186
Tokyo, Japan, 76–136
    bars and cabarets, 60, 61–62, 88, 112–117
    baseball, 127–129
    coffee shops, 115–117
    department stores, 85–86, 88, 110–111
    entertainment, 112–127
    gangsters, 112
    geishas, 96, 117–119
    girls' operas, 86–87, 122–123, 182
    golf, 132–133
    historic places, 80–82, 84–85, 87, 89, 90, 91
    horse racing, 132
    hotels, 66–67, 91–95
    inns, 95–96
    Kabuki plays, 120–122

long trips from, 156–165
map, 77
massage parlors, 88, 125–126
movie theaters, 86, 124–125
museums, 81–83, 89–90
musical events, 123–124
neighborhoods, 78–80
Noh plays, 105, 119–120
ping-pong, 132
puppet drama, 122
rental cars, 64
restaurants, 70–71, 96–101
shopping, 85–86, 101–112
short trips from, 135–156
sightseeing, 82–91
special places of interest, 80–82
sports, 127–135
stage shows, 87, 123
strip shows, 88, 123
subway system, 62, 83–84
sumo wrestling, 90, 129–131
taxis, 62–64
theaters, 84, 86–87
tours, 82–83
weather, 57–58
Tokyo International Airport (Haneda), 67
Tokyo International Airport, New (Narita), 66–67
Topazes, buying (Sri Lanka), 439
Tortoise-shell ware, buying (Japan), 189–190
Tours, conducted, 7–10
Towada-Hachimantai National Park (Japan), 195
Transportation. See Air travel; and under names of cities and countries
Traveler's checks, 38–40
Traveling
by air. See Air travel
by conducted tours, 7–10
currency, 38–40
diet during, 43–44
document and regulation checklist, 16–18
health data, 40–45
independently planned, 10–11
inoculations for, 16–18, 40–43
itineraries, 12–13
jet lag and, 22, 44–45
making arrangements for, 7–8
on your own, 11–14
passports, 14–15
ship, 1–2
time change, 29–33, 44–45
traveler's checks, 38–40
U.S. Customs, 45–49
visas, 14–21
weather, 33–38
what to take, 22–28
Trichinopoly, India, 423
Tsuen Wan, Hong Kong, 272
Typhoid-paratyphoid vaccinations, 40, 42
Typhus vaccinations, 40, 42

Udaipur, India, 409–411
Ukkuwella, Sri Lanka, 441
Unzen Park (Japan), 190–191
Unzen Spa (Japan), 190
Utsunomiya, Japan, 192

Vaccinations, 16–18, 40–42
Varanasi, India. *See* Benaras, India
Victoria, Hong Kong, 264–272
hotels, 265, 278–279
Visas, 14–21
list of sources, 20–21
See also under names of countries

Watches, buying
Japan, 104
Singapore, 465
Water. *See* Drinking water
Weather, 33–38
See also under names of countries
Wood carvings, buying
Burma, 367
Indonesia, 491, 494

Sri Lanka, 441
Taiwan, 246
Thailand, 354
Woolens, buying (India),
  403
World Health Organization (WHO),
  40, 41
Wuhan, China, 321
Wulai, Taiwan, 250

Yami aborigines (Taiwan), 253
Yashima, Japan, 186
Yellow fever vaccinations, 40, 41, 42
Yokohama, Japan, 136
Yoshiwara, Japan, 148
Yuen Long, Hong Kong, 272–273
Yukatas, buying (Japan), 105

Zushi, Japan, 136